INCLUSION IN
EARLY CHILDHOOD PROGRAMS

CHILDREN WITH EXCEPTIONALITIES

INCLUSION IN
EARLY CHILDHOOD PROGRAMS
CHILDREN WITH EXCEPTIONALITIES

Sixth Canadian Edition

K. Eileen Allen
Glynnis E. Cowdery
Carol L. Paasche
Rachel Langford
Karen Nolan
Bernice Cipparrone

NELSON

NELSON

**Inclusion in Early Childhood Programs,
Sixth Canadian Edition**

by K. Eileen Allen, Glynnis E. Cowdery,
Carol L. Paasche, Rachel Langford,
Karen Nolan, and Bernice Cipparrone

**Vice President, Editorial
Higher Education:**
Anne Williams

Publisher:
Lenore Taylor-Atkins

Marketing Manager:
Terry Fedorkiw

Developmental Editor:
Lisa Berland

**Photo Researcher/Permissions
Coordinator:**
Lisa Brant

**Senior Production Project
Manager:**
Imoinda Romain

Production Service:
Cenveo Publisher Services

Copy Editor:
Marcia Gallego

Proofreader:
Kavitha Ashok

Indexer:
BIM Indexing Services

Design Director:
Ken Phipps

Managing Designer:
Franca Amore

Interior Design:
Lisa Delgado

Cover Design:
Cathy Mayer

Cover Image:
SuslO/Shutterstock

Compositor:
Cenveo Publisher Services

**Library and Archives Canada
Cataloguing in Publication**

Allen, K. Eileen, 1918-, author

Inclusion in early childhood
programs: children with
exceptionalities/
K. Eileen Allen, Glynnis
E. Cowdery, Carol L. Paasche,
Rachel Langford, Karen Nolan,
Bernice Cipparrone. — Sixth
Canadian edition.

Revision of: Inclusion in early
childhood programs: children with
exceptionalities / K. Eileen Allen
... [et al.]. — 5th Canadian ed. —
Toronto : Nelson Education,
©2011.

Includes bibliographical references
and index.
ISBN 978-0-17-653177-5 (pbk.)

1. Children with disabilities—
Education (Preschool)—Canada.
2. Inclusive education—Canada.
3. Children with disabilities—
Development—Canada.
4. Early childhood special
education—Canada.
I. Cowdery, Glynnis Edwards, author
II. Paasche, Carol L., 1937-, author
III. Langford, Rachel, author
IV. Nolan, Karen, author
V. Cipparrone, Bernice, author
VI. Title. VII. Title: Early childhood
programs.

LC4019.2.A46 2014 371.9'0460971
C2014-906360-1

ISBN-13: 978-0-17-653177-5
ISBN-10: 0-17-653177-7

Brief Contents

Contents

Preface to the Sixth Canadian Edition

The sixth Canadian edition of *Inclusion in Early Childhood Programs* contains a number of organizational and content changes. We have sought to incorporate recommendations from professionals who have used the text with students. A major focus in this edition has been on incorporating recent research and updating Canadian content. We continue to include material from earlier research, which serves as a foundation for current theory and practice.

Basic Approach

As in previous Canadian editions of this text, we believe that regardless of what special need a child has, he or she is still first of all a child. Therefore, whenever possible, a child with special needs should be able to attend and be included in neighbourhood early childhood programs and schools. We are aware that, in order for inclusion to be effective for all children within a group, additional support staff resources and specialized equipment may be necessary.

An inclusive approach to working with children who have exceptionalities has at its foundation knowledge of child development theory. In this edition of the book, we have continued to include brief synopses of theoretical child development information, recognizing that extensive development content can be acquired from other texts and is included in other courses.

Our approach to working with young children continues to focus on supporting, encouraging, and responding to the developmental needs of all children. We have tried to provide information that will enable teachers to feel comfortable teaching children with special needs and to successfully include them in their early childhood programs.

We view the early childhood teacher as a member of a dynamic team that includes the teacher, the child, the child's family, and other children in the centre, supported by consultants—such as the early childhood interventionist/resource teacher, physiotherapists and other specialists, the personnel of the school that the child will eventually attend, and the members of the community in which the child lives.

The historical background of the treatment of children and adults with special needs has been somewhat different in Canada than it has been in the United States. Whereas the United States now has federal legislation that designates specific rights and services for young children with special needs, Canada's legislation is mainly provincial and territorial. This text promotes primarily a Canadian perspective.

In most of Canada, it was only in the 1990s that a team approach toward inclusion was recognized as the most effective way of providing support and services to children with special needs and their families. At one time, programming for Canadian children with special needs took place only in segregated settings. It is now recognized in most areas of Canada that an inclusive approach is most effective, providing models for those who need them, and giving all children an opportunity, through interacting with those who may be different from themselves, to develop openness, acceptance, and appreciation for individual differences. We are aware that there are circumstances in which some children need to begin their preschool or school experience in a specialized setting, with the goal of moving into an inclusive setting as soon as special skills (behavioural or otherwise) are acquired and necessary supports are available.

We strongly urge those working with children with special needs to seek additional postsecondary training specifically geared to understanding and gaining knowledge that will help them to be most effective in creating a positive environment for all children in the group. It is also recommended that those who took training in special needs continue to attend workshops and short updating courses as new strategies and materials are constantly being developed.

New to This Edition

We have made a number of revisions in this edition. Research has been updated throughout the book, including more Canadian-based information and providing Canadian sources wherever possible.

 A new icon in the margin alerts readers to the many recommended strategies throughout the book.

New to each chapter is a Connection piece highlighting current research relevant to inclusive practices. The new larger trim size and beautiful colour design with outstanding colour photos makes this sixth Canadian edition even more engaging and accessible.

Significant changes include the following:

Chapter 1—An Inclusive Approach to Early Childhood Education

▶ A recent joint position statement on inclusion from the U.S. Division for Early Childhood (DEC) of the Council for Exceptional Children (CEC) and the National Association for the Education of Young Children (NAEYC) (2009)

▶ A discussion by two professionals on the use of the terms *special needs* and *disability*

Chapter 2—Canadian Legislation: Support for Children through Early Intervention

▶ Current information drawn from a paper by Halfon and Friendly (2013) on provincial and territorial child care policy related to children with special needs

Chapter 3—Partnership with Families

▶ Up-to-date definition of the family from the Canadian census

▶ New statistics and information on family abuse and the child with special needs

▶ New information on family-centred care/practice

Chapter 4—Preparing Teachers for Inclusive Programs

▶ Information on specialized training programs for working with children with a range of developmental differences in Canadian provinces and territories

▶ A sense of humour is added as a characteristic of effective teachers in inclusive settings

▶ A clearer definition of *scaffolding*

Chapter 5—An Overview of Developmental Differences

▶ A chart that identifies how provinces and territories classify developmental differences

Chapter 6—Children with Cognitive Delays

▶ Updated definition of intellectual and developmental disabilities

▶ Updated discussion on alcohol and substance abuse and the impact of poverty on infant and child development

Chapter 7—Advanced Cognitive and Developmental Abilities: Children Who Are Gifted

▶ Updated information on characteristics of children who may be gifted

Chapter 8—Sensory Impairments: Hearing and Vision

▶ The section on hearing impairments has been significantly revised in consultation with Dr. Kristen Snodden to reflect current research and understandings of the competencies of children who are deaf

Chapter 9—Orthopedic and Other Health Conditions

▶ New detailed information on how to support children with asthma

▶ More examples to illustrate the MOVE (Mobility Options via Education/ Experience) approach

▶ Additional examples on how to incorporate principles of universal design in the classroom

▶ New terminology for dwarfism

▶ Resources to deepen children's understanding of diabetes and how to address daily life

▶ Strategies to increase children's level of physical activity

▶ Updated data on sickle-cell disease, Tourette syndrome, and hemophilia

Chapter 10—Social, Adaptive, and Learning Disorders

▶ Updated information on autism spectrum disorder, anxiety, and depression based on the *DSM-5*, as well as resources and strategies to support children with daily life

▶ A detailed definition of ADHD to deepen understanding

▶ A section on mental health promotion and prevention

Chapter 11—The Developmental Behavioural Approach

▶ Expanded coverage and illustration of task analysis

Chapter 12—Identification and the Individual Program Plan (IPP)

▶ Discussion of how educators can engage in appreciative inquiry to guide their work

▶ Expanded discussion on the role of families in contributing to the IPP

Chapter 13—Planning Transitions to Support Inclusion

▶ Findings from current research on what makes transitions to support inclusion effective

▶ A new section on the role of team members—the sending program, the receiving program, and the parents—in a child's transition to a new program

Chapter 14—Intervention with Specific Age Groups: Infants, Toddlers, and School-Aged Children

▶ Updated Canadian definition of early intervention

▶ New information on social policy regarding provinces/territories linking early years services with educational services

▶ New goal for infant/toddler intervention from NAEYC

▶ New information on a universal early learning and care project

Chapter 15—Arranging the Inclusive Learning Environment

▶ Updated references to pedagogical approaches

Chapter 16—Facilitating Social Development

▶ New and updated information on promoting the development of social skills in an inclusive program

▶ Timeline of social development for the typical child

Chapter 17—Facilitating Positive Behaviour (Managing Challenging Behaviours)

▶ Additional information on how to understand functional behaviour

▶ Updated definition of conduct disorder and oppositional defiant disorder

▶ New information on resources and programs available to support children, families, and educators

Chapter 18—Facilitating Cognitive Learning

▶ Expanded coverage of emerging literacy and effective early literacy instruction

Chapter 19—Facilitating Language, Speech, and the Development of Communication

▶ Updated information on alternative language systems, including new information on PECS (Picture Exchange Communication System), voice synthesizing, and signing

▶ Expanded discussion on augmentative communication systems

▶ Updated Communication Checklist for children from birth to age five

▶ A new section on the Hanen Centre's Learning Language and Loving It program, an evidence-based program for promoting enriched language environments for young children

► Information on the development of English as a second language and bilingual education has been removed. Throughout the history of this textbook, there was little literature on second-language learning in the early years, bilingual education, and Aboriginal early childhood education and care in the Canadian context. For this reason, previous editions provided content focused on these areas. More recently, however, several books by Canadian scholars have comprehensively addressed these gaps in the literature, and on this basis we decided to remove these content areas from Chapter 19.

Comments

We continue to strive to present a comprehensive text that will meet the needs of those who want to learn more about ways to understand and work with infants, toddlers, preschool, and school-aged children who have developmental differences.

Working on this updated Canadian edition continued to be very challenging. Though research exists, much of it is published and disseminated on a local or provincial and territorial basis. The Child Care Resource and Research Unit located in Toronto has made major efforts to develop, obtain, and publish Canada-wide research and resource materials on inclusive child care. Although a number of innovative and inclusive education and early childhood programs have been developed in Canada, we have concluded that it has been difficult for many of these programs to get publicity, ongoing funding, and recognition.

In summary, in this edition we have sought to obtain as complete an updated record as possible of current trends in Canada and to provide useful information for teachers who will be working with young children with special needs in inclusive settings. We have contacted, wherever possible, Canadian organizations in an attempt to strengthen the Canadian content in the text by using these organizations' definitions and research.

Ancillaries

Ancillaries for Instructors

ABOUT THE NELSON EDUCATION TEACHING ADVANTAGE (NETA) The **Nelson Education Teaching Advantage (NETA)** program delivers research-based instructor resources that promote student engagement and higher-order thinking to enable the success of Canadian students and educators. To ensure the high quality of these materials, all Nelson ancillaries have been professionally copyedited.

Be sure to visit Nelson Education's **Inspired Instruction** website at **www.nelson.com/inspired** to find out more about NETA. Don't miss the testimonials of instructors who have used NETA supplements and seen student engagement increase!

All NETA and other key instructor ancillaries are provided on the Instructor Companion Site at **www.nelson.com/inclusion6ce/instructor**, giving instructors the ultimate tool for customizing lectures and presentations.

NETA POWERPOINTS Microsoft® PowerPoint® lecture slides for every chapter have been created by one of the book's authors, Bernice Cipparrone of George Brown College. There is an average of 20 slides per chapter, many featuring key figures and tables from *Inclusion in Early Childhood Programs*, Sixth Canadian

Edition. NETA principles of clear design and engaging content have been incorporated throughout, making it simple for instructors to customize the deck for their courses.

INSTRUCTOR'S MANUAL An online instructor's manual accompanies this book. It contains information to assist the instructor in designing the course, including comments and suggestions, discussion possibilities, in-class and out-of-class activities, selected journals, and selected audiovisual materials.

COURSEMATE Nelson Education's **CourseMate** to accompany *Inclusion in Early Childhood Programs,* Sixth Canadian Edition, brings course concepts to life with interactive learning and exam preparation tools that integrate with the printed textbook. Students activate their knowledge through quizzes, games, and flash-cards, among many other tools.

CourseMate provides immediate feedback that enables students to connect results to the work they have just produced, increasing their learning efficiency. It encourages contact between students and faculty: You can select to monitor your students' level of engagement with **CourseMate**, correlating their efforts to their outcomes. You can even use **CourseMate's** quizzes to practise "Just in Time" teaching by tracking results in the Engagement Tracker and customizing your lesson plans to address their learning needs.

Ancillaries for Students

COURSEMATE *Inclusion in Early Childhood Programs,* Sixth Canadian Edition, includes **CourseMate**, which includes the following interactive teaching and learning tools:

▶ an interactive ebook, with highlighting, note-taking, and search capabilities

▶ quizzes

▶ case studies

▶ flashcards

▶ videos

▶ ... and more!

Visit NELSONbrain.com to start using CourseMate. Buy instant access at NELSONbrain.com

Acknowledgments

We are grateful to K. Eileen Allen and Glynnis E. Cowdery of *The Exceptional Child* for having written an excellent text, and we have sought to include some of the new research and resource materials found in the eighth edition of that text. In addition, we are most grateful for the opportunity offered to us by Nelson Education Ltd. throughout this project. We thank Publisher Lenore Taylor-Atkins; Developmental Editor Lisa Berland; Senior Production Project Manager Imoinda Romain; and our copyeditor, Marcia Gallego. We also thank our Project Manager, Sangeetha, and our proofreader, Kavitha Ashok, at Cenveo Publisher Services.

We also want to give special thanks to the children, families, and early childhood educators who have permitted us to use photographs of them. Many of the photos for this edition were taken at Bloorsview-Scarborough Site and Ryerson Early Learning Centre. Special thanks go to Jennifer Leung at Nelson Education and to Sandy Matos for taking many of the photographs for this edition.

We want to give thanks to all those who have supported us in writing this edition. These include the many agencies and people who have contributed pictures and expertise in previous editions.

We would also like to give special thanks to the following contributors, without which this edition and previous editions would not be possible:

- Dr. Kristen Snodden, associate professor, School of Linguistics and Language Studies, Carleton University, who significantly contributed to revisions in Chapter 8 and the section on hearing impairments

- Susan Mace, manager of Infant and Child Development Services in Durham, Ontario, and Kathryn Underwood, associate professor in the School of Early Childhood Studies, Ryerson University, for contributing to the ongoing debate about the use of the term *special needs* versus *disability* for identifying children with developmental differences

- Janice Greenberg, who contributed the new piece on the Learning Language and Loving It program from the Hanen Centre for Chapter 19

- Pearl Rimer from Boost Child Abuse Prevention and Intervention, who provided current research on the prevalence and risk of violence against children with disabilities

- Cindy Smith, professor of early childhood education at Seneca College, for making recommendations on the content of the book and for providing feedback from early childhood education students

- Rita Barron, Maxine Brown, and Debbie Vanzuylen, professors at the School of Early Childhood at George Brown College, for providing recommendations and feedback on the content

Rachel Langford, Bernice Cipparrone, and Karen Nolan (2014)

About the Canadian Authors

Carol L. Paasche was a professor and coordinator of Early Childhood Education at Seneca College, Toronto, for 30 years. Since taking early retirement, she has established a counselling and consultation practice, primarily focused on working with parents and children. She also consults with early childhood centres. Carol has been an executive on the board of a nonprofit community-based, parent-participating, inclusive child care centre and is the author of the book *Children with Special Needs in Early Childhood Settings* (New York: Delmar, 2004), a resource book for teachers of young children with special needs.

Before teaching adults, Carol taught in an integrated cooperative nursery school, worked with children with special needs, and did counselling with elementary and junior high school children.

Carol Paasche has a B.A. in psychology and child development from Antioch (College) University and an M.Ed. from Harvard Graduate School of Education. She also completed a year of doctoral studies in educational psychology at the University of Michigan.

Rachel Langford is the director of the School of Early Childhood Studies at Ryerson University. After receiving an elementary school teacher certificate and early childhood certificate, she worked for 18 years in a variety of primary and early childhood settings in British Columbia. For 10 years, she taught Ontario ECE diploma students and is the recipient of George Brown College's Crystal Apple Award for teaching excellence. She edited the *Checklist for Quality Inclusive Education: A Self-Assessment Tool and Manual for Early Childhood Settings* for the Early Childhood Resource Teacher Network of Ontario. Her research and publications focus on early childhood professional preparation and work, early learning curriculum frameworks, and child care advocacy. She is the principal investigator of a SSHRC-awarded project that examines professionalism as a Canadian child care movement strategy in last decade. She is the current president of the board of directors of the Association of Early Childhood Educators, Ontario, and is a frequent presenter, provincially and nationally, on a range of early childhood issues.

Rachel Langford has a B.A. and an M.Ed. from the University of British Columbia, and a Ph.D. in sociology and equity studies in education from the Ontario Institute for Studies in Education at the University of Toronto. She received the 2005 George L. Geis Award for the most outstanding Canadian doctoral dissertation in higher education.

Karen Nolan is a professor and coordinator in the School of Early Childhood Education at Seneca College in Toronto. Before 1998, Karen worked in a variety of early childhood settings, supporting children with special needs and their families. She was a teacher at Bloorview McMillan Children's Centre in two programs: Play and Learn and Play Haven. Karen was also an early childhood consultant for Adventure Place, a mental health agency in Toronto.

Karen Nolan has a diploma in early childhood education from Seneca College, a B.A.A. in early childhood education from Ryerson University, a B.Ed. from York University, and an M.Ed. from Brock University.

Bernice Cipparrone McLeod has been in the field of early childhood education for over 30 years. She worked in children's mental health, specializing in infant mental health, trauma, and supporting child development. In addition, during her professional and personal time she has been committed to collaborating with others in creating inclusive, accessible communities. Bernice has served on the board of several nonprofit organizations, most recently as the board chair of a community health centre. Bernice has developed three cultural competency evaluation tools for the Ministry of Children and Youth Services. These tools have been well received by the community, which led to a number of local and national presentations. Bernice also worked at a senior level for the Ontario Trillium Foundation (an agency of the government of Ontario) for three years while she was an instructor with George Brown College in the ECE continuing education department, before becoming a full-time professor and coordinator in 2011.

Bernice McLeod graduated from York University with a B.A in psychology before receiving her diploma in early childhood education from Seneca College. She completed graduate studies at the University of Toronto's Institute of Child Studies.

An Inclusive Approach to Early Childhood Education

1

OBJECTIVES

After studying the material in this chapter, the student will be able to

- Define inclusion.
- Trace society's changing attitudes toward children with special needs.
- Discuss inclusion in terms of early development, critical learning periods, and teachable moments.
- Discuss the benefits of inclusion for all children in an early childhood setting.
- Identify the challenges associated with implementing inclusive early childhood programs.

KEY CONCEPTS AND TERMS

advocacy group

handicappism

inclusion

individual family service
  plan (IFSP)

individual program plan (IPP)

integration

mainstreaming

peer imitating

peer tutoring

people-first language

reverse integration

sensitive or critical periods

teachable moments

zero reject

Introduction

Inclusion children are included, with additional assistance and resources, regardless of ability in early childhood settings, educational environments, and community programs

This book is about inclusion in the lives of young children such as Chanda, Devon, and Jonathan. **Inclusion** means that children with special needs attend preschool, child care, educational, and recreational programs with their peers. Inclusion is about belonging, being valued, and having choices. Inclusion is about accepting and valuing human diversity and providing the necessary support so that all children and their families can successfully participate in the programs of their choice.

Mainstreaming children with special needs have to "be ready" for integration into the mainstream

For the past 30 years, families and professionals have worked to provide appropriate and quality education for all children. The first attempt at implementing this goal was called **mainstreaming**. The term **integration** is also used to describe the placement of children with special needs in education programs. Some professionals argue that there are clear-cut differences between mainstreaming and integration; others use the terms interchangeably. Currently, many early education professionals use the term *inclusion*. The difference between mainstreaming or integration and inclusion is philosophical. In mainstreaming, children with special needs have to "be ready" for integration into the mainstream. The emphasis is placed on helping the child with special needs meet the existing classroom expectations. Sometimes the child who is "integrated" is withdrawn from the regular program for part of the day and provided with separate support. However, this separation from other children can result in fewer opportunities for the development of social relationships between the child with special needs and those without special needs. In inclusive education, children with special needs are full-time members of the educational setting. The emphasis is on providing the support necessary so that the children are accommodated and can participate in a meaningful way in ongoing social and educational activities. Support may include adaptation of the curriculum, materials, and educational practices. Support may also include additional staff, consultation, or specialized training for the existing staff. Support services, such as speech therapy and physical therapy, are part of the daily activities and routines within the early childhood program (see photo, page 5).

Integration children with special needs are given extra support so that they can be integrated into a regular setting and meet the existing expectations of the classroom

Inclusion Defined

Since the early 1990s, researchers and professionals have developed and refined definitions of inclusion. In 1993, Ehlers described three ways to view inclusion: through beliefs and values, through experiences, and through outcomes. The *beliefs and values* that every family brings to inclusion are a reflection of their unique history, culture, and family relationships (Frankel, Gold, & Ajodhia-Andrews, 2010). Family choices must drive the inclusion process. The family identifies the community to which it belongs and in which the child is to be included. The concept of "goodness of fit" first developed by Thomas and Chess (1977) is important when developing inclusive programs. An inclusive program must consider the unique experiences of every child and family, and how the program can address the child's strengths and needs as well as family priorities.

The beliefs and values that influence inclusion occur at the levels of the family, the community, and the society. A family's belief system has a direct impact on their views about inclusion. The sociopolitical context in which children and families live and work also affects inclusion. This includes how our society views high-quality early childhood care and education for all children. In other words, if providing high-quality child care for children of working parents is not a societal priority, providing high-quality child care for children with special needs will not be a priority either.

The *experience* of inclusion varies from child to child and from family to family. The goal is to create a match between the program and the child and family. Inclusive classrooms are caring communities that support the ongoing development of participants (Frankel, 2004). Inclusion requires planning, teamwork, and support. Teacher values and beliefs define experiences with inclusion and these experiences, in turn, influence future values and beliefs (Odom et al., 2004).

The *outcomes* observed and reported by the parents and teachers of children in inclusive programs are broad based and *holistic*. The outcomes include some of the developmental changes observed in specialized (segregated) special education programs (e.g., improved communication skills, improved motor skills). They also include important changes in social behaviour and a general sense of belonging. Many parents of children in inclusive educational programs report that their child received his or her first invitation to a birthday party or to play at a friend's house after being involved in inclusive programs. Some parents

Inclusion supports the right of all children, regardless of individual abilities, to participate in early childhood programs.

Courtesy of Ryerson Early Learning Centre

report feeling more included in the community because their child is attending a "regular" school.

Billingsley, Gallucci, Peck, Schwartz, and Staub (1996) proposed a three-domain conceptualization of inclusive education outcomes. These three interlocking domains are membership, relationship, and development:

1. The *membership domain* includes the child's interactions with groups. This includes being a member of a class, of a small group within a class, and of non-school-related groups (e.g., children's choir at place of worship.) The defining criterion of this domain is that other members of the group are willing to make accommodations for the child with special needs to support inclusion and membership.

2. The *relationship domain* describes peer relationships—that is, relationships with playmates and classmates. This domain looks at the different roles that the child plays in his or her relationships with peers. For example, in the majority of interactions with peers, is the child with special needs receiving help? Does the child have opportunities to be in a role of helping other children? Are there reciprocal or play and companionship types of interactions? Looking at relationships this way allows us to provide rich descriptions of the peers in the child's social network and the many different roles each peer plays.

3. The *development domain* looks at more traditional types of early childhood special education outcomes: changes in participation in classroom routine and rituals, social-communicative behaviour, functional skills, pre-academic skills, and other goals that are included in a child's individual program plan (IPP) or individual family service plan (IFSP).

Together, these three domains provide a tool for teachers and families to use to describe the unique outcomes found in inclusive educational settings. This outcome framework can guide the development of goals and objectives for inclusive educational programs (see the discussion of IPPs in Chapter 12 and IFSPs in Chapter 3).

A recent joint position statement from the United States Division for Early Childhood (DEC) of the Council for Exceptional Children (CEC) and the National Association for the Education of Young Children (NAEYC) (2009) articulated a clear, comprehensive definition of inclusion in early childhood:

> Early childhood inclusion embodies the values, policies, and practices that support the right of every infant and young child and his or her family, regardless of ability, to participate in a broad range of activities and contexts as full members of families, communities, and society. The desired results of inclusive experiences for children with and without disabilities and their families include a sense of belonging and membership, positive social relationships and friendships, and development and learning to reach their full potential. The defining features of inclusion that can be used to identify high quality early childhood programs and services are access, participation, and supports. (p. 2)

Inclusive Language: Changing Terminology

In the past, the term *handicapped* was applied to individuals who were noticeably different, either physically or intellectually. Usually, they were referred to as "deaf and dumb," "blind," "crippled," or "retarded." Society provided

Individual program plan (IPP) an approach to providing services to individuals with special needs: the process involves developing a written plan based on the child's strengths, needs, and interests; implementation and evaluation are part of the IPP process

Individual family service plan (IFSP) similar to the IPP, the IFSP is a written plan that describes services for families with young children with special needs; it is written collaboratively with parents and describes the child's current strengths and needs "homes for crippled children" and "institutions for the mentally retarded" (a then-common term used for individuals judged to be of lesser intellectual abilities). Now, we vigorously question the appropriateness of such terms, especially when describing a given individual. Later, terms covering a broader but more individualized range of disabilities came into use: *Behaviour disordered*, *learning disabled*, and *mentally deficient*, along with *handicapped*, *deviant*, and so on, were commonly used to describe both children and adults. Individual identities were locked into differences: "He's Down syndrome"; "She's autistic"; "These boys are mentally retarded." This language devalued people and reflected prejudice and stereotyping toward people with diverse abilities. When society and individuals act on prejudice and stereotyping, discrimination and handicappism result. **Handicappism** is "a set of assumptions and practices that promote differential and unequal treatment of people because of apparent or assumed physical, mental, or behavioural differences" (Bogdan & Biklen, 1993, p. 69).

Handicappism assumptions and practices based on physical, mental, or behavioural differences that foster differential and unequal treatment of people

In this text, a people-first approach to describing children who require extra support will be used. Such statements as "She is a special needs child" highlight the "problem" rather than the child; whereas "This child has special needs" puts the focus on the child. The new word order and terminology is referred to as **people-first language**. Incidentally, the people-first approach highlights a fundamental assumption of inclusion—that all children are children and our practices should reflect that reality (Snow, 2005). Moreover, all children have multiple identities; identifying a child solely by his or her exceptionalities (e.g., "He is an autistic child") may overlook other aspects of the child, such as the importance

People-first language language that focuses on the person instead of the disability

of cultural and linguistic heritage in the child's life. The way a child is described may depend on the context and, in some situations, the child's disability may not be relevant (see photo, right). Using people-first language consistently requires self-monitoring. For example, although we strive to use people-first language, instead of describing "the child who is gifted," we put the descriptor before the child, saying the "gifted child." This practice likely reflects different (e.g., more positive) attitudes toward giftedness in contrast to other categories of disabilities.

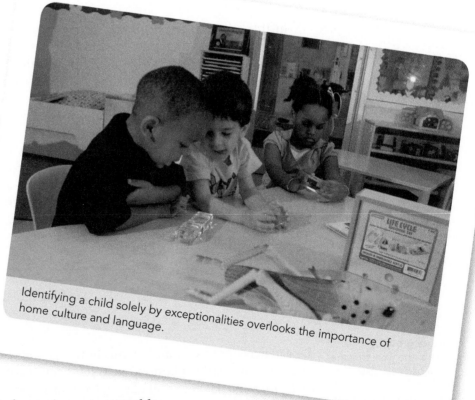

Identifying a child solely by exceptionalities overlooks the importance of home culture and language.

© Cengage Learning

The term *handicapped* is becoming unacceptable. What are acceptable terms is under considerable debate by everyone committed to inclusive early childhood education and care (see Box 1-1).

When talking to parents of young children with developmental challenges, I never use the term *disability*, which can get in the way of seeing the real child and his or her potential. Our role as interventionists is to help each child achieve optimal development, and that path is unique to each child, dependent upon a complex interplay of genes expressed through environmental interaction. Recent research in the neurosciences provides powerful evidence for the influence of the early years on children's later competence and coping skills. These influences will affect learning, behaviour, and health throughout the lifespan. Young children are extremely resilient, and there are many protective factors and environmental influences that can mitigate diagnosis or adverse circumstances at birth. To me, the label *disability* puts limitations on a child.[*]

Many practitioners continue to use the term *special needs* because they believe that this term is broader than *disability*. Many people perceive the term *special needs* to be a more positive term than *disability*. The term *disability*, however, is consistent with international rights-based language. Further, it avoids the term *special*, which is often used to justify education and care provisions for this group of children as an addition to regular care provisions, undermining the argument that all children have an equal right to care and education. When we consider the term *disability* as it has evolved in sociology, it is very broad. The United Nations Convention on the Rights of Persons with Disabilities (UNCRPD, 2006) defines persons with disabilities to "include those who have long-term physical, mental, intellectual, or sensory impairments which in interaction with various barriers may hinder their full and effective participation in society on an equal basis with others" (article 1, p. 2). This definition includes the interaction and barriers that are in a society as part of the experience of disability. In addition, the term *disability* refers to the experience of having barriers, as well as the individual experience of impairment. Impairment can be a result of genetic or biological conditions, or social conditions such as poverty. Additionally, the term *disability* is important in that it is well developed as a sociological theory that has informed human rights law within Canada at the provincial level and internationally (Canadian Human Rights Act, 1985; UNCRPD, 2006).[†]

[*],[†] Source: Reprinted by permission of Susan Mace and Kathryn Underwood.

In this text, the term *child with special needs* is used because this language helps identify that some young children need extra support to reach their full potential. Nevertheless, it is recognized that the language used to describe an individual's abilities is a living language, and we need to be constantly aware of changes in usage and the reasons for these changes. Early childhood professionals must decide based on the various positions presented here the language they will use to respectfully describe differences in children's abilities. This text avoids comparing children (e.g., atypical versus typical; abnormal versus normal) so that the range and diversity in human growth and development can be recognized as a source of enrichment rather than as divisiveness among people. However, when historical references are made, the language used to describe children with special needs at that time will be retained.

Best Practices for Inclusive Early Childhood Programs

Advocacy group a group of individuals who work together for a particular cause; the Epilepsy Association works to ensure equal access, opportunity, and acceptance within society for persons with epilepsy

Researchers, professional organizations, parent organizations, and **advocacy groups** in the early childhood field have put forth general principles for inclusive programs (Frankel et al., 2010; Guralnick, 2008; Irwin, 1997; Irwin, Lero, & Brophy, 2000; Langford, 1997; Odom, 2002). These principles are equally useful when discussing quality early childhood education programs for *all* children. They can be used to identify the *best practices* for meeting the needs of young children with special needs in early childhood programs. Practices have to reflect or be compatible with the following principles:

- research-based and value-based
- family-centred
- bias-free
- transdisciplinary approach to programming
- chronologically age-appropriate
- allow for full participation

The following is a brief description of each of these principles.

Research-Based and Value-Based

Accountability must be a cornerstone practice for teachers working with all young children and their families. Inclusive practices, strategies, and techniques used in early child education require empirical research support. Research shows, for example, that teachers who practise inclusive education flexibly use a range of strategies that are responsive to children's individual needs (Underwood, Valeo, & Wood, 2012). At the same time, inclusive education is driven by social values so that "it is not simply about placement, but about having access to education that optimizes each child's potential through teaching practices, as well as fair treatment from other children, families, staff, and community members who are part of the school" (Underwood et al., 2012).

Family-Centred

In family-centred or family-focused intervention, practices are designed with, rather than for, the child and family. This view of intervention acknowledges that the child is part of a dynamic family system and that any change in the system (e.g., intervention or change in programs) affects all parts of the system. Families should have the right to choose their involvement level in program planning and advocacy.

Recognition and Appreciation of Differences

Recommended practices embrace a perspective and celebrate the concept of family uniqueness. *Family uniqueness* encompasses ethnic, racial, linguistic, and socioeconomic differences, as well as the unique structure and traditions of individual families. This is especially important as our society becomes more diverse, with families that may encompass unique blends of backgrounds. This perspective recognizes and respects the different needs and value systems of the children and families. Educators translate this perspective into practice by developing programs that naturally integrate the recognition and appreciation of differences into everyday activities. Educators supporting inclusive practices question their attitudes toward differences. They acknowledge bias and prejudice in themselves and others and work effectively to intervene in situations of discrimination.

Transdisciplinary Approach to Programming

Early childhood and early childhood special education programs should involve professionals from different disciplines working as a team on behalf of young children and their families. Disciplines often represented on early childhood teams include speech pathology, audiology, occupational therapy, physical therapy, nursing, medicine, art therapy, nutrition, psychology, music therapy, and social work. Team members share expertise in their own disciplines and work cooperatively with other professionals. (Chapter 3 provides additional information about transdisciplinary teams.)

Chronologically Age-Appropriate

For children with developmental differences, the issue of chronologically age-appropriate practices is crucial. This principle challenges researchers and practitioners to consider an individual child's unique learning needs while developing an intervention program within a chronologically age-appropriate environment. In other words, a five-year-old child with special needs should be using materials and exploring environments that his or her peers are using and exploring, regardless of the child's developmental levels.

Full Participation

Full participation refers to opportunities for individuals with special needs to go to school and participate in education experiences, as do other children and youth. For young children these experiences may include preschool, child care, swimming lessons, play groups, trips to the movies, religious training, and dance lessons. A family with a child with special needs should have the same range of activities and services available to them as any other family. At the same time, extra supports (e.g., financial grants, lower staff-to-child ratios) are provided, enabling children with special needs to participate in all activities. Irwin (1997) referred to the principle of **zero reject**, in which no child is ever excluded for reasons of level or type of special need from participating fully in a program or service. Using this principle, children with special needs are never limited to shorter days or excluded from some types of programs (see photo, left). The 2009 SpeciaLink Early Childhood Inclusion Quality Scale is a Canadian developed tool for measuring inclusion quality in child care settings. The tool consists of two sections, an inclusion practices profile and an inclusion principles scale; the examples in Tables 1-1 and 1-2

Zero reject no child is ever excluded for reasons of level or type of special need from full participation in a program or service

Inclusion increases awareness and promotes acceptance.

© Cengage Learning

TABLE 1-1

Principle 1: Zero Reject

In fully inclusive child care centres, *all* children are welcome, regardless of type or level of disability. Many child care centres referred to as "inclusive" actually integrate only children with mild to moderate disabilities, or children with a single disability. Children who are not toilet-trained, who are not ambulatory, who have behavioural disorders, or who have special health care needs are most likely to be excluded. (Read this statement to the Director as you begin to discuss Principle #1 in a non-judgmental tone. Then use probe questions, as necessary, and record comments.)

Some probe questions: (1) Have you been, or would you be, unable to accept children with any particular level or type of disability? If "yes," what type of disability(ies) or level(s) are these? (2) Children with what types of disability and levels of disability (mild/moderate/ severe/profound) have you been able to accommodate in your centre? Record as "comment."

Inadequate 1	Minimal 3	Good 5	Excellent 7
1.1 ☐Y ☐N Director describes previous and present inclusion of children with disabilities in terms of very subjective criteria, such as "very nice parent," "seemed easy to include," "we were forced to."	3.1 ☐Y ☐N Director specifies some[1] types[2] and levels of disability that the centre can accommodate.	5.1 ☐Y ☐N Director specifies many[1] types[2] and levels of disability that the centre can accommodate.	7.1 ☐Y ☐N Director specifies that the centre will enroll children with all levels and types of disability—actively following the principle of zero reject.
1.2 ☐Y ☐N Lead ECE is not aware of previous or present enrollment of children with disabilities in her classroom.	3.2 ☐Y ☐N Lead ECE is aware of previous or present enrollment of some[1] children with disabilities in her classroom.	5.2 ☐Y ☐N Lead ECE is aware of many[1] children with disabilities, previously and presently enrolled, including some specifics about accommodations and modifications to include them.	7.2 ☐Y ☐N Lead ECE, another ECE, a support staff (such as secretary or cook), and a parent[3] all articulate zero reject principle as their own and as the centre's.
1.3 ☐Y ☐N The centre has no written or verbal policy on inclusion.	3.3 ☐Y ☐N The centre has an informal policy on inclusion (evidenced by Director's comments and supported by such evidence as accessible materials on diversity including pictures, books, dolls with disabilities, or by the presence of information and training opportunities on inclusion being available to staff).	5.3 ☐Y ☐N The centre has a written policy statement that supports inclusion.	7.3 ☐Y ☐N The centre has a written inclusion policy statement that affirms the zero reject principle, with a phrase such as *all children.*"

[1] "Some" means three or fewer; "Many" means four or more.

[2] "Types of disability" refers to diagnosis, such as autistic, intellectual, physical, visual, auditory. "Levels" refers to intensity, such as mild, moderate, or severe.

[3] "A parent" means the first parent (or close family member) of a child with special needs whom you see—in the locker room, at arrival or departure, or identified through probe question. A telephone call to a parent, initiated by the Director, can also be used for this indicator.

POINTS OF CLARIFICATION:

- All *Principles* are about the entire centre: the *Practices* are about an individual classroom. In all instances, you will interview the Lead Educator (or the most senior ECE in the classroom) as well as the Director.
- Some observers confuse "zero reject" (Principle 1) with "natural proportions" (Principle 2). Principle 1 should NOT be understood to be about "how many children with special needs are enrolled?" That question is taken up under Principle 2. Principle 1 is about possible limitations of types and levels of disability, not about numbers.
- 7.2 If there is no support staff, interview a third ECE, preferably from another classroom. If there is only one staff in the classroom, ignore the section about support staff. If no parent of a child with special needs is present, ask the Director to telephone one and ask permission for you to speak with him/her.

Source: *SpeciaLink Early Childhood Inclusion Quality Scale*, Breton Books (2013). Irwin, S.H. Reprinted with permission.

TABLE 1-2

Practice 9: Involvement of Typical Children

Note frequency and intensity of play that involves children with special needs and typically developing children—especially in dramatic play area, block area, out of doors, and during free play times.

Inadequate 1	Minimal 3	Good 5	Excellent 7
1.1 ☐Y ☐N Typically developing children rarely interact with children with special needs. 1.2 ☐Y ☐N Staff take no active role in encouraging social inclusion. 1.3 ☐Y ☐N Competition is used frequently to motivate children to perform.	3.1 ☐Y ☐N Typically developing children sometimes[1] interact with children with special needs in group social play situations. (That means that during at least 25% of the time when children with special needs are in group play situations such as the Dramatic Play area and the Block area, they are not ignored and left out of the play.) 3.2 ☐Y ☐N Staff make comments or gestures to promote social inclusion. 3.3 ☐Y ☐N Cooperation is motivated occasionally, by adult requests.	5.1 ☐Y ☐N Children with special needs are often[1] included in group social play. 5.2 ☐Y ☐N Staff suggests appropriate roles or dramatic situations that are inclusionary. 5.3 ☐Y ☐N Cooperation is stressed through planned activities that require more than one child to accomplish.	7.1 ☐Y ☐N Children with special needs are included in group social play most of the time.[1] 7.2 ☐Y ☐N Staff systematically use techniques of scripting, cooperative learning, valued object sharing, etc., to promote social inclusion. 7.3 ☐Y ☐N Staff receive specific training in promotion of inclusive social play. 7.4 ☐Y ☐N Cooperation is motivated frequently by adult verbal statements AND by activities that need more than one child to accomplish.

1 "Sometimes" means 25% of the time; "Often" means 50% of the time; "Most of the time" means over 75% of the time.

POINTS OF CLARIFICATION:

7.2 "Scripting" is a peer-mediated strategy designed to teach a socially advanced peer to promote the involvement of another child—often one with autism.

7.3 This indicator would be met by workshops such as *Making Friends* and by other workshops also based on M. Guralnick's *Assessment of Peer Relations*. Other workshops of at least 8 hours duration that focus on facilitated social play, such as SpeciaLink's *Social Play in Inclusive Child Care Settings* and the training, planning, and use of *Social Stories*™, would also meet this indicator.

Source: *SpeciaLink Early Childhood Inclusion Quality Scale*, Breton Books (2013). Irwin, S.H. Reprinted with permission.

illustrate how the full participation of children with special needs can be assessed in an early childhood setting.

Reverse integration is the term used to describe programs in which children without special needs participate in programs originally established for children with special needs. In reverse integration programs, the number of children who require extra support is equal to or more than the number of children who do not require extra support. Rafferty and Griffin (2005), drawing upon the perspectives of parents and teachers, documented the benefits and risks of reverse inclusion for preschoolers with and without disabilities. Some professionals and researchers believe that the optimal situation is one in which the percentage of children with special needs in an inclusive program is the same as the percentage found within the specific community. Irwin referred to this as the principle of naturally occurring proportions (Irwin, 1997).

Note that all provinces and territories in Canada have their own legislation pertaining to the education of children with special needs. Children in the public education system have the right to access services under the Canadian Charter of Rights and Freedoms. Because early childhood programs are optional, equal access and participation are not guaranteed. Thus, in Canada the move toward including all children is voluntary. Funding, training, and resourcing have often followed decisions by programs to include children with special needs, but without cohesive legislation and regulatory or financial support, it can be easier to find barriers than to create opportunities for inclusion.

Though some of these problems still need addressing, there is fairly general agreement at this time that inclusion of children with special needs is a sound and ethical policy.

Reverse integration programs in which children without special needs participate in programs originally established for children with special needs

Inclusion in Perspective

Early Attitudes

The number of children with diverse abilities participating in community programs has increased steadily over the past 30 years. This is in marked contrast to the way children with special needs were viewed in the past. In 1973 Caldwell described three stages that North American society has gone through in its treatment of children with special needs, and we have included a fourth stage to describe the current approach.

FORGET AND HIDE Until the middle of the twentieth century, families, communities, and society in general seemed to try to deny the existence of people with disabilities. As much as possible, these children were kept out of sight. Families often were advised to institutionalize immediately any infant who was born with a disability.

In 1958, the Canadian Association for Retarded Children (now called the Canadian Association for Community Living) was established. One person in Canada who contributed much to the process of changing attitudes toward those with special needs was Jean Vanier, son of the Right Honourable Georges P. Vanier, governor general of Canada. Jean Vanier began by working with people who had intellectual impairments. He was inspired by Gandhi's love and acceptance of the underprivileged and the untouchables in India. In 1964, through Vanier's efforts, a small home known as l'Arche was opened in the village of Trosly-Breuil, France, for patients who lived in local institutions for the mentally retarded. Supported by volunteers from Canada and other countries, the people who lived in l'Arche actively joined in village life and were accepted by its citizens. The l'Arche model became the basis for a movement that developed similar centres throughout Europe and North America. The first Canadian l'Arche community was founded in the early 1970s.

SCREEN AND SEGREGATE The purpose of the "screen and segregate" period was to identify individuals with disabilities and provide them with a program separate from their peers without special needs. This movement grew partly out of the belief that individuals were better served within the segregated or specialized group setting.

In the 1960s and early 1970s, parents, through their local advocacy associations, began pressing provincial and territorial governments to fund early childhood programs for their children with disabilities. Often, mothers of children with disabilities became activists leading campaigns to close segregated institutions and secure human rights for their children (Panitch, 2008). Some provinces took legislative action.

For example, in 1972, the Day Nurseries Act in Ontario was amended to provide a funding mechanism for services for children with developmental handicaps. At this time, the Ministry of Community and Social Services also provided funding to open programs for school-aged children excluded from local public school programs due to the severity of their intellectual impairment.

As a consequence of this process, a segregated system was developed, separate from the one available to other same-aged children (see photo, below).

It was not until the early 1980s that the Ontario Ministry of Education provided educational services for all school-aged children.

IDENTIFY AND HELP The "screen and segregate" period lasted for 20 years or more, at which point the rights of people with disabilities began to be recognized. The "identify and help" period began in the 1970s because of social and political activities. Wolf Wolfensberger at the National Institute on Mental Retardation (later known as the G. Allan Roeher Institute, York University, Toronto) advocated for the integration of persons with special needs into all aspects of the "normal" social system (Wolfensberger, 1972). This movement included

Programs designed exclusively for children with special needs were developed in the late 1960s and early 1970s.

advocating for the integration of young children with special needs into regular early childhood settings. In the mid-1970s, large institutions for intellectually impaired and emotionally disturbed children were downsized or closed and residents returned to mainstream society. The philosophy of normalization and integration at that time was broadened to include all children with special needs, not just those defined as mentally retarded. By 1982, the federal government had adopted the Charter of Rights and Freedoms; this helped to prevent discrimination on the basis of disability (see Chapter 2).

INCLUDE AND SUPPORT This stage came after Caldwell's stages. The underlying assumption of the "include and support" period is that people with special needs should be included as full members of society and that they should be provided with appropriate supports, such as education and accessible environments, to ensure their full and meaningful participation.

Rationale for Early Intervention and Inclusion

Early childhood education has been gaining widespread acceptance in our society since the middle of the twentieth century. The formal inclusion of all young children regardless of ability is relatively new to the early education scene, though the acceptance of children with special needs has occurred informally within many programs. The rationale for early childhood inclusion will be discussed in terms of ethical issues, socialization concerns, developmental considerations, and cost-effectiveness problems.

The Ethical Issue

The right of children with special needs to live as full a life as possible has been a major ethical force among integration and inclusion advocates. It was Dunn (1968) who first brought into public consciousness the unfairness of segregated education for people with disabilities. He asserted that special classes, for the most part, provided inadequate education for children with disabilities and developmental delays. Advocacy for the inclusion of children with disabilities runs parallel to advocacy for bias-free early education. The goal these two social movements have in common is to gain acceptance in our educational system for all children—those with cultural, gender, racial, socioeconomic, intellectual, or physical differences. Until this is accomplished, ethical issues related to any kind of segregation in our child care and educational systems remain unresolved.

The Socialization Issue

Including young children with diverse abilities implies that these children will be given equal social status with all other children. Inclusion promotes awareness of human differences. Members of the community become more accustomed to children with diverse abilities; this leads to greater acceptance. It cannot be overemphasized that young children with special needs are entitled to the same kinds of enriching early experiences as all other children. As Haring and McCormick (1990) pointed out, "separating young children with handicaps from normal experiences creates distance, misunderstanding, and rejection.... Moreover, separating these youngsters from the real world means that there must be reentry. Reentry problems can be avoided by not removing the child from normal settings" (p. 102).

Young children with special needs who play and interact only with other children with special needs will not learn a range of developmentally and culturally appropriate social skills. Play with all children must be an integral part of any program designed to promote healthy development in young children with special needs (Lieber, Schwartz, Sandall, Horn, & Ashworth Wolery, 2003).

All children, during their preschool years, should have the opportunity to get to know children with diverse abilities, especially children whose differences are obvious—children who are blind or deaf, those who have physical disabilities, and those who have cognitive disabilities. During their very early years, all children, unless otherwise influenced, will accept children who are developmentally different. In fact, a difference may not even figure in a child's efforts to describe a classmate. One parent tells the following story:

> Andrea came back from preschool saying she wanted to invite Katie home for lunch the next day. I could not figure out who Katie was. Andrea tried to describe Katie's hair, then her new jacket, then her paintings. I still couldn't place her. Finally Andrea said, "Katie's the one who comes with shiny ribbons in her hair," and I knew immediately who Katie was. She was the child in the wheelchair who always had big colourful bows at the ends of her braids! Apparently, being confined to a wheelchair was not one of Katie's outstanding characteristics for my child.

The Developmental Issues

The significance of the early years in laying the foundations for lifelong learning is all but indisputable. As described in Chapter 5, it is then that children acquire a broad range of skills in all areas of development. Figure 1-1 lists these skills.

A quality early childhood program can assist all children in acquiring the developmental skills outlined in Figure 1-1. The experience is of special benefit to children with developmental differences or children at risk for developmental problems. For these children, it is like opening a door to both the present and the future. An inclusive early childhood program may be their *only* access to appropriate early learning experiences. They will encounter a variety of challenging materials and equipment, as well as planned and unplanned activities. There will be interactions with all kinds of children who serve as models to imitate and to play with, children who will help and who will need help. There will be teachers who understand differences in development and will assist all children, regardless of their developmental abilities, in taking advantage of sensitive learning periods and teachable moments.

Sensitive or critical periods a time when a child is especially responsive and able to learn a particular skill

SENSITIVE OR CRITICAL PERIODS The majority of young children acquire basic developmental skills on their own. Some of these skills, however, seem to come about more readily at particular times. These are referred to as developmentally **sensitive or critical periods**. During these periods, children appear to be especially responsive and able to learn from specific kinds of stimulation (see Box 1-2). The same stimulation at other times is thought to have little impact on development. It is important that all children be in an enriched and responsive

FIGURE 1-1

Basic Developmental Skills

1. They learn to move about, to get from one place to another independently, to explore and experiment.

2. They become skilled at grasping, holding on to, releasing, and manipulating evermore complex objects.

3. They become increasingly able to take care of their personal needs: toileting, dressing, eating.

4. They acquire their native language and use it in a variety of ways to get what they need (and prefer) from others in their environment.

5. They develop the ability to think, generate ideas, solve problems, make judgments, and influence others.

6. They respond with increasingly sophisticated words and gestures when others speak to them or attempt to influence them.

7. They discover ways of getting along with and interacting with others—those who are like themselves and those who are different.

Source: © Cengage Learning

BOX 1-2

THE IMPORTANCE OF RELATIONSHIPS

Research has shown that secure, loving family relationships contribute significantly to a child's developing brain. As cited in Dann (2011), Cairns stated,

> It is now clear that the brain of the developing infant is more radically shaped and structured by the quality of interactions between the infant and the environment than we had previously thought. Children whose environment is hostile or lacking in nurture end up thinking with a very different brain. (Cairns, 2002, p. 46)

If children are not given adequate stimulation, there may be fewer connections being made in the brain. For young children who experience disruption in attachment due to abuse or trauma, the brain is affected biochemically. When children experience trauma, this can lead to stress. Increased stress levels produce high levels of hormones, which alter the neurobiology of the brain and central nervous system. The caregiver's role is to reduce the impact of stress; if a child does not receive this support from a caregiver, the child is likely to have difficulties controlling stress levels. This will lead to the child either dissociating or shutting down to avoid being totally overwhelmed by the high level of stress. These responses are likely to become part of the brain's response in the future, resulting in more extreme fight, flight, or freeze reactions related to stress.

Dann also stated that it may be tempting to say that the damage is already done and that these children will always struggle with their learning and their relationships, but this fails to recognize the importance that future teaching and learning may have on the child's ability to cope with stress and to learn. She went on to state that evidence is still emerging within neuroscience research. She cited Wilson (2002, 197), who contended that "the notion of the first three years as a critical period for brain development is not as yet substantiated by the research." The brain retains plasticity well beyond the early years, and "even in situations of child neglect there can often be recovery." This hope of recovery makes the need for quality programs and well-trained educators even more significant.

Your Turn

Relate the idea above to the issue of sensitive or critical periods as described in the book. Why does this information make the need for quality programs even more significant?

Sources: Cairns, K. (2002). *Attachment, trauma and resilience: Therapeutic caring for children*. London, England: British Association for Adoption and Fostering; Dann, R. (2011). Look out! "Looked after"! Look here! Supporting "looked after" and adopted children in the primary classroom. *Education 3-13: International Journal of Primary, Elementary and Early Years Education, 39*(5), 455–465; Wilson, H. (2002). Brain science, early intervention and "at risk" families: Implications for parents, professionals and social policy. *Social Policy and Society, 7*(3), 191–202.

learning environment during these periods. For children with developmental differences, it may be even more essential (UNICEF, 2012).

A developmental disability often prevents a child from reacting in ordinary ways during a sensitive period. Parents, especially new parents, on their own in the home setting, may not recognize signals from their child that a critical learning period is at hand. By contrast, teachers in an inclusive setting, where there is a range of developmental differences among children, tend to pick up on all kinds of subtle behavioural variations and many forms of communication.

Critical learning periods that are not recognized and not utilized are common among infants and children who are visually or hearing impaired. Think of the learning experiences so readily available to most children: hearing the difference between the doorbell and the telephone; puzzling over a birdcall, a flash of lightning, or an angry face. These children turn automatically, dozens of times a day, to look and listen and learn specific things at specific times.

These same cues, quite literally, are *not there* for the child with a sensory impairment. Without special assistance and opportunities to follow the lead of other children who are responding to what is going on, the child with a sensory impairment is isolated from everyday events.

Language acquisition appears especially linked to a critical period in development. A child with a hearing impairment may never acquire adequate communication skills if the hearing loss is not treated before what is thought to be the critical period for language development. Conversely, a child whose hearing impairment is identified early may experience fewer difficulties in language development. A combination of appropriate treatment and a special education program for the hearing impaired or an inclusive preschool (or a combination, depending on the child's age and severity of loss) allows for building on critical learning periods as they occur.

Children with physical differences are also denied critical learning opportunities, but for different reasons. Many cannot move themselves about. They cannot explore their environment. They may not be able to open doors, get into cupboards, run to the window—or learn by simply getting into mischief. Contrast this with children who are physically able and on the move from morning to night. They are touching, reaching, running, tumbling, climbing, and getting into this and that. They try adults' patience at times, especially during critical learning periods when they seem to be in constant motion, as in the following example.

The infant who is learning to walk is forever on the go. Once walking is mastered, a great cognitive advance seems to take place. Then comes another surge of motor development. The child learns to run, jump, and climb, practising these skills relentlessly, all day long. Conversely, those who do not walk until late childhood may have continuing challenges. They may never become skilled at activities that involve sustained running, jumping, and climbing. Even more serious, they may have missed other critical aspects of early learning during the sensorimotor stage when cognitive development and motor activity are so interdependent.

TEACHABLE MOMENTS For teachers in an inclusive setting, another concept of developmental significance is that of **teachable moments**. These are points in time (perhaps associated with critical periods) when a child is highly motivated and better able to learn particular skills, such as walking, riding a tricycle, or learning to count. All children, including those with a severe impairment, have many such teachable moments (see photo, page 19). They can occur any time throughout daily routines and activities. It is important that teachers recognize these opportunities and ensure they lead to appropriate learning activities. Teachers also can

Teachable moments a specific points when a child's level of readiness and interest come together to create the best milieu for new teaching help parents understand the significance of teachable moments and guide parents in recognizing them and finding ways of responding. The inclusive program is an especially suitable place for parents to observe teachers and try out various ways of working with their child.

The infant who is blind and getting ready to learn to walk is a good illustration of a teachable moment. First, though, think about developmental sequences and the infant who is sighted. Walking usually is preceded by a period of just standing, then holding on to furniture, and finally cruising about. Most infants do this spontaneously; no teaching is necessary, and no special arrangements are needed.

On his or her own, the baby who cannot see may barely progress beyond the standing stage. What is needed is someone who recognizes pulling-to-stand as a teachable moment and helps the baby build on it. Experienced parents usually recognize the sign; inexperienced parents may not. The teacher in an infant program should be geared to such moments and ready to adapt the environment and provide specific supports. The more the infant who is visually impaired (or any other infant) moves about, the more the infant progresses in every area of development. In fact, a major reason for using teachable moments as often as possible is to keep the child involved in the process of learning.

Throughout the program day, all children have teachable moments.

Courtesy of Bloorview—Scarborough Site

IMITATION Another important rationale for inclusion is that young children with special needs will observe and imitate more advanced skills modelled by peers (Charlesworth, 2014). The logic is sound—**peer imitating** is a major avenue of learning for everyone, old and young alike.

Young children learn by doing. If children with developmental differences are to learn to play appropriately, they must have children around them who play appropriately and whom they can imitate. If children with poor social skills are to learn to share and take turns, they must have opportunities to imitate and interact with children who know how to share and take turns. If a young child who is hearing impaired is to learn to initiate conversations, there must be peers available who are interesting and appropriate conversational partners. In a segregated setting where there are only children with hearing impairments, it is unlikely that children will do much talking or modelling of appropriate language skills for one another. This is a powerful argument for inclusion of all children in group settings. Totally segregated programs can lead to even greater developmental disruption. When there are no appropriate behaviours to imitate, inappropriate and purposeless behaviours tend to dominate.

Until the late 1950s, for example, many children with Down syndrome were institutionalized soon after birth. Though they often were in an early childhood wing of a residential building, their playmates were children like themselves. The playmates, too, had been institutionalized at an early age. They, too, had never had opportunities to learn even the most basic developmental skills. And so the myth was perpetuated for generations that children with Down syndrome were unteachable.

What many of these children did learn through imitation was a variety of bizarre or self-destructive behaviours. As noted, their only models were other institutionalized children who had few appropriate social behaviours. Today an infant with Down syndrome is rarely institutionalized; many are included in

Peer imitating young children with special needs observe and imitate more advanced skills modelled by peers community early childhood programs. Most will acquire basic developmental skills and attain varying degrees of academic achievement.

The Cost Issue

In Canada, the cost of a full-day child care space varies greatly across provinces and territories, depending on a number of variables, including the age of the child. However, in general, most Canadian parents struggle to meet their child care costs. Because of the greater number of adults required for infant group care, infant programs are more costly than group care for preschool and school-aged children. To address these challenges, child care advocates have long pushed for a publicly funded system of early childhood services.

Most programs serving young children with special needs use specifically trained early childhood educators or persons with parallel training. In addition, many consultants are used, such as physiotherapists, occupational therapists, speech pathologists, registered nurses, behaviour consultants, and others, including those trained in signing or orientation and mobility skills. Since the staff required for children with special needs is usually greater than regular staff requirements, the cost of operating quality inclusive programs is relatively higher. Because of government grants, the actual fee paid by parents of children with special needs should be no different from that paid by other parents.

The fees vary across provinces and territories, as do the program options (for example, full- or half-day, segregated or integrated programs). In many areas throughout Canada, there are waiting lists for services for all children, including children with special needs.

Another aspect of the cost issue is the large number of children with special needs who continue to go unserved or who are cared for in unsupervised settings. Simply put, there are not enough inclusive, affordable, quality early childhood programs to go around. Investing public money in additional segregated, rather than inclusive, programs would be a setback—philosophically and financially—in meeting the developmental needs of all young children (Halfon & Friendly, 2013). In the case of children with special needs, it is vital to begin to support parents and begin the intervention process, as well as to provide an inclusive environment for the child, at an early age. The cost to the public of a "late start" may be substantial as the child grows older. (See Chapter 3 regarding the role of parents.)

Supporting Inclusion: Implications for Teachers

The mere act of placing children with special needs into inclusive environments is not enough. Teachers must take responsibility for ensuring that effective socializing and learning occur among all the children. Particular teacher skills are needed. Many of these skills stem from knowledge of child development (see photo, page 21). Effective inclusion requires responsibilities listed in Figure 1-2.

Structuring Child–Child Interaction

The effectiveness of inclusion depends on the interactions between children who require extra support and those who do not. Peer interactions do not necessarily

FIGURE 1-2

Teachers' Responsibilities for Effective Inclusion

- Individualizing programs and activities to meet each child's specific needs and abilities
- Arranging a highly engaging learning environment that encourages appropriate behaviour
- Recognizing that all children belong and that although a specific behaviour may be inappropriate in a particular setting, the goal is to support the child in learning a more appropriate alternative for that behaviour
- Recognizing the value of play as a major avenue of learning for all children; at the same time, recognizing that play skills often have to be taught to children with disabilities, many of whom neither know how to play nor play spontaneously
- Arranging a balance of large- and small-group experiences, both vigorous and quiet, so that all children, at their own levels, can be active and interactive participants
- Structuring a learning environment in which children with diverse abilities are helped to participate together in a variety of activities related to all areas of development
- Creating a nurturing environment by providing a curriculum that emphasizes friendship, caring, and respect for diversity
- Assessing children's progress periodically and using this information to adjust curriculum and instruction
- Providing a flexible curriculum by making adjustments to the instruction and environment to address children's needs
- Supporting the development of all children by creating a learning and playing environment that includes a range of materials and activities to ensure that all children can successfully engage with and be challenged in this environment
- Collaborating with other team members (i.e., speech therapists, parents, occupational therapists, paraprofessionals) regarding progress and intervention

Source: © Cengage Learning

occur. Guralnick and his colleagues (Guralnick & Neville, 1997) continue to conduct research on this issue. Their research indicates that all children play together when *the teacher structures the environment to promote such interaction.* (Chapters 4 and 15 discuss ways for teachers to accomplish this structure.)

In another study that focused on imitation in an inclusive classroom, Garfinkle and Schwartz (1998) demonstrated that children with autism can learn to imitate their peers during small-group activities. After the imitation training, the amount of time children with autism played together with peers in small groups during free-choice time increased. From these and other research studies, it is apparent that teacher-structuring of play activities is essential. Curriculum planning for an inclusive early childhood program must focus on activities that lead to all children in an inclusive environment working and playing together (see Chapter 15).

Planning Classroom Activities

Curriculum planning for inclusive classrooms also requires teachers to integrate the goals identified

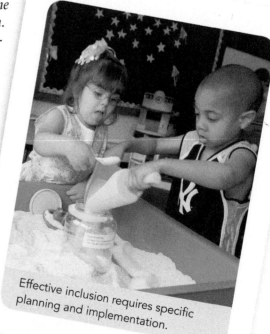

Effective inclusion requires specific planning and implementation.

© Cengage Learning

Members of the transdisciplinary team plan together.

© Cengage Learning

on the children's IPP/IFSP in ongoing classroom activities. This approach allows teachers to use learning experiences in dramatic play, art, nature walks, and water play to address specific goals and objectives across developmental domains (e.g., cognitive, social, communication, motor, self-help/care).

Professional Collaboration

In addition to classroom practices, full inclusion of all children requires integrating professional efforts. Administrators, teachers, aides, volunteers, health-care and social-services professionals, and members of the transdisciplinary team need to work together (see photo, above). Within an inclusive setting, professional growth comes with the collaborative search for ways to provide for children who have developmental differences. Part of the search has to do with looking for paths that lead to a genuine partnership with parents. As discussed in Chapters 3 and 11, this means listening to parents, consulting with them, and learning from them. In fact, everyone—children, parents, teachers, classroom staff, and clinicians—can learn from one another in an inclusive early childhood setting. Early childhood teachers, however, receive a special bonus: In learning to meet the needs of children who require extra support, they become more skilled at meeting the needs of all children. By learning to build on the capabilities of children with special needs, they become better attuned to the special capabilities of all children.

Benefits of Inclusion for Young Children

Benefits for Children with Special Needs

In addition to the philosophical and legal issues discussed earlier, there are a number of specific benefits of educating young children with special needs in inclusive programs. Children with developmental differences are likely to benefit from a quality, inclusive early childhood environment because it provides

- more stimulating, varied, and responsive experiences than do segregated classrooms, where all the children have special needs;

- developmental scaffolding for curriculum activities, rather than a *deficit curriculum model* in which the major emphasis is on children's limitations rather than their strengths;

- opportunities to observe, interact with, and imitate children who have acquired higher-level motor, social, language, and cognitive skills;

- implicit motivation to "try a little harder," in that more skillful children expect and encourage improved behaviours from those children with lesser skills; and

- opportunities to learn directly from other children. It appears that certain skills are learned more easily from other children—their explanations and demonstrations are often closer to the capabilities of the child with special needs than are those of the adults.

Benefits for All Children

DEVELOPMENTAL PROGRESS Children who are developing at an expected pace benefit from inclusive programs "at least to the same degree and sometimes to a greater degree than would have been expected if they had attended non-integrated preschools" (Thurman & Widerstrom, 1990, p. 39). There is no evidence of negative effects on any children who are in inclusive programs (Odom, Buysse, & Soukakou, 2011). In studies that have compared the amount of teacher attention to individual children, and children's rate of engaged learning time—in classrooms with and without children with special needs—there are no differences, again suggesting no negative impact on child development (see photo, below). Another safe conclusion to draw from the current research, according to these authors, is that *the developmental outcome for children in inclusive programs depends on the quality of teaching* and on how well the teacher is provided with special supports when needed, rather than on the process of inclusion itself.

Peer tutoring one child instructing or assisting another

PEER TUTORING A well-documented benefit of inclusion for all children is **peer tutoring**—one child instructing another. It appears that both the child being tutored and the child doing the tutoring receive significant benefits from the experience. The common sense of this is readily apparent; most of us have discovered that, given an unpressured opportunity to teach someone else something we know (or are learning), our own skill and understanding are increased. The same is true of children. As pointed out by Spodek, Saracho, and Lee (1984), voluntary peer tutoring among young children of all developmental levels can promote

- social interactions among children with and without special needs;

- acceptable play behaviours; and

- appropriate and enhanced use of materials.

Peer tutoring (a child demonstrating to another child how to do something) should not be confused with peer modelling (the unconscious process that occurs when a child observes and interacts with

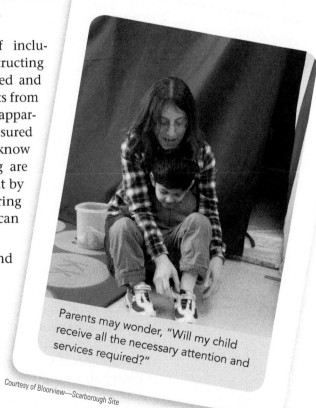

Parents may wonder, "Will my child receive all the necessary attention and services required?"

Courtesy of Bloorview—Scarborough Site

other children). Both peer tutoring and peer modelling enhance the development of children with special needs.

DEVELOPMENT OF SENSITIVITY Rafferty, Boettcher, and Griffin (2001) surveyed 244 parents of children who attended a community-based preschool in New York. Almost all parents surveyed reported that inclusion helped typically developing children to understand differences in others. The children developed sensitivity and became increasingly aware of their own strengths and weaknesses.

Benefits for Families

In general, parents' attitudes about inclusion were influenced by their experiences with inclusion (Lamorey & Bricker, 1993; Palmer, Fuller, Arora, & Nelson, 2001). Parents of children with special needs were most often positive in their responses, although they did identify some concerns. Attitudes of parents of children without special needs improved as experience with inclusion increased. In a study involving 125 parents of children who attended inclusive preschool programs, Peck, Carlson, and Helmstetter (1992) found that parents perceived their children's experience as generally positive and were supportive of inclusive education. Additionally, Peck and his colleagues found that parents reported that their children were more accepting of human differences and had less discomfort with people with developmental differences and people who looked or behaved differently from the way they did.

Benefits for Society

Not only does inclusion have positive effects on all children, but it also appears to be of long-term benefit to society. Children who grow up with opportunities to interact with children with special needs are likely to be more tolerant in later years. They tend to mature into adults with greater understanding and respect for those who have diverse abilities in our society. Many teachers report that most young children, unless influenced by inappropriate adult attitudes, have a natural acceptance of individual differences. They are unlikely to make negative judgments and comparisons of children who are developmentally different. When they do comment or ask questions, they are doing so because they need to learn about whatever it is that is unfamiliar about the child who requires extra support.

The Concerns and Challenges of Inclusion

As noted repeatedly, the inclusion of young children with special needs in a preschool setting appears to be of general benefit to everyone. Even so, concerns continue to be voiced. This section reviews arguments for and against the practice. Such arguments, however, must be based on the assumption that the studies were conducted in a quality program with well-trained and caring adults in a ratio appropriate to the number of children enrolled (Friendly & Prentice, 2009). A poorly structured, poorly staffed program can have a negative effect on any child, from the most delayed to the most gifted. In the United States, inclusion is the law. In Canada, though not required by law, the inclusion of young children with special needs in early childhood community programs is recognized as a preferred practice. The pros and cons of early inclusion continue to be raised and to be the focus of considerable research. The discussion that follows has to do with identifying the most common concerns and providing brief glimpses of research findings that address those issues.

Case Study ▪ How much to share? ▪

One of the challenges faced by parents of children with special needs is how much information to share about their child with potential early childhood programs. Some parents have faced rejection from care providers when they hear the child has special needs, often before they have even met the child. On the other hand, once parents have found a program, it is critical that the staff have the information needed to provide proper care and effective teaching. Think about how you would approach this issue as a parent. What types of questions could you ask a program to determine whether it is a good fit? What are the potential problems, if any, of not sharing enough information or sharing too much information?

Will Special Needs Be Served?

Parents and teachers have expressed concern that the special needs of children with developmental differences may not be met adequately in a community early childhood program. They feel that teachers may not have the time or the skills needed. The opposite is of concern, also: If a program is meeting the special needs of some children, then what about the other children who do not require extra support? Are they going to be shortchanged?

This concern has been addressed in a number of research studies. By and large, the data indicate that most parents believe that their children benefit from inclusive programs (see photo, below). Again, the findings are based on well-structured programs with knowledgeable teachers. Little parent satisfaction is found in poor programs, integrated or otherwise. There is agreement that professionals need

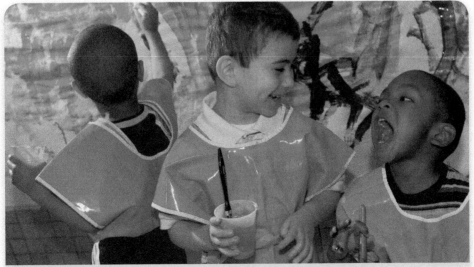

Most parents believe that inclusive programs benefit their children.

© Cengage Learning

additional knowledge to work collaboratively to deliver high-quality inclusive early childhood programs (Wiart, Kehler, Rempel, & Tough, 2011).

Many researchers have documented that the parents of children without special needs report that their children are learning important social and academic lessons from their experiences in inclusive classrooms (e.g., McGregor & Vogelsberg, 1998). A similar reaction is found among parents of children with special needs. Guralnick (1994) reported the following:

> Particular benefits to children with special needs were noted in relation to promoting the acceptance of children with disabilities in the community, preparing the child for the real world, encouraging children with special needs to learn more, and providing opportunities to participate in a wider variety of interesting and creative activities. (p. 180)

Another parent concern is the possible rejection of children with special needs by their peers. Palmer, Borthwick-Duffy, Widaman, and Best (1998) and Palmer et al. (2001) found that parents whose children display the most significant disabilities are less likely to favour inclusion. Parents opposing inclusion wrote statements indicating that the severity of their child's disability precluded the child from benefiting from inclusion, or that the general education program would not be accommodating or welcoming. Researchers have demonstrated and assert that there does not appear to be any basis for the fear of children being slighted, as an examination of successful programs at the preschool level demonstrates (Rafferty, Piscitelli, & Boettcher, 2003).

In general, teachers' attitudes are favourable toward inclusion, once they have actually worked with children with special needs in an inclusive setting. However, teachers' attitudes toward inclusion and the quality of an inclusive program can be affected by the amount and regularity of professional development opportunities focusing on working with children with disabilities (Irwin & Lero, 2008).

Concerns about Inappropriate Behaviours

Another frequently expressed concern is that children will learn immature or inappropriate behaviours from classmates who show less skilled behaviours. Again, this is an unfounded fear. This is not to imply that children do not imitate other children. They do. They should. As noted earlier, imitation is an important avenue for learning. But children learning new skills tend to imitate peers who have comparable or more skills. Rarely (and then only briefly) do they imitate less skilled behaviours of another child. The exceptions are those children who get undue attention from teachers and parents for imitating inappropriate behaviours.

Will Children with Special Needs Be Teased?

One of the important reasons to pursue inclusion is for the potential impact it can have on the attitudes of peers without special needs in regards to their classmates with special needs. It is believed that children without special needs who grow up with the opportunity to interact with children with special needs are more likely to show greater understanding of human differences (Daley, 2002).

Friendship and interactions do not just happen magically. Teachers must set up opportunities and model behaviour for all children. Adults must answer children's questions about differences in abilities openly and honestly (Dybvik, 2004). They must model accepting behaviour. This encourages children with and without special needs to form friendships and encourages children without special needs to assist their peers with special needs (Daley, 2002).

Case Study ▪ A caring community of learners ▪

Hayden is a four-year-old attending a community preschool. He has a diagnosis of autism. A classmate, Miles, came to school and announced that what Hayden has is contagious. For the last week, some of Hayden's classmates have refused to sit beside him at circle, and have been teasing him during playtime. Hayden is very upset by the change in his classmates.

Hayden's teacher has done her best to explain to the students that Hayden is not contagious and all the children are friends. Hayden has reported to his parents that Miles is mean, causing the parents to ask the teacher what is going on. What can the teacher do to change the class climate and create a caring community of learners?

Summary

Including young children with special needs in regular early childhood programs is the preferred practice in Canada. The degree to which a child is included in an early childhood program depends on his or her special needs and the intensity of the services that are required. The reasons for inclusion are based on ethical, social, developmental, and cost considerations. No longer is it acceptable, as it once was, to keep children with special needs out of the social and educational settings.

For children with and without developmental differences, the early years are critical years. A variety of learning seems to be *programmed* at particular times as a part of the developmental plan. These types of learning may never again be acquired as readily or as well. An abundance of *teachable moments* occur during infancy and the preschool period. These are best used in an inclusive setting with teachers who are trained to recognize such developmental opportunities. An inclusive early childhood program also provides opportunities for children with developmental disabilities to imitate their more skilled peers. At the same time, the peers of children with special needs are provided with significant learning experiences in helping children who are less able to acquire a variety of skills—motor, social, and intellectual. However, in inclusive settings, all children do not necessarily work and play together of their own accord. Teachers should structure the program so that interactions can occur and be reinforced.

A number of concerns about the advisability of inclusion continue to be voiced. A common one, expressed by both parents and teachers, is that the special needs of children may not be adequately met in an inclusive program. Another is that other children will receive less than their share of attention if children with special needs are properly served.

There is also the concern that some children will learn inappropriate and bizarre behaviours from children with special needs. Numerous research studies conducted over the past 15 years have demonstrated that these anxieties are largely unfounded. In fact, the opposite is true: The advantages of inclusion, for all children, are numerous and well documented.

Resources

The Canadian Abilities Foundation

http://www.abilities.ca

This website provides an opportunity for everyone to engage in dialogue around issues that are pertinent to people with disabilities, and has a variety of relevant resources and information.

Canadian Association for Community Living

http://www.cacl.ca

The Canadian Association for Community Living promotes the well-being of people with developmental disabilities and their families. Links to the organization's various provincial and territorial chapters are available at this site.

Marsha Forest Centre

http://www.MarshaForest.com

The centre focuses on developing future leaders and advocates for inclusion through programs, materials, and research to create a world where everyone belongs.

SpeciaLink: The National Centre for Child Care Inclusion

http://www.specialinkcanada.org

This organization's goal is to expand the quality and quantity of opportunities for inclusion in child care, recreation, education, and other community settings to young children with special needs and their families. Access the SpeciaLink Early Childhood Inclusion Quality Scale at this website.

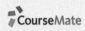 Access an interactive ebook and chapter-specific interactive learning tools, including flashcards, quizzes, videos, and more, in the *Inclusion in Early Childhood Programs* CourseMate. Visit NELSONbrain.com to log in, register, or purchase access.

Canadian Legislation: Support for Children through Early Intervention

2

OBJECTIVES

After studying the material in this chapter, the student will be able to

- Describe influential legislation on the history of child care in Canada.
- Describe how the Canada Assistance Plan Act influenced the growth of Canadian child care.
- Recognize the impact of the Canada Health and Social Transfer Act on child care in Canada.
- Understand the differences between legislation for children with special needs in Canada and legislation for children with special needs in the United States.
- Identify key differences between a social model and a medical model for understanding disability.
- Describe the importance of advocacy.

KEY CONCEPTS AND TERMS

advocacy   medical model   social model

Introduction

Public policy on behalf of infants and children with special needs (and children at risk for needing extra support during the developmental years) has been expanding steadily over the past several decades in North America. Beginning in the early 1960s, the Congress of the United States passed a number of laws that supported early identification, prevention, and treatment of developmental problems. Shortly thereafter, parallel legislative action took place in Canada.

At this time, Canadian activists—many of whom had disabilities or had children with special needs—began to question society's use of a **medical model** for understanding disabilities. They introduced a **social model** as an alternative.

To gain an appreciation of the differences that influenced the field of early childhood education in Canada and the United States, it is important to review the historical background against which Canadian early childhood legislation developed. The education and care of young Canadian children are the responsibility of provincial and territorial governments and not, as in the United States, the responsibility of the federal government. The chapter concludes with a discussion on the importance of advocacy in the field of inclusive early childhood education.

Medical model an approach to understanding disabilities that individualizes and pathologizes a disability as a biological impairment, a deficit, or a dysfunction residing within the person

Social model an approach to understanding disabilities that identifies the barriers that prevent the social inclusion of people with disabilities, and then focuses on the capacity of people with disabilities to change these barriers, with the help of others

Federal Legislation in Canada

The Influence of the British North America Act

The legislation of any young country influences the development of the services that it provides to its population. In Canada, the British North America Act of 1867 established that the federal government should take responsibility for those matters affecting all provinces, such as national defence. Provinces were to be responsible for local matters, such as education and social services (Friendly & Prentice, 2009). Therefore, child care and care for children with special needs (when it became available) were regarded as provincial and territorial concerns. A variety of child care centres and related services evolved in an informal manner as the need arose in each province and territory.

The War Measures Act: Its Impact on Child Care

It was not until World War II, with the passing of the War Measures Act, that the federal government provided funds for child care. Since more female workers were required to replace male workers in essential industries, the provision of child care became a priority legislative issue. The provincial governments and the federal (sometimes called "Dominion") government were asked to participate in the provision of daycare for those children whose mothers were employed in an essential industry.

The Dominion–Provincial Wartime Day Nurseries Agreement, under the War Measures Act, provided for shared funding between the federal government and any province that was interested in developing daycare for children (see photo, above). Thus, in 1942, a mother working in an essential industry in Ontario paid about 33 percent of the cost of daycare for her child or children, while the remainder of the cost was shared on a 50–50 basis between the federal and provincial governments (Stapleford, 1976, p. 2). This was the first time that child care was included in Canadian legislation.

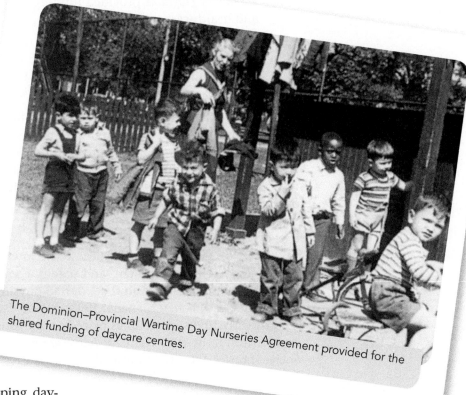

The Dominion–Provincial Wartime Day Nurseries Agreement provided for the shared funding of daycare centres.

Victoria Day Care Centre

Federal funding for child care was withdrawn after World War II when the War Measures Act expired. With the termination of the War Measures Act and the return of men to the workforce, it was expected that mothers would resume caring for their children in the home. Any continued cost sharing for child care was limited to agreements between local municipalities and provincial governments. Provincial legislation evolved as a result of pressures from women who wanted to continue to work outside the home. An example was the 1946 Day Nurseries Act in Ontario. More than 20 years passed before the federal government would once again provide a mechanism for the funding of child care.

The Canada Assistance Plan Act (1966–1996): Federal Support for Social Services

Despite public interest in continuing some form of cost sharing for child care services through federal legislation, it was not until the passing of the Canada Assistance Plan (CAP) Act in 1966 that certain welfare programs, including subsidized child care, entered the federal cost-sharing picture. Under this open-ended legislation, the federal government offered to share with any province or territory the cost of up to half the financial assistance required for children in child care whose families were deemed to qualify through a needs test or income test.

Note that funding specifically for children with special needs was not addressed in this legislation.

The Canada Assistance Plan Act had two major sections:

1. *Assistance programs* provided funding in such categories as food, shelter, and health-care services.

2. *Welfare services* focused on reducing, removing, or preventing the causes and effects of poverty, child neglect, and dependence on public assistance. Some services included under this legislation were rehabilitative programs, adoption, and community development.

For many years after the introduction of the CAP, there was slow but steady growth within the child care system and its related services, including specialized programming for infants and young children with special needs. Child care for low-income working families continued to be supported across Canada through federal cost sharing. The number of full-day child care spaces (daycare and home daycare) for both subsidized families and those paying the full fee rose approximately 500 percent between 1973 and 1984, going from 28 373 to 171 654 (Health and Welfare Canada, 1986).

The 1970s saw a move toward the active involvement of parents through the Parent Cooperative movement, and parent associations for children who were gifted, were emotionally disturbed, or had physical and developmental disabilities (Health and Welfare Canada, 1990).

The early 1990s saw ceilings placed on the funds available to some provinces and territories. In 1996 the CAP Act was repealed and the Canada Health and Social Transfer Act was established.

The Canada Health and Social Transfer Act (CHST) of 1996

During times of economic flux, at both the federal and provincial or territorial government levels, there is often an impact on funding formulas for health and social services for children and families, such as has been revealed in the Canada Health and Social Transfer (CHST) Act. The elimination of the Canada Assistance Plan Act and the introduction of the Canada Health and Social Transfer Act signalled that the federal government had transferred social responsibilities, such as welfare and child care, to the provinces and territories. Under the new legislation, the federal government guaranteed an annual, though shrinking, "lump sum" contribution to each province or territory, to be spent on health and social services, including welfare. Unlike the CAP, which refunded provinces and territories 50 percent of the cost for child care to families in need, there was no requirement that any of the annual lump sum under the CHST be allocated to child care. Some provincial and territorial governments with growing child care services were forced to consider transferring larger welfare costs, including those for child care, to the local governments. The local government was then responsible for determining how to obtain enough funding to meet their child care costs. Increasingly, public opinion, especially from working parents, indicated the need for both provincial or territorial and federal funding for child care. This will require the introduction of a new method of federal child care funding to relieve financial pressure on provincial and territorial governments.

Children's Rights: The Impact on Children with Special Needs

The phrase "least restrictive environment" became popular in the 1970s as part of the development of normalization and integration activities throughout

Canada. Those who followed the normalization philosophy agreed that children or adults with special needs should not be placed in an institution but should remain in their own community, preferably in their own homes. Similarly, children with special needs should not be segregated but should be included in early childhood programs in order to experience a full range of activities and to interact with their peers in the neighbourhood (see photo, below).

The Charter of Rights and Freedoms became a part of the Canadian Constitution in 1982. Section 15 of the Charter guarantees equal rights for all citizens. It has been argued that there is a right to education implicit in the Charter. Since the responsibility for both school-age and preschool education lies with each provincial or territorial government, it is up to the provinces and territories to show that any lack of service that limits these rights (e.g., lack of service to a child with special needs) is due to the child's excessive needs, which go beyond the "reasonable limits" clause as stated in section 24 of the Charter of Rights and Freedoms.

The equality rights in the Charter did not come into force until 1985, providing time for provincial and territorial ministries and local school boards to plan for the integration of children with special needs into the regular school system. Although education for school-aged children is mandatory under provincial and territorial legislation (usually starting at six years of age), early childhood education, including kindergarten or child care, is not mandatory. Therefore, under the Charter of Rights and Freedoms, parents of school-aged children with special needs who are denied access to education have the right of legislative appeal (i.e., parents are able to take their provincial or territorial ministry of education to court and demand equal educational opportunities for their children). However, parents of a preschool child who has a special need are unable to use the power of the courts, since early childhood education is optional, not a legislated requirement. Therefore, the courts cannot regard it as a right under the Charter of Rights and Freedoms. Nevertheless, Halfon and Friendly (2013) noted that "the child care sector has led the way in early years' inclusion" and "since the 1980s, community-based child care centres have voluntarily expanded their mandate (often with the support of provincial/ territorial funding) to include children with disabilities" (p. 12).

In January 1990, the Canadian government signed the United Nations Convention on the Rights of the Child (CRC). This was interpreted as a

Children with special needs have the right to be included in community early childhood programs.

© Cengage Learning 2015

sign that the federal government continues to be committed to recognizing the rights of all children (Friendly, 2006), including children with special needs. CRC General Comment No. 7 outlines children's vulnerability to poverty as well as different types of discrimination, including "discrimination in access to quality services for young children" (UNICEF Innocenti Research Centre, 2008, p. 24).

Following input from provincial and territorial governments, as well as Aboriginal self-governing groups, in March 2010 Canada signed the United Nations (UN) Convention on the Rights of Persons with Disabilities. In 2012 the World Health Organization (WHO) and UNICEF declared that

> the *Convention on the Rights of the Child* (CRC) and the *Convention on the Rights of Persons with Disabilities* (CRPD) highlight how children with disabilities have the same rights as other children—for example, to health care, nutrition, education, social inclusion and protection from violence, abuse and neglect. Ensuring access to appropriate support, such as early childhood intervention (ECI) and education, can fulfil the rights of children with disabilities, promoting rich and fulfilling childhoods and preparing them for full and meaningful participation in adulthood). (p. 5)

By signing the convention, the Government of Canada promises to advance the rights of all people. Yet Mayer (2009) noted that "despite all the language about inclusion, access to inclusive early childhood education is not an entitlement for children with disabilities and is not mandated through federal government legislation" (p. 161) as it is in the United States.

Mayer (2009) added that "a *change of attitude in society* is necessary if persons with disabilities are ever to achieve equal status" (p. 161) in Canadian society. Bach (2002) also cautioned against an "exclusive reliance on human rights law to secure equal recognition and dignity in society" (p. 10) for children with disabilities. Bach proposed a social inclusion agenda which he described as

> the process of rewriting the rules, recasting our cultural images and resources, and instituting practices to accord equal value and status to those who have assigned a place of lesser value and status in Canadian society—its education systems, workplaces and communities. Valued recognition of others entails respecting their differences and identities in ways that enable them to speak their voices, exercise their rights, and secure their own path to well-being. (p. 13)

In recent years, the educational philosophy of an educators' group in Reggio Emilia, Italy, has influenced an understanding of the child with special needs as having "special rights" (Fraser, 2012). The child with special rights is viewed as having strengths rather than needs. Fraser (2012) wrote that "educators in Reggio Emilia have become world leaders in their advocacy for the rights of *all* children to experience a quality early childhood education" (p. 38) that enables them to reach their full potential.

Provincial and Territorial Legislation for Child Care

There continued to be a lack of any federal child care legislation beyond the subsidy arrangements in the Canada Assistance Plan and, as a consequence, most provinces and territories began developing their own child care legislation, either through separate acts or through inclusion in existing provincial or territorial laws. Some provinces may have an explicit policy of inclusion in relation to child care legislation (see Table 2–1).

TABLE 2-1

Policies of Inclusion in Canadian Provinces/Territories

Province	Is there an explicit policy of inclusion? How is inclusion defined?
Newfoundland and Labrador	The policy manual states that "inclusion of children with special needs in child care entails much more than children being able to access and be physically present in a child care centre/home: the program and practices must be able to foster the development of all children, including those with special needs, to help ensure their optimal overall development" (p. 5).
Prince Edward Island	No explicit policy.
Nova Scotia	Grant guidelines state that "inclusion means that as a value, supports the right of all children, regardless of their diverse abilities, to participate actively in natural settings within their communities. A natural setting is one in which the child would spend time had he or she not had a disability" (p. 12).
New Brunswick	No explicit policy. Curriculum framework states: "we emphasize the need for a curriculum that is responsive to differences, with the capacity to provide additional support as required to ensure each child's right to full participation" (p. 5).
Québec	No explicit policy.
Ontario	No explicit policy.
Manitoba	Regulations require that centres have an inclusion policy, provide a daily inclusive program, have an IPP for each child in the inclusion support program, and ensure staff are aware of policy and IPP process. The government website states that "inclusion in early learning and child care is the practice of educating and caring for children of all abilities together in the group setting. The goal is to enhance each child's development within the regular daily program and foster positive social attitudes toward all abilities."
Saskatchewan	No explicit policy.
Alberta	The inclusive child care program overview states that "an inclusive child care setting is one where children with and without special needs participate in the same routines and play experiences as their peers. It is a setting where the staff or providers recognize children as distinct individuals with special strengths and needs and continually make modifications to routines and activities so that each child benefits from participating."
British Columbia	The policy and procedure manual for the funding program states that "inclusive refers to the active participation of children with special needs with typically developing children in the same child care setting" (p. 9).
Northwest Territories	No explicit policy.
Nunavut	No explicit policy.
Yukon	Child care regulations state that children with special needs in mainstream child care programs must be integrated to the fullest extent possible and IPPs must be developed for each child.

Source: Table 4 from Halfon, S., & Friendly, M. (2013). *Inclusion of young children with disabilities in regulated child care in Canada: A snapshot: Research, policy and practice* (Occasional Paper 27). Toronto, ON: Childcare Resource and Research Unit.

As a result of inconsistent inclusion policy across provinces and territories, Irwin (1997) noted,

> Most Canadian child care centres include *some* children with special needs *some* of the time. Generally speaking, though, this inclusion is on an *ad hoc* basis—responding on a child-by-child basis, admitting or excluding a particular child depending on the resources and skills currently available to that centre. (p. 15)

Table 2–2 provides a list of provinces and territories with a description of their services or funding for children with special needs.

TABLE 2-2

Provincial/Territorial Services and Funding for Children with Special Needs

Province/ Territory	Program Name	Department Responsible for Policy	Administrative Responsibility	Eligibility	Supports
Newfoundland and Lab rador	Inclusion supports	Health and Community Services	Regional inclusion consultants	Licensed child care providers apply to the program for funds and support. - Child eligibility definition: Child has a delay and/or exceptional ability in any of the developmental domains and/or presents with emotional, behavioural, sensory, and/or learning difficulties unrelated to a particular diagnosis or condition.	Various services provided by regional consultants; staff training in inclusion and special needs; and grants to support replacement staffing for individual support services plan (ISSP) meetings, funded spaces, ratio enhancement, and child-specific support.
Prince Edward Island	Special needs grant	Education and Early Childhood Development	Department of Social Services and Seniors	Licensed child care providers apply to the program for funds and support. - Child eligibility: Child must have a diagnosed disability and, in order to attain the usual developmental goals, requires additional and/ or specific types of stimulation/care.	The role of these grants is to lower ratios to allow for more successful inclusion into early childhood settings for children with special needs.
Nova Scotia	Supported Child Care Grant (SCCG)	Department of Community Services	Regional early childhood development consultants	Licensed child care providers apply to the program for funds and support. Following consultation with the Department's Regional Early Childhood Development Consultants	SCCG funding can be used for specialized training and professional development for early childhood educators, *(continued)*

				(ECDC), facilities may access funding support creation or enhancement of existing inclusive child care program. Both the application process and use of SCCG funding are the responsibility of the facility. Funding is not attached to a child or diagnosis, and must be used to enable provision of inclusive care.	additional staff to enhance ratios for the delivery of a facility's inclusive program, and to purchase educational and resource materials directly related to inclusive programs.
New Brunswick	Integrated Daycare Services	Social Development (Early Childhood Initiatives)	Regional health authorities	Licensed child care providers apply to the program for funds and support. - Child eligibility: Children from birth to 4 years with identified special needs in 1 of 3 categories: a confirmed diagnosis at birth, developmental issues after birth, or family risk factors.	Funding is primarily to provide a support worker; may also be used for transportation, materials and equipment, and nutritional needs of the child.
Québec	Enfants ayant des besoins particuliers Funding to CPEs, garderies, and family child care for integration of a child with a disability	Ministère de la Famille et des Aînés	Ministère de la Famille et des Aînés	Licensed child care providers apply to the program for funds and support. - Child eligibility: Child has a diagnosed disability, or meets the ministry definition of a "disabled" child.	A one-time grant of $2200 (of which $1800 is for equipment or improving the set-up to meet the child's needs); and an additional $37.30/day/child. There is also an assistance measure to promote integration of children with "significant" special needs.
Ontario	Support for children with special needs	Ministry of Education	Consolidated Municipal Service Manager (CMSM) or District Social Services Administration Board (DSSAB) (municipal or regional governments)	Licensed child care providers apply to the program for funds and support. - Child eligibility: Child with special needs up to 18 years.	Special needs resourcing to pay for staff, equipment, supplies, and other services to support inclusion of children.

(continued)

Province/ Territory	Program Name	Department Responsible for Policy	Administrative Responsibility	Eligibility	Supports
Manitoba	The Inclusion Support Program	Department of Family Services and Labour	Children's disABILITY Services	Licensed child care providers apply to the program for funds and support; only nonprofit centres are eligible for funding. - Child eligibility: Children must have an eligible cognitive, developmental, or physical disability or a behavioural or emotional issue, and need additional accommodation or support to meaningfully participate in the program.	Most additional support needs funding for staff; also may be grants for renovations, equipment, training, or professional services. As well, may be funds for nursing support for medically fragile children.
Saskatchewan	Child care inclusion program	Ministry of Education	Regional early learning and child care offices	Licensed child care providers apply to the program for funds and support. - Child eligibility: A referral (not necessarily a diagnosis) is needed; the child must attend the program for a minimum of 20 hours per month.	Basic grants provide support and consultation to the child, family, and staff. An additional staff person may be provided if necessary. Enhanced Accessibility Grant—up to $2000/month to support the inclusion of a child with "exceptionally high diverse needs." As well, there is a grant for adapted equipment and for staff training and resources.
Alberta	Inclusive child care program	Ministry of Human Services	Child and Family Services Authorities	Licensed child care providers apply to the program for support. - Child eligibility: Child's needs are significantly higher than his/her peers in the same group, present a barrier to successful inclusion in the program. Child's parents must be working/ going to school.	Consultation, information and referral, program professional development, funding supports for ratio enhancement. Day home agencies can apply for funding to compensate for taking fewer children or for other additional supports. (continued)

British Columbia	Supported Child Development Program (SCDP)	Ministry of Child and Family Development (MCFD)	Local SCD agencies, or local MCFD office	Licensed child care providers apply to the program for funds and support. -Child eligibility: Children 0–19 years (priority 0–6), with documented disability and/or diagnosed or documented need.	Individualized planning, training, information and resources, referrals to other specialized services, and when required, staffing supports.
Northwest Territories	Higher operating grants	Department of Education, Culture and Employment (Early Childhood and School Services)	Department of Education, Culture and Employment (Early Childhood and School Services)	Licensed child care providers apply to the program for funds and support. - Child eligibility: Medical referral from a recognized health-care professional.	
Nunavut	Daily operating grants increased by c. 50% for child with identified special need	Department of Education	Regional early childhood services offices	Licensed child care providers apply to the program for funds and support. - Child eligibility: Letter from a recognized health-care professional is required for the centre to receive the additional funding for a child.	Centres may apply for funding to the Healthy Children's Initiative for adaptive equipment or for a one-on-one worker if necessary.
Yukon	Supported child care fund (Whitehorse Child Development Centre provides special needs programming and supports across Yukon)	Health and Social Services	Health and Social Services	Licensed centres and family day homes apply to the program for funds and support. Child eligibility: A child is designated special needs on the assessment of a child care professional.	Adaptive equipment, transportation, programming support, and additional staff.

Source: Table 2 from Halfon, S. & Friendly, M. (2013). *Inclusion of young children with disabilities in regulated child care in Canada: A snapshot: Research, policy and practice* (Occasional Paper 27). Toronto, ON: Childcare Resource and Research Unit.

Educational Legislation in Canada

In Canada, the responsibility for the education of school-aged students with special needs lies with the provincial and territorial governments. Although all provinces and territories recognize the right to education for all children, the legislation varies across jurisdictions.

The U.S. public law clearly recognizes the importance of parent contributions to the child's progress.

© Cengage Learning

Differences exist in provincial and territorial educational legislation with respect to the diagnostic categories of identified exceptionalities. How an individual student is designated as eligible for special services also varies. However, in some provinces, diagnostic categories such as "orthopedically impaired," "visually impaired," and "educable mentally retarded" are used for determining program designation.

Some ministries of education assume responsibility for servicing preschool age children with special needs. For example, in Ontario, children who are hearing impaired are eligible from two years of age for special education services at no extra cost, even though they are much younger than the entry age for the public education system. Overall, a 2011 Canadian Association for Community Living national report card concluded that "a pattern of exclusion still starts early ... families still face tremendous challenges in obtaining inclusion for their children in early childhood and educational systems" (p. 4).

The Impact of U.S. Legislation on Canada

In contrast to Canada, in the United States the provision of services to young children with special needs is required by federal legislation (see photo, above). Many of the service components required under U.S. legislation—and the extensive research used in the development of program resources and strategies—have significantly influenced services and program practices across Canada. The *Portage Guide to Early Education* is an early example of the many U.S. resources now widely used in Canada. More recent programs, such as the Brigance Diagnostic Inventories, which enable ongoing record keeping of children's development, are also now widely used.

Table 2–3 provides a brief overview of major U.S. legislation that has directly influenced the resources and services available to young Canadian children with special needs and to their families. Box 2–1 looks at the shift from using a medical model to understand disabilities to using a social model.

TABLE 2-3

U.S. Legislation for the Education of Children with Special Needs

Year	Public Law	Title and Significance
1968	90-538	Handicapped Children's Early Education Assistance Act (HCEEAA). Federal funds support improvements in early intervention services for children with disabilities, children who are at risk of disabilities, and their families. Renamed as the Early Education Project for Children with Disabilities in 1992. This program no longer exists.
1972	92-424	Head Start Amendments. Although Head Start programs always included children with special needs, these amendments mandate that 10 percent of enrolment be reserved for children with special needs. In 1974, the regulations were changed to ensure service to children with more severe disabilities. In 1990, Head Start was reauthorized at its highest funding level ever through the Child and Development Block Grant and continues to be one of the primary programs that include children with special needs.
1973		Rehabilitation Act of 1973. Section 504 of this act is a civil rights law that promotes equitable opportunities for children and adults. (continued)

1975	94-142	**Education for All Handicapped Children Act.** This law guarantees that all children and youth, regardless of the severity of their disability, have the right to a free and appropriate public education. The law gives specific support to early education programs. Special funds, called incentive monies, are authorized to encourage states to locate and serve preschool children in need of early intervention services (also referred to as ChildFund). This law has a number of important rulings: • **Zero Reject:** Local school systems must provide an appropriate free education for all children regardless of the severity of their special needs. • **Nondiscriminatory Evaluation:** All children must be fully assessed before placement in a special education program. Tests must be appropriate to the child's language and cultural background. • **Appropriate Education:** Local school districts must provide educational services appropriate to each individual child. • **Least Restrictive Environments/Mainstreaming:** To the greatest extent possible, children with special needs will be educated in regular programs. • **Due Process:** This legal procedure enables parents to call a special hearing when they do not agree with the removal process. This further ensures that a child cannot be removed from a classroom simply because of annoying or inconvenient behaviour. • **Parent Participation:** The importance of parents' contributions to their child's progress is recognized. Parent participation was further encouraged by IDEA-1997 (see below), and then in the reauthorization of 2004.
1986	99-457	**Education of the Handicapped Amendments.** These amendments to the Education for All Handicapped Children Act are the most comprehensive legislation ever enacted on behalf of infants and young children. This law has several parts or Titles. Title I and Title II focus on the very young (up to the age of three): • **Title I:** A state may serve children who are experiencing developmental delays or who are at risk from birth through two years of age if it chooses. An exception is that any state serving infants and toddlers without disabilities must serve infants and toddlers with disabilities. Very young children do not need to be labelled as having a particular kind of disability to receive services. An individualized family service plan must be provided. • **Title II:** States receiving federal funds for early intervention programs must serve young children with developmental disabilities. Parent-support services are allowable as "related services."
1990	101-176	**Individuals with Disabilities Education Act (IDEA).** This amendment to PL 94-142 changes program emphasis from providing segregated programs for specific conditions to providing support to individuals with special needs in community settings.
1990	101-336	**Americans with Disabilities Act Law (ADA).** This law gives civil rights protection to individuals for private employment, all public services and accommodations, transportation, and telecommunications.
1992	93-112	**Developmental Disabilities Act (DDA).** This law requires that everyone with a disability be given access to jobs, education, housing, and public buildings. This law also rules that states offering preschool services to children without disabilities must offer comparable services to those with disabilities. Schools are also required to make accommodations for children who have disabilities but do not qualify for special education.
1997	105-17	**Reauthorization of the Education for All Handicapped Children.** The name was changed to the Individuals with Disabilities Act (IDEA) to reflect people-first terminology. IDEA-1997 requires educators to deal with challenging behaviours proactively.
2002	107-110	**No Child Left Behind.** The 2001 No Child Left Behind Act (NCLB) is federal legislation founded on a standards-based education philosophy. As part of the requirements of the NCLB Act, each state must administer a standard test to all public schools as a measure of growth in accountability. The results from these tests are used to assess each school's progress from year to year in order to establish eligibility for Title 1 funding (originally set up for school programs that support families with a low income) and number of teachers (United States Government Accountability Office, 2005).

(continued)

Year	Public Law	Title and Significance
2005	108-446	Individuals with Disabilities Education Improvement Act (IDEA). This revision maintains the integrity of IDEA, with a few significant modifications: • Special education teachers are required to hold at least a B.A. and obtain full state special education licensure or equivalent, and not hold temporary or emergency licensure. • Extensive provisions are included for children with special needs who are homeless or otherwise members of highly mobile populations. The provisions require the school to appoint a surrogate within 30 days of the request for placement so that there is no lapse in services for the child. • Significant changes have been made to procedural safeguards. • Authority is granted to extend Part C services for infants and toddlers beyond the age of two, until the child enters kindergarten. • Short-term objectives and benchmarks are no longer required sections in the IEP, and are used according to the extent decided upon by each state.

BOX 2-1

UNDERSTANDING DISABILITY FROM A SOCIAL MODEL PERSPECTIVE

In the past two decades, people with disabilities, influenced by the civil rights and women's movements, have dramatically revised the way disability is understood. Activists with disabilities and academics shifted the focus away from the more traditional emphasis on individual deviancy and pathology, and toward an exploration of social issues, such as inaccessible buildings, exclusionary policies and practices, and prejudice, as the "real" or sociological problems of disability.

This new focus is frequently called the "social model" of disability. It is distinct from a "medical model" of disability, which individualizes and pathologizes the disability as a biological impairment, a deficit, or a dysfunction residing within the person. Disability rights activists believe that an overemphasis on the medical model has detracted from full citizenship for people with disabilities. The social model is also characterized by the identification of the barriers that prevent the social inclusion of people with disabilities. It allows for an analysis of these barriers, on the one hand, and the capacity of people with disabilities and their allies in changing them on the other. In this struggle for social justice, hundreds of activist parents launched national organizations, including the March of Dimes, Easter Seals, the Muscular Dystrophy Association, and the Associations for Community Living. Mothers of children with disabilities have been at the forefront of this activism. For example, the social model approach turns the focus away from examining how individual families react to having a child with a disability and focuses instead on the social and historical factors that influence these reactions. It considers what resources are available to families, and examines the interconnection between the organizational resources that can or cannot be accessed, and the way families interpret the meaning of a child's disability. So the question becomes not "How do families respond to disability?" but rather "How does society respond to families?" It is only by asking questions from this social perspective that we can create new knowledge about disability that takes into account its various and richly textured social dimensions.

Source: Melanie Panitch, School of Disability Studies, Ryerson University. Prepared for this text.

National Health Care and Prevention in Canada

Although people criticize the lack of child care legislation and educational legislation at the federal level in Canada, it is to the credit of the federal government that a national health-care system was introduced in 1966. The Medical Care Act offered medical care to all Canadians, with the cost shared between the federal and provincial governments. Services provided specifically for children included childhood immunization at the request of the child's parents. With this legislation came an increase in the provision of screening and assessment services for children (including those with special needs) at hospitals and health centres in major Canadian cities. Such procedures as amniocentesis and other pregnancy-related health-care services became more readily available. Although a variety of funding mechanisms now exist for the provision of health care across provinces and territories, every family is entitled to receive medical assistance and care.

Efforts have been made to establish and implement community prevention programs that encourage families to use the local health services and centres. Therefore, assistance, such as support services for infants, may be provided through either provincial or territorial health or social service legislation (see photo, below). The source of funding, whether from the Ministry of Health or the Ministry of Social Services, influences the model of service delivery (medical versus social services) and the required educational background of the service providers (e.g., nurse, early childhood educator, therapist).

The Push for Federal Child Care Legislation in Canada

During the 1990s and 2000s, the provinces and territories continued to struggle to develop sufficient child care services to meet the needs of a growing population of young children and their families. Many young families emigrating from other countries to Canada have needed more initial support. Federal and provincial or territorial agencies and many advocacy groups representing both parent users and professional early childhood educators have come together to demand that the federal government enact specific child care legislation. This legislation is needed to address universal concerns, such as the quality of child care, accessibility of education and care, professional training, affordability, and the full inclusion of children with special needs in child care centres.

Organizations that have Canada-wide representation through provincial or territorial and local chapters, and that are actively involved in advocating for these concerns, include the Canadian Child Care Federation, the Canadian Association for Young Children, the Canadian Council for Exceptional Children, the Canadian Rehabilitation Council for the Disabled, and the Child Care Advocacy Association of Canada. Other associations with broad membership, such as the Canadian Association for Community Living (formerly the Canadian Association for the Mentally Retarded), are also working on behalf of children with special needs.

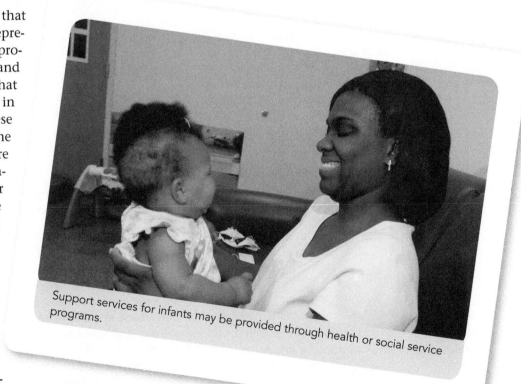

Support services for infants may be provided through health or social service programs.

Early childhood educators have always been strong advocates for young children (see Box 2–2).

Several detailed reports, such as the *Canadian National Child Care Study* and the *You Bet I Care!* study (Doherty, Lero, Goelman, Tougas, & LaGrange, 2000a, 2000b; Flanagan, Beach, & Varmuza, 2012), have confirmed that existing services do not meet the needs of many young children, including those with special needs, and that services struggle to recruit and retain qualified professionals. Therefore, the Canadian goal is to have federal legislation that would give support to all children within child care programs rather than having separate provincial and territorial legislation for children with special needs.

In the mid-1990s, the federal government introduced new services for early childhood development, such as Aboriginal Head Start (a targeted early intervention program) and Community Action Programs for Children (e.g., Brighter Futures). A new program to support research and developmental projects related to child care, Child Care Visions, was announced in 1995. In 1999, the federal, provincial, and territorial governments issued a National Children's Agenda that proposed a "new vision" for children in Canada. At the same time, the Social Union Framework Agreement confirmed that consensus of a majority of provinces and territories is necessary to initiate a new national social program like child care.

BOX 2-2
EARLY CHILDHOOD EDUCATORS AS ADVOCATES

Advocacy is speaking and acting in support or on behalf of people or ideas. Early childhood educators have a long tradition of being advocates. Our commitment to providing high quality care and education for young children has compelled many educators to take action at different times in their professional careers. Sometimes, the power of one educator (personal advocacy) positively changes practices in the care and education of children. Other times, the power of many (collective advocacy) changes government policies. There are different levels of advocacy that vary in factors such as degree of involvement and time commitment. All levels of advocacy are courageous and important.

Low-Level Advocacy

- Intervene in situations of discrimination, speak out in opposition to bias and defend people discriminated against.

- Support the inclusion of a child and act on behalf of the family.

- Join local, provincial, national and international professional organizations concerned with the inclusion of children with special needs.

Mid-level Advocacy

- Initiate networking with community groups who are committed to inclusive ECE (e.g., parent groups, cultural organizations).

- Raise a concern about exclusionary practices in your setting and provide leadership in making changes.

- Share information about inclusive practices with coworkers and promote the value of them.

High-Level Advocacy

- Submit a grant proposal to fund inclusive programming in your setting.

- Present information about the benefits of inclusion to community groups, government bodies and organizations.

- Join an advocacy group lobbying governments for supportive policy, funding and social change.

- Provide a workshop about inclusive practices.

Sometimes our advocacy efforts are successful; sometimes our efforts may result in only some small measure of success. Personal and collective advocacy are long, hard processes. However, inspiring gains have been made in inclusive care and education as a result of activism and advocacy by many committed educators and groups. Fortified by the strength of our convictions, educators will continue to advocate in support of inclusion, human respect and dignity.

Source: Early Childhood Resource Teacher Network of Ontario. (1997). Resource Sheet Unit V, Checklist for Quality Inclusive Education: A Self-Assessment Tool and Manual for Early Childhood Settings, Ontario. Used with permission.

An indication of the future of child care in Canada came in September 2001, when the prime minister and premiers signed an Early Childhood Development (ECD) Accord that provided more funding for services and programs for families and children, from prenatal to age six. Under the ECD Accord, the federal government planned to invest $2.2 billion in early childhood development over five years through CHST. Increased services included infant screening programs, family resource programs, and early development centres. Soon after, other national policy initiatives, including the *Multilateral Framework on Early Learning and Child Care* (Federal/Provincial/Territorial Ministers Responsible for Social Services, 2003), recognized the importance of learning and care in the early years. In 2004, the Organisation for Economic Co-operation and Development (OECD), in its 20-nation Thematic Review of Early Childhood Education and Care, reported that Canadian "national and provincial policy for the early education and care of young children in Canada is still in its initial stages" (p. 6). In the spring of 2005, the federal Liberal government and provincial and territorial governments began negotiations on a national early learning and child care system based on four principles: quality, universality, accessibility, and developmentally appropriate programming (Friendly & Beach, 2005). With the 2006 election of a Conservative government, the Liberal plan for a national child care program was replaced with the Universal Child Care Benefit, a monthly taxable payment of $100 per child in the family (birth to age six). Friendly and Prentice (2009) reported that following the cancellation of the national child care plan, child care space expansion showed the smallest increase in regulated child care in some years, an increase of only 26 661 spaces since 2006. At the end of 2008, Canada, among other industrialized countries, received UNICEF's lowest ranking on 10 benchmarks for quality, accessible early childhood education, and care (UNICEF Innocenti Research Centre, 2008). Friendly and Prentice (2009) concluded that Canada's history with child care is a problem of politics and policies, and early childhood education and care (ECEC) is still "trying to find a place on the national policy agenda during an era of political and social shift" (p. 103). In the absence of a national focus on child care, some provinces and territories have assumed greater responsibility for developing an early childhood education and care system through the implementation of full-day kindergarten programs and the integration of child care and education within one provincial ministry. Many provinces have also initiated innovative early learning curriculum frameworks that recognize the specific needs of diverse groups, including those of children with disabilities (Langford, 2012).

Advocacy speaking and acting in support or on behalf of people or ideas

Summary

Canadian legislation supporting the inclusion of children with special needs has been influenced by U.S. federal legislation. In the United States, a number of federal laws, specifically PL 94-142 and PL 99-457, have been passed that support the identification, prevention, and treatment of developmental differences in young children. Though there is no comparable federal legislation in Canada, a parallel development has occurred through the inclusion of children with special needs within provincial and territorial educational and child care legislation. In addition, an alternative social model for understanding disabilities has led to increased advocacy efforts to ensure social justice and inclusion for children with disabilities and their families.

The British North America Act established a structure whereby each province would be responsible for developing its own child care and educational legislation. This included responsibility for services for children with special needs. Through the

Canada Assistance Plan Act, provinces and territories entered into cost-sharing agreements with the federal government for child care services. The Medical Care Act ensured health care for all Canadians, including support for the prevention and treatment of developmental disabilities. This legislation was cancelled in March 1996 and was replaced by the Canada Health and Social Transfer Act of 1996. Through this legislation, the federal government transferred responsibility for health and welfare to the provinces and territories, along with a guaranteed, but decreasing, annual monetary contribution. At the same time, agreements in recent years between the federal and provincial or territorial governments point to a new federal role in social programs and collaboration between these governments to establish joint initiatives in early childhood services. Early childhood educators must continue to advocate in a variety of ways for inclusive programs within a national early learning and child care system.

Resources

Canadian Association for Young Children

http://www.cayc.ca

This is a national association concerned with the well-being of children up to age nine.

Canadian Child Care Federation

http://www.cccf-fcsge.ca

This member-based organization is committed to excellence in early learning and child care.

Child Care Advocacy Association of Canada

http://www.ccaac.ca

This Canadian organization is dedicated to promoting publicly funded, inclusive, quality nonprofit child care that is accessible to everyone.

Council of Ministers of Education, Canada

http://www.cmec.ca

This site provides a link to the Ministry of Education in each province and territory, with access to information on special education.

UNICEF

http://www.unicef.org/crc

UNICEF's mission is to advocate for the protection of children's rights, to help meet their basic needs, and to expand their opportunities to reach their full potential.

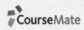 Access an interactive ebook and chapter-specific interactive learning tools, including flashcards, quizzes, videos, and more, in the *Inclusion in Early Childhood Programs* CourseMate. Visit NELSONbrain.com to log in, register, or purchase access.

Partnership with Families

3

OBJECTIVES

After studying the material in this chapter, the student will be able to

- Identify issues that are common among families of children with developmental differences.
- Describe family-centred care/practice.
- Outline the major components of an individual family service plan (IFSP).
- Define the concepts *enabling* and *empowering* as related to families of children with developmental differences, and explain the social significance of the concepts.
- List a number of ways for teachers to communicate with parents.
- Draw up a format for holding a conference with parents that includes follow-up.
- Discuss how the concept of cultural sensitivity affects interactions between teachers and families.

KEY CONCEPTS AND TERMS

case manager

cultural mediators

culturally competent

culturally sensitive

empowerment

failure to thrive

family uniqueness

family-centred service (FCS)

individual family service plan (IFSP)

nonintrusive

reciprocal relationships

reconstituted (or blended) family

resource consultant/resource teacher/early interventionist

service coordinator

transactional relationships

transdisciplinary team

Introduction

Family involvement has long been a tradition in early childhood education for many years. With the advent of intervention programs for children with developmental disabilities, family involvement now is viewed as required, as well as essential to the progress of the child (see photo, below) . The success of early intervention and early childhood special education programs can be directly attributed to the service providers' ability to work cooperatively with each family and with one other (Noonan & McCormick, 2006). Contrast this with earlier times when parents were advised, almost routinely, to institutionalize a child who had a disability. Professionals and parents alike agreed that institutions could not offer the individualized support and nurturing that were needed to facilitate early development. Today, relatively few children are institutionalized: Most live in their family's home; others may live in residential or group homes within their family's community. However, it was not until the 1970s that family support and involvement in their children's special education programs, as well as intervention services, were aided through provincial and territorial funding. Shonkoff and Phillips (2000) described this evolution: "As its knowledge base has matured, the field of early childhood intervention has evolved from its original focus on children to a growing appreciation of the extent to which family, community, and broader societal factors affect child health and development" (p. 339). Providers of preschool services need to build relationships between home and school to optimize learning potential (Dearing, Simpkins, Kreider, & Weiss, 2006).

The role of families in the planning, implementation, and evaluation of early childhood special education programs has changed dramatically over the past 30 years as early intervention services moved from a child-centred to a family-centered approach. Turnbull, Turnbull, Erwin, and Soodak (2005) described this shift:

> The pendulum has swung in many ways: from viewing parents as part of the problem to viewing them as a primary solution to the problem, from expecting passive roles to expecting active roles, from viewing families as a mother–child dyad to recognizing the presence and needs of all members, and from assigning generalized expectations from the professionals' perspective to allowing for individual priorities defined from each family's perspective. (p. 21)

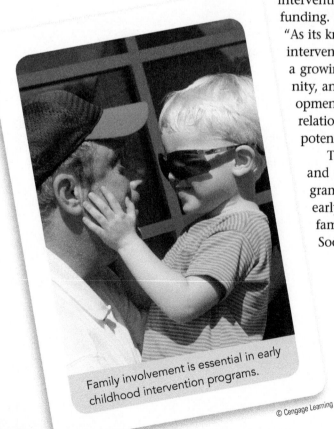

Family involvement is essential in early childhood intervention programs.

© Cengage Learning

The major trends examined in this chapter are the following:

- involvement of families in planning and implementing intervention services and educational programs for their infants and young children with developmental differences
- the rights and options of families
- avoidance of professional intrusion into family affairs
- **empowerment** of the family
- family roles and responsibilities in case management
- development of **culturally competent** early intervention services

As background, various aspects of family living will be touched on, starting with the many types of families in today's society. Having an infant with a disability and the impact this has on parents and on the family as a whole will be described. The rationale and justification for family involvement will follow, with emphasis on the family as a system of interactive, **reciprocal relationships.** Strategies that early childhood teachers engage in when working with parents of children with special needs will conclude the chapter. (Throughout the chapter, primary caregivers are referred to as "parents," even though it is not always the case that a parent is the primary caregiver.)

Empowerment planning and carrying out intervention activities in ways that pass as much control and decision making as possible on to the family

Culturally competent classroom activities, materials, and curricula that acknowledge and respect the different ethnicities that are represented in the classroom and community

Reciprocal relationships interactions between individuals in which each person gives and receives in response to the giving and receiving of the other

Family Patterns and Expectations

The makeup of families, and their expectations regarding the behaviour of family members, varies from family to family and from culture to culture. The emotional climate within families varies, too. Often it is characterized by the way parents interact with their children (which is not a one-way street, as we shall see later in the chapter). As we develop strategies and programs to facilitate family involvement, it is important to understand the families with whom we work. Our society is becoming increasingly diverse, and the families with whom we work come from different cultures and speak different languages. There may also be cultural differences in what people know and believe about disabilities and child rearing. We must understand and respect these differences as we work to build **culturally sensitive**, reciprocal, and responsive programs (Kalyanpur & Harry, 1999).

The concept of **family uniqueness** recognizes that every family is a distinct collection of individuals who have come together to create a new whole. Although many families may share similar characteristics, it is important not to assume that these families share common beliefs and practices. For example, not all Jamaican-Canadian families share common views on child rearing, nor do all Jewish families have the same priorities when it comes to early intervention goals, nor do all families headed by lesbian couples express their spirituality in similar ways. The concept of family uniqueness requires that practitioners learn how to work with families as individuals, how to communicate with families effectively, and how to develop cultural self-awareness to understand the ways our own beliefs influence our work (Harry, 1992).

Culturally sensitive classroom activities, materials, and curricula that acknowledge and respect the different ethnicities that are represented in the classroom and community

Family uniqueness a perspective that recognizes that every family is different

What Is the Family?

Parents are their child's first and best advocate. By knowing children's strengths and needs, understanding the basic special education process, and being able to work collaboratively with school people, parents can be instrumental in shaping a successful experience for their children in school, and help prepare them for life as full members of their communities. (Anderson, Chitwood, Hayden, & Takemoto, 2008, p. x)

Today's families come in all shapes and sizes. The most prevalent definition that is used in Canadian research and policymaking is Statistics Canada's *census family*. This unit includes a married couple with or without children living with them, or a single parent or grandparent sharing a dwelling with only his or her children or grandchildren. These children may be any age and be brought into the household through birth, marriage, or adoption, but they cannot have their own offspring living with them. Cohabiting couples living together for longer than one year are considered to be married, although separate statistics are kept for legally married and cohabiting couples. Today, a married couple can be opposite or same sex (Statistics Canada, 2013).

As noted by Sager (2010), "truly understanding what it means to be a family in Canada ... requires looking beyond our own immediate experience to include the diverse spectrum of relationships and responsibilities that make up family life from coast to coast to coast" (p. 5). Thus, early interventionists must become culturally competent. One of the first steps to increase our sensitivity to the values and practices of the families who are in our care is to be aware of the ways our own culture and upbringing influence our expectations of children (Marshall, 2001). Lynch and Hanson (2004) recommended a number of steps early interventionists could take to become more culturally competent, starting with learning about the families in the community. **Cultural mediators** can help with learning about the "interaction styles, childrearing practices, and cultural beliefs about disability" (456) from a family's culture. Communication is a key part of cultural competency that early interventionists can enhance by learning to greet family members in their own language, working with interpreters, and using means of communication that are acceptable to the family. Cultural competency also requires recognizing that "the collaboration assumed in family-centred early intervention programs may not be comfortable for families from different cultures" (Lynch & Hanson, 2004, p. 456).

When early childhood educators acknowledge and respect children's home languages and cultures, ties between the family and program are strengthened. This atmosphere provides increased opportunity for learning because young children feel supported, nurtured, and connected, not only to their home communities and families, but also to teachers and the educational setting. In addition to the cultural, ethnic, and linguistic diversity represented by the families in most early childhood programs, social factors affect families and add to their diversity. For example, divorce and remarriage continue to be common. The majority of divorced men and women remarry. When children are involved, the arrangement is often referred to as a **reconstituted or blended family**. It is not uncommon for her children, his children, and their children to be living under one roof.

Cultural mediators individuals who help mediate between the culture of the school and the culture of the family; they share information and enhance understandings so that the family can participate fully in the assessment and education process

Reconstituted (or blended) family each parent bringing children into a new household

Families of Children with Exceptionalities

Having a child with special needs presents unique challenges to parents, and for some, the initial discovery can be an intense and traumatic event. Studies reported by Heward, Cavanaugh, and Ernsbarger (2005) indicated that parents of children with disabilities go through an adjustment process similar to grieving in working through their feelings. Initially, parents may experience shock, denial, and disbelief. These feelings may be followed by periods of anger, guilt, depression, shame, and rejection or overprotection of their child. Eventually most parents accept their child's disability, and some grow to appreciate the positive impact their child has on their lives (Hanson & Lynch, 2004). The vast majority of research about families is actually research about mothers of children with disabilities. Yet, some research has shown that fathers demonstrate feelings similar to those of mothers, although fathers often are more concerned about long-term care issues and less concerned about day-to-day issues (Meyer, 1995).

When we talk about families, we usually mean parents. However, it is important to consider the needs of other family members in adapting to a child with special needs, including grandparents. Although early childhood teachers may have limited contact with grandparents, teachers may serve as a support and resource to families who are dealing with difficult reactions from family members, including the child's grandparents (see photo, right) .

Another important group that must be considered is siblings. Siblings will have lifelong relationships with their brothers or sisters with special needs, and they can benefit from special support and honest information about the special need. As Tozer (2001, p. 35) pointed out, "certain issues often arise for a sibling of a child with special needs, although each sibling, even in the same family, will be different." According to Tozer, there are typical stressors for siblings:

Grandparents are major caregivers in the families of many children.

© Cengage Learning

- jealousy about the time and attention the child with special needs gets from parents or caregivers
- guilt about being angry with a sibling with a special need
- embarrassment about a brother or sister
- stress at home
- worry about bringing friends home
- restrictions of family activities
- teasing or bullying about a brother or sister
- protectiveness about a dependent or ill brother or sister
- concerns about the future*

Family Abuse and the Child with Special Needs

A 2012 review on the prevalence and risk of violence against children with disabilities found that children with disabilities are almost four times more likely to experience violence than children without disabilities (Jones et al., 2012). The review indicated that children with disabilities are

3.7 times more likely than non-disabled children to be victims of any sort of violence; 3.6 times more likely to be victims of physical violence; and

* Tozer, R. (2001). Spotlight on Siblings. *Interations*, *15*(1). Used with permission.

2.9 times more likely to be victims of sexual violence. Children with disability associated with mental illness or intellectual impairments appear to be among the most vulnerable, with 4.6 times the risk of sexual violence compared with their non-disabled peers. (WHO, 2012, para. 2)

Although we are still learning about the complex interactions between abuse and disabilities, two facts are well documented:

1. Children with disabilities are more likely to be abused than other children (Govindshenoy & Spencer, 2006; Hershkowitz, Lamb, & Horowitz, 2007; Jaudes & Mackey-Bilaver, 2008; Sobsey, 1995; Sobsey & Varnhagen, 1988; Sullivan & Knutson, 2000).

2. Some childhood disabilities result from child abuse, including traumatic brain injury as a result of shaking an infant and violence during pregnancy (Campbell, Garcia-Moreno, & Sharps, 2004; Cherniak, Grant, Mason, Moore, & Pellizzari, 2005; Cook & Bewley, 2008; Sarkar, 2008).

Adequate and appropriate support systems are a key factor in ensuring the well-being of families of children with developmental disabilities (Janko,1994). Support is often taken for granted when a family has regular income, extended health insurance, adequate housing, and caring family and friends. Even so, additional support is usually required as soon as a newborn is identified as having serious developmental issues. Families do not plan to have a child with a disability. They expect a healthy infant who will grow, slowly but surely, into an independent and productive adult. From the start, parents of children with disabilities are often faced with disappointments and adjustments. These will affect every member of the family and every aspect of the family's life together.

Family Adjustment

Grief is the usual reaction when parents first realize that they have an infant with disabilities. Even when an older child is diagnosed with a disabling condition, grieving is the normal response of most parents. It is almost as if their child has died. In a way, it is so. Ken Moses (1987) suggested that parents of children with disabilities experience a grieving process that is strikingly similar to that of people who experience a death. Working with groups of parents, Moses saw anxiety, anger, denial, guilt, depression, and fear expressed over and over again. Gradually he came to understand that the parents were grieving the *loss of the dream* of what their child was to be for them. Emily Perl Kingsley's (1987) timeless *Welcome to Holland* (Box 3–1) illustrates this sense of loss and points out what Moses believes is essential in the recovery process—to separate from the lost dream and to generate new, more attainable dreams.

Families who are dealing with the kind of loss associated with a child who has disabilities have complex and often conflicting feelings that surface and resurface throughout the years (see photo, page 57). As early childhood educators, we will find ourselves listening and responding to this type of grief as our centres and classrooms become inclusive. If we listen and respond to family needs, we will recognize the dynamics that affect all members.

Families need to begin the process of adapting to the realities of caring for a child with special needs. Almost immediately, they will have to begin making

Families need to adapt to the realities of caring for a child with special needs.

© Cengage Learning

urgent decisions and solving complicated issues affecting the family unit. These might include the following:

- extensive (and perhaps painful or life-threatening) medical treatment and surgery or hospitalization that may occur repeatedly and for extended periods

- heavy expenses and financial burdens other than medical ones, such as the cost of special foods and equipment

- frightening and energy-draining crises, often recurring, as when the child stops breathing, turns blue, or has a major seizure

- transportation problems, babysitting needs for the other children, time away from jobs to get the child with a disability to consultation and treatment appointments

- lack of affordable, available, or appropriate child care for families with children who have developmental differences

- continuous day-and-night demands on parents to provide what are routine but difficult caregiving tasks (e.g., it may take an hour or more, five to six times during a single day and night, to feed an infant with a severe cleft palate condition)

- constant fatigue, lack of sleep, and little or no time to meet the needs of other family members

- little or no opportunity for recreational or leisure activities; difficulty (and additional expense) locating babysitters who are both qualified and willing to care for a child with a disability, especially if the child has severe problems (medical or behavioural)

- lack of, limited, or restricted respite care facilities

- jealousy or feelings of rejection among brothers and sisters who may feel that the child with special needs gets all the family's attention and resources

- marital problems arising from finances, fatigue, differences about management of the child's disability, or feelings of rejection by husband or wife who feels passed over in favour of the child

- choosing among different interventions or approaches

BOX 3-1
WELCOME TO HOLLAND

By Emily Perl Kingsley

I am often asked to describe the experience of raising a child with a disability—to try to help people who have not shared that unique experience to understand it, to imagine how it would feel. It's like this....

When you're going to have a baby, it's like planning a fabulous vacation trip—to Italy. You buy a bunch of guide books and make your wonderful plans. The Coliseum. The Michelangelo David. The gondolas in Venice. You may learn some handy phrases in Italian. It's all very exciting.

After months of eager anticipation, the day finally arrives. You pack your bags and off you go. Several hours later, the plane lands. The flight attendant comes in and says, "Welcome to Holland."

"Holland?!?" you say. "What do you mean Holland?? I signed up for Italy! I'm supposed to be in Italy. All my life I've dreamed of going to Italy."

But there's been a change in the flight plan. They've landed in Holland and there you must stay.

The important thing is that they haven't taken you to a horrible, disgusting, filthy place, full of pestilence, famine and disease. It's just a different place.

So you must go out and buy new guide books. And you must learn a whole new language. And you will meet a whole new group of people you would never have met.

It's just a *different* place. It's slower-paced than Italy, less flashy than Italy. But after you've been there for a while and you catch your breath, you look around … and you begin to notice that Holland has windmills … and Holland has tulips. Holland even has Rembrandts.

But everyone you know is busy coming and going from Italy … and they're all bragging about what a wonderful time they had there. And for the rest of your life, you will say "Yes, that's where I was supposed to go. That's what I had planned."

And the pain of that will never, ever, ever, ever go away … because the loss of that dream is a very very significant loss.

But … if you spend your life mourning the fact that you didn't get to Italy, you may never be free to enjoy the very special, the very lovely things … about Holland.

When these problems are further compounded by social isolation and poverty, the subsequent development of a child with a disability, as well as the growth and well-being of the rest of the family, is doubly jeopardized. Such problems further emphasize how nearly impossible it would be to provide effective intervention for a young child without including the child's family.

Bronfenbrenner (2006) convinced developmentalists of the range of environmental and family influences on a young child's development. The mother–child relationship, once thought to be the major determining factor, has proven to be but one of many. Innumerable strands of **transactional relationships**, both cultural and personal, are at work (Sameroff & Chandler, 1975). They form the system, or ecological niche, into which the child is born and reared. A child's ability to cope or adapt depends on understanding his or her larger social system, made up of family function, support of friends and community, and cultural beliefs.

> **Transactional relationships** the understanding that children and adults influence each other in their ongoing relationships and that both children and adults learn from these interactions; future interactions are influenced by earlier interactions

The Individual Family Service Plan (IFSP)

Many early intervention programs in Canada have begun to put into place a service focused on the family. This is modelled after the requirements of the U.S. law PL 99-457, which amended the Education for All Handicapped Children Act (see Chapter 2). This U.S. legislation emphasizes family support, thereby recognizing that infants and young children are best served in the context of a strong and healthy family. In Canada, many intervention agencies use a family-centred approach. **Family-centred service (FCS)**

recognizes that each family is unique; that the family is the constant in the child's life; and that they are the experts on the child's abilities and needs.

> **Family-centred service (FCS)** a set of values, attitudes, and approaches to services for children with special needs and their families. In FCS, the family works with service providers to make informed decisions about the services and supports the child and family receive.

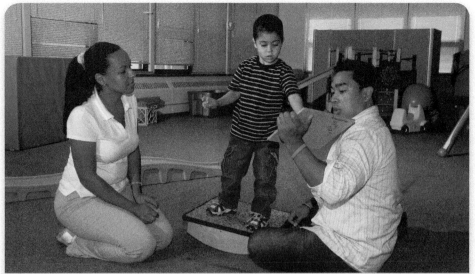

Family members are essential members of the child's IFSP team.

The family works with service providers to make informed decisions about the services and supports the child and family receive. In family-centred service, the strengths and needs of all family members are considered. (CanChild Centre for Childhood Disability Research, 2014, para. 2)

The investment of the family in the early intervention process highlights the need for professionals to work effectively with family members. An important first step in establishing a family–professional partnership is for the interventionist to learn culture-specific information about the various groups living the family's immediate community, particularly related to the family's attitudes and beliefs regarding appropriate roles for parents in the education of the children (Wong & Hughes, 2006). It is essential for effective educators to invest time in understanding each family's background to gain insight into how it affects the family's goals and aspirations for the child. For example, different cultures have varied perspectives on beliefs and feelings about children with special needs. Perceptions of what constitutes a special need may vary widely among different cultures, as well as within the same culture. It is important for educators to become aware of these differences and use these understandings about the family to individualize the program for the child and to support the family with an individual family service plan (IFSP).

The entire IFSP process—developing, implementing, and evaluating—must be conducted in a culturally sensitive manner, including the use of an interpreter whenever needed.

Woods and McCormick (2002) offered the following recommendations for supporting the family's role in the assessment process:

- provide the family with choices in the assessment process
- conduct the assessment in the child's natural environment, with everyday materials and activities
- avoid professional jargon and acronyms
- present results in a strengths-based and a family-friendly manner, using interpreters as needed
- provide time for questions

Individual family service plan (IFSP) a written plan that describes services for families with young children with special needs; it is written collaboratively with parents and describes the child's current strengths and needs

- provide information to parents on such things as development, the child's disability, or legislation

- provide information on resources, such as respite

- encourage participation of the extended family or other family supports in the assessment and team meetings*

Individual Family Service Plan Components

The purpose of an IFSP—a term that some service providers use interchangeably with individual program plan (IPP)—is to identify and organize resources to assist families in raising their children who have developmental disabilities (see Chapter 12). These are some of its major features:

Help is provided in a form that meets the unique needs of each child and family.

- It is an ongoing process that supports but *does not take the place of* parents' natural caregiving roles.

- Family-centred as well as child-centred services are provided through a **transdisciplinary team** approach.

- Family members are equal participants in the team (see photo, page 59).

- A **case manager** is identified and assigned the task of coordinating services and keeping the program moving.

- An outline of specific steps is provided, ensuring a smooth transition to the next intervention program.

Transdisciplinary team the team that shares the responsibilities for assessment, program planning, implementation, and evaluation across members

Case manager the member of the IPP team who assumes responsibility for coordination of the program and services for the child

IDENTIFICATION OF NEEDS Each infant and toddler with special needs should first receive a transdisciplinary assessment. In addition, the family is asked to participate voluntarily in a transdisciplinary identification of its strengths and unique needs. Families should receive the necessary services for their child even if they are unable to participate, or choose not to participate, in the identification process. Services designed to meet the assessed needs of the child and the identified needs of the family should be organized into an IFSP by the transdisciplinary team. The parents, other family members (grandparents, aunts, uncles, etc.), or an appointed guardian should be represented on the team. Encourage the family to invite an advocate, counsellor, or friend for assistance or support in presenting the family's position.

An important point, to be stressed again and again, is that the initial step in preparing an IFSP is *not* an assessment of the family. It is the family's *voluntary identification* of its strengths, resources, needs, and concerns, as these relate to *enhancing the development* of the child. Those who make up the intervention team need to recognize family issues that are beyond the scope of an early intervention program and advise the parents of appropriate resources.

Nonintrusive professionals respecting the privacy of families and not intruding into families' lives or lifestyles without an invitation to do so

NONINTRUSIVENESS Constant care is needed to ensure that families are benefited, rather than weakened or demeaned, by participation in the IFSP. Professionals involved in the IFSP process should be **nonintrusive**: that is, they should not intrude into a family's life or lifestyle without the family's invitation to do so. Family members are not to be prodded into discussing private or sensitive matters. Personal information gleaned from professional probing usually has little or no bearing on the special needs of the child.

* By Wood, J. J. & McCormick, K. M. *From Exceptional Children, 5*(3) (April 2002). Published by Sage Publications Inc. Journals. Used with permission from Copyright Clearance Centre.

IFSP EVALUATION The IFSP should be evaluated at regular intervals by the team. The purpose of the evaluation and review is to appraise the progress made by the child and family toward the objectives identified in the IFSP. If progress is unsatisfactory, program revisions are in order.

SERVICE COORDINATION (CASE MANAGEMENT) A transdisciplinary team approach to early intervention implies that a number of professionals are dealing with the same child and family. It is strongly recommended that one particular person be designated as **service coordinator** (case manager). The service coordinator may be chosen because of his or her professional expertise in the child's exceptionality or because it is anticipated that the service coordinator will have longer contact and more frequent involvement with the family. The communications specialist might be the service coordinator when the main concern revolves around speech and hearing, the physiotherapist when there are evident motor delays, and the nutritionist in cases of **failure to thrive**. In addition to providing clinical skill, the service coordinator needs to be a sensitive listener, a child and family advocate, and a linkage agent (getting families linked to needed services). In many areas, the **resource consultant/resource teacher/ early interventionist** serves as the service coordinator.

The service coordinator is essential to team functioning as well as to family functioning. Without a liaison or go-between, both the team and the family tend to become confused. When there is a duplication of efforts (the family was put through three or four intake interviews, for example), intervention services lose continuity and coherence, and whole programs can fall into chaos and disintegration.

Generally speaking, the duties of the service coordinator/case manager are decided by each team. Assigned tasks might include these:

- coordinating the individual child's assessments and identification of family needs with prescribed services
- chairing team and family conferences
- making sure that records are kept up to date, paperwork gets done, and appointments are made (and kept)
- arranging the child's transitions to other programs and providing follow-up services
- serving continually as a source of contact, interpretation, and support for the family

Families, to the maximum extent possible, should have the opportunity to select their own case manager/coordinator. In some instances, family choice cannot be an option and a service coordinator must be assigned. A family that feels that its needs are not met adequately by the assigned case manager must be helped to find a more acceptable one.

FAMILY MEMBER AS CASE MANAGER/COORDINATOR A family member who may want to serve as case manager should be encouraged and supported by other members of the IFSP or IPP team. Training should be provided for family members in how the system and the network of backup services operate. Gathering the necessary resources and assistance should not add to the family's burdens. Instead, the family should reap positive benefits and become stronger and more capable through the case management process. When the family assumes responsibility for getting needed assistance, it serves to reduce overdependency on the team service system. Parent associations for specific disabilities will often help parents to locate resources that will prepare them for the case management role.

Service coordinator the member of the IPP team who assumes responsibility for coordination of the program and services for the child

Failure to thrive refers to undersized infants whose bodies, for various reasons (organic, genetic, or environmental) either do not receive or cannot use the nurturance necessary for proper growth and development

Resource consultant/resource teacher/early interventionist a professional with special training and expertise in planning and implementing developmentally appropriate programs for children who have developmental problems

PROGRAM-TO-PROGRAM TRANSITIONS The transdisciplinary team should provide support for the child and family during transitions from one program to another. The hallmark of effective early intervention is the child's graduation into a more challenging program—frequently a program that is in a different setting. The transition between programs calls for special kinds of planning and support. The focus of Chapter 13 is on planning and implementing transitions.

Enabling and Empowering Families

A major public concern about the individual family service planning process was that it would promote increased dependency. Many feared that families would become less able to function independently. Out of this public concern grew the major philosophical thrust of IFSP, the *enabling and empowering* of families. Deal, Dunst, and Trivette (1989) suggested the following definitions of the terms:

> Enabling families means creating opportunities for family members to become more competent and self-sustaining with respect to their abilities to mobilize their social networks to get needs met and attain goals.
>
> Empowering families means carrying out interventions in a manner in which family members acquire a sense of control over their own developmental course as a result of their own efforts to meet needs. (p. 33)

The intent of the *enabling* and *empowering* concepts is to strengthen families without taking away their ability to cope. The IFSP aims to support and build on those things the family already does well. Professionals believe that this can be accomplished by providing families with the information and skills that will enable them to try to solve their own problems and meet their own needs. The case manager should play the pivotal role in fostering and overseeing the empowerment of families. According to Dunst and Trivette (1989), "Case management may be considered effective only to the extent that families become more capable, competent, and empowered as a result of the help-giving acts of case managers" (p. 99).

The Family–Teacher Partnership

Families and teachers should be partners in facilitating children's development. It is important to recognize that families must maintain the right to have the final word. They bear the ongoing and primary responsibility during the long years of their child's growth and development (frequently, many additional years when a child has a disability). Numerous research studies have described the benefits of active parent involvement in a child's early intervention program. Without it, children tended to regress or slip back once the program ended (Simeonsson & Bailey, 2000). Collaboration among parents, teachers, and specialists is a cornerstone of high-quality inclusion (Odom, Schwartz, & ECRII Investigators, 2002). Parent involvement has two major functions: (1) it provides an ongoing reinforcement system that supports the efforts of the program while it is underway, and (2) after the program ends, the child's gains are maintained and expanded on as a result of the family members' increased knowledge and confidence in their ability to support the changing developmental needs of their child.

Rationale for Parent Participation

Many reasons can be given for encouraging parents' involvement in their child's early education and intervention program (see photo, right):

- Families are the major socializing agents for their child, as transmitters of cultural values, beliefs, and traditions.

- Families know their child better than teachers or clinicians do; thus, families have a source of information that is available from no one else.

- Family members can help the child transfer knowledge from school to home and neighbourhood: Only a few hours a day are spent in school; many more hours are spent at home.

- Consistency of adult expectations can be maintained. Young children become anxious when important adults do not agree on expectations. Confusion and even resistance may result if, for example, teachers expect a child to put on his or her own coat while parents always do it for the child.

- Pleasing parents is important to young children in that the parents are the source of many pleasant and necessary reinforcers for their young child—food, warmth, comfort, outings, playthings, and so forth.

- Children with disabilities acquire developmental skills more quickly when parents learn to participate in home teaching.

- Involvement in an early intervention program offers families access to support from other families and a better perspective on their own child's strengths and needs.

Truly effective early intervention includes parents.

© Cengage Learning

Degree of Participation

The extent to which parents can be actively involved in their child's program depends on a number of factors:

- work schedule and job constraints
- additional young children at home who need care
- availability of transportation
- parental health (both physical and psychological)
- parental maturity and understanding of the child's needs
- attitudes and comfort level of the parent with medical personnel, teachers, and authority figures
- the program's ability to accommodate to the primary language of the family
- cultural and linguistic match with the program

It is important to recognize that simply *maintaining a child's enrolment in a program is a form of parent involvement.* Lack of active participation does not imply lack of interest in the child or the program. Instead, as Ray, Pewit-Kinder, and George (2009) suggested, it may be a form of energy conservation. Family life with a child who has a disability is a marathon rather than a sprint. A crucial aspect of supporting families during the early years is to empower them with coping strategies that can help them to run the full course with their son or daughter and to avoid the trap of investing their energies heavily for a short period of time and then burning out.

Establishing Trust

To ensure ongoing effective communication, teachers and parents must first establish and maintain a trusting relationship. According to Klein, Cook, and Richardson-Gibbs (2001),

> Perhaps the most important ingredient in the process of creating a true partnership with families is the development of mutual trust. Trust will not develop unless families feel safe. Their right to privacy, to confidentiality, to ask questions and to make choices for themselves and their children must be respected. (p. 254)

As stated, one key to forming this trust is maintaining confidentiality. Parents must know that information about children or their families will not be discussed with other parents or with other staff in a casual setting, such as the lunchroom, or with other community members without the parent's written permission.

Confidentiality—in combination with acceptance of the child and his or her family, respect and value for the child's home culture, and encouragement or participation of all families—becomes a strong foundation for a positive working relationship.

Communicating with Families

The teachers' approach to parents should be the same as the teachers' approach to children: respect and appreciation for individual differences in culture, values, attitudes, and learning styles. When mutual understanding is established between parents and teachers, children are more likely to experience a good learning environment. When communicating with parents, it is important to do the following:

- Establish two-way communication.
- Talk *with*—rather than *to*—parents.
- Simultaneously try to share knowledge and obtain feedback.
- Share information that may address the expressed and unexpressed concerns of the parents. Unexpressed concerns may be one of the biggest obstacles to communication. With some parents, it may be a long while, for example, before they are able to talk about their child's exceptionality or even to express openly that a concern exists.

It is helpful to talk with parents about how they would like to communicate with the teacher and the school staff. For example, do they prefer phone calls, email, or notes home? If they prefer phone calls, is there a time that is most convenient and when they will be able to give the call their full attention? How often would parents like to hear from classroom staff? Teachers must work with the family to set up expectations for ongoing communication that meet family needs and are sustainable by staff (Davern, 2004). When considering how to communicate with various families in an early childhood classroom, issues of culture, language, and literacy must be taken into consideration: Who in the family will be the primary contact? If the family has limited English, is there a member of the classroom staff who speaks their native language? Is it acceptable for this staff member to be their primary contact in the classroom?

The following sections describe the various ways that teachers can communicate with families.

INFORMAL EXCHANGES A tremendous amount of information can be exchanged during informal encounters (see photo, below). The quick conversations that occur in programs where parents pick up and deliver children are especially fruitful. Positive comments made by teachers to parents in the presence of the child are important when working with any family. This is especially true when working with families who have a child with special needs. Often people focus on the negative or inappropriate behaviour of the child, so parents come to realize that seemingly small events have developmental significance. Children learn that their accomplishments have merit; otherwise, why would the teacher pass on the news? And why would both of these important adults, parent and teacher, look so pleased? Appreciative comments have another function, too. They serve as models for parents. Hearing them helps parents learn to put into words their own recognition and appreciation of their children's efforts.

PARENT OBSERVATIONS In all programs for young children, parents should be welcome at any time. Since parents are the primary partners in their child's development, they have the right to see and question everything that goes on in the classroom. This is especially true when working with families who have children with special needs. Firsthand observations offer one of the best ways of providing indirect parent education. Watching their child interacting with other children and adults, with materials and activities, provides insights that can be obtained in no other way. The following ideas should be kept in mind when parents are observing:

- Every parent observation is followed by at least a brief discussion with a teacher.

Arrival and departure times are not the time to discuss concerns about the child.

© Cengage Learning

- If possible, the teacher should be the one in the activity area where the parent observes for the longest period.

- When a conversation cannot take place on the spot, a follow-up telephone call is important to answer questions parents might have or share information regarding why certain play or group situations were handled as they were.

  - Help parents recognize the positive aspects of their own child's uniqueness and developmental progress.

  - Describe the appropriateness of individualized curriculum activities in enhancing the child's development and meeting their child's special needs.

- Parent observations may be regularly scheduled or held on the spur of the moment.

- When a formal observation is planned, it is best for teachers to provide some type of structure. A clipboard with a simple observation form works well. Parents are asked to note the child's activities, playmates, and special interests, as well as avoidances, if relevant.

- Focused observation helps parents note what is actually going on with their child. Taking notes helps parents see the subtleties of their child's involvement. This enables the parents to be a part of the programming process while not interfering in their child's activities. A parent engaged in close observation and note taking tends to discourage the child from staying too close to his or her side.

- Video-recorded observations may be used in place of on-site parent observations. Recordings are also useful when parents need translators for interpretation. Follow-up discussions can then take place afterward.

Case Study ■ Sofia's mom ■

Sofia and her mother just moved into the area and enrolled in your preschool class. Sofia's mom is a single parent who works two jobs to make ends meet. She drops off Sofia one to two times a week, but on most days Sofia is transported back and forth by a babysitter. Sofia's mom speaks primarily Spanish and some English. What are some things that you, as the teacher, can implement in order to develop a trusting relationship with Sofia's mom?

TELEPHONE CALLS Telephone calls help keep communication going between teachers and parents. When children arrive by bus and parents work, the telephone may become the chief means of maintaining contact. Phone calls may be used for the same kinds of casual reporting as arrival and departure contacts. Many parents prefer a convenient day and time of day arranged in advance so that they can plan to have a few minutes to talk freely. When teachers' calls become a regular event, most parents welcome them—a call from school no longer signals trouble. Usually, the focus is on routine matters, such as the outcome of a visit to the audiologist, the progress of an illness, or the reason for an absence of several days. For children who are not picked up by their own parents, the teacher should phone to report any unusual happening at school: torn or soiled clothing;

a scrape, fall, or rash; or an unexplained change in a child's behaviour. The teacher should always try to reach the parent before the child arrives home. The advance call can allow parents time to think of the best way to handle the situation before they see their child.

WRITTEN NOTES If immediate reporting and feedback are not essential, written notes sent home with the child can be useful. Once a relationship has been established between a teacher and parent, a written note often is preferred to a telephone call. Parents can read the note at a convenient time. Written notes can be used to request items from home, such as extra clothing, beautiful junk, and so on. Notes home can also provide parents with exciting news of a child's progress (see photo, above). Notes of this kind give parents something specific and positive to talk about with their child. In addition, notes are one more way for teachers to help parents recognize the developmental significance of a child's seemingly routine accomplishments.

A written note sent home with the child might say, "Your child managed to eat by herself today."

© Cengage Learning

CLASS WEBSITES A class website can provide a place for teachers to post information about activities, permission forms, the parent handbook and school calendar, and ideas for at-home activities. A website can also be a place to post student artwork (with the parent's permission). Care must be taken not to post recognizable pictures of students unless they are posted on a password-protected portion of the website, and then only with the parent's permission.

Many schools and programs maintain websites to which a teacher can post a class section. For teachers without this option, tools to create web pages, such as Google Sites and Facebook, are free and accessible from any computer.

While a website is a great way to foster communication, it can also raise an equity issue, as not all families will have access to or knowledge of how to use a computer, let alone navigate a website. The following are strategies to increase access to technology for all families (Mitchell, Foulger, & Wetzel, 2009):

- Continue to provide print copies of newsletters and information posted on your website to families who are unable to access the website.

- Help families increase their comfort with technology by providing a brief orientation to your website during open house or another family evening.

EMAIL Communicating via email might be very convenient for many parents and teachers. It is important to discuss with parents the type of information they want to receive by email. Because of security implications, highly confidential information should neither be composed nor sent through email unless it is possible to attach a file encrypted with a password.

THE TWO-WAY JOURNAL (OR COMMUNICATION BOOK) Some settings take the brief written note idea a step further and use a journal system. Parents and teachers both write in the journal. It travels back and forth between school and home on a frequent and fairly regular basis. Once such a system becomes established, it may become a relatively effortless but rewarding method for keeping the communication lines open between home and school.

NEWSLETTERS Most parents appreciate having newsletters sent home. One of the major purposes of a newsletter is to describe the everyday events and learning experiences that go on at school. A newsletter can also serve as a reminder to parents of upcoming events or situations that involve all families (e.g., cold weather and the need for warm clothing). Newly enrolled children and families, teachers, and volunteers can be introduced in the newsletter. Whenever possible, try to include children in the process. They can dictate special events or provide drawings for the newsletter.

A newsletter must be written in plain language at the reading level of the families receiving it. In many programs, newsletters need to be written in two or more languages.

Parent–Teacher Meetings

Meeting together has been the traditional form of parent–teacher interactions. Usually held on the premises of the school or program, the meetings provide opportunities for all parents to see their children's work, interact with teachers, and compare notes with other parents.

LARGE-GROUP MEETINGS Group meetings can be very beneficial to families. Group meetings usually focus on issues of general interest or concern to the parents, such as aspects of child development, curriculum, or behavioural challenges. A recognized expert in a particular area may be invited to speak. Time for questions and open discussion is an important part of any family–teacher get-together. An informal social time or open house often precedes or follows the group discussion. Casual socializing helps parents get to know teachers and other parents better. Parents should have many opportunities to visit their child's classroom, where paintings, clay work, woodworking, or other projects are on display. Parents of children with an identified special need should also be encouraged to attend workshops or meetings offered by disability-specific organizations.

PARENT CONFERENCES In addition to IFSP planning, regular parent conferences should be scheduled two or three times a year, or more often in some instances. Conferences should have the purpose of building parent–teacher communications. A positive note must be established at the onset. Conferences with parents require a quiet place with comfortable seating. After greeting the parents cordially and exchanging social pleasantries, conversation should focus on a review of the purpose of the conference. This should be followed by a brief progress report. The report should combine both parent and teacher observations, interspersed with many examples of how the child is gaining (or has mastered) particular developmental skills, both at home and at school. Throughout, parents should have ample opportunity to comment, ask questions, and express their concerns. Strategies that work at home and school should also be discussed. The conference should close with a brief summary of the discussion, a restatement of long- and short-term learning goals for the child, and a restatement of the child's unique and valuable qualities. A date for the next conference should be set.

In every parent conference, the focus must be on issues related to the child's development and learning. Teachers should avoid counselling parents on deeply personal concerns but still attempt to help the family find an appropriate resource.

Ethical issues are a concern of many teachers in their work with parents (Feeney & Kipnis, 2005; Howard, Williams, & Lepper, 2009). What should be done, for example, when a child has serious health problems that the parent appears to neglect? or behaviour problems that parents apparently do not recognize? Before going into such a conference, the teacher must make extensive observations and, when appropriate, take frequency counts of the behaviour in question. The teacher should also consult with other teachers. This will ensure staff agreement that a serious problem exists and that it cannot be handled through rearrangement of particular aspects of the program. No matter how carefully the teacher sets a positive note at the outset of such a conference, or how tactfully he or she brings up the problem, parents may feel threatened. Inevitably, they feel that whatever is "wrong" with their child is their fault (or is perceived by teachers as the parents' fault). At first mention of their child's shortcomings, parents may feel alienated, defensive, and even angry. Little can be accomplished in that kind of an emotional climate. Teachers, therefore, should bring up difficult problems only when the child's present or future well-being is at stake and teachers cannot help the child without the parents' help.

It would be unconscionable for teachers not to bring up certain problems—for example, ongoing excessive drowsiness. The teacher must discuss this with the parents immediately. After brief greetings, the opening statements should have to do with the frequency of the problem as observed and documented. It should be pointed out to the parents how much the child is missing because of his or her lethargic state. At no point should the teacher back down. The teacher should advise the parent to consult immediately with the child's doctor. Should the condition continue, the teacher should contact the public health nurse or the case manager for support.

Family Support Groups

Families with a child with special needs have individual concerns and need information regarding their child, services, and community resources.
Parent support groups provide parents with the opportunity to talk to and support one another.

Many different parent groups have been formed, and their structure may vary according to their purpose. Some might offer education and parent training, some might help parents learn to become advocates for their child, and others might be an informal exchange of information. Almost all groups focus on developing relationships and friendships for support and exchange of resources. It is important that programs also remember the fathers' needs. Some programs offer "dad-only" support groups, which give fathers their own forum to discuss issues that are specific to them. It is important that early childhood educators be aware of the support groups that they can refer families to. The following websites provide information regarding support groups for families with children with a variety of challenges.

- The Canadian Association for Community Living, http://www.cacl.ca. Provides support and resources and strives for the full inclusion of people with intellectual disabilities

- Geneva Centre for Autism, http://www.autism.net. Offers a wide range of services designed to support families who have a child diagnosed with autism spectrum disorder

- Canadian Down Syndrome Society, http://www.cdss.ca. Provides support and resources for families who have a child with Down syndrome

Parent Feedback

Most feedback from parents is obtained indirectly. Much of it comes from incidental comments during informal parent–teacher exchanges. Parents' responses are most useful if questions relate to specific aspects of the program; creating a questionnaire for written responses is often the most effective. In addition, questions should be designed so that parents can rate the degree of satisfaction of each item, rather than having to give a yes or no answer. Suggestion boxes can also be helpful. Parents can make their comments anonymously if they are supplied with the form. Teachers' responses to parents' suggestions can be posted on the bulletin board. If parents are given acknowledgment that comments are not only wanted but acted on, they are more likely to continue to contribute their ideas and suggestions.

HOME VISITS Home visits have a long tradition of bridging the gap between school and home. Getting to know a family in its own setting enables teachers to work more effectively with children in the school setting.

During home visits, teachers can discover the interests, concerns, and needs of new children, and prepare the environment and curriculum to reflect these needs. Through home visits, the process of establishing a positive connection with each child begins. Educators will also benefit from meeting different family members and learning something about their roles within the family.

During home visits, personal biases may influence the impressions and judgments about diverse socioeconomic conditions, child-rearing practices, and child behaviour. It is important to question personal assumptions and reflect on how they can affect interactions with children and families. When discussing home visits with other staff members, be sure to focus on family strengths and the benefits of visits. Home visits provide teachers with an initial understanding of a child and family; as the relationship with them deepens, understanding will change and broaden.

In conducting home visits the following strategies may be helpful:

- Spend time playing with children and looking at the toys and books they value.

- Follow the child's lead in play.

- Bring a special book or toy from the classroom setting (particularly one that reflects diversity and inclusion) to share with the children—it may add to the home visit. However, children may prefer to show their teacher every single toy or book they possess!

- Ask children, using different communication strategies, what they like to do and indicate how activities in the classroom setting are like the ones they enjoy. By doing so, teachers show the children that they are people who care about and value what children think and feel.

Teachers should always remember the parents' role in their child's learning. Not only are parents the child's first teachers, but they are also the child's most frequent teachers. With appropriate support, parents can make their home a significant learning environment for their children. "The goal is to find ways to build on what the family is already contributing to their child's learning and growth" (ERIC/OSEP Special Project, 2001). Home is the place where all developmental skills can be practised over and over, in a real-life setting, with those who have a personal stake in the child's development.

Summary

The family, regardless of its makeup, is a young child's most important teacher. Although early childhood teachers are partners with parents in the teaching process, parents are always the primary partners. With children who have developmental differences, parents' involvement in their child's early intervention program is especially important. Involvement takes many forms. Simply keeping their child in the intervention program may be the only involvement some parents can manage.

An ecological approach to understanding early development is fundamental to the individual family service plan. The first underlying assumption is that children who are young and special can be helped best in the context of their family and culture. The second is that family members, including grandparents and siblings, are as likely to be in need of special services as the child. The IFSP is an interdisciplinary team effort that includes parents as team members. Appointing a case manager keeps the program organized and running. The emphasis is on helping families become stronger and more able through the IFSP process.

The teacher–parent partnership is fostered in a variety of ways. A relationship that benefits children is based on open communication and teachers' respect of the range of individual differences among parents. Many of the most effective teacher–parent exchanges are brief and informal chats—for instance, when a parent brings the child to school or observes in the classroom. Telephone calls, written notes sent home with children, emails, newsletters, classroom websites, and group meetings keep the lines open between teachers and parents. Formal conferences are another means of communicating with parents, as are home visits. Teachers may also seek parent feedback about the program itself through questionnaires and suggestion boxes.

Resources

The Canadian Association of Family Resource Programs

http://www.frp.ca

FRP Canada promotes the well-being of families by providing national leadership, consultation, and resources to those who care for children and support families.

Canadian Child Care Federation

http://www.cccf-fcsge.ca

The site offers a virtual library of articles on parenting, child development, health, social concerns, safety, and family issues.

Child and Family Canada

http://www.cfc-efc.ca

The site offers information on 800 toy libraries, parent resource centres, and related services.

Contact a Family

http://www.cafamily.org.uk

This British charitable organization helps families who care for children with any disability or special need.

Kinark Child and Family Services

http://www.kinark.on.ca

Kinark Child and Family Services is a children's mental health organization in Ontario that provides help to children and families.

Vanier Institute of the Family

http://www.vanierinstitute.ca

The Vanier Institute is an acknowledged leader on issues affecting families.

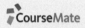 Access an interactive ebook and chapter-specific interactive learning tools, including flashcards, quizzes, videos, and more, in the *Inclusion in Early Childhood Programs* CourseMate. Visit NELSONbrain.com to log in, register, or purchase access.

Preparing Teachers for Inclusive Programs

4

OBJECTIVES

After studying the material in this chapter, the student will be able to

- Describe the knowledge and training needed to work in early childhood inclusive programs with children who are developmentally different.
- Justify the statement that all young children, regardless of their abilities, need enriched learning experiences.
- Discuss early education arrangements for children who have severe and multiple disabilities.
- Compare contingent stimulation, teachable moments, spontaneous teaching, and incidental teaching; identify developmental principles they have in common and their significance to children's learning.
- List 10 or more characteristics demonstrated by effective teachers working in inclusive environments.

KEY CONCEPTS AND TERMS

contingent stimulation	dual placements	readiness
coordinated teaching	incidental teaching	scaffolding
developmental disequilibrium	mediated learning model	teachable moments

Introduction

Qualified early childhood teachers should be the central element in programs for infants, toddlers, preschool-aged, and school-aged children. These teachers should be supported by assistants who are trained or in the process of being trained, or by caregivers who have had on-the-job experience. Qualified early childhood education personnel should supervise caregivers providing child care in family-home daycare settings. Program quality is determined by the teachers' skills in managing the learning environments. Quality is further determined by teachers' personal attitudes about children and themselves, and by their beliefs regarding how children learn. In the inclusive classroom, the need for quality teaching is critical. The developmental diversity among children calls for skilled and sensitive teachers who will respond to children's special needs with a range of individualized programs. At the same time, inclusive classrooms call for teachers who recognize that young children with developmental disabilities are more like other children than they are different from them.

All children need learning activities and experiences geared to their level of development and interests. Children who are meeting developmental expectations within their particular culture need such experiences; children who are gifted need them; children with developmental differences need them. Effective early childhood teachers use a developmental approach as the basis for every aspect of their teaching. They recognize that all children have basic needs and all children have special needs. They recognize further that special needs cannot be met unless basic developmental needs also are met.

This chapter focuses on those general teaching skills and general developmental and behavioural principles that apply to all young children and all early childhood teachers. The point to emphasize is this: *If children with developmental differences are to benefit from special approaches, learning experiences must take place within a developmental framework.* In other words, teachers must make particular adaptations. These adaptations are then incorporated into each child's individual developmental program.

The Teacher Experience in an Inclusive Setting

Teaching in an inclusive early childhood program is both challenging and rewarding. In these settings, teachers encounter the richest and widest range of developmental likenesses and differences among children. Skilled teachers enjoy this diversity once they are convinced of the underlying developmental similarities among children of varying abilities (see photo, below).

At the mention of inclusion, many teachers are concerned about having to work unassisted with children with challenging behaviours or disabilities. Flanagan and Beach (2010) found that although Canadian early childhood educators support the philosophy of inclusion, they struggle in their understanding of "what it means to work in a truly 'inclusive' environment" (p. 16). Odom (2000) reported similar findings with preschool teachers who were concerned about their lack of knowledge of children with special needs. These concerns are understandable; however, in many cases support services are available to the teacher. Blasi and Priestley (1998) concluded that teachers need to be willing to seek out information and resources that will help them understand the special challenges. Kilgallon (2003) found that as teachers got to know a child with special needs, they were better able to plan for and teach the child. She found that the teachers did have an understanding of the child's needs and effective teaching strategies, but that factors such as lack of resources, access to information, support, and opportunities for collaboration, training, and time affected the teachers' perceived competence, as well as their attitudes and ability to include children with special needs in the classrooms successfully. This research confirms that in many cases it may be the teachers' responsibility to seek out the knowledge they need.

No one professional can meet the needs of all the diverse learners in an inclusive early childhood program. Teachers in an inclusive classroom are members of a team of professionals who work together to meet the needs of all the children in the program. Each member of the team brings specialized knowledge to planning and implementing an appropriate developmental program for a child with special needs. Teamwork is especially important in providing the systematic and specialized instruction that is necessary to meet the needs of children with challenging behaviour or severe disabilities. The expertise that the early childhood educator brings to the team is in creating a classroom environment and learning activities that are fun, motivating, safe, interesting, responsive, and supportive.

To ensure successful inclusion, the challenge for early childhood teachers is to make adaptations that accommodate the developmental needs of the range of children in the group. Program adaptation is not a new or unusual challenge for early childhood teachers. Adjusting curriculum and teaching strategies to individual differences and developmental variations has long been the heart of early childhood education. The full implications of this philosophy tend to be overlooked, however, where children with special needs are concerned.

A study conducted by several Canadian researchers (Irwin et al., 2000) found that most of the frontline staff and directors who participated in the study showed positive attitudes toward the inclusion of children with special needs. Factors that enabled teachers to be most successful with inclusion were support from resource teachers and consultants, external therapists, and co-workers, as well as emotional support. The researchers suggested that these ongoing resources strengthen team efforts within centres and built on staff strengths and motivation (Irwin et al., 2000). Directors of child care centres identified several factors that made it more difficult to develop inclusive programs,

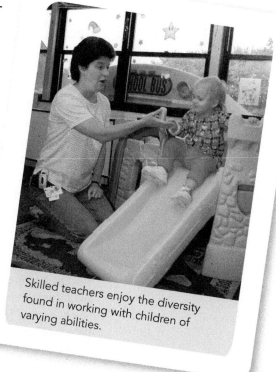

Skilled teachers enjoy the diversity found in working with children of varying abilities.

© Cengage Learning

such as reduced general funding for child care programs, reduced funding or subsidies for children with special needs, and reduced access to specialists. Killoran, Tymon and Frempong (2007) found in their study on inclusive practices within Toronto preschools that a significant number of these centres lacked the support of extra staff and/or resource teachers, and "directors may be inclined to turn away children based on this limitation" (p. 93). Irwin, Lero, and Brophy (2004) described a virtuous cycle of inclusion in which the supports in place allow directors and early childhood educators to have positive experiences with, and to learn from, inclusion; they begin to include a broader range of children with special needs and become more confident about working with all children.

Training Programs for Early Childhood Teachers

People who want to prepare themselves to work with children with developmental differences will find a range of training options:

- Some provinces and territories have early childhood departments, child development and public health agencies, and university- or college-based institutes or centres that offer in-service and on-the-job training.

- Universities, two-year colleges, and vocational/technical schools are sources of early childhood training and basic courses on special needs. Also offered are specialized, post-diploma courses for those wanting to receive more advanced training in special needs and in inclusive programming strategies.

- Some provinces and territories have colleges and universities that offer distance education and Internet courses in early childhood education and related areas.

- Workshops and seminars sponsored by agencies, such as the Learning Disabilities Association of Canada (formerly the Association for Children with Learning Disabilities) and the Association for Community Living (formerly the Association for the Mentally Retarded), are available in many communities.

Specialized Training for Early Childhood Teachers

Post-diploma and degree programs offering specialized training for work with a range of developmental differences are available in a number of provinces and territories. The resource teacher/early interventionist post-diploma certificate program provides specialized training for early childhood education teachers in working with children with special needs and their families. With the expansion of the number of children included in community programs, the need for persons with additional knowledge and specialized training has greatly increased (Halfron & Friendly, 2013). If we are to be successful in accomplishing inclusion as an option for *all* children, regardless of ability, greater recognition of the need for specially trained personnel, as well as greater financial support, must be forthcoming from all levels of government. Table 4–1 identifies how Canadian provinces and territories currently fund programs to provide specially trained personnel.

All early childhood educators should undertake ongoing professional development. Workshops that provide additional knowledge about the specific

TABLE 4-1

Provincial/Territorial Guidelines and Funding for Inclusion of Children with Disabilities

Does the province/territory have a specific approach or guidelines for how children with disabilities are included in the program? What is it? Are there specific guidelines/categories that set out how funding directed toward inclusion is used?	
Newfoundland and Labrador	Yes, the policy manual uses an itinerant consultant model to support providers and administer inclusive initiatives. Individual supports services plans (ISSPs) are used to promote integrated/coordinated services with other agencies and support providers. Funding can be used to bring in other professionals for support, staff training, reducing ratios, reducing group size, child-specific support person.
Prince Edward Island	No specific guidelines for inclusion. Extra funding can only be used to bring in an extra staff person and lower ratios. Funded early years centres may not refuse to admit a child with special needs.
Nova Scotia	Yes, the grant includes six principles of inclusion. An itinerant consultant model is used to facilitate inclusion for individual centres. Funding is to be used for wages for additional staff, approved professional development, and approved education or resource materials directly related to the delivery of an inclusive program.
New Brunswick	Beginning in 2012–13 the province will use community-based facilitators to support inclusion in regulated child care. Available funding is primarily to provide a support worker. The funding may also be used for transportation, materials and equipment, and/or additional nutritional needs of the child.
Québec	n.a.
Ontario	An itinerant consultant model is used to facilitate inclusion for individual centres. Funding is used for consultation, training, hiring extra staff, materials, etc.
Manitoba	Yes, the inclusion policy guidelines include principles of inclusion. Centres have to use IPPs to plan and monitor inclusion. Itinerant consultants are used to coordinate and place children into child care programs, and to facilitate the transition to school. Most of the funding is for staff. There may also be grants available for necessary renovations, equipment, training, or professional services.
Saskatchewan	Program is guided by inclusion principles set out in the application. To apply for extra funding there must be a meeting that includes the parents, child care director, supporting professionals, early learning and child care consultant, and individuals who will be working with the child, including the school teacher if applicable. Family involvement and a team approach to inclusion are promoted. Funding for inclusive child care is intended to support the centre as a whole and not to provide a worker allocated to a specific child. Grants provide support and consultation to the child, family, and staff. An additional staff person may be provided if necessary.
Alberta	Program overview provides guiding philosophy. Funding is used for consultation, information, and referral; program professional development; funding supports for ratio enhancement (home agencies can apply for funding to compensate a provider for taking fewer children to reduce the ratio); or other additional supports (programs may apply for funding to offset the additional or extraordinary costs related to providing care to children with disabilities).
British Columbia	There are no strict guidelines. Supported child development (SCD) consultants help determine the family and child's needs and match these with the resources available in their community. Parents are involved at every step as the key partners in their child's success. In addition, SCD local advisory committees (LACs) involve parents and other key government and community partners in many aspects of program planning and service delivery. Funding is used for individualized planning, training, information and resources, referrals to other specialized services, and, when required, staffing supports.
Northwest Territories	No specific guidelines for inclusion. Operating grants are increased to facilitate inclusion.
Nunavut	No specific guidelines for inclusion. Daily operating grants increased by approximately 50% for a child with an identified special need. In addition, centres may apply for funding to the Healthy Children's Initiative for adaptive equipment or for a one-on-one worker if necessary.
Yukon	An individual program plan (IPP) must be developed for the child in consultation with staff, parents, and professionals in the community, which outlines goals and objectives for the child. The guidelines make clear that children with disabilities must be able to participate in all aspects of the program. Funding may be provided for adaptive equipment, transportation, programming support, and additional staff.

Source: Adapted from Table 5 from Halfon, S., & Friendly, M. (2013). *Inclusion of young children with disabilities in regulated child care in Canada: A snapshot: Research, policy and practice* (Occasional Paper 27). Toronto, ON: Childcare Resource and Research Unit.

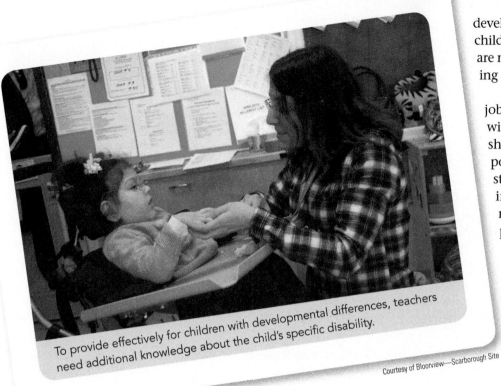
To provide effectively for children with developmental differences, teachers need additional knowledge about the child's specific disability.

Courtesy of Bloorview—Scarborough Site

developmental disability of each child who is about to be enrolled are necessary for effective teaching (see photo, left).

Teachers also need on-the-job experience with children with special needs, but they should always have support from specially trained staff, such as resource/early interventionist teachers, resource consultants, and program advisers. Teachers must also work in close partnership with the parents of each child with special needs. The kinds of information offered in this text will provide a useful and comprehensive starting point for working in inclusive settings with children who have special needs.

Dual Placements and Coordinated Teaching

Coordinated teaching when a child with special needs is in dual placements, staff from the specialized program and those from the inclusive early childhood setting provide coordinated programming for the child

Dual placements when children with special needs spend a part of the day in a specialized program and part in an inclusive child care setting

A child with severe impairments should be provided with various kinds of inclusive experiences whenever possible and appropriate for the child and the child's family. For some children in specialized programs, this may mean frequently scheduled visits to inclusive settings. Other children may spend a part of each preschool or child care day in an inclusive setting. With careful **coordinated teaching** between the two staffs—those from the specialized program and those from the inclusive early childhood setting—these **dual placements** can be of benefit to all children. It is important that early childhood teachers become aware of the special community support services available to families and child care staff in their area. With written permission from the child's parents and the centre's supervisor, the child's teacher may find it helpful to contact one or more local services for a child needing special support. For example, if a three-year-old is observed as having no verbal communication skills, the local hospital might be asked for an assessment by the speech pathologist. The speech pathologist might recommend a language-stimulation program.

In rural areas where specific agencies and organizations are often not yet established, it is helpful to contact a national organization and ask to be referred to the nearest local agency in that province or territory. Local elementary school principals and public health nurses are usually good sources of information on the availability of social services or special consultants in a given area. Some remote regions are visited once a year by a travelling clinic or team of consultants. Most of these consultants will give support if requested in writing before their visit. Retired specialists may also be willing to volunteer or offer support and advice. The child care centre should consult any services that are involved with the child's family in his or her home.

Agencies and service organizations that focus on specific developmental differences can recommend or provide DVDs, articles, books, and other kinds of information. (See the Resources section at the end of each chapter for the websites of many of these organizations.) These materials describe the disabilities and the challenges that confront the child and family. If a child who has a vision impairment, for example, is to be included in a program, it is imperative that teachers begin immediately to find out about blindness and how it affects early development. The Canadian National Institute for the Blind or any of several other organizations with expertise in the area of vision impairments, such as departments of health, are best able to provide helpful materials. To be truly effective, such materials should be used along with background information provided by the family. It should not be forgotten that parents are the most important source of information about their children and their children's disabilities. No amount of special coursework or special training can take the place of the unique information that parents have to offer about their child with a developmental disability.

The Applied Developmental Approach

A Child Is a Child

In an inclusive early childhood setting, teachers need a particular mindset: seeing each child as a child, rather than as a "stutterer" or an "epileptic" or a "Down syndrome child." By viewing every child first as a child, teachers come to realize that many behaviours are not necessarily related to a child's disability. Blaming a child's tantrums or excessive shyness or aggressiveness on his or her disability is commonplace but seldom justifiable. More accurate and certainly more helpful to the child is to view behaviours from the developmental perspective: as developmental commonalities, developmental irregularities, or cultural differences that are seen in all children to a greater or lesser degree. Children's speech is a prime example. Individual children speak differently, just as communities speak differently. Consider the many ways the English language is used in this country; obviously, a difference in language use does not necessarily imply a developmental disorder.

Review of Developmental Principles and Practices

Teachers who work with children with developmental differences need, first and foremost, a thorough foundation in child development. It is nearly impossible to recognize or evaluate many developmental differences without an understanding of the range and variations of behaviours and skill levels found among all children.

DEVELOPMENTAL SEQUENCES Noting sequences of developmental accomplishments rather than of chronological age is a key factor in working with young children. Effective teachers have learned that it is more useful to know that a child is moving steadily forward than to know that the child is above or below the so-called norm.

> *Example:*
>
> *A 39-month-old child with Down syndrome is just beginning to pull up to a standing position. The child's teachers are predicting that she soon will be walking and are planning her program accordingly. How can the teachers be so confident? It's easy—they know this child has passed, in order (though later), each of the preceding large gross motor skills milestones.*

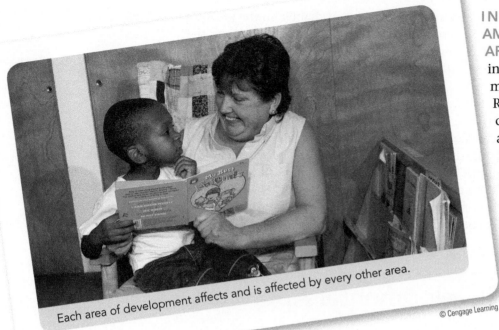
Each area of development affects and is affected by every other area.

© Cengage Learning

INTERRELATIONSHIPS AMONG DEVELOPMENTAL AREAS Understanding the interrelatedness of developmental areas is important, too. Recognizing that each area of development affects, and is affected by, every other area is essential when teaching young children (see photo, left).

Example:

A four-and-a-half-year-old boy with a developmental delay had refused solid foods throughout his life. Clinical findings indicated that the prolonged soft diet, requiring little chewing, had contributed to poorly developed muscle tone, hence poorly controlled movement of the mouth and tongue. The result was almost unintelligible speech, which in turn played a part in the child's cognitive and social development. Teachers and clinicians agreed that the child needed help in acquiring speech, social, and cognitive skills. They also agreed that even with treatment it was unlikely that there would be much improvement in any of the developmental delays unless the child learned to eat solid foods. That probably would not happen until the parents were supported in modifying their child's diet.

DEVELOPMENTAL INCONSISTENCIES Though not all children go through exactly the same sequence of development, there is a sequential pattern that children can follow: Typically, they go from lying on their back or stomach to turning over, to sitting, to crawling, to pulling up, to standing, to walking. However, development is an irregularly paced process—even among children developing within cultural expectations. A period of rapid development often is followed by an unsettled period known as a time of **developmental disequilibrium**. During such periods, children seem developmentally disorganized: calm and capable one moment, screamingly frustrated (and frustrating) the next. Some children may even regress, or appear to go backward, for a while.

Developmental disequilibrium a period of inconsistent behaviour, which often follows a spurt of rapid development

Example:

A three-year-old with a nine-month-old sister competing for attention may revert to babyish ways. He displays tantrums for no apparent reason, loses the bladder control that seemed to be well established, and demands the bedtime bottle that had been given up months ago. Teachers can help parents understand that their child is continuing to progress well in every other aspect of development and, therefore, it is unlikely that the current problems will persist. They might recommend that the parents attempt to give some individual time to this child, away from the baby who is perceived as getting so much attention. It may be agreed that there is no need for a clinical assessment of the child for the time being, that the situation is likely to be but a temporary regression to earlier behaviours. It is further agreed that both parents and teachers will continue to observe the child carefully, in the event that the situation does not change within a reasonable period.

TRANSACTIONAL ASPECTS OF DEVELOPMENT Continual interplay goes on between children and their environment. The process is referred to as the *transactional aspect of development*. The concept recognizes the young child as a dynamic individual who is affected by, and has an effect on, almost everyone and everything that he or she comes in contact with (Horowitz, 1987). Learning can be both positive and negative, reflecting the consequence of both direct and indirect or unintended teaching. It is easy for teachers to recognize their role in promoting intentional learning: They set up appropriate curriculum experiences, interact frequently with children, respond to children positively, and allow children to explore and experiment. Seldom, however, are teachers aware of inappropriate learning that may be promoted unintentionally. For example, the experience of having a single wagon or a single pegboard for a large group of three- and four-year-olds may teach more about shoving, pushing, waiting endlessly, and doing without than about the fine and gross motor skills the materials were intended to promote.

The following frequently cited case study (Allen & Goetz, 1982) illustrates efforts to help a child expand his attention span. The situation demonstrates how an inappropriate behaviour may be learned from the way teachers' well-intentioned efforts combine with the transactional nature of teacher–child interactions. In other words, the very behaviour a teacher wants to eliminate may be unintentionally reinforced by the way the teacher responds to the child:

> James was a five-year-old who seldom stayed with an activity more than a moment or two. Teachers were constantly intercepting him, trying to settle him down, get him interested in something. As the weeks went by James continued to flit, more than ever, it seemed. What was he learning from the teachers' efforts? Certainly not to focus his attention, which was their goal. Instead, he was learning, at some unrecognized level, that flitting about was a sure way to get the teacher attention he needed and could not seem to get in any other way. Unfortunately, this constant flitting maintained a short attention span that interfered with James's acquiring other developmental skills.

Fascinating accounts of this transactional process are found in a number of research studies. One older but still relevant example is Fraiberg's (1974) comments on unsettling transactions between infants who are blind and their mothers. The infants' inability to see their mothers' face interferes with their

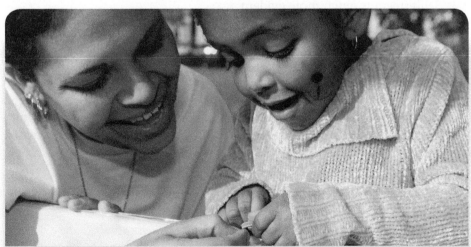

Adult–child transactions have powerful potential for promoting healthy development.

© Cengage Learning

Every day, children show interest in exploring and acquiring new knowledge.

Courtesy of Bloorview—Scarborough Site

ability to respond to their mothers' smiles. The unresponsiveness often is perceived by the mother as rejection. Without her realizing it, her behaviour changes: She smiles less and less because her infant provides her with less delight. Both mother and baby, through no fault of their own, promote a mutual unresponsiveness. This comes at a critical developmental period when both need to be engaging in mutually reinforcing behaviours that lead to a strong parent–child attachment.

Conversely, adult–child transactions have an equally powerful potential for promoting *healthy* development (see photo, page 83). Negative examples were cited here because of a general tendency for adults to overlook or underappreciate their everyday responses to children. Many of these responses carry the unsuspected potential for inappropriate learning emerging from routine interactions between children and adults. It must be remembered that children are learning *something*, for better or worse, from every environmental encounter.

Contingent stimulation responding to a child in a way that prompts further learning

CONTINGENT STIMULATION Closely related to transactional processes is the principle of **contingent stimulation**. In the context of child development, *contingent* implies a kind of dependency or conditioning in which new learning comes about because of the prompt responses of another. With young children, in particular, it refers to the ways in which parents and other significant adults respond to cues from the child. Adults who react to an infant's cooing, gurgling, and babbling stimulate the infant's continuing efforts to communicate. Contingent stimulation is readily observable in the simple give-and-take games that both parents and their babies initiate and take such delight in: peek-a-boo, pat-a-cake, chase-and-hide, and toss-the-toy-out-of-the-crib. When adults make their responses at least partially contingent on what the infant or child says and does, specific developmental benefits result:

- Language development is earlier and better.
- Cognitive development is accelerated and richer.
- Self-esteem is much more evident.
- Attachments are more secure.

Readiness the point when a child has the necessary prerequisite skills to engage in specific new learning

Teachable moments specific points when a child's level of readiness and interest come together to create the best milieu for new teaching

READINESS AND TEACHABLE MOMENTS **Readiness** is a useful concept when appropriately defined as a combination of genetic and environmental factors: *maturation*, *motivation*, and *opportunity*. When these three come together, the child is often *ready* to learn a new skill and a *teachable moment* is likely to occur. **Teachable moments** are those naturally occurring opportunities when a child is most likely to learn a new skill. Consider the following two examples:

An infant reaches for the spoon while being fed, a cue that he or she is ready— that is, mature enough and has acquired the necessary perceptual motor skills—to reach for and hold a spoon (though not always right side up). The reaching also indicates readiness to begin to explore the difficult business of self-feeding. What is needed now is opportunity. Opportunity tends to come in the form of a patient adult who is willing, for many meals running, to scrub the floor, the high chair, and the child after every meal.

Toddlers often get to the point where they demand to be changed, or they pull off their wet diapers by themselves. These children are giving clear cues that they are moving toward the idea of learning to use the toilet.

Observant teachers attuned to developmental differences among children easily translate the concepts of readiness and teachable moments into practice. Every day, children show interest in exploring and acquiring new knowledge and skills (see photo, page 84).

Examples:

A two-year-old trying to put on a shoe heel-to-toe.

A three-year-old struggling to make an upside-down coat stay on the hook.

A four-year-old asking, "Where did the ice go?"

A five-year-old trying to balance a teetering block structure.

In each case, based on knowledge of the individual child, the teacher makes decisions about how to use the moment to a child's best advantage.

Incidental Teaching Opportunities

In many ways, **incidental teaching** is similar to contingent stimulation and teachable moments. All three depend on child-initiated contacts. An incidental teaching episode, however, is *always* initiated by the child. The child approaches the teacher, asking for help, materials, or information. Because the contact is child initiated, the teacher knows that the child is interested and therefore likely to be receptive to a brief learning experience about whatever it is that prompted the contact.

Incidental teaching using a spontaneous teaching opportunity, which is always initiated by the child when he or she asks for help, materials, or information

Incidental (also referred to as milieu) teaching moments represent the systematic application of principles compatible with both a developmental and a behavioural approach to early learning (Kaiser, 2000; Warren & Kaiser, 1988). They also exemplify quality teaching practices that include

- meeting a child where his or her interests lie;
- responding in a way that matches the child's skill level; and
- introducing the bit of novelty that provides challenge for the child.

From the behavioural perspective, the incidental teaching process is a combination of the shaping, prompting, and reinforcement procedures that are central to effective teaching. (Reinforcement procedures, including shaping and prompting, are discussed in Chapter 11.) In spite of being child initiated, every incidental teaching episode occurs in a planned environment, one that teachers have arranged so as to make good use of children's contacts.

The effectiveness of incidental teaching depends on teachers' efforts at

- providing an interesting classroom environment in which children can be busy, active, and inquiring;
- selecting appropriate objectives for each child that match his or her skill levels and interests;
- answering a child's initiation of contact with a request for a response from the child related to a developmental objective for that particular child; and
- responding to the child with whatever is most appropriate in terms of his or her initial contact.

These practices are illustrated in the following example having to do with a child with muscular dysfunction. One of the IPP objectives for André was to increase his ability to reach:

> Teachers had observed André over several days and had identified a number of his play interests. On the physical therapist's recommendation, his preferred toys were put in full view but out of reach. Whenever André asked for, or otherwise indicated interest in, a toy or material, a teacher held it out to him slightly out of reach, but close enough so that he could get it with a little effort. When he got his hands on the object, his efforts were applauded: "You reached for the truck and now you are going to play with it." As André's reach improved, teachers gradually increased the distance. Later, to facilitate the development of overhead reaching, teachers held things just a bit above André's eye level. This, too, they increased gradually.

Incidental teaching opportunities are particularly evident in a curriculum approach referred to as *emergent curriculum*, because one source of curriculum emerges out of the child's contacts and interests and what adults know is necessary for the child's education and development. Gestwicki (2010) described emergent curriculum as "a very organic process, growing from real actions and interactions" (p. 55) between adults and children. In Chapter 15, emergent curriculum as an approach for teaching children with special needs is explored further. In Chapters 16 and 19, the specific use of the process of incidental teaching to promote social and language development is described.

Characteristics of Effective Teachers in Inclusive Settings

In addition to a thorough knowledge of child development, several other traits characterize effective teachers in an inclusive setting. Teaching styles and interactions with children reflect a teacher's own unique personality; nevertheless, effective teachers seem to have a number of characteristics in common. These are described in the following nine points.

Awareness of the Big Picture

Effective teachers of young children have an interest and a social view that extends beyond just the early childhood setting (Gestwicki & Bertrand, 2012). These teachers are linked professionally in many ways to a community, city, province or territory, and country. Teachers who are aware of the "big picture" know about community, municipal, and provincial or territorial services for children with special needs and their families. They value their role as advocates for the inclusion of children with special needs in society and see themselves as part of a larger movement toward social change.

Every early childhood program should have a written policy on inclusion (Langford & Kotsopoulos, 2008). Creating an inclusion policy is a complex process that requires everyone—teachers, families, and children—to be involved. Exploring different understandings of concepts and terms such as "fairness" and "special needs" is a large part of writing an inclusion policy. The policy needs to have adequate information about processes and protocols to demonstrate that the program will exhaust every avenue to put an inclusive philosophy into practice.

Enthusiasm That Supports Learning

Teachers of young children need unlimited enthusiasm to support children's progress and accomplishments, great and small (see photo, right). This is especially important for children with developmental disabilities, who may learn at a slower rate and in smaller steps. A teacher's enthusiastic support becomes a major motivation to wanting to learn more. Every child, regardless of his or her abilities, is quick to catch enthusiasm for almost any activity from a patient, skillful teacher who rejoices with the child over each step or partial step forward.

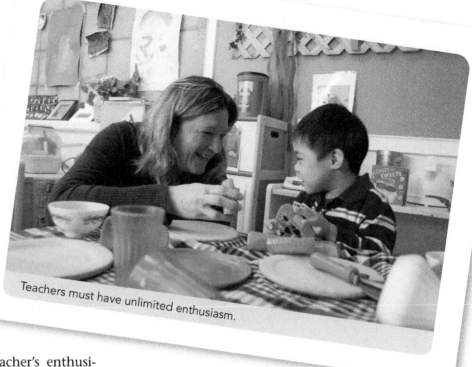
Teachers must have unlimited enthusiasm.
Courtesy of Bloorview—Scarborough Site

Enthusiasm is a reciprocal or mutually supportive process. The teacher's enthusiasm stems from the child's accomplishments, small as they sometimes are. The child's accomplishments, in turn, are supported by the teacher's skills and enthusiasm in promoting the child's learning. It is imperative, therefore, that teachers of young children know how to carry out task analysis, the process of sequencing developmental tasks into small, incremental steps. Small-step successes give both child and teacher many opportunities to enjoy their work together. (Task analysis is discussed in Chapter 11.)

Consistency That Provides Security

The effective teacher is consistent and can be depended on to provide a predictable and stable environment. In addition, expectations need to be communicated in ways that all children can understand. The teacher then can be confident about keeping to expectations, knowing that they are culturally, developmentally, and individually realistic and understood by all. Consistency provides children with security, an especially important factor for children with challenging behaviours. Children who feel secure tend to be more self-confident. They learn to make sound judgments when they are sure of what is expected of them and know that things will remain the same unless teachers give fair warning of a change.

Consistency does not rule out change. Children change throughout their developmental years. Teachers' expectations also must change. What remains consistent is the developmental and cultural appropriateness of the changing expectations and the teachers' care in communicating the changes to the children. Consistency, however, must never be confused with rigidity or inflexibility. An inflexible teacher is not an effective teacher.

Flexibility for Supporting Individuality

The ability to be flexible, to improvise, to adapt an activity to individual or group needs at any given moment is a hallmark of effective teaching. A flexible teacher knows when to cut an activity short if it turns out to be too difficult or if it fails to hold children's interest. The opposite is also true. A flexible teacher knows how and when to extend and elaborate on an activity that has developed into an especially absorbing and worthwhile experience for one or more children. *Flexibility does not rule out consistency.* Truly effective teachers are a blend of consistency and flexibility. They are good judges of when to *bend the rules*. They know when to overlook a minor transgression when a child is trying to handle frustration or work through any other kind of learning experience, as in the following examples:

> *Jana's physical attacks on other children were frequent. Never had she been heard to tell anyone what she wanted; instead, she hit, grabbed, or shoved. One day, however, she stunned teachers by shrieking, "Get out, you stupid!" The rudely shouted command and name-calling were directed at an approaching child who obviously meant no harm. The teacher, though regretting the verbal assault on a well-intentioned child, ignored the inappropriateness of Jana's response. Instead, the teacher supported Jana for talking, not hitting. This was done in the presence of the other child, to promote the child's understanding that Jana was learning to replace hitting with talking.*
>
> *The teacher's flexibility indicated responsiveness to the most urgent priority for Jana as well as to the child who had been rebuffed. It let the child know that classroom expectations were operating, in spite of occasional exceptions. As for the unacceptable verbal behaviour, even if it should accelerate for a while, teachers should not be unduly concerned. When verbal requests dependably replace physical assaults, a new goal, polite requesting, can be written into Jana's IPP.*

The second example focuses on a five-year-old who is gifted, engaging in a block-building activity:

> *The classroom rule was that block structures could be built only as high as the builder's head. Toward the end of the school year, a capable five-year-old had discovered a balancing principle that enabled her to build the tower she was working on higher and higher. At one point she stood on a stool so as to continue building. (Technically, when she was standing on the stool, the blocks were not as high as the child's head.) The teacher's decision to be flexible about the height of the block structure was based on the purposefulness of the child's experimentation. The teacher's continuing presence conveyed consistency about classroom rules: that one child may not endanger another.*

Ability to Build Trustworthiness

The more that children can trust the consistency of teachers' expectations, the more trustworthy children themselves become; hence, the more flexible teachers can be. Teachers who respect children and their need to develop initiative can give children even greater freedom to explore and experiment with their own behaviour. The consistent teacher knows that children know what is expected of them. The teacher knows, too, that children usually can be trusted to stop themselves before a situation gets dangerously out of bounds. Consistency on the part of the teacher allows mutual trust to flourish as a teacher–child relationship grows.

Sense of Humour

Young children need to know that learning is fun and often joyful. Teachers best convey this through their sense of humour, joy, and playfulness. Effective teachers enjoy what they are doing and are willing to laugh at things that are funny even when they laughing at their own mistakes and or when the joke is on them (Colker, 2008).

Provision of Positive Child-Guidance Techniques

Everyone needs limits, especially young children who are trying so hard to learn the many things expected of them. Limits, in the form of culturally appropriate expectations, allow children to relax, to know that they can depend on someone else to make some of the decisions. Expectations, in general, should be limited to health and safety issues and stated positively as much as possible.

Limits should be established to cover situations in which a child is likely to

- hurt himself or herself;
- hurt another person; or
- damage or destroy property.

Whatever expectations there are *must be enforced*. Therefore, the number of rules should be kept to a minimum because enforcing rules is not an especially productive role for teachers.

A typical set of rules, designed to clearly govern teachers' decisions about situations in which children must be redirected, might include the following:

- children are not allowed to push other children when in high places
- children are not to hit other children
- children may not throw sand, toys, books, or other objects
- teachers' cupboards (out of children's reach, we hope) are to be opened only by teachers
- children are not to leave the classroom or play yard without a teacher or other authorized adult

Rules should be stated to clarify the desired outcome behaviour, for example,

- "The sand stays in the sandbox."
- "Books are to read and looked at."
- "Those are the teacher's cupboards; children's cupboards are down there."

Only when a child fails to heed a reminder or redirection should the teacher give negative and emphatic commands: "Kelly, I can't let you throw sand." Rules apply to every child in the group. "No sand throwing" means *NO sand throwing*. This includes children with developmental differences.

There should be no double standards. Double standards do the child with a special need a disservice by not helping him or her learn acceptable behaviour. Furthermore, double standards can lead to resentment and dislike among children who try to abide by the rules. Fortunately, there is no need for double standards. Every child can learn to abide by the few safety rules that are necessary in an early childhood setting.

On many occasions, children truly do not understand what is expected of them from teachers' efforts at positive redirection. When a teacher advises,

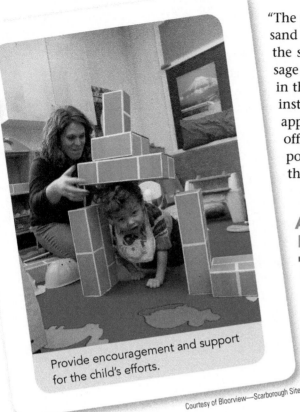
Provide encouragement and support for the child's efforts.

Courtesy of Bloorview—Scarborough Site

"The sand stays in the sandbox," a child may continue to throw sand about while carefully keeping within the boundaries of the sandbox. Clearly, the child does not understand the message the teacher had intended; neither are the other children in the sandbox receiving the protection they deserve. In these instances, specific statements of expectations may be more appropriate right from the start. Clear and indisputable limits offer security to children who may not grasp the subtleties of positive redirection or who may be disciplined differently in their home environment.

Ability to Facilitate and Support Children's Efforts

Though teachers must set limits and hold to them, their major role is that of *facilitator*, a person who makes things happen. Therefore, the facilitative teacher

- provides a range of interesting and appropriate materials and activities;

- presents materials and activities in ways that are attractive and conducive to children's learning;

- offers the right amount and kind of assistance—not too much, but never refusing to assist;

- is aware of what the next step is for each child on each developmental task; and

- responds to each child with ample feedback as to the effectiveness of his or her efforts (see photo, above).

Case Study ■ One preschool teacher's inclusion experience ■

Last fall, a four-year-old boy with Down syndrome enrolled in our program. With the exception of a few biting incidents in the beginning (something we might witness in any young child regardless of whether or not they have special needs, because it often depends upon their language skills), he thrived in our setting. And once he was acclimated and comfortable with the routine, he began attending independently. He participated in everything with the typical zest of a four-year-old, was in every way an integral member of the class, and was gentle and loving.

Although I originally had concerns about how to deal with our students' questions about him, I quickly realized that I had underestimated their ability to accept the differences between themselves and other children. I also discovered that as long as we kept our answers truthful and simple ("Jacob is screaming

because he does not know how to use his words yet"), it seemed to be enough for them. In fact, their immediate response was usually in the form of self-reassurance: "I know how to use my words" or "My legs work."

This experience was not without challenges, however. I often felt ill-equipped when dealing with some behaviours such as tantrums. It was at these times that I enlisted the help of the parent, or other members of the transdisciplinary team.

- What aspects of this teacher's experience relate to the characteristics of an effective teacher?

- What did this teacher do to meet the challenges she faced?

- What else could she have done?"

Facilitation and support, in just the right degree, are especially important during children's play. As Gordon and Williams Browne (2010) pointed out, it can be difficult for teachers to decide when to join children at play and when to remain outside the activity. The important question is whether their presence will support what is happening or whether it will inhibit the play. In an inclusive classroom, teachers tend to find it appropriate to join in more frequently but as unobtrusively as possible. Supportive teacher participation can go a long way toward fostering play relationships among children with or without disabilities, especially when the teacher quietly fades in and out, depending on the progress of the activity (Kontos & Wilcox-Herzog, 1997). Children with special needs tend to have lower self-esteem; it is important for the teacher to work on supporting the building of self-worth and to offer opportunities for independence.

Ability to Integrate Therapeutic Recommendations into Everyday Learning Experiences

Supporting a child with special needs in an inclusive early childhood program includes environmental arrangement, curricular adaptation, and systematic use of teaching strategies to help the child be as effective as possible in interactions with the environment.

> *Example:*
>
> *The speech therapist was working with a five-year-old on beginning B, M, and P sounds. At the small-group breakfast table, the teacher improvised a riddle game based on the therapist's objectives. The teacher described and gave the beginning sounds of various foods the children had encountered over the year. Children supplied the words or labels. The cues for the child in speech therapy had to do with such things as bananas, milk, and pears; butter, muffins, and plums. Everyone at the table participated and learned from the game and had fun with it. No one was the wiser (including the child with special needs) that speech therapy was going on.*

Everyday activities of this kind actualize and integrate the therapy sessions; in other words, they provide a bridge that allows the child to practise, generalize, and consolidate what is learned in therapy sessions to functional, everyday situations.

The Teacher as Mediator

According to social-constructivist theorists such as Vygotsky (1978) and Feuerstein, Rand, Hoffman, and Miller (1980), it is essential that teachers of young children serve as mediators between the child and the learning environment. These theorists emphasize the role of the adult in helping children learn to solve cognitive and social problems.

The strategy is to provide decreasing levels of support while placing higher demands as the child progresses toward the goal of independent problem solving. This part of the teaching/learning process is described as **scaffolding**.

> Scaffolding can take a variety of forms: for example, giving the child a hint, adding a cue, modeling the skill, or adapting the materials and activities.
> It can be provided in a variety of contexts, not only in planned learning

Scaffolding a teaching and learning process in which the teacher provides decreasing levels of support while placing higher demands as the child progresses toward the goal of independent problem solving experiences but also in play, daily routines and outdoor activities. (National Association for the Education of Young Children [NAEYC], 2009, p. 19)

Example:

An objective written into Maya's IPP was that she learn to talk to other children. She had the prerequisite language skills but was not using these with peers. The teacher began the scaffolding process by bringing children together in a group and asking Maya to say "Hi" to each child (high support, low demand). When Maya became successful in this kind of interaction, the teachers arranged opportunities away from group time for Maya to greet peers (higher demand). Gradually, the teacher reduced the amount of assistance and support. Before long, Maya was spontaneously saying "Hi" (and a good deal more!) when she encountered other children.

Mediated learning model based on the teaching premise that cognitive and social processes are interdependent factors in all learning

The **mediated learning model** theorizes that cognitive and social development are intertwined. The teacher's role is to foster children's awareness of their own thought processes by asking them to predict outcomes, test reality, and communicate their thoughts. Most importantly, the teacher emphasizes generalization by encouraging children to think about how a given skill could be used in a different situation: for example, "What might you say to Julie when she doesn't want to play with you?" According to Mills and Cole (1999), teachers who practise mediated teaching create an environment that is conducive to learning by

- thinking through the purpose of an activity;
- assessing the current skill levels of each child;
- providing support and placing demands that reflect the appropriate developmental goals for a child;
- demonstrating intentionally—that is, organizing the experience in ways that clearly communicate what is to be learned;
- helping children generalize new learning to situations beyond the immediate setting;
- taking cues from children's interests and responding to child-initiated learning situations; and
- providing activities that have meaning or function in the everyday life of the child.

In other words, the role of the teacher as mediator is to highlight significant aspects of the environment, emphasize social context, and encourage the child to explore the options.

The foregoing discussion of the attitudes and attributes of effective teachers in an inclusive early childhood program is by no means complete. Teachers also need to know how to do these things:

- integrate behavioural and developmental principles when teaching young children
- work with parents and members of other disciplines
- arrange and present materials and equipment
- schedule the daily program to provide children with an appropriate balance of child-initiated and teacher-structured learning experiences

Summary

In the inclusive classroom, the need for quality teaching and appropriate learning experiences is critical. Effective teachers make ongoing adaptations to the learning environment to meet the developmental needs of all children. Teachers who work with young children who have severe impairments should have the support of a resource consultant available to them. Many children with special needs may initially benefit from dual placements, with one program highly specialized to ensure the intensive treatment the child requires and the other providing opportunities to use newly learned skills as spontaneous opportunities occur.

Early childhood teachers in inclusive classrooms need ongoing professional training. Knowledge about particular disabilities is available, as needed, through various workshops, training programs, organizations, and resource centres. It is also available from resource teachers/specialists who can assess children and consult with early childhood teachers, and from the parents of children with particular developmental differences. What teachers in an inclusive preschool or child care setting need most is knowledge and experience in working with young children in general. To this end, this chapter briefly reviewed significant developmental principles and practices: developmental sequences, the interrelatedness of developmental areas, inconsistencies in development, the transactional aspects of the developmental process, and contingent stimulation.

Special mention was made of readiness and incidental teaching opportunities. Use of incidental teaching moments is effective in teaching all children. It is especially effective when working with children with developmental differences. Because an incidental teaching opportunity is child initiated, it signals to a teacher that the child is ready and interested in learning whatever he or she has contacted the teacher about. The teacher's responsibility is to *be ready* to take advantage of this teachable moment. Other characteristics of effective teachers in an inclusive early childhood program are awareness of the "big picture," enthusiasm, consistency, flexibility, sense of humour, trustworthiness, the ability to limit children as necessary, the capability to integrate therapy-prescribed activities into the regular curriculum, and the skill to mediate children's learning opportunities.

Resources

Canadian Abilities Foundation

http://www.abilities.ca

This site provides access to a wide range of disability information and resources, including provincial and territorial advocacy and support groups.

Center on Inclusion and Early Childhood Care and Education, Western Oregon University

http://www.wou.edu/tri/COI.php

The mission of the Center on Inclusion and Early Childhood Care and Education is to enhance and expand inclusive opportunities for children with disabilities and their families through the study, development, and demonstration of innovative models of service.

Government of Manitoba

http://www.gov.mb.ca/fs/childcare/pubs/writing_inclusion_policy_aug_2009_en.pdf

This site offers a Government of Manitoba publication on how to write an effective inclusion policy for child care centres.

CourseMate Access an interactive ebook and chapter-specific interactive learning tools, including flashcards, quizzes, videos, and more, in the *Inclusion in Early Childhood Programs* CourseMate. Visit NELSONbrain.com to log in, register, or purchase access.

An Overview of Developmental Differences

5

• •

OBJECTIVES

After studying the material in this chapter, the student will be able to

- Describe characteristics of children who are meeting developmental and cultural expectations and those who are not.
- Provide three reasons to justify this statement: "To work effectively with children with special needs, teachers need to have a thorough knowledge of the range of individual and cultural differences in development."
- Distinguish between developmental sequences and developmental milestones, recognizing the impact of a child's culture on these aspects of development.
- Describe biological and environmental factors that can put infants and young children at developmental risk.
- Discuss the arguments both for and against labelling young children as having developmental differences and support each argument with examples.
- Recognize the major categories of developmental differences that are likely to affect children.

KEY CONCEPTS AND TERMS

adventitious deafness

auditory

biological risk

blindness

chronic

communication and language disorders

congenital deafness

developmental delay

developmental deviation

developmental disability

developmental milestones

developmental sequences

dysgraphia

dyslexia

emotional disturbance

environmental risk

handicap

health impairments

hearing impairment

multiple disabling conditions

orthopedic impairments

resilience

special needs

specific learning disabilities (SLD)

tactile

traumatic brain injury

visual impairment

vulnerability

Introduction

Young children are alike in many ways. They also are different in just as many ways. Too often, the strengths of children with special needs are overlooked. The focus is on remediation of their delays or differences. Such perceptions are undergoing change, however, especially in light of recent findings of developmental pathologists (Cohen & Cicchetti, 2006). They argue that both typical and atypical development emerge from the same basic processes, that we need to learn how to respond to the diverging developmental pathways among children of essentially the same age. Remember:

● A child is first of all a child, regardless of his or her individual difference.

● Every child is unique and therefore exceptional in one or more ways.

In small, closely knit societies, the fact that some children are different is not an issue. This seldom holds true in complex societies, such as ours. Setting some children apart, even excluding them from society, seems to have been built into our system almost from the start. As we have seen, however, change is happening. Inclusive educational programs are a major step in the right direction. The underlying issue of classification is still with us. Having to distinguish between those children said to be developing within developmental and cultural expectations, and those who are developing differently, continues to plague us. Policymakers, early childhood teachers, early childhood consultants, and special education administrators often use categories of exceptionality that vary from area to area and across province and territories.

Definitions of normalcy and of developmental differences vary among physicians, psychologists, educators, and many other professionals associated with the growth and development of young children (Bee & Boyd, 2009). The variations come from each professional's training, clinical practices, and traditions. Government policymakers, for example, may use their own specific guidelines to identify particular disabilities, whereas educators may use different guidelines. In other words, there is little consensus as to which children are to be classified as developmentally disabled, which are classified as gifted and talented, and which are classified as developmentally normal (see photo, page 97). The result is confusion for everyone and especially for students and newcomers to the field of early childhood education and early intervention. This chapter will provide an overview of characteristics of children who are meeting developmental and cultural expectations and those children who show exceptionalities within these expectations. In this book, children who are at risk, who have disabilities, who are gifted, and who are of different language backgrounds will be included in the term *exceptional*. Recent research on brain development and the concept of *normal development* will be discussed first, as background. The rationale is obvious: To work effectively with infants and children with special needs, teachers must have a thorough knowledge of growth and development within particular cultural norms. All early intervention programs should have as a main goal the facilitation of a child's overall development. A parallel goal is to implement strategies that promote the inclusion of all children. This chapter will also include and identify categories of developmental differences.

Research on Brain Development

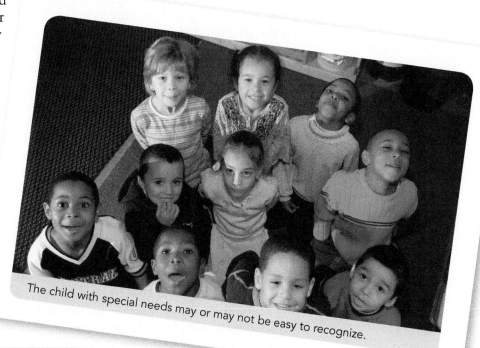

The child with special needs may or may not be easy to recognize.

© Cengage Learning 2015

Recent research on the brain has important implications for learning and development. Only one-quarter of its potential size at birth, the brain is particularly spongelike in the first few years. It is during this time that the brain forms a "network of neural pathways" (Shore, 2003). A major developmental task in the first three years of life is to form and reinforce these links (called synapses) so that they become a permanent part of the brain's "wiring." These synapses occur through continual and repeated use, primarily as a child experiences his or her surroundings, adult care, responsiveness, and teaching (Shore, 2003). By the time the child is a year old, there are trillions of synapses. The pathways they form make up the wiring of the brain. The number and organization of these connections influences all the individual's intellectual and social functioning. Neurons develop rapidly before birth. After birth, brain development consists of "wiring and rewiring" the connections. Within each brain millions of neurons (nerve cells) form and are connected to one another by synapses. After a child's first birthday, new synapses continue to form, while unused synapses are discarded more quickly. By 10 years of age, a child has nearly five hundred trillion synapses, which is the same as the average adult. The brain maintains flexibility for future learning, continually discarding those synapses that have not been used. Simply stated, the growth of the brain operates on a use-it-or-lose-it principle. Thus, children's brains need to be stimulated in order to be protected from this process of elimination. (See Chapter 18 for further discussion of brain research.)

What Is Normal or Typical Development?

As noted above, there are many interpretations of terms used to describe the developing child. One of the most common and frequently used terms, *normal development*, has long been the subject of dispute. What is normal for one child may be quite different for another. For example, most early childhood teachers expect children to make eye contact when spoken to. Teachers tend to be concerned if a child fails to do so. Yet, in certain other cultures, such as some Canadian Aboriginal groups and some areas in the West Indies, children are considered disrespectful if they look directly at the adult who is speaking to them. Drawing on the works of Vygotsky (1978) and Rogoff (1990), Bernhard (2012) stated that it is important for early childhood professionals to question theories and assumptions of human development because cross-cultural evidence suggests that there may be more than one pathway of normal development. In North American culture, a growing independence during the preschool years is expected from a child, whereas in Latin American cultures, what is valued is the child's demonstration of affection and strong ties to parents. Without this understanding of multiple pathways of normal development, Bernhard (2012, p. 65) argued, professionals may consider a preschool child from a Latin American culture delayed if the child does not demonstrate autonomy. One goal for professionals is to distinguish between behaviour that is typical for the culture in which the child and family live and behaviour that is atypical for that culture and suggests a disability that will alter development. Trent, Artiles, and Englert (1999) summarized this goal in another way: A theory that takes into account sociocultural contexts "affords us the possibility to also view 'competence,' 'ability,' and 'disability' ... in new ways" (pp. 299–300).

In addition to culturally defined differences within what is considered normal, there are individual differences among children. No two children grow and develop at the same rate, even within the same culture. Some children walk at 8 months; others do not walk until 18 months. Most children begin walking somewhere in between. All children within this range, and even a bit on either side of it, are normal with respect to walking. The same is true for every other area of development. In summary, broad variations and significant differences in child development are evident within every culture.

Developmental Sequences

Developmental sequences an ongoing process of moving step by step toward mastery of each developmental skill in every area of development

Some principles of human development can serve as guidelines for describing characteristics of children who are progressing in their development and those who are progressing differently. One is that the **developmental sequences** of child growth and development within particular cultures are predictable. Well-trained early childhood teachers (and experienced parents) know that each normally/typically developing child can be expected to move step by step toward mastery of each developmental skill in every area of development. Normal/typical development in this sense implies an ongoing process of growing, changing, and acquiring a range of complex skills. As children develop, individual differences begin to show. Each child will accomplish a specific step but will do so at his or her own rate. Furthermore, no matter how quickly or slowly a child is developing, in most instances, each preceding step occurs before practice on the next step begins. A child rolls over before learning to sit, sits before standing, and stands before walking. Exceptions are common, even to this basic principle of developmental sequencing. For example, most infants crawl before they walk, but some do not. A few infants move about by sitting up and hitching forward with one foot. Others lie flat on their back and push with both feet. Such self-propelling methods of getting about are quite appropriate, even though less common. In some cultures, children are carried on the mother's back all day, and when children are expected to walk, they do so without crawling before walking.

It must be remembered, too, that no two children grow uniformly and at the same rate. Nor do they move forward in all developmental areas at the same time. Rarely is developmental progress smooth and flowing; irregularities and slowdowns are typical (see photo, below). In fact, progress in one skill may actually stop when the child is attempting to learn a new skill in a different area of development. A common example is the infant who talked early and then quit talking for a time, while learning to walk. Some children even regress, that is, slide backward, under certain conditions—for example, the three-year-old who temporarily loses bladder control with the arrival of the new baby. Almost all children experience "special needs" on a short-term basis at one time or another. It may appear that the toddler who walks or talks early is somehow "better" than those who walk or talk several months later. We now know that a developmental lead is not necessarily retained. By Grade 1, the later walkers and talkers are often equally skilled in both language and motor performance.

Special needs challenges in learning and functioning in one or more areas of development and increased vulnerability to environmental and non-environmental stresses

Developmental Milestones

Regardless of variations that may occur, certain behaviours or skill sequences can be seen in a fairly predictable order in almost every child who is developing normally. These significant points or events at certain ages often are referred to as **developmental milestones**. If we take into consideration "cultural context," we may find in various developmental pathways different milestones at different ages (Bernhard, 2000). However, a child who does not reach or is seriously delayed in reaching one or more developmental milestones needs attention. It could be a warning signal that something may be amiss in the child's development. Thus, it is necessary for everyone working with very young children to have a thorough knowledge of different cultural and developmental milestones and sequences in each area of development. If all goes well, the developing child passes milestone after milestone in every area of development. Nevertheless, the question posed at the start, "What is normal?" has not been given a truly complete answer. What about a child who is developing normally in some areas but is delayed, even disabled, in others? What about children with severe orthopedic disabilities, for example, who cannot walk, let alone run and jump and climb as other children do? Many children with orthopedic impairments are developing normally otherwise and can be gifted in language, intellectual, or artistic development. The opposite may also be true: Children who are delayed in language or cognitive development may have well-developed motor skills. It is helpful to look more closely and examine why some children are identified as having exceptionalities.

Developmental milestones points at which specific skills are acquired in a fairly predictable order

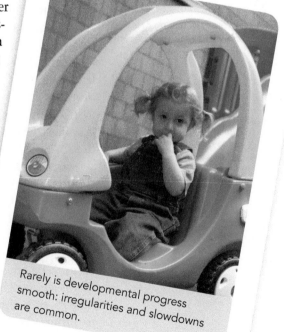

Rarely is developmental progress smooth: irregularities and slowdowns are common.

Who Are Children with Exceptionalities?

Efforts to decide which children have exceptionalities have been going on for decades. At times, the term has been all-inclusive. Its use has ranged from children with the mildest of speech differences to those who were outstandingly brilliant (but different). The term has been used most frequently in the field of education. Other terms that are frequently used to identify children who are in need of additional support services include the following:

- *Special or challenging needs.* These are the preferred terms used by early childhood educators, service providers, and advocates for children who

  1. face barriers in their learning and functioning in one or more of the following areas of development: physical, social, emotional, communication, intellectual, behavioural; and

  2. have increased vulnerability to environmental and non-environmental stresses, including those related to family, social, economic, and cultural circumstances.

- **Handicap.** This relates to environmental or functional demands that, when placed on a person with a disability, are not met (Winzer, 2007).

- *Impairment.* This refers to incapacities or injuries, especially those having to do with the sensory and neural systems; thus, we speak of children with visual impairments, orthopedic impairments, and speech and hearing impairments.

- *Atypical.* This is a much broader term that covers almost any variation from what is considered normal; often it is a matter of degree: How different or how far behind must a child be to be considered atypical? Seldom is this term used in reference to children who are gifted.

- **Developmental disability.** This term usually refers to a variety of conditions that interfere with the child's physical, sensory, or cognitive development and originate between conception and 18 years of age.

It can be useful to think of developmental disabilities as taking two basic forms: delays and deviations. What is the difference? A **developmental delay** is present when a child is performing like a developing child of a younger age. As an example, consider Josh, a three-year-old just beginning to put together two-word sentences. Josh has moved steadily through each earlier milestone in language development. It is evident that this three-year-old is experiencing a language delay; normal language will come, though later than for other children his age. By the age of eight or ten, it is unlikely there will be any hint of Josh's earlier delay. A **developmental deviation** is present when some aspect of a child's development is different from what is seen in other developing children. Another language example will be used—this time, a three-year-old with severe oromuscular dysfunction because of cerebral palsy. The child makes many sounds and tries very hard to talk but cannot be understood. This is a deviation. It is likely that this child will continue to have speech problems.

Developmental deviations, however, are not necessarily handicapping. Individuals with six toes on each foot have a physical deviation, yet they most surely would not be thought of as having a handicap. Conversely, what may seem to be an equally nondisabling deviation can be a handicap if it is a source of anxiety for the person. Such things as a large birthmark on the cheek, missing fingers, or a shortened leg might be a handicap for some but of little concern to others. The impact depends on how well the child, especially in the early years, is helped to adapt to and accept the deviation. Recognizing a child with a developmental disability is not always easy to do. Whereas a severe spinal cord malformation, present at birth, is easily identified, other disabilities, such as a severe hearing loss in a newborn, may be nearly impossible to recognize

Handicap relates to environmental or functional demands that, when placed on an individual with a disability, cannot be met

Developmental disability one of a range of conditions that interfere with any aspect of the normal development of the child

Developmental delay development of a skill progresses at a slower rate so that a child demonstrates the skill as a younger child would

Developmental deviation some aspect of a child's development is different from what is seen in other developing children

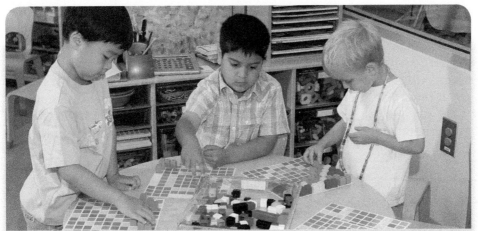

At one time a child who did not speak English or French was considered to have a "handicap."

unless the infant is receiving high-quality medical screening or is in an intensive neonatal health-care facility. We must also consider whether a child who speaks a language other than English or French in either an English or French classroom is "exceptional." Haring and McCormick (1994) referred to this as an "environmentally related limitation." It should be noted that the same child may well be highly capable in the language of his or her home environment (see photo, above). Note, too, that the child's preschool teacher might be considered to have a handicap in the child's own community if the teacher speaks only English or French. Therefore, in this textbook, the child who speaks a language other than English or French in either an English or French classroom is not considered to have a developmental disability. Rather, this child has additional needs that may require extra support until he or she has mastered the necessary linguistic skills to function in the classroom.

Children at Risk

Many infants and young children are said to be at risk or at high risk. This means there is reason to believe that serious problems are likely to develop. For example, mothers who were heavy drinkers or chemically addicted during pregnancy often bear children who are at risk developmentally. Their newborns may or may not show immediate special needs. Infants who are born addicted and at a very low birthweight are likely to be considered children with high-risk needs; they may be in grave developmental danger. These children are more likely than others to exhibit learning disabilities, emotional disorders, and attention deficits. Another less dramatic, but all too frequent, example of children at risk are those born into serious poverty. Developmental risk is likely to occur in cases of malnutrition, inadequate shelter, and poor health care. An important characteristic of children who are at risk is that the potential for healthy development is there. The majority of infants and children at risk have a good chance of overcoming initial setbacks. What is required is early and comprehensive intervention services: medical treatment, ample nurturance, and in many cases, family support services (see Chapter 3). Risk factors, including those already discussed, can be grouped into two major categories: biological risk and environmental risk.

Biological risk infants and children whose systems have undergone some kind of biological insult, such as an accident, injury, or severe stress, are at risk for developmental disabilities

BIOLOGICAL RISK The term **biological risk** applies to infants and children whose systems have undergone some kind of biological insult, such as an accident, an injury, or severe stress. The incident may have occurred before birth (prenatal), at birth (perinatal), or following birth (postnatal). For example, a newborn with respiratory distress syndrome (RDS) is at risk but likely to recover if given immediate treatment. Premature birth or low birthweight (5.5 pounds or 2500 grams or less) are risk factors that require immediate, intensive intervention. Without it, many infants suffer severe developmental complications.

Environmental risk factors in a child's environment, such as poverty, child abuse, family beliefs, and inaccessibility of medical care, that put the child at risk for developmental disabilities

ENVIRONMENTAL RISK Poverty is the greatest single factor associated with **environmental risk**. As noted earlier, families who live in severe poverty are often seriously undernourished and may lack adequate shelter. In addition, they may have little or no way to learn about caring for their infants and may not know how to obtain appropriate social services and medical care. At the same time, Polakow (1992) reminds us, as well, that as early childhood educators "we need to recognize that the lack of entitlement to health care, housing, nutrition, and childcare create stressful and powerless lives; that the problems that are often diagnosed as emotional impairments and learning disabilities are very real reactions to concrete conditions of want." (p. 144). As will become evident in Chapter 6, the effects of poverty produce many biological risk conditions. However, poverty is not the only environmental factor that puts infants and young children at risk. Other factors include

- child abuse and unfit living conditions because of addicted or dysfunctional family members;
- family beliefs that prohibit urgently needed medication, medical treatment, or surgery; and
- the inaccessibility of medical care when families live in remote areas.

Resilience and Vulnerability

Resilience the ability to "come back" after a damaging or traumatic experience

Vulnerability lack of resistance to or ability to recover from a damaging or traumatic experience

Biology and environment (nature/nurture) may not interact in the same way for every child. The degree of inborn and learned **resilience** and **vulnerability** appear to make a difference (Steinhauer, 1998). Horowitz (1990) concluded that given a facilitative environment, vulnerable children often have a good developmental outcome and that resilient families and children in a poor environment also may do quite well, because they learn to use whatever resources are available to them. Child care professionals who interact with children daily are in a unique position to promote optimism and resiliency (Kordich Hall, 2000). However, the vulnerable child raised in an unfavourable environment is in greater jeopardy of developmental risk.

The Disadvantages of Labelling

Convincing arguments can be made for not putting a specific diagnostic label on infants, toddlers, and preschoolers who are developmentally different. Many young children who are developmentally different in one way or another resemble their peers far more than they differ from them. With the exception of children with severe impairments, children with developmental disabilities go through the same sequences of development as do other children, though at different rates. It should not be assumed that a disability in one area of development means that special programming is required in all areas (see photo, page 103). Furthermore, many infants and young children start out with serious challenges that they

Special needs in one area of development do not mean that special programming is required in other areas.

© Cengage Learning

are able to overcome if they receive appropriate early intervention services. Premature infants are a good example. Often they are delayed in acquiring early developmental skills. Yet by age two or three, many of these children, with adequate care and nutrition, are catching up. Freedom from developmental delay does not hold true for all low-birthweight babies, but many show no long-term disability. This is in contrast to those born a generation ago, when treatment of premature infants was less advanced (Bee & Boyd, 2009). Some impairments, even though serious, may never be handicapping if the child receives appropriate support and intervention services. The condition may continue to exist, but the child finds ways to compensate and so learns to function in spite of it.

Example:

Bret was a child born with one short arm and a malformed hand. The family, from the start, had referred to this as his "little hand." At preschool, there was nothing Bret could not do as well as any other child, be it puzzles, form boards, or block building. In kindergarten, he was among the first to learn to tie his shoes. By Grade 7 he was a champion soccer player.

Individuals like Bret seldom consider themselves to have a handicap, nor do their families view themselves as having a child with a handicap. It is unlikely that this positive attitude could be maintained if the label "handicapped" (with the inevitable differences in attitude that accompany the term) had been attached to this child in infancy. Those opposed to labelling or categorizing argue that it can be harmful. The harm may be especially great when young children are concerned. The very young may get locked into categories that are developmentally unsuitable or put into programs that compound their delay, as in the following example.

Example:

At three, Jodie was talking very little, had difficulty following simple directions, and demonstrated few play skills. She scored low on an IQ test and was placed in a preschool for children who had intellectual impairments. It was not until age seven that a severe hearing loss was discovered. Between three and seven, crucial developmental years, Jodie functioned as a child with an intellectual impairment. Why? Because she had been labelled as having an intellectual impairment and consequently had not been identified as a candidate for deaf education services, she was not receiving the stimulation needed to develop language and cognitive skills.

Chapter 5 | AN OVERVIEW OF DEVELOPMENTAL DIFFERENCES

The Advantages of Labelling

Labelling is useful and at times necessary for

- enhancing public awareness of developmental differences;

- gaining access to public funds from provincial, territorial, and federal governments;

- advocating for support services and changes;

- clarifying and facilitating communication between professionals (e.g., in research); and

- identifying specific medical conditions (such as hemophilia and anaphylaxis).

Classification of Developmental Differences

Disagreement has long revolved around classifying individuals with developmental differences. Should we label children who are developmentally different according to categories, such as *deaf, blind, emotionally disturbed*, or *intellectually impaired*? In the United States, government legislation (PL 99-457) recognizes the potential harm of prematurely classifying children under the age of six. For this reason, funding by categories has been discontinued in this legislation for children under age six. Instead, the more flexible concept of *developmental delay* is used to cover all developmental differences. Such an approach is more in keeping with the tremendous variability of development among young children.

There is no comparable federal legislation in Canada. At this time, some provinces and territories are developing and others are adapting legislation that provides for young children with special needs. The current direction in Canada is to focus on providing funding for all children who are experiencing developmental challenges during the early years. Table 5–1 identifies how (or if) each Canadian province/territory defines "a child with special needs."

Some policymakers believe that to qualify for specific treatment programs and services, young children need to be assessed and in many instances categorized. In their view, it is in such instances that having a classification system becomes important. Classification, labelling, and categorization are also necessary in situations where medical doctors and other professionals communicate with others by using research and sharing case information. Those doing research into various disabilities need to have a common vocabulary. To make important decisions, those in favour of categorizing argue that questions, such as the following, need to be raised:

- How many individuals have a particular disability? (Is it widespread? increasing? decreasing?)

- Does it occur mostly in particular areas or among certain groups (urban, rural, immigrant, itinerant farm worker, etc.)?

- How many teachers, clinicians, and facilities are needed to provide services for children in this category?

- What proportion of public money should be allocated to serve each of the different groups of developmental disabilities?

- Which individuals are eligible for government financial assistance?

TABLE 5-1

Definitions of Special Needs

Newfoundland and Labrador	Policy manual states that "special needs refers to delay and/or exceptional ability in any of the developmental domains (social, cognitive, language, physical and/or self-help)."
Prince Edward Island	Special needs grant guidelines state that "a child with special needs is defined as a person who is under the age of 12 years, has a diagnosed disability and, in order to attain the usual developmental goals, requires additional and/or specific types of stimulation/care."
Nova Scotia	Early intervention program (EIP) describes a child with special needs as a child who has " a developmental delay of 6 months or more, in two or more areas of development or is at risk for developmental delay due to a diagnosis or health history."
New Brunswick	Three categories of special needs: 1. a confirmed diagnosis at birth; 2. developmental issues after birth; 3. family risk factors.
Québec	No
Ontario	No
Manitoba	Children's disABILITY Services serves children with a mental disability; a developmental delay; autism spectrum disorder; a lifelong, physical disability that results in significant limitations in mobility; or a high probability of developmental delay due to a pre-existing condition, significant prematurity with medical and/or biological factors, or a parent who has a mental disability.
Saskatchewan	Children with special needs are "children with diverse and intensive needs."
Alberta	No
British Columbia	Supported child development program policy and procedures manual defines disability as a condition that persists over time and limits the activities of the person
Northwest Territories	No
Nunavut	No
Yukon	No

Source: Table 3 from Halfon, S., & Friendly, M. (2013). *Inclusion of young children with disabilities in regulated child care in Canada: A snapshot: Research, policy and practice* (Occasional Paper 27). Toronto, ON: Childcare Resource and Research Unit.

Definitions of Categories

In spite of disagreements, categorization does exist. A major problem is that the systems vary. The medical profession may group the individuals with disabilities one way, special education programs another way, and government agencies still another way. Brief descriptions of each category are given in the following discussion. In later chapters, developmental differences are regrouped and discussed in greater detail, focusing on early identification, assessment, and intervention.

COMMUNICATION AND LANGUAGE DISORDERS

Communication and language disorders among young children vary greatly. It is difficult to define clearly what is and what is not a disorder because so many factors affect language development:

- individual differences in temperament
- rate of development
- cultural expectations

Communication and language disorders difficulties with speaking or learning language, which can lead to serious disruptions in cognitive and social development

- general health and well-being
- opportunity to hear language and talk to others

Also, a number of typical or frequently experienced irregularities are common in the course of language development. These need not become problems unless the child is unduly pressured. Communication and language disorders are likely to accompany other developmental disorders. Children with cerebral palsy often have serious speech disorders, as do children with hearing impairments and severe emotional disturbances. Whatever the cause, it is important that communication and language disorders receive attention as early as possible (Photo 5–5). Problems in this area can lead to serious disruptions in cognitive and social development.

It is important that communication and language disorders receive attention as early as possible.

Courtesy of Bloorview—Scarborough Site

SPECIFIC LEARNING DISABILITIES Like communication and speech disorders, **specific learning disabilities (SLD)** or learning disabilities (LD) are difficult to define satisfactorily. In the school-aged child, the label is often one of exclusion—what the child does *not* have, such as

- an intellectual impairment;
- a hearing impairment;
- a visual impairment; or
- an identifiable neurological problem, such as cerebral palsy.

Specific learning disabilities (SLD) a difficulty in any of the following areas: attention, memory, reasoning, coordination, communicating, reading, writing, spelling, calculation, social competence, and emotional maturation

Dyslexia an impaired ability to read and understand written language

Dysgraphia difficulty with or inability to express thoughts in writing and/or to identify the written symbols of language

In spite of no observable or identifiable disabilities, these children have trouble acquiring basic academic skills. The Learning Disabilities Association of Canada's (LDAC) definition states that school-aged children with learning disabilities include those with potentially average, average, or above-average intelligence. Nevertheless, these children may have difficulties in any of the following areas: attention, memory, reasoning, coordination, communicating, reading, writing, spelling, calculation, social competence, and emotional maturation (LDAC, 2002). The largest group of children characterized as having a learning disability are those having difficulty with reading. The problem is often referred to as **dyslexia**. Other children may have trouble learning to print and write. This may be referred to as **dysgraphia**. More than 100 different labels have been assigned to children whose learning problems baffle clinicians and educators. The labels, it should be noted, do little to help children with their learning disability.

COGNITIVE DELAYS Generally speaking, it is unwise to assign the label of cognitive delay to a young child. Children change; they evolve. The younger the child, the more likely it is that changes will occur. The range of "normal" intellectual functioning is enormous. Furthermore, a child's family circumstances may change, health problems may clear up, or the child may enter an early intervention program. Any one of these has the potential to produce dramatic change in a child's cognitive skills. Issues related to cognitive development and mental functioning are addressed in Chapters 6 and 19.

GIFTED Children described as gifted or talented do exceptionally well in one or more areas of development. They often are a good fit with the concept of multiple intelligences. Gardner (1993) theorized six types of intelligence: linguistic, logical-mathematical, musical, spatial, bodily kinesthetic, and personal-social. Children who are gifted show accomplishments that seem to appear spontaneously, as part of their own unique developmental process. It is unlikely that these early and outstanding abilities emerge because of special training or parental pressure. Parents of especially bright or talented children often are surprised when told of their child's remarkable abilities (Robinson, 1981).

MULTIPLE DISABLING CONDITIONS A number of children have **multiple disabling conditions**, meaning more than one disability (Photo 5–6). It is estimated that 20 percent to 50 percent of children with serious hearing deficits have additional disabilities. The same is true of children with cerebral palsy. Many of the syndromes are also characterized by several disabilities occurring together. It is not uncommon, for example, for a child with Down syndrome to have a heart defect, respiratory problems, a marked hearing loss, and hard-to-understand speech.

The number of children with multiple disabilities is rising. Three possible reasons for the increase are as follows:

> **Multiple disabling conditions** the condition of having more than one disability

1. Increasing numbers of pregnant women are using alcohol and drugs.

2. Many of the diseases that cause both prenatal and postnatal disabilities in infants and young children have not yet come under modern medical control. In other words, we do not yet know how to treat a number of the medical problems that occur at the same time.

3. Advanced medical practices now allow us to keep babies alive who have serious disabilities or have a very low birthweight. A major concern is that we do not know how to treat many of the disabilities with which these children are born.

> **Orthopedic impairments** developmental differences that interfere with walking or other body movements

ORTHOPEDIC IMPAIRMENTS

Developmental differences that interfere with walking or other body movement are considered **orthopedic impairments**. In many instances, orthopedic and neurological impairments are closely related, one example being cerebral palsy. The term *orthopedic impairments* includes

Some children may require multiple supports in their development.

- impairments caused by congenital anomalies and structural deformities such as club foot, absence of a limb, or paralysis;

- impairments caused by diseases, such as polio;

- neurological and spinal cord damage resulting in problems, such as paralysis of major muscles; and

- impairments from other causes, such as incidents that result in severely fractured bones, amputations, or burns.

It is commonly thought that neurological problems are evident at birth. Often the opposite is true. It may be weeks or months (even well into the first year) before the infant gives evidence of a neurological impairment. The problem may become noticeable only when certain very early reflexive (primitive) behaviours do not drop out on schedule, interfering with the acquisition of new and more mature responses. For example, most newborns automatically grasp a finger placed in their hand. However, unless this primitive grasp reflex disappears between one and four months of age, infants will not be able to learn to release objects at will.

Courtesy of Ryerson Early Learning Centre

EMOTIONAL DISTURBANCE **Emotional disturbance** has no formally agreed-on definition and is thus subject to much controversy. One proposed definition is that the disability is characterized by behavioural or emotional responses so different from appropriate age, ethnic, and community norms that the responses adversely affect educational performance, including academic, social, vocational, or personal skills (McClelland, Morrison, & Holmes, 2000). Whatever the definition, emotional disturbance is a label that *should not be assigned to young children*. The reasons are similar to those given earlier for avoiding the label of intellectual impairment with young children. Alternative terms for emotional disturbance (which are more appropriate, developmentally) might be *behaviour disorders*, *behaviour problems*, or *behaviour challenges*. The term *social adjustment problems* is also used. These terms will be used interchangeably in this text. Even so, they are used with caution. Why? One reason is that children's behaviour during the early years is heavily influenced by child-rearing practices, cultural values, and expectations of the family and community. Parents who are aggressive, for example, tend to have children who also behave aggressively. Thus, the child's aggressiveness is perfectly "normal" in the light of the family environment.

The social and emotional characteristics of young children also are highly influenced by particular stages of development. (In times gone by, early childhood educators and pediatricians even used such terms as "the terrible twos" to describe the toddler's struggle for independence.) Behaviour difficulties often arise out of the frustrations a young child experiences in trying to master basic developmental skills, such as learning to feed himself or herself, learning culturally acceptable bowel and bladder practices, and learning what to fear and what not to fear. In most cases, therefore, a child's behaviour should be judged by what is developmentally appropriate for his or her particular age range and cultural background. The majority of behaviour problems occurring in early childhood do not carry over into adult life. Note: There are other developmental disorders that have symptoms that involve severe behaviour disorders. These include autism spectrum disorders (ASD) and attention deficit hyperactivity disorder (ADHD). These conditions are discussed in Chapter 10.

DEAFNESS AND HEARING IMPAIRMENTS As defined by U.S. legislation (PL 94-142), the deaf are individuals whose hearing loss is so severe they cannot process spoken language, even with hearing aids or other forms of amplification. Children with a **hearing impairment** are those whose loss may have a delaying effect on a young child's cognitive, social, and language development. Because of the age factor, deafness and hearing impairments often are labelled according to when the damage occurred:

- **Congenital deafness** is experienced by individuals who have been deaf since birth.
- **Adventitious deafness** is experienced by individuals who are born with normal hearing but lose it through injury or disease.

HEALTH IMPAIRMENTS Young children with severe **health impairments** often have limited strength, vitality, and alertness. They also may experience pain and discomfort much of the time. A regular childhood may be nearly impossible because of frequent hospitalizations or intensive medical treatment.

Health disorders can take many forms, including

- heart problems (weak or damaged heart);
- leukemia (cancer of the bone marrow);
- asthma (disorder of the respiratory system);

Emotional disturbance characterized by behavioural or emotional responses so different from appropriate age, cultural, and community norms that the responses adversely affect educational performance

Hearing impairment a hearing loss that can have a delaying effect on a child's cognitive, social, and language development

Congenital deafness deafness present at the time of birth

Adventitious deafness deafness acquired through injury or disease after birth

Health impairments chronic or acute disorders, such as heart problems, leukemia, and asthma, that threaten a child's overall development

- sickle-cell disease (red blood cell malformation);
- hemophilia (a bleeding disorder);
- diabetes (faulty metabolism of sugar and starch); and
- cystic fibrosis (lung and digestive problems).

Health disorders may be described as **chronic** or acute (although a chronic problem can develop into an acute state). In either case, the child's overall development is threatened. Although poor health problems may not be the actual cause of other developmental differences, they can create situations that lead to other concerns.

Chronic a health problem of long duration and frequent recurrence

Example:

A child who is physically weak and unable to run and jump and play with children of the same age may be socially isolated. Brothers and sisters may resent having to play with the child instead of their own playmates. They also may resent that so much of the parents' attention and resources seem to be focused on the sick child. This may lead to the sick child feeling lonely, rejected, anxious, guilty, and even more isolated.

BLINDNESS AND VISUAL IMPAIRMENTS There is no clear-cut definition of **visual impairment**. A legal-medical definition proposed by the U.S. National Society for the Prevention of Blindness is currently accepted in Canada, and it includes the following:

Visual impairment vision loss that includes the following conditions: blind, partially sighted, and low vision

- *Blind.* Visual acuity of 20/200 or less in the better eye with the best possible correction; or a much reduced field of vision (at its widest diameter, a visual arc of 20° or less).
- *Partially sighted.* Visual acuity between 20/70 and 20/200 in the better eye with the best possible correction.

The American Foundation for the Blind offers these educational definitions:

- *Blindness.* Visual loss is severe enough that it is not possible to read print, requiring the child to be educated through the use of Braille and other **tactile** and **auditory** materials.
- *Low vision (partially seeing).* Residual vision is sufficient to allow the child to read large print or possibly regular print under special conditions and to use other visual materials for educational purposes.

Tactile refers to what is learned or perceived through touch

Auditory refers to what is experienced through hearing

Total **blindness**, whether congenital or occurring after birth, is readily identified. The baby simply does not respond to people or objects within its range of vision. Less severe visual disorders may be more difficult to identify. Frequently, the difference does not show up until it is time to learn to read and write. By this time the child may have developed a number of other problems in trying to compensate for the undiagnosed vision loss.

Blindness vision loss severe enough that it is not possible to read print, requiring the child to be educated through the use of Braille and other tactile and auditory materials

COMBINED DEAFNESS AND BLINDNESS Children who are described as being both deaf and blind have a combination of vision and hearing problems so severe that they require highly specialized intervention programs. Two such serious sensory deficits in combination usually result in a number of other differences in language, cognitive, and social development.

AUTISM SPECTRUM DISORDER Autism spectrum disorder is a serious disturbance evident in the first three years that affect a child's verbal and non-verbal communication skills, reciprocal social interaction, or ability to engage in imaginative play. Autism spectrum disorder includes autism, Rett's disorder, childhood disintegrative disorder, and Asperger's disorder (see Chapter 10).

Traumatic brain injury includes injuries to the head that cause tearing of the nerve fibres, bruising of the brain against the skull, or bruising of the brain stem

TRAUMATIC BRAIN INJURY The category **traumatic brain injury** includes injuries (either open- or closed-wound) to the head that cause tearing of the nerve fibres, bruising of the brain against the skull, or bruising of the brain stem. The most common consequences as far as learning is concerned are

- confusion in spatial orientation and directionality;
- marked distractibility and short attention span;
- problems in both short- and long-term memory; and
- impulsivity and sometimes aggressiveness.

Summary

Decisions as to which children are developing normally and which children have exceptional development vary among child development theorists, government agencies, and the various professions involved with young children. The terminology used to refer to children who are exceptional has gone through a series of changes over time, reflecting changes in societal attitudes. Normal development is difficult to define because it is so complex a process, particularly in light of recent brain research. Normal development includes a range of developmental skills and may take a different developmental pathway within cultural environments. Certain guidelines are available, based on knowledge of developmental sequences and developmental milestones. Because young children are in a constant state of change, it is preferable to think of them as having a developmental delay or difference—not a handicap. Children at developmental risk are those who are likely to develop a developmental delay if they do not receive special services as early as possible. Risk factors—biological, environmental, or both—may occur prenatally, at the time of birth, or during the early developmental years. Classifying or categorizing children in terms of particular developmental differences is a common educational and administrative practice. Most professionals argue against categorizing, especially for young children, because infants and children change rapidly during the early years. Nevertheless, a classification system seems necessary from both the funding and the professional training standpoint.

Resources

Council of Ministers of Education, Canada

http://www.cmec.ca

This site provides a link to the Ministry of Education in each province and territory, with access to information on special education.

Learning Disabilities Association of Canada

http://www.ldac-acta.ca

This website provides LDAC's official definition of learning disabilities as well as links to related sites.

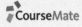 Access an interactive ebook and chapter-specific interactive learning tools, including flashcards, quizzes, videos, and more, in the *Inclusion in Early Childhood Programs* CourseMate. Visit NELSONbrain.com to log in, register, or purchase access.

Children with Cognitive Delays

6

OBJECTIVES

After studying the material in this chapter, the student will be able to

- Explain why it is especially inappropriate to label a young child as "mentally retarded."
- Specify several possible underlying causes of cognitive delays and give examples.
- Discuss the correlation between poverty and cognitive delays in young children.
- Identify major conditions that are likely to affect the development of the young child.
- Discuss basic programming considerations for a child with developmental delays.

KEY CONCEPTS AND TERMS

amino acid

anoxia

asymptomatic

at risk/high risk

autosomal recessive gene disorder

biological insult

biological risk

cognitive delay

congenital

first trimester

metabolic disorders

muscle tone

neurological

perinatally

postnatally

prenatally

protein deficiency

respiratory distress syndrome (RDS)

stigmata (stigma)

syndrome

CONNECTIONS

- Graham and Bart are three-year-olds with similarly diagnosed hearing loss. Graham is talking almost at age level. Bart has two distinguishable words among the songs and signs that he makes.
- As a newborn, Noah was characterized as a "floppy baby"; that is, he had little muscle tone. Therapists have worked with Noah and his parents since early infancy. His condition has not been specifically diagnosed.
- Clarrissa is four and speaks only one or two words. She communicates using signs and gestures.

Introduction

Cognitive delay intellectual growth that does not follow the expected rate of development due to genetic or environmental conditions or a combination of both

Determining the cause of any developmental difference is a complex process. The cause of a **cognitive delay** is at times difficult to recognize; at other times, the reasons may be clearly evident. Cognitive delays may have their origins in the prenatal, perinatal, or postnatal period of development. It is important to try to determine the extent of the delay and then work with specialists to develop effective strategies for supporting the child and the child's family. Consider the following examples of questions that might arise when we attempt to determine the cause of a cognitive delay in a child:

1. Two three-year-old boys display hearing impairments: One is talking well; the other is not talking at all. Why?
   - Do they have different kinds of hearing losses?
   - Has one child had more frequent or more severe ear infections?
   - Is one child in a better early childhood program?
   - Do cultural and family differences account for the developmental differences?
2. What might account for performance differences among three preschool children who have been labelled as "cognitively delayed" but who have no recognizable physical disabilities?

Questions such as these are common among child developmentalists, clinicians, and educators. Though the issues are not new, there are no ready answers. The best response, so far, is that the causes of cognitive delays appear to be a combination of factors: heredity, biology (physical makeup), temperament (personality style), and a long list of environmental factors that interact in complex ways.

The range of both normalcy and individual differences is broad. Furthermore, all children develop at slightly different rates, excelling more quickly in some areas of development than others. It is important to observe children fully and refer them for professional assessments before jumping to the conclusion that an observed deviation from normal growth and development is serious or permanent. One thing is certain: More harm than good comes from prematurely labelling a child.

The term *mental retardation* has been used primarily by the medical community. Early childhood professionals are urged to use the term *cognitive delays* because of the historical negative connotations associated with the term *mental retardation*.

Because a child has a cognitive delay does not mean that the child cannot learn. Every child has the potential to learn, and the base point at which learning starts depends on the degree of delay. Some children may acquire cognitive skills more slowly than others do. Some may never acquire higher-level thinking skills. What we need to keep in mind is that none of us can fully know the potential of any child.

Assessment tools and tests can guide us in determining an appropriate level at which to start programming to support cognitive development. In spite of the difficulties associated with assigning categories to—and specifying the causes of—cognitive delays, some guidelines are available. Practical knowledge about the causes of developmental irregularities is accumulating rapidly. In addition, classification systems have been designed that can be used under prescribed conditions with some infants and young children. These issues—causes and characteristics of cognitive delays—are the focus of this chapter.

Characteristics of Cognitive Delays

We must remember that as children grow, they will develop at their own pace and the range of normal is quite wide. Health experts also remind us that it is helpful to be aware of the red flags for potential developmental delays in children. These delays are significant lags in one or more areas of emotional, mental, or physical growth.

The areas of development where delays might be observed include

- language or speech;
- vision;
- movement—motor skills, including **muscle tone**;
- social and emotional skills; and
- thinking—cognitive skills.

Muscle tone the interaction between the central nervous system and motor activity; the term does not mean the same thing as muscle strength; without muscle tone there is no voluntary movement

Sometimes, a delay occurs in many or all of these areas. When that happens it is called *global developmental delay*.

As attitudes in both Canada and the United States have shifted to reflect greater awareness and recognition for individuals with intellectual and developmental disabilities, the former American Association of Mental Retardation has changed its name and website in 2013 to the American Association on Intellectual and Developmental Disabilities (AAIDD). The organization defined *intellectual disability* as "a disability characterized by significant limitations both in intellectual functioning ... and in adaptive behaviour, which covers a range of everyday social and practical skills" (AAIDD, 2013, para. 1).

The Merck Manual website stated, "The previously used term mental retardation has acquired an undesirable social stigma, so health care practitioners have replaced it with the term intellectual disability" ("Intellectual Disability (ID)," 2009, para. 2).

Causes of Cognitive Delays

Causes of a cognitive delay can occur at any stage of development: before the child is born (**prenatally**), during the birth process (**perinatally**), or any time following birth (**postnatally**). Any condition present at the time of birth is referred to as **congenital**. Congenital problems may or may not be genetically related. Deafness, for example, can be caused in one child by an infection the mother

Prenatally occurring or existing before birth

Perinatally occurring or existing at the time of birth

Postnatally occurring or existing after birth

Congenital refers to a physical condition that originates during the prenatal period

A healthy infant "hooks" parents into responding.

© Cengage Learning

had during early pregnancy; in another child it may be genetically linked to parents who are deaf. Some of these differences can be recognized at birth; others may not be detected or do not manifest until much later. Generally speaking, the more severe the disabling condition, the earlier it is recognized. There are, however, many exceptions. For example, a serious hearing loss may not be identified until the child enters group care.

Research indicates that biology and environment each have an equal impact on human development. Without exception, environmental factors have an impact on a child's biological foundation, influencing the developmental outcome. Environment affects and is affected by heredity in two ways. Parents with high IQs tend to produce children with high IQs and also tend to provide a rich and stimulating environment for their children. In addition to this, behaviour geneticists state that children are born with particular types of temperaments that affect the way the environment responds to them. Thus, some children may actually create for themselves a more responsive learning environment because of their more responsive temperaments. A healthy infant, as we will see, "hooks" parents into responding (see photo, left). Strong, early bonding is the usual result. An ill, low-birthweight infant may have little or no energy to expend on any activity and so the outcome may be less positive. These complex interactions and transactions, with the child as the pivot point, need to be kept in mind in the discussions that follow.

Risk Factors

Risk factors, including those already discussed, can be grouped into two major categories: *biological* and *environmental*.

Biological Risk

Biological insult interference with or damage to an individual's physical structure or functioning

First trimester the first three months of prenatal development

Biological risk infants and children whose systems have undergone some kind of biological insult, such as an accident, injury, or severe stress, are at risk for developmental disabilities

Respiratory distress syndrome (RDS) a problem commonly found among premature infants because of the immature development of their lungs; it may also occur in about 1 percent of full-term infants during the first days of life

At risk indications (either physical or environmental) that an infant or child may develop serious problems

BIOLOGICAL INSULT Biology plays a major role in determining both healthy and at-risk development. **Biological insult** refers to interference with or damage to an individual's physical structure or functioning. The biological insult may occur at the time of conception, during pregnancy (often within the **first trimester**, because of health problems in the mother), during the birth process (from complications, such as the umbilical cord becoming wrapped around the baby's neck), or following birth (from respiratory distress, viral infections, and so on). All of these, singly or in combination, together with environmental factors, can lead to cognitive delays. The stages of typical fetal development are documented in Figure 6–1.

Some examples of a **biological risk** are the following:

- A newborn with **respiratory distress syndrome (RDS)** is at risk—in serious trouble medically—but likely to recover if given immediate and appropriate treatment.

- Premature birth or low birthweight (5 pounds [2500 grams] or less) are risk factors that require immediate, intensive intervention. Without it, many of the infants affected will suffer irreversible developmental damage.

FIGURE 6-1

Typical Fetal Development

2 weeks
- Cell division results in an embryo consisting of 16 cells.

3–8 weeks
- Structures necessary to support the developing embryo have formed: placenta, chorionic sac, amniotic fluid, and umbilical cord.
- Embryonic cell layers begin to specialize, developing into major internal organs and systems, as well as external structures.
- First bone cells appear.
- Less than 1 inch (2.54 cm) in length at 8 weeks.

12 weeks
- Weighs approximately 1 to 2 ounces (0.029–0.006 kg) and is nearly 3 inches (7.6 cm) in length.
- Sex organs develop; baby's gender can be determined.
- Kidneys begin to function.
- Arms, legs, fingers, and toes are well defined and movable.
- Forms facial expressions (e.g., smiling, looking around) and is able to suck and swallow.

16 weeks
- Weighs about 5 ounces (0.14 kg) and is 6 inches (15.2 cm) in length.
- Sucks thumb.
- Moves about actively; mother may begin to feel baby's movement (called "quickening").
- Has strong heartbeat that can be heard.

20 weeks
- Weighs nearly 1 pound (0.46 kg) and has grown to approximately 11 to 12 inches (27.9–30.5 cm) in length (approximately half of baby's birth length).
- Experiences occasional hiccups.
- Eyelashes, eyebrows, and hair forming; eyes remain closed.

24 weeks
- Weight doubles to about 1.5 to 2 pounds (0.68–0.90 kg) and length increases to 12 to 14 inches (30.5–35.6 cm).
- Eyes are well formed, often open; responds to light and sound.
- Grasp reflex develops.
- Skin is wrinkled, thin, and covered with soft hair called lanugo and a white, greasy, protective substance called *vernix caseosa*.

28 weeks
- Weighs about 3 to 3.5 pounds (1.4–1.6 kg); has grown to approximately 16 to 17 inches (40.6–43 cm) in length.
- Develops a sleep/wake pattern.
- Remains very active; kicks and pokes mother's ribs and abdomen.
- Able to survive if born prematurely, although lungs are not yet fully developed.

32 weeks
- Weighs approximately 5 to 6 pounds (2.3–2.7 kg) and is 17 to 18 inches in length (43–45.7 cm).
- Baby takes iron and calcium from mother's diet to build up reserve stores.
- Becomes less active as a result of larger size and less room for moving about.

36–38 weeks
- Weighs an average of 7 to 8 pounds (3.2–3.6 kg); length is approximately 19 to 21 inches (48–53.3 cm).
- Moves into final position (usually head down) in preparation for birth.
- Loses most of lanugo (body hair); skin still somewhat wrinkled and red.
- Is much less active (has little room in which to move).
- Body systems are more mature (especially the lungs and heart), increasing baby's chances of survival at birth.

Source: © Cengage Learning 2015

The most readily recognized chromosomal disorder is Down syndrome.

Courtesy of Bloorview—Scarborough Site

- Other biological risk factors include genetic disorders, such as Tay-Sachs syndrome, and chromosomal disorders, such as Down syndrome (see photo, left), which may have accompanying physiological problems, putting the child at greater risk developmentally.

GENETIC DISORDERS

The genetic makeup of every individual is determined at the moment of conception. Each parent contributes 23 chromosomes on which there are thousands of genes. In a process called cell division (involving two processes, *meiosis* and *mitosis*), the chromosomes from each parent divide and recombine. Physical characteristics, such as size, body build, eye and skin colour, and sex, are determined at that moment. Genetically determined abnormalities also become evident at this time. They may be caused by deviations in chromosomal structure or by abnormal single genes. Chromosomal abnormalities are usually biological accidents that occur one time and do not affect future pregnancies. They occur in all races with similar frequency.

Single-gene disorders, however, are hereditary, often show racial variations, and are found in healthy carriers. When both parents have the same recessive abnormal gene, statistically, one in four of their children will be affected by the disorder.

Syndrome a grouping of similar physical characteristics

Stigmata (stigma) an identifying mark or characteristic; a diagnostic sign of a disease or disability

SYNDROMES Various syndromes make up a major class of genetic abnormalities. The term **syndrome** refers to a grouping of similar physical characteristics called **stigmata**. When several stigmata are found in a recognizable pattern (having a similar chromosomal error), the child is said to have the syndrome. In many instances, children with a given syndrome have similar physical characteristics, which may make them look somewhat alike.

Down syndrome The most widely recognized chromosomal disorder is Down syndrome (Trisomy 21). It occurs approximately once in every seven hundred births, with the risk slightly higher among young teenage mothers and greatly increased in women over 45, at 1 in every 20 births (Rozien, 2007).

The individual with Down syndrome has 47 rather than 46 chromosomes. On chromosome 21, there is an additional chromosome, hence the term Trisomy 21. Children with Down syndrome are often easy to identify because of the following physical characteristics:

- a small, round head that appears somewhat flattened in the back
- a low-set bridge of the nose, giving a flat mid-face appearance
- low-set, small ears with unusually shaped earlobes

- a protruding tongue due to poor muscle tone

- short fingers and toes with the little fingers and little toes curving inward

- a simian crease (a single, almost straight line across the upper part of one or both palms, instead of the usual pair of parallel lines)

- curving folds of skin at the inner corners of the eyes, which give an almond shape to the eyes

That said, the Canadian Down Syndrome Society (2014) also urges us to remember that while people with the syndrome often share some physical disabilities, individuals will look like their family members and will have their own unique personality, just as the general population includes diverse personalities.

About 50 percent of children with Down syndrome have congenital heart defects and intestinal abnormalities. Hearing impairments, often from severe cases of ear infection, such as otitis media, are also common. Some degree of cognitive delay, ranging from mild to severe, becomes increasingly apparent as these children grow older.

Fragile X syndrome (FXS) Fragile X syndrome is caused by a marker on the X chromosome of some males. Because boys inherit their X chromosome from their mothers (and the Y chromosome from their fathers), this disorder often shows a sex-linked pattern with one mother having more than one affected son, even if the sons have different fathers. The consequences of this condition are cognitive deficiencies varying from mild to severe, language delays, behavioural problems, repetitive speech and autistic-like behaviours (including poor eye contact and hand flapping), large or prominent ears, hyperactivity, delayed motor development, and/or poor sensory skills. Fragile X syndrome can cause some disability in both sexes, but boys tend to be more seriously affected physically, mentally, and behaviourally. According to the National Fragile X Foundation (n.d.), a number of studies have determined that the prevalence of FXS is approximately 1 in 3600 to 4000 males and approximately 1 in 4000 to 6000 females. In the United States it is considered a leading known familial cause of intellectual/cognitive deficiency.

METABOLIC DISORDERS **Metabolic disorders** cause a breakdown somewhere in the complex chemical activities needed to metabolize food. The breakdown can destroy, damage, or alter cells. Metabolic disorders are single-gene defects. Two of the more common genetically related metabolic disorders are phenylketonuria and galactosemia.

Metabolic disorders single-gene defects that cause a breakdown somewhere in the complex chemical activities needed to metabolize food

Phenylketonuria (PKU) Phenylketonuria occurs in about 1 in 10 000 births. It is caused by a breakdown somewhere in the complex chemical activities needed to metabolize food. It is most common in people of Northern European ancestry and uncommon among African Americans. The infant born with PKU lacks the liver enzymes needed to digest the **amino acid** known as phenylalanine. Phenylalanine is present in milk, wheat, eggs, fish, and meat. The mother's normal metabolism protects the infant before birth, but as soon as the infant is fed milk, toxic (poisonous) substances build up, leading to irreversible brain damage. Today, blood tests are available and all newborns should be routinely screened for this disorder. If placed immediately on a highly restricted diet, the child can usually be saved from serious intellectual impairment. The diet, low in phenylalanine, must be continued during most of the child's developmental years. It is also recommended that a woman who has PKU stay on the diet throughout her child-bearing years. If an affected woman does not, any baby she carries will be

Amino acid one of the chief components of proteins; amino acids are obtained from the individual's diet or are manufactured by living cells severely brain damaged because the fetus will be exposed to an abnormal metabolic environment in utero. The control of PKU demonstrates how environmental manipulation can modify genetic disorders successfully.

Galactosemia Galactosemia is a metabolic disorder in which milk cannot be digested. Infants with galactosemia tend to appear normal at birth. The moment milk is introduced, vomiting, diarrhea, and enlargement of the liver begin. Without treatment, death usually occurs within the first few months of life. Should the infant live, intellectual impairment is inescapable. Again, the problems can be avoided with screening of the newborn. If milk intolerance is detected in the early days of life, a special diet, started immediately, will prevent intellectual impairment.

ABNORMAL GENE DISORDERS

Autosomal recessive disorder a gene carried by healthy parents on any one chromosome except the sex chromosomes that, if inherited from both parents, results in a child with a medical condition not present in the parents

Tay-Sachs Tay-Sachs is a rare **autosomal recessive disorder** occurring most commonly in children of Eastern European Jewish descent. Research by the National Human Genome Research Institute (2011) has revealed that non-Jewish French Canadians and the Cajun community of Louisiana also have a higher incidence of Tay-Sachs. A faulty enzyme of fat metabolism is the cause of this disorder. Fatty accumulations in the brain interfere with neurological processes. The result is a rapid degeneration of the nervous system from birth on, with death usually occurring in early childhood.

Some other gene disorders do not affect the brain directly, but result in frequent absences from school, affecting the child's learning (see Chapter 9). These include cystic fibrosis, sickle-cell disease, and muscular dystrophy.

PRENATAL CONDITIONS, INFECTIONS, AND INTOXICANTS Most developmental abnormalities, especially those that occur prenatally, cannot be explained by genetics. Less than 3 percent of all birth defects are thought to be purely genetic in origin. Diseases that have a negative effect on a mother's health during pregnancy are responsible for 25 percent or more of all developmental deviations.

A few of the conditions and infections that can occur prenatally in utero are described below.

Rubella Rubella (also known as German or three-day measles) can have a devastating effect on the fetus (unborn infant). If contracted during the first trimester, rubella can lead to severe and lifelong disabilities. Fortunately, childhood immunizations have now drastically reduced the incidence of congenital rubella.

CMV virus CMV virus (cytomegalic inclusion disease), which can be contracted by the mother through intimate contact, is a frequent cause of severe damage to infants. Often, the pregnant woman has no symptoms. Ninety percent of infants with CMV are **asymptomatic** at birth; that is, they show no problems. It is only later that intellectual impairment, deafness, diseases of the eyes, and other disabilities begin to show up.

Asymptomatic showing no signs of a disease or impairment, which nevertheless may be present

Herpes simplex Herpes simplex is an incurable viral disorder that can cause recurring severe to mild genital sores. Even when it is in remission, a woman can pass it on to her unborn infant. The results can be devastating, even fatal, as in cases of inflammation of the infant's brain and spinal cord. Less damaging results include periodic attacks of genital sores.

AIDS (acquired immune deficiency syndrome) AIDS is a condition that interferes with the body's ability to ward off diseases such as respiratory disorders and certain types of cancer. Transmission of AIDS is through sexual contact, shared hypodermic needles, and blood transfusions. An infected mother can pass AIDS on to her unborn infant (see Chapter 9).

Diabetes Diabetes in the pregnant mother puts the infant at **high risk** for serious developmental problems, even death. Today, a woman with diabetes has a better chance of bearing a healthy baby because of medical advances. Nevertheless, maternal diabetes must be monitored throughout pregnancy.

High risk a high probability of developing serious problems

Toxemia Toxemia is a frequent complication of pregnancy, which produces a variety of symptoms, including swelling of the mother's arms and legs, poorly functioning kidneys, and high blood pressure. Women with toxemia often deliver babies who are premature or of low birthweight, putting the baby at medical risk.

Drugs, alcohol, and other chemical substances Maternal use of any chemical substance during pregnancy, whether for medicinal purposes or as a "recreational" substance (e.g., crack cocaine, alcohol, and some prescription drugs), often results in serious abnormalities in the unborn infant. These range from deformed arms and legs to mild to severe intellectual impairment. Similar problems can be the result of alcohol intake during pregnancy. Still relevant is the years of research by Streissguth, Barr, and Sampson (1990) indicating that alcohol consumption, even in moderate amounts, or occasional binge drinking, can damage the developing fetus. Research consistently continues to suggest that risk is cumulative; that is, children who have more risk factors (e.g., drug exposure, low birthweight, poor prenatal care, poor nutrition) are more likely to have developmental delays than children with fewer risk factors (Ackerman, Riggins, & Black, 2010; Decoufle, Boyle, Paulozzi, & Lary, 2001).

Alcohol and drug intake have been linked to a variety of developmental problems now grouped under two headings: fetal alcohol syndrome (FAS) and fetal alcohol effect (FAE). The potential for subnormal IQ is three times greater among children whose mothers drink during pregnancy. The major symptoms of FAS include growth deficiency before and after birth; damage to the central nervous system, leading to learning disabilities; and facial and cranial malformation. The chance of intellectual impairment and pervasive developmental problems is greatly increased in children who have the physical abnormalities associated with FAS, including a smaller head, droopy eyes, a wide space between the nose and upper lip, the occasional cleft palate, and heart problems. It is believed that any amount of drinking during pregnancy can affect the developing fetus and that even occasional binge drinking can have a devastating impact. Health Canada (2009) discussed the secondary disabilities of FAS/FAE, including mental health problems like depression or obsessive-compulsive disorder, dropping out of or disrupting school, trouble with the law, chronic unemployment, alcohol and drug problems, and homelessness.

A number of drugs used by pregnant women for medicinal purposes also can cause serious birth defects. Pregnant women should not take medications without consulting a physician. This is particularly important in terms of over-the-counter drugs. Illegal drugs—cocaine and its many variations, for example—used during pregnancy can put the unborn infant at high risk for both short-term and long-term developmental problems. Many such infants are born prematurely, have very low birthweight, or are stillborn; others die of SIDS (sudden infant death syndrome), otherwise known as "crib death," during the first year. Research conducted by Kartin, Grant, Streissguth, Sampson, and Ernest (2002) demonstrated that the developmental performance of preschool children exposed to alcohol and drugs prenatally was, on average, substantially lower for their age. Children who are exposed to cocaine prenatally are often underweight, have smaller head circumferences, and are at greater risk for developmental delays than are children who have not been exposed. These delays are seen in the areas of attention, information processing, learning, and memory (Shore, 2003).

It is not known how much drug use is too much. However, as indicated above, no drug is safe for a developing fetus. In light of this information, the only safe course is for women to refrain from all alcoholic and drug intake during pregnancy. It should also be noted that the fetus is most vulnerable in the earliest stages of pregnancy, and the mother may not even realize at this time that she is pregnant.

Rh blood incompatibility In Rh blood incompatibility, the mix of the mother's blood type and the father's causes serious problems. The mother's body may reject the fetus, or the fetus's red blood cells may be destroyed. The danger of Rh incompatibility can be controlled with early medical treatment. Rarely does the problem occur with a first child.

Protein deficiency a factor in maternal malnutrition when the mother's diet is lacking in milk, cheese, eggs, meats, and so on, which can result in premature or seriously low-birthweight babies

Poor nutrition Maternal malnutrition due to poor diet and **protein deficiency** due to lack of milk, cheese, grains, eggs, fish, chicken, and meat can result in premature and seriously low-birthweight babies. These infants are at high risk for a number of developmental problems, including limited brain cell development, illness, and a higher risk of death during the first year. Stunted growth throughout childhood is often another consequence. (Note: there are many reasons other than poor nutrition that also are responsible for premature and low-birthweight infants.) The effects of poor diet are particularly damaging during the last trimester of pregnancy, when significant maturing of the brain and nervous system takes place. It is now recommended that a pregnant woman gain 25 to 30 pounds (10 to 15 kilograms) during pregnancy—and more if she is underweight to begin with.

Anoxia a shortage of oxygen to the brain that can cause physical damage to the brain before, during, or at any time after birth; anoxia is one of the major causes of physical and cognitive dysfunction

Neurological refers to the functioning of the nervous system

BIRTH COMPLICATIONS Birth itself can result in trauma—that is, injury or shock. An infant, perfectly healthy until the moment of birth, can experience damage during the birth process. For example, **anoxia**, lack of oxygen available to the brain cells, can occur because of labour complications. Brain damage or severe **neurological** problems, such as cerebral palsy or intellectual impairment, may result. Recent evidence, however, indicates that a healthy newborn may be able to withstand a fairly substantial shortage of oxygen without suffering major damage. When damage does occur, it may not come from a newborn's inability to breathe immediately. Instead, the failure to start breathing may have been caused by earlier, perhaps unsuspected, damage in utero. This is one example of how difficult it is to be certain about the cause of a developmental problem.

Complications at birth may necessitate a Caesarian section (C-section) delivery. This type of delivery may be required when the typical vaginal delivery is impossible or when the lives of the mother, infant, or both are threatened. The most common reasons for the procedure are signs of fetal distress, such as a weak infant heartbeat, or breech presentation of the about-to-be-born infant.

Premature infants, especially, are subject to another kind of trauma: hemorrhaging or bleeding into the brain. These immature newborns are also at higher risk for breathing problems, heart failure, and infections. Even less severe problems at birth can result in later trouble. It is now thought that some school-age learning disabilities may be associated with low birthweight or seemingly minor disturbances at the time of birth (Mayo Clinic, 2011b).

COMPLICATIONS AFTER BIRTH Following the birth process, other events can lead to developmental problems. Among these are physical injuries from falls or bumps that involve severe trauma to the brain; ingesting of poisonous substances, such as bleach, and other household cleaning products; viral and bacterial infections, including meningitis and encephalitis; lead poisoning; and poor nutrition.

Meningitis Meningitis is a viral or bacterial infection that causes inflammation of the protective covering of the brain and the spinal column. When meningitis-related death occurs in newborns, the cause usually is organisms found in the intestines or birth canal of the mother. The results of meningitis are unpredictable. Some children show no serious effects; others experience major neurological damage.

Encephalitis Encephalitis is an infection that attacks the brain itself. The symptoms are so many and so varied that the infection often is not diagnosed correctly. A range of after-effects is possible, from no damage to identifiable neurological damage and later learning problems.

Lead poisoning Lead poisoning can cause grave damage to young children whose bodies and nervous systems are still developing. According to Pimento and Kernested's *Healthy Foundations in Early Childhood Settings*, "Scientists now know that even low-level lead exposure can affect a child's brain development and nervous system, leading to possible behavioural and learning difficulties and reduced intelligence" (2010, p. 426).

Pimento and Kernested warned that

> exposure to lead in dust and soil is a main concern because preschoolers are likely to ingest dust and soil every day. Houses and apartments and early childhood settings situated near industries that have used lead, or are situated on busy streets, may contain high levels of lead because lead can remain in the soil for decades and contaminate vegetables grown in that soil. (p. 426)

A child who has been exposed to high levels of lead over a long period of time may not show any physical evidence of lead poisoning but may develop intellectual, developmental, and behavioural abnormalities associated with lead poisoning.

In 2005, Health Canada established Children's Jewellery Regulations, making it illegal to import, advertise, or sell lead-based jewellery for children. Pimento and Kernested (2010) stated that one can tell if a toy or jewellery contains lead by the following:

- appearance of metal that is dull and grey-looking
- pieces that seem heavy for their size
- jewellery or toys that leave a grey line if rubbed against a sheet of paper
- soft plastics—lead is used as a stabilizer to keep the plastic soft

There are several lead-testing kits available through paint stores and large hardware store chains.

Children who eat well-balanced diets are at less risk of lead poisoning than are children who are malnourished or have calcium or iron deficiencies.

Additional sources of lead include

- lead-glazed ceramics (utensils and pots made of lead-glazed ceramics should not be used for cooking or serving food or beverages, especially acidic ones, such as tomatoes, fruit juice, and so on);

Chapter 6 | CHILDREN WITH COGNITIVE DELAYS

- old painted toys and furniture (see photo, below);
- recent toys made with lead or painted with lead-based paint;
- folk medicines;
- cosmetics from Asia; and
- imported earthenware toys.

Lead-based paint—which can be found in older (circa World War II and later) homes and buildings constructed and/or painted into the 1950s—also presents a risk to young children who may chew on and ingest peeling paint or plaster.

In conclusion, because young children put almost everything into their mouths, it is particularly important that early childhood centres be vigilant about ensuring that the physical environment and the contents of the environment in which young children are placed is lead-free.

The Impact of Poverty

Many cognitive delays, regardless of when they occur—before, during, or after the birth of the baby—can be directly or indirectly related to poverty. Families living in poverty experience the highest rates of infant death, failure to thrive, and birth defects. The same holds true for subsequent developmental problems, including intellectual impairment, learning disabilities, and social and emotional deviations.

The link between poverty and developmental delays cannot be denied. Consider the following:

- Poor nutrition during pregnancy, as well as during infancy and early childhood, can have a major impact on the overall development of the child.

- Children who are poor are likely to be living in unhealthy environments that are beyond their control to change. Poverty usually means having food insecurity, living in housing that is often substandard (cold, damp, drafty, or crowded) and in unsafe areas, having inadequate clothing, and not having access to safe play and recreation opportunities (Pimento & Kernested, 2010).

- Pimento and Kernested (2010) cited information from the *2007 Report Card on Child and Family Poverty in Canada* stating that 11.7 percent of all children in Canada live in poverty: "People living in poverty are much more likely to develop health problems, including chronic illnesses such as heart or lung disease" (p. 26).

- "Children who live in persistent poverty are less likely to be academically prepared to start school. When they get there, they have less positive, less successful school lives—with poorer scores in reading, math, science, and writing. They are more likely to have emotional problems and to exhibit anxiety and aggressive behaviours, and hyperactivity" (Canadian Council on Social Development, 2006, p. 16).

The *Campaign 2000 2012 Report Card on Child and Family Poverty in Canada* stated that "more recent statistics

By law, play equipment and toys are no longer painted with lead-based paint.

indicate that 979,000 or 14.5% of children in Canada live in poverty as of 2010, compared to 912,000 or 13.7% in 1989" (p. 4). The report also reached the following conclusions:

- Disproportionately high child poverty rates among marginalized children are linked to structural discrimination experienced by parents who have difficulty finding employment.

- Children in lower-income schools are at a double disadvantage, with less access to learning-enhancing resources both at home and at school.

- Income inequality compromises children's physical and mental health.

- Inadequate housing, directly linked to higher morbidity and mortality, often exposes children to conditions that lead to chronic health issues like asthma.

- Household stress caused by financial strain affects children's emotional and behavioural well-being. Not having enough food or a safe place to live and being excluded from social activities may negatively affect mental health in childhood and adulthood.

It is important to note that not every child living in poverty will have developmental problems. Many parents find ways to cope, to raise bright and healthy children despite severely challenging circumstances.

Case Study ▪ Helping Tanisha ▪

Tanisha is a three-year-old girl. She has been attending a community-based preschool program for the past six months. She is the youngest of three children in her family. Tanisha responds well to one-on-one interactions with teachers. When successfully completing activities, Tanisha smiles broadly; however, it is very difficult to understand her as her articulation skills are not clear. She often points and gestures to communicate her needs. Tanisha is easily distracted by noises in her environment and by peers playing near her. She seems to enjoy water, sand, and other sensory activities, as well as tabletop activities. Outdoors, Tanisha demonstrates difficulty with a number of gross motor activities. What intervention would you recommend for her to increase her future success in school?

Strategies and Ideas for Programming

Because of the range of differences in cognitive delays, there is no set "program" to recommend. However, the following general guidelines should be helpful:

- Break down tasks into small steps, focusing on one step at a time.

- Use repetition until a child accomplishes the desired response.

- Support the child's efforts by verbally reinforcing positive steps.

- Use a variety of resources, such as music, movement, and sensory materials, to support exploration and stimulate learning.

- Guide the child's actions, using hand over hand when appropriate.

- Support the child's involvement in music and movement by modelling or, when necessary, by sitting behind the child and guiding his or her arms, legs, and so on, with your own motions and touch.

- Work from simple to complex, and concrete to abstract, when teaching a new idea. Use physical or concrete examples whenever possible.
- In group games and activities, try to find a role that is developmentally appropriate and can enable a child with cognitive delays to participate actively with his or her classmates. This role might include distributing equipment, helping to rearrange furniture, erasing a blackboard, and so on.
- Use predictable schedules and routines. When changes are pending, try to prepare the child in advance.

While implementing the above recommendations, it is important to keep in mind the importance of inclusion, of enabling the child with a special need to participate in the ongoing curriculum and to be as much a part of it as possible.

Summary

In summary, for the purposes of this text, the term *cognitive delays* is used to refer to a continuum of cognitive differences, ranging from those children who have a mild delay to those who have a severe impairment in their cognitive functioning.

A cognitive delay may or may not be permanent, depending on the cause, level of severity, and timing and effectiveness of intervention. There are a range of factors that may influence the cognitive development of a child, including the conditions that occur prenatally, usually caused by problems during the first trimester, as well as some conditions that may be caused by an as-yet-unidentified deviation in the child's genes or chromosomes. Prenatal, perinatal,

and postnatal factors that may influence cognitive development include

- certain viral and bacterial infections, as well as parasitic organisms;
- environmental conditions affecting the diet and living environment of the mother or child, or both;
- physical injuries from falls or bumps that involve severe trauma to the brain; and
- ingesting of poisonous substances.

Programming for a child with a developmental delay must be based on individual needs and should be implemented in a way that supports the inclusion of the child within the preschool program of his or her class.

Resources

Canadian Association for Community Living (CACL)

http://www.cacl.ca

The CACL offers a range of resources for information on developmental delays. This site also provides links to all the provincial and territorial chapters of the CACL.

Canadian Down Syndrome Society

http://www.cdss.ca

This site provides information and support to families who have children with Down syndrome.

Children's PKU Network

http://www.pkunetwork.org/Childrens_PKU_Network/Home.html

This nonprofit organization provides education, public awareness, programs, and assistance for individuals and families living with PKU.

Down Syndrome Association of Toronto

http://www.dsat.ca

This site provides information and support to families who have children with Down syndrome.

Independent Life Resources

http://www.ilresources.com

This site provides a wide range of links to North American resources and organizations concerned with developmental delays.

National Fragile X Foundation

http://www.fragilex.org

This site provides information, support, and advocacy to families and practitioners.

TASH: Equity, Opportunity and Inclusion for People with Disabilities

http://www.tash.org

TASH is an international grassroots leader in advancing inclusive communities through research, education, and advocacy.

CourseMate Access an interactive ebook and chapter-specific interactive learning tools, including flashcards, quizzes, videos, and more, in the *Inclusion in Early Childhood Programs* CourseMate. Visit NELSONbrain.com to log in, register, or purchase access.

Advanced Cognitive and Developmental Abilities: Children Who Are Gifted

7

OBJECTIVES

After studying the material in this chapter, the student will be able to

- Define giftedness in young children and explain the factors that contribute to giftedness.
- Identify the characteristics of young children who are gifted.
- Give reasons why potential giftedness and talents may not be identified in young children with disabilities and children from different cultural backgrounds.
- Develop programming strategies that support children who are gifted as well as all children in the class.

KEY CONCEPTS AND TERMS

advanced psychomotor ability	genetic predisposition	precocious
emergent curriculum	gifted and have ADHD	special ability in art
environmental influences	giftedness	special ability in music

Introduction

Children who have advanced cognitive and developmental abilities are usually referred to as *gifted* or *talented*. These children demonstrate abilities that are advanced in one or more areas of development when compared with their peers of the same age, maintain this advanced state throughout their developmental years, and continue to outperform children of the same age and socioeconomic status. Other children neither catch up to them nor overtake them.

Preschool children who are gifted are often not recognized as requiring specialized individual programming. However, when specialized programming is not provided, these children may become bored and uninterested, at times creating behaviour challenges for their teachers. In Canada there is no formal identified process for evaluating children who may be gifted in the preschool years.

Origins of Giftedness

Giftedness evidence of superior or unusual ability in areas such as intellect, creativity, artistic talent, physical agility, or leadership

Environmental influences the impact of environment on the development of the child

Genetic predisposition a child is born with genetic characteristics that predispose them to certain abilities and/or tendencies

What is the source of **giftedness**, especially when it takes the form of a high IQ and general intellectual competence? The child's **environmental influences** seem to be a major factor; however, of equal importance is the genetic makeup of the child. When a child with the **genetic predisposition** for giftedness enters an enriched environment, that giftedness is more clearly identified and encouraged. In general, better-educated families are better off financially. This enables them to provide the daily, taken-for-granted enrichment that is a key element in their children's performance. Given two children with equal genetic endowment, the child in the enriched environment almost surely would be observed as and labelled as "brighter" than the poorly nourished child raised in a nonstimulating environment. In other words, giftedness, most likely, is a combination of "good genes" and a stimulating environment. Unfortunately, standard methods used to identify children who are gifted are often culture- and class-bound, and not sufficiently sensitive to recognize future performance potential.

Characteristics of Young Children Who Are Gifted and Talented

Precocious the term used to describe young children who appear remarkably bright or unusually verbal and who may demonstrate outstanding talents in some specialized area, such as art, music, math

Precocious is a term often used to describe young children who appear to be remarkably bright or unusually verbal. Precocious children tend to demonstrate outstanding talents, far beyond what would be expected for their age. The precocity may show up in some specialized areas, such as painting or music or math.

In the child who is truly gifted, the accomplishments seem to appear spontaneously, as a part of the child's own unique developmental process. They appear to occur without special training or parental pressure. It should be noted that some children are extremely bright—but not gifted.

The characteristics that identify young children who may be gifted are a combination of advanced verbal skills, curiosity, and the ability to concentrate, learn rapidly, and enjoy problem solving. In addition, researchers have identified the following characteristics (Clark, 2007; Coleman & Cross, 2005; Renzulli et al., 2002; Roedell, Jackson, & Robinson, 1980; Rogers, 2001):

- has a detailed memory
- possesses a large vocabulary and experiments with new words
- uses language to give suggestions, express ideas, pass on information, and ask content questions: "How did the fox know the baby rabbit was there?"
- uses metaphors and analogies: "the moss on the tree is like an old man's beard"
- modifies his or her language to meet the comprehension level of younger children
- invents songs, stories, rhymes; plays with the sound and rhythm of words
- uses blocks, play dough, or drawing materials to make interesting patterns; creates unusual and well-thought-out designs; thinks through the steps in what he or she is creating ahead of time (see photo, page 132)
- asks intelligent questions
- learns information quickly
- uses logic to arrive at commonsense answers
- has a broad knowledge base—a large quantity of information
- understands abstract concepts such as time, family relationships, cause and effect, and connections between past and present
- has complex classification and discrimination skills; spontaneously groups items such as toy cars, boats, airplanes, and trucks; arranges objects according to size and colour
- finds and solves difficult and unusual problems
- wants to learn, is curious
- is able to easily follow task steps
- is skilled in putting together new and difficult puzzles; appears to examine puzzle pieces first and then put them in place, rather than depending on trial and error
- becomes absorbed in particular topics, such as dinosaurs, astronomy, animals, mechanical objects
- has good orientation skills and sense of spatial relationships
- is aware of what is new and different in the environment: rearrangement of equipment, a teacher's new hairstyle
- is aware of the feelings of others; comments when a teacher is not feeling well or another child appears withdrawn or especially happy
- shows a sense of humour (tells about the new kitten falling in the fruit bowl), makes up jokes and riddles

Preplanning is one characteristic of children who are gifted.

Needless to say, no child is likely to show all of these traits; many, however, will show two, three, or more, in various combinations. What is also important is to note the child's ability to

- process abstract concepts (e.g., comprehending the humour in a situation or understanding the quantity that a numeral stands for);
- comprehend the consequences of actions;
- solve problems (e.g., how to make a series of blocks balance, how to fit the pieces of a difficult puzzle together);
- learn new songs quickly;
- use a new toy, game, or computer program appropriately, with little learning time; and
- show curiosity in new situations, asking questions that show insight.

Some children demonstrate special talent in a specific area, such as art, music, or psychomotor coordination. The following information, adapted from Saunders and Espeland's *Bringing Out the Best* (1991), identifies a number of behaviour patterns in children that may indicate special talents in these areas. By recognizing special talent or ability, a teacher of young children may be able to develop and provide appropriately challenging and stimulating learning opportunities, ones that can be enjoyed by all the children but that will enable the inclusion of those who are more advanced.

Special ability in art an indication that a child may be potentially gifted in this area

Children who have **special ability in art**

- demonstrate eye–hand coordination that is developmentally advanced;
- are able to include fine detail in pictures, clay, or play dough objects;
- are able to remember and replicate detail in objects, pictures, and scenes they have seen;
- recognize and respond to differences in textures and colours (hues and tones);
- show an interest in and respond to photos, paintings, and sculptures; and
- express their feelings, emotions, and moods in their drawings, paintings, and sculpted creations, such as in play dough, collages, and so on.

Children who have **special ability in music**

- often request and initiate music-related activities and show the ability to respond emotionally to different pieces or types of music;
- can label the name of a familiar song from hearing the tune or beat;
- can carry a tune when singing;
- can sing in key with a song that is within their range;
- can recognize the sounds of particular instruments within a group instrumental performance and can label the familiar instruments by name;
- can dance, move, clap, and tap in time with music and rhythms;
- can respond to poetry that has a rhythmical flow and rhyming words; and
- may spontaneously make up their own tunes, songs, or rhythmical chants.

Special ability in music an indication that a child may be potentially gifted in this area

Children with **advanced psychomotor ability**

- demonstrate a well-developed sense of balance: hopping; climbing on a jungle gym, showing early ability in gymnastics, skating, and so on;
- show advanced abilities in sport-related activities: can throw and catch a ball, dribble a basketball, skate, and so on;
- have advanced coordination as is evident in their running, jumping, climbing, and tumbling skills;
- compete easily with older children in sport-related activities; and
- are able to create vigorous dances involving active coordinated movement: rolling, jumping, hopping, twisting, and so on.

Advanced psychomotor ability eye–hand or eye–foot coordination is at the level of a much older child, as found in some children who are gifted

Children from Minority Backgrounds Who Are Gifted

Many of the characteristics of children who are recognized as gifted relate to high-level language skills. Bright children from minority cultures and different ethnic backgrounds often are not recognized because they lack the language skills of the dominant culture (see photo, page 134). This difference should never be interpreted to mean that a child has less potential. Rather, it is usually due to the fact that the child has had less opportunity to acquire sophisticated language. Often, the child's home-language skills, which are not observed, may be advanced (see Chapter 19).

Other influences that tend to work against the identification of preschoolers from racialized backgrounds who may be gifted include

- having the attitude that giftedness does not exist among children from low-income backgrounds;
- defining giftedness in ways that reflect only the dominant culture's values;
- using identification procedures that are unfavourable to children from low-income and racialized groups (as will be discussed in Chapter 12); and
- providing few environmental opportunities for enhancing intellectual or artistic achievement in children from racialized backgrounds who are young and bright (no one can excel at anything without the opportunity to try).

Clearly, there are children who are gifted from every ethnic and racialized background and all socioeconomic levels. Thus, early identification and appropriate preschool education for children without economic advantages is critical as a means of identifying and nurturing those with special gifts and talents. Through observations of children's strengths, needs, and interests, appropriate curriculum planning can be undertaken to help all children reach their potential.

Children with Disabilities Who Are Gifted and/or Talented

Children from different backgrounds often are not recognized as gifted because of the teachers' inability to understand the children's home languages.

© Cengage Learning 2015

The fact that a child with a disability also may be a child who is gifted and/or talented is often overlooked (see photo, below). For example, a child with a learning disability may have superior intelligence or outstanding artistic or mechanical talents. The same is true of children who are deaf, children with cerebral palsy, or those with almost any other kind of developmental disability. The potential for intellectual or artistic giftedness in these children seldom receives much attention. Educational emphasis and energy tends to be narrowly focused on helping children overcome physical or sensory "deficits." As Gallagher (1988) pointed out, rarely do we even search for potential giftedness in special populations.

Identifying children who are gifted among children with disabilities may be difficult. Conventional assessment instruments often fail to pick up on these children's strengths, let alone their giftedness. Wolfle (1989) suggested using direct observation in a natural setting as a valuable way of discovering the special talents that a child with special needs may have. The importance of this recommendation is borne out by the following story of a situation that occurred with a four-year-old in an inclusive preschool, Benjamin, who was introduced in the Connections box at the beginning of the chapter:

One teacher began sitting down with Benjamin with musical instruments. One time it was a ukulele, then an autoharp, another time a recorder. After a brief period of experimentation, Benjamin would "find" tunes he could play on any one of the instruments. Next the teacher took him to a classroom that had a piano. Again, with only limited exploration of the instrument, Benjamin began to improvise recognizable tunes. The teacher shared these experiences with Benjamin's parents, who were able to buy a piano. Benjamin spent hours at the piano and became an eager piano student. By the age of 16, he was regarded as a gifted young pianist.

The special talents of a child with special needs often go unnoticed.

© Cengage Learning 2015

Many young children with disabilities and sensory

impairments have high potential for both intellectual and creative achievement. Attention needs to be directed toward these children in early childhood programs so that their curiosity and eagerness to learn are encouraged rather than allowed to wither.

Children who are **gifted and have ADHD** differ in cognitive, social, and emotional ways from children who are of average intelligence and have ADHD. Lovecky (1999) stated that on intelligence and achievement tests, children who are gifted and have ADHD show a greater degree of inter- and intra-test variability, with greater amounts of scatter in their performance scores. They miss many easier items and are correct on much more difficult items. Children who are gifted and have ADHD, although deficient in many of the supporting work skills needed to succeed in school (note taking, outlining, organization of ideas, writing skills), are often more proficient at learning things rapidly when compared with other same-aged peers with ADHD.

Furthermore, children who are gifted and have ADHD are more proficient in such things as grouping by category, using mnemonic devices, using recall of one thing to trigger another, and organizing by pattern or spatial characteristics. However, unlike most children who are gifted, children who are gifted and have ADHD have trouble effectively using these strategies. They know them and forget to use them. When they remember to use the strategies they know, their work is superior. As with many children who are gifted, children who are gifted and have ADHD are highly sensitive to both the external environment and their internal feelings. Because of the ADHD, children who are gifted and have ADHD can have more extreme reactions, because they do not have the emotional resilience to cope with fearful or upsetting situations (Lovecky, 1999).

Gifted and have ADHD unlike most children who are gifted, these children have trouble effectively using the strategies and skills they have, and their giftedness is not recognized

Strategies for Supporting Young Children Who Are Gifted and/or Talented

It is important to *support* and *challenge* children who are gifted, while at the same time not draw attention in such a way as to give the children a false sense of importance or the message that they are expected always to achieve at the highest level. Too much "emphasis on success may result in children avoiding situations that may lead to failure" (Elkind, 1981).

We must not forget the importance of supporting *all* areas of the young child's development. It should not be assumed that advancement in one area of development (for example, cognitive or language skills) necessarily precludes the need for support in another (such as gross or fine motor abilities).

Yewchuk and Jobagy (1991), in an article about the importance of recognizing the emotional needs of children who are gifted, stated,

> Pressure to succeed, personal expectations, emotional sensitivity, lack of support from parents and peers—all may have a detrimental effect on the emotional development of the gifted child. Educators are finally becoming aware of the advanced academic needs of the gifted child, and programming is finally taking place. What is now required is that teachers and counsellors become aware of the social and emotional needs of the gifted child, as these can have a profound effect on the academic ability of the child.

Recent research seems to indicate that children who are *truly* gifted develop best in an environment that *recognizes* and *responds* to their special needs. Thus, very young children who show an interest in ideas and concepts beyond those of other children of the same age should be encouraged and given opportunities to explore and expand their particular area of interest. Providing greater access to libraries, museums, and computer programs may enable these children to find answers to their questions and motivate them to further inquiry. Children who excel in psychomotor, music, and creative art abilities may need challenging and varied opportunities for expanding their particular talent. The child care setting might provide obstacle courses, opportunities for creative dance, time for music improvisation, and materials for sculpting, constructing, and handicraft work.

In our experience, the following techniques and methods have worked successfully with young children who are gifted and/or talented:

1. Observe *all* children, especially those with identified special needs, for their unique strengths, abilities, and talents.

2. Plan small-group activities that may require all children, including the child who is gifted, to work as a team and to help one another reach a shared goal—for example, a cooking activity that requires eye–hand coordination for pouring and stirring, physical strength for beating and mixing, intellectual ability for interpreting a recipe, social skills for sharing, and language skills for reporting. Through such activities, all children take part and support one another.

3. Make sure stimulating activities and materials are always available in the classroom. These may include

   - a terrarium-building activity;

   - CD's, music from smartphones or tablets to listen to

   - a range of recorded music and props for creative movement;

   - smartphones or tables for children to use for their own compositions

   - computer programs that challenge creative thinking and problem solving, abilities that do not simply require "yes/no" or "right/wrong" answers, and do not preclude opportunities for the child to play interactively with other children;

   - different types of creative art materials (frequently augmented and changed) that allow opportunities to explore colour, form, and texture;

   - a range of different types of building blocks, unit blocks, Lego, and so on, that require balance, form spatial relations, and stimulate creative construction and play;

   - new props that will stimulate creative role-playing—for example, new hats, makeup, jewellery, uniforms, and supplies for "community helper" play—as well as props that can be used to expand building projects: farm and forest animals, family figures, electrical (battery and bulb) hookups, and so on; and

   - opportunities for trips supported by specific preparation and follow-up: scrapbooking, drawing things they saw, and recording or writing (with teacher support) about the trip.

4. Use volunteers who can provide unique learning experiences; often, they can help keep the gifted child intellectually stimulated and involved.

5. Help parents recognize ways in which they can support their child's abilities, interests, and talents. Teachers might suggest

   • trips to exhibits, museums, street festivals, and building sites; and

   • hands-on experiences, such as fixing broken things, creating three-dimensional structures, and exploring new media.

   According to Wolfle (1989), "The gifted child is a child who should be treated like a child. ... Like their peers, [gifted children] love drawing, going on field trips, playing in the housekeeping area, but [they] seem to want to delve into everything deeper." For this reason, it is important for teachers to provide time, often over a number of days or weeks, for children to fully explore and expand on their interests and projects.

6. Develop interesting and enriching special program opportunities—for example, arranging for visitors with special skills (musicians, scientists, artists/sculptors, chefs, tailors, etc.), taking trips to interesting places and events, and locating people who will donate time or materials that will enhance learning opportunities for the whole class. Be sure to call on the children's parents for contributions. Kitano (1989) stressed that "offering learning activities at a range of levels hurts no one and helps gifted children, as well as many others." She urged teachers to be flexible and offer choices that will appeal to all children.

7. Provide specific guidance to the children to help them pursue and expand on special interests. Teachers might try to find times in which they can cluster children who share similar interests and who are able to do more extensive work on a specific interest or group project. Teachers can then guide them in how to do basic research to find answers to their questions, challenge them with new and interesting questions and ideas, and give them opportunities to discuss their insights.

Emergent curriculum curriculum that is developed from a variety of sources, including children's play activities and questions, and that is personally meaningful, intellectually engaging, and socially relevant

Children who are gifted are creative thinkers and often make connections between what appear to be dissimilar topics or ideas. Therefore, it is important that teachers be responsive and follow the child's lead. Planning curriculum that builds on children's interests and involves them in developing and planning long-term projects is critical (see photo, right). It is often a good idea to begin by working with the children to draw a web of the knowledge that the children have, and then to set up a process for investigating new information, documenting the process and the children's findings with photographs, pictures, videos, audiotapes, and so on. Gestwicki (1999) referred to this kind of programming strategy as **emergent curriculum**.

In conclusion, when programming for young children, it is important to support the development needs of all the children in the group. The breadth of needs that teachers must accommodate varies from group to group. The process of inclusion—whether it is with a child who is developmentally delayed, has specific physical needs, or is developmentally accelerated in one or more areas—challenges the teacher to plan program and learning opportunities in which all the children can participate and from which

Planning curriculum that builds on children's interests and involves them in developing and planning long-term projects is critical.

Courtesy of Ryerson Early Learning Centre

all can benefit. The teacher should work to facilitate the inclusion of the child who is cognitively and developmentally advanced as a member of his or her peer group. Teachers need to be flexible and willing to consider and respond to the questions and observations of the children in their group, especially those of young children who are cognitively advanced and who may need more pervasive challenges and cognitive stimulation.

Summary

Young children who are gifted and/or talented are those with exceptionally advanced skills in one or more areas of development. Characteristics that identify young children who may be gifted are a combination of advanced verbal skills, high levels of curiosity, and the ability to concentrate and remember. Many children who are potentially gifted and who are from culturally different backgrounds or low-income families are not identified because of restricted learning opportunities and culturally biased identification procedures. Many children with developmental disabilities are gifted; however, their potential often goes unrecognized because of the focus placed on overcoming their deficit areas.

It is of prime importance that teachers plan daily programs that meet the needs of all the children in their group, providing a broad range and variety of intellectually challenging and creative opportunities for play and learning.

Resources

Alberta Associations for Bright Children

http://www.edmontonabc.org/aabc

This organization provides information and advocacy for children who are gifted and talented, their families, and their teachers.

Association for Bright Children of Ontario

http://www.abcontario.ca

Numerous links and resources on children who are gifted and talented are available at this site.

Gifted Development Center (Denver, Colorado)

http://www.gifteddevelopment.com

A great deal of statistical data is available at this American website.

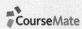 CourseMate Access an interactive ebook and chapter-specific interactive learning tools, including flashcards, quizzes, videos, and more, in the *Inclusion in Early Childhood Programs* CourseMate. Visit NELSONbrain.com to log in, register, or purchase access.

Sensory Impairments: Hearing and Vision

8

OBJECTIVES

After studying the material in this chapter, the student will be able to

- Discuss hearing and vision impairments and their impact on the learning needs of young children.
- Identify warning signs indicating that an infant, toddler, or young child may have a hearing loss.
- Identify signs of a possible hearing loss for a child with spoken language abilities.
- Indicate some strategies useful in helping a child make the transition into an inclusive program.
- Discuss the possible effects of a visual impairment on a child's language, cognitive, motor, and social development.
- Describe strategies that teachers may use in preschool activities to facilitate the learning of children with visual impairments who are in an inclusive environment.

KEY CONCEPTS AND TERMS

amplification device

auditory brainstem response (ABR)

auditory nerve

cochlea

cochlear implant

conductive hearing loss

cortical/cerebral visual impairment

deaf

deafblind

earmould

intermittent hearing loss

occlusion

peripheral vision

preorientation and mobility skills

refractive errors

residual hearing

residual vision

sensorineural hearing loss

sensory impairments

sign language

strabismus

tactile sign language

visual acuity problems

The authors wish to acknowledge the significant contributions of Dr. Kristen Snodden to this chapter.

Introduction

From the moment of birth, almost everything that children learn about themselves and their world comes through their five senses—hearing, vision, touch, taste, and smell. The most prevalent **sensory impairments** are hearing and vision losses. Most of what infants and children are expected to learn is acquired through these two senses. Children with sensory impairments related to hearing and vision often need supports in order to reach their learning potential.

Hearing loss almost always has implications for supporting language acquisition. While language does not fully determine cognition, it is related to cognition in several ways. As noted in earlier chapters, development of cognitive skills is tied closely to both receptive and expressive language skills.

Children who are blind learn spoken language with considerably less difficulty than do children who are deaf. Children who are blind can benefit from the many incidental learning opportunities available every day. They hear environmental sounds, footsteps, doors closing, and other sounds that, when tied to the child's concrete experiences, provide the basis for cognitive insight. All of this gives children who are blind a great potential for academic success. Children who are deaf have equal potential for academic success and social learning when they have full access to language.

Infants and young children with severe hearing or vision impairments require teachers and support people who are trained to meet their special needs. Sometimes this special care may be necessary in an intensive, highly specialized program or, as in the case of children who are **deaf**, a bilingual program that supports learning of American Sign Language (ASL) or another **sign language** used by deaf communities. The normal activity level of an early childhood program may be both confusing and frightening for children who are **deafblind**. For

Sensory impairments differences in the ability to sense the environment through a specific sensory modality, such as hearing or sight

Deaf having a hearing loss so severe that the individual cannot process spoken language even with amplification

Sign language a visual/gestural language, such as American Sign Language (ASL). Sign languages are full languages displaying the same levels of linguistic organization found in spoken languages. Sign languages include fingerspelling.

Deafblind being both blind and deaf

successful inclusion to occur, highly specialized support services and teaching staff who are fluent in **tactile sign language** may be necessary. Users of tactile sign language may hold the hands of their conversational partner and feel their partner's hand movements. Children who are deafblind with some visual ability may use but use tactile sign language when lighting is poor or when their vision deteriorates further (Mesch, 2002).

Tactile sign language sign language used by children who are deafblind

The developmental needs of children who are blind or deaf are the same as those for all children. Therefore, it is important to try, whenever possible, to ensure that they are in inclusive early childhood programs and are involved in all the social, physical, and cognitive experiences available.

Hearing Impairments

Causes of Hearing Impairments

Hearing impairments may be caused by prenatal, perinatal, or postnatal factors. Prenatal causes include those that are genetic in origin, as well as viral infections the mother experienced during the first trimester of pregnancy, such as rubella. Perinatal (at birth) causes are mainly due to a lack of oxygen at birth. Postnatal causes of hearing deficits include accidents, prolonged high fevers, measles, rubella, mumps, meningitis, and, sometimes, reactions to medication. Injuries that affect the ear drum, ear and sinus infections, and any other circumstances that result in blockage of the eustachian tubes also cause impairment to hearing. Fluid buildup in the middle ear is a major cause of temporary hearing loss.

Definitions and Types of Deafness and Hearing Loss

Hearing loss is defined as follows:

- *Prenatal:* Occurring before or at birth.
- *Postnatal:* A hearing loss occurring after birth.
- *Unilateral:* A hearing loss involving only one ear.
- *Bilateral:* A hearing loss involving both ears.
- *Conductive:* Loss of hearing sensitivity caused by problems involving either the outer or middle ear. Common causes of conductive losses are: holes in the eardrum, infection in the middle ear, build-up of ear wax, problems with the three little bones in the middle ear, atresia, and stenosis. Atresia is the complete closing off of the ear canal as in congenitally absent or malformed outer ears. Stenosis is the narrowing of the canal. Many of these problems can be treated by medication or surgery and hearing can be restored.
- *Sensori-neural:* Loss of hearing sensitivity caused by damage to the hair cells in the inner ear or along nerve pathways to the brain. The loss is permanent and cannot be cured by medication or surgery. The causes are many: German measles or other viral infections in pregnancy, damage or lack of oxygen at birth, prolonged high fevers, illnesses such as measles, rubella, mumps and meningitis, toxic effects of some drugs and injury to the skull. There are also a number of inherited forms of hearing loss. In about half the cases, no cause can be identified.

- *Mixed:* A combination of sensori-neural and conductive hearing loss. Medical treatment can improve the conductive difficulty, but the nerve damage cannot be repaired. Hearing is worse when a conductive hearing loss exists on top of a sensori-neural loss, for example, having an ear infection on top of a permanent hearing loss.*

Children with hearing impairments are usually classified in two ways, as deaf or as hard of hearing. Children who are deaf are those with severe to profound hearing losses, typically at the 70 to 90 decibel range and above. Children who are classified as hard of hearing span a wide range of audiological thresholds, from 30 to 90 decibels of hearing loss (Blamey, 2003).

Hearing losses can be prenatal (occurring before or at birth) or postnatal (occurring after birth). Spoken language is not accessible for many children who are deaf, and the impact this has on development is significant when access to sign language is not adequately supported.

Types of Hearing Loss

Hearing losses are categorized in various ways, through various kinds of assessments. To ensure valid results, both screening and testing should be done by audiologists who are specially trained to work with infants and young children. The results of hearing tests usually are plotted on what is called an *audiogram*. A hearing loss is classified according to where the loss occurs:

- Problems in the outer or middle ear produce a **conductive hearing loss**.
- Problems in the inner ear (in the **cochlea** or the **auditory nerve**) produce a **sensorineural hearing loss**.
- Problems in the higher auditory cortex produce central deafness.
- A combined loss involves two or more of the above.

In most instances, a conductive hearing loss interferes with audibility (the ability to hear), not understanding. If the sound is loud enough to be heard, the child can understand the message. Therefore, this type of hearing loss can be helped relatively easily by amplification of sound. In many instances, this type of loss can be corrected or greatly reduced with appropriate medical treatment.

A young child with chronic ear infections, such as *otitis media*, may suffer a hearing loss that comes and goes a number of times in the course of a year, as the infection flares up and clears up. These infections often cause a buildup of fluid, which leads to what is called an **intermittent hearing loss**. Because of recurring hearing losses, children's language development and learning abilities may be delayed. Once the infection is cleared up permanently, language is likely to improve. It is important to observe children closely and impress on the parents the importance of seeking medical treatment and/or learning sign language if the condition persists, in order to prevent long-term developmental delays. It should be remembered that even after an ear infection has been eliminated, residual fluid may remain, resulting in distorted hearing.

Identifying an intermittent hearing loss is difficult. The condition is often missed entirely in routine screening tests because the child is hearing adequately and therefore responding appropriately at the time of testing. These children may be diagnosed as having speech problems or categorized as having a learning disability. On careful study of their health records, most of the children have

Conductive hearing loss refers to problems in the mechanical transmission of sounds through the outer or middle ear, which in turn reduce the intensity of sound vibrations reaching the auditory nerve in the inner ear

Cochlea a snail-shaped structure in the inner ear that allows hearing to occur

Auditory nerve the nerve along which the sensory cells (the hair cells) of the inner ear transmit information to the brain

Sensorineural hearing loss a hearing loss that involves a malfunctioning of the cochlea or auditory nerve

Intermittent hearing loss hearing comes and goes because of a buildup of fluid caused by repeated ear infections

---

* Mackenzie, K. (Ed.). (2004). *Starting point: A resource for parents of deaf or hard of hearing children.* Toronto, ON: The Canadian Hearing Society. Used with permission.

histories of chronic otitis media, yet the resulting hearing loss was not identified in general screening procedures. Recently, some schools have begun providing screening programs that check for both conductive hearing loss and sensorineural hearing loss. This testing has been effective in identifying hearing loss (Roeser, 2000). Once a hearing loss is identified, it is important that the child is immediately referred for further diagnosis and appropriate treatment.

Unlike conductive hearing problems, sensorineural hearing losses and central deafness do not respond readily to medical intervention. Sensorineural hearing losses can cause inaudibility and sound distortion. With a sensorineural loss, even if sound is made loud enough to be heard, the child may still have difficulty understanding speech. A child whose loss is too severe to be helped by a hearing aid may benefit from a cochlear implant (Discolo & Hirose, 2002). See the section on the cochlear implant and its advantages and disadvantages in this chapter on pages 152 and 153.

Warning Signs

Soon after birth, most infants make a variety of responses to various noises. The whole body may move in a *startle response*, eyes may blink, or a rapid increase in sucking may occur. At about three to four months, infants begin to *localize*—that is, turn their heads in the direction of sounds. Over the next several months, they get better and better at localizing. Early use of hearing becomes refined to the point that infants can discriminate among voices and indicate a preference for their mother's voice, as contrasted to that of a stranger (Allen & Marotz, 2010).

When infants do not make such responses, hearing loss is a definite possibility. However, all infants make so many random movements that the infant who is hearing impaired may be difficult to identify. Furthermore, if the infant has some **residual hearing**, the loss may be all the more difficult to identify. This infant may be hearing just enough to be able to respond appropriately some of the time, giving the appearance of normal hearing. Another complication is that even infants who are profoundly deaf babble, at least for a while. It is interesting to note that studies have found that infants who are exposed to sign language also babble—with their hands (Petitto & Maramette, 1991).

Residual hearing the degree of hearing of a person who is deaf or hard of hearing

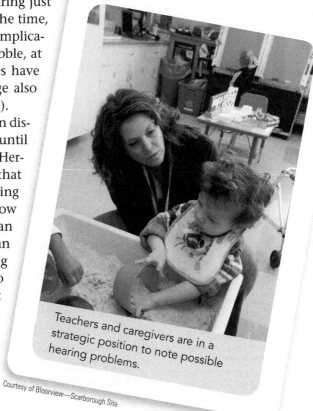

Though hearing losses are one of the most common disabilities present at birth, they are often not detected until a child is between one and three years old (Mason & Herrmann, 1998). Parents are usually the first to sense that something is wrong, but they may not suspect a hearing loss. Physicians and health-care workers are often slow to diagnose a hearing impairment—yet the earlier an impairment is detected, the earlier intervention can begin. Early intervention and sign language learning can minimize the negative effects of lack of access to language on all aspects of a child's development. It is now possible to screen hearing shortly after birth, using an automated *auditory brainstem response* measurement (Pickard, 2002).

Infant caregivers and early childhood teachers are in a strategic position to notice possible hearing impairments and risk conditions (see photo, right).

Teachers and caregivers are in a strategic position to note possible hearing problems.

Courtesy of Bloorview—Scarborough Site

Amplification device devices, such as hearing aids, that make sound louder and clearer for a child with a hearing impairment

Persistent ear infections, discharge from the ears, or constant poking or pulling at the ears often indicate a possible impairment. If a parent or teacher suspects a hearing loss, it should be checked by a medical specialist immediately. The earlier a hearing loss is recognized, the earlier the child can be treated and, if need be, fitted with **amplification devices** (hearing aids). It should be emphasized that most children with hearing impairments have some *residual hearing*. To maximize the use of residual hearing and ensure access to language, it is important that intervention by a trained specialist or sign language educator occur as early as possible. Remember, it is only when the child has access to language that language will begin to develop.

Children with a conductive hearing loss may drop certain initial consonants (the ones that are described as voiceless: p, h, s, f). They simply do not hear these sounds and so they do not reproduce them. With sensorineural hearing loss, a marked delay in speech and language development is a major warning sign.

With children who have acquired some spoken language, teachers need to be alert to a child who displays the following behaviours:

- does not respond when spoken to
- does not understand, or looks puzzled, when addressed directly with a simple question or request
- cocks his or her head to one side, studies the speaker's face, or watches the speaker's mouth
- asks for frequent repetitions ("Huh?" "What?")
- turns one ear to the source of sound or speech
- seems overly shy, avoids children and teachers
- is inattentive
- makes inconsistent or irrelevant responses
- complains of ringing or buzzing in the ears
- has an articulation or voice-quality problem
- speaks too loudly or too softly

Further signs of a potential hearing impairment are shown by a child who displays the following:

- has a speech delay or slow response to usual sounds
- does not participate or concentrate or both during activities based on speech (e.g., story time, show-and-tell), especially if the child is not directly facing the speaker
- persistently withdraws from the other children and is moody
- has an unexplained personality change, especially during a cold or following an ear infection
- always wants the radio, TV, music, or video player on high volume
- pulls at his or her ear(s)

When teachers become aware of a possible hearing loss, the first step is to speak with parents about seeking clinical help. Because any degree of hearing loss has an impact on language development, early detection is extremely important. For this reason, it is also a good idea to have annual screening of every child's hearing.

A frequently used procedure called **auditory brainstem response (ABR)** is now being used effectively to provide an objective measure of the degree of hearing

Auditory brainstem response (ABR) a procedure that measures the brain's response to high-frequency sound in infants and young children suspected of hearing impairment. This procedure involves placing surface electrodes on the child's forehead, as far back as the ear. It is most effective in determining high-frequency impairment. Whereas other screening devices require a child to respond to stimuli, this process, by monitoring involuntary brain activity, is independent of the child's participation and is, therefore, extremely useful in identifying high-frequency hearing deficits in infants and preverbal children.

The Impact of Hearing Loss

Many children who are deaf and hard of hearing are at risk for delays in their language development regardless of the degree of their hearing loss (Spencer, 2004). There is nothing in hearing loss that inherently restricts language development. Rather, delayed language development is often a result of delayed access to language, particularly a visual language that children can process effectively. As children who have hearing impairments grow older, without adequate access to language some fall even further behind as a result of the increasing complexity of school and community expectations.

EFFECTS ON LANGUAGE DEVELOPMENT The most serious and far-reaching effect of a hearing impairment is on early language development. Language acquisition appears to be tied to certain periods in a child's development (the *critical period* idea, as discussed in Chapter 1).

According to this theory, a child who does not receive adequate linguistic input in a signed or spoken language at certain points in development may never fully master language. Children exposed to ASL or another native sign language from birth acquire this language on a similar developmental course as children who are hearing learn a language (Petitto, 2000). Inadequate linguistic input during early development almost always leads to serious delays in language acquisition. Delayed early language development may also be caused by a lack of responsiveness from family and teachers. Unwittingly, they may fall into the habit of not talking to the young child who has impaired hearing. It is easy to see how this happens. The child's range of responses is limited when the child lacks access to a full language, thus providing inadequate feedback for family and friends. Consequently, the child's language skills become even more delayed.

EFFECTS ON COGNITIVE DEVELOPMENT Once the typically developing child is beyond the sensorimotor stage, cognitive skills, as mentioned at the outset, become inseparably intertwined with language skills. Thus, children with hearing loss who lack access to sign language often perform less effectively than do hearing children when it comes to language-based cognitive activities. As noted earlier, many children with severe hearing impairments are often several years behind in their education. Their educational delay, however, is seldom due to poor cognitive potential. Usually, the cause is the inadequate linguistic input; in other words, the child has been denied a major channel for cognitive development.

EFFECTS ON SOCIAL DEVELOPMENT Children with hearing impairments often experience some degree of social isolation when their access to sign language communities is not supported. They may begin to be left out of things, even within the family, at a very early age. The child with a hearing impairment may be in the room where a family activity is going on, but nevertheless, he or she is often unintentionally excluded, for a very simple reason: The child is not able to enter into the verbal give-and-take if family members do not use sign language and so has no way of figuring out what is going on. Unless sign language learning is supported for helping the child understand everyday family and school events, the child will often remain a passive and silent observer. Poor communication between the child and others frequently leads to social adjustment difficulties. Reports of impulsivity, aggressiveness, or low self-esteem begin during the preschool years. Children whose parents use sign language do not exhibit the same behaviour problems, which supports the view that these problems result from a lack of frequent, sustained communication between children and parents (Calderon & Greenberg, 2003). Sign language, visual attention, and touch strengthen bonds and communication between parents and children who are deaf and hard of hearing.

EFFECTS ON FAMILY LIFE Having a child with a hearing loss can dramatically change the tenor of family life. With proper early intervention and support, such as taking ASL classes and enrolling in home-visiting services provided by a sign language educator, families can be introduced to the deaf community and begin learning ASL or another native sign language. Children who are deaf have the same social and emotional needs as hearing children.

Families often need support to help them to adapt to their deaf child's visual learning needs (Sass-Lehrer, 2011).

Communication

With the help of a trained specialist teacher of the deaf, some children with hearing impairments, even those with a severe loss of hearing, can be taught to speak and to understand speech. In recent years, more and more infants and toddlers have been fitted with special hearing aids as soon as their impairment is identified. However, for many children who are deaf, speech is an acquired skill that must be taught. It is important that the desire for a child to acquire speech not take precedence over the child's need for accessible linguistic input, such as sign language.

Once a hearing loss is identified, the child, regardless of age, can be immediately fitted for hearing aids and other equipment that will maximize the use of any residual hearing. (This may also involve having the child's teachers and caregivers wear special microphones that enhance the sound the child receives through his or her hearing aid.)

It should be noted that lip reading is only a very limited means of accessing speech for children who are deaf or hard of hearing. The success of lip reading depends on the child already knowing spoken English and having some degree of residual hearing. Thus, lip reading does not often provide an effective means for promoting language acquisition in children who are deaf or hard of hearing.

Early and easy communication between a child and the people in his or her environment is critical not only to language development, but also in the areas of cognitive and social development (Malloy, 2003). It is crucial that different modalities of language be used with children who are deaf and hard of hearing to help them reach their optimal developmental potential. These modalities include a sign language such as ASL or another sign language that is native to a deaf community. *Langue des signes québécois* (LSQ), or Quebec sign language, is another sign language used by deaf communities in francophone regions of Canada. While sign systems such as signed English or total communication are sometimes promoted by professionals working with children who are deaf, these systems are not natural languages. Research has shown that children who are exposed exclusively

FIGURE 8-1

Sign Language around the World

The status of sign language varies in each country. The first country in the world where sign language was recognized and passed into parliament was Uganda in 1995 (World Federation for the Deaf, 2012). No one form of sign language is universal. American Sign Language (ASL) is one of the most commonly known forms of communication for the deaf, and many people assume that it is *a universal language*. They would be incorrect. Different sign languages are used in different countries or regions. For example, there are two sign languages in Belgium (French Belgian Sign Language and Flemish Sign Language) and in Spain (Spanish Sign Language and Catalan Sign Language). Also, there are different sign languages in countries that have the same spoken language, such as in the United Kingdom and Ireland. Some languages, such as Japanese Sign Language, incorporate more mouthing of words than other sign languages such as ASL. A person who is deaf travelling to a foreign country would not necessarily understand the sign language used there.

Source: © Cengage Learning 2015

to sign systems instead of ASL exhibit delays in their language development and do not acquire the grammar of either ASL or English (Schick, 2003). Refer to Figure 8–1 for a description of sign language around the world.

WHICH METHOD? There is a long-standing controversy concerning which modality to use in teaching language to a young child. Parents must be informed of the advantages of exposing their children to both signed and spoken language. The Canadian Hearing Society's (2013) position on access to language and language acquisition for children who are deaf and hard of hearing is as follows:

> The right to language access and language acquisition is a necessary prerequisite for exercising the right to human dignity, freedom of expression and all other human rights. Deaf children and children with hearing loss have the right to barrier-free access to language acquisition during the early years when language is readily acquired. They have the right to acquire signed language in addition to spoken language. (para. 5)

Professionals and teachers working with parents and children need to provide accurate information about the language learning needs of children who are deaf and hard of hearing and work together to provide the child with the best learning environment possible.

Early Intervention with Children with Hearing Impairments

The importance of early language stimulation and training for infants and young children who are hearing impaired cannot be overemphasized. Language delays among older children with hearing impairments may be the result of failure to begin language learning activities during the infant and toddler years. The longer the delay in starting language intervention, the less likely it is that the child will develop fully functional language skills. Without preventive measures, even a mild hearing loss can result in a permanent loss in language ability.

Guidelines for Teachers

Throughout the years, early childhood teachers have worked successfully with children with hearing impairments. Effective programming usually incorporates

Children with hearing loss need to be spoken to face to face.

the skills of a specially trained early childhood consultant for the hearing impaired and/or a sign language educator. The specialists should assist both teachers and parents in providing children who have hearing impairments with an education tailored to their special language learning needs. The following guidelines from specialists are often recommended for working with children with hearing impairments:

1. Sit, kneel, or bend down to the child's level to talk. Look directly at the child when talking or communicating with him or her. Children with hearing impairments need to be spoken to face to face (see photo, above).

2. Talk in a normal voice. Avoid an overly loud voice and do not overenunciate. Overenunciation makes speech reading difficult.

3. Use a clear voice and talk at a slightly slower pace.

4. Use gestures when appropriate.

5. Use brief, but complete, sentences when the child who is hearing impaired has reached that stage of language development. As with hearing children, *holophrastic* and *telegraphic* language (Chapter 19) belong to particular stages of language development.

6. Always try to seat the child directly across from the teacher. This gives the child the best possible position for lip reading.

7. Face the light when talking to a child who has a hearing impairment. The light needs to be on the speaker's face, not on the child's. Glaring light in the child's eyes interferes with bringing the speaker's face and mouth into full focus.

8. To get the child's attention, gently touch or tap a child on the shoulder or hand. Always be aware of the possibility of startling a person who does not hear.

9. When talking about something in the room, point to it, touch it, hold it up. For example, if the teacher picks up the scissors and demonstrates the cutting task while giving the instructions, the child has a better chance of understanding what is expected.

10. Include children who are hearing impaired in all music activities. Provide many opportunities for them to participate by

- putting their hands on various instruments so they can feel the vibrations;
- allowing them to play the instruments;
- having frequent rhythmic activities, such as clapping, jumping, rolling, and twirling; and
- pairing a child who has normal hearing with a child who is hearing impaired for various musical games.

11. Involve children with hearing impairments in story time. Choose books with bright, clear pictures that tell the story. Gesture when telling the story, and use facial expressions that give clues to the moods in the story. Consider inviting a adult who is deaf to tell stories in ASL and/or read picture books through ASL.

12. Keep to a regular schedule of activities each day. To feel secure, young children, and especially children with hearing impairments (who often do not pick up on environmental signals), need to know what comes next.

13. Provide opportunities for the whole class to learn ASL from a trained ASL educator. Some early childhood environments have hired early childhood educators who are deaf to maximize ASL learning by all children and teachers.

14. When a sign language interpreter is present, allow the child who is hearing impaired and the interpreter to choose the most favourable seating.

Though many of the preceding guidelines focus on the child who has a hearing impairment, the early childhood teacher should constantly be working toward full inclusion—planning for group activities that will enable the full and equal participation of *all* children. Special adaptations can and should be planned, if necessary, so that a child who has a disability can participate in group activities as fully as he or she is able.

Case Study ▪ Supporting a new child ▪

You have just learned that a new child will be entering your preschool classroom on Monday. She cannot hear and does not speak. She knows a few signs, including "potty" and "hungry." What resources would you need to support her development in all domains? Identify local resources in your area that provide assistance to you (as the teacher) and the child's parents.

Amplification Devices (Hearing Aids)

Electronic hearing aids are a great help, especially for people with a conductive hearing loss. A hearing aid has three basic parts: a microphone, an amplifier, and a receiver (Figure 8–2). Most young children are fitted with hearing aids that are placed on the bone directly behind the ear or inserted into the ear canal. In most cases, plastic tubing carries the amplified sound to an **earmould** made especially for each child. The hearing aid may have On/Off switches and volume controls.

In spite of the great benefits of hearing aids, problems can occur. The fact that a child is wearing a hearing aid does not mean that the child is hearing. Teachers and parents need to be aware of possible minor breakdowns in the system:

- *Improperly fitting or damaged earmould.* If the earmould does not fit properly, it can cause irritation and discomfort. The same holds true if the earmould becomes chipped or cracked. A cracked or poorly fitted earmould also can make a squealing feedback sound, which can be extremely annoying.

Earmould that part of an amplification device (hearing aid) that is fitted to the individual's ear

FIGURE 8-2 Hearing Aid That Fits Behind the Ear

VOLUME CONTROL

EARMOULD

BATTERY CASE

- *Feedback.* This irritating, high-pitched squealing sound can be caused by an earmould that is cracked or improperly seated in the ear.

- *Dead or feeble batteries.* Batteries die with amazing frequency. Teachers and parents should know when batteries are dead because the child will stop responding. However, batteries should be replaced well before they are dead so that children do not have to cope with periods of diminishing sound.

- *Switched-off device.* Teachers must check regularly to make sure a child's hearing aid is turned on. Young children tend to turn the devices off, sometimes repeatedly. This happens most frequently when they are first learning to wear their aid. Eventually, most children become accustomed to wearing the device and leave it turned on all the time. At this point, children can begin to check its working order for themselves. Nevertheless, adults should continue to spot-check at least once a day.

- *Sore ears.* The earmould should never be inserted into a sore, cracked, or infected ear. At the first sign of irritation, the child should see a health-care provider.

FM SYSTEMS Many children can use an additional amplifying system that helps reduce background noise. These devices work like miniature radio stations. They can be connected directly to hearing aids, or the child may wear a small plastic neckloop. Teachers clip a microphone and transmitter to their clothing and transmit their voices directly to the receiver, which is worn by the child.

Because so many things can go wrong with hearing aids and FM systems, it is important that teachers, in conjunction with parents, make sure that all hearing devices are tested on a daily basis. They should receive special instructions from an audiologist on how to examine the devices to make sure that they are functioning properly.

Cochlear implant a device, surgically placed by opening the mastoid structure of the skull, that allows electrical impulses (sound) to be carried directly to the brain

COCHLEAR IMPLANTS With **cochlear implants** an electrode (computerized device) is surgically inserted into the inner ear (cochlea). A cochlear implant bypasses the damaged hair cells in the inner ear and directly stimulates the auditory nerve (National Institute on Deafness and Other Communication Disorders, 2002).

Cochlear implants can now be used in children under a year old. There are more than 14 000 children age 18 years or younger with implants in the United States (Smith, 2006). Research has demonstrated that children who are deaf who receive cochlear implants before 30 months of age are better able to integrate auditory and visual information than those who receive their implants when they are older (Schorr, Fox, van Washove, & Knudsen, 2005). While the increased use of cochlear implants is changing education of the deaf, their use is not without problems. The following problems can occur:

- Cochlear implants can malfunction and are difficult to program.
- There is background noise and sounds are heard differently.
- Their use has impacts on lifestyle because the external portion of the device must not get wet and is easily damaged.

There are no long-term data regarding the use of cochlear implants (U.S. Food and Drug Administration, 2014). Both the Canadian Hearing Society and the Canadian Association of the Deaf maintain that children who receive cochlear implants should not face restrictions on exposure to and acquisition of ASL.

In conclusion, whether a child has a cochlear implant or is prescribed hearing aids, it is important to remember that sign language learning also needs to be supported (Kushalnagar et al., 2010).

Blindness and Vision Impairments

Types of Vision Impairments

Vision impairments vary as to cause, type, and severity. They are usually grouped in terms of physical abnormalities, visual acuity, and muscular imbalances.

PHYSICAL ABNORMALITIES Physical problems resulting in impaired vision are fairly common. These may develop prenatally, or the damage can occur at birth or any time thereafter. The cause may be diseases, such as maternal rubella, inherited disorders, injury, or drugs taken by the mother during pregnancy. Even some medically prescribed drugs, such as Accutane (used to treat acne), may produce toxic reactions in the fetus. Some of the disorders that teachers are most likely to encounter include the following:

- *Cataracts*. Cataracts cause progressive clouding of the lens of one or both eyes. This is a prenatal disorder.
- *Glaucoma*. Also a prenatal disorder, glaucoma is caused by a gradual destruction of the optic nerve because of the buildup of pressure caused by poor circulation of the fluids of the eye.
- *Retinopathy of prematurity (ROP) or retrolental fibroplasia*. This disorder occurs at birth and is due to the formation of a kind of scar tissue on the retina of one or both eyes. This used to occur more frequently as it is caused by an excessive concentration of oxygen administered to premature infants. At present, ROP is mainly found in extremely low-birthweight infants, even if the oxygen concentration has been ideal. Treatment is available if the condition is identified early. Ophthalmological screening of the premature infant is essential.

- *Retinal blastoma.* Retinal blastoma is a type of cancer of the eye. Infants may have an eye removed to prevent the spread of cancer. A prosthetic eye can usually be fitted.

- *Physical problems within the brain.* Some types of visual impairments are caused by physical problems within the brain. Infections or injuries that occur before, during, or following birth may damage the optic nerve or the visual cortex (portion of the brain where messages from the eyes are processed). Although vision is altered, the eyes appear normal.

- *Cortical/cerebral visual impairment.* Cortical/cerebral visual impairment is vision loss that is due to damage to the parts of the brain that receive and interpret the visual information from the eye. This type of impairment is often accompanied by other developmental disabilities.

Cortical/cerebral visual impairment visual impairments originating in the brain

VISUAL ACUITY Visual acuity problems usually are caused by refractive errors (Figure 8–3). Eyes that appear normal may have refractive errors. Refraction is the bending of light rays, necessary to make a focused image at the back of the eye. When there is even a minor malformation of the eye or certain parts of it, refractive errors can occur. The most common refractive errors are discussed below. Refractive errors are correctable with eyeglasses.

Visual acuity problems problems in how well an individual is able to see

Refractive errors problems, such as astigmatism, hyperopia, and myopia, caused by a minor malformation of the eye that influences the bending of light rays

- *Astigmatism.* Astigmatism is a defect of the lens that is caused by uneven refractions in different planes of the eye, causing blurred vision.

- *Hyperopia.* Hyperopia is also known as farsightedness. With this disorder, objects that are close up are seen less clearly.

- *Myopia.* Myopia is commonly known as nearsightedness. With this condition, faraway objects are seen less clearly.

MUSCULAR IMBALANCES When the major eye muscles are not working together, double vision and other problems may result. The following are among the most common muscular imbalances:

- *Amblyopia.* A common term for amblyopia is lazy eye. In an older person, amblyopia causes double vision. In young children, the brain may choose to develop the eye that can see more clearly and repress the image received from the other eye, eventually destroying that eye's ability to function. Unfortunately, there are often no observable signs associated

FIGURE 8-3 Structure of the Eye

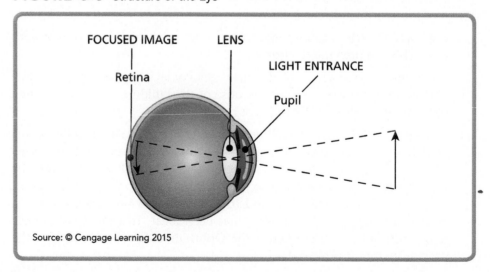

FOCUSED IMAGE LENS LIGHT ENTRANCE Retina Pupil

Source: © Cengage Learning 2015

with amblyopia. The alignment of the eyes appears normal unless the child has strabismus. Amblyopia causes a lack of depth perception and also increases the risk of long-term visual impairment.

- *Strabismus.* When **strabismus** exists, the two eyes are unable to focus together on the same image. There are several forms of strabismus: cross-eyed, wandering eye, or one eye that turns in or outward (wall-eyed). To avoid seeing double, the brain in young children shuts off the nondominant eye. This eye will not develop if it is not being used to see. This will gradually lead to permanent loss of vision in that eye if it is not corrected. If the child sometimes focuses with the left eye, sometimes with the right eye (alternate strabismus), both eyes may continue to work well.

- *Nystagmus.* Nystagmus is characterized by quick, involuntary, jerky up-and-down or back-and-forth eye movements as the child tries to obtain a single image. These movements seriously interfere with the ability to see. This condition is usually caused by neurological abnormalities and not by problems with the eye muscles. This condition improves with age.

Strabismus eye muscle imbalance problems, which are correctable with eyeglasses

Identifying Vision Impairments

Congenital blindness and severe low vision can be identified in the first year of life. It is usually the parents who first become aware that their infant does not look at them or at objects that they wave or offer to their child. Partial vision losses are more difficult to recognize. Often they go undetected until the child is in school. Even then, there are children with vision problems who are not identified until Grade 3 or 4, when the print in schoolbooks gets smaller, pictures are fewer, the print becomes more densely packed, and the children become aware that they cannot see what the teacher has written on the board.

Accurately assessing the visual function of a young child with disabilities is essential in determining appropriate intervention and educational strategies (Koenig et al., 2000). Many children with visual impairments are identified through routine screening in preschool and child care settings or by their parents, who suspect a possible vision problem. The Snellen Illiterate E Test for identifying visual acuity and muscle imbalance (e.g., amblyopia) is widely used for young children, beginning at about two years of age. Teller Acuity Cards, a preferential-looking procedure (Teller, McDonald, Preston, Sebris, & Dobson, 1986), can be used in younger children and low-functioning older children. The Teller Acuity Cards test for pediatric visual acuity without requiring a verbal response. The professional judges an infant's attention to a series of cards showing stripes of different widths. This allows the professional to perform accurate infant vision screening and avoid the more complex, time-consuming laboratory testing that would otherwise by necessary.

Photoscreening is a relatively new technique being used to detect amblyopia, strabismus, cataracts, and significant acuity conditions in infants, toddlers, and children with developmental delays in situations that were previously difficult to screen (American Academy of Pediatrics, 2002).

A major difficulty in trying to assess vision is that children with visual impairments have no idea what they are supposed to be seeing. In other words, they really do not know that what they see is imperfect and different from what others are seeing. For this reason, parents and early childhood teachers are often the first to suspect possible vision problems in young children.

Warning Signs

The following list of warning signs, or alerts, is adapted from material published by the U.S. National Society to Prevent Blindness. The alerts are grouped according to children's behaviour, appearance, or verbal complaints:

- rubs eyes excessively
- shuts or covers one eye
- tilts head or thrusts it forward
- has difficulty doing work or playing games that require close use of the eyes
- blinks excessively or becomes irritable when doing close work
- is unable to see distant things clearly
- squints, squeezes eyelids together, frowns
- has crossed eyes or eyes that turn outward
- has red-rimmed, encrusted, or swollen eyelids
- has inflamed, infected, or watery eyes
- has recurring sties
- has itchy, burning, or scratchy-feeling eyes
- is unable to see well—holds objects close to the eyes or trips easily
- experiences dizziness, headaches, or nausea following close work
- has blurred or double vision

An ophthalmologist may prescribe eyeglasses for a child with visual problems.

© Cengage Learning 2015

If parents' and teachers' observations or a vision screening suggests an impairment, the next step is for parents to obtain medical assistance. The best qualified consultant is a pediatric ophthalmologist. The ophthalmologist can arrange for the child to receive a visual evoked potential test. This procedure involves placing surface electrodes on the child's scalp and then showing the child different visual patterns. This evaluation process measures involuntary brain activity and is very useful in identifying visual impairments in infants and young children. The ophthalmologist may also prescribe eyeglasses, medication, surgery, eye exercises, occlusion (covering) of one eye, or some combination of these (see photo, above).

A note of caution: If a screening test does not reveal an impairment but the symptoms continue, it is wise to refer a child for a medical checkup anyway. Marotz, Cross, and Rush (2009) explained that false positives can occur. This means that in screening a child with a visual impairment (or any other kind of impairment), the child may still pass a general screening test. In the case of vision screening, there may have been unintended coaching by the examiner, or the child may have peeked around the occluder during testing. Test results (of all kinds) should always be regarded with caution, especially when a teacher or parent has reason to believe that a child's behaviours indicate a potential impairment.

Children with severe visual impairments, especially school-aged children with weak **residual vision**, may be referred to a low-vision clinic. Specialists can determine if the child will benefit from using magnifiers, telescopic lenses, specific electronic devices, or closed-circuit greatly magnified television. As children

Occlusion an obstruction; as used here, something to prevent vision; an occluder is the object the examiner uses to prevent a child from seeing (usually one eye at a time)

Residual vision vision remaining after disease or damage occurs to a person's visual system advance in the elementary grades, a number of other sophisticated reading and writing devices are available.

The Impact of Vision Impairments on Development

Poor vision has an impact on overall development. The more severe the visual impairment, the greater the developmental delay is likely to be. A lot of what a young child learns comes from scanning the environment, then focusing on particular stimuli (Erin, 2000) and pondering on what is occurring. Learning also comes from watching others, imitating them, and observing what follows. For these reasons, poor vision affects a child's language development, large and small motor development, and cognitive and social development. Why? Because the child's ability to interact with people, objects, and activities is seriously curtailed. Children with visual impairments may fail to recognize the presence of amusing events, such as a kitten scampering about. Children with visual impairments may be unaware of the consequences of their behaviour (such as spilled juice staining a bedspread). They may be unable to enter into new experiences because they have an inaccurate sense of what is going on. A card game, such as Go Fish, cannot be understood just by listening to it being played.

The inability to play is also a hindrance to the development of a child with visual impairments. Whereas babies who are sighted begin deliberately reaching for and playing with nearby objects, infants who are blind remain passive. They continue to hold their hands at shoulder height, a posture typical of very young children. Babies with visual impairments play alone a lot of the time because they are not able to be motivated by seeing play activities and other stimuli in the environment (see photo, above). In addition, they have fewer of the play challenges that children who are sighted exchange among themselves. Therefore, parents and teachers have to create structured play opportunities for children who are visually impaired in order to provide opportunities for them to acquire the cognitive, social, language, and adaptation skills that are repeatedly practised in play and are necessary preparation for higher-order skills.

EFFECTS ON LANGUAGE DEVELOPMENT Language acquisition depends on discovering and identifying objects and actions. This is difficult for children who cannot see the objects and the actions. They must depend almost entirely on what can be touched or heard, which reduces their learning opportunities. Once the child with a visual impairment begins to understand how to explore objects and formulate ideas about them, it is very important that a parent or teacher model descriptive language for the child. This facilitates more rapid development

Tactile exploration of the environment is essential for children with severe vision loss, who may receive fewer invitations to play. Using real objects supports this exploration.

© Cengage Learning 2015

of language in the child. It may take a child who is visually impaired at least a year longer to develop a full range of language skills. By school age, most are using language within developmental and cultural norms.

EFFECTS ON COGNITIVE DEVELOPMENT Children who are blind or have low vision generally lag behind children who are sighted in cognitive development and concept formation. For example, an infant who is sighted, in play with adults, will learn quickly that everyone has a nose. The toddler who is blind can learn to identify his own nose and those of his parents, but may not be aware, unless taught, that all people have noses. Delays are more noticeable during the first three or four years of life (Hatton, Anthony, Bishop, Gleason, Greeley, Miller, … Tompkins, 2003). However, with adequate nurturing and early intervention, the preschool child who is blind can develop the functional skills for academic learning.

EFFECTS ON MOTOR DEVELOPMENT Although a visual impairment is not the cause of differences (delays or deviations) in motor development, it can exert an influence. The greater the vision loss, the greater the delays in reaching, crawling, and walking. In fact, a child who has limited vision does not develop the ability to localize sound and move toward it until the end of the first year. Many children who are blind do not walk until they are two years old. Motor development may be further delayed by the child's difficulty in learning skills related to judging distance, direction, body position, and objects' positions in space. Children who are blind often develop awkward patterns of walking and positioning themselves, because they have no visual reference points or models. It is therefore very important that children who are blind receive appropriate programming to facilitate developmentally normal body posturing and movement patterns.

EFFECTS ON SOCIAL DEVELOPMENT Young children with visual impairments frequently are unable to participate in the interactions that build good social skills and interpersonal relationships. They may, because they are often focusing on listening to sounds in the environment, appear to be quiet and passive as infants. Parents, as noted earlier, must be helped to both stimulate and respond to their infant's developmentally different ways of interacting. Play skills, as previously mentioned, develop more slowly in children who are visually impaired. Toys, for example, are used less creatively, and play is often stereotyped because of the lack of visual models necessary for expanding the imagination. Furthermore, the young child with a vision impairment will often find it more challenging to interact with peers because he or she is unable to pick up on the nonverbal cues in interactive play. For this reason, adult support in interpreting play, giving a running verbal commentary of what is happening, pointing out available alternatives in the environment, and so on, is extremely important for the young child with a visual impairment in an inclusive program.

EFFECTS ON FAMILY LIFE Children who have vision impairments tend to be identified earlier than children with other impairments. Many vision difficulties are the result of prematurity, so vision tests are done on very young premature infants. Reactions from the parents to the infant and the infant to the parents may affect the parents' emotional state. If parents know that their child cannot see them, they may not smile at their baby. The baby then does not coo back at the parents, because it cannot "feel" the emotion. It is like talking to a friend on the telephone. Your friend can tell you are smiling even though he or she cannot see you. Your friend's tone of voice then changes and the conversation continues. The infant can sense the smiles and affectionate gazes of the parents and respond. Parents need to be encouraged to look at, engage, and interact with their baby as if the baby can see (Hatton, McWilliam, & Winton, 2002).

Intervention Programs

Intervention programs serving infants and toddlers who are blind and visually impaired often focus on the parent as teacher. During the first year of life, as with many early intervention programs for children with other special needs, programs for children with visual impairments are often home based. A specially trained person visits the home on a regular basis and may focus on **preorientation and mobility skills**. In Canada, many provinces and territories have specific early intervention programs for young children with visual impairment provided through the Ministry of Social Services or Ministry of Education. Throughout Canada, the Canadian National Institute for the Blind (CNIB) provides ongoing support to families of young children with severe visual impairments *as long as they are registered as visually impaired*. The visiting specialist provides information about the effects of vision impairment on all aspects of development and coaches parents in special techniques for interacting with their infant or toddler. The specialist also is likely to provide instructional play materials, demonstrate teaching strategies, and help parents record their child's progress.

Preorientation and mobility skills the ability of a child who has a visual impairment to map out and travel in a room safely

In some areas there are intervention programs for older toddlers and preschoolers. The toddler program often includes parents. Older preschool children are likely to stay at school without a parent. Even so, parents should continue to be an integral part of their child's learning activities. Many school-aged children, depending on the severity of the visual impairment and their progress, will be able to make the transition from a segregated early childhood or kindergarten classroom (if available) to an inclusive setting. Other children, needing further specialized training, may continue in the segregated setting part time and for the remainder of the school day participate in an inclusive classroom.

When teachers model appropriate ways to interact with a child who is visually impaired, supporting their activity to build feelings of competence and independence, other children learn to do the same. They learn to call the child's name or touch the child's shoulder to attract his or her attention. They learn to put things directly into a child's hands, naming each object at the moment. They learn to help the child move about by describing things specifically: "Here are the lockers. Jenny's locker is the second one. You can put her truck on the bottom shelf." Children who serve as helpers need to enjoy the job and feel positive about being able to provide assistance.

General Guidelines for Teachers

A number of conditions causing visual impairments are responsive to treatment procedures. It is important that teachers be alert to any signs that might indicate a change in a child's vision. It is the teachers' responsibility to alert parents and professionals if they note any changes.

A resource teacher/early interventionist or a specially trained consultant can help early childhood teachers arrange the classroom and develop curriculum activities that support the inclusion of a child with a visual impairment. This will ensure effective learning experiences throughout the program for the child with a visual impairment. The broad goal of early education for children with visual impairments is to strengthen their intact sensory channels (Pogrund, Fazzi, & Hess, 2002) and provide activities that require hearing, touch, taste, and smell.

The hardest part, for many adults, is to refrain from overprotecting a child who has little or no vision. Like all young children, children who have visual impairments need to explore their environment if they are to learn. In the process, they may bump into a wall, fall down, get up, start out again, have another mishap, and another, and another. To make sure the child does not experience unnecessary harm, the classroom and play yard must be kept safe and orderly. Pathways need to be clear of toys and misplaced equipment that the child with a visual impairment (and the teachers and the other children) may trip over. Most importantly, children with low vision may need to continue to be helped with their mobility skills throughout the day.

Learning to get about efficiently and safely on their own will be of prime importance throughout life. If furniture is to be rearranged, the child with a visual impairment should be alerted ahead of time and then physically guided over the new pathways. This enables the child to avoid the frustration of not knowing his or her way around and the embarrassment of bumping into things.

Teachers must also avoid the tendency to deny the child's right to learn self-defence and the right of possession. One way is to refrain from speaking out prematurely on behalf of the child. On many occasions, however, the teacher may need to supply the words: "Melinda, say, 'No! My eggbeater!'" Another time it may be necessary to tell the child who is visually impaired that he or she is about to lose a turn. For example: "Marcie, Khalil has been waiting for a turn on that swing. He is next. Khalil, tell Marcie, 'My turn.'" At this point, the teacher must be sure to follow through. It is important that the child who is sighted yield the swing, give back the eggbeater, or respond to any other reasonable request made by the child who is visually impaired.

GUIDELINES FOR WORKING WITH CHILDREN WHO HAVE VISUAL IMPAIRMENTS It is important to determine the degree of residual vision. Find out from the child's parents and the vision specialist what and how the child sees. Many children with visual impairments see shadows, colour, and large pictures or objects. Some children's **peripheral vision** may be their best vision. For this reason, a turned-away head does not necessarily signal inattention.

Orientation and mobility skills should be a major initial teaching priority. The following suggestions should support children with visual impairments in adjusting to an early childhood program:

- Familiarize the child with the classroom layout and storage of materials, placing as many toys as possible on low shelves where they can be easily touched.

- Be sure to reorient the child whenever changes in the room occur (e.g., moved furniture, shift of toys from one shelf to another, or a change in schedule).

- Put identifying material or subtle noisemakers on the floor, doors, room dividers, and lockers, such as
  - a wind chime near the door to the play yard;
  - tile in the creative arts and sensory play areas;
  - carpeting in the blocks area and large-group area;
  - rough matting by doors to the outside;

Peripheral vision that degree of vision available at the outer edges of the eyes

- a patch of velveteen glued to the child's locker; and

- cork or raised tape along certain walls or furniture to guide the child by touch.

• Use specific words when giving directions, to tell the child what to do: "Put the book on the table"; or "I'm sitting by the piano. Bring your shoes to me." Avoid nonspecific phrases, such as "Come here," "Put it there," or "Be careful."

• Talk to the child about everything in the immediate environment. Give the names, over and over, for everyday objects, such as ball, dog, cup, and brush. Naming the object is not enough. For a child who is visually impaired to understand the meaning of "watering can," for example, the child must hold one, feel what is inside, pour from it, and handle it empty and filled with water.

• Give the child action words. Tell the child many times over what he or she is doing: "You are *running on* the grass." "You are *brushing* your teeth." "You are *drinking* juice."

• Help the child localize and sort out sounds. Tell the child what the classroom sounds are and where they are coming from: the guinea pig squeaking *by the window*, the faucet dripping *in the sink*, the fan whirring *on the ceiling*. Help children learn to identify the sound of an eggbeater, the tick of a timer, the swishing of sandpaper blocks rubbing together.

• Play sound-guessing games. The teacher (or another child) can make the sound of one of several objects on a tray (tearing paper, closing a book, dropping a marble in a cup). The child who is visually impaired then must locate the correct object(s) by touch. To make the game challenging for children without visual impairments as well, the teacher can turn away from the children while making the sound, or can make the sound under a cloth or in a large box open only on the teacher's side.

• Teach sounds that may signal danger in contrast to those that are simply frightening. The sound of the power mower in the playing field is something to stay away from. The drone of the vacuum cleaner signals something the child can help push. The fire alarm indicates STOP whatever is going on and stand by the door. The squeak of chains warns children to stay back because the swings are in motion.

The teacher's goal should be to plan activities that involve all children and incidentally are of specific benefit to the child with a visual impairment:

• Offer several opportunities each day to learn through smelling, touching, and tasting.

• Vary the consistency of paint by adding sand, soap, cornstarch, and so on. Introduce different sizes and weights of paintbrushes, rollers, or markers; different types of paper; textures; and so on.

• Use actual objects, rather than plastic replicas, for teaching—for example, in a session on fruit, a real banana and orange should be used for feeling, cutting, peeling, smelling, tasting, and comparing. (Be sure to check whether any children have food allergies.)

• Plan cooking or baking experiences that involve measuring, smelling, tasting, touching, before-and-after cutting, mixing, and so on.

• Offer sorting activities that support learning categorizations—for example, same versus different, or seriation from small to large, cold to hot, smooth to rough, different odours, and so on.

- Use touch, hearing, smell, or taste to tell the difference between shapes, sizes, textures, and odours.

- Provide left-to-right training. Informal practice in working from left to right is a skill all preschool children need in preparation for reading English. The child who is visually impaired is no exception; Braille and other academic activities follow the same format. When using pegboards, for example, there can be teacher-initiated activities in which the child is encouraged to fill the board systematically by placing pegs in left-to-right and top-to-bottom progression.

- Provide access to materials such as Braille books and auditory stories to promote emergent literacy skills.

Special considerations for children with visual impairments include the following:

- Use the child's name before speaking to the child, thus signalling that the statement is directed to him or her.

- Ensure your tone of voice communicates the tone and mood of the message. Many verbal statements are accompanied by nonverbal gestures, facial expressions, and other types of body language the child cannot see.

- Encourage as much active participation as possible, as this will ensure the greatest amount of opportunity for obtaining sensory information.

- Seat the child close to the teacher in situations where support may be necessary—such as circles.

- Provide real three-dimensional objects as often as possible. Many toys are one-dimensional visual representations of a real object and thus do not provide sufficient tactile information about the object (Stewart & Cornell, 2004).

- Provide many physical prompts. This is especially important in music times when the child may need to be physically guided in hand or body gestures. Having the child place his or her hands on yours during hand movements will also support learning.

- Help the child with a visual impairment to feel more secure by ensuring that during gross motor circle activities, certain parts—such as marching, jumping, and so on—can be done in one place.

- Make sure that teacher demonstrations take the form of subtle physical assistance and hand-over-hand guidance.

- Have the teacher guide and support the child from behind, gradually reducing assistance as the child masters the successive steps required to accomplish the task (see the Task Analysis section in Chapter 11).

- Make sure that whenever possible materials are introduced that have high contrast in colours—this will help the child with low vision.

- Explain ahead of time to the child any new ideas or experiences being planned for a group or circle time.

- Keep an eye on the child when he or she is playing with other children, making sure that they are including the child who is visually impaired in their play in as equally important roles as those they take for themselves.

- Help the child with basic social skills; for example, the child should learn to turn his or her face toward people when talking, use appropriate physical posture, and so on.

In addition, teachers may find it useful to consult a resource person, who can assist them in arranging the classroom and developing curriculum activities. A resource person can also assist parents and teachers in achieving the broader goal of strengthening children's intact sensory abilities through touch and sound (Pogrund et al., 2002).

MANNERISMS OF CHILDREN WHO ARE BLIND Rhythmic, seemingly purposeless mannerisms may occur almost continually among some children who are blind, especially when they are left too long on their own. They may rock back and forth for long periods, poke their eyes, flip their hands about in front of their face, or spin around and around. These movements may be accompanied by strange noises or high-pitched squeals. It is speculated that these behaviours develop because of reduced stimulation. Lacking vision, infants receive less motivation and challenge from their environment. In turn, they do not learn to explore their environment the way infants who are sighted do. It is almost as if these behaviours are the infants' efforts to create their own stimulation and so have something to respond to.

Whatever their causes, these behaviours can interfere with the development of social skills. They make the child stand out as uncomfortably different. As teachers help children who have severe visual impairments learn appropriate play skills and movement patterns, the children will spend less of their developmentally valuable early learning time in nonpurposeful spinning, poking, and twirling. Other children can be of help, too, especially with prompts from the teacher—for example, "Come, Sarah, let's go and get Mila and I'll pull you both in the wagon."

Summary

Hearing or visual impairments may greatly interfere with overall development. Infants who are blind or have an identified hearing loss should receive early intervention services and programming in the first months of life. In fact, early intervention planning and programming should begin as soon as the condition is identified. It is important to include parents in this process. Some children with visual and hearing impairments need to be educated in the most stimulating and enhancing environment possible. This may require a specialized setting, at least in the very early years, if these children are to develop the basic skills necessary and prerequisite to adapting effectively to a group setting.

Hearing losses are classified in three ways: conductive hearing loss, sensorineural hearing loss, and problems originating in the higher auditory cortex. (Combined losses can also occur.) Chronic ear infections, especially otitis media, which may come and go, are responsible for impairments in both hearing and language. Infants who do not startle or blink their eyes in response to loud noises may be hearing impaired. A hearing loss may be suspected in children who have acquired some language, especially if they begin asking to have things repeated or behave in ways that suggest difficulty with understanding.

Specially trained teachers can teach speech to children with hearing impairments; also available are a variety of language systems, including American Sign Language (ASL). However, the long-standing controversy continues: Should the child be taught to communicate only through speech? Or should the child be allowed to use all forms of communication? The Canadian Hearing Society states that children who are deaf or hard of hearing have the right to acquire signed language in addition to spoken language. Early childhood teachers are important agents in facilitating language development and cognitive learning in young children with hearing impairments. Part of the teacher's responsibility can be to make sure each day that a young child's hearing aid is working effectively.

Children classified as educationally blind do not have functional vision. For educational placement, children who are low visioned or are partially sighted will often be able to learn by using specially presented printed or other visual materials. In the preschool child, identification of a visual impairment may be difficult, because screening tests cannot be relied on to identify all vision problems. Therefore, parents and teachers need to be alert to behavioural signs that a child may have a vision problem. If not identified and treated, poor vision affects all areas of development.

Learning for children with visual impairments requires more time, more practice, more verbal mediation, and more encouragement from adults.

Many early intervention programs serving infants and toddlers are home based and focus on training parents as teachers. Young children, even those who are visually impaired, are more readily included in an early childhood setting if a specially trained consultant is available to assist the teacher. It is important that teachers and parents restrain themselves from overprotecting the young child who is visually impaired, because children with vision impairments need to learn how to be self-reliant in order to cope with daily challenges.

Resources

The following resources have been compiled as the most useful sites on which to find relevant research and information related to children with vision and hearing disabilities.

Canadian Association of the Deaf

http://www.cad.ca

Canadian Hard of Hearing Association

http://www.chha.ca

The Canadian Hearing Society

http://www.chs.ca

Canadian National Institute for the Blind (CNIB)

http://www.cnib.ca

National Association for Parents of Children with Visual Impairments

http://www.spedex.com/napvi

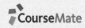 Access an interactive ebook and chapter-specific interactive learning tools, including flashcards, quizzes, videos, and more, in the *Inclusion in Early Childhood Programs* CourseMate. Visit NELSONbrain.com to log in, register, or purchase access.

Orthopedic and Other Health Conditions

9

....

OBJECTIVES

After studying the material in this chapter, the student will be able to

- Define and give examples of orthopedic and other health impairments.
- Explain the general effects of orthopedic and health impairments on overall development (including physical, cognitive, and social development).
- Describe the role of the early childhood teacher in working with children with orthopedic and health conditions.
- Discuss the implications of both obesity and undernourishment in young children in general and in young children who have health concerns.
- Outline classroom procedures to consider in preparation for emergency situations related to orthopedic and health impairments.

KEY CONCEPTS AND TERMS

adaptive equipment

anaphylactic shock

anoxia

ataxia

athetosis

cerebral palsy

chemotherapy

contractures

genetic mutation

health conditions

hydrocephalus

hypertonicity

hypotonicity

immune system

incontinence

meningocele

metabolize

myelomeningocele

orthopedic conditions

Prader-Willi syndrome

primitive reflexes

prostheses/prosthetic devices

radiation

regeneration

seizures

shunting

spasticity

spina bifida

wedges, bolsters, and
    prone-boards

CONNECTIONS

- Beth was nearly four years old and not walking when her grandparents became her guardians. From early infancy, she had been seriously neglected by her parents and had been without adequate medical care despite her obvious physical and developmental problems. Soon after Beth moved in with her grandparents, they made appointments for her to be seen by the pediatric team at a nearby medical centre, and they enrolled her in a preschool program associated with the centre. Within a year and a half, Beth was showing marked improvement: walking, riding tricycles, and climbing on playground equipment along with the other children.

- Jack has asthma, which is controlled with daily breathing treatments he receives at home. His Grade 1 teacher, the principal, and the yard-duties and office manager have all been trained to look for signs of breathing difficulty and are familiar with his Emergency Treatment Plan. Jack's parents communicate about how Jack is doing and how changes in seasons and activities are affecting Jack's asthma. Because of this careful planning and ongoing communication, Jack's parents know he is well cared for at school and able to participate with his peers.

Introduction

Physical activity and general good health are essential for optimal early development. Infants and young children who eat well, sleep well, and move about freely are likely to acquire a well-integrated range of cognitive, language, social, and physical skills. Problems with health and motor control, however, tend to interfere with everything a child tries to do or learn. Since young children's learning is activity based, a physical impairment may affect overall development because it interferes with the ability to move about, explore, rearrange play materials, and seek out playthings and playmates. Even casual observation indicates that innumerable times a day, children who are able-bodied will move about, rearranging their own learning environment.

> *Example:*
>
> *A nine-month-old tires of playing with familiar toys. She crawls to the bookcase and soon discovers the fun of taking books off the shelf. This infant has found a challenge for herself and a match for her rapidly developing motor skills. Of course, pulling books off the shelf may be viewed as mischievous by parents or caregivers. If so, they need to challenge themselves to find new play materials that both stimulate the child and meet their adult standards of appropriateness.*

In this chapter, the discussion will focus on the two broad categories of physiological disabilities: orthopedic challenges and other health conditions. Their definitions, given below, have helped reduce confusion about the meaning of the term *physical disability*.

Orthopedic conditions involve the skeleton, joints, and muscles. Included are the following:

- missing or malformed limbs, or paralysis
- structural problems, such as clubfeet
- congenital hip dislocations
- damage caused by diseases, such as polio and bone tuberculosis
- **contractures** (muscular and/or joint tightening) caused by fractures, burns, or amputations

Orthopedic conditions conditions involving the bones, joints, and the associated muscles and ligaments

Contractures permanent tightening of muscles and joints

Neurological disorders that have orthopedic consequences include **cerebral palsy** and **spina bifida**, resulting in such problems as paralysis of major muscles.

Other **health conditions** are defined generally as limited strength, vitality, or alertness due to chronic or acute health problems. Among them are the following:

- heart conditions
- epilepsy
- asthma
- leukemia
- sickle-cell disease
- diabetes
- hemophilia
- cystic fibrosis
- HIV/AIDS
- nutritional problems

Actual boundaries between physical disabilities and other health impairments frequently overlap. Furthermore, neurological problems may complicate many conditions. Physical and neurological impairments may both be present, as in cerebral palsy, spina bifida, and other childhood conditions.

This chapter will also consider the impact of nutritional problems on the development of young children.

Orthopedic Conditions

Orthopedic conditions cover a wide range of impairments. In general, they include any condition that interferes with the normal functioning of bones, joints, and muscles (see photo, right). The conditions may be evident at birth, as with the physical manifestations of cerebral palsy, hip dysplasia, and clubfoot, or they may be identifiable later in childhood, as in the case of muscular dystrophy, a multi-system disorder.

Cerebral Palsy

Cerebral palsy (CP) is a neurological condition that involves the inability to coordinate muscle action, as well as limited ability to sustain normal posture, achieve balance, and control normal movements and skills. CP is the most common source of physical disabilities among infants and young children. The basic cause is damage to the brain occurring before, during, or after the infant's birth. Cerebral palsy is a nonprogressive disorder resulting from oxygen deprivation (**anoxia**), injury, infection, hemorrhage (excessive bleeding), or malformation of the brain. The exact cause can seldom be specified. The extent of the damage to the brain, and the corresponding impact on the child's ability to control physical movement, will

Cerebral palsy a condition that affects muscular control; it is caused by damage to various parts of the brain. Its effects range from very mild (nonincapacitating) to moderate (involving fine or gross motor skills, or both), to pervasive (involving almost all areas of the body's physical activity)

Spina bifida the imperfect development of the spinal cord and spinal column that occurs during the first 30 days of fetal development; it can cause severe disabilities

Health conditions refers to the range of health problems a child might have and how these affect their growth, development, and everyday lives

Anoxia a shortage of oxygen to the brain that can cause physical damage to the brain before, during, or at any time after birth; anoxia is one of the major causes of physical and cognitive dysfunction

Children with orthopedic impairments can participate when provided with specialized equipment.

Courtesy of Bloorview—Scarborough Site

determine how well the child will function. One way of classifying cerebral palsy is by the type of abnormal muscle tone displayed; the other is by how the various parts of the body are affected.

It is frequently thought that neurological conditions are evident at birth. Often the opposite is true. Neurological symptoms in young children change with the rapid maturation of the brain in early infancy and therefore it may be weeks, months, or well into the first year before the infant gives evidence of a neurological impairment. The condition may become noticeable only when certain very early reflexive (primitive) behaviours do not disappear on schedule and so interfere with the acquisition of new and more mature responses. For example, most newborns automatically grasp a finger placed in their hand. However, unless this primitive grasp reflex disappears between one and four months of age, infants will not be able to learn to release objects at will. Early identification of any behavioural dysfunction or developmental difference is extremely important, because the sooner a disability is identified, the sooner therapeutic remediation and special programming can begin.

CLASSIFICATIONS BASED ON MUSCLE TONE Muscle tone may be described in terms of *hyper* (high) or *hypo* (low) muscle tension. The child who displays **hypotonicity** is one who has too little muscle tone. The result is an inability to move about or maintain postural control (the rag doll syndrome). Infants with this type of condition are often referred to as "floppy babies." Many have difficulty simply holding up their heads. This deprives them of the learning experiences that most infants get from being held in an upright position. The child with **hypertonicity** is one who has taut muscle activity, preventing fluid movements. The following conditions, which often accompany cerebral palsy, are associated with muscle tone.

Spasticity Most children with cerebral palsy fall into the category of **spasticity**. They usually are considered to be hypertonic. Without early intervention, a child may become locked into certain positions because muscles become permanently contracted. These muscle contractures occur frequently in the hips, knees, ankles, elbows, and wrists, as well as in the child's fingers and toes, which may become irreversibly curled or clenched.

Athetosis Fluctuating or uneven muscle tone is called **athetosis**. Muscle control that goes from one extreme to the other (either too low or too high) is typical. Children with this condition tend to retain **primitive reflexes** past the normal time. This interferes with the development of voluntary motor responses.

Ataxia A lack of motor coordination, **ataxia** is characterized by poor balance and a lurching kind of walk, reflecting a lack of voluntary muscle control. Purposeful activity such as feeding themselves, cutting with a pair of scissors, or picking up small objects is extremely difficult. For example, a teacher's carefully organized collage materials are swept off the table as a result of involuntary muscle responses as the child strives to participate.

Mixed Approximately 30 percent of children with cerebral palsy have a mixture of spasticity and athetosis or ataxia.

CLASSIFICATIONS BASED ON BODY PARTS A second way of classifying cerebral palsy is according to the parts of the body that are affected. Figure 9–1 lists the terms used to describe the location of the involvement.

Hypotonicity too little muscle tone; "floppiness"

Hypertonicity abnormally high muscle tone

Spasticity abnormal muscle tone—evident in taut muscle activity or too little muscle tone, both of which prevent fluid movements, as seen in cerebral palsy

Athetosis fluctuating or uneven muscle tone; muscle control that goes from one extreme to the other (either too low or too high) is typical

Primitive reflexes the responses the infant is born with, such as grasping, stepping, rooting, and sucking. Most of these disappear around four months of age and are replaced by similar but voluntary behaviours, as in the sucking response

Ataxia a lack of motor coordination, ataxia is characterized by poor balance and a lurching kind of walk, reflecting a lack of voluntary muscle control

FIGURE 9-1

Terms That Describe the Location of the Body Affected by CP

- *Diplegia:* Involvement of all four extremities with the legs more severely affected than the arms.

- *Hemiplegia:* Only one side of the body is involved.

- *Paraplegia:* Involvement of the legs only.

- *Quadriplegia:* Involvement of both arms, both legs, trunk, and the muscles that provide head control.

Source: © Cengage Learning 2015

The extent of motor impairment varies in children with cerebral palsy. Some children have disabilities so severe they cannot hold their heads still or straighten their arms or legs. Others have control problems so slight as to be scarcely noticeable. Many children with cerebral palsy, like children with other developmental disabilities, fail to meet major motor milestones at expected times. A distinction must be made, however. Children with general developmental differences usually have delays in all areas. In contrast, children with cerebral palsy may have developmentally appropriate cognitive and receptive language ability (see photo, below), but their motor skills, including those affecting speech production, may be poorly developed.

Young children with cerebral palsy, especially those with mild to moderate involvement, usually benefit from an inclusive early childhood classroom experience. All children with a motor dysfunction should receive ongoing evaluation.

The parents and early childhood teachers should participate in developing a program for the child, while at the same time receiving appropriate training on physical management techniques and special programming strategies. The success of the early childhood program experience will depend on the teachers and child receiving adequate assistance and support from the interdisciplinary team, which should include a resource teacher, a pediatric physiotherapist, and an occupational therapist, as well as a speech and language therapeutic consultant.

Children with cerebral palsy often have excellent cognitive and receptive language abilities.

© Jaren Wicklund/Fotolia

Spinal Cord Injuries/Damage

Spinal cord damage presents motor problems quite different from those associated with cerebral palsy. When the spinal cord is injured or severed, muscles below the point of damage become useless or severely impaired because these muscles no longer receive messages from the brain. Furthermore, sensations normally experienced below the point of injury are no longer transmitted back to the brain. It is important to note that the brain itself is not affected. However, because of interruption in neural communication between the brain and certain parts of the body, there are no sensations as to where the limbs are or what is happening to them. A child may suffer serious burns, cuts, or broken bones without knowing it. Parents, teachers, and caregivers of young children must be aware of this and constantly be alert to protect a child who has nonfeeling extremities and trunk. It should be noted that regeneration (repair or renewal) of the spinal cord is not possible at this time, but huge scientific advances are being made in this area. The use of stem cells to regenerate injured spinal cords or repair congenitally malformed spinal cords is currently being researched in a number of countries. Initial findings are very positive (Canadian Stem Cell Foundation, 2013).

The most familiar of spinal cord injuries is spina bifida (myelomeningocele and meningocele). The damage comes from imperfect development of the spinal cord and spinal column during the first 30 days of fetal development. Children with spina bifida experience a number of problems in addition to paralysis of the affected limbs. The two most common problems are hydrocephalus and incontinence.

1. **Hydrocephalus.** Blockage of the circulation of the spinal fluid in the cranial (brain) cavity. This is usually corrected through shunting, whereby tubes are surgically inserted in the back of the neck to drain spinal fluid from the brain to another area of the body, often the abdominal cavity. Without shunting, the spinal fluid will accumulate in the head cavity, enlarging the head and damaging the brain.

   Occasionally, shunts may become blocked. It is important that teachers be aware of the symptoms related to blocked shunts. These symptoms involve dizzy spells, nausea, sleepiness, and vomiting. The child's parents are the most appropriate resource for identifying their child's specific symptoms. Parents should also indicate to the teacher what action should be taken if any of these signs should occur.

   Dr. Benjamin Warf at the Boston Children's Hospital (2011) has pioneered a promising new treatment for hydrocephalus in infants that replaces the need for shunting. This minimally invasive surgical technique has been taught to surgeons around the world.

2. **Incontinence.** Lack of bladder or bowel control. Many children with myelomeningocele cannot feel the urge to urinate. Often they are unable to receive messages from the urinary sphincter muscles. The result is that the child has little or no control of urinary functioning. The same may be true of bowel activity. Although these problems are difficult to overcome, many children who experience them can be helped to learn techniques for managing their own bowel and bladder needs. Liptak (2002) pointed out that competence in toileting is necessary for social growth toward independence and that prevention of soiling, wetting, and odour enhances the child's self-esteem (p. 544). As the team evaluates the child's developmental skills, adaptive behaviours, and emotional strengths, they can also begin to determine the child's readiness to learn toilet skills and other everyday tasks.

Regeneration the regrowth, repair, or renewal of the spinal cord or other parts of the body

Myelomeningocele a congenital protrusion of the spinal cord through the vertebrae; paralysis and lack of sensation below the protrusion (usually the lower trunk and legs) are often the result

Meningocele a congenital protrusion of the spinal cord through the vertebrae; it is limited to the covering of the spinal cord and usually causes little or no neurological impairment

Hydrocephalus a condition that occurs as the result of a buildup of cranial spinal fluid in the head; if not corrected (shunted), can lead to an enlargement of the head and, ultimately, pressure on and deterioration of the brain

Shunting a process for implanting a tube (shunt) into the brain to allow proper circulation and drainage of fluids from within the skull into one of the body cavities

Incontinence a lack of bladder or bowel control

Muscular Dystrophy

Progressive weakening of the muscles is the major characteristic of muscular dystrophy—a neurological condition—and related muscular disorders (see photo, below). As children with muscular dystrophy get older, they lose their large motor skills first. Loss of fine motor skills comes later. Several types of muscular dystrophy exist; each type involves specific muscle groups. The most common is Duchenne muscular dystrophy, a sex-linked disorder that affects boys almost exclusively. In Duchenne, progressive muscle weakness begins at the hips and shoulders and gradually moves out to the arms and legs. Children with this condition often walk on tiptoes and have large calf muscles but weak legs. Children with muscular dystrophy tend to move slowly and become easily tired. Hand skills are often retained, even when the limbs are severely impaired. Onset is usually between the ages of 3 and 5 years of age. Some cases are very mild and the condition progresses very slowly over a normal life span. In many cases, however, the disorder progresses more quickly and steadily, and by the age of 12, most children with this condition are unable to walk and may need a ventilator to breathe (Muscular Dystrophy Association of Canada, 2009). Early childhood teachers should encourage as much activity as the child can manage. Physical participation should be encouraged, but not forced. Teachers need to be aware of the extent of a child's ability and set up the environment to optimize his independence. For example, one child was able to string small wooden beads in complicated patterns if the beads were placed in a basket in his lap. However, when he ran out of beads he was unable to lift his arms to get more beads from the nearby table. Teachers need to be aware of the child's abilities and limitations. While still mobile and able to get around, a child with muscular dystrophy must be encouraged to move about the classroom frequently as exercise is helpful. Prevention of muscle contractures is a major goal of both therapy and classroom activity for these children.

Osteogenesis Imperfecta

Brittle bones is the common term for this congenital condition. The child's bones do not grow normally in length or thickness and they break easily. Joints, too, are involved and may show excessive range of motion, as in children who can bend their thumb backward to touch the wrist. Short stature, dental defects, and hearing problems also may be associated with this bone disease. The child's hearing often gets progressively worse, adding another dimension to teachers' planning. Generally, the child's cognitive skills are not affected, but a child may seem to be "behind" because of frequent hospitalization and absences from school. The Osteogensis Imperfecta Foundation (2012) stated that people born with this disorder may also experience the following health issues:

Progressive weakness of the muscle structure characterizes several early childhood disabilities.

© Rich Legg/iStockphoto.com

- bleeding, easy bruising, frequent nose bleeds and in a small number of people heavy bleeding from injuries

- breathing problems, higher incidence of asthma plus risk for other lung problems (Types section, para. 1)

Osteomyelitis

Infection of the bones is the simple definition of osteomyelitis. It can be a physically disabling disease if not treated promptly and properly. Medication (antibiotics) and surgery are used to treat this condition in children.

Hip Dysplasia

This condition—once called congenital dislocation of the hip (CDH), but now referred to as developmental dislocation of the hip (DDH)—is the result of abnormal development of the hip joint. The head of the thigh bone (femur) may be out of the hip socket or may move in and out at random. This condition is found much more often in females than in males. Hip displacement can occur in utero or may occur after birth. It is usually diagnosed soon after birth and treated nonsurgically, frequently through the use of casts and braces. Without treatment, the child will usually not be able to walk normally and will usually develop a waddling kind of gait.

Dwarfism

Dwarfism is a condition of short or small stature. "It is defined by the advocacy group Little People of America (LPA) as an adult height of 4 feet 10 inches and under, as a result of a medical or genetic condition" (WebMD, 2012, para. 1). It is caused by a variety of hereditary and metabolic disorders. There are many different types of dwarfism. The main types are

- *Hereditary*. Achondroplasia is one of the more common forms of dwarfism. In this condition, the arms and legs are extremely short, while the body trunk is of normal size. The head tends to be large. Hypocondroplasia, another common form of dwarfism, is similar in appearance to achondroplasia, except the head is of normal size. A third type of hereditary dwarfism is Diastrophic. In this condition, there is a progressive crippling caused by skeletal deformities.

- *Pituitary*. Pituitary dwarfism is the main endocrine type of dwarfism. It can be hereditary, and is caused by a dysfunction of the pituitary gland.

- Dwarfism resulting from inadequate nutrition during the early developmental years.

Most children with dwarfism are of normal intelligence and able to participate in all aspects of an early childhood education program. Teachers should be alert to times when they may need to rearrange or adapt classroom furniture, and/or adapt gross motor activities so that children of smaller stature or with shorter limbs can participate equally and without difficulty.

Juvenile Arthritis (JA) (Sometimes Referred to as Juvenile Rheumatoid Arthritis)

Juvenile arthritis is characterized by continuous painful inflammation of one or more joints and the tissue surrounding the joints. It may last for as little as several months to a year; however, many children experience it for a number of years. Most children will go through periods of flare-ups and then remissions.

The inflammation of the joints resulting in stiffening of the joints, problems sleeping, and difficulty walking are also characteristic of the illness. Some children also develop a fever and rash, and/or inflammatory eye disease. It is important for children with juvenile arthritis to have regular eye examinations by an ophthalmologist as there are often no recognizable eye symptoms prior to the onset of loss of vision. At no time is this condition contagious. Severe inflammation of some joints may affect the growth of some children. Physiotherapy and occupational therapy, as well as medication to ease pain and reduce inflammation, are major parts of the treatment for this condition. Sitting for long periods, though often less painful for the child than physical movement, causes further stiffening of the joints. Therefore, children with juvenile arthritis need both the freedom and the encouragement to move about a great deal, at home and at school. Symptoms often disappear by the time a child is 18 years old. The teacher's major goal must be to help the child keep his or her motor skills functional and to be aware of providing alternative group activities, if the activities being provided are too painful for the child to participate in.

Program Implications of Orthopedic Conditions

It is generally agreed that early and appropriate intervention has a positive effect on the acquisition of motor skills in young children with orthopedic conditions. Children with orthopedic disabilities, in spite of great individual differences, have basic classroom needs in common:

- the service of allied health professionals working as a team with classroom teachers
- **adaptive equipment** designed to meet each child's physical needs.
- environmental adaptations to facilitate and support each child's learning efforts in all parts (indoor and outdoor) of the early childhood program.

Adaptive equipment mobility devices, prostheses, and prescribed alterations of standard furnishings to meet the needs of children with special needs

Team Effort

The teacher's need for input from various health professionals in carrying out individualized early intervention programs has been discussed elsewhere in several contexts. A brief review, related to orthopedic and neurological conditions, is presented here.

As noted repeatedly, good motor skills are critical to every aspect of children's development. The pediatric physiotherapist or occupational therapist, trained to focus on early motor skills, is often selected as case coordinator/manager. The early interventionist/resource teacher, however, may be the key person in developing a specific program for the child. The early interventionist needs to work closely with parents, teachers, and others involved in the care of the child, establishing and adapting goals and specific objectives as the child's skills and behaviours change. The early interventionist often is the person who must coordinate the roles and responsibilities of the various team members who are meeting the ongoing needs of the child. For example, in drawing up an intervention program for a child with cerebral palsy who also has a feeding issue, the early interventionist may make use of a nutritionist, a social worker, and, perhaps, a dentist to provide consultation or direct assistance. If the child also has a speech or language issue, the services of a speech and language pathologist, an audiologist, and a psychologist should be enlisted.

In order for early learning and care settings to effective, it is vital that the members of the interdisciplinary team work collaboratively to achieve identified goals. This includes shared knowledge, perspectives, and expertise both at home and in the centre.

The ways in which a child who has a physical disability is positioned and helped to move about, at home and at school, are crucial to the child's development. Depending on the therapists' assessments, individual remediation activities are mapped out for each child. The classroom teacher should never be expected to put a child through stressful exercises. In fact, current practice tends to consider such exercises counterproductive for most children. Activities that are pleasant for both the child and the teacher (and often fun for other children as well) are the usual recommendations. *Under no circumstances should teachers initiate positioning exercises or remedial motor activities without specific guidance from a certified therapist.*

Adaptive Equipment

Prostheses/prosthetic devices artificial devices replacing body parts that are damaged, missing at birth, or later removed

The pediatric therapist also guides teachers in the use of special mobility devices, demonstrates how **prostheses/prosthetic devices** are used, and shows ways in which to adapt regular play equipment. Some of the more common prostheses are discussed below.

MOBILITY DEVICES Braces, crutches, walkers, and wheelchairs are among the mobility devices prescribed for children who cannot move about easily. Young children with paraplegia may use a low, small-wheeled flat cart. They lie "tummy-down" on the cart and propel themselves from one activity to another by pushing with their hands and arms. These devices are frequently referred to as scooter-boards or tummy-boards. Power wheelchairs are increasingly in use even by two- and three-year-olds. For stand-up activities, children with poor balance are often fastened into a standing board—also known as a prone-stander. Children with uncertain motor skills, even though they are able to walk, tend to fall more frequently than do other preschoolers. The falls are likely to distress adults more than they do the child. Usually, the child has become quite accustomed to falling down. Many children with conditions that impair their physical functioning are given training in how to fall and how to get themselves up again. The latter is especially important. Adults must restrain themselves from "rushing to the rescue," picking the child up before he or she has a chance to get up independently. Adults who restrain themselves save the child from being unnecessarily and additionally disabled through *learned helplessness*. Children who fall frequently are often fitted with a helmet to prevent serious head injury.

Neurological and medical factors first must be evaluated by a physician or other accredited specialist before walking becomes part of the developmental programming for this child.

Children with poor balance and poor motor control sometimes can hold on to and push a piece of play equipment as a means of getting about. A doll carriage or stroller or a large wooden box with a handle bar attached works well. If the box does not slide readily, wooden slats can be attached to the bottom. If the piece of equipment is too light, it can be loaded with bags of sand or large unopened juice cans, thus providing a feeling of greater security. Some children who lack precise hand control may need prosthetic devices, such as on-head sticks to enable them to operate computers and battery-operated toys. These devices enable children who are unable to be understood by other means to communicate.

POSITIONING DEVICES Motor and neurological disability are often accompanied by muscular weakness that interferes with head and trunk control. Maintaining a sitting position becomes difficult, as does grasping and hanging on to objects. The pediatric therapist can help teachers reduce the hampering effects of motor problems by recommending (or even procuring) specially designed equipment, such as **wedges, bolsters, and prone-boards** (see photo, right). *Cautionary note:* The inappropriate use of adaptive equipment may do *more harm* than good. It is essential that therapists and early interventionists/resource teachers explain to teachers of young children the purpose of each piece of equipment, and provide guidance in the proper use of the equipment for each individual child. Specialists must also help early childhood teachers be aware of situations that might arise and suggest precautions that should be taken while a child is using the equipment.

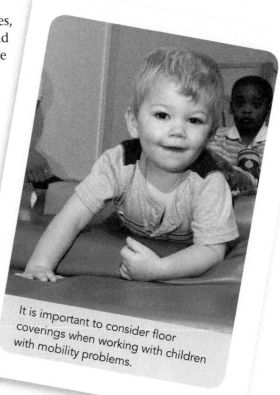

It is important to consider floor coverings when working with children with mobility problems.

Adaptations of Materials

Ingenious teachers have adapted almost every ordinary preschool material to fit the needs of children with motor impairments.

Wedges, bolsters, and prone-boards therapeutic positioning devices prescribed for use by physiotherapists and occupational therapists in treating children with impaired motor skills

MOVE (MOBILITY OPTIONS VIA EDUCATION/EXPERIENCE) MOVE is a program designed for children with physical conditions that limit the child's ability to fully participate in daily activities. This international program is designed to systematically teach independence in sitting, standing, transferring, walking, and toileting, with a strong emphasis on team collaboration between trained professionals and families. The approach includes researching, assessment, teaching, and practice in order to build skills. According to Move International (n.d.),

> The MOVE program is designed to use six-step process to assist the learner, family, and/or care provider in helping the learner advance in their gross motor skills.
> - Step One determines the learner's skill level through an interview assessment;
> - Step Two uses the learner's MOVE team to determine the functional goals needed to work toward promoting independence;
> - Step Three creates meaningful, functional activities and embeds appropriate skills into the activity for the learner to be successful in reaching their goals;
> - Step Four looks at the support the learner currently needs;
> - Step Five reduces the prompts the learner currently needs; and
> - Step Six defines and schedules teaching of the skills throughout the learner's typical day. ("MOVE Is …," para. 2)

UNIVERSAL DESIGN Universal design for learning (UDL) is a framework for supporting all young learners. The principles of universal design were introduced in the area of architecture to address the challenges associated with designing physical spaces for all people, including individuals with physical and cognitive disabilities.

The universal design of early learning suggests that "children enter classrooms with different experiences, backgrounds, interests, emotional, social, and academic strengths and needs. Planning for this diversity by intentionally creating accessible teaching processes and materials will allow more children to learn successfully" (University of Maine Center for Community Inclusion and Disability Studies, 2014, para. 2).

A universal design approach to learning follows good practice in early education (Conn-Powers, Cross, Traub, & Hutter-Pishgahi, 2006) and includes the following three principles:

1. providing multiple means of representation;
2. providing multiple means of action and expression; and
3. providing multiple means of expression (CAST, 2011).

Figure 9–2 provides a description of each of these principles in the classroom.

The following is an example of UDL in a preschool class where the teacher adapted a classroom routine so that all students could participate, despite their varied abilities.

Jonathan teaches in a classroom with children ages three to five. They range in language abilities from typical to nonverbal. Some of his students use words, while others use signs or a picture exchange program (described in Chapter 19). Each morning during circle, Jonathan gives his students the chance to choose the closing song. On a small flannel board, he places a choice of four small cards, each bearing a symbol for one of the class's favourite songs. He rotates the songs regularly. Throughout the week, the children each get a chance to choose their favourite song card. The children all shout out encouraging words as their peer make a selection. Children who are verbal not only pull a song card off the board and hand it to Jonathan, but they are also asked to tell their class which song they have chosen. Likewise, students who are nonverbal choose a card and hand it to Jonathan. He will then either announce the song or ask another student to announce the song. This simple strategy of a song board enables all his students to participate in what is now the class's favourite part of circle.

FIGURE 9-2

The Three Principles of UDL

Multiple means of representation	Multiple means of expression	Multiple means of engagement
• Provide instructions and learning opportunities in multiple formats • Vary level of complexity • Highlight critical features • Provide background information • Support vocabulary	• Give plenty of options to express what they know • Provide models and feedback for differing levels of proficiency	• Provide choices that fuel student's interest and independence • Teach them to risk making mistakes and learn from these mistakes

Source: CAST. (2012). UDL at a glance. Retrieved from http://www.cast.org

Teachers should make every attempt to design their classroom with universal design in mind. Once this is complete, adjustments and adaptations to learning materials may still be necessary. Examples of possible adaptations follow.

MANIPULATIVE MATERIALS For children who must spend a lot of their time standing or in wheelchairs, interesting materials can be mounted on a board fastened to the wall. Wall displays allow children to grasp and manipulate objects they otherwise might not be able to manage. These arrangements also give a new dimension to materials for normally developing children, and all children should be encouraged to use them. Items that can be mounted on a playboard include the following:

- bolts, such as those used to lock doors
- bicycle bells
- light switches
- old-fashioned telephone dials
- touch-tone phones
- doorknobs that turn
- clothespins
- metal boards with magnetic pieces
- large-holed pegboards with large pegs
- Lego or Duplo boards with a bag or container to hold extra blocks
- felt boards with pockets for storing felt pieces
- Velcro tabs on which the child can place sequential story pictures or other pictures or items that are tabbed with Velcro

CREATIVE MATERIALS For children with impaired fine motor skills, creative materials can be adapted in a variety of ways:

- Provide large crayons, chalk, and paintbrushes. Even these may be too small for some children to hang on to. If so, a section can be wrapped with layers of securely taped-down plastic material, enabling the child to get a firmer grip.
- Pencils, crayons, and coloured markers can be pushed through a small sponge-rubber ball or pencil grip, or wrapped in sponge material. These will enable the child to have a firm enough grasp to scribble or draw.
- Paper can be taped to the table. This prevents it from sliding away when a child is colouring, painting, or pasting.
- Thick-tipped felt pens can be provided for children with weak hand and wrist control. They require less pressure than crayons but result in the rich, bright colours that please children.
- Fingerpaint, potter's clay, and water play can be made available more frequently. These materials require a minimum of fine motor control but make a major contribution in the improvement and strengthening of small-muscle function.

SELF-HELP/CARE DEVICES Many devices (available through special education catalogues) assist children in feeding, grooming, and dressing themselves. In addition, low-cost adaptations can be devised:

- Put a small suction device under a child's plate to keep it from sliding out of reach or off the table.

- Build up a spoon handle by taping a hair roller or piece of foam rubber in place to give the child better control of the spoon.
- For a child who cannot hold a spoon, make a cuff that keeps the spoon in the palm of the hand. The cuff is a wide strap that has a pocket for the spoon and is fastened around the hand with a Velcro closure.
- Use Velcro to replace buttons, zippers, and snaps. In many cases, the Velcro can be put on over existing buttons and buttonholes.
- Skid-resistant shelf paper can be placed on a table to keep plates, papers, and other items from skidding.
- Magnets are also useful on some surfaces for holding items together, hanging items, or affixing them to metal surfaces.
- Hang other devices—for feeling, touching, smelling, examining, and manipulating—at the child's level from fixtures like those used in hanging mobiles. These fixtures can also be adapted so that they can be lowered or raised depending on the appropriate height for the individual child.

Adaptations of the Classroom

Alterations may be needed in the classroom and play yard if children with motor challenges are to have a safe and appropriate learning environment. Examples of possible adaptations are described below.

WHEELCHAIR ACCOMMODATION Space to manoeuvre a wheelchair, in and out of activities, and to turn it around, is essential. Toileting areas must be clear so that a child can wheel in and out of the bathroom easily and pull up parallel to the toilet. Handrails mounted on the wall are needed so that the child can learn to swing from the wheelchair onto the toilet seat. Ramps can be constructed to facilitate movement in and out of the building and classroom, and onto the playground area.

RAILINGS Attached in strategic places, indoors and out, railings help children with poor balance and inadequate coordination to move about more independently. Railings can serve all children. They can also be used as exercise and ballet bars.

FLOOR COVERINGS Carpeting, if it is well stretched and securely fastened down, is good for children with mobility challenges. It also provides a warm and comfortable play surface for the many activities that all children engage in on the floor. When carpeting is not possible, crutches must have nonskid tips; the shoes of a child with a motor impairment should have nonskid soles. Nonskid soles can be devised by gluing textured rubber onto the child's shoe soles.

EYE-LEVEL MATERIALS Teachers need to ask themselves, How does this room appear at a child's level? Are there interesting things (such as manipulative wall hangings) for all children to watch, touch, and work with? What is available at eye level for a child on a scooter-board or in a wheelchair, or one who gets about only by crawling?

ORDERLINESS AND VISIBILITY These concepts, and a number of others related to environmental arrangements, are discussed in considerable detail in Chapter 14. All are of major importance when designing learning environments for young children, and especially so when the program includes children with motor disabilities.

Case Study ■ Helping Clarissa ■

Clarissa is a very petite four-year-old with severe language delays, as well as physical delays. The physical delays, in combination with her small stature (she is closer to the size of a two-year-old), present many challenges in her child care classroom. The physical environment alone, including the toilets, sinks, and chairs, is oversized for her. What might her teacher do to modify both the physical environment and the classroom curriculum to help Clarissa feel safe and be successful in her development and learning?

Other Health Conditions

Most children experience a variety of health issues during infancy and early childhood. For the most part, these are relatively mild and do not interfere appreciably with growth and development. However, there are children who are chronically ill and have to live their everyday lives with serious health conditions. These present the child and his or her parents and teachers with ongoing obstacles that must be dealt with throughout the developmental years.

Asthma

Asthma is among the most common chronic health problems in children. It is defined as a "chronic inflammatory disease of the airway" (Asthma Society of Canada, 2013, para. 3). All students with asthma need to be identified at the school in both the classrooms and the office so that all staff know how to respond in the event of an asthma attack.

It is important for the school and all teachers/staff to receive a written student asthma action plan and to meet with the parents and student to discuss the action plan so that they are aware of the steps to be taken if a student experiences an asthma attack.

All staff need to be aware of the symptoms of an asthma attack. The symptoms of asthma include cough, wheeze, difficulty breathing, shortness of breath, and/or complaining of chest tightness. Most often these symptoms occur when a student is exposed to their trigger. A trigger is anything that can cause asthma symptoms, for example, dust, mould, cold air, exercise, and strong smells. Students should be allowed to carry their rescue inhaler with them as soon as they are capable of using it themselves.

If a student experiences these symptoms, he or she needs to be removed from the trigger and the rescue/reliever inhaler needs to be administered. The number of "puffs" of inhaler required will be listed on the inhaler and on the student asthma action plan. If the symptoms do not improve within five minutes an additional two puffs of the reliever/rescue inhaler need to be administered and the teacher must seek medical attention by activating 911. Teachers should not hesitate to call 911, and it is not recommended that a student ever be taken to the emergency room by car.

Everyone working with young children must be taught ways in which they can effectively respond to a child with asthma. Figure 9–3 provides a guideline for both children and educators of what action to take when dealing with asthma.

Before the actual onset of an attack, the child's nose might run and/or a dry, hacking cough might start. Breathing (wheezing) may become loud and

FIGURE 9-3

What to Do if Your Asthma Gets Worse

The Asthma Society of Canada (2014) categorizes symptoms for children and the appropriate response into three zones similar to traffic lights:

If it's green, you're good to go.

- You have no trouble breathing, even when you're laughing, playing, and having fun.
- You don't cough or wheeze, and you don't get short of breath.
- You only need to use your reliever medication (blue puffer) less than 4 times a week.
- Your breathing is fine, so you can go to school.

If you're in the green zone, you're probably doing all the right things: taking your controller medication every day, staying away from your triggers, and using your puffer properly. Keep it up!

If it's yellow, take it slow.

When your asthma is in the yellow zone, it's telling you to take care. You know you're in the yellow zone when
- You have trouble breathing when you're laughing, playing, and having fun.
- You start to cough, or wheeze, or feel that tight feeling in your chest.
- You wake up in the morning or in the middle of the night coughing or wheezing.
- You need to use your reliever medication more than three times a week to help you breathe better.
- You have to stay home from school because of your asthma.

If you're in the yellow zone, your asthma is probably not letting you do all the things you want to do. Take your reliever medication when you need it, but you also need to find out why you need it so much.

   You may not be using your puffer properly, or you may need to change the medication you take. A doctor can help you find these answers so you can get back in the green where you belong.

If it's red, STOP!

When your asthma is in the red zone, you'll know right away. You'll feel terrible, you'll have trouble breathing, you may even have trouble talking. And it can be scary!
- Your reliever medicine does not seem to be helping you breathe better.
- You are breathing hard and fast.
- You can't walk or talk well, or it's hard to lie down and sleep.
- Your lips or nails are turning a blue colour.
- You're scared!

Asthma Agents never want to be in the red zone, but if you are, you need to know what to do. If you're in the red zone

1. If you're running around or doing some sort of activity, STOP!
2. Sit down and stay still.
3. Use your reliever every 10 minutes
4. Tell someone to get help.

You might need an ambulance so a doctor can help you breathe!

Source: Asthma Society of Canada. (n.d.). "About Asthma: What to Do if Your Symptoms Worsen" Retrieved from http://asthmakids.ca/about/attack.php. Reprinted with permission.

 laboured. Lips and fingertips may take on a bluish look because of a lack of air. At the start of the attack, the child should be encouraged to follow these steps:

1. Relax, rest, try to stay calm, and breathe easily.
2. Remain sitting in an upright position.
3. Sip warm water (avoid cold liquids)—this may help to prevent a full-blown episode.

The Asthma Society of Canada website (http://www.asthma.ca) also provides a template that can be used to create an individualized action plan for children.

If medication or special equipment—such as a Ventolin mask or inhaler—is available for the child, it should be used at first sign of increasing severity (see photo, right). The Asthma Society of Canada (2013) recommends removing the child from any possible triggers (e.g., stopping exercise, coming in from the cold, taking away pets) and administering the child's bronchodilator medication. If the child's condition does not improve after two treatments of medication, medical attention should be sought immediately. It is further recommended that on enrolment of a child with asthma, the teachers meet with the parents and obtain specific instructions as to how to recognize and respond to that child's condition. Consultation with the child's physician or the community public health nurse is also advisable. If no special medication or equipment is available and a child appears to be having an asthma attack, it is important to quiet the child and follow the three steps above. If the symptoms seem to be increasing in severity, the child should be taken without delay to the nearest medical facility and the parents and physician notified immediately. Teachers should not hesitate to call in paramedics if a medical facility is not near. A child can die from a combination of oxygen deprivation and exhaustion (Marotz, 2012).

Administration of asthma medication should become part of the daily routine.

© Cengage Learning 2015

Cystic Fibrosis

Cystic fibrosis is a genetic disease. Among Caucasian children, cystic fibrosis is the most common inherited single-gene disorder (in contrast to other racial groups, among whom it occurs infrequently). According to Cystic Fibrosis Canada (n.d.),

> cystic fibrosis is a genetic disease that occurs when a child inherits two abnormal genes, one from each parent. Approximately, one in 25 Canadians carry an abnormal version of the gene responsible for cystic fibrosis. Carriers do not have cystic fibrosis, nor do they exhibit any of the symptoms of the disease. (para. 6)

The disease is incurable, but with modern medical care, many people with this disorder live into their 30s and 40s. Cystic fibrosis is the most common fatal inherited disease affecting young Canadians (Cystic Fibrosis Canada, n.d.).

Cystic fibrosis is characterized by excessive mucus, progressive lung damage, and the body's inability to absorb fats and proteins appropriately. Children have trouble gaining weight and tend to have chronic coughs, an excessive appetite (even though they do not gain weight), frequent foul-smelling bowel movements, and unusually salty perspiration. It is this excessively salty perspiration, detected through a medical sweat test, that confirms the diagnosis of cystic fibrosis. Research has provided much information. For instance, scientists at the Hospital for Sick Children in Toronto have identified a region on chromosome 19 that contains a gene that modifies the severity of cystic fibrosis (Hospital for Sick

Children, 1999). Though there is still no known cure for cystic fibrosis, advances in treatment continue to take place:

- In 1991, significant progress in CF treatment was made with successful experiments in the aerosol administration of Dnase, an enzyme that breaks down human genetic material. When Dnase was administered to CF lungs, it acted to break down "junk" DNA in lung secretions and reduce the thickness of these secretions, which otherwise plugged the airways and encouraged infection (Canadian Cystic Fibrosis Foundation, 2000).

- The transplanting from live donors of single lung lobes (we have five lobes in each lung) into a child with CF is life prolonging (Canadian Cystic Fibrosis Foundation, 2000).

- In Calgary, new approaches to treating CF are emerging. Current research involves innovations and effective ways of treating children with CF. Indications are that there is rapid progress occurring at this time in treating this disorder.

In the 1960s, most children with cystic fibrosis did not live long enough to attend kindergarten; today half of all Canadians with CF are expected to live into their 40s and beyond (Cystic Fibrosis Canada, n.d.).

The rate of deterioration in children with CF varies from child to child. Symptoms may be minimal in one five-year-old and severe in another. In general, teachers should encourage physical activity as long as the child is reasonably well. As the child gets older, health problems tend to worsen and more frequent hospitalizations are sometimes required. Both the child and the family are likely to need considerable emotional support from teachers.

Hemophilia

Another inherited disorder is hemophilia, experienced primarily by males. Females usually do not have the disease; they are the carriers or transmitters. Hemophilia occurs when the blood clots too slowly or not at all.

> The chief danger is not bleeding to death from accidental injury. ... It is internal bleeding that poses the greatest threat to life and health. Bleeding into the joints, especially knees, ankles, and elbows can cause severe and constant pain, and eventually permanent crippling. ... Internal bleeding episodes, particularly in children, can be triggered by what seem to be trivial bumps, falls and minor injuries. Often they occur without any known injury at all. (Apgar & Beck, 1973, p. 295).

 It is important to encourage young children with hemophilia to be as active as possible without exposing them to unnecessary risks. If a teacher suspects a joint bleed, the child's doctor should be contacted because clotting factor therapy is often the only effective treatment.

It is important to know that joint bleeds do not necessarily cause bruising. A physician should be consulted immediately if a child

- is irritable or appears to be in pain;
- favours one limb over another;
- has a warm feeling around a joint;
- walks with a limp or refuses to walk or crawl; or
- has one joint that appears swollen when compared with the same joint on the other limb.

Ice should be applied to relieve pain, the child's activity should be limited, and the affected joint should be elevated until the swelling goes down. If a child has a small cut or scrape, applying pressure and a bandage will generally stop the bleeding (Mayo Clinic, 2011a).

It is sometimes necessary for children with hemophilia to have blood transfusions or clotting factor replacement therapy. The development of clotting factors, made in the laboratory, has virtually eliminated the danger of HIV or hepatitis infection by transfusions. Regular home-based infusions have helped to reduce chronic joint problems.

Active children with hemophilia who are in good physical condition seem to have fewer episodes of bleeding than do inactive youngsters with a similar degree of clotting deficiency. Sometimes, an increase in physical activity results in a decrease in bleeding.

Despite some increased risk, most children with hemophilia grow up to lead normal adult lives. To ensure this outcome, teachers and parents must avoid treating an affected child as overly special or so fragile that the child becomes excessively dependent or excessively concerned about personal health and well-being. Padding corners of furniture as well as the knees and elbows of the child's clothing will enable the child to move more actively without fear of personal harm from bumping into things.

The Canadian Hemophilia Society (2013) created the Passport to Well-Being program "aimed at empowering people with bleeding disorders, at all stages of their lives, to maximize their quality of life" (para. 1). The program has been revised to tailor its various aspects to each particular stage of life, including childhood.

Leukemia

Leukemia is one of several forms of cancer found among young children. It is a disease that destroys bone marrow through an overproduction of white blood cells. It was viewed as a fatal disease up until a few years ago; now, **chemotherapy** and **radiation** have proved very effective in the treatment of this condition in children. Fatigue, consistent aching of joints, and easy bruising are symptoms related to leukemia. They should be checked by a physician if they are observed in a child.

A child with leukemia—whether treatment is administered in a hospital or at home—is likely to have associated physical discomfort, and may be experiencing emotional upset because of both the disorder and the stresses associated with treatment. Teachers must be sensitive to what the child is experiencing.

- The child's teacher should keep in close contact with the child's parents in order to know how treatment is progressing and how the child is feeling.

- The child should be supported and encouraged to join activities as much as possible.

Sickle-Cell Disease (Sickle-Cell Anemia)

Sickle-cell disease, another genetically transmitted, recessive condition, is found predominantly among black children and in varying degrees of severity. It is also common in people whose families come from Africa, South or Central America (especially Panama), Caribbean islands, Mediterranean countries (such as Turkey, Greece, and Italy), India, and Saudi Arabia (National Institutes of Health, 2012).

Chemotherapy the treatment of cancer by using drug therapy to kill cancer cells

Radiation the use of high-energy penetrating rays to damage cancer cells, stopping them from growing and dividing

Whereas in Africa the **genetic mutation** was probably an advantage—offering protection against malaria—in North America, many generations later, this once-useful sickle-shaped red blood cell has led to a chronic, painful health problem that can result in death during childhood. A crisis occurs when a number of the "sickled" cells stick together and cause a blockage. The result is severe pain in the abdomen, legs, and arms; swollen joints; fainting; and overall fatigue. Special therapy can help a child to adapt and have a fairly normal existence, but there is no cure for this disorder. Research indicates that because malaria is not a threat in North America, the number of children with this condition is steadily decreasing, and it is felt that this genetic mutation has almost died out through natural selection (Jorde, Carey, Bamshad, & White, 2009).

Given that children with sickle-cell disease are often particularly vulnerable to infection, parents should ensure that teachers and medical practitioners work collaboratively to reduce the child's risk for infection in order to allow participation in early childhood settings. A child with a mild case of sickle-cell disease should continue to participate in regular preschool activities. Teachers should cooperate with the parents and the physician in preventing a sickle-cell crisis by helping the child avoid fatigue, stress, and exposure to cold, and by making sure the child has adequate fluid intake.

Cardiac Disorders

Heart disease is a common term for cardiac disorders. Many heart defects result in death during the infant's first year. Other defects can be surgically repaired, allowing the child to lead a normal life. Causes of congenital heart problems range from genetic abnormalities, to the mother's exposure to rubella during the first trimester of pregnancy, to maternal alcoholism. Children with heart disease may complain of shortness of breath, and physical activity may be more tiring than it is for other preschoolers. Some children experience cyanosis—a blueness of the skin, lips, and fingernails—that is due to poor oxygenation of the blood.

The child with chronic heart problems should not be pressed to participate in activities that bring on excessive fatigue. Most children with cardiac problems are fairly reliable monitors of their own exertion tolerance. Children who have had complete surgical correction should be able to participate in all preschool activities. Teachers, parents, and health-care providers, however, need to exchange information on a continuing basis. Based on the current status of a child's condition, they should jointly work together to plan activity levels for home and school.

Diabetes (Mellitus)

TYPE 1 DIABETES—JUVENILE DIABETES (MELLITUS)
This form of diabetes is found in children under the age of 16. Type 1 diabetes is an autoimmune disorder—a problem with the body's immune system. The immune system mistakes beta cells for invaders and attacks them. When enough beta cells have been destroyed, symptoms of diabetes appear. Problems arise because the pancreas (a gland located behind the stomach) fails to produce enough of a natural chemical called *insulin*. Insulin is required if the body is to **metabolize** glucose (a form of sugar). Without insulin, cells cannot use the glucose already in the bloodstream. The result is insufficient nourishment to carry on the body's functions. Children with Type 1 diabetes must receive insulin on a regular basis. However, adverse

Genetic mutation an alteration in the chromosomal materials (genes) that control inherited characteristics

Metabolize the chemical process within living cells by which energy is manufactured so that the body systems can carry out their functions reactions to insulin are a constant threat. One such threat is *hypoglycemia*, or excessively low levels of sugar circulating in the blood. Another is *hyperglycemia*, or too much sugar circulating in the bloodstream. Hypoglycemia can result in a diabetic coma (unconsciousness). The person experiencing hypoglycemia will exhibit some of the following signs:

- cold, clammy, or sweaty skin
- pallor
- shakiness or lack of coordination
- irritability
- hostility and poor behaviour
- staggering gait
- fatigue
- eventually fainting and unconsciousness

Furthermore, the child may complain of nervousness, excessive hunger, headache, blurred vision and dizziness, abdominal pain, or nausea. It is important to immediately (as long as the child is conscious) get the child to eat sugar, or drink fruit juice or regular nondiet pop . . . anything that will get some sugar into his or her system. The "administration of sugar can cause no harm, while withholding sugar could have serious consequences" (Katz, 2004, p. 78).

Teachers and caregivers will need to be involved in other ways too, including

- carefully regulating food intake;
- monitoring the child's exercise and activity level;
- observing the child for changes in behaviour and signs of infection; and
- assisting in blood-glucose monitoring.

It is important that teachers, parents, and health-care providers be in partnership and communicate regularly. This ensures the best possible care, with the fewest complications for the child (Canadian Diabetes Association, 2005–2009).

A recent research study by Koller and Khan (2013) determined that young children with diabetes were found to have very little knowledge about their disease. In response, these authors designed an online toolkit, which they refer to as a "playkit," aimed at increasing children's and adolescents' knowledge and reduce the stress that can be associated with managing diabetes.

TYPE 2 DIABETES Type 2 diabetes is the more common form of diabetes and, until recent years, was found mainly in adults. It results from insulin resistance (a condition in which the body fails to use insulin properly), combined with relative insulin deficiency. Genetics and environmental factors such as obesity and lack of exercise appear to play a role in this type of diabetes. An increase in this type of diabetes in children has been observed in North America in recent years.

Seizure Disorders

The terms *epilepsy*, *seizure*, and *convulsions* are used somewhat interchangeably to describe disturbances in the normal electrical discharges in the brain. The term *epilepsy* refers to recurrent seizures. **Seizures** may be focal (partial), localized to one muscle group (or sensory system), or generalized with loss of consciousness. Sometimes focal seizures may spread and become generalized. What happens, in simple terms, is bursts of electrical energy in the brain result in partial or total

Seizures bursts of electrical energy in the brain that cause uncontrolled muscular movement and reduced or total loss of consciousness, as in epilepsy loss of consciousness. Uncontrolled muscular movements, ranging from brief twitching of the eyelids to massive shaking of the entire body, accompany these bursts or episodes. These random motor movements have been categorized in various ways:

- *Febrile seizures.* Febrile seizures are the most common. They occur in 3 to 5 percent of children under the age of five. In general, the seizure is brought on by a high fever. Usually, it lasts less than 15 minutes and stops by itself. Rarely are these seizures harmful, and children who experience them do not develop epilepsy.

- *Absence (petit mal) seizures.* Absence (petit mal) seizures are those in which there is momentary loss of consciousness. This may occur many times a day with some children. The lapses are so brief that they may go unnoticed, even though there could be slight twitching of the eyelids, neck, or hands. The child is often accused of daydreaming.

- *Tonic-clonic (grand mal) seizures.* Tonic-clonic (grand mal) seizures usually cause children to lose consciousness and fall to the floor with violently jerking muscles. They may stop breathing temporarily, lose bowel or bladder control, and bubble saliva about the mouth.

- *Partial or psychomotor seizures.* Partial or psychomotor seizures, found only rarely in young children, sometimes resemble a temper tantrum or an episode of bizarre behaviour characterized by lip-smacking, repetitive arm and hand movements, or aimless running about. Though there is the appearance of consciousness, the child is usually unaware of behaving strangely.

A variety of medications are used to control seizures in children. The medication may have an adverse effect, especially in the beginning, causing the child to be drowsy or inattentive. An important role for teachers is to observe and record changes in the child's behaviour. Behavioural observations assist the child's physician in altering the medication or dosage as needed. In general, the anticonvulsant medications prescribed for a child are effective in preventing seizures. Rarely does the early childhood teacher encounter a tonic-clonic (grand mal) seizure. However, it is important to know what to do should there be an episode. The following recommendations are adapted from material published by Epilepsy Ontario (2013) and Marotz (2012):

- Remain calm. Children will react the same way as teachers do. The seizure itself is painless.

- Do not try to restrain the child. Nothing can be done to stop a seizure once it has begun. It must run its course.

- Clear the space around the child so that no injury from hard objects occurs and there is no interference with the child's movements.

- Do not try to force anything between the teeth.

- Loosen tight clothing, especially at the neck; turn the child's head to the side, and wipe away discharge from the mouth and nose to aid breathing.

- When the seizure is over, allow the child to rest.

- Medical assistance should be called for if the seizure lasts more than five minutes or is followed by another major seizure. Many things can trigger seizures in young children: poisoning, infections, severe electrical jolts, and allergic reactions. If unsure about whether to call for medical help, it is always better to err on the safe.

- The child's parents must always be informed of a seizure. Teachers and parents should plan together on how best to handle future seizures for that particular child.

The child with epilepsy should not be restricted from participating in the full program, unless specific limitations are imposed by the child's physician. It would be useful for the child's teacher to know what may trigger a seizure for this particular child (e.g., flashing lights, fatigue).

A seizure episode can be turned into a learning experience for the children in the class. Teachers can explain in simple terms what a seizure is. They can assure children that it is *not catching* and that children need not fear for themselves or for the child who had the seizure. Epilepsy Ontario suggests that it is important for teachers to help other children understand, but not pity, the child who has seizures so that he or she remains "one of the gang." It is important that the child not feel self-conscious on regaining consciousness. Other children in the class should be encouraged to continue in their ongoing activities.

Making sure that the child receives the prescribed medication regularly and in the proper amounts is the best approach to preventing seizures. Teachers who are asked to administer medication must follow the guidelines described later in this chapter.

In concluding this section on epilepsy, it seems important to reiterate two points. The first is a repeat of the cautionary note: Never attempt to force anything between the child's upper and lower teeth. This procedure, once thought necessary, was discontinued years ago. Children's teeth can be damaged and adults' fingers severely bitten. The second point that bears repeating is that *teachers should remain calm*. In the interests of everyone, a teacher must not panic. Young children rarely become unduly alarmed about anything if their teachers do not appear anxious or upset. Children's anxieties over a seizure episode are reduced almost immediately if adults are confident and matter-of-fact in assuring them that the child soon will be all right. In fact, the teacher's quiet care of the child having the seizure can be a valuable experience in human concern that is of benefit to all children.

Tourette Syndrome and Behavioural Tics

"Tourette Syndrome (TS) is a neurological disorder characterized by tics: involuntary, rapid sudden movements or vocalizations that occur repeatedly in the same way. The cause has not been established and as yet there is no cure" (Tourette Syndrome Foundation of Canada, 2014, para. 1). Tourette syndrome is often not recognized until the child is five years old or older. It is found more frequently in boys. Typical symptoms include uncontrollable head jerking, facial grimacing, repetitive eye blinking or squinting, repetitive nose movement, tongue clicking, body scratching, leg jerking, foot tapping, and/or vocal sounds. The tic behaviour is likely to become more pronounced during times of excitement. The movement and noises that a child with Tourette syndrome makes can be disturbing to other children. It is up to the teachers to try to redirect the child with Tourette syndrome into a new activity, while at the same time communicating to other children that this child has no control over this part of his or her behaviour. Often, using an example that other children are familiar with—such as coughing or sneezing, over which they have no control—will help them to be more understanding and accepting of the child with Tourette syndrome. There are now some medications available that can help control the symptoms.

According to the Tourette Syndrome Foundation of Canada (2013), students with Tourette syndrome often have added or associated conditions such as attention deficit disorder (ADD), attention deficit hyperactivity disorder (ADHD), and obsessive-compulsive disorder (OCD) (see Chapter 10). The teacher can facilitate the child's ability to develop some self-awareness and self-management as he or she matures by providing predictable, empathetic interventions.

AIDS (Acquired Immune Deficiency Syndrome)

Immune system that aspect of body functioning responsible for warding off diseases

AIDS stands for acquired immune deficiency syndrome. It is a disease that leaves a person open to contracting illnesses that a healthy **immune system** might otherwise overcome. It is caused by the human immunodeficiency virus (HIV). Individuals may be infected without knowing it and without showing symptoms of the infection. Children who are infected may seem delayed or small for their age, or they may display neurological problems, *before they display visible symptoms*.

AIDS is transmitted primarily through intimate sexual contact, through blood-to-blood contact (as through shared hypodermic needles), or from an infected mother to her baby (prenatally or through breast milk). It is estimated that one-third to one-half of the infants born to infected mothers will be infected. However, all infants of HIV-infected mothers will test positive for the disease in the first year or so of life. Why? Because infants are still operating on their mothers' antibody systems, while their own are gearing up and getting ready to function.

There is no evidence of casual transmission by sitting near, living in the same household with, or playing with a person with clinical AIDS (American Academy of Pediatrics, 2005). According to the National Association for the Education of Young Children (NAEYC) Information Service (personal communication, 1991), HIV is not transmitted through urine, stool (diarrhea), vomit, saliva (mouthing of toys and other objects), mucus, sweat, or any other body fluid that does not contain blood. All children with HIV infection or AIDS should be admitted to the program as long as their own health and developmental status allow them to benefit from the program. According to the Committee on Pediatric AIDS (2000),

> The spread of HIV infection in school has not been documented, and fear of its communicability must be allayed by appropriate education of all school personnel. Participation in school provides a sense of normalcy for children and adolescents with HIV infection. (p. 1358)

Some children who have AIDS are quite ill and unable to be in a child care program or a preschool classroom. Also, children with AIDS are highly vulnerable to all of the many childhood infectious illnesses; enrolment in an early childhood group of any kind may be against their best interest.

For those children who are well enough to be in a program, strict hygiene precautions are required of caregivers:

- thorough handwashing
- wearing disposable gloves when dealing with bodily secretions
- cleaning caregiving surfaces with bleach-and-water solution

Health Canada (2010) continues to promote these universal practices. As put forth by Best, Bigge, and Sirvis (1994), "because these precautions constitute good hygiene for anyone who requires physical care, their universal adoption allows protection for care providers while preserving the privacy of the student with AIDS" (p. 314).

It remains good practice that in an early childhood centre, no children or adults should be attending or working in the program if they have open, oozing sores that cannot be covered or kept under control with medication. Nor should they be in the program if there is any bloody discharge accompanying diarrhea. This applies to everyone, those with and those without known HIV infection. The foregoing recommendations are in accord with medical, technical, and legislative findings as originally reviewed by Dokecki, Baumeister, and Kupstas (1989) and the NAEYC Information Service. Once again, a reminder: Information on AIDS/HIV is changing continually. Therefore, it is essential that everyone working with infants, young children, and families keep abreast of current findings. Public health organizations in cities across Canada provide many resources to their local communities.

Nutritional Conditions

Obesity (Overweight)

Obesity is not necessarily a handicapping condition. It is a developmental health disorder that affects one in five children and youth in North America. Unchecked, obesity may lead to significant long-term health problems, as well as social and psychological problems. "Increasingly, obese children are being diagnosed with a range of health conditions previously seen almost exclusively among adults, including type-2 diabetes and high blood pressure" (Public Health Agency of Canada, 2013, para. 1). Overweight children are often unable to keep up physically with their peers and may be teased by others or excluded from play activities. This can lead to poor self-image, decreasing physical fitness, and fewer opportunities to build satisfying social relations (Marotz, 2012).

Obesity is related to chronic disequilibrium between energy output and caloric intake. In other words, children who eat too much also tend to have reduced activity levels. Obesity is quite common among children with disabilities, and tends to further reduce their activity levels. According to the American Academy of Pediatrics (2010), children with obesity have a high potential risk for

- high cholesterol and blood pressure levels, which are risk factors for heart disease;
- sleep apnea (interrupted breathing while sleeping), which in some cases can lead to problems with learning and memory;
- a high incidence of orthopedic problems, liver disease, and asthma; and
- becoming overweight or obese adults (70 percent chance).

Fat babies do not necessarily become fat adults; substantial evidence exists, however, that overweight preschoolers are not likely to outgrow the problem. As weight increases, children move less vigorously and so continue to put on more weight. This further compounds both their physical and psychological problems. The increase in obesity in children has risen dramatically in the past few decades. It is understood that the increase correlates with reduced physical activity and increased consumption of convenience foods and fast foods, which tend to be high in fat and sugar. Research indicates that genetics plays a major role in predisposing a person to obesity. Two controllable factors contribute to excessive weight gain that teachers can help to prevent:

- *Overeating.* The consumption of too many calories, or at least too many calories from the wrong kind of food. Often an overweight person eats

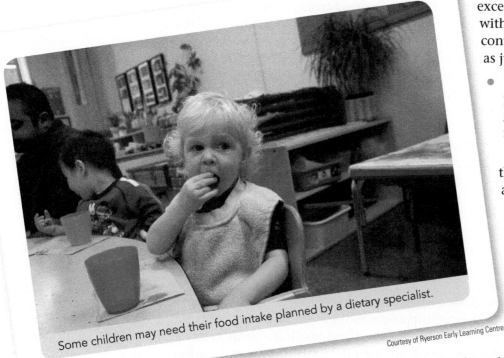

Some children may need their food intake planned by a dietary specialist.

Courtesy of Ryerson Early Learning Centre

excessive amounts of foods with poor nutritional content, popularly known as junk food.

- *Underexercising.* Lack of physical activity is often given as a major reason for obesity.

All children, including those who are obese, need an adequate number of calories each day, but the calories need to come from the right kinds of foods—fruits, vegetables, grains, lean meats, fish, milk, and cheese. Through responsible menu planning, early childhood educators can introduce children to a variety of nutritionally sound foods.

Interestingly enough, many children who are overweight are undernourished. The early childhood teacher should work closely with parents and a nutritionist or health-care nurse to make sure that a child with a weight problem is getting a daily intake of appropriate foods in appropriate amounts.

Teachers can also focus parts of the early childhood curriculum on helping children understand the role of good nutrition and exercise in everyday life.

Some children with developmental problems may require the concentrated supervision of a nutritionist or dietary specialist (see photo, above). Situations requiring intensive nutritional intervention vary. Sometimes patterns of excessive food intake may have been established unintentionally by parents and caregivers. By providing an abundance of food, parents may seek to compensate for the many ordinary life experiences they are unable to provide for the child. For example, a parent who works long hours may lack the energy to interact with the child in the evening. Providing the child with a sugary treat not only pleases the child but also alleviates the parent's feelings of guilt.

Physical activity is of major importance for all children (see photo, left). This is especially true for children who have a tendency to put on extra weight. These children should be monitored daily to ensure that they are encouraged to participate in gross motor activity. It is the responsibility of the early childhood teacher to make sure that the daily curriculum provides for ample outdoor/physical activity. Figure 9–4 provides a framework that is useful to consider when incorporating physical activity and healthy eating into the program.

Frequently, children with conditions that limit regular physical activity may require a diet with fewer calories. Children with other conditions, such as the genetic

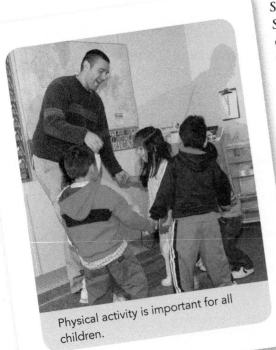

Physical activity is important for all children.

© Cengage Learning

FIGURE 9-4

School Health Guidelines to Promote Healthy Eating and Physical Activity

1. Use a coordinated approach to develop, implement, and evaluate healthy eating and physical activity policies and practices.

2. Establish school environments that support healthy eating and physical activity.

3. Provide a quality school meal program and ensure that students have only appealing, healthy food and beverage choices offered outside of the school meal program.

4. Implement a comprehensive physical activity program with quality physical education as the cornerstone.

5. Implement health education that provides students with the knowledge, attitudes, skills, and experiences needed for lifelong healthy eating and physical activity.

6. Provide students with health, mental health, and social services to address healthy eating, physical activity, and related chronic disease prevention.

7. Partner with families and community members in the development and implementation of healthy eating and physical activity policies, practices, and programs.

8. Provide a school employee wellness program that includes healthy eating and physical activity services for all school staff members.

9. Employ qualified persons, and provide professional development opportunities for physical education, health education, nutrition services, and health, mental health, and social services staff members, as well as staff members who supervise recess, cafeteria time, and out-of-school time.

Source: Centers for Disease Control and Prevention. (2011). School health guidelines to promote healthy eating and physical activity. *Morbidity and Mortality Weekly Report, Recommendations and Reports, 60*(5). Retrieved from http://www.cdc.gov/mmwr/pdf/rr/rr6005.pdf

syndrome Prader-Willi, engage in uncontrolled and obsessive food consumption. Refrigerators must be kept locked. Food cannot be left out, even in a pet's dish. Teachers must keep uneaten food, even leftovers on other children's plates, securely out of the way of the child with **Prader-Willi syndrome**.

Prader-Willi syndrome a genetic disorder characterized by obesity, short stature, disorders in sexual development, and a tendency toward behavioural and cognitive disabilities

Undernourishment

Consuming too few calories is as damaging to a growing child as taking in too many. Many children with physical impairments burn far more calories each day than they are able to take in. One example is children with severe cerebral palsy. They use up tremendous amounts of energy on the unwelcome but constant and uncontrollable muscular reactions characteristic of their disability. Often these children are far below ideal body weight. The same disability and muscle impairment that burns so many calories can also lead to other nutritional problems. Some affected children have trouble holding food in their mouth or chewing and swallowing. Parents, teachers, and caregivers need specialized help in learning to provide easy-to-swallow foods that are high in nutritional value (see photo, page 194).

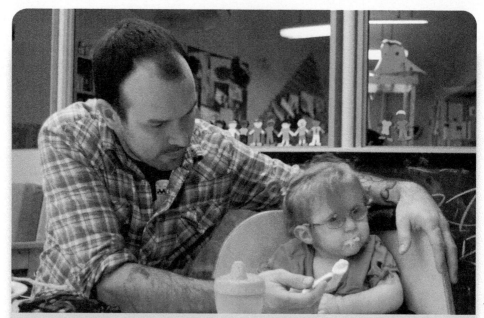

Parents, teachers, and caregivers may need specialized help in learning to feed a child with a physical disability.

© Cengage Learning

Although young children with physical disabilities may be undernourished due to eating difficulties, poor children also may be malnourished because their parents cannot afford to buy and prepare nutritious food on a daily basis. It is imperative, therefore, that meals provided by child care staff and parents, whether in centres or in private homes, follow Canada's Food Guide (Health Canada, 2011) in detail. The Food Guide has been revised in order to reflect the many food preferences selected by the various cultural groups reflected in the nation. Many centres now offer breakfasts as well as hot lunches and snacks. Elementary schools in impoverished areas may also provide breakfast and lunch for school children.

Anaphylactic Shock

Anaphylactic shock a rapid allergic reaction that can be life-threatening if not treated immediately; it is caused by an intense overreaction of the body's immune system to a trigger

Anaphylactic shock is a rapid allergic reaction that can be life-threatening if not treated immediately. It is caused by an intense overreaction of the body's immune system to a trigger. The usual triggers are peanuts, tree nuts, bee or wasp stings, and in some cases fish, penicillin, spices, or latex. Not every case has an obvious trigger and specific triggers don't produce specific reactions. The symptoms of anaphylactic shock include

- tingling, itching, swelling
- throat tightness, swelling
- difficulty swallowing
- wheezing, coughing, difficulty breathing
- chest tightness
- sense of fear
- flushing of face and body
- weakness or dizziness

- hives or a nettle-like rash
- stomach cramping, vomiting, diarrhea
- feeling faint

Coma or death may result if treatment does not occur. Current treatment for an anaphylactic shock reaction is adrenaline (epinephrine). This is supplied in the form of an EpiPen.

It is important that teachers are taught how to use the EpiPen properly. When teachers have a child in the class with a known anaphylactic trigger, it is essential that the EpiPen be kept on the premises at all times and brought along on any trips, walks, and so on. The EpiPen should be administered as soon as there is evidence of a reaction and before there is a lot of deterioration. Do not hesitate to administer epinephrine if any anaphylactic symptoms appear. Always accompany the child to the hospital, even if symptoms seem to go away after the first injection. The effects of epinephrine can wear off 10 to 20 minutes after the injection. Determine how long it will take to get to a hospital and be sure there is enough epinephrine to get to an emergency room. If the child appears to be okay after exposure to a known trigger, monitoring of the child must continue for at least six hours, as there may be a delayed reaction. The child's parents and doctor must be notified right away (Paasche, Gorrill, & Strom, 2004).

Some provinces now have legislation that requires the training of school staff on dealing with life-threatening allergies, having school administration put into place prevention plans that will protect at-risk students, and setting up emergency procedures to be taken if a child has an allergic/anaphylactic reaction (e.g., Sabrina's Law was enacted in Ontario in 2005).

Health Conditions and Classroom Practices

Early childhood teachers sometimes feel anxious, inadequate, even threatened, when first asked to include a child with a serious health problem or a disabling physical condition in their class. However, teachers find that the more they work with children with disabilities, the more natural it seems. *Healthy Young Children* (NAEYC, 2002) advises teachers that having relevant information is one of the best ways to know how to handle situations, feel confident and in control. When you know what to do—whether it is taking a temperature, giving first aid, or keeping a child relaxed during an asthma attack—both you and the child are going to benefit from your knowledge. Lack of information often leads to panic in emergencies or improper care, such as spreading disease by not washing hands when necessary. You need to be able to provide the necessary immediate care, remain calm, and maintain control.

Useful information for teachers comes from many sources in addition to parents and the interdisciplinary team members who are involved in the child's intervention program. The most important are up-to-date health records on each child and complete knowledge about a child's medication program. Teachers also must be sure they know what they will do in both routine and emergency situations related to specific health problems among the children in their classes. Every time a child with a health condition is to be enrolled, teachers must have a careful briefing by both the child's parents and a health-care professional before the child enters the program.

Health Records

A complete and frequently updated health record must be maintained on every child in the group. To provide the best possible support to the child and family, the health record should contain the following essential information:

- telephone numbers where parents and other emergency contacts can be reached at all times
- name of the child's regular physician, health-care provider, or clinic, with address and telephone numbers
- permission slips authorizing emergency health care and transportation, and the administration of prescribed medications
- health insurance information, where relevant
- child and relevant family health history
- immunization information with dates
- results of medical assessment or physical and dental examinations and treatment
- results of special testing, such as vision or hearing assessments
- dated reports, signed by the attending teacher, on all injuries or illnesses that occur while the child is in the classroom, in the playground, or on a school-sponsored excursion
- notations on allergies, special diets, treatment procedures, medications, prosthetic devices, or other health concerns
- notations on health-related communications with parents and health-care providers, including referral recommendations and follow-up
- ongoing records of medications given to the child while at school

Administering Medication

Regulations regarding the administration of medication by teachers should follow provincial guidelines. These guidelines, as well as those for recording this procedure, vary across provinces and territories. It is important that teachers familiarize themselves with the regulations in their specific area.

Teachers may be required to administer medication during program hours. All medication should be stored in a child-resistant container and labelled with the following information:

- child's name
- physician's name and phone number
- name of the medicine
- dosage to be given to the child
- schedule for administering dosages

Requests for the administration of medication should be put in writing and signed by the parents. Each time medicine is given, the time and date must be recorded on the child's record sheet and initialled by the person who did the medicating. Medication must be kept in a locked cupboard or refrigerator and out of reach of all children.

Emergency Considerations

All programs serving young children should have carefully laid-out plans for emergency situations. When children with health problems and physical disabilities are enrolled, individual plans need to be formulated for each child:

- Confer with parents (or the child's doctor) to plan in advance for an emergency health crisis.

- Understand the cause of a crisis and how often it is likely to occur.

- Learn how a child may behave before, as well as during and after, a crisis.

- Know what to do during and following the crisis, and understand when to call for additional help.

Marotz (2012) recommended that all teachers, if they are expected to administer first aid to children, complete first aid and CPR training, preferably before they begin work.

Preventing a health crisis is important, too. For example, it is wise to prepare a list of classroom activities. Give this list to the child's parents or physician and ask them to indicate activities that should be avoided or modified. In addition, the other children need to be prepared for possible health crises of classmates. Teachers can give simple explanations. They also can assure children that the teachers will be able to take care of all the children, not just the child who has the problem.

Summary

Physical disabilities in children include a wide range of orthopedic and other health impairments. Neurological involvement often accompanies both types of conditions. The physical disabilities that teachers are most likely to encounter were described briefly in this chapter in terms of characteristics, causes, program recommendations, and the responsibilities of teachers, including crisis management, as needed.

Children with both orthopedic and health conditions are likely to benefit from being enrolled in a regular early childhood classroom if the staff has adequate support. Early interventionist/resource teachers and other specialists must be used to support teachers in planning and implementing a range of appropriate activities. The specially trained interventionist/resource teacher or physiotherapist is essential in cases of orthopedic involvement, though a variety of other disciplines also play significant roles, depending on the nature of the child's condition.

Early childhood educators and other members of the transdisciplinary team should work together to integrate therapeutic recommendations into everyday activities. Teachers should never initiate any kind of therapeutic activity without specific instruction and supervision from a certified specialist.

Regular classroom activities, materials, and equipment often can be adapted to meet the needs of children with physical disabilities. A major responsibility of teachers is to help the child with a physical disability keep active and involved to the maximum extent possible. Teachers need to help children with physically handicapping conditions or disabilities learn how to do as much as possible for themselves so that their medical condition or disability does not take over their lives. Another responsibility of teachers is to prepare themselves to meet emergency situations. When teachers remain calm and quietly in charge, young children do not panic.

Resources

The following organizations provide information as well as written and physical resources for parents, professionals, and children. Canadian resources are identified with an asterisk (*).

Anaphylaxis Canada*

http://www.anaphylaxis.org

The Arthritis Society*

http://www.arthritis.ca

Asthma Society of Canada*

http://www.asthma.ca

Canadian Diabetes Association*

http://www.diabetes.ca

Canadian Hemophilia Society*

http://www.hemophilia.ca

Cystic Fibrosis Canada*

http://www.cysticfibrosis.ca

Epilepsy Canada*

http://www.epilepsy.ca

FARE Food Allergy Research and Education

http://www.foodallergy.org

Muscular Dystrophy Canada*

http://www.mdac.ca

My Diabetes Playbox

http://www.mydiabetesplaybox.com

National Hemophilia Foundation

http://www.hemophilia.org

Spina Bifida and Hydrocephalus Association of Canada*

http://www.sbhac.ca

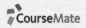 Access an interactive ebook and chapter-specific interactive learning tools, including flashcards, quizzes, videos, and more, in the *Inclusion in Early Childhood Programs* CourseMate. Visit NELSONbrain.com to log in, register, or purchase access.

Social, Adaptive, and Learning Disorders

10

OBJECTIVES

After studying the material in this chapter, the student will be able to

- Recognize the symptoms of anxiety disorders found in young children.
- Describe eating and toileting concerns sometimes associated with behavioural disorders, and discuss appropriate adult attitudes toward these types of situations.
- Describe the characteristics of a child with autism spectrum disorder.
- Discuss attention deficit hyperactivity disorder and effective strategies for inclusion.
- Discuss the use and misuse of the term *hyperactivity*.
- Identify a children's mental health promotion and prevention program.
- Recognize the major warning signs in a preschool child that suggests the potential for learning disabilities related to later reading, writing, and math skills.
- Provide a convincing argument against labelling or diagnosing a preschool child as having a learning disability.

KEY CONCEPTS AND TERMS

anxiety disorder

applied behaviour analysis (ABA)

attention deficit hyperactivity disorder (ADHD)

autism spectrum disorder (ASD)

behaviour disorder (BD)

discrete trial teaching (DTT)

echolalia

emotional disturbance

encopresis

enuresis

hyperactivity

hyperkinesis

learning disability

learning disorders

perseveration

phobias

pica

pivotal response training (PRT)

tangible reinforcers

CONNECTIONS

- Tyra is a toddler with autism spectrum disorder. She does not make eye contact easily, but she smiles and watches attentively when her teacher produces her favourite stuffed-dog toy.
- Anthony is a second grader diagnosed with attention deficit disorder. He is better able to stay on task now that his teacher has taught him how to monitor his behaviour and use a schedule to predict what is going to happen during the day.
- Ken is a kindergartner with very challenging behaviour. He is aggressive and destructive when asked to participate in activities that are not his choice. Through the use of simple behavioural contracts, however, he is demonstrating more appropriate behaviour in the classroom.

Introduction

Disorders associated with behaviour and with learning have been linked to various developmental conditions. In this chapter, we will discuss those that are not a result of a primary disability, such as intellectual developmental disabilities or blindness. The behaviours discussed here are qualitatively different. Behaviours such as occasionally not following directions or finding it hard to sit still for 20 minutes are common behaviours of young children.

In this chapter we will examine behaviour disorders, learning disorders, attention deficit hyperactivity disorder (ADHD), and autism spectrum disorder (ASD). The diagnosis of all four of these types of disabilities is based on a professional's diagnosis of a child's behaviours. There are standard diagnostic criteria for these disabilities, based on criteria set out in the *Diagnostic and Statistical Manual of Mental Disorders* (5th ed.; *DSM-5*; American Psychiatric Association [APA], 2013). In May 2013 the manual was revised based on a comprehensive review of scientific advancements, targeted research analyses, and clinical expertise (APA, 2013). Several types of professionals can diagnose these types of disabilities, including physicians, psychologists, neurologists, and psychiatrists. However, there is no blood test or other physical procedure or examination that confirms or refutes the diagnosis. For this reason, it is especially important that the family or primary caregiver is involved in the assessment process; that the assessment instruments used are culturally relevant, bias-free, and in the child's home language; and that at least part of the assessment is conducted in an environment that is familiar to the child. The terms *behaviour disorder*, *ADHD*, and *learning disability* should be used with extreme caution when describing a young child.

The label *behaviour disorders* is widely used to classify a variety of social and **emotional disturbances** ranging from mild to severe. Children who are identified as having a **behaviour disorder (BD)** are those whose behaviour is extreme, chronic, and unacceptable. Defining and diagnosing behaviour disorders are ongoing challenges in special education and are extremely problematic in early childhood. Sometimes drawing the distinction between developmentally and culturally appropriate behaviour and behaviour that impedes a child's development in one or more areas is difficult for even the most skilled teacher or parent.

The term **learning disorders** is often applied to children with average IQs and reasonable adaptive functioning who nevertheless have difficulty learning to read, write, or do math. A behaviour or learning disorder may be a child's major or *primary* special need, or it may be a *secondary* problem. There are some children who function successfully in most areas of development but exhibit

Emotional disturbances characterized by behavioural or emotional responses so different from appropriate age, cultural, and community norms that the responses adversely affect educational performance

Behaviour disorder (BD) a chronic or pervasive challenging behaviour

Learning disorders the name given to a group of problems that can cause children who have average IQs and reasonable adaptive functioning to nevertheless have difficulty learning to read, write, do math one or more inappropriate behaviour patterns. In these cases, the behaviour disorder is the primary concern.

The inability, or lack of opportunity, to learn appropriate behaviours or to understand routine expectations may be the cause of secondary behaviour concerns. The frustrations the child experiences in trying to perform everyday developmental tasks and engage in effective social exchanges are often a factor. Children with developmental special needs tend to get relatively little positive feedback from parents, caregivers, and teachers; yet their maladaptive behaviours, such as head banging, shrill squealing, eye poking, or hitting of other children, draw a great deal of attention. Thus, the maladaptive behaviours become more dominant, making it even more difficult for these children to acquire necessary positive developmental skills.

When working with young children who present challenging or inappropriate behaviours, it is essential to keep in mind what is developmentally appropriate within various cultures. Most three- and four-year-olds do not follow all directions, they challenge adults occasionally, and they can go from laughter to tears in a few seconds. For this reason, the term *behaviour disorder* should be used with extreme caution when describing the behaviour of young children.

There is general agreement among most child developmentalists that preschool children (with few exceptions) *should not be labelled as emotionally disturbed or having a learning disability*. Early development is characterized by constant change. Therefore, the labels *emotionally disturbed* and *learning disabled* are premature, nonfunctional, and likely incorrect.

Emotional and Psychological Disorders

Separation Difficulties

Infants and young children are frequently fearful of strangers and unwilling to separate from a parent or major caregiver. The behaviour tends to peak between 12 and 15 months of age and then lessen gradually. Children in families in which there is general instability may be especially fearful of strangers and, throughout the preschool years and beyond, have trouble separating.

Entering preschool or a childcare centre for the first time can be intimidating for young children. Young children with disabilities may experience even more anxiety. They are likely to have had fewer play experiences away from home than other children have. Also, they often have been the focus of intensive adult care and concern to a degree that may not be possible in a school situation. Separation anxiety is common. In most cases it does not need to become a major problem if the first days of school are carefully planned by teachers and parents.

In a few instances, a child and parent may have prolonged and severe difficulty in separating. At the least hint that the parent might leave, the child has a severe emotional reaction that may be a consequence of the parent trying to slip away without saying goodbye after agreeing to stay.

In these cases, teachers must involve parents in a plan to help the child learn to separate. Discussions of the difficulties the child is experiencing should take place away from the classroom and out of the child's hearing. The separation process should focus on the parent's gradual withdrawal, usually over several days. The amount of time required depends on the child and the degree of difficulty. Throughout the parent's separation efforts, teachers should encourage and appreciate the child's participation in the program. Gradually, the teacher's support will replace the parent's support.

Occasionally, a child who likes coming to the program may use protest as a way to keep the parent at school. These children often engage in every activity and play happily as long as the parent stays. As soon as the parent tries to leave, however, the child starts to cry or scream and strongly protest. Parents in these situations often complain about the child's behaviour. Yet, after saying goodbye they have a tendency to pause and look back, as if waiting for the child to begin to protest. At times, it is the parent who is having difficulty separating.

In these cases, the teacher may have to assist the lingering parent in leaving swiftly with only a brief and matter-of-fact goodbye. The child almost always settles back into play after a token protest.

Overdependency

The early childhood teacher may be the target of a child's efforts to get extraordinary amounts of attention. Sometimes this is the child who has had difficulty separating from his or her parents, but not always. The child who is overly dependent may cling to a particular teacher, hang on to the teacher's clothing, and shadow the teacher's every move. Complaining, whining, and tattling may be accompanying behaviours. Working with a child who is overly dependent requires the teacher to walk a fine line between giving too much attention and too little. Too much attention is likely to increase the child's dependency problems; too little may lead the child to feel disliked or rejected, or even distrustful of the situation.

To receive the full benefit from the program, a child must be helped to relate to all teachers and, eventually, to children. Once the child is familiar with the program and the routines, the *weaning* process can begin. It is not a question of reducing the amount of attention; it is one of making decisions as to when to give attention in order to help rather than hinder the child's progress. Consider the following examples:

The teacher watches for those moments when the child is not clinging and immediately gives attention: "It looks as if you are enjoying that book. Let's read the pictures together. What do you suppose is going to happen to the kitten?"

When a child is pulling at the teacher's clothing or person, the teacher should resist the impulse to react or respond. Hard to do, yes; but it is to the eventual benefit of both the child and the teacher. As always, preventive measures are best: As the child approaches, the teacher can reach out and put an arm around the child or take the child's hand before the clinging or clutching starts.

Teachers should support the child in taking personal responsibility, beginning with non-threatening situations: "If you want to play in the rocking boat I'll go with you while you talk to Sherri. If you ask, I know she'll stop rocking so you can get in."

Finding ways to get the child to allow another teacher to respond to his or her needs is another step in solving a difficult situation. The teacher should choose those times when the child really wants something, as when one teacher says to another, "Ms. Kaur, Charles wants the red truck. Will you get it out for him?" or to the child, "I can't read your book because I have to set up fingerpainting. Let's ask Mr. John to read it to you."

Occasionally, a teacher finds it flattering to be singled out for undivided devotion and unintentionally reinforces the child's overly dependent behaviours. In these instances, both child and teacher need the help of other staff members.

Children who are overly dependent or anxious may also complain of headaches, stomach aches, or nearly invisible cuts and scrapes. Though the hurt is real to the child, it also has become a sure way of getting focused attention from an important adult. Most young children can be expected to have these kinds of complaints sometimes. When the complaints go on day after day, it is cause for concern.

The first step is to check with parents to make sure that there are no physical problems. Classroom procedures then become the same as for other problematic behaviours: minimum attention to the aches and scrapes, as well as additional attention when the child is actively engaged in play activities. This helps the child focus on the fun times at school.

Withdrawal and Shyness

Some children seem to be alone most of the time. They rarely engage in social play activities. Often, they turn away when other children approach. In structured, large-group activities, they may be there in body but appear too remote and not there emotionally. Teachers seldom express the degree of concern over these children that they do with children who show extreme emotional reactions and aggressive behaviour. The behaviours of the child who is withdrawn are easily overlooked; those of the child who is disruptive seldom go unnoticed. Yet the child who is withdrawn may be in greater developmental jeopardy than the child who displays disruptive behaviours.

Withdrawal problems and their causes may be so complex as to require clinical treatment and a segregated, therapeutic classroom. However, most children who show signs of withdrawal in early childhood settings are likely to have less serious problems with less obscure origins. The cause may be a recent upheaval at home, such as a parent leaving or a serious illness in the family. It may be a change of neighbourhood where the new children's ways seem strange, even frightening or bullying. It may be the first venture of an only child or a child with a disability into a play setting with other children. These children may have been overprotected unwittingly, due to the parents' efforts to keep them from getting hurt or catching a childhood disease. There are also those children who are simply shy. All children experience shyness off and on to some degree. In some children, shyness becomes a long-standing habit. Whatever the cause, teachers usually can help these children become more involved.

Careful observation is the required first step. Specific questions should be asked:

- Does the child engage in particular activities when playing alone?
- Are there materials and equipment (see photo, page 206) that the child appears to enjoy or prefer?
- Does the child spend time watching certain children or certain activities more than others?
- Is the child likely to leave an activity if certain children approach? Does the child avoid these children consistently?
- Are some children less threatening for the child to sit next to in group activities or to play next to in parallel play situations?

When a child's preferences (and avoidances) have been noted, plans can be made to gradually reduce the child's isolation. The following are three examples of first approximations to social interactions for Jeanine, a child whose isolated behaviours were of concern.

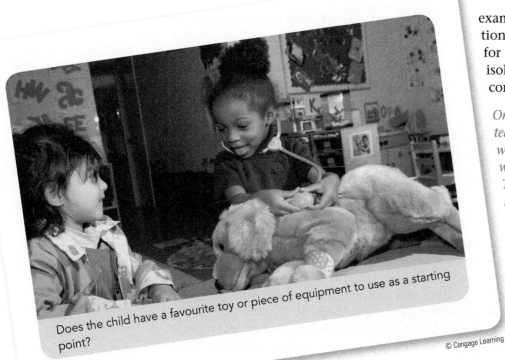

Does the child have a favourite toy or piece of equipment to use as a starting point?

© Cengage Learning

On several occasions the teacher had observed Jeanine watching housekeeping play with apparent interest. The teacher arranged that he and the child together would deliver additional materials to the activities in progress. The teacher announced, "Jeanine and I have brought some more birthday candles. We'll put some of them on the cake, too, okay?"

Jeanine seemed fascinated by the rocking boat. A quiet but friendly child asked the teacher for another ride. The teacher responded, "Yes, Jon, but let's give Jeanine a ride, too. Here, Jeanine, you sit across from Jon." Another time a third child was invited, who also was seated across from Jeanine, and then a fourth who sat next to Jeanine. In each of these early steps, the teacher selected quieter, less rambunctious children to share the ride.

Jeanine was watching two children working with pegboards. The teacher said, "Jeanine, I'll put a pegboard down here for you." The teacher placed the pegboard at the end of the small table near, but not between, the other children. "All three of you can reach the basket of pegs."

Having Jeanine take pegs out of a common basket was a step forward from the week before. At that time, the teacher had seated her near the other children but had given her a small basket of pegs of her own.

Sometimes, the child who is shy will focus almost exclusively on one or more of the adults in the program. Overdependency does not seem to be the problem; it is as if some children prefer the company of adults. They always find ways to sit next to the teacher. They linger during transitions to help the teacher clean up. They engage the teacher in long, one-to-one conversations. This may be pleasant for the teacher, but it does not promote the kinds of social development that come with learning to interact with other children.

The teacher's job becomes one of consciously involving another child or two in the conversation or the cleanup operation. If no other children are about, the teacher should respond to the child pleasantly but briefly, and then move to an area where there are other children. Usually the child who is shy will follow. This increases the opportunity for the teacher to involve other children.

Anxiety and Depression

Depression, fearfulness, and anxiety occur in young children, though to a lesser degree than found in preadolescents and teenagers. Young children are seldom thought of as having severe depression. However, today experts agree that severe depression can occur at any age. This disorder is marked by changes in emotion, motivation, physical well-being, and thoughts. The causes of depression are unclear. There is some evidence that if the children's parents are depressed, there is a greater likelihood that the child will have bouts of anxiety or depression. If a sustained, severe depression is suspected, referral to a pediatric specialist is strongly advised (Canadian Mental Health Association [CMHA], 2013a).

Studies have shown that about 8 percent of teens aged 13 to 18 have an anxiety disorder, with symptoms commonly emerging around age 6. However, of these teens, only 18 percent received mental health care (National Institute of Mental Health, 2013). Common **anxiety disorders** in the early years revolve around separation problems, overdependence, and withdrawal or avoidance of social contacts. Some young children are more prone to being overly anxious than are others. "Although researchers don't know exactly why some people experience anxiety disorders, they know that there are various factors involved. Like many other mental health conditions, anxiety seems to be a result of a combination of biological, psychological and other individual factors" (CMHA, 2013b, para. 1). These children may need extra support and reassurance when entering new situations. It is important to build self-esteem in young children, to give them a strong sense of their own worthiness. Anxiety in preadolescent and adolescent children often results in low self-esteem, which can lead to depression.

Anxiety disorder an extreme and lasting concern and fearfulness in certain situations, which other children their age do not experience; these commonly include separation problems, overdependence, withdrawal from social interactions, and so on

Phobias

Fears that result in excessive and unrealistic anxiety about everyday happenings are called **phobias**. The individual with a phobia may go into a panic reaction at encountering a feared object or event, or at the mere thought of encountering it. For example, there are people who take extreme measures, such as climbing 20 flights of stairs to avoid riding an elevator, or walking a kilometre out of the way, every day, rather than passing a well-fenced yard in which there is a small, securely tied dog that barks at passersby. A certain amount of fear is appropriate. Fears are natural adaptive mechanisms in young children and are built in for survival purposes. No child should be laughed at or shamed for his or her fears. As with all developmental issues, there is a fine line between too much and too little attention. Adaptive fears can become unrealistically stressful if adults are overly attentive to (thereby reinforcing) the child's fearful responses. Conversely, not receiving enough attention can make the child feel insecure and rejected. These feelings may lead to other kinds of maladaptive behaviours and stressful reactions.

Phobias fears that result in excessive and unrealistic anxiety about everyday happenings

CMHA (2013b) and APA (2013) both make reference to social anxiety disorder (formerly referred to as social phobia), where individuals experience panic at the thought of performing in public. Children may become extremely self-conscious about themselves, and fearful of being judged or evaluated. In these cases, individuals will make every attempt to avoid any situation where they will be surrounded by other people.

Eating and Elimination Disorders

Eating problems associated with particular disorders, as well as with being overweight and underweight, were described in Chapter 9. Incontinence associated with spinal cord damage also was discussed. This section will look at several other eating and elimination disorders sometimes found among young children in group settings.

Pica

Pica craving to eat nonfood substances

The uncontrollable craving and eating of nonfood substances is called **pica**. In pica, the young child eats nonfood substances, such as clay, dirt, animal feces, bits of paint, glass, hairballs, and so on, without discriminating these nonfood items from food. Early childhood teachers may encounter children who constantly *taste* substances considered inedible, such as dirt, tar, grease, chalk, paper, fingerpaint, paste, play dough, or clay. Though sometimes a health threat, most young children experiment with the tasting of inedible materials. This should *not* be confused with pica. In pica, the intake of this material is frequent and at times in great quantities. It can lead to malnutrition, cuts in the mouth, and intestinal obstructions.

Whether it is pica or simple experimental tasting, this random intake of nonfood substances should be discouraged, with an explanation to the child that it can make him or her sick. If the child continues, the problem usually is solved by removing the material with the simple statement "I can't let you play with the play dough if you eat it. It will make you sick." If everything fails to work, a specialist should be consulted. Effective management of this disorder typically involves the expertise of a multidisciplinary team.

Children also may go on food jags. They insist on certain foods to the exclusion of all others. Except in extreme cases (or if too much pressure is put on the child to "eat right"), the jag usually disappears in a reasonable time. Some children eat excessive amounts of a certain food. One four-year-old was known to eat whole heads of lettuce, almost ravenously. At times, this eating behaviour may indicate a nutritional deficit.

Whenever a teacher is concerned about a child's eating, the parents and public health nurse should be consulted.

Soiling and Wetting

It is not uncommon for early childhood teachers to encounter children who are not toilet trained, or are not reliable about getting themselves to the toilet in time. The same holds true for young children with developmental disabilities, many of whom may not be toilet trained when they reach preschool age. The reasons vary. Often, conflict has resulted in a toilet-training impasse between the child and parents. In the early childhood program, where emotional involvement is at a minimum, toilet training usually can be accomplished quickly. Effective training guides include *Steps to Independence* by Baker, Brightman, and Heifetz (2004) and *Self-Help Skills for People with Autism spectrum disorder* by Anderson, Jablonski, Thomeer, and Knapp (2007). It is the rare child, even among children who are severely intellectually impaired, who cannot be trained to use the toilet.

Even after they are toilet trained, young children, including those with disabilities, may have soiling or wetting episodes on occasion. They often give clues of an impending accident by jiggling or clutching themselves.

What is needed is a quiet instruction from the teacher *before* the accident occurs: "Run in and use the toilet. I'll save the swing until you get back." When a toilet accident does occur, a child should never be ridiculed or made to feel guilty. Even the most conscientious child can slip up. Clothing should be changed matter-of-factly. Every young child should have spare clothes at school, rotated from home if possible.

Chronic soiling or wetting sometimes occurs in an older preschool or primary-age child who has been reliably toilet trained. It is important to be aware of the following:

- Persistent wetting, especially in girls, may be related to a chronic urinary tract infection.

- A child may have a recurring low-grade intestinal virus causing loose or runny bowels.

- Children with diabetes may have failure of urine control at times.

- Some children are anxious about using a strange bathroom or may have been trained to greater privacy than is available at school.

- Some school bathrooms have a toilet that flushes much more loudly than the home toilet, and children become fearful of using the bathroom due to the sound.

Once in a while, even when all physical disorders have been ruled out, a child may continue to have toileting problems. **Encopresis** (chronic soiling problem) and **enuresis** (chronic wetting problem) are the clinical names often assigned to such conditions. Though there are a number of possible reasons, earlier difficulties associated with elimination or toilet training may have become intertwined with anxiety, fear, and other emotional reactions. These can result in a child's unpredictable and hard-to-control soiling or wetting accidents.

In these cases, as in all others, the clothes should be changed matter-of-factly, without reprimand or moralizing. Working together, teachers, parents, and the appropriate team member(s) can help a child with enuresis or encopresis gain reliable control.

Encopresis chronic soiling problem

Enuresis chronic wetting problem

Social/Learning Adaptation Disorders

Autism spectrum disorders, attention deficit hyperactivity disorders, and schizophrenia are three conditions that, to varying degrees, interfere with the child's ability to

- initiate and maintain relationships with others;
- concentrate for any length of time; and
- assimilate new material into his or her existing framework of knowledge.

Autism Spectrum Disorder (ASD)

Autism spectrum disorder (ASD) refers to a group of childhood disorders usually evident by age three. The newly released *DSM-5* (APA, 2013) now includes within the ASD category disorders previously referred to as early infantile autism, childhood autism, Kanner's autism, high-functioning autism, Asperger's disorder, childhood disintegrative disorder, pervasive developmental disorder (not otherwise specified), and childhood disintegrative disorder. Figure 10–1 provides the characteristics of autism spectrum disorder as outlined in the *DSM-5* (APA, 2013).

According to an APA news release (2012), the change indicates that the symptoms of these disorders represent a continuum from mild to severe, rather

Autism spectrum disorder (ASD) persistent impairment in reciprocal social communication and social interaction and restricted, repetitive patterns of behaviour, interests, or activities

FIGURE 10-1

APA Definition of Autism Spectrum Disorder

A. Persistent deficits in social communication and social interaction across multiple contexts, as manifested by the following, currently or by history (examples are illustrative, not exhaustive: see text):

1. Deficits in social-emotional reciprocity, ranging, for example, from abnormal social approach and failure of normal back-and-forth conversation; to reduced sharing of interests, emotions, or affect; to failure to initiate or respond to social interactions.

2. Deficits in nonverbal communicative behaviours used for social interaction, ranging, for example, from poorly integrated verbal and nonverbal communication; to abnormalities in eye contact and body language or deficits in understanding and use of gestures; to a total lack of facial expressions and nonverbal communication.

3. Deficits in developing, maintaining, and understanding relationships, ranging, for example, from difficulties adjusting behaviour to suit various social contexts; to difficulties in sharing imaginative play or in making friends; to absence of interest in peers.

Specify current severity:

Severity is based on social communication impairments and restricted repetitive patterns of behaviour.

B. Restricted, repetitive patterns of behaviour, interests, or activities, as manifested by at least two of the following, currently or by history (examples are illustrative, not exhaustive: see text):

1. Stereotyped or repetitive motor movements, use of objects, or speech (e.g., simple motor stereotypes, lining up toys or flipping objects, echolalia, idiosyncratic phrases).

2. Insistence on sameness, inflexible adherence to routines, or ritualized patterns of verbal or nonverbal behaviour (e.g., extreme distress at small changes, difficulties with transitions, rigid thinking patterns, greeting rituals, need to take same route or eat same food every day).

3. Highly restricted, fixated interests that are abnormal in intensity or focus (e.g., strong attachment to or preoccupation with unusual objects, excessively circumscribed or perseverative interests).

4. Hyper- or hyporeactivity to sensory input or unusual interests in sensory aspects of the environment (e.g., apparent indifference to pain/temperature, adverse response to specific sounds or textures, excessive smelling or touching of objects, visual fascination with lights or movement).

Specify current severity:

Severity is base on social communication impairments and restricted, repetitive patterns of behaviour.

C. Symptoms must be present in the early developmental period (but may not become fully manifest until social demands exceed limited capacities, or may be masked by learned strategies later in life).

D. Symptoms cause clinically significant impairment in social, occupational, or other important areas of current functioning.

E. These disturbances are not better explained by intellectual disability (intellectual developmental disorder) or global developmental delay. Intellectual disability and autism spectrum disorder frequently co-occur; to make comorbid diagnoses of autism spectrum disorder and intellectual disability, social communication should be below that expected for general developmental level.

Source: Reprinted with permission from the *Diagnostic and Statistical Manual of Mental Disorders*, Fifth Edition, (Copyright © 2013) American Psychiatric Publishing. All Rights Reserved.

than being distinct disorders (see Table 10–1). The new category is designed to help clinicians more accurately diagnose people with relevant symptoms and behaviours by recognizing the differences from person to person. It was felt that previous criteria led to providing general labels that tended to be inconsistently applied across different clinics and centres.

TABLE 10-1

Severity Levels for Autism Spectrum Disorder

Severity level	Social Communication	Restricted, Repetitive Behaviour
Level 3 "Requiring very substantial support"	Severe deficits in verbal and nonverbal social communication skills cause severe impairments in functioning, very limited initiation of social interactions, and minimal response to social overtures from others. For example, a person with few words of intelligible speech who rarely initiates interaction and, when he or she does, makes unusual approaches to meet needs only and responds to only very direct social approaches	Inflexibility of behaviour, extreme difficulty coping with change, or other restricted/repetitive behaviour markedly interfere with functioning in all spheres. Great distress/difficulty changing focus or action.
Level 2 "Requiring substantial support"	Marked deficits in verbal and nonverbal social communication skills; social impairments apparent even with supports in place; limited initiation of social interactions; and reduced or abnormal responses to social overtures from others. For example, a person who speaks simple sentences, whose interaction is limited to narrow special interests, and who has markedly odd nonverbal communication.	Inflexibility of behaviour, difficulty coping with change, or other restricted/repetitive behaviour appear frequently enough to be obvious to the casual observer and interfere with functioning in a variety of contexts. Distress and/or difficulty changing focus or action.
Level 1 "Requiring support"	Without supports in place, deficits in social communication cause noticeable impairments. Difficulty initiating social interactions, and clear examples of atypical or unsuccessful responses to social overtures of others. May appear to have decreased interest in social interactions. For example, a person who is able to speak in full sentences and engages in communication but whose to-and-fro conversation with others fails, and whose attempts to make friends are odd and typically unsuccessful.	Inflexibility of behaviour causes significant interference with functioning in one or more contexts. Difficulty switching between activities. Problems of organization and planning hamper independence.

Source: Reprinted with permission from the *Diagnostic and Statistical Manual of Mental Disorders*, Fifth Edition, (Copyright © 2013) American Psychiatric Publishing. All Rights Reserved.

These disorders have identifiable characteristics and behaviours that can be exhibited in children to extremely varying degrees—hence the concept of a "spectrum." The primary characteristics include

- deficits in social communication and social interaction; and
- restricted, repetitive patterns of behaviour, interests, and activities.

Research indicates that the prevalence of autism in North America has increased significantly in recent years, jumping from 40 to 60 cases per 10 000 people, which represents approximately 190 000 Canadians (Fombonne, 2009). Professionals from the Hospital for Sick Children AboutKidsHealth resource centre (Mulligan, MacCulloch, Roberts, & Steel, 2009) stated that

ASD is the most common developmental condition. Based on Canadian research by Fombonne and colleagues from 2006, one out of every 165 people have ASD. More recent U.S. data from the Centers for Disease Control, 2009) show that this incidence may be closer to one in 100. Four out of five people with ASD are male. ASD affects people from all parts of the world. It affects people of every social economic background and race. ("How Common Is ASD?" para. 1)

It is not yet clear whether this huge increase is due to a greater recognition and detection of autism, or whether environmental conditions have affected the prenatal or postnatal development of the child. Girls with the disorder tend to have more severe symptoms and greater cognitive impairment (Yeargin-Allsopp et al., 2003). Children with autistic spectrum disorder exhibit a moderate to severe range of communication, socialization, and behaviour problems.

There are several problems and syndromes that may accompany ASD. They include sensory problems, intellectual disabilities, seizures, fragile X syndrome, and tuberous sclerosis sensory problems. Many children with ASD are extremely sensitive to certain sounds, textures, tastes, and smells. Some children find the feel of clothes touching their skin unbearable. This discomfort may result in tantrums, screaming, and other avoidance behaviours. Some children with ASD are oblivious to extreme cold or pain. A child may experience severe injury and not cry or seek help.

Uneven cognitive development is also found in some children with autism spectrum disorder. For example, they may excel at completing puzzles and fine motor tasks, but may lag behind their peers in receptive and expressive language, often exhibiting signs of echolalia, or repetition of words and sentences that do not convey meaning.

Echolalia describes a condition in which language is characterized by repetition of words and sentences that do not convey meaning; this condition is often associated with autism

One of the earliest signs of autism is resistance to being held or cuddled. The infant tends not to mould to the parent's (or caregiver's) body, as do most infants. Sally Ozonoff and her colleagues (2010) reported that while such babies begin life appearing relatively normal in terms of social responsiveness (e.g., eye contact, smiling), there was an observed decline in this responsiveness, with symptoms beginning to emerge between six and twelve months. This finding is of particular note given that the average age of diagnosis is four and a half years. Due to this relatively late age of diagnosis, the CDC launched a campaign to stress the importance of recognizing milestones. Autism Speaks is funding a three-year research project to assess the effect of proposed revisions to the criteria used to diagnose autism. The new study will be conducted at one of the sites currently used by CDC to estimate prevalence of ASD. The study will provide important information regarding how the changes in diagnostic criteria will influence estimates of prevalence (Autism Speaks, 2012).

As toddlers and little children, children with autism spectrum disorder treat others as inanimate objects. Rarely do these children make eye contact (see photo, left).

Since there is currently no physical or medical test for autism, a thorough assessment completed by an interdisciplinary team is warranted. This team should include a physician, psychologist, teacher, language specialist, and the parent(s).

Teachers of young children should be aware that not all but rather a cluster of the above symptoms may be found in a child with an autism spectrum disorder.

If teachers suspect autism spectrum disorder, they should contact a specialist as soon as possible. The earlier the intervention, the greater the likelihood of positive changes in the child's behaviour.

Many children who are diagnosed with autism spectrum disorder rarely make eye contact.

Courtesy of Ryerson Early Learning Centre

There are a number of successful early intervention programs for children with autism spectrum disorder. Some have been validated via research; others have not. Among these treatments, **applied behaviour analysis (ABA)** has become widely accepted as an effective treatment. ABA refers to the process of teaching skills systematically using interventions that are based on the principles of learning, and through this systematic process demonstrating that the interventions are responsible for learning or changes in behaviour. There are several types of treatment strategies that fall under ABA, including **discrete trail teaching (DTT)**, a teaching strategy that enables the learner to acquire complex skills and behaviours by first mastering the subcomponents of the targeted skill; incidental teaching; and pivotal response training (PRT).

Incidental teaching has the same principles of learning as found in discrete trial training, following the same technical conditions:

- The intervention is composed of operant conditioning techniques;
- The intervention goals are socially significant; and
- The intervention results are analyzed objectively by assessing each child's progress before, during, and after the intervention. (AutismConnect, n.d., para. 1)

PRT is "play based and child initiated. Its goals include the development of communication, language and positive social behaviors and relief from disruptive self-stimulatory behaviors" (Autism Speaks, 2014, para.1).

The most successful programs for children with autism spectrum disorder include predictable routines, use of effective instructional strategies, and curricular content that is developmentally appropriate for the individual child. When possible, teacher training in any of the above described techniques will also contribute to providing inclusive settings.

The following are useful strategies:

- Keep messages simple and direct.
- Use real objects and actions along with words (e.g., show the child a shoe and demonstrate how to lace it).
- Emphasize spoken language by having the child ask for things by name rather than by gesturing.
- Seek to maintain eye contact with the child, redirecting his gaze by gently turning his head, if necessary.
- Give the child opportunities to interact with younger children who are at a more comparable level in language and social development.
- For behaviour management programs, use **tangible reinforcers** (small toys, stickers, music, or favoured foods, if all else fails) and pair these with adult attention.
- Establish and maintain a predictable environment, including teacher's language and behaviours, daily schedule, and classroom furnishings and materials.
- Rearrange the environment, placing highly desired items out of reach and using teaching strategies that motivate the child to request these items.
- Provide opportunity for the child to generalize new skills by ensuring the opportunity to practise these skills in a variety of settings (home, school, and park) and with a variety of people (several teachers, parents, siblings, peers).

Applied behaviour analysis (ABA) a teaching approach used with children with autism spectrum disorder that involves observation, assessment, breaking skills down, and teaching skills systematically; progress is closely monitored through ongoing data collection

Discrete trail teaching (DTT) a teaching strategy that enables the learner to acquire complex skills and behaviours by first mastering the subcomponents of the targeted skill

Tangible reinforcers material things that the individual likes; in children, favourite foods and drinks, toys, stickers, and so on (older children usually like money)

- Focus on improving the child's communication skills perhaps by using a communication device, such as a picture exchange communication system (PECS). In PECS, the child identifies a desired object in a picture and gives the teacher the picture in exchange for the item. PECS are being used in more and more early childhood environments (see photo, below). By using PECS, the child learns to initiate communication.

- Reduce class or group size whenever possible and provide appropriate seating for the child to help minimize distractions.

- Modify the curriculum according to the child's strengths and weaknesses.

- Provide frequent communication with parents and other care providers.

Parental involvement has also emerged as a major factor in treatment success. Parents should be involved in intervention and work with teachers and therapists to identify the behaviours to be changed and the skills to be taught. Parents should be trained to deal with behaviours and teach new skills so that intervention occurs across environments throughout the day.

It is important, when working with families of children who have autistic behaviours, to support the parents in every way possible and to work with other members of the transdisciplinary team to help parents find specialized help, as well as *respite care*, as required by the family.

Another urgent need of parents is frequent assurance that the autism spectrum disorder was not caused by a lack of love or caring on their part. Parents of children with autism spectrum disorder have often been greatly wronged. Without valid evidence, for many years professionals implied that parents (more often than not the mother) were somehow responsible for their child's autism. According to Bee and Boyd (2012), children are born with the disorder: "Whatever the specific origin, the evidence jointly points to the conclusion that autism reflects different brain functions of some kind."

RETT'S DISORDER This disorder, also known as Rett syndrome, has been identified as stemming from a rare genetic disorder (Beers, 2005). It is diagnosed

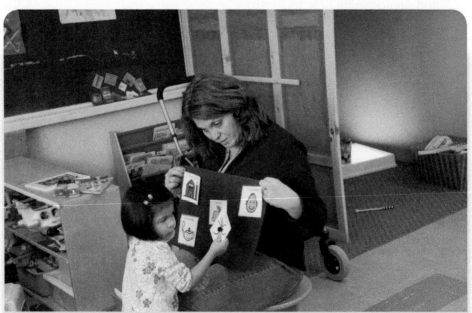

Picture exchange communication systems are being used more in early childhood environments.

Sarah is a second-year kindergarten teacher. Her principal has just told her that a student is moving into her classroom next week. The child has autism and will be accompanied by an aide. This is her first experience with a child with autism and with having an aide in her classroom. Think about the following questions: What will she need to do to prepare for the student's arrival? Should Sarah do anything to prepare the other students? If so, what? What can she do to develop an effective working relationship with the aide?

primarily in girls. Incidence is one in 10 000 children; in the United States approximately 16 000 children and women are affected (Rett Syndrome Research Trust, 2013). Parents report normal development over the first 18 months followed by a loss of abilities, especially in the area of gross motor skills. This regression continues in the areas of speech and hand use. According to the Ontario Rett Syndrome Association (2013), other medical issues include epileptic seizures, muscle stiffness, osteoporosis, and scoliosis. Diagnosis is often made based on the repetitive gestures and hand movements often described as hand-wringing. Behaviours in children with Rett's disorder are often confused with those found in the autism spectrum disorder. Better information about this disorder will enable medical practitioners to diagnose children much earlier and likely stop the progress of the symptoms with effective treatment. Children diagnosed with this disorder are also encouraged to engage in physical and cognitive activities to avoid further deterioration due to inactivity. Teachers supported by occupational, speech and language, and physical therapists can design appropriate individual program plans to meet the needs of the child and family. Current technology, as well as a variety of communication devices, will assist the child in participating in early learning and care settings.

OTHER INTERVENTIONS In an effort to do everything possible to help their children, many parents of children with ASD continually seek new treatments. Some treatments are developed by reputable therapists or by parents of a child with ASD. Although an unproven treatment may help one child, it may not prove beneficial to another. One has only to search for treatments on the Internet to see the confusing array of treatment options and to hear conflicting reports of what is effective and what is not. To be considered proven, the treatment should undergo clinical trials (preferably randomized, double-blind studies) that compare treatment and nontreatment groups.

This following list of questions still has relevance for parents to use to help determine the appropriateness of an intervention for their child and family:

- Will the treatment result in harm to the child?
- Is the treatment developmentally appropriate for the child?
- How will failure of the treatment affect my child and family?
- Has the treatment been validated scientifically?
- How will the treatment be integrated into the child's current program?*

The following are among interventions that have been reported as helpful to some children but whose efficacy or safety has *not* been proven (Strock, 2004).

* *Journal of Autism and Developmental Disorders*, 27 (641–561) Guidelines, 1997. B. J. Freeman. Reprinted with kind permission from Springer Science and Business Media.

Dietary interventions Some feel that food allergies and an insufficiency of a specific vitamin or mineral may cause autistic symptoms. Some parents report results from a diet that is gluten free and casein free. Gluten is a protein that is found in the seeds of various cereal plants, such as wheat, oats, rye, and barley. Casein is the principal protein in milk. Since gluten and milk are found in many of the foods we eat, following a gluten-free, casein-free diet is extremely difficult.

Numerous inconclusive studies discuss the use of various vitamin therapies such as vitamin B as a supplement that some parents feel is beneficial to their child with ASD. The results vary from one child to the next.

Chelation An unproven theory claims that by removing the heavy metals from the blood of a child with autism, symptoms can be reversed. Chelation is used on the premise that there is a link between the use of thimerosal, a mercury-based preservative used in the measles-mumps-rubella (MMR) vaccine, and autism. Mercury is no longer found in childhood vaccines in the United States. Many well-done, large-scale studies have failed to show a link between thimerosal and autism. While some may have considered chelation therapy as a suitable alternative remedy, a cautionary note is that "children, pregnant women, and people who have heart or kidney failure should not have chelation therapy at any dose" (WebMD, 2011).

Childhood Schizophrenia

There is less scientific knowledge about childhood schizophrenia than there is about autism spectrum disorder. However, it is understood by the medical community to be a brain disorder where genetics and environment appear to play a role. According to the Schizophrenia Society of Ontario (2013),

> schizophrenia affects 1 in 100 people and occurs in every race, culture, and socio-economic group. It occurs equally in males and females. In Canada, approximately 300,000 people live with the disease, of whom 120,000 live in Ontario. The disease usually begins when people are in their teens or early twenties, although it can occur later in life. Because it strikes young people in their formative years, it is often referred to as "youth's greatest disabler." (para. 1)

Childhood schizophrenia is characterized by loss of ego boundaries and an impaired sense of reality. Major characteristics of the disorder include tantrums and repetitive or otherwise bizarre behaviours or postures. Other characteristics are rejection of and withdrawal from social contacts and unpredictable mood swings. The child frequently is described as "cut off from reality" and given to hallucinations. Children with schizophrenia usually have normal language development, though the language may be used for noncommunicative purposes. Many of these children talk to themselves in a private language that no one can decode. Children with schizophrenia tend to have more varied symptoms than do children with autism. They are also more likely to have contact and interactions with other people. Early childhood teachers rarely encounter a child with schizophrenia because the onset of the condition usually occurs after the preschool years. However, if a child with this condition were enrolled in an early childhood program, as with other conditions, a team approach involving specialists should be used in developing an intervention program for this child.

Attention Deficit Hyperactivity Disorder (ADHD)

Hyperactivity (or hyperkinesis) is a catch-all diagnosis and label that is much over-worked. It is used to refer to children who are highly active, energetic, impulsive, and distractible and who have a hard time waiting their turns or listening to instructions. These children may be described as showing "excessive motor activity." Regardless of particular behaviours, these children have two things in common:

1. Many adults find their behaviours challenging.
2. An identifiable physical or neurological cause is seldom found for their high activity level.

Attention deficit hyperactivity disorder (ADHD) is a term that has come into popular use over the past several years. It is classified as a subsection under "Neurodevelopmental Disorders" by the APA (2013), which uses "attention deficit/hyperactivity disorder," but also recognizes that some children have ADHD without hyperactivity. Figure 10–2 provides a comprehensive description of the disorder, as outlined in the *DSM-5*.

It is estimated that 3 to 5 percent of children have ADHD (Strock, 2006). Longitudinal data published by Barkley (2005) indicate that the mean onset is between three and four years of age. In addition, it appears that more boys than girls (approximately 3:1 ratio) have the disorder. It was once thought that children outgrew ADHD in adolescence, but it is now believed that only the hyperactivity decreases during the teen years. Many symptoms do continue into adulthood, affecting approximately 4 percent of adults (Chaban & Tannock, 2009). This means that in a classroom of 25 to 30 children, it is likely that at least one or two will have ADHD (Barkley, 2005; Stock, 2006).

Many of these same behaviours are also characteristic of young children diagnosed as having a learning disability. The attention deficit hyperactivity disorder label, authoritative as it may sound, does little to lessen the problems associated with supporting a young child who is constantly on the move. It should also be noted that those children who have ADHD without hyperactivity have trouble focusing and may appear to be "daydreaming."

CAUSES OF ADHD Research has yet to reveal one specific cause of ADHD. Several hypotheses have been offered, one or two of which are backed up by fairly sound evidence. One is the possible role of genetic transmission. Bee and Boyd (2012) reported a study in which one-fourth of the subjects with ADHD had parents with a history of hyperactivity. Researchers continue to work on the brain and its various functions, or malfunctions, to explain ADHD. A correlation has also been found between ADHD and a mother's smoking or drug and alcohol use during pregnancy (Markussen Linnet et al., 2005). Barkley's (2005) publication of longitudinal data also indicated that the mean age of onset of ADHD is between three and four years, and it appears to be a universal disorder.

THE HYPERACTIVE LABEL The term *hyperactivity* is both misused and over-used, especially when applied to young children. Among children of preschool and primary school age, there is a broad range of activity levels. Some seem to be on the move continually. Teachers often feel as if these children never settle into any activity for any length of time.

Yet few of these children have any organic problems. A child who can stay with any activity for several minutes at a time is not clinically hyperactive. The child may be difficult to entertain, not interested in typical learning tasks, easily distracted by activity in other areas of the room, or perhaps worried and

---

Hyperactivity or hyperkinesis refers to children who are highly active, energetic, impulsive, and distractible and who have a hard time waiting their turns or listening to instructions

Attention deficit hyperactivity disorder (ADHD) behaviour that is characterized by consistently short attention span, inattentiveness, distractibility, impulsivity, and heightened levels of movement and physical activity (hyperactivity)

FIGURE 10-2

APA Definition of ADHD

A. a persistent pattern of inattention and/or hyperactivity-impulsivity that interferes with functioning or development, as characterised by (1) and/or (2);

1. Inattention: six (or more) of the following symptoms have persisted for at least 6 months to a degree that is inconsistent with developmental level and that negatively impacts directly on social and academic/occupational activities:

   Note: The symptoms are not solely a manifestation of oppositional behaviour, defiance, hostility, or failure to understand tasks or instructions. For older adolescents and adults (age 17 and older), at least five symptoms are required.

   a. often fails to give close attention to details or makes careless mistakes in schoolwork, at work, or during other activities (e.g., overlooks or misses details, work is inaccurate).
   b. often has difficulty sustaining attention in tasks or play activities (e.g., has difficulty remaining focused during lectures, conversations, or lengthy reading).
   c. often does not seem to listen when spoken to directly (e.g., mind seems elsewhere, even in the absence of any obvious distraction).
   d. often does not follow through on instructions and fails to finish schoolwork, chores, or duties in the workplace (e.g., starts tasks but quickly loses focus and is easily sidetracked).
   e. often has difficulty organizing tasks and activities (e.g., difficulty managing sequential tasks; difficulty keeping materials and belongings in order; messy, disorganized work; has poor time management; fails to meet deadlines).
   f. often avoids, dislikes, or is reluctant to engage in tasks that require sustained mental effort (e.g., schoolwork or homework; for older adolescents and adults, preparing reports, completing forms, reviewing lengthy papers).
   g. often loses things necessary for tasks or activities (e.g., school materials, pencils, books, tools, wallets, keys, paperwork, eyeglasses, mobile telephones).
   h. is often easily distracted by extraneous stimuli (for older adolescents and adults, may include unrelated thoughts).
   i. is often forgetful in daily activities (e.g., doing chores, running errands; for older adolescents and adults, returning calls, paying bill, keeping appointments).

2. Hyperactivity and Impulsivity: six (or more) of the following symptoms have persisted for at least 6 months to a degree that is inconsistent with developmental level and that negatively impacts directly on social and academic/occupational activities:

   Note: The symptoms are not solely a manifestation of oppositional behaviour, defiance, hostility, or a failure to understand tasks or instructions. For older adolescents and adults (age 17 and older), at least five symptoms are required.

   a. often fidgets with hands or feet or squirms in seat.
   b. often leaves seat in classroom or in situations in which remaining seated is expected (e.g., leaves his or her place in the classroom, in the office or other workplace, or in other situations that require remaining in place).
   c. often runs about or climbs excessively in situations in which it is inappropriate. (Note: in adolescents or adults, may be limited to feeling restless.)
   d. often unable to play or engage in leisure activities quietly.
   e. is often "on the go" acting as if "driven by a motor" (e.g., is unable to be or uncomfortable being still for extended time, as in restaurants, meeting; may be experienced by others as being restless or difficult to keep up with).
   f. often talks excessively.
   g. often blurts out answers before a question have been completed (e.g., completes people's sentences; cannot wait for turn in conversation).
   h. often has difficulty awaiting for his or her turn (e.g., while waiting in line).
   i. often interrupts or intrudes on others (e.g., butts into conversations, games, or activities; may start using other people's things without asking or receiving permission; for adolescents and adults, may intrude into or take over what others are doing).

B. Several inattentive or hyperactive-impulsive symptoms were present prior to age 12 years.
C. Several inattentive or hyperactive-impulsive symptoms are present in two or more settings (e.g., at home, school, or work; with friends or relatives; in other activities).
D. There is clear evidence that the symptoms interfere with, or reduce the quality of, social, academic, or occupational functioning.
E. The symptoms do not occur exclusively during the course of schizophrenia or another psychotic disorder and are not better explained by another mental disorder (e.g., mood disorder, anxiety disorder, dissociative disorder, personality disorder, substance intoxication or withdrawal).

Source: Reprinted with permission from the *Diagnostic and Statistical Manual of Mental Disorders*, Fifth Edition, (Copyright ©2013) American Psychiatric Association. All Rights Reserved.

TABLE 10-2

Disorders that Sometimes Accompany ADHD

Disorder	Prevalence
Learning Disability	20–30%
Oppositional Defiant Disorder (ODD)	35%
Conduct Disorder (CD)	25%
Anxiety Disorder	18%
Depressive Disorder	18%

Source: © Cengage Learning

unhappy, but the child is *not* hyperactive as per the accepted *DSM-5* (APA, 2013) definition.

There are several disorders that sometimes accompany ADHD. These include learning disabilities, oppositional defiant disorder, conduct disorders, and bipolar disorder. Table 10–2 indicates the prevalence in children with ADHD.

INTERVENTION STRATEGIES FOR MANAGING ATTENTION DEFICIT HYPERACTIVE BEHAVIOUR Attention deficit hyperactive behaviour in young children does place them at a greater risk for accidents because they do not anticipate the consequences of their actions. Also, adults become more frustrated by excessively active, impulsive children who must be watched constantly.

There can be serious consequences for children who do not receive adequate treatment for ADHD. These may include poor self-esteem, academic failure, and poor social development and interactions. Treatment plans should be developed with the parent or caregiver to best meet the individual needs of the child and family.

The most effectively used approaches to helping children diagnosed as having ADHD are medication and behaviour management, often best used in combination with one another.

Medication In assessing highly active children, it is argued that distinctions should be made between (1) the child whose high activity level is truly organic and (2) the child who is simply overly active. The reason for making the distinction is that some children in the organic group may benefit from prescription drugs, such as Ritalin or Dexedrine, in addition to behavioural intervention strategies. Psychostimulants, such as Ritalin or Dexedrine, are the most widely used class of medication for the management of ADHD. Between 70 and 80 percent of children with ADHD are said to respond positively to these medications. However, this medication may have undesirable side effects, including weight loss (loss of appetite), insomnia, or increased blood pressure; individual children may respond differently to medication therapy. In 2003 nonstimulants were approved for treating the disorder in the United States. Nonstimulants are reported to have fewer side effects than stimulants and can last up to 24 hours (CDC, 2011).

Medication should be used only under the supervision of a physician and only when there is indisputable evidence that it is the most beneficial treatment. Sometimes, it is parents and teachers who come to rely on the medication. In other words, they may become "addicted" to having the child on medication because the child is much less troublesome when medicated. Kopelwicz's (1996) reminder to us still rings true about the limitations of medication:

> Ritalin (the most commonly prescribed drug for children with ADHD) lets a kid pay attention more. It does not force kids to do their homework, it doesn't teach social skills, it doesn't make them smart, it just makes them more accessible to perform in these areas. (p. 15)

Special diets Special diets should be viewed with skepticism. The controversial Feingold diet (introduced during the 1970s), for example, linked artificial food colouring and food additives with hyperactivity. Dr. Feingold (1975) asserted that many children labelled as hyperactive would improve if synthetic colours and flavours and natural salicylates were removed from their diets. Research studies investigating his claims found no clinically significant differences between untreated groups of children and those on the Feingold diet (Conners, 1980). True, no harm can come from feeding children foods that are nutritious and additive free. However, even if a curative diet is nutritious (and some are not), looking for a diet as the sole cure for a behaviour disorder often results in ignoring challenging behaviours that require a different treatment.

Classroom management of hyperactive behaviour Drugs and special diets do not teach. Children whose behaviour is controlled by medication are still in need of special, individually designed behaviour management strategies.

Teachers must think about preparing the environment carefully, looking for positive behaviours to reward, and treating the child as one who is learning to develop self-control and socially positive interactive behaviours. Beware of statements such as, "Oh, you forgot to take your pill this morning. I guess this will be a bad day." Too many children and parents come to believe that the child's improved concentration is totally the result of medication. In fact, without special planning by adults, and special effort on the part of the child, improvement in behaviour would not be possible. The more a child feels responsible for improved behaviour and experiences a sense of accomplishment, the more likely he or she will continue the behaviours that lead to greater self-control. Once a child has developed more control over his behaviour, the more likely he is to develop positive social interactions with peers.

Systematic classroom observations a few times a week are extremely useful in helping teachers to recognize areas that seem to interest and involve the child. Observations as short as 3 minutes or as long as 30 minutes usually reveal one or more activities that engage even the most overly active child. Such observations are important. They give teachers a place to start a positive behaviour-management program designed to increase the child's span of attention. Even briefly focusing on an activity—any activity—sends a signal to teachers. Now is the time to give positive attention to the child while the child is engaged in this purposeful activity. This is in contrast to what teachers (and parents) often do—that is, giving their attention when the child is flitting about, thus reinforcing the negative behaviour.

It is, therefore, important that teachers watch for those times when a child is appropriately involved in an activity. It is then that they should go to the child with a relevant comment, supportive interest, or a gentle challenge: "I bet you can fill that pail full of sand all the way to the top. I'll watch while you do it." Few children can resist staying with a task when so challenged by an interested and responsive adult. Furthermore, a child's span of attention often can be extended by calling attention to unexplored aspects of the activity or by asking questions (see photo, page 221). While supervising the water table, the teacher might ask, "I wonder what would happen if we put a little yellow food colouring in the blue water?" (Or some nontoxic soap powder? Or a drop or two of glycerine?) At the fingerpainting table the teacher can pose questions such as, "What can your thumbs do? the tips of your fingers? the backs of your hands?" Offering additional but related materials may also enhance an overly active child's "stick-to-itiveness": "Here are some new cookie cutters to use with the dough when you get it all rolled out. Do you want to start with the heart or the diamond?" Or, "The big doll looks as if it needs a bath, too." The key is to try to offer the ideas and materials while the child is still engaged in the activity—before the child loses interest and leaves.

A child's attention span can often be extended by calling attention to unexplored aspects of the activity.

© Cengage Learning

When they appear to be getting ready to quit an activity, overly active children should be helped to plan where they will play next. Noting that a child is about to leave an area, the teacher can say, "Let's decide where you want to play now." If the child seems unable to make the decision, the teacher can offer choices: "There is room for you in the block corner or at the water table." Once a choice has been made, it is best for the teacher to accompany the child to the chosen area. If there is a teacher in the block area, for example, the first teacher can say something like, "Julie has come to work with blocks. Will you help her get started?" Otherwise, the accompanying teacher should help the child get involved.

Children who are overly active often display impulsive behaviours. These behaviours can include

- abruptly grabbing something;
- suddenly hitting a child or throwing something; and/or
- unexpectedly and suddenly leaving an activity.

Anticipation and intervention before the impulsive behaviour occurs is a key element in the behaviour management of impulsive behaviours. Children with ADHD often need to be guided in developing prosocial alternatives.

To further reduce overactive and impulsive behaviours in young children, teachers may want to try the ideas listed below. These suggestions are readily carried out in any early childhood program:

- Observe the child in various activities over several days. If observations indicate, for example, that a child's attention begins to wander after five or six minutes of music time, plan to end that child's participation as it gets toward the five-minute mark. A second teacher can quietly draw the child away and provide another activity before the child wearies of music. The child can be given crayons or a puzzle, or might assist the teacher setting up the snack tables. It is important that a special activity not be offered if the child has already disrupted the music group.

- Keep the classroom and play yard neat and orderly. Limit the quantity of materials that are out at any one time. Encourage the children to restore (tidy up) each play area before they leave it. A disorganized environment encourages nonfocused behaviour, especially with overly active children.

- Alternate active and quiet experiences, large and small groups, and teacher-initiated and child-initiated activities. Extended free-play periods can be especially difficult for overly active children. For many children who are very active or who have attention deficits, the amount of free-play time and the number of play choices usually need to be limited.

- Transition times should be as consistent as possible. Externally imposed transitions are frequently difficult for children with ADHD; therefore, forewarning a child of an impending transition is helpful in that it allows the child some time to prepare for the upcoming change.

When working with a child who is overly active, teachers frequently need to review the following questions:

- Are the classroom activities interesting, varied, attractive, and lively? In other words, are they fun and are they challenging?

- Are the activities a good match to the child's skill levels?

- Are activities and interest centres adapted on a regular basis to reflect the changing interests and developmental levels of the children?

- Is the child getting attention when focusing on an activity, or involved in prosocial behaviour, even for a moment or two, rather than for flitting about or infringing on another child's territory?

Working toward positive answers to these questions is essential in reducing hyperactivity. When behaviour-management strategies and knowledge of what is appropriate curriculum are laced together with care and concern for the child's well-being, hyperactivity inevitably lessens. The same four-pronged approach also works effectively with children who display a variety of other behaviour concerns.

It is always important to consider the following:

Most children who are diagnosed by competent mental health professionals as having attention-deficit hyperactivity disorder, do; but as early childhood educators, we must always ensure that our classrooms are developmentally appropriate and that children are not being inappropriately labeled because our classroom is inappropriate. (Landau & McAninch, 1993, p. 53)

Mental Health Promotion and Prevention

Over the years children's mental health practitioners have recognized the importance of mental health promotion and prevention as a strategy to support families with young children. Accordingly, early childhood educators have played an instrumental role in reaching out to families and communities, given their expertise in working in this context. An example of two mental health promotion and prevention programs are the following:

- Kids Have Stress Too! Preschool Program (KHST!) "is designed to influence young children's social and emotional development. The program teaches practitioners to help preschool children enhance their physical, mental, emotional and behavioural coping skills, thinking styles and key abilities during the important window of opportunity of the preschool years" (KHST!, 2009, p. 10).

- "Handle with Care training program was prepared as an extension of the Early Childhood Care and Mental Health Project, completed in 2005 by the Canadian Mental Health Association, National Office and the Hincks-Dellcrest Centre/Institute. The purpose of that project was to explore the ways that the mental health of young children from birth to 6 years can be promoted in community-based child care centres. In this context, mental health promotion was seen as development of age-appropriate and culturally relevant life skills that benefit all children's social and emotional development" (Handle with Care, 2007, p. 3).

Learning Disabilities

Children with **learning disabilities**, to varying degrees and in varying combinations, may display the following:

- constant motion and purposeless activity
- poor perceptual motor skills
- low tolerance for frustration
- frequent mood swings
- poor coordination, in both large and fine motor activities (see photo, right)
- distractibility and short attention span
- poor auditory and visual memory
- a variety of language deficits

From the above list, it is obvious that learning disabilities encompass a wide range of behavioural disorders. Efforts at clinical classification are continuing. Some textbooks discuss learning disabilities in conjunction with attention deficit disorders. Others may group learning disabilities with cognitive disorders or impaired mental functioning. Other classifications are motor dysfunction and impaired motor planning. In this text, learning disabilities are discussed as a separate category. The decision is based on the extensive overlap of learning disabilities with other behaviour disorders and related developmental disabilities. Providing a separate discussion may serve to clarify some of the issues. Nevertheless, the overlaps remain, as is evident in the sections that follow.

Learning disability one of a number of disorders that may affect the acquisition, organization, retention, understanding, or use of verbal or nonverbal information, even though the individual is of at least average intellectual ability (thinking, reasoning, or both)

Fine motor control is often more poorly developed in children suspected of having a learning disability.

Courtesy of Bloorview—Scarborough Site

Learning Disabilities Defined

What is a learning disability? Two answers come immediately to mind: first, the many things that it is; second, the many other things that it is not. This is the official definition adopted by the Learning Disabilities Association of Canada:

"Learning Disabilities" refer to a number of disorders which may affect the acquisition, organization, retention, understanding or use of verbal or nonverbal information. These disorders affect learning in individuals who otherwise demonstrate at least average abilities essential for thinking and/or reasoning. As such, learning disabilities are distinct from global intellectual deficiency.

Learning disabilities result from impairments in one or more processes related to perceiving, thinking, remembering or learning. These include, but are not limited to: language processing; phonological processing; visual spatial processing; processing speed; memory and attention; and executive functions (e.g., planning and decision making).

Learning disabilities range in severity and may interfere with the acquisition and use of one or more of the following:

- oral language (e.g., listening, speaking, understanding)
- reading (e.g., decoding, phonetic knowledge, word recognition, comprehension)
- written language (e.g., spelling and written expression)
- mathematics (e.g., computation, problem solving)

Learning disabilities may also involve difficulties with organizational skills, social perception, social interaction and perspective taking.

Learning disabilities are lifelong. The way in which they are expressed may vary over an individual's lifetime, depending on the interaction between the demands of the environment and the individual's strengths and needs. Learning disabilities are suggested by unexpected academic under-achievement or achievement which is maintained only by unusually high levels of effort and support.

Learning disabilities are due to genetic and/or neurobiological factors or injury that alters brain functioning in a manner which affects one or more processes, related to learning. These disorders are not due primarily to hearing and/or vision problems, socio-economic factors, cultural or linguistic differences, lack of motivation or ineffective teaching, although these factors may further complicate the challenges faced by individuals with learning disabilities. Learning disabilities may co-exist with various conditions including attention, behavioural and emotional disorders, sensory impairments or other medical conditions.

For success, individuals with learning disabilities require early identification and timely specialized assessments and interventions involving home, school, community and workplace settings. The interventions need to be appropriate for each individual's learning disability subtype and, at a minimum, include the provision of:

- specific skill instruction;
- accommodations;
- compensatory strategies; and
- self-advocacy skills.*

* Learning Disabilities Association of Canada. (2013). Official definition of learning disabilities. Ottawa: Author. Retrieved from http://www.ldac-acta.ca/learn-more/ld-defined/official-definition-of-learning-disabilities. Used with permission.

Therefore, as defined, a learning disability is *not* the result of the following list of conditions, although it may occur concurrently with any one of them:

- visual, hearing, or motor impairments
- cognitive delays
- emotional disturbance
- environmental, cultural, or economic disadvantages
- second-language learning

During the last 35 or 40 years, hundreds upon hundreds of studies have been conducted on learning disabilities. Competent researchers in the fields of psychology, neurology, education, and educational psychology have attempted to come up with definitive answers to the elusive question of how to define (and diagnose) learning disabilities. Diagnosing learning disabilities in preschool children is particularly difficult (see photo, right).

As described in the formal definition given in U.S. law PL 101-476 (formerly known as PL 94-142), learning disabilities are related primarily to academic performance: "the imperfect ability to listen, think, speak, read, write, spell, or do mathematical calculations." Because most early childhood educators consider it developmentally inappropriate for preschool-aged children to be spending their school hours in such pursuits, we might ask whether young children should *ever* be considered to have a learning disability. "No," seems to be the logical response; yet not all teachers are comfortable with that, and for good reason. Many young children show behaviour patterns similar to those associated with learning disabilities in older children. They may include being distractible, easily frustrated, excessively active, or poorly coordinated. These behaviours already are interfering with their everyday learning activities in a variety of ways. A number of early childhood educators believe that early intervention is in the best interest of these children, helping them to deal with their behaviours during the preschool years, before the consequences have an opportunity to compound and create additional difficulties for the child. The type and timing of such intervention is a recurring issue in early childhood education.

What is a learning disability? There is no agreed-on answer, especially where young children are concerned.

© Cengage Learning 2015

Predicting Learning Disabilities in Young Children

Is it possible that certain behaviours in a young child may be predictive of subsequent trouble with academic tasks? The answer seems to be yes, as long as it is understood that the judgment is based on *hunch* and educated guesswork. Teachers of young children frequently identify a child whose behaviours appear to put him or her at risk for learning disabilities and, perhaps, later academic problems. The next question: Is it possible that these worrisome behaviours can be eliminated, or at least reduced, before they have a serious impact on later academic performance? Again, the answer seems to be yes. During the past several years, early identification of young children who may potentially have a learning disability has gained strong support. Child developmentalists, parents, and professionals from other disciplines, such as medicine and psychology, believe that a range of environmental, biological, genetic, and perinatal conditions may be associated with adverse developmental outcomes (Shonkoff & Phillips, 2000) and may be risk indicators (i.e., warning signs) for learning disability. Figure 10–3 is a

FIGURE 10-3

Risk Indicators for Learning Disabilities

Perinatal conditions

1. Low Apgar scores

2. Low birth weight and/or preterm birth

3. Hospitalization for longer than twenty-four hours in a neonatal intensive care unit

4. Difficulty with suckling, sucking, and swallowing

5. Chronic otitis media that may result in intermittent hearing loss

Genetic or environmental conditions

1. Family history of LD

2. Child is adopted

3. Family history of language problems

4. Exposure to environmental toxins or other harmful substances

5. Limited language exposure in home, child care, and other settings

6. Poverty

Developmental milestones

1. Delay in cognitive skills

   a. Not demonstrating object permanence

   b. Lack of symbolic play behaviour

2. Delay in comprehension and/or expression of spoken language

   a. Limited receptive vocabulary

   b. Reduced expressive vocabulary

   c. Difficulty understanding simple (e.g., one-step) directions

   d. Monotone or other unusual prosodic features of speech

   e. Reduced intelligibility

3. Delay in emergent literacy skills

   a. Limited phonological awareness (e.g., rhyming, syllable blending)

   b. Minimal interest in print

   c. Limited print awareness (e.g., book handling, recognizing environmental print)

4. Delay in perceptual-motor skills

   a. Problems in gross or fine motor coordination

   b. Difficulty colouring, copying, and drawing

Attention and behaviour

1. Distractibility/inattention

2. Impulsivity

3. Hyperactivity

4. Difficulty changing activities or handling disruptions to routines

5. Perseveration (i.e., constant repetition of an idea)

Source: © Cengage Learning 2015

partial listing of risk indicators for infants, toddlers, and preschoolers (National Joint Committee on Learning Disabilities, 2006).

Exercising caution is necessary in the identification of young children at potential risk for later learning disabilities. The first step is observation of the child in a number of activities. The next step is matching the observed performance to performance expectancies in all areas of development. At the same time, it must be remembered that all young children are unique and have different rates and patterns of development; furthermore, young children often demonstrate marked differences or delays in their development. These are some of the reasons for considering learning disabilities an inappropriate diagnosis for a young child. In most instances, it is more beneficial to the child to view early differences as developmental deviations calling for learning experiences that meet individual needs. This is a more effective use of professional energy than trying to decide whether to pin (or not to pin) the label "learning disabled" on a child.

SIGNS OF POSSIBLE FUTURE LEARNING DISABILITIES A cue in preschool children that learning problems may lie ahead is a lack of what are sometimes called *readiness* or *prerequisite skills*. As described in Chapter 18, these are skills thought to be necessary for academic success once the child enters grade school. However, simply waiting for the unready child to become ready rarely helps the child. Readiness comes through experiences, learning, and the opportunity to practise and master developmental skills (see photo, below). What follows are examples of particular deviations or delays in various areas of development that are thought to be related to potential learning disabilities and may be more easily identified by early childhood teachers.

1. Indicators of visual-sensory gross motor difficulties Many developmentalists theorize that all early learning is sensorimotor based. Children about whom teachers express concern in terms of future academic performance invariably show some kind of sensorimotor problems. In addition, they often show generalized delay in reaching basic motor milestones and exhibit one or more of the following characteristics:

- *Imperfect body control* results in poorly coordinated or jerky movements and trouble with running, throwing, catching, hopping, or kicking.

- *Poor balance* may cause the child to fall off play equipment, fall down, or fall into furnishings or other people. (An inability to walk a balance beam is almost always a symptom in a Kindergarten or Grade 1 child.)

- *Uncertain bilateral and cross-lateral movements* are often a telltale sign of future difficulties with academic tasks. The child with a bilateral problem may not be able to use both arms simultaneously or in synchrony, as children do when catching a ball or jumping off a wall. Or a child may not use opposite legs and arms in opposing harmony (cross-laterality), as seen in agile children climbing to the top of a jungle gym. The clearest example of cross-laterality is crawling: left leg and right arm moving forward, alternating with right leg and left arm moving forward.

Readiness comes through appropriate early learning experiences and many unhurried opportunities to practise.

- *Inability to cross body midline* has long been viewed as a possible predictor of future academic difficulty. In such cases the child has trouble using the right hand to work on a task where any part of the task lies to the left of the midpoint of the child's body or vision. The same holds true of the left hand and the right-side focus. A common example is a child painting on a large piece of paper at the easel. The child transfers the brush from the right hand to the left when painting on the left half of the paper and back again when painting on the right.

- *Faulty spatial orientation* interferes with children's ability to understand where they are in space, in relation to their physical surroundings. For example, a child may walk into a wall; poor orientation interferes with the child perceiving the wall as being *right there*. Or the child may gear up for a mighty jump only to land with frightening force because the ground was much closer than the greater height the child had anticipated. Putting clothes on inside out or backward, or having difficulty going up and down stairs, also may indicate difficulties with spatial orientation.

2. Indicators of fine motor difficulties (poor fine motor/eye–hand coordination skills) Difficulties in buttoning, lacing, snapping, cutting, pasting, and stringing beads are characteristics of older preschool children thought to be at future academic risk. Often these children are unable to draw a straight line or copy simple shapes, such as a circle, cross, or square. When they manage to draw a crude imitation, the circle seldom is closed, the corners on the square are rounded or irregular, and the cross is crossed far off centre. Tasks of this kind and others, such as cutting with scissors, are virtually impossible for these children to master without extensive training and practice.

3. Visual-perception difficulties Visual-perception difficulties refer to how well the child's processing mechanism handles the information that comes in visually—that is, how well the child makes sense of what is seen. Various aspects of perceptual motor skills are described in Chapter 18; here the focus will be on other aspects related specifically to the current topic of learning disabilities, where difficulties take several forms.

Poor visual perception has nothing to do with blindness or impaired vision. In other words, there is no *physical disability*. The following issues are of concern in this area:

- *Visual discrimination* is the ability to look at objects or pictures and note how they are alike or how they are different. Children with poor visual discrimination may have trouble sorting objects according to colour, size, or shape. They may not be able to match lotto pictures, copy block designs, or tell the difference between the smiling and the frowning clown pictures. Often they can be seen trying to fit a large object into too small an opening or container.

- *Visual orientation* is related to spatial orientation. The child with visual disorientation may recognize three-dimensional objects, such as a head of lettuce, a cap, or a paintbrush, but not recognize the same items in two-dimensional pictures (see photo, page 229).

Another example of visual disorientation is recognizing objects in their normal or upright positions but failing to recognize them when they are turned over or lying sideways. One child insisted that an overturned wooden armchair was a cage; the moment it was turned right side up, he labelled it as a chair. Even

Visual discrimination and visual orientation skills go together.

when the chair was turned over while he watched, he insisted it was a cage the moment it was overturned.

- *Visual memory* involves remembering what was just seen, at least for a few seconds. Children with poor visual memory may not remember the name of the animal on their card, for example, even though the picture has been face down for only a moment. Or, in the familiar take-away game, they cannot recall what was removed even though there were only three or four articles on the tray when it was presented just a moment before.

- *Visual tracking* involves the ability to follow objects visually. Children with difficulties in tracking may have trouble keeping an eye on the ball, following the flight of a bird, or buttoning buttons in order, from top to bottom. Visual-tracking ability is likely to be associated with reading skills, in that reading requires systematic eye movements from left to right and from top to bottom.

- *Visual–motor integration* is a skill that can also be thought of as eye–hand coordination. Children with these kinds of problems may have trouble with almost every motor task that requires vision: fitting appropriately shaped pieces into a puzzle box, cutting on the line, drawing around a form, or tracing a simple shape. It is as if the child's hands cannot do what the eyes say needs to be done.

4. Auditory-perception difficulties Many young children who are at risk for future learning disabilities have trouble processing what they hear (see photo, page 230). Again, this is not a physical problem; deafness or being hard of hearing is not the cause of the child's difficulty. Basically, the problem results from the inability to tell the difference between sounds—lack of auditory discrimination. *Hat* and *mat* may sound the same to these children. Often, they cannot tell the difference between high and low musical tones, especially as the range lessens. Localization of sound is usually a problem, too. The child may have to look in two or three directions when trying to locate a whistler or a barking dog.

5. Language delays Children at risk for learning disabilities frequently have trouble with receptive or expressive language, or both (see Chapter 19). Acquiring the more advanced grammatical forms and the ability to formulate organized sentences tends to come considerably later for children with potential

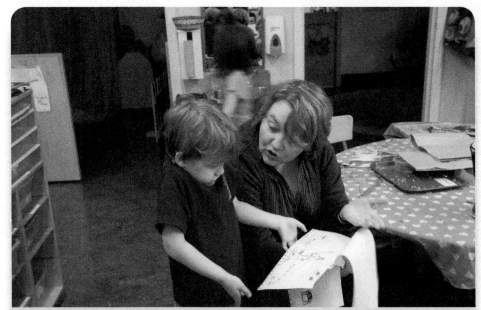
A child may have trouble making sense out of what people are saying.

learning disabilities than for most children. Although vocabulary is not necessarily more limited, trouble can arise, for example, when the child tries to recall a well-known word to describe a familiar concept. Carrying out directions that include common prepositions such as *in, on, under,* and *over* is often baffling. If the teacher says to put the block *on top of the box*, a child may look at the teacher questioningly while putting the object *in* the box. Many of these children have trouble repeating short sentences, rhymes, and directions. In addition, they often have difficulty imitating sounds, gestures, body movements, facial expressions, and other forms of nonverbal communication.

6. Cognitive disorders Trouble in organizing thoughts and processing information with logic is characteristic of many young children with potential learning disabilities. They tend to operate only in the here and now, to think concretely, demonstrating little or no ability to deal with any kind of abstract thought or event. Although concrete thinking is characteristic of young children, most older preschoolers are able to deal with a certain amount of abstraction.

Cognitively disorganized children may also have trouble carrying out simple directions or remembering what it was they were supposed to do, even while they are working on the task. Trouble generalizing from one event to another is also common. A rule about no running indoors may not generalize to no running in the classroom or in the halls or in the library, even though all are indoors within the same building. Especially frustrating for adults, as well as the child, is that the same mistakes are made again and again, simply because there is no carryover from one event to the next.

Perseveration repeating the same act over and over with no discernible intention (in an obsessive, ritualistic manner)

7. Perseveration Perseveration (repeating the same act over and over, seemingly endlessly) is found in some children who seem likely to develop a future learning disability. These children appear unable to stop what they are doing of their own accord. A child may scrub back and forth with the same crayon, or draw the same shape for minutes at a time, until stopped by a teacher or parent. Some children chant the same words or make the same hand gestures repeatedly until someone succeeds in diverting them to something else. It usually is difficult for the child who perseverates to change activities. Even when a change is accomplished, there may be carryover from the preceding activity. For example, the child who has been scrubbing with a crayon may have been moved into block play. Here the back-and-forth scrubbing continues on the floor, with the child using a block rather than a crayon to make the back-and-forth motions.

8. Social skills delay Children who appear to have the potential for later learning disabilities tend to have more than their share of social difficulties. They may be bullying or aggressive, withdrawn, or overly dependent. Their behaviour often confuses other children and so they have trouble making friends. When they do succeed in forming a friendship, they tend to have difficulty keeping it. Sometimes the child puts too many demands on the friend, or has such inadequate play skills that the friend loses interest. Also, their impulsiveness may cause them to say and do inappropriate things. They may not foresee the possibility of negative consequences, such as hurt feelings or the unintentional destruction of a friend's favourite toy. When a child loses two or three friends (for reasons the child neither understands nor seems able to change), feelings of rejection are likely to follow. Rejection increases frustration, a sense of incompetence, and low self-esteem. These feelings, in turn, lead to a tendency to break into tears at the slightest provocation, to strike out for what seems to be little or no reason, or to withdraw even more.

PROGRAM CONSIDERATIONS In concluding this section on possible learning disabilities in young children, one concept bears repeating. Characteristics associated with learning disabilities can be observed in all young children, at one time or another. Many preschool teachers have watched a child do a lovely painting only to see it overlaid from edge to edge and top to bottom with endless coats of paint. The teacher may mourn the loss of the painting (having mentally earmarked it for display at the parent meeting), but this once-in-a-while behaviour is no cause for concern and should not (because it is an isolated event) be considered perseveration. As noted before, in connection with all developmental differences, teachers must look for clusters of behaviours and note the degree to which a behaviour occurs. Questions that are appropriate to ask are these: Are the behaviours happening excessively? Do they interfere with the child's development and general well-being? Age, too, must be a consideration. It is always a warning sign when a behaviour is extreme and persists significantly beyond appropriate age levels.

In working with children whose behaviours seem predictive of future learning disabilities, careful re-examination of the learning environment is essential (see Chapter 14), as is a thorough review of effective teaching strategies. These strategies have been described throughout the text in regard to various developmental issues. Many of the strategies have special relevance in work with preschool children whose behaviour disorders put them at risk of future failure at school.

Here are some strategies for teachers of preschool children with behaviour disorders to consider:

- Be consistent in the use of positive reinforcement to increase behaviours that facilitate the child's development, thereby decreasing behaviours that interfere with development.

- Provide the child with encouragement and descriptive praise for each step forward, regardless of how small.

- Provide learning activities that support the child's home language and culture.

Be patient. Provide a lot of support and encouragement.

© Cengage Learning 2015

- Remember that every child has strengths and does positive things; concentrate attention on these rather than on the child's needs and misbehaviours (see photo, left).

- Use task analysis (see Chapter 11) to teach whatever skills the child is having trouble with, whether learning to imitate, to focus attention, to say no instead of hitting, or any other skill or behaviour.

- Give directions one at a time and allow adequate time for the child to comply. Verify the child's understanding of the request; rehearse (walk the child through) the required response as often as necessary.

- Teach new concepts and skills in short sessions with concrete materials that allow a child to use several sensory modalities: seeing, hearing, moving, and manipulating.

- Be patient. Children with learning disabilities may have to be told or shown many times in many different ways how to accomplish a simple task. Do not expect learning to generalize from one situation to another. Each situation *may seem new* to the child.

- Help parents understand that their child is not being difficult or inattentive on purpose. Tell them of their child's accomplishments, no matter how small. To enhance the child's self-esteem, describe his or her accomplishments to the parent in the presence of the child, whenever possible.

Summary

Teachers of young children with social and adaptive disorders may encounter a number of behavioural difficulties:

- excessive dependency on adults or general withdrawal from social contacts

- fears that result in excessive and unrealistic anxiety about everyday happenings

- withdrawal problems

- eating problems—the most serious of which is pica, the eating of inedible substances (lead-based paint flakes are likely to pose the greatest risk: intellectual impairment, even death, may follow excessive eating of this toxic substance)

- soiling and wetting that continues past the expected age for toilet training

Social learning/adaptation disorders include

- autism spectrum disorder (ASD), formerly known as pervasive developmental disorders (PDD), the most severe form of which is autism

- childhood schizophrenia

- attention deficit hyperactivity disorder (ADHD)

These are all conditions that require a professional diagnostic assessment and specialized program support.

Learning disabilities are classified under a variety of headings, depending on the researcher's, the clinician's, or the teacher's theoretical background. Confusion arises at times because some definitions of learning disabilities refer to them as being specific to reading, writing, or math. For early childhood educators, this raises a number of questions. For example, is it ever appropriate to diagnose a preschool-aged child as having a learning disability? If not, what about the many behaviours (distractibility, short attention span, visual-perception problems, and many others) that are excessive in some preschool children and that resemble the behaviours of older children who have serious problems with academic tasks? Is it not important to deal with these non-academic behaviour disorders in the early years, before they become greater problems that are likely to have a negative impact on subsequent academic learning? The answer seems to be yes, and the question then becomes, how? Strategies for teaching young children with all kinds of behaviour disorders and potential learning disabilities are found throughout this chapter and the other chapters in Section II.

Throughout this chapter, there is a cautionary theme: Behavioural difficulties of every type are common among young children. Every child exhibits a number of them during the developmental years. It is only when certain behaviours begin to become so excessive that they interfere with a child's developmental progress that they are of great concern. Even then, to label or prematurely classify a young child who has so much development yet to come often does the child a grave injustice. It is not how a child is classified but how the child is cared for and taught—as an individual—that is the important issue in working with young children who are demonstrating a range of behavioural and learning difficulties.

Resources

The following organizations provide useful information for parents and early childhood educators. Canadian resources are identified with an asterisk (*).

Autism National Committee

http://www.autcom.org

Autism Ontario*

http://www.autismontario.com

Autism Society

http://www.autism-society.org

Autism Society Canada*

http://www.autismsocietycanada.ca

Autism Society of British Columbia*

http://www.autismbc.ca

Children and Adults with Attention-Deficit/Hyperactivity Disorder (CHADD)

http://www.chadd.org

Families for Early Autism Treatment (FEAT)

http://www.feat.org

Geneva Centre for Autism*

http://www.autism.net

Hincks-Dellcrest Centre*

http://www.hincksdellcrest.org

Hospital for Sick Children*

http://www.aboutkidshealth.ca/En/ResourceCentres/AutismSpectrum Disorder/DevelopinganASDProgramforYourChild/Pages/default.aspx

Indiana Resource Center for Autism

http://www.iidc.indiana.edu/irca

Kids Have Stress Too! The Psychology Foundation of Canada*

http://www.psychologyfoundation.org/index.php/programs/kids-have-stress-too

Learning Disabilities Association of Canada*

http://www.ldac-acta.ca

Learning Disabilities Association of Ontario*

http://www.ldao.ca

National Center for Learning Disabilities

http://www.ncld.org

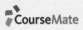

Access an interactive ebook and chapter-specific interactive learning tools, including flashcards, quizzes, videos, and more, in the *Inclusion in Early Childhood Programs* CourseMate. Visit NELSONbrain.com to log in, register, or purchase access.

The Developmental Behavioural Approach

11

OBJECTIVES

After studying the material in this chapter, the student will be able to

- Describe some early education practices that are a blend of developmental and behavioural principles.
- Define positive reinforcement and describe how skilled early childhood teachers use it in working with young children.
- Identify behavioural approaches used with young children within a variety of situations.
- Define preventive discipline and punishment and state how these do or do not support developmentally appropriate practices with young children.
- Explain task analysis and its importance in working with all children, especially children with developmental differences.
- Explain how task analysis can be applied in the learning of self-help/care skills for all children.
- Demonstrate forward and backward chaining in teaching a self-help/care skill.

KEY CONCEPTS AND TERMS

backward chaining

behaviour modification

descriptive praise

didactic materials

forward chaining

intrinsic motivation

learning theory

manual prompts

maturation

modelling

nonambulatory

operant conditioning

preventive discipline

reinforcement

renewal time

task analysis

Introduction

These examples of changes in children's behaviour are essential testimony that developmental progress is taking place. From earliest infancy, behaviour changes in every area of development are critical benchmarks—conclusive evidence of development.

The changing behaviours of infants and children in early childhood programs attest to the quality of the program and the effectiveness of the teaching. For Miriam, Joel, and Avron, the accomplishments their teachers were reporting in a staff meeting represented achievement of short-term objectives written into the child's individual program plan (IPP). In other words, teaching has been considered effective as indicated by positive changes in the three children's behaviours. It must be emphasized that healthy developmental progress does not occur unless there are changes in a child's behaviour.

The developing child is in a state of continual behaviour change. Developmental or behavioural changes range from the simple to the complex. They come about because of physical growth, **maturation**, experience, and observational learning of peers and adults (**modelling**) within diverse social and cultural environments.

Basic developmental principles have been discussed specifically in Chapter 5 and elsewhere throughout this text. This chapter will provide a brief analysis of behavioural principles, especially those that have particular relevance for teachers of young children. It will focus on reinforcement procedures, discipline and punishment, modelling, and task analysis, with emphasis on the role of adult social reinforcement. Positive reinforcement practices are emphasized as the first and preferred approach to effective discipline. This chapter will apply the concept of task analysis to the development of self-help/care skills.

The terms *self-care* and *self-help skills* are used interchangeably; therefore, we use the term *self-help/care skills* in this text. Self-help/care is the ability of individuals to manage personal needs and to adapt their behaviours to social expectations. The specific skills and adaptive behaviours that children are required to learn are determined by the culture in which they live. Though patterns differ, all cultures prescribe ways of eating, toileting, dressing, behaving sexually, sleeping, resting, and keeping public places orderly. The chapter also includes the application of the concepts of forward and backward chaining in teaching a self-help/care skill.

Maturation developmentally, maturation is often defined as an internal process that governs the natural unfolding of innate ("preprogrammed") skills and abilities

Modelling learning by watching and imitating another's actions; also called observational learning

Early Education: Developmental and Behavioural Principles—A Blend

Effective early childhood teachers rely on developmental principles and show an awareness of behavioural principles when deciding how to program for young children. They know that one of the best measures of the effectiveness of their teaching is a change in children's behaviour.

Historical Influences

A developmental-behavioural approach to teaching has been evolving for at least 40 years. By the middle of the twentieth century, developmentalists were in the majority. Researchers, such as Gesell et al. (1993), believed that development was independent of experience, a natural *unfolding* of innate or inborn abilities. The role of teachers (and parents) was neither to unduly restrict nor to push the child. Then came theorists like Hunt (1961), who argued that development was *not* independent of external influences. Rather, it was controlled to some unknown extent by environmental experiences. Hunt was greatly influenced by Piaget (1992). Piaget had theorized that though there was a natural progression that was developmentally based, changes in a child's thinking (cognitive structure) were direct results of exploration of the environment. Hunt went one step further. He suggested that learning depended on a good *match* between the child and the experiences available to the child.

THE PROBLEM OF THE MATCH In early childhood education *the problem of the match* became a central issue. Teachers were trained to provide play materials and learning opportunities that attracted and held children's attention. At the same time, the materials were to include new and intriguing elements (see photo, below). These were to be just a bit beyond the child's current skill level. Providing exactly the right match was the way to produce pleasure and continuing eagerness (motivation) to learn. There was no need for teachers or parents to push.

Intrinsic motivation feelings of pleasure and personal satisfaction derived from working on or accomplishing a task, discovering something new, or solving a problem

The *joy of learning*, often referred to as **intrinsic motivation**, would take over. Children would seek out additional learning of their own accord, simply because they wanted to.

LEARNING FROM SUCCESS The role of environmental influences was also central to the developmental ideas of Bijou (1959, 1993). He believed that the results (consequences) of a child's behaviour were the crucial element. According to Bijou, children tend to learn the behaviours that result in success and positive consequences. They avoid those that result in failure or negative consequences. Teachers were trained to present tasks step by small step and to provide positive consequences for each successful step. The result: a learning

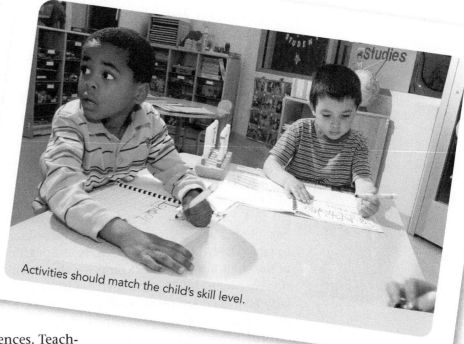

Activities should match the child's skill level.

Chapter 11 | THE DEVELOPMENTAL BEHAVIOURAL APPROACH **239**

environment in which children had frequent success and were motivated to learn more.

ENVIRONMENTAL ARRANGEMENTS Arranging the learning environment so as to help a child take the next step in skill development is a long-established and fundamental principle in early childhood education. The following are three examples from different periods in the history of early childhood education:

- Friedrich Froebel (1782–1852), hailed as the founder of the kindergarten movement, is likely to have been the first to propose that early learning experiences be broken down into their smallest components. Froebel also argued that young children need hands-on experiences: materials to enjoy, examine, and manipulate (Froebel, 1911).

- Maria Montessori (1870–1952), a gifted physician, was a champion of the educational potentials of children with developmental delays and differences. She spent her life designing and demonstrating systematic and sequential learning activities based on what she called **didactic materials** (Montessori, 1912). Many of these materials, as well as her ideas about a prepared environment, are central to today's early education practices.

- John Dewey (1859–1952) is often given the title of founder of the *progressive education* movement. He, too, put major emphasis on the learning environment, especially as represented by the teacher, who was to respond, support, and guide children's exploration of everyday materials (Dewey, 1950).

Didactic materials manipulative materials in which the child's errors and successes are self-evident—the material, not the teacher, provides the information; Montessori was the originator of many such materials

In each of these approaches to early education, the route to sound learning reflects similar principles, a developmental and behavioural blend that includes these elements:

- a prepared learning environment matched to children's current skill levels (in behavioural terms, preparing the environment is referred to as the *arrangement of antecedent events*, a topic yet to be discussed)

- materials and activities sequenced in small enough segments so as to provide both success and challenge

- emphasis on learning through play and active involvement with appropriate materials

- responsive teachers who serve as guides and facilitators

Behavioural Principles and Practices

Misinformation, faulty implementation, and abuse of behavioural practices have led to a knee-jerk reaction in many early childhood educators whenever the behavioural approach is mentioned, according to Wolery (1994), who went on to say, "The behavioral perspective, although often seen as stressing the impact of the environment, in fact proposes that learning occurs from dynamic interactions between children and their environment" (p. 98). He then added, "Particularly beneficial are those child-environment interactions that are initiated and directed by children and in which they are highly engaged" (p. 99).

The behavioural approach to early intervention is based on arranging the environment and implementing teaching strategies in ways that enhance children's learning experiences. Although this approach is important when working with all children, it has been particularly effective in facilitating learning among children with special needs.

All Children Can Learn

In an inclusive classroom, the most significant and useful behavioural principle for teachers is one that emphasizes the point that *every child can learn*. Some children learn faster than others. Some children learn more than others. Some children learn some things easily and other things only with great effort or not at all. Some children learn from one type of approach; others from a different approach. But all children can learn.

To make the *teachability* of all children a day-by-day reality, teachers need to understand and practise basic behavioural principles. In the inclusive classroom, these procedures are especially important. Each child can be provided with a responsive and reinforcing learning environment matched to his or her developmental level and special interests. Children who are gifted can be provided with learning opportunities that neither push nor hold them back but instead foster their interests and talents. Children with developmental differences, though they may learn more slowly or with greater effort, need to be provided with a responsive and reinforcing learning environment matched to their developmental skill levels. The essence of the approach is to start where the child is, developmentally, and build from there (see photo, below).

Children who have severe disabilities may have few observable behaviours to build on. Skilled observation is important here. Teachers need to be able to pick up on subtle cues that indicate a child's possible interest and awareness. For example, a child's eyes may widen as the caregiver approaches the crib, even though the child cannot raise or turn his or her head in the caregiver's direction. In some instances, teachers, parents, and caregivers themselves may have to decide what should be the starting point for learning. An example might be a child with multiple impairments who displays few behaviours of any kind. Simply getting the child to look in a given direction may be a first priority. Even

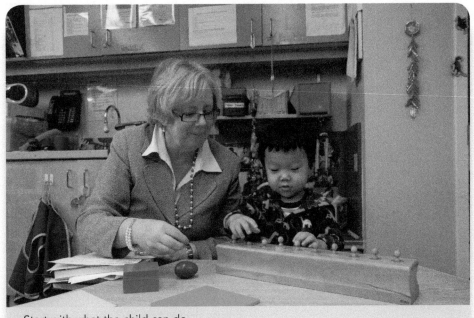

Start with what the child can do.

to accomplish this, a teacher often has to structure the environment so as to evoke (trigger) an attending response from the child: the sight or fragrance of a favourite food or the sound of a loud bell—whatever will attract the child's attention and give the teacher a behaviour to reinforce and expand on.

Reinforcement Procedures

Operant conditioning a teaching strategy in which the child's behaviour is shaped as the result of a planned response designed to reinforce a specific behaviour

Behaviour modification a system by which particular environmental events are systematically arranged to produce specified behaviour changes

Learning theory emphasizes the dominant role of environment and reinforcing experiences in all learning; social learning theory adds other dimensions—that learning also occurs through observing and imitating and that individuals can generate their own satisfactions (intrinsic reinforcement)

Reinforcement procedures come from research related to **operant conditioning**, **behaviour modification**, and **learning theory**. Volumes of studies demonstrate that behaviour is triggered by antecedent events and then increases or decreases according to its consequences (reinforcers). The principles can be put into a simple ABC format:

A: *Antecedent event* (that which precedes or comes before a behaviour—see photo, below)

B: *Behaviour* (response of the individual)

C: *Consequence* (that which follows a behaviour)

A and C are environmental events, planned and unplanned, that both precede and follow a behaviour.

Example:

A: *Teacher slices apples.*

B: *Child looks and says, "I want apple."*

C: *Teacher hands child a slice of apple.*

The child's request (B) was triggered by seeing the teacher slicing the apple (A). It is likely the child will ask for an apple (B) every time the teacher is cutting apples (A), because the request resulted in a piece of apple being given to the child (C).

If specific learning (B) is to occur (or not to occur as in the case of inappropriate behaviours), then A and C must be decided on and systematically arranged. In simple terms, A is what teachers do *before* they want a child to respond. This includes the selection, arrangement, and presentation of activities and materials (and playmates, in some instances). Then, C (consequence) is what teachers do immediately following a child's behavioural response, such as providing or withholding reinforcers (the next topic to be discussed). Whatever adults do in A and C (or fail to do) will

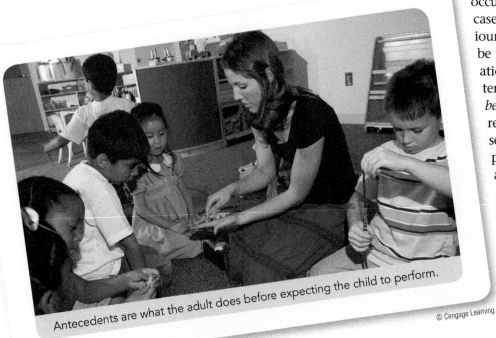

Antecedents are what the adult does before expecting the child to perform.

© Cengage Learning

242 SECTION 3 | PLANNING FOR INCLUSION

NEL

have some kind of an effect on the child's behaviour and learning (Allen, 1974; Chance, 2006).

Reinforcement is a response to a behaviour that increases the likelihood that the behaviour will occur again. Reinforcement takes two main forms: *positive* and *negative*. Reinforcement, as we will see, may also be both *external* and *intrinsic*. In this text, the focus will be mainly on positive reinforcement because of its effectiveness in supporting young children's learning and development.

POSITIVE REINFORCEMENT In simple terms, a positive reinforcer is a pleasant consequence of a behaviour; therefore, it has a high probability of increasing whatever behaviour preceded it. (Note: In the following example, A refers to *antecedent*, B refers to child's *behaviour*, and C refers to social *consequences*.)

Example:

A: *Teacher announces it's time to tidy up so children can go outside.*

B: *Ari runs over and begins to put toys away.*

C: *Teacher praises Ari for working with everyone to clean up quickly.*

Reinforcers that are usually successful with young children are

- toys, play, and other favourite activities; and
- the attention of certain adults.

Different children like different things. A reinforcer for one child may be of little value to another. Hugging is a good example. It is generally assumed that all children like to be hugged. Not true: Some children may be selective as to whom they like to be hugged by. Therefore, hugging may not be an effective reinforcer for these children.

NEGATIVE REINFORCEMENT The strengthening of a behaviour by the removal of an unpleasant consequence is called negative reinforcement. Negative reinforcement is a confusing concept that has been explained in a variety of ways. Bee and Boyd (2009) gave one of the more easily understood definitions:

Negative reinforcement occurs when something *unpleasant* is stopped. Suppose your child is whining and whining at you to be picked up. You pick him up. What happens? He stops whining. So your picking up behaviour has been *negatively reinforced* by the cessation (stopping) of the child's whining and you will be *more* likely to pick him up the next time he whines. At the same time, his whining has been *positively reinforced* by your attention and picking up, so he will be more likely to whine on other occasions. (emphasis added; p. 289)

Chance (2006) defined negative reinforcers even more simply: "Negative reinforcers: A reinforcing event in which something is removed following a behaviour" (p. 102). (Note: Negative reinforcement is not the same as punishment, which will be discussed later.)

Example:

A: *Teacher asks children to tidy up.*

B: *Patrick continues to play.*

C: *Teacher says, "When you have tidied up you can go outside to play."*

In the example above, the teacher wants Patrick to tidy up. Her statement indicates the removal of something the child likes if he doesn't comply.

Intrinsic reinforcement: a sense of pleasure, satisfaction, and self-esteem.

Because Patrick wants the thing that the teacher states she will remove, he complies with the behaviour she desires. It should be noted that overuse of negative reinforcement as a child-management technique places the teacher in a power role that may lead to fear in the child, and for this reason should be avoided.

INTRINSIC REINFORCEMENT Positive inner feelings of pleasure and personal satisfaction describe intrinsic reinforcement. This form of reinforcement comes from working on or accomplishing a task, discovering something new, or solving a problem (see photo, above). For those who love to play with water, playing with water is always intrinsically reinforcing; that is, the very act of playing with water provides hour after hour of pleasure, stimulation, and satisfaction. For children who fear getting wet, there is little or no intrinsic reinforcement; water play is taxing, something to be avoided. The same holds true whether it is riding a tricycle, building with blocks, or working with puzzles.

EXTERNAL REINFORCEMENT One reinforcer that is both powerful and universally appealing to young children of every culture is adult social reinforcement. Adult social reinforcement is made up of the attention of significant adults: parents, teachers, grandparents, other family members, and nurturing caregivers. Generally, adult attention is readily available and potentially plentiful. More than 30 years of research provides conclusive evidence that adult attention is likely to increase those behaviours that it immediately and consistently follows. The opposite is also true: When adult attention is consistently and immediately withheld (ignoring the behaviour) or withdrawn, the child's behaviour decreases. The following excerpt from a classic case study points out the appropriate and systematic use of teachers' attention in helping a child acquire a needed behaviour—improved attention span (Allen, 1974):

Concerns about James's lack of attention span led teachers to make a series of observations. It was obvious that James was getting a great deal of attention from teachers, yet there was no increase in his attention span. Teachers agreed, therefore, to focus their attention on James only on those moments, no matter how brief, when he was engaged with a material or activity. They agreed, further, not to interact with him just as he was leaving an activity or when he was flitting

about. That is, they refrained from doing what they usually did at those times, which was to attempt to steer the child into an activity. Teachers consistently held to their plan as to when they would provide attention and when they would withhold it. James's span of attention soon began to increase.

Many research studies demonstrate how powerful teachers are as sources of reinforcement for young children. Most important, the studies indicate how simple reinforcement procedures may bring out the best in each child. All that has to be done is what good teachers do so well: respond to children in encouraging and positive ways and provide materials and activities matched to children's interests and skill levels (see photo, below). The following are brief descriptions of everyday teacher behaviours that serve as powerful reinforcers for almost any young child:

- *Verbal responsiveness.* Example: producing relevant comments, interested questions, answers to children's questions, exclamations of approval (such as "Great!"), and **descriptive praise** or encouragement that focuses on some aspect of what the child is accomplishing, such as "Paula, you laced your shoe all by yourself!"

  Descriptive praise feedback that lets children know specifically what it is they are doing well

- *Physical proximity.* Example: quietly standing or sitting close to a child and showing genuine interest by watching, nodding, smiling, or listening.

- *Physical contact.* Example: touching, hugging, holding a child's hand, tussling, rocking, or otherwise physically comforting a child. (Teachers must note and discuss the occasional child who avoids or shrinks from adults' touches.)

- *Physical assistance.* Example: providing support on the climbing frame, pushing a swing, helping a child achieve balance on a walking beam, and so on.

- *Providing things that children want.* Example: providing a favourite nutritional snack, play materials, activities, or mini-excursions, such as riding in the elevator or crossing the road to watch the carpenter.

The essence of a reinforcement procedure is responding to children in positive and encouraging ways.

Courtesy of Bloorview—Scarborough Site

Descriptive praise, because it is so central to children's learning, is discussed in several places in this text. Praise statements need to be specific. It is of little value, in terms of children's learning, to make statements such as "Good boy," "Good work," "That's nice." In contrast, descriptive praise gives the child specific feedback, which is always an aid to further learning. When the teacher says, "You're putting all the red blocks on the red squares," the child knows exactly what it is that he or she is doing well. Such information is useful to the child in learning the rest of the colour-matching task. Furthermore, the focus is on the child's effects and accomplishments. In recent years, articles and books have been published on the issue of too much praise and too many rewards (Kohn, 2001). The issue has been raised as to whether we are causing children to become dependent on adults to measure their worth, rather than children doing things for their own pleasure. The phrase "good job" has been overused in many classrooms, and as stated previously is of little value. When giving attention to children, two things can be kept in mind:

- A simple statement, free of your evaluation, tells the child you noticed.
- A question about the child's activity tells the child you are interested.

Competition Is Inappropriate

Descriptive statements carry no implications that any one child is better than another. Promoting competition among young children establishes an uneasy learning environment. Children cannot appreciate the process of learning, or their own uniqueness, if adults imply that they should try to be better than someone else. The only competition or comparison that enhances development occurs when a child's progress is measured against that child's own earlier performance: for example, "You are really learning colours. Now you know all the colour names of the blocks."

Withholding or Withdrawing Reinforcers

Another form of adult social reinforcement, much less pleasant to practise, is taking away (withdrawing or withholding) something that is important to a child—a favourite toy, activity, playmate, or the attention of an important adult. Withholding reinforcement is used when an inappropriate behaviour is not decreasing in spite of teachers' efforts. (Recall the staff's first efforts to redirect James, with the resulting increase in flitting about.) Though punishment itself will not be discussed until later, withdrawing or withholding reinforcement, in one sense, is a form of punishment. It has less damaging side effects than does physical or verbal punishment, however. It is also more effective. Equally important, it cuts down on the emotional conflict between adult and child that so often accompanies other forms of punishment. In early childhood settings, withholding attention and other reinforcers can be accomplished in several ways:

- Teachers may ignore an incident and act as if they do not see the undesirable behaviour (as long as the child is not endangering himself or others). Ignoring can be accomplished by turning away for the moment and showing interest in another child or activity.
- Teachers may remove materials or equipment if a child continues to misuse them.
- Teachers may remove the child from play with other children or from an activity.

It will be stressed again and again in this book that in a well-arranged and developmentally appropriate early learning environment, the need for any kind of negative procedure should be rare. Hence the rationale for including in this text an entire chapter (Chapter 15) on appropriate environmental arrangements and the consequent positive effect on children's behaviour.

Incompatible Behaviours

Incompatible behaviours are two or more responses that cannot occur together. An inappropriate behaviour cannot occur at the same time that an appropriate behaviour is occurring. For example, it is impossible for children to walk and run at the same time. Therefore, if the rule is "Walking in the classroom," teachers should turn their attention (social reinforcement) to children who are remembering to walk. The child who runs, after a first reminder, receives no further teacher attention until the running stops (withholding attention). Rules should always be stated in a positive manner; that is, teachers should state the behaviour they want to see rather than the behaviour they are trying to eliminate. Here are some other examples: listening is incompatible with talking; making a neutral comment is incompatible with teasing; waiting for the cookie basket to be passed is incompatible with snatching cookies. In other words, whenever a child is not behaving inappropriately, he or she is engaging in some kind of appropriate behaviour (even if it is only standing and watching for a moment). Recognizing this gives teachers the opportunity to respond to something appropriate rather than wasting their time and emotional energy on behaviours that are inappropriate.

Withholding attention from behaviours that are maladaptive or inappropriate need not (and should not) result in a child getting appreciably less adult attention. Children who misbehave tend to be attention seekers; ignoring them along with their inappropriate behaviours often results in more varied and even greater inappropriateness as they increase their efforts to get attention. The strategy is for teachers to attend to other, more appropriate (or at least, less objectionable) behaviours in which the child engages. The best behaviours for teachers to reinforce are those that are incompatible with the inappropriate behaviours. James, once again, will be the example:

James's constant flitting about the classroom prevented him from focusing on any one activity. In other words, flitting and focusing are incompatible behaviours. Teachers therefore stopped attending to his flitting and instead paid attention to those moments, brief as they might be, when he became engaged in an activity. The teacher in charge of the activity provided interest and support as long as James was engaged. When he left, that teacher and the others immediately turned their attention elsewhere, until such time as he lingered again, even briefly, with another activity. As noted earlier, James's attention span soon began to show rapid and marked improvement.

SUPPORT THE CHILD WHEN THE CHILD IS DOING SOMETHING POSITIVE

One problem that often occurs in early childhood settings is that the focus on punishment is too strong. Adults tend to remain fairly neutral until a child does something the adult considers inappropriate. *Then* the child is likely to get a great deal of attention, but of a punishing kind that will do little to eliminate the unacceptable behaviour. It is important to respond positively to a child who is engaged in positive or appropriate behaviours. An important phrase that still remains true is "Catch the child being good" (Harris, Wolf, & Baer, 1964).

Chapter 11 | THE DEVELOPMENTAL BEHAVIOURAL APPROACH

Case Study ▪ Marie's behaviour ▪

Marie is a four-year-old child with autism. Her language has improved significantly in the past year, but she still exhibits inappropriate behaviour on occasion. Marie is eating lunch at home while watching her favourite television show. Her mother asks her to take one more bite. Marie says no and dumps her remaining lunch on the floor. Her mother keeps her cool, walks over to turn off the television, hands Marie a paper towel, and calmly requests that Marie clean up the food. What makes this an effective strategy? What does Marie's mother need to do after Marie cleans up the food? What if Marie whines and says no?

Adults should freely and spontaneously respond to (reinforce) the many appropriate things that children do all day long. It is almost impossible for a child to be good and bad at the same time. Appropriate behaviours, therefore, have the potential of crowding out inappropriate behaviours. The strategy is to focus very little attention on what adults have agreed are inappropriate acts. The same amount of attention is directed instead to almost anything else the child does. Adults need spend no additional time on the child. They simply spend the time in ways that are more effective and certainly more pleasant for all (see photo, below).

Preventive discipline a child-management procedure for arranging the environment in ways that reduce the occurrence of inappropriate behaviours and increase the occurrence of appropriate behaviours

Discipline versus Punishment

The goal of discipline is self-discipline. Discipline techniques used by teachers should support the child in developing control of his or her own behaviour. As children mature, they become more aware of the range of consequences that may result from their actions, enabling them to adapt their behaviour on their own.

Children with challenging behaviours need guidance that reduces prejudice and promotes positive outcomes (Neilson, Olive, Donovan, & McEvoy, 1998). Discipline is most effective when it is based on anticipation. Through their observations of children and their knowledge of child development, teachers can anticipate potential trouble spots and deal with them *before* they occur. In other words, adults prevent mishaps; hence the often used term **preventive discipline**.

Preventive discipline depends on what teachers do and say to forestall trouble (in behavioural terms, this is referred to as *arranging antecedents*). How the learning environment is arranged can be one form of preventive discipline (see Chapter 15). By placing the drying rack next to the easel, for example, teachers help children avoid the many problems (and tension-provoking reminders) associated with carrying a dripping painting across the floor.

By providing a parking place for wheel toys (instead of letting children abandon them "mid-road"), teachers help children avoid injuring others or getting into

It is important to respond positively when children are engaged in positive behaviours.

Courtesy of Bloorview—Scarborough Site

angry exchanges as to which child really owns a piece of equipment. The point to be underscored is this: *Environmental arrangements are a major determinant of children's behaviour and of children's learning.* Preventive discipline accomplishes the following:

- It communicates to children how to behave according to developmentally appropriate expectations, and then facilitates children's efforts to do so.

- It makes it easy for children to learn the vast number of behaviours and skills necessary to grow up to be confident and competent in a world that expects so much of young children and the adults who care for them.

- It helps children avoid unnecessary and ego-deflating errors that squander children's time and self-esteem.

- It ensures a positive environment in which teachers enjoy teaching and children enjoy learning.

Punishment, in terms of its common definition, consists of those adult behaviours that emotionally or physically hurt children—scolding, nagging, yelling, ridiculing, criticizing, isolating, slapping, shaking, and spanking. As noted earlier, punishing children is *not* an effective way of managing them. True, punishment often stops an undesirable behaviour at the moment. However, it usually is a short-lived victory for the adult and one that tends to backfire. Yelling at children is an example. Most children will stop, for the time being, whatever they are doing that is causing them to be yelled at. That behaviour, however, is almost sure to return again and again under various circumstances and often as soon as the adult who was yelling at them leaves the scene.

In many instances, punishment has undesirable side effects. In the yelling example, the behaviour that the adult does not like is stopped at the time. This reinforces the adult for yelling at the child. The result? The adult yells at the child all the more. In addition, the adult is modelling yelling, literally teaching inappropriate yelling behaviour to the child: "Children who are yelled at yell back on other occasions. So, to a considerable degree, you get back what you give" (Bee & Boyd, 2012, p. 499).

The same holds true of spanking or other forms of physical punishment. In a classic study by Bandura (1973), it was found that children who are spanked frequently, or otherwise physically punished, become highly aggressive. Other children react very differently. Some behave as though they were tightly coiled springs. They often behave well at home or school, but once out from under adults' eyes, they seem to explode into a range of forbidden behaviours. Still other children appear troubled, turn inward, hold back, and become passive. It is as if they fear that whatever they do will result in ridicule, criticism, or some form of physical punishment. In general, punishment leads to loss of self-confidence and self-esteem. Children who are frequently punished (either verbally or physically punished) do not feel good about themselves or their world. Such feelings have a negative effect on all aspects of their development.

Stopping a Harmful Behaviour

All children must be stopped (i.e., have limits set) on occasion. Children who are endangering themselves or others, or causing serious disruptions at home or in the classroom, must be controlled. For many children, a reminder or a mild verbal reprimand is enough. This is especially effective in classrooms and homes where preventive discipline is practised, where children receive adequate amounts of positive attention for the good things they do all day long. When a child does not respond to ordinary reminders, the teacher may need to use a firmer tone of voice and more definitive words.

Example:

"No! Janie, I can't let you push Tammy off the tricycle. That can hurt Tammy."

When none of this works, the child may have to be removed from this activity—a form of discipline *that seldom needs to happen.*

Withdrawing the Child

Renewal time a discipline technique that gives a child the message that he or she needs some time to calm down and to gain some inner control

Clare Cherry (1983) used the term **renewal time**, stating that "time out is a widely used term, but it tends to be overused, as it can be applied to many different kinds of situations. It often characterizes punitive isolation" (p. 137). Cherry went on to say, "I prefer the term renewal time. It is easy to say and it means what I really want—a chance for the inner self to become renewed, as opposed to the whole self being 'out.'"

In this form of discipline, the message given to the child is that he or she needs some time to calm down and to gain some inner control. Examples of renewal time are contained in these statements:

- "Playing alone for a little while will help you settle down."
- "You may read a book quietly or play quietly, but you need time by yourself because you were hurting (disturbing, etc.) other children."
- "You need some time to calm down. You were getting too wild and excited. You need to play quietly on your own for a while until you are calmer."

Giving choices also empowers a child:

- "You need to sit and watch, or you can play quietly somewhere."

The goal is (as it should be with all forms of discipline) to help children become self-managing. The process to follow in positive discipline is this:

1. Tell the child what is problematic about the child's behaviour, explaining why he or she is being asked to change what he or she is doing.

2. If the child does not respond, the teacher needs to tell the child again, this time explaining the consequences to the child if the inappropriate behaviour continues.

Example:

A child is throwing sand at another child. The teacher says, "Please keep the sand in the sandbox, Tony. If you throw the sand it could get in someone's eyes and hurt them." Tony continues to throw the sand. The teacher then says, "Tony, the sand needs to stay in the sandbox. If you keep on throwing sand, I am going to have to ask you to leave the sandbox. I don't want any of your friends to get hurt."

The teacher clearly explains to Tony *what* is inappropriate about his behaviour, *why* she feels that this behaviour cannot continue, and the *limit* she will have to place if he does not stop the behaviour on his own. Children often realize that they have made a mistake in self-management but may not yet have developed the inner control needed to change their behaviour. When they are asked to leave a play situation, the adult is letting them know that it is important to work on developing this control if they want to remain in their chosen play situations. To help children remember, the teacher can talk with the children about what happened and how they could have handled the situation more effectively.

Basic guidelines for withdrawing a child include the following:

- The behaviour is harmful to the child (this includes physical hurt as well as situations in which a child is becoming emotionally overstimulated).

- The behaviour is likely to be harmful to another child.

- The behaviour is likely to harm property.

Time-out should be used only as a last resort. It is the extreme form of withdrawing reinforcement. *Time-out* means removing the child from all reinforcement, including teacher attention, other children, materials, and equipment. *Time-out should be used only with the permission of the parent and the consultants.* It should be reserved for seriously inappropriate behaviours (habitual antisocial behaviours, extreme temper tantrums, etc.) that have not responded to less severe forms of behaviour management. Children who do not comprehend verbal and problem-solving strategies for changing behaviour may need time-out to define the limits being set. (Note: Many provinces and territories have specific guidelines that must be followed for use of specific behavioural practices, including time-out.)

On those occasions when time-out has to be used, the time-out period should be short. After the child has begun to self-regulate, the amount of minutes for time-out should not exceed the child's age (e.g., for three-year-olds, three minutes would be the maximum). During the time-out process, adults in the room do not respond to the child. The child should be in a safe area with minimal stimulation and in clear view of the teacher. Other children should be reassured that the child will rejoin the group when he or she is calm. *A written plan that monitors the frequency and duration of time-out should be maintained.*

An important reminder: Children do not learn *what to do* in time-out; they learn only *what not to do*. If children are to learn how to work and play with each other and with materials, they need to be involved (Schickedanz, Schickedanz, & Forsyth, 1982). It is in the classroom, *not in time-out*, that teachers can help children learn appropriate ways of responding (see photo, below). Good teachers seldom need to use time-out or any other punishment procedure when preventive discipline is the practice and all children receive adequate amounts of positive

It is in the classroom, *not in time-out*, that teachers help children learn appropriate ways of behaving.

Courtesy of Bloorview—Scarborough Site

attention. It must be remembered, however, that what is an *adequate amount* will vary from child to child, depending on individual differences.

Task Analysis

Task analysis the process of breaking down a complex task into smaller units so that learning can occur more easily

Task analysis is a teaching procedure that grew out of the behavioural concept of *shaping* new responses. It is a particularly important teaching strategy to use when a child is unable to accomplish a task within a time period that is considered appropriate for the child's development. Shaping of behaviour is the process of reinforcing *successive approximations* (a series of small steps) toward the eventual mastery of a complex behaviour. In analyzing any kind of a task—tying shoes, counting bears, printing letters, defending possessions, making friends—the first requirement is to break the task down into its step-by-step components. The steps must be small and logical. They also must be in sequence, progressing from the known, simple, and easy to the more difficult and complex. Small steps provide frequent opportunities for success. Many small steps, and therefore many small successes, help the child avoid unnecessary frustrations. Too many frustrations are defeating to young learners and even more defeating for children who have special needs.

Observation and Task Analysis

In preparing to analyze a task, early childhood teachers often find it helpful to watch a young child perform the task first. It is especially instructive to watch a child who has only recently mastered a particular skill. The child's motor coordination and general approach to the problem are likely to be more finely sequenced and developmentally appropriate than are those of an older child or an adult performing the same task. When adapting a procedure to an individual child, the starting point is determined by observing that child. The rule is to start where the child is, with what the child can do. This provides the child with a successful experience at the start. It also enables the teacher to make positive comments immediately, thus getting the new learning off to a good start.

It is true that the first step may be far removed from what is seen as the end behaviour. Many times it is nothing more than a child standing and watching an activity that has been targeted as a developmentally necessary skill for that child; this, however, is but a first step, an opportunity for a teacher to reinforce a first approximation to a more complex skill. A teacher can stand companionably close, watch with the child, and comment briefly on some aspect of the activity. An example of a task analysis for hanging a coat appears in Figure 11–1.

FIGURE 11-1

Task Analysis for Hanging a Coat

1. Child walks to cubby
2. Child removes coat (able to do this)
3. Child finds loop in coat
4. Child puts finger in loop
5. Child puts loop onto hook

Source: © Cengage Learning

The ability to break a task down into small steps and teach it in a systematic manner is a critical skill for early childhood educators. This is especially valuable when working with children with special needs. A teacher can use the task analysis to collect information (data) on the progress a child is making. These data can be used to determine the level of prompting the child needs to complete the task. This allows the teacher to plan effectively how to move the child toward completing the task independently. See Figures 11–2 and 11–3 for

FIGURE 11-2 Task Analysis and Data Sheet Illustrating Level of Prompting Required for a Task

Child: Ricky

Prompts: V = verbal   G = gesture   P = physical   I = independently

STEPS	DATES	1/12	1/14	1/20	1/22
Child walks to cubby		V	V	V	V
Child removes coat (able to do this)		I	I	I	I
Child finds loop in coat		P	P	P	P
Child puts finger in loop		P	P	G	I
Child puts loop onto hook		P	G	G	I

Source: © Cengage Learning

FIGURE 11-3 Blank Task Analysis Data Sheet

Child: _____

Prompts: V = verbal   G = gesture   P = physical   I = independently

STEPS	DATES			

Source: © Cengage Learning

an example of a data sheet that can be used for listing the steps of a task and collecting data.

The following case study describes the application of the task analysis process.

TASK ANALYSIS: LADDER-CLIMBING SEQUENCE
Planning Process

1. Assess child's abilities and needs.
   Before a task can be selected for a child to perform, a careful assessment of the child's current abilities and skills must be completed.

Case History

Matthew would soon be four years old. He was a pale, slow-moving child who seldom played with other children. He rarely engaged in the vigorous outdoor play activities typical of the rest of the group. Teachers agreed, based on a series of observations, that it would help Matthew's overall development if he were to learn to use the climbing equipment. However, he resisted all of their efforts to involve him in climbing activities. Below is a condensed account of the step-by-step procedures that resulted in Matthew's becoming not only an active climber, but also a more sociable four-year-old.

2. Set a goal, objectives, and the task.
   a. *Set a goal.* Set a goal and then identify the task to be performed by the child. The goal in the above example might be developing motor skills for outdoor play.
   b. *Identify objectives.* For example, the child will independently climb up to the top of the slide in the playground.
   c. *Set the task.* The task in this case is climbing a ladder.

3. Determine the sequential steps necessary for performing the task.
   The child follows this sequence of steps when climbing a ladder:
   a. looks at ladder
   b. approaches ladder
   c. places hands on rails of ladder
   d. places dominant foot on lower rung
   e. pulls body up with arms while at the same time pressing down with the dominant foot
   f. places other foot on bottom rung
   g. moves dominant hand up one rung
   h. moves dominant foot up to the next rung
   i. repeats above steps

4. Decide on an implementation plan.
   Develop a plan and decide on how this plan will be carried out. Teachers need to agree on the following:
   a. the step in the sequence with which to begin
   b. the teaching strategies that are most appropriate for this child
   c. the type of reinforcement to be provided
   d. when and where the task will be performed

5. Implement the plan.

   A short ladder with broad steps was set up against play equipment that Matthew often wandered past. A teacher was stationed near the ladder, supervising children playing in the area.

   a. Whenever Matthew wandered by, the teacher spoke to him and chatted with him. Often he drew closer, watching the children climbing about. When he stopped watching the children and looked as if he were about to move away, the teacher became busy with the other children.

   b. As Matthew stopped to chat more frequently and for longer periods of time, he sometimes leaned against or put his hand on the ladder. Soon the teacher began to chat with Matthew only when he was touching the ladder.

   c. Next, whenever Matthew was leaning on the ladder, the teacher made up a game, placing one of Matthew's feet on the lowest rung and then taking it off. Matthew delighted in the game. Soon he was putting his own foot on the ladder.

   d. Before long, Matthew himself was putting both feet on the bottom rung of the ladder. The teacher then changed the game to feet on and off the second rung.

   e. In this game-like atmosphere, where the teacher provided both physical and verbal reinforcement, Matthew was soon climbing up and down the ladder.

   f. The ladder was later moved to different locations. Matthew continued to climb on it with only occasional attention from teachers. It appeared that the activity itself had become fun for Matthew and therefore self-reinforcing.

   g. The next step was to place the ladder against another big piece of climbing equipment. As Matthew began to make the transition from the familiar ladder to the big piece of equipment, teachers once again provided an abundance of physical and verbal support.

By the ninth day of the program, Matthew was spending more than half of the outdoor play time in a variety of climbing activities. At mid-year he was as active and involved outdoors as any child in the group. Presumably, vigorous outdoor play with other children had become a pleasurable activity that would continue to be self-reinforcing.

Using Task Analysis for Toilet Training

As noted at the outset, all self-help/care skills are learned. It follows, then, that all self-help/care skills can be taught. Success depends, in part, on physiological maturity, especially of the sphincter muscles, when toilet training a child.

Toilet training, once thought to be totally dependent on maturation, can be *task analyzed* and taught in its component parts. With some children, *each part*, in turn, may need to be task analyzed and taught step by step. Ordinary toilet training includes many steps. It starts with getting into the bathroom, pulling the pants down, and getting up onto the toilet. It concludes with getting off the toilet, pulling clothes up, and flushing. What could be simpler? Yet, for many young children, one or more of the steps may present great difficulty. Even the seemingly simple task of getting on and off the toilet may need to be broken down into smaller steps. For sure, using toilet tissue effectively is a challenge for all young children! Teachers may require additional information on toilet training children who are **nonambulatory** or have other special concerns.

STEP-BY-STEP PLANNING In teaching any self-help/care skill, the teacher must know exactly where each child is in that particular skill sequence. This can be accomplished by asking a simple question about each step: Can the child do it? If yes, the teacher can proceed to the next step; if no, the teacher figures out the substeps appropriate for that child at that point in the sequence. Figure 11–4 shows the procedure for the first two or three steps in the toilet-training tasks listed above.

Chaining in Task Analysis

Self-help/care tasks, such as toileting, shoe lacing, and feeding oneself, are all examples of tasks comprising a set of smaller behaviours (skills), chained (sequenced) together and organized into what seems to be a single task. When the chaining concept is adapted to teaching self-help/care skills, the child is helped to learn one response, one link of the skill chain at a time. Once the child is performing the first component in the chain, the next step (or link) is introduced. Single components of the chain are added one by one until the child can perform all of them, in order, from start to finish.

Step-by-step learning can be made easier if the child can see the entire chain being performed (see Chapters 16 and 18 for learning through observation and modelling).

FIGURE 11-4 Skill Sequence for Independent Toileting

On many tasks, forward chaining and backward chaining are equally successful. The choice depends on the particular task and level of skill the child displays. In **forward chaining**, the teacher helps the child learn the first step in the chain, then the second, and so on. In **backward chaining**, instruction begins with the last step and progresses in reverse to the first component.

The child in the following example of zipping has fairly well-developed fine motor skills; the teacher, therefore, has broken the task into only six component parts (a six-step task analysis). The steps are suitable for teaching the task with either a forward- or a backward-chaining approach. Throughout both forward and backward chaining, the teacher will demonstrate or provide **manual prompts** as needed.

Step 1. With both hands, the bottom front edges of the coat are brought together at the bottom.

Step 2. The zipper foot is inserted into the zipper catch.

Step 3. The zipper foot is seated in the catch by pushing up and down with opposing movements of each hand.

Step 4. The tab on the zipper is grasped between thumb and forefinger.

Step 5. The bottom of the coat at the zipper catch is held with one hand while the zipper tab is pulled to the top, with the other hand holding the zipper tab.

Step 6. The zipper tab is pushed down firmly into locked position.

In backward chaining, the child would first master step 6, then 5, and so on, back to step 1. The major advantage of backward chaining is that the child is always reinforced by task completion, even in the first lesson. Accomplishing the last step sends a reinforcing message to the child that the time has come to move on to something more interesting. At some point, for most children, the chain becomes one integrated skill they scarcely need to think about.

Forward chaining breaking a task down into a series of small steps and teaching the first step first

Backward chaining teaching starts with the last step of a learning sequence

Manual prompts when the teacher's hand is around the learner's and actually putting the learner through the motions (may also be referred to as "hand over hand")

Practical Considerations When Using Task Analysis in Teaching Self-Help/Care Skills

In many other dressing and self-help/care tasks, it is important that the adult work from behind the child. This ensures that the teacher's hands are performing the hand and finger movements in the same way that the child will be expected to reproduce them. Young children do not have a well-developed sense of spatial orientation or a concept of reversibility. Teachers' demonstrations, therefore, must be conducted from the child's perspective. For this reason and others, the use of lacing, buttoning, and zipping boards for children to practise on has been questioned. It is too confusing for many children to try to reverse and transfer the motions learned in practice sessions to their own bodies (Cook, Tessier, & Klein, 2004).

A word about the importance of suitable clothing when learning self-help/care skills: Children who are being toilet trained need both underpants and outer pants with elastic at the top so that they can be pulled down easily. Children who are learning to dress themselves can learn more easily if their clothing has big, sturdy zippers that work; large buttons and unrestricted buttonholes; and simple fastenings, such as Velcro on belts, shoes, and overalls. When children are having prolonged difficulty in learning to dress themselves, temporarily providing clothing a size or two too big is sometimes a help. Obviously, teachers should never presume to tell parents how to dress their children. However, parents often welcome suggestions that help their children learn more easily.

Prompting, Cueing, and Fading

Task analysis often needs to be accompanied by, and reinforced with, physical and verbal assistance referred to as *prompting and cueing*. Prompts and cues help all children, and especially children with developmental differences, acquire a skill they may be having trouble with. *Fading* is the process of gradually and systematically reducing assistance (the prompting and cueing) as much and as soon as possible without interfering with the child's progress. The goal is for the child to learn to perform the task as independently as is feasible. To illustrate these procedures, the task of learning to hang up a coat is described here:

1. The teacher accompanies the child to the cubby or locker and gives verbal cues: "Here is your locker. Here is the hook for your coat."

2. The teacher explains and demonstrates: "This is the loop that keeps your coat on the hook. It goes over the hook like this."

3. Taking the coat off the hook but holding it open, the teacher prompts, "Can you find the loop?"

4. When the child finds the loop, the teacher says, "Right. Now you can put your finger into it, just as I did."

5. The teacher continues, "Now, slip the loop over the hook." If the child cannot yet coordinate the necessary movements, the teacher guides the child's hand (provides a manual prompt).

6. After a few tries the teacher is able to withdraw physical assistance the instant before the loop goes over the hook and so can say to the child, "Look at that! You hung up your coat. Good for you."

In this example, physical assistance was gradually reduced while verbal prompts and cues and positive comments were continued. As the child got better at the task, verbal help was also reduced but only as the child showed near mastery of each step. Some tasks and some children need even smaller, more specific steps and special kinds of assistance.

Manual prompting is a common form of special assistance leading to skill mastery. Manual prompting, sometimes referred to as *hand over hand*, consists of positioning the adult's hand around the child's and actually putting the child through the motions. Once the child has the feel of the movements, manual prompting is gradually reduced.

Teachers must guard against overwhelming children with directions when helping them learn a complex task. Directions, like rules, should be kept to a minimum. They should be given only if the teacher is prepared to help the child carry through with additional prompting, cueing, and physical assistance. As with rules, *directions are more effective if worded positively*. It is more informative and helpful to say, "Hold tight with both hands" than it is to say, "Be careful. Don't fall." The latter statement provides children with no information about what they *should* be doing. In all cases, the primary goal is to encourage children's independence, especially in children with special needs. Therefore, teachers provide just enough assistance to ensure children's success but not so much as to promote overdependence.

And now a few words of caution: Slow down. Be patient. Adults best promote children's independence by waiting, allowing children adequate time to figure out what they are going to do next and how they will do it. This is in contrast to what happens all too often: The adult says, "Put on your sock." The young child is still trying to figure out which is the open end of the sock when the adult grabs it and expertly puts it on the child's foot. What message does this convey to the child?

Amount and Timing of Reinforcement

How much reinforcement is enough? The answer varies from child to child and task to task. Almost continual reinforcement—feedback—may be needed when a child is beginning to learn something new. Every time the new behaviour (or an approximation to the new behaviour) occurs, the adult tries to respond in some way. At times, smiling and nodding may be all a teacher can take the time to do (see photo, right). As in the shaping and prompting examples, adult attention is gradually reduced as the child becomes more able. The goal, as always, is that the child's success (intrinsic motivation) takes over, keeping the child eager to continue learning. To accomplish this, a balance must be achieved: not so much adult attention that the child becomes dependent, but enough so learning continues until the skill is well established and intrinsically reinforcing.

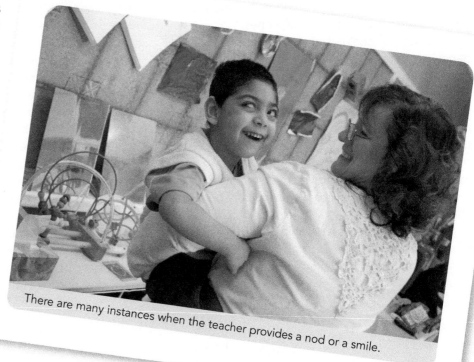

There are many instances when the teacher provides a nod or a smile.

Courtesy of Bloorview—Scarborough Site

Summary

Developmental concepts, such as the "problem of the match" and "learning from success," as well as behavioural principles, have blended into today's well-articulated early childhood teaching practices. The effectiveness of an early education program is demonstrated by changes in children's behaviour. To have healthy development, ongoing changes in behaviour must occur. The blend of developmental and behavioural principles and practices is good for all children and particularly important in inclusive environments where the range of skill levels is extensive. The blend of practices demonstrates that all children can learn; if a child is not learning, the responsibility is placed squarely on the program, not on the child.

In the behavioural perspective, systematic reinforcement procedures—if imposed within an appropriate structure—account for children's learning (or failure to learn). The principles can be put into an ABC format (A stands for antecedents; B stands for the child's behaviour; C stands for consequences). Reinforcements (consequences) are negative or positive. Positive reinforcement is the teacher's best tool. It is readily available through teachers' assistance, genuine interest, and positive reactions to each child and each child's activities. Positive reinforcement also resides in the interesting and appropriate materials and activities provided by teachers.

In some instances, reinforcers must be withheld or withdrawn so that a child does not get attention for behaviours that are detrimental to his or her development. When teachers must withhold reinforcement for an inappropriate behaviour, it is important that they double their efforts to give the child positive attention for useful behaviours. When they do so, inappropriate behaviours are likely to be *crowded out* by more appropriate ones.

Preventive discipline supports appropriate behaviour by guiding children before problems occur.

Renewal time involves removing a child from a situation that he or she is not able to cope with and directing him or her to a quiet area to play alone until he or she is able to rejoin the group. This is the preferred form of withdrawal. Time-out is used only in those infrequent situations where systematic positive practices have failed to produce necessary behaviour changes.

Punishment is the least desirable and least effective of all forms of child management. Though the punished behaviour may stop for the moment, it usually returns again and again. Frequent punishment has many undesirable side effects, including heightened aggressiveness and diminishing self-esteem.

Other educational practices related to reinforcement procedures include task analysis and learning through observation (modelling), a principle derived from social learning theory. Task analysis is the process of breaking a learning task into small sequential steps for those children who need special help in the form of reduced frustration and more frequent successes. Step-by-step learning is further facilitated with prompting and cueing, which can be reduced gradually as the child gains mastery of a task. Self-help/care skills can be taught effectively through task analysis using either forward or backward chaining. In every kind of learning situation, teachers provide encouragement and descriptive praise to the degree that is appropriate for individual children, rather than foster competitiveness.

Resources

Adventure Place

http://www.adventureplace.ca

Adventure Place is a child and family centre that provides prevention, early intervention, and treatment services to children and their families.

Child Development Institute

http://www.childdevelop.ca

The Child Development Institute (CDI) is an accredited children's mental health agency providing a range of services for children up to age 12 and their families.

Children, Youth and Family Consortium

http://www.cyfc.umn.edu

The Children, Youth and Family Consortium's electronic clearinghouse is a forum for sharing information and exchanging ideas. The wide range of topics include resources for children and families; youth; violence; children's health; chemical dependency; ADHD; disabilities; family economics; gay, lesbian, transgender, and bisexual issues; child care; statistics on children; and government resources.

Medbroadcast Corporation

http://www.medbroadcast.com

This Vancouver organization specializes in providing online medical information and services. It covers a wide range of topics relevant to families.

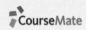 CourseMate Access an interactive ebook and chapter-specific interactive learning tools, including flashcards, quizzes, videos, and more, in the *Inclusion in Early Childhood Programs* CourseMate. Visit NELSONbrain.com to log in, register, or purchase access.

Identification and the Individual Program Plan (IPP)

12

....

OBJECTIVES

After studying the material in this chapter, the student will be able to

- Explain why scores obtained on all tests given to young children should be viewed with caution, even skepticism.
- Discuss the role of the early childhood teacher in the identification of developmental differences and in the IPP process.
- Identify different observational recording techniques and give appropriate examples for application.
- Summarize each of the major components of an IPP.

KEY CONCEPTS AND TERMS

appreciative inquiry process

bias-free screening and assessment

criterion-referenced tests

individual program plan (IPP)

interdisciplinary

norm-referenced tests

portfolio

reliable and valid tests

transdisciplinary

Introduction

The identification of developmental differences is a responsibility of everyone associated with infants and young children and their families. Though some provinces and territories in Canada provide screening of newborn babies and follow-up home visits by public health nurses, no federal legislation requires early screening and assessment of an infant's development. Brain studies by McCain and Mustard (1999) and their follow-up reports, including the *Early Years Study 3* (McCain, Mustard, & McCuaig, 2011), give us powerful evidence that the early years of development from conception to age six, particularly the first three years of life, set the competence and coping skills that will affect future learning, behaviour, and health. Early identification of special needs is critical in order to access early intervention and specialized programming.

The focus of this chapter is on these two issues: early identification of developmental differences and the delivery of special services through the individual program plan (IPP).

The Process of Early Identification

Identification of developmental differences can take place any time from a few weeks after conception to adulthood (age 18). These years are formally recognized as the developmental period. Early identification of differences is not limited to the first five to eight years of life. A child may appear to be healthy up to age 12 or 15, and then show first-time symptoms of a "disability" that has an impact on development (juvenile rheumatoid arthritis, for example). The older child is as much in need of early identification of an emerging condition as is a two-year-old showing first-time symptoms of any kind. In both cases, early identification should lead to prompt treatment. In turn, prompt treatment can reduce the level of involvement and prevent the condition from affecting other areas of development.

The identification of developmental differences or potential developmental differences involves several steps: screening, assessment, diagnosis, and evaluation. The first two of these steps in the identification process will be discussed in this chapter.

Early Identification

In Canada, because of the universal health-care program, the identification of children who have developmental differences falls mainly on the shoulders of the medical profession:

- The doctor or midwife who delivers the baby.
- The nurses who observe the baby directly after birth.
- The family physician or pediatrician who usually sees the child at regular intervals.

Programs and services available through community public health departments, medical centres, and community early intervention services seek to identify those children who may require further assessment to ensure early identification of developmental differences.

Screening is the process of identifying *possible* differences in a child's development that may indicate the need for a more thorough assessment or specific support (see photo, below). Screening can be carried out by people without highly specialized training and is based on various observation techniques and screening tools. *Assessment* is the process used to measure a child's performance or development, which may be based on observations, tests, or the child's behaviour. Specially trained early childhood resource teachers/early interventionists are often able to conduct informal functional assessments that can provide information to support appropriate programming. However, the use of standardized assessment techniques to obtain a more definitive diagnosis requires a licensed clinician.

Screening

Screening is important in the identification of developmental differences (or potential differences). Screening tests describe a child's level of performance, but *only at that point in time* (Allen & Marotz, 2012). Comprehensive screening evaluates the child's current abilities and needs in all areas of development. If areas of concern are identified during routine developmental screening, clinical assessments are indicated.

Several points should be emphasized:

- Accurate screening results can be achieved only with tests that are **reliable and valid** and that are developed specifically for use with young children. In the absence of valid instruments, testing is of no value (National Association of Early Childhood Specialists, 2003; NAEYC, 1988).

- Results from screening tests should not be confused with assessment. They do not constitute a diagnosis and should never be used as a basis for planning an intervention program.

- Follow-through is essential. "Identifying children with potential problems is only the first step; encouraging families to seek further assessment for their child is the next" (Lynch & Hanson, 2011).

PARENTS AS PARTNERS IN SCREENING Parents have a wealth of firsthand knowledge about their children. They know what their child can and cannot do in everyday life. Often, they are the first to suspect an issue with their child's development even if unable to specify its nature clearly. It is not unusual to encounter parents who question the development of their child as they compare their child's progress to that of siblings, playmates, or other family members. They do not necessarily recognize, for example, a hearing loss, but they might report to the health-care provider that their child acts strange or "talks funny."

A hearing loss, as well as a number of other subtle differences, may not show up during a routine medical checkup. When a developmental difference

Reliable and valid tests reliability relates to consistency—how accurate, dependable, and predictable a test is; validity refers to how accurately a test measures that which it purports to measure

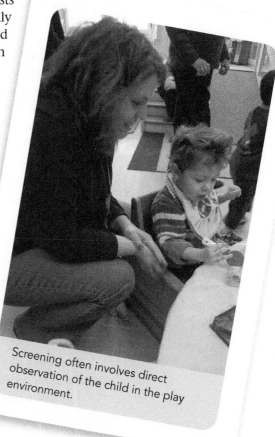

Screening often involves direct observation of the child in the play environment.

Courtesy of Bloorview—Scarborough Site

cannot be pinpointed by the clinician, parents sometimes are led to believe that "nothing is wrong with their child." They are often advised to go home and relax, to get over being so anxious. Ignoring parents' observations, however, is not in the best interest of the child. It is crucial that professionals pay close attention to the concerns raised by parents, which will contribute to a successful experience for the child within a child care setting. Parents are more likely to work collaboratively with teachers if they believe their input is valued by the team. Failing to recognize a parent's concern in its early stages may result in a long-range negative impact on the child's development.

CULTURAL, ETHNIC, AND LINGUISTIC DIFFERENCES Family customs, beliefs, and language influence a child's performance on screening tests (Lynch & Hanson, 2011). A child's responses may be scored as wrong even when they are right according to the family's values. The result may be an invalid (false) evaluation, suggesting that there is cause to be concerned about the child's development when no issue exists. Invalid assessment results became dismayingly apparent in the early days of special education reform, and they continue to be apparent in the overrepresentation of minority students in special education. These were the children who functioned perfectly well in their own communities and in their own language but had few skills and little background for functioning in schools designed to accommodate only the majority culture. As stated in the *Checklist for Quality Inclusive Education* (Langford, 1997),

> Age guidelines must also be looked at from a cultural perspective. Age guidelines suggest what is normal development during an age range. For example, a developmental checklist may state that children are expected to drink from a cup with one hand, unassisted between the ages of 13 and 24 months. However, in some cultures, children receive assistance with drinking until the middle years because interdependency between a mother/father and child is expected and encouraged. In this case, a developmental checklist item has not been sensitive to a wide range of child-rearing practices that influence the behaviour of a child. An educator may interpret a child's inability to drink from a cup independently as a problem rather than as a reflection of a cultural norm. As well, educators need to know that all children progress at vastly different rates of development or may lack experience with particular activities. (Resource Sheet Unit 13, p. 2)

To avoid similar errors, safeguards must be built into every step of the screening and assessment process. Dotsch (1992) made the following suggestions, which are still considered effective practice:

- Conduct assessments in the child's dominant language or in the first *and* second language.

- Rely on nonbiased observations and anecdotal information, as well as on formal modes.

- Adapt assessment methods for the specific diverse child/family from family input.

Examples of these safeguards are evident in the Nipissing District Developmental Screen (NDDS, 2011), in which some of the developmental outcomes are rated as not common to all cultures (see Figure 12–1).

TYPES OF SCREENING AND ASSESSMENT INSTRUMENTS Early childhood screening tests take many forms (see Figure 12–2). Some, like the Peabody Picture Vocabulary Test, focus on only one aspect of development and must be

FIGURE 12-1 Developmental Screen: 30 Months

Child's Name _____

Birth Date _____ Today's Date _____

The Nipissing District Developmental Screen is a checklist designed to help monitor your child's development.

✓   ✓

By _30 Months_ of Age, does your child ...

Yes No

☐ ☐ 1. Usually have healthy ears and seem to hear well?
☐ ☐ 2. Put a toy _in_ and put a toy _under_ when asked?
☐ ☐ 3. Join three words together, like "Me want ball"?
☐ ☐ 4. Recognize the names and pictures of most common items (i.e., "Show me the ball")?
☐ ☐ 5. Use pronouns I, you, me, and mine?
☐ ☐ 6. Lift and drink from a cup and replace it on the table?*
☐ ☐ 7. Imitate drawing vertical and horizontal lines? (Picture A)
☐ ☐ 8. Remove clothing already unzipped or unbuttoned?
☐ ☐ 9. Run without falling most of the time?
☐ ☐ 10. Kick a ball forward?
☐ ☐ 11. Jump off the floor with both feet? (Picture B)
☐ ☐ 12. Try to join in songs and rhymes with you?
☐ ☐ 13. Listen to simple stories?
☐ ☐ 14. Act out daily routines with toys (e.g., feed doll, sweep floor)?
☐ ☐ 15. Wait briefly for needs to be met (e.g., when placed in high chair at meal time)?
☐ ☐ 16. Recognize self in mirror or picture?

* Item may not be common to all cultures.

A   B

Always talk to your health care or child care professional if you have questions about your child's development or well-being.

Source: From Wylie, *Observing Young Children.* © 2004 Nelson Education Ltd. Reproduced by permission. www.cengage.com/permissions.

administered by a professionally trained speech pathologist. Others tests, such as the Denver Developmental Screening Test II (DDST), Diagnostic Inventory for Screening Children (DISC), and the NDDS attempt to assess all developmental areas.

Screening tests also are available that assess newborns and older infants (see photo, page 269), such as the APGAR (which assesses a newborn's colour, heart rate, reflex, muscle tone, and respiratory effort) and the Baley Scales of Infant Development. Other tests assess vision (Snellen Illiterate E), hearing (Pure Tone Audiometry), and cognitive skills (the Wechsler Preschool and Primary Scale of Intelligence, or WPPSI).

FIGURE 12-2

Developmental Preschool Screen

Materials	Starting Point by Month	Does the Child . . . . . ?			
Crayon, paper	36 & 37 months	Imitate both vertical and horizontal lines. Demonstrate. 1/3 trials	YES	NO	REFUSE
	38 months	Repeat phrases. "little boy" _____ "big red truck" _____ "nice warm coat" _____ 2/3 phrases	YES	NO	REFUSE
6 cubes	39 months	Match colours. "Find another one like this one—the same colour." blue _____ red _____ green _____ 2/3 matches	YES	NO	REFUSE
Picture book p.1	40 & 41 months	Answer questions using related words. "What is the boy/girl doing?" girl crying _____ boy swinging _____ girl sleeping _____ girl skipping _____ boy sitting _____ boy reading _____ 3/6 answers	YES	NO	REFUSE
	42 months	Stand on one foot for at least three seconds. Demonstrate. 1/3 trials	YES	NO	REFUSE
Picture book pp. 2–3	43 months	Discriminate pictures apple _____ cup _____ doll _____ baby _____ 3/4 pictures	YES	NO	REFUSE
Crayon, paper	44 months	Imitate a cross (+). Demonstrate. 1/3 trials	YES	NO	REFUSE

Source: Reprinted by permission of Marian Mainland. President, Mainland Consulting

A screening instrument noted for its interdisciplinary capabilities is the DIAL-3 (Developmental Indicators for the Assessment of Learning, third edition). DIAL makes the classroom teacher central to the screening process. The advantage is obvious: Except for parents, no one knows a child, or can interpret a child's responses, better.

Although there is no single test that identifies children who may be gifted, teachers play a major role in screening for giftedness. Several measures must be used. IQ scores, level of motivation, and creativity (which is difficult to define and measure) may be useful when backed up by a teacher's observations and insights into a child's developmental skills (see Chapter 7).

Criterion-referenced tests Some screening instruments are criterion-referenced tests; that is, a child's performance on each task is compared with a preselected standard (*criterion*). A child's performance is not compared with the performance of other children. Criterion-referenced test items might ask, for example, "Can the child lace and tie his or her own shoes? walk seven consecutive steps on a balance beam? match five shapes and colours in one minute?" The Brigance Diagnostic Inventory of Early Development is one example of a criterion-referenced test. It is used to assess children (birth to age seven) in 11 developmental domains. This test is developed to assist teachers in program planning rather than determining a child's eligibility or diagnostic category. The DASI (Developmental Assessment Screening Inventory) is useful for testing nonverbal children because it strictly focuses on evaluating performance.

Norm-referenced tests With norm-referenced tests the question becomes: How well does the child do, *compared with other children of the same age*, on tasks such as counting pennies, naming letters of the alphabet, or stacking six small cubes? Norm-referenced tests provide standardized information intended to relate to children's abilities at various ages. In other words, the norm-referenced test provides scales that compare the performance of one child with the averaged performance of other children of approximately the same age. Throughout the years, practitioners have come to realize that these tests are not necessarily reflective of the diverse cultural communities they may encounter, given that the tools were originally created for a fairly homogeneous culture at the time. The Battelle Developmental Inventory is an example of a norm-referenced assessment tool. It is useful because it is curriculum based. In other words, we can test a child, find the areas where the child lacks knowledge or ability, teach to that gap, and then retest to see if the missing information or skill has been acquired.

Several screening tests are available for assessing older infants as well as newborns.

Courtesy of Ryerson Early Learning Centre

Criterion-referenced tests assessments that describe a child's developmental level and progress according to a prescribed set of skills, tasks, and activities

Norm-referenced tests instruments that compare a child's developmental level with a normative sample of same-age peers

IQ tests Most intelligence tests (IQ tests) are norm referenced. Tests such as the Wechsler Intelligence Scale for Children (WISC) and the Stanford-Binet Intelligence Scales are sometimes given to young children. The purpose is to attempt to determine

- how much the child knows;
- how well the child solves problems; and
- how quickly the child can perform a variety of cognitive tasks.

The scores from IQ tests must be viewed with caution, even skepticism. A number of factors may lead to poor performance on an IQ test (or any other test, for that matter). The child may be tired, hungry, or unwell at the time. He or she may be anxious about the unfamiliar testing situation and the unfamiliar person giving the test. The child also may be answering in ways appropriate to his or her own language or culture but inappropriate in terms of standardized test responses (recall the earlier discussion on cultural differences). Furthermore, some children are hampered by an unidentified developmental or sensory impairment. A partial vision or hearing loss, for example, can interfere with a child's ability to respond appropriately; thus, the child's IQ score may falsely indicate an impairment of intellectual functioning.

IQ scores of young children *do not predict future intellectual performance.* In fact, they are not even good at assessing a young child's current intellectual capabilities. The major problem with IQ scores is that they do not account for the child's learning opportunities (or lack of learning opportunities). Neither do they reflect the quality of the learning experiences a child may have had. The use of a single test score to determine a child's intellectual competence must always be challenged. In fact, *more than one instrument* should be used in any screening program to ensure a valid picture of the child's development. Every child has the right to appropriate assessment. Assessment must be ongoing, developmentally appropriate, and supportive (Hyson, 2002).

The Teacher's Role in Early Identification

The teacher's role is critical in the identification of developmental differences in infants and young children (see photo, below) . It is teachers' recorded observations of children in many situations, over time, that provides a valid picture of each child's skills, capabilities, and special needs.

Teachers' Qualifications

Teachers have special qualifications and opportunities for experience in identifying children with diverse abilities. They should have knowledge of early development and understand its regularities and irregularities, enabling them to recognize developmental differences. Teachers also should have had sufficient training

Systematically recorded observations are extremely useful in identifying children with possible developmental differences.

© Cengage Learning

to allow them to provide infants and young children with sound developmental activities that bring out the best in each child during the assessment process.

Teachers are further advantaged in that they see children in a natural environment. In the classroom, a child is likely to be comfortable and spontaneous. Furthermore, teachers can observe children of similar ages and interests; this enables them to evaluate each child's development in the context of an expected developmental range. Teachers also have extended periods and many situations and activities in which to informally observe children. Contrast this with clinicians, such as the doctor, the audiologist, and the psychologist, who usually see the child only on brief and tightly scheduled visits. At these times the child may be ill at ease and behave quite differently from when they are in a familiar home or school environment.

THE TEACHER AS OBSERVER According to Wylie and Fenning (2012), "observation is the most important investigative tool we have to discover the world of young children" (p. 5). The search for developmental differences should always begin with systematic observation of children as they work and play in the preschool or child care centre.

Observers must be *objective*—that is, they should write down only what a child actually does and says. *Subjective* recording, by contrast, occurs when teachers put their own interpretations on children's behaviour. Note the differences in the following statements:

- *Objective:* Susie smiled and laughed frequently throughout the morning; she cried only once.
- *Subjective:* Susie was happy and carefree today.
- *Objective:* Mark stamped his feet and screamed "No!" each time he was asked to change activities.
- *Subjective:* Mark gets angry all the time.

At the same time, Wylie and Fenning (2012) encourage educators to consider that the process of watching and learning about young children requires professional educators to engage in an **appreciative inquiry process**, an approach that highlights the importance of open-mindedness and objectivity, curiosity, and inclusivity in observation. In essence, the process prompts educators to be self-reflective, collaborative, and equitable to ensure that each child's uniqueness is valued and there is respect for the child.

Appreciative inquiry process an approach that highlights the importance of open-mindedness and objectivity, curiosity, and inclusivity in observation

> Appreciative inquiry is a strength-based approach to change focusing on people's energy and passion; it brings an openness to seeing new potentials and possibilities from collective knowledge. ... Engaging in a systematic and appreciative inquiry approach when observing and recording not only considers the child's learning and development but also includes contextual factors that impact children's learning such as development, temperament, relationships, culture, environment, ability, family or diversity, language, gender, philosophy, and values. Each of these factors in its own way will impact what we observe, how interpret and reflect upon what we see and hear, and finally how we respond.*

SYSTEMATIC OBSERVATIONS Most teachers are used to observing children; few, however, record their observations in an organized way. Observation-based assessment is essential to providing curriculum and interactions that are individually age appropriate. It should be completely integrated with curriculum and

*Wylie and Fenning, Observing Young Children, 2012, p.235 (Nelson Education).

instruction or interactions (Gestwicki, 2014). Each observation should start with these four parts:

1. child's name or initials (confidentiality of information is essential)
2. date and time of day
3. setting (and, in some instances, names or number of children and teachers present)
4. name or initials of the observer

Teachers' observations take many forms. The questions teachers need to have answered determine the observation strategy they will select. In most cases, it is best if more than one person observes the child, especially if there is a hint of a serious problem. When two people agree that they are seeing the same thing, personal bias and misinterpretation of a child's behaviour are reduced.

Observational Recording Techniques

Here we discuss a sampling of the many kinds of observation tools that are useful in working with all young children, including those with special needs. For a comprehensive overview of observation strategies, see Martin (2010) and Wylie and Fenning (2012).

CHECKLISTS "Checklists record the presence or absence of particular predetermined behaviours such as skills, attributes, competencies, traits, reactions, achievements, or stages of development" (Martin, 2010, p. 138).

- Checklists are a quick and effective way of collecting systematic information on one or many children.
- They can be used by teachers, aides, parents, volunteers, and children.
- They can be relatively simple or designed to give much more information (as in the teacher observation form and checklist shown in Figure 12–3).
- They are most useful when teachers design them to answer their own questions about children and the program.

NARRATIVES Narrative observations include anecdotal records, running records, and logs, journals, and diaries. "The open method of recording spontaneous behaviour is flexible and unstructured. It suits the catch of the day: unanticipated behaviours … the uniqueness of each child will be reflected in the observations and, ultimately, in the documentation created and the decisions made" (Wylie & Fenning, 2012, pp. 102–121).

Anecdotal records

- Anecdotal records are brief written, objective observations, each recorded individually.
- They allow observers to choose what is significant to record.
- They may focus on an individual child or group of children.
- They can form useful information regarding significant behaviours and development.

Running records

- Running records are objective narrative recordings.
- They are written observations that capture everything the child does and says during a specific time.

FIGURE 12-3

Teacher Observation Form and Checklist for Identifying Children Who May Require Additional Services

Child's Name: _____   **Birth Date:** _____

Date: _____   **Recording Teacher's Name:** _____

LANGUAGE	YES	NO	SOMETIMES
Does the child:			
1. use two- and three-word phrases to ask for what he or she wants?	_____	_____	_____
2. use complete sentences to tell you what happened?	_____	_____	_____
3. when asked to describe something, use at least two or more sentences to talk about it?	_____	_____	_____
4. ask questions?	_____	_____	_____
5. seem to have difficulty following directions?	_____	_____	_____
6. respond to questions with appropriate answers?	_____	_____	_____
7. seem to talk too softly or too loudly?	_____	_____	_____
8. Are you able to understand the child?	_____	_____	_____

PRE-ACADEMICS	YES	NO	SOMETIMES
Does the child:			
9. seem to take at least twice as long as the other children to learn pre-academic concepts?	_____	_____	_____
10. seem to take the time needed by other children to learn pre-academic concepts?	_____	_____	_____
11. have difficulty attending to group activities for more than five minutes at a time?	_____	_____	_____
12. appear extremely shy in group activities; for instance, not volunteering answers or answering questions when asked, even though you think the child knows the answers?	_____	_____	_____

MOTOR	YES	NO	SOMETIMES
Does the child:			
13. continually switch a crayon back and forth from one hand to the other when colouring?	_____	_____	_____
14. appear clumsy or shaky when using one or both hands?	_____	_____	_____
15. when colouring with a crayon, appear to tense the hand not being used (for instance, clench it into a fist)?	_____	_____	_____
16. when walking or running, appear to move one side of the body differently from the other side? For instance, does the child seem to have better control of the leg and arm on one side than on the other?	_____	_____	_____

(continued)

FIGURE 12-3

Teacher Observation Form and Checklist for Identifying Children Who May Require Additional Services (Cont.)

MOTOR	YES	NO	SOMETIMES
Does the child:			
17. lean or tilt to one side when walking or running?	_____	_____	_____
18. seem to fear or not be able to use stairs, climbing equipment, or tricycles?	_____	_____	_____
19. stumble often or appear awkward when moving about?	_____	_____	_____
20. appear capable of dressing self, except for tying shoes?	_____	_____	_____

SOCIAL	YES	NO	SOMETIMES
Does the child:			
21. engage in more than two disruptive behaviours a day (tantrums, fighting, screaming, etc.)?	_____	_____	_____
22. appear withdrawn from the outside world (fiddling with pieces of string, staring into space, rocking)?	_____	_____	_____
23. play alone and seldom talk to the other children?	_____	_____	_____
24. spend most of the time trying to get attention from adults?	_____	_____	_____
25. have toileting problems (wet or soiled) once a week or more often?	_____	_____	_____

VISUAL OR HEARING	YES	NO	SOMETIMES
Does the child:			
26. appear to have eye movements that are jerky or uncoordinated?	_____	_____	_____
27. seem to have difficulty seeing objects? For instance, does the child:	_____	_____	_____
• tilt head to look at things?	_____	_____	_____
• hold objects close to eyes?	_____	_____	_____
• squint?	_____	_____	_____
• show sensitivity to bright lights?	_____	_____	_____
• have uncontrolled eye-rolling?	_____	_____	_____
• complain that eyes hurt?	_____	_____	_____
28. appear awkward in tasks requiring eye–hand coordination such as pegs, puzzles, colouring, etc.?	_____	_____	_____
29. seem to have difficulty hearing? For instance, does the child:	_____	_____	_____
• consistently favour one ear by turning the same side of the head in the direction of the sound?	_____	_____	_____
• ignore, confuse, or not follow directions?	_____	_____	_____
• pull on ears or rub ears frequently, or complain of earaches?	_____	_____	_____
• complain of head noises or dizziness?	_____	_____	_____
• have a very high, very low, or monotonous tone of voice?	_____	_____	_____

(continued)

GENERAL HEALTH	YES	NO	SOMETIMES
Does the child:			
30. seem to have an excessive number of colds?	___	___	___
31. have frequent absences because of illness?	___	___	___
32. have eyes that water?	___	___	___
33. have frequent discharge from:			
• eyes?	___	___	___
• ears?	___	___	___
• nose?	___	___	___
34. have sores on body or head?	___	___	___
35. have periods of unusual movements (such as eye blinking) or "blank spells" that seem to appear and disappear without relationship to the social situation?	___	___	___
36. have hives or rashes?	___	___	___
37. wheeze?	___	___	___
38. have a persistent cough?	___	___	___
39. seem to be excessively thirsty?	___	___	___
40. seem to be ravenously hungry?	___	___	___
41. Have you noticed any of the following conditions:	___	___	___
• constant fatigue?	___	___	___
• irritability?	___	___	___
• restlessness?	___	___	___
• tenseness?	___	___	___
• feverish cheeks or forehead?	___	___	___
42. Is the child overweight?	___	___	___
43. Is the child physically or mentally lethargic?	___	___	___
44. Has the child lost noticeable weight without being on a diet?	___	___	___

- They can produce a well-rounded picture of a child's overall behaviour and development.
- They are a very useful form of observation, as well as the most time consuming of the narrative records.

Logs, journals, and diaries

- Logs, journals, and diaries are similar to running records but are less comprehensive.
- They may be kept in a loose-leaf notebook with a section for each child.
- They are notes jotted down during class time or immediately after children leave for the day.
- They may be general notes about a child or focused notes on some aspect of the child's behaviour and development.
- They may contain contextual information that could help explain certain behaviours.

SAMPLINGS Sampling observations are those in which (a) examples of behaviour are recorded as they occur or (b) behaviours are recorded as they are demonstrated at previously decided intervals or (c) "work" samples are gathered (Martin, 2007, p. 97).

Time samples

- Time samples are periodic and momentary observations to determine the presence or absence of behaviour.

- They focus on the behaviour of one child.

The familiar classroom is a good place to obtain language samplings.

© Cengage Learning

- They identify behavioural patterns.

- They record behaviours on a chart that can be analyzed to determine the needs of the child. For example, information may show that a child was engaged with materials in only 3 out of the 15 samples. This could mean that the child needs different materials or help in expanding his or her attention span.

Language samples

- Language samples are verbatim recordings (word for word, or sound for sound) of exactly what the child says or what sounds the child makes (see photo, above).

- They should be recorded phonetically (e.g., if a child says "du gul," it is written "du gul" even if the recorder knows the child is referring to "the girl").

- They should include physical gestures a child makes while communicating (e.g., pointing to the juice while squealing "Eeeeee").

Frequency counts

- Frequency counts keep track of how often a certain behaviour occurs.

- They assist educators in establishing how often a behaviour occurs:

  – excessively?

  – infrequently?

  – only under certain circumstances?

- They provide significant information as to whether a given behaviour is actually a problem, as well as how significant the problem is. For example, every time a behaviour occurs, a tally mark is made on a piece of paper. Over several days, the tally marks will show the frequency of behaviour.

Example:

One teacher was concerned about John's safety because of what she thought were his frequent attempts to climb over the fence during outdoor play. The other teacher thought it seldom happened. An actual frequency count showed that the fence-climbing attempts occurred four or five times each play period. Teachers now could agree that there was a problem. They assessed the play yard and realized that there was not much for John to climb on. They began to set up climbing activities several days a week. John's fence-climbing dropped to one or no episodes per day. On days when no climbing activities were set up, John's fence-climbing was again high. The frequency counts gave teachers clues to the extent of the problem as well as to their success in reducing the unsafe behaviour.

Duration measures

- Duration measures indicate how long an event or a behaviour lasts.
- They note the start and stop time of a child's activities.
- They show how long a child's attention span is or how much time the child spends in either appropriate or inappropriate behaviours.

Example:

Teachers were concerned about Omar's poor attention span. They decided to find out how many minutes at a time he spent at various activities. Several days' observations indicated that he spent many minutes (15 to 20) with hands-on activities (painting, block-building, puzzles). In contrast, he had a short attention span—only a minute or two—for activities that required listening (music, stories, conversation). These duration measures were invaluable as teachers planned Omar's program, conferred with his parents, and participated in the team meetings.

CHARTS A chart is developed from observed information that is recorded onto a prepared format.

- Charts allow observers to record behaviours quickly and efficiently.
- They may be recorded during or after observation.
- They include routine information as well as behaviours like feeding and diapering.
- They may identify behavioural patterns (as in Figure 12–4, which shows a social skills chart).

PICTORIAL REPRESENTATIONS A pictorial representation is any visual interpretation of recorded observations. Mapping is one example of pictorial representations.

- Mappings can focus on one child or a group of children.
- They are efficient and easy to use.
- They can identify traffic patterns, safety concerns, and use of space.

MEDIA TECHNIQUES According to Martin (2010), "a media technique is any method of recording or storing observational data that is achieved by mechanical, electronic, or technical means" (p. 205). Photography and video and audio recordings are examples of media techniques used to observe children. All these techniques can be used to support any traditionally recorded observations, as well as to become part of a child's development portfolio.

Photography can be used in many ways to enable educators to learn more about children. Photography can be useful in

- demonstrating evidence of changes in a child's physical appearance and growth;

FIGURE 12-4

Social Skills Chart

Child's Name: _____ D.O.B: _____ Age:_____

Observer(s):_____ Date(s):_____ Time:_____

Behaviour	Frequency	Duration	Comment

- helping a child remember situations; and
- recording specific aspects of a child's activity.

Video recording a child's activities or environment can be used for several purposes, such as to

- use as a review when time permits for greater analysis;
- provide information to parents regarding their child's development;
- use for research purposes; and
- assist in assessing the child's environment.

Audio recording may be used for any of the following purposes:

- sharing recordings with parents.
- recording and keeping records of a child's language, music, or reading skills.
- recording a child's expressive language for analysis.

Portfolio a carefully selected collection of a child's work that is used to document growth and development

PORTFOLIOS AND CHILD STUDIES A **portfolio** is a record-keeping device in which observations, health and social information, test results, work samples, and other significant information about an individual child are stored. "Portfolios present primary resources for consideration by parents, teachers and children ... the work itself is presented as tangible evidence of progress ..., rather than relying on teacher's reactions to the work, as might be presented in anecdotal reports" (Gestwicki, 2014, p. 435).

A child study is a thorough analytical document. It contains observations and collected information about a child, and it may include a variety of other information collected over time (see photo, page 279).

Early Identification: Cautionary Notes for Teachers

Observation is a useful and important tool in providing high-quality education and care for all children. It is important to remember, however, that if teachers or other

Teachers should be aware of environmental factors that may affect children's behaviour.

Courtesy of Ryerson Early Learning Centre

FIGURE 12-5

Teachers' Dos and Don'ts

Teachers should avoid

- making diagnoses;
- using labels to describe children (remembering that all children in their program are children first);
- raising parents' anxiety;
- telling parents what to do; and
- jumping to conclusions without adequate observational data.

Teachers should

- develop good working relationships with families;
- voice concerns to parents about possible developmental differences in their child;
- listen carefully and respectfully;
- be knowledgeable about local resources and be able to make helpful and appropriate referrals;
- be culturally sensitive and take cultural and linguistic differences into consideration when evaluating behaviour;
- remember that development encompasses a broad spectrum of individual differences; and
- be aware of environmental factors.

© Cengage Learning

caregivers have a concern about a possible developmental difference in a child in their care, they must demonstrate caution, sensitivity, and respect in how these concerns are shared with families. Teachers should not keep concerns to themselves, but they should be careful not to raise concerns based on inference rather than actual observation. Some issues for teachers to consider are listed in Figure 12–5.

The Individual Program Plan (IPP)

The **individual program plan (IPP)** is an approach to providing services to individuals with special needs. The written plan provides the structure and direction for the services and activities to be provided to the child and family by the early

Individual program plan (IPP) an approach to providing services to individuals with special needs: the process involves developing a written plan based on the child's strengths, needs, and interests; implementation and evaluation are part of the IPP process intervention program. (Note: *Individual education plan* [IEP] is sometimes used by service providers interchangeably with IPP.)

Teachers are essential throughout the IPP process: in their observations of children's behaviour, in their implementation of the classroom aspects of the individual programs, and in their evaluations. Teachers should be responsible for integrating classroom practice and program recommendations by the child's IPP team. Furthermore, the ongoing evaluation of the appropriateness of each child's daily program is largely dependent on the teacher. In other words, teachers are central to the entire IPP process. The written plan provides the structure and direction for the services and activities to be provided to the child and family by the early intervention program.

The IPP Team

The IPP is developed by a team consisting of the child's parents or parent surrogates and professionals from the various disciplines involved with the child and family (such as resource teachers, early childhood teachers, physiotherapists, a speech and language pathologist, and/or the case coordinator). The types of teams and the disciplines involved are varied. Several models for IPP teams have emerged in the last few years:

- *Multidisciplinary.* Professionals work independently of one another in a parallel format; each professional is viewed as important but takes responsibility only for his or her own area of clinical expertise. Within this model, a child may be withdrawn for individual therapy.

- **Interdisciplinary.** Professionals and parents collaborate in decision making around the program and service needs of each child and family, with individual team members contributing in their area of expertise. In most instances, extra support for children is provided within the group environment.

- **Transdisciplinary.** Professionals share expertise, model, and instruct other team members on how to implement specific practices within the group setting. (The term *transdisciplinary* is used in this text.)

Interdisciplinary refers to several different professions working together on a common problem, sharing information, and exchanging roles, depending on the case

Transdisciplinary professionals sharing expertise, modelling, and instructing other team members on how to implement specific practices within the group setting

Components of the IPP

The IPP should be based on developmentally valid, **bias-free screening and assessment**. Program and placement decisions are to be formulated from information from multiple sources: test scores, observation in situations in which the child is comfortable and at ease, and input from significant persons in the child's life (parents, grandparents, teachers, out-of-home caregivers). For an example of one aspect of a child's IPP focusing on motor skills, see Figure 12–9 on page 286.

The components of an IPP are the following:

1. observation and assessment.
2. identification of strengths, needs, and interests.
3. setting of goals and objectives.
4. creation of an implementation plan.
5. evaluation.

Bias-free screening and assessment selecting and administering screening and assessment tools that ensure a child is given the opportunity for optimum performance

OBSERVATION AND ASSESSMENT Before an IPP is written, a child's developmental skills must be assessed. As described earlier, this is an information-gathering (nondiagnostic) process. It is not, however, a one-time occurrence; instead, it should be an ongoing process throughout the year so that the child's progress can be tracked and programs adjusted as needed. Ongoing observation and assessment provide a comprehensive description—a developmental profile—of a child at particular points in time.

Depending on the results of earlier screening tests, the child may need to receive specialized assessments from specific disciplines (audiologist, nutritionist, physiotherapist/occupational therapist, and others). The early childhood teacher is responsible for collecting the general information that often provides the "glue" to hold together the overall developmental picture of the child (see photo, below).

Numerous assessment instruments have been developed over the past 20 years. In addition, there are developmental profile forms that many teachers of young children find even more useful. A separate chart or profile should be kept for each child. Periodic observations should be made and recorded for each child in all developmental areas: gross and fine motor skills, cognitive abilities, self-help/care, social and play behaviours, and receptive and expressive language.

A child's developmental profile should be updated periodically on the basis of observations and notes made by teachers as they work with children. Emerging skills show up clearly on the preschool profile. Mastering a skill in a particular area of development often depends on specific achievements in other areas. For example, a child cannot perform certain self-help/care tasks, such as buttoning and unbuttoning, until the *pincer grasp* is well established. Developmental delays also show up clearly. Delays may accumulate because of unrecognized relationships among developmental areas. By keeping a child's profile up to date, teachers can pinpoint a delay in one area and so explain issues in other areas. Language difficulties, for example, often lead to challenges with play relationships because of the inability to express ideas and preferences adequately. Limited verbal skills also may delay cognitive development or have a negative effect on intellectual performance because inadequate language interferes with formulating and expressing thoughts.

The information about the child's performance in the early childhood setting is a valuable part in the overall assessment process. The early childhood teacher should be able to provide information about the child's current skill level, as well as information about activities in which the child has interest and preference.

Teachers provide the "glue" that holds together the overall developmental picture of each child.

IDENTIFICATION OF STRENGTHS, NEEDS, AND INTERESTS Teachers can use information gathered from observations and assessments to identify a child's strengths, needs, and interests. Information gathering may be informal, from parents, psychologists, physiotherapists, speech and language pathologists, and so on, or obtained in a more formal method, as discussed earlier in this chapter. Once information has been compiled, it may be useful to summarize the child's strengths, needs, and interests in a child profile chart (see Figure 12–6). Information summarized in the child profile chart will lead to the development of goals and objectives.

If families have access to the Internet, teachers can use blogs and other interactive media for sharing information about infants and toddlers. Teachers can

FIGURE 12-6

Child Profile Chart

Child's Name: _____	D.O.B: _____	Age: _____
Setting: _____	Observer(s): _____	Date: _____

Developmental Area	Strengths	Needs	Interests
Physical:			
Gross Motor			
Fine Motor			
Communication:			
Receptive Language			
Expressive Language			
Cognitive			
Social/Emotional			
Self-care:			
Toileting & Hygiene			
Dressing/Undressing			
Eating & Drinking			

connect families directly to important resources and have online conversations. If the teachers and families agree on this method of communication, it is important that these blogs are private between users and deny general public access. Teachers must also ensure confidentiality by using secure settings and privacy features on blog sites (Elicker, Benson, & McMullen, 2013).

SETTING OF GOALS AND OBJECTIVES

Long-term goals The IPP should include written statements specifying expected learning outcomes for each child each program year. Long-term goals are usually presented as broad general statements about what can be expected of the child within six months to one year, depending on the child's age.

Example:

Erin will be able to

1. move about the room independently throughout the day;

2. play cooperatively with other children during small group activities; and

3. use verbal skills to communicate her needs.

Long-term goals centre on priorities essential to the child's overall development, as agreed on by the child's IPP team. Cook, Klein, and Chen (2012) referred to the U.S. practice of working in partnership with families and professionals to identify outcome statements within the Individual Family Service Plan (IFSP), which become integrated into the IPP:

These IFSP outcome statements are to reflect changes the family want to see for their child or themselves. Each outcome is to be stated functionally in terms of what is to occur (process) and what is expected as a result of these actions (product). (p. 92)

The statements are based on the developmental needs of the child, representing practical activities that support the development of skills to support daily life. For every child, the number and kinds of goals will vary. Goals for a child should be reasonable and manageable in number so as not as to overwhelm the child and family; additional goals can always be added at a future date when the child has achieved identified goals. Furthermore, self-sufficiency goals, as important as they are, should not rule out goals that help improve the child's self-esteem and enjoyment of life.

Example:

Melinda was a bright and lively child born with severely malformed hands. Even as an infant, it was obvious that she had a talent and love for music and rhythm. Although long-term goals for this child must include learning to use a prosthesis on each hand (a major priority), her musical development is important, too. At least one goal related to music should be written into Melinda's IPP.

Short-term objectives Every IPP should include a list of short-term objectives. These are mini-programs—step-by-step lessons that enable the child to achieve the designated long-term goals. Short-term objectives usually focus on skills or behaviours that can be measured (counted or timed) and acquired within one week to one month. The data give objective evidence of a child's progress. Learning to wear and become adept at using her prostheses might be a long-term goal for the child mentioned above. Exactly how this will be accomplished and measured is spelled out in the short-term objectives.

Enhancing the child's musical talents might also be worked into the goals and objectives.

Example:

Melinda will pick out tunes using single notes on the piano while wearing her prostheses, with encouragement from the teacher, for 15 minutes each day.

The amount of time spent playing the piano and the numbers of tunes learned might be the measurable aspects of this objective. Furthermore, learning to play tunes on the piano is likely to be reinforcing for Melinda in her efforts at wearing her prostheses.

Objectives should answer the following questions:

- **Who** will be engaged in acquiring the behaviour?
- **What** specifically is the behaviour?
- **When** and **where** is the behaviour to be exhibited? Under what conditions? (Where, how, when, with what kinds of support?)
- **How well** is the behaviour to be performed? For how long? How many times?

Example:

May-lin is a three-year-old child who has a severe visual impairment. She currently is able to climb stairs, but places both feet on one stair before proceeding to the next stair. The goal set for May-lin was that she be able to navigate her environment. After completing a task analysis (see Chapter 11) for stair climbing, it was determined that the next step in May-lin's program should be that she be able to climb stairs with alternating feet, using the railing for support.

The objective would be written as follows:

- Who? (May-lin)
- What? (climb stairs)
- When and Where? Under what conditions? (during free play time in the gym, using alternating feet, while holding the banister)
- How well? (for a minimum of five consecutive steps)

Example:

Stefano is a three-year-old child with a diagnosis of Down syndrome. When requested, he uses single words to label objects, but only in imitation of an adult. Stefano's IPP team set the following goal for him: Stefano will speak in simple sentences to express his needs and wants. The task analysis for this goal identified the use of single words to express needs and wants as the first step in a program for Stefano.

The objective would be written as follows:

- Who? (Stefano)
- What? (use single words spontaneously)
- When and Where? (during free play time to indicate his preference when offered choices)
- How well? (each time a choice is offered)

Graphing (transferring the measurements to a chart), as shown in Figures 12–7 and 12–8, brings progress into focus. Displaying children's progress in graphic form is beneficial because it provides a visual record of change over time. Behaviour changes, even when slow, appear more clearly on a graph. The visual display may also help both teacher and child be more aware of progress and so feel more

FIGURE 12-7 May-lin's Stair-Climbing Program

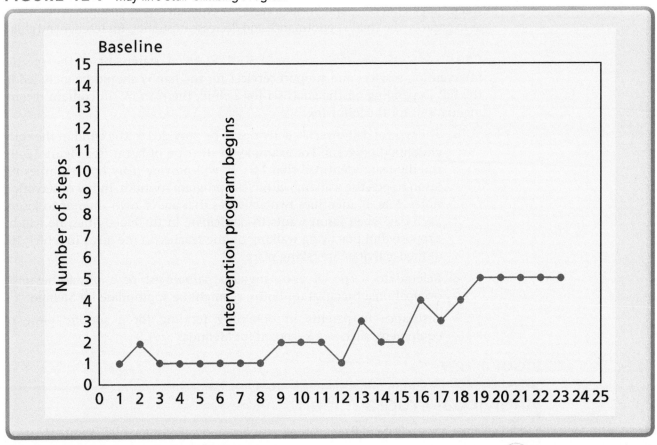

FIGURE 12-8 Stefano's Verbal Response Program

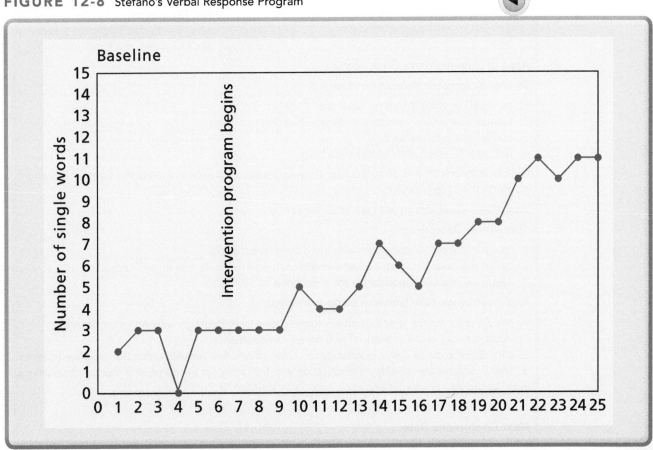

successful. Success always leads to increased motivation. Lack of progress also is readily apparent on a graph. In such cases the program can be changed promptly so as to improve the child's performance and decrease frustration for teacher and child.

CREATION OF AN IMPLEMENTATION PLAN A statement of the specific intervention services and support services for the family should be included in the IPP. Depending on the goals set for a child, the plan might contain recommendations for the following:

- The type of daily/weekly activities to be provided to the child in the early childhood program. For example, in the case of Jason (see Figure 12–9), the IPP team identified that Mrs. B. will provide daily opportunities for Jason to practise walking within the program routines. In her observation notes, Mrs. B. identifies two activities that are of high interest to Jason. Each day when Jason wants to participate in these activities, he will be supported in practising walking by the teacher to the areas in which his desired activities are taking place.

- Referral to a speech and language pathologist or a physiotherapist/ occupational therapist (or both), as might be appropriate for Stefano.

- Assistance to parents in obtaining funding for a specific piece of equipment, such as a keyboard for Melinda.

FIGURE 12-9

Individual Program Plan

Child's Name: Jason **Date of Birth:** _____ **Program:** ABC Preschool

Conference Date: _____ **Team Members Present:**
Ms. M.—Parent
Mrs. B.—Early Childhood Education
Mr. G.—Resource Consultant

Area of Development: Gross Motor

Strengths (present level of functioning):

1. pulls self to standing using furniture
2. stands momentarily without support, lowering to sitting
3. cruises around furniture
4. will take 10 steps with both hands held

Child's interests in this area include: throwing balls, rolling balls across the floor, and being pushed in the big plastic car.

Long-Term Goal: Jason will walk independently.

Short-Term Objectives:

1. Jason will walk 10 steps with one hand held by an adult.
2. Jason will take 4 to 5 steps without support, walking between familiar adults.
3. Jason will walk independently for a distance of 10 feet.

Implementation Plan (services to be provided):

1. Ms. G. will provide specific written suggestions to encourage walking, which can be implemented in the preschool and home environments.
2. Mrs. B. will provide daily opportunity for Jason to practise walking within the program routines.
3. Mrs. B. will maintain weekly communication with the family, for the purpose of sharing observations.

Evaluation: Ms. G. will conduct biweekly observations, documenting Jason's progress.

Next Conference Date: _____

Projected starting dates should be specified for each service prescribed for the child, and the person responsible for carrying out the specific objective should be identified.

Example:

Josh will receive ongoing speech and language consultation services from the community speech pathologist beginning October 1.

The projected starting date assists the team members in implementing the plan. A reasonable length of time must be allowed for accomplishing the objectives and goals stated in the child's IPP. See Figure 12–9 for an example of an individual program plan.

The completed IPP includes statements about

- the child's present level of skill development and the quality of performance;
- long-term (six months to one year) goals for the child and short-term objectives that will accomplish the long-term goals;
- specific services to be provided, with target dates and team member responsible for carrying out the service; and
- accountability (evaluation) to determine whether objectives are being met.

EVALUATION (STATEMENT OF ACCOUNTABILITY) At least once a year (more frequently for younger children) the IPP should be evaluated to see whether the stated objectives are being met. Evaluations should be based on specifically described procedures, such as developmental assessment results and written observations. In actual practice, evaluations should be conducted more often. As mentioned earlier, an in-place system of ongoing assessments simplifies the procedure. The preschool developmental profile, for example, provides both ongoing assessment and program evaluation. Every item on the profile describes a specific child behaviour; its presence or absence can be noted by a teacher. Graphs also provide program accountability. By using the preschool developmental profile to assess a child periodically and by keeping graphs of a child's progress, a convincing evaluation process is always in operation.

Case Study ▪ An IPP dilemma ▪

You are an educator and have sent an IPP parent notification letter about a child's progress. The parent did not respond. You sent a second letter and made a phone call. The child is continuing to regress. You decide to hold the IPP meeting without the parent.	What consequences, if any, do you foresee from your actions? At what point can the teacher decide to hold the IPP meeting without the parent? Research your province's rules and regulations regarding parent contact and participation in IPP meetings.

Summary

The identification of developmental differences can take place any time, beginning with the first several weeks after conception. The earlier an area of concern is identified, the more likely it is that it can be treated effectively and that associated problems can be prevented. All young children (except those with obvious disabilities) should be screened; many differences are subtle and difficult to recognize.

Many kinds of screening instruments are available. Some are geared to overall development; some to specialized areas, such as hearing and vision; and some to particular ages or developmental domains. Whatever the test, for reliable results it must be given in the child's first language, with scrupulous regard for the customs of the child's family and the child's physical and biological state. More than one instrument should be used in the assessment process. Even then, the results of many tests must be viewed with extreme caution, especially IQ tests. Most early childhood educators view standardized IQ tests as being of little value when working with young children.

Teachers are major agents in the early identification process. Direct observation is a teacher's best tool in determining a child's developmental status and the suitability of specific classroom activities for the group and for individual children. Appreciative inquiry has an impact on what we observe, how we interpret and reflect upon what we see and hear, and, finally, how we respond. Observation forms and checklists, especially those that teachers devise themselves, help teachers answer questions about children's behaviour and classroom practices. Teachers should always use their information with care and in the best interests of the child and family.

The individual program plan is a major and logical outcome of early identification and intervention procedures. A child's teacher and parent(s) are an essential part of the IPP planning process, along with other members of the transdisciplinary team. The IPP must be in written form. It should be based on bias-free tests and observations, and should specify long-term goals and short-term objectives. Services that will be provided and their starting dates should also be specified. Finally, the IPP should describe the accountability component: how the effectiveness of the implementation plan will be measured.

RESOURCES

Childcare Resource

http://www.childcare-resource.com

This site provides resources related to the advocacy and education of young children, with information on the importance of observing young children, including those with a variety of special needs.

CITYKIDS

www.mothercraft.ca/index.php?q=ei-citykids

This is a network of agencies working together to provide single-point access, coordinated intake, and service delivery to children with special needs and their families in the Toronto. This site also provides resources to service providers.

The Nipissing District Developmental Screen

http://www.ndds.ca

The Nipissing District Developmental Screen is a Canadian innovative developmental screening tool available to health-care or child care professionals working with infants and children up to six years of age.

Ontario Ministry of Education, Individual Education Plans

http:www.edu.gov.on.ca/eng/general/elemsec/speced/iep/iep.html

This site provides information on developing, implementing, and evaluating individual education plans.

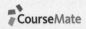 **CourseMate** Access an interactive ebook and chapter-specific interactive learning tools, including flashcards, quizzes, videos, and more, in the *Inclusion in Early Childhood Programs* CourseMate. Visit NELSONbrain.com to log in, register, or purchase access.

Planning Transitions to Support Inclusion

13

OBJECTIVES

After studying the material in this chapter, the student will be able to

- State the major goals of an early childhood transition-planning process.
- Identify possible accommodations that need to be made by children, families, and service providers during the transition process.
- Describe a transition-planning format that includes program and personnel responsibilities.
- Discuss strategies that enable a child with special needs to ease into a new program.
- Suggest support services that could assist a child in adjusting to a new program.

KEY CONCEPTS AND TERMS

accommodations

inclusive

transition coordinator

transition plans

CONNECTIONS

- Sophie's third birthday is tomorrow, and her family is busy making plans for the big day. They are having a birthday party with all of her friends to mark the special occasion. There is another reason the family is excited. She gets to start preschool. Sophie was born with Down syndrome and has been enrolled in a early intervention program since she was an infant, which included home services once a week.

- It is February and Carlos is turning five. He is very excited about attending kindergarten in the fall. For the past two years he has been attending ABC Preschool program, where he also receives special education services from a consultant and speech and language services from a therapist with the local early intervention agency. Carlos entered preschool with a diagnosis of developmental delay and has shown substantial gains across the two years of preschool services. Carlos's parents are worried about the expectations they will face in a kindergarten program within the school system.

Introduction

Inclusive equitable access is offered to all children, regardless of ability

Transition plans the plans developed to ensure a comfortable and positive transition for the child and family as they move from one educational setting to a new educational setting

It is necessary to plan for the services required to assist young children with special needs as they move from one early childhood program to another or into an **inclusive** school setting. Transitions occur for a variety of reasons. The most common reason is the child's age. Other reasons include the child's developmental needs, a family relocation, or a newly identified diagnosis (Minor, 2002). **Transition plans** should be an essential element of the child's individual program plan (IPP), ensuring that services to meet the specific needs identified by the family are addressed. To formulate such plans, early childhood educators need to develop specific skills and procedures for facilitating both the child's and the family's transition into a new program.

As children and families move from one type of program to another, whether it is a new preschool program or a kindergarten program, they encounter new faces, new environments, and new procedures. Planning for these transitions into newness is critical. It is, however, an often-neglected component of early intervention programming, especially for children with special needs who are moving into inclusive environments. Each change may require numerous **accommodations** on the part of the child, the family, and the service providers (Bohan-Baker & Little, 2004; Janus, Lefort, Cameron, & Kopechanskil, 2007). The child may need more time than his or her peers to adjust to the new environment, as well as learn how to play and work more independently. The family may need to alter their before-school child care arrangements to fit the schedule of the new program. The early childhood teacher may need to redesign small-group activities to accommodate a new child with a specific special need.

Accommodations adjustments on the part of the child, family, or service providers that enable a successful transition to a new environment for the child

Planning for the changes required by the transition and developing ways to maintain the changes are critical components in ensuring a successful transition. If careful planning is not undertaken and followed through, the outcome may be an unsuccessful placement for the child and family.

There are three specific steps to take when trying to ensure a successful transition:

1. Identify possible challenges that may arise during the transition.
2. Plan strategies for supporting the child, the family, and the receiving teacher(s).
3. Maintain ongoing support following the transition.

Transition Goals

The purpose of transition planning is to lay out a process that enables the family and the child to make a comfortable and positive change from one program to another. Ideally, the process produces minimum disruption in family routines, while supporting the child's developmental progress. The following is an example of the accommodations required of a child, a family, and a teacher during one transition program:

> *Abby, who was born with spina bifida, had gotten about in a wheelchair for most of her life. Psychological assessments indicated average to above-average intelligence. She had been in a private special education preschool and child care centre since infancy. Both parents worked full time. As Abby neared her fourth birthday, her parents decided she was ready to attend an inclusive community program. After four months of planning and working with their early intervention specialist, Abby began attending a full-day inclusive program.*
>
> *The community program teachers had concerns, too. They redesigned some of the materials and activities so that Abby would be able to participate during the first critical days of the transition. The teachers wondered, though, whether they would have the time or energy to continue to adapt materials and learning experiences. They wondered, too, whether they could consistently include Abby in large motor activities, given the demands on teachers' time made by a group of active four-year-olds.*

The success of the transition into the community program ultimately would be measured by the extent to which Abby, her family, and her teachers were able to manage the many accommodations required of them. It is the ability to handle and adjust to a range of accommodations (the transition's *sustainability*) that determines the success of a transition (Rice & O'Brien, 1990).

Transitions in Perspective

The transition process requires systematic planning and evaluating (see photo, below). It also requires ongoing modification to keep it in tune with the needs

The transition process requires systematic planning.

© Cengage Learning

of individual children, their families, and the service providers who are involved (Haines, Rosenkoetter, & Fowler, 1994). The perspectives of all must be considered in identifying the accommodations needed. A particular mother, for example, may believe that she should be consulted about every aspect of her child's education and that she should be the one to make the decisions about her child's transition to another program. In the same family, the father may believe it is best to leave such decisions to the teachers. The professionals involved in the transition may have ideas quite different from those of either parent about the decision-making process and who should decide what. Respect for, awareness of, and responsiveness to these several perspectives are critical for a successful transition for the child and the family.

The Child's Perspective

A child's developmental progress is the main reason for a transition from one program to another. The change in services may be agreed on because of the child's age (entering kindergarten, for example, is usually based on chronological age). The change also may be called for on the basis of clinical evidence—an updated diagnosis or a change in diagnostic findings, as when an intermittent hearing loss is identified. Another factor may be that the child has acquired new and functionally significant skills. Whatever the reason, the child's ability to adapt to the next program is the central issue in determining the success of the transition (Rous, Hallam, Harbin, McCormick, & Jung, 2007).

The accommodations required of a child during a transition will depend on the individual child and the *sending* and *receiving* programs. The child will need to make new friends, generalize old skills to new situations, and learn unfamiliar routines while attempting to explore a new environment. Children often have difficulty transferring even well-established skills to new situations. What looks like a similar set of expectations to professionals may not look at all the same to a child who has learned to respond to distinct cues or events that are not present in the new program. A child, for example, may be used to only one teacher or one particular type of instruction. That child may do well in a tightly structured, individualized program but have difficulty in a loosely structured program. Therefore, as professionals and parents prepare a child for a transition, they need to ask three questions:

1. What will be different for the child?
2. What skills does the child already have that will be useful in the new setting?
3. What skills does the child need to learn before a transition is attempted?

A child's strengths, needs, and interests should be identified before the transition plan is developed. Which accommodations will be easy for the child? Which will be difficult? To answer these questions, each child must be assessed in terms of

- his or her current skills;
- the conditions under which the child demonstrates particular skills (e.g., does the child demonstrate them at home but not at school, or vice versa?); and
- the skills the receiving program expects the child to have before entering the program.

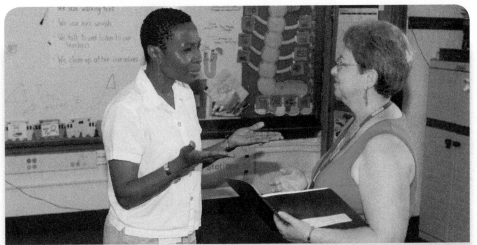

Successful transition planning depends on recognizing and respecting the diversity that each family brings to the planning process.

The Family's Perspective

Family involvement is a critical component of transition planning (Janus et al., 2007; Villeneuve et al., 2013). A family must adjust to differences between programs by adapting to new schedules, finding new services, and accepting new responsibilities. Families may have to educate new school personnel about their child's special needs. They may be expected to set new goals for their child. They may need to adjust to fewer contacts with their child's teacher. Plans for the family component in a child's transition will vary, depending on family structure, characteristics, and stressors.

Developing successful transition activities depends on recognizing the diversity that each family brings to the planning process (see photo, above). Professionals should not assume that all families have the capacity, desire, or ability to participate in the same ways. A number of factors influence how the family participates in the transition planning. These include characteristics of the family, the nature of the child's disability, the family's culture and beliefs, and the family's priorities and concerns (Lynch & Hanson, 2011; Villeneuve et al., 2013). In general, families are concerned about questions such as these:

- What services and supports will be available in the next setting, and how can they obtain these services and supports?
- How will their child adjust to the new program, both academically and socially?
- How will the new teacher or teachers adjust to their child, and vice versa?
- What changes in daily routines will be required?

Families need adequate time to address these questions if they are to make logical decisions about their level of involvement in the transition planning. Some families choose to let professionals make the decisions, while others want to make the decisions themselves; most families fall somewhere in between.

Transition Planning

Planning is the key to successful transitions for the child, family, and teachers. As noted earlier, the accommodations required of everyone during a transition tend to be stressful. Careful planning reduces stress by putting the focus on specific issues related to the child's and the family's needs and preferences. When parents and professionals work as partners in developing a plan acceptable to all, it is likely that everyone will be more comfortable about what they are to do. It is likely, too, that everyone will find the time (or the help) necessary to accomplish the mutually agreed-on tasks.

Successful transition planning should be an ongoing and integral part of every child's program. Planning an individual transition requires ongoing commitment. Time must be built into the regular program schedule for staff and parent meetings, for visits to the sending and receiving programs, and for exchange of child and program information. Ten basic steps (described in the following pages) are identified as central to the transition-planning process.

Step 1: Coordinate the Transition

When several people work together to plan a child's transition, it is essential to appoint one person to coordinate efforts and take responsibility for getting things done. The **transition coordinator** may be the director of a program, a resource teacher/early interventionist, a consultant, an infant development worker, another member of the staff, or the case manager of the IPP or individual family service plan (IFSP; see Chapters 3 and 12). The professional background of the transition coordinator is likely to vary from child to child. A transdisciplinary team may rotate the coordinator's position among its members, depending on the child's and the family's special needs. In addition to a transition coordinator, a recent study discussed the need for a key facilitator in the school context who can support families throughout the first year of the child's transition (Villeneuve et al., 2013). Regardless of professional training, a major responsibility of the transition coordinator is to be familiar with

Transition coordinator the team member who is responsible for coordinating the transition from one educational setting to a new educational setting

- the transition procedures of both the sending and the receiving programs; and
- the resources, placement, and service options available in the community.

Step 2: Visit Alternative Programs

Early childhood professionals within a community need to be familiar with one another's programs. Familiarity creates understanding and cooperation. For example, the infant development worker should be familiar with the preschool options available in the child's community. He or she should therefore be able to inform the parents of the choices available and support the parents in investigating the range of available settings. This provides parents with opportunities to become more knowledgeable and better able to make the most appropriate choices with respect to their child and family. Similarly, when the community early childhood staff know what social and academic skills are expected from five-year-olds by the local kindergarten teacher, they are better able to develop successful transition strategies. Learning about the specific expectations of a program or classroom helps the current teacher and the family decide whether the child

- will be ready for the program under consideration;
- needs additional skills;
- is likely to need special help from the sending program before the transition; and
- will need certain changes in the receiving program in order to succeed.

Coordinators can assist families in the transition process by arranging visits to new programs.

The transition coordinator (or individual teachers) should visit the programs where their children are most likely to be enrolled. If possible, visits should extend through a full session. Only by sitting in on a program in its entirety can the observer become familiar with the schedule in action, the range and tempo of activities, and teacher–child interactions.

Visits can be arranged by contacting the future program setting (see photo, above). An increasing number of school boards have an early childhood or kindergarten specialist whose job is to arrange meetings to discuss a program-to-program transition.

While observing, the coordinator and parents should make written notes. Features of the program that might create problems for the child or family should be underscored. Observation notes often are arranged under the following headings:

1. *Environment/physical setting:* the physical arrangement of the classroom (including accessibility for the specific child), the number of teachers and aides, and the daily schedule

2. *Staff–child interaction:* what children and teachers do and how they interact

3. *Program approach:* the learning opportunities provided for the children and the range of available supports

4. *Parent involvement:* the range of opportunities for involvement/participation by parents within the program (see Figure 13–1, which shows an example of a checklist that can be used by parents and professionals to plan for young children's transitions from one program to another)

Step 3: Hold Meetings among the IPP Team

After the coordinator and family have visited several programs, the IPP team should meet and discuss the information obtained from the visits. Attention should be directed toward evaluating how each program may or may not be able to meet the priority needs of the child and his or her family.

Minor differences in approach are not likely to cause problems. However, when major differences exist, the staff of the child's current centre should consider adapting their program to reflect the expectations of the new setting.

FIGURE 13-1 Choosing a Child Care Program

Section A: Staff/Children Relationships	Appropriate for My Child and Family		
	YES	NO	UNDECIDED
The children come to the teachers for help, information, and comfort.	_____	_____	_____
The teachers spend time interacting and playing with the children in a respectful manner.	_____	_____	_____
When interacting with the children, the teachers get down to the child's physical level.	_____	_____	_____
I am comfortable with the approach used by the staff to manage the children's behaviour.	_____	_____	_____
All children are included and/or encouraged to participate in all aspects of the program.	_____	_____	_____
The children play with others in the group and work cooperatively with each other.	_____	_____	_____
My impression of teacher–child interactions is a positive one.	_____	_____	_____
Teachers are qualified with training in "child use" and "First Aid/CPR."	_____	_____	_____
I am comfortable with the number of adults in the group.	_____	_____	_____

Section C: The Program Approach	Appropriate for My Child and Family		
	YES	NO	UNDECIDED
The centre has a written Parent Handbook with information on the program approach and policies.	_____	_____	_____
Daily activities are planned based on the needs of the group.	_____	_____	_____
The children are provided with a choice of activities.	_____	_____	_____
The children are interested and involved in the activities.	_____	_____	_____
The staff is open to consultation or support from other agencies.	_____	_____	_____
The selection of toys and activities is appropriate for my child.	_____	_____	_____
The room is set up to promote social interaction between children.	_____	_____	_____
Sensory play experiences are a daily part of the program (e.g., water play, sand play, music circles).	_____	_____	_____
There is a balance between small group, large group, and individual activities.	_____	_____	_____
The program activities address the priority areas in which my child needs to learn and develop.	_____	_____	_____
There are opportunities for the staff to meet for information sharing and planning on a regular basis.			
Comments:			

Section E: Staff/Parent Relationships	Appropriate for My Child and Family		
	YES	NO	UNDECIDED
Staff communicates with parents on a regular basis.	_____	_____	_____
I felt comfortable and welcomed by staff during my visit.	_____	_____	_____
The staff members encourage full parent participation in their child's program.	_____	_____	_____
The staff takes into consideration the concerns of parents.	_____	_____	_____
Parents are informed of upcoming events, changes about the centre/agency through a parent board, newsletter, etc.	_____	_____	_____
Activities are planned that encourage parent involvement (e.g., meeting with guest speakers, social activities).			
Comments:			

Source: www.connectability.ca/en/, Community Living Toronto. Reproduced by permission.

Step 4: Develop a Transition Plan

Ideally, the transition coordinator and the teacher meet with the family 9 to 12 months before the child's transition. This gives the family time to learn about and prepare for the transition. A meeting should be held in advance of the IPP meeting so that transition-related goals may be identified. During the meeting the following should happen:

- The transition coordinator should introduce the topic of transition and explain the process.
- The family should identify their preferences, concerns, support needs, and other agenda items for their child.
- The teacher should summarize the child's progress and include suggestions for future goals.
- The family should begin to identify how much time they can devote to being involved, what they are able to do to prepare for the transition, and other issues they may want to address, such as hours of operation, program fees, and transportation arrangements.
- The minutes of this meeting should be circulated in a written report.

After the meeting, the teacher and family need to work together to develop ideas for specific goals related to the transition, and the family will need to begin to identify their strengths and needs, as well as the child's.

Two additional tasks of the transition coordinator are to (1) help the family determine the level of involvement best for them and (2) develop appropriate strategies with the families to achieve involvement goals.

Figure 13–2 provides specific suggestions as to the kinds of information families like to have regarding their child's transition. Information that families may want to share with new providers can be found in Figure 13–3. Figure 13–4 provides ideas that will help families prepare preschool children as they make the transition from one program to another.

Step 5: Determine the Responsibilities of the Sending Program

Classrooms in different programs vary greatly in their physical arrangements, the structure of learning opportunities, and the style, knowledge, and attitude of the teacher. To the best of their ability, teachers will want to prepare the child for the next environment, especially if it is quite different from the current one. For example, a child leaving a flexible preschool and entering a regimented classroom would be sure to benefit from learning some of the specific skills needed in the next classroom.

Once the transition goals have been identified, the sending program can create activities for working toward those goals. The specific activities will depend on the skills needed for the next program. For example, if the receiving setting is a kindergarten classroom, the early childhood program can incorporate the following ideas into its current curriculum:

- Gradually give children more responsibility for their personal and classroom possessions.
- Teach children to ask for attention in nondisruptive ways.
- Help children learn to follow directions given to the group in general.
- Teach children to care for their toileting needs independently.

- Teach children the difference between boys' and girls' toilet facilities (if this differentiation is made in the new setting).

- Gradually reduce the number of prompts from teachers to children during all kinds of tasks.

- Gradually increase the amount of time children work and play independently, without teachers' involvement.

- Teach children to line up and move in lines, if this is the practice in the new setting.

- Help children learn to complete one task before starting another.

FIGURE 13-2 Ways That Families May Be Involved in the Transition-Planning Process

- Learn about the transition process.
  - How are children evaluated?
  - When will my child make the transition?
  - When will decisions be made?
  - What are the differences between early intervention and preschool?
  - What are my child's and family's legal rights related to special education?
- Be an active member of the transition-planning team.
- Participate in evaluating the child.
- Help amend the IFSP to include a transition plan.
- Work on goals to prepare the child and family for change.
- Help identify goals for the IEP.
- Visit potential programs.
- Participate in placement decisions.
- Share information about the child with new program staff.

FIGURE 13-3 Information That Families May Want to Share with New Providers

- Types of things that the child enjoys doing.
- Things that are easy and difficult for the child to learn.
- The child's favourite toys and activities.
- How the child gets along with other children.
- Types of rewards that the child prefers (e.g., praise, hugs, stickers).
- Types of discipline that work best with the child.
- Kinds of support that the child needs during routine activities such as eating, dressing, toileting, etc.
- Things the child was working on in the previous program that families would like to see continued in the new program.
- Additional goals that the family would like to see addressed in the new program.

FIGURE 13-4 Preparation of the Child

- Talk with the child about the impending changes.
- Provide opportunities for the child to make new friends.
- Teach the child to care for personal belongings.
- Teach the child to share toys and materials.
- Teach the child to use toys and equipment appropriately.
- Help the child acquire as many self-care skills and as much independence as possible.
- Encourage the child to ask for help when needed.
- Allow the child to practise working independently.
- Teach the child to follow directions.
- Read with the child more frequently, encouraging increased attention and involvement in the stories.
- Help the child learn his or her full name, address, and phone number.
- Help the child learn his or her new teacher's name and the name of the school.
- Take the child to visit the new program and the new teacher.
- Talk with the child about rules and activities in the new program.

- Teach children to recognize their printed name and to claim ownership of materials and possessions.
- Teach children to follow classroom routines and change-of-activity patterns (as much as possible, introduce the routines of the new program).
- Vary the length of activities.
- Vary the amount of help provided during and between tasks.
- Vary the type and number of instructions given to children.
- Teach everyday safety rules.
- Role-play meeting new children and ways of making new friends.

Step 6: Hold Placement Meetings

Several meetings may be necessary to determine the appropriate placement for a child. It is important that the transition coordinator, the teacher, and any other professionals who worked with the child attend these meetings (see photo, page 302). Personnel from the receiving program may include the transition coordinator, a member of the program's special service staff, and a teacher representing the classroom program. The family also must be present and be encouraged to invite others involved with the child (a grandparent who frequently provides care for the child, perhaps). Ideally, those from the receiving program would have observed the child in the current program before the placement meeting.

The group as a whole should discuss the child's overall performance and future needs. Information prepared by the sending teacher and the family regarding the child's abilities and progress toward transition goals should be circulated. This information provides the format for the discussion of what services the child needs and the potential sources of such services. There must be ample opportunity to ask questions, request further information, and receive clarification of particular issues. The service and placement decisions are based on the discussion at the meeting and on observations of the child. The child's parents should be equal partners in the decision-making process. When thinking about an appropriate placement, it is important to keep these considerations in mind:

- special services and supports available in the new program
- related services, such as transportation options between programs
- ratio of adults to children
- total size of group
- number of children in the group needing additional support
- availability of paraprofessionals, classroom aides, teacher assistants, or volunteers
- enrolment procedures and prerequisites
- date on which the child can enter the new program
- classroom requirements (e.g., special equipment)
- accessibility for children with physical disabilities
- medical or other clinical personnel available on the premises—if required

Once the appropriate placement has been determined, the parents, transition coordinator, and the teacher should meet with the new teacher, principal, or program director and the special service staff who will be involved with the child during and after the transition. The purpose of this meeting should be to review the child's current performance and special needs, as well as future goals for the child. Arrangements also should be made for the receiving teacher to visit the sending program and for the child and parents to visit the new program.

Step 7: Transfer Records

Transferring a child's records is essential to ensure that the staff members in the new learning environment receive relevant information. A clearly defined process for transferring records needs to be made between the transition coordinators. Written procedures for transferring records ensure that the right records are sent to the right persons in a timely manner. *Parental approval must be obtained before sending records of any kind to another person or program.* Parents must be informed about the records to be sent, to whom they will be sent, and when they will be sent. Ideally, parents should receive copies of any teacher reports that are to be sent to the receiving centre. The following questions can serve as a guide when planning the transfer of records:

- What method does each program use when getting parental consent for transfer of records?

The transition coordinator and the child's teacher are but two of the key people at the placement meeting.

© Cengage Learning 2015

- To what extent do the sending and receiving programs use the same types of records?
- What information collected by the sending program does the receiving program need?
- When and how will additional information be obtained?
- Who is responsible for sending the records?
- Who in the receiving program will accept and be responsible for the records?
- When and how will the records be sent?

Step 8: Have the Child and Family Visit the New Program

A visit to the new program by the child and parents should be planned as early as possible, so that they can see what the new program is like. The transition coordinator can make the appointment. The visit should include a tour of the building, time to explore the classroom, and time for the child to play in the play yard (see photo, below). It is of great value if the new teacher can arrange to spend a few minutes with the child and family. This kind of informal visit should help both the child and the family experience the new program and possibly reduce anxieties about the impending change. *The purpose of this visit is not for parents or teachers to discuss the child's abilities or specific needs.* A meeting without the child must be scheduled when such issues can be discussed.

Step 9: Move into the New Program

For some children, especially those with a developmental delay or other special need, a full session in the new setting may be too much at first. Scheduling arrangements should vary, depending on each child. Program flexibility is critical when young children, with or without developmental differences, are starting a new program.

The following are three suggestions for children who are not ready to start out independently or with a full session:

1. The child might attend the new program for only one hour a day for the first week or so; the time then can be extended. How quickly it is extended depends on how quickly the child adjusts.

2. The sending teacher, transition coordinator, or parent might accompany the child for the first few days. As the child becomes comfortable in the new classroom, adult support can gradually be withdrawn.

3. The child might continue to attend the old program part time while starting to attend the new program the rest of the time.

The child should visit the new program and be given time and support to explore the environment.

Courtesy of Bloorview—Scarborough Site

With systematic planning and cooperation among staff and family, the new experience can be made comfortable for all children as they make the transition from one program to another. Some ideas to help receiving children are as follows:

- Talk with the children about the new program, how the children are growing up, and how the new program is different (and even a little scary, perhaps—but that it will be fun, too).

- Initially, provide additional time for self-directed play so that children can become familiar with one another.

- Give simple one- and two-step instructions; gradually get children used to longer and more complex instructions.

- Vary the duration and type of activities more frequently at first.

- Vary the amount of teacher help during academic tasks, but always be available for a child who needs help.

- Throughout the transition period, review classroom rules and routines each day (more often for some children).

- Assign experienced children as *buddies* for new children.

Step 10: Offer Support Services

During the first weeks—even months—of a new program, the child may need extra assistance. This may be in the form of support services offered by the transition coordinator, the previous teacher, or the special service staff. Many receiving teachers welcome such offers. Others are not interested. Whether or not the support services are provided depends on individual teachers. If a teacher is interested, the coordinator should plan to maintain communication. Four services that might be made available to the receiving teacher are described below.

1. Teacher conferences Regularly scheduled meetings can be a critical part of the support services. They provide an opportunity for teachers to follow the child's progress. Suggestions can be offered as needed. During the first days of school in the new setting, the transition coordinator, who is familiar with the child's special needs and challenges, can help. If trouble develops, the coordinator can suggest solutions based on the child's former program experiences. It is important that the coordinator also be available by phone, as problems can come up without warning.

Teachers sometimes want to schedule a few meetings with the transition coordinator after school, or they may want the coordinator to come and observe after the new child is enrolled. Sometimes the coordinator can provide the most help by simply listening quietly to a teacher describe the program day. Talking about a problem often leads to a solution. These meetings also can provide opportunities for teachers to express their feelings—both the challenges and the pleasures of working with children who have special needs.

2. Family input The child's family is a prime resource. Regular contact between the teacher and the parents allows for the sharing of a child's progress, opportunities to express concerns, and identification of solutions.

3. Sharing of materials and activity ideas Transitions can be eased if the new classroom offers experiences familiar to the child. The sending program might lend a favourite learning or play material to the receiving program. Something familiar to use or hang on to tends to promote a child's sense of security. With familiar objects and activities are readily available during the first weeks of the transition, the classroom, the teachers, and classmates may seem less strange.

4. Teaching assistants Providing a teaching assistant for short periods several times a week often helps both the receiving teacher and the child during the transition period. The teaching assistant can supplement the regular teaching activities in the classroom (which is especially useful when a child needs intensive instruction or supervision during the adjustment period, however long that may be). A teaching assistant can work individually with the specific child or work with a small group that includes the child. Teaching assistants may be regular classroom aides, or they may be older children whose own learning will be enhanced by working with younger children. Teaching assistants also may be arranged through parent groups, community volunteer agencies, and community college or university early childhood programs.

Roles of Team Members

THE ROLE OF THE SENDING PROGRAM The sending program is the major support system for the child and family during the transition. It assists the family in gathering information about the new program(s) and provides recent reports and evaluations to the receiving program. One critical component of transition planning is for the sending program to work with the child and family to identify any skills the child may need to learn to succeed in the new program (see the following section on preparing children for transitions). This might include experience with sitting on a carpet square for circle versus a chair, being able to attend for longer periods of time, being able to write his or her name, or walking down a hall to use the bathroom. When these skills are identified before the transition, current service providers can spend time preparing the child for the receiving program's expectations. Figure 13–5 lists the role of the sending program.

THE ROLE OF THE RECEIVING PROGRAM The receiving program may or may not have much experience with a child with special needs. Depending on their experience, they may be anxious about being able to meet the needs of the child. To ensure a successful transition, the receiving program should meet with the family and child before the child begins. The family should be provided with brochures, tours, and program times. Before the child starts, it is important to hold a meeting with the parents, teachers, program director (if applicable), and current providers. The purpose of this meeting is to answer any questions, identify potential problems, and share strategies found to be effective in working with the child. If an aide or a paraprofessional will be shadowing the child, his or her role in relation to the other adults in the room should be clarified. It is also important for the receiving program to identify the parents' desires with regard to how to handle questions from other parents. Parents of children with special needs have varied wishes, ranging from wanting no one to know that their child has special needs to wanting to share all they have learned with fellow parents. According to parent wishes, staff should have a plan on how to handle questions when they arise.

Before the child's start date, the receiving program should ensure that all staff, including volunteers, have the information they need to work effectively with the child. Ongoing consultation from specialists or additional in-service training may be required throughout the year. Finally, the receiving program,

FIGURE 13-5 Role of Service Providers and Parents during Transitions

Role of Sending Program	Role of Receiving Program	Role of Parents
• Gather information about the new program (i.e., contact person, telephone numbers, and population of children attending the program)	• Make arrangements to meet the family and child before the child begins	• Learn about the transition process: – How are children evaluated? – When will my child make the transition? – When will decisions be made? – What are the differences between early intervention and preschool? – What are my child's and family's legal rights related to special education?
• Provide copies of recent reports and evaluations	• Provide pictures, brochures, tours, times for observation for the family and/or previous service providers	
• Support the family during the process	• Identify physical barriers that may impede the child's access	
• Determine if the child needs to learn a new skill prior to the transition	• Identify and supply special materials and equipment needed (adaptive seating, eating utensils, colourful and musical toys, trikes)	• Be an active member of the transition planning team
• Determine if the new program has special materials that the child might need	• Arrange the classroom environment so that children feel safe to explore and socialize	• Participate in evaluating the child
• Provide a contact person and telephone number from the sending agency to maintain contact and provide assistance as needed	• Provide the staff information about the child's specific diagnosis and needs	• Help amend the IFSP to include a transition plan • Work on goals to prepare the child and family for change • Help identify goals for the IEP
• Share information about the child that will help the new program understand the child's previous services and his ways of communicating and interacting with the environment	• Learn strategies used in previous program • Provide ongoing in-service training and information on young children with special needs	• Visit potential programs • Participate in placement decisions • Share information about the child with the new program staff
• Provide the new program with adaptations and supports needed to support the child's play (i.e., materials used to keep toys within the child's reach, adaptive utensils, visual schedules, communication systems)	• Work with family to develop system for ongoing feedback and communication • Evaluate the child's adaptation to the new program and participation in classroom activities	• Prior to transition: – Visit the new program with their child – Arrange play dates with children from the new program

Sources: Adapted from Minor, L. (2002, Summer). Effective practices in early intervention planning transitions to preschool. *See/Hear Newsletter.* Retrieved from http://www.tsbvi.edu/seehear/summer02/planning.htm; © Cengage Learning 2015

in collaboration with the parents, should determine how to provide ongoing feedback and communication. This is key, because often a transition can result in a change from parents having daily contact and communication with their child's provider to seeing the teacher only on an occasional basis. Figure 13–5 lists the role of the receiving program.

THE ROLE OF PARENTS Throughout their children's early intervention years, families are taught to become their advocates. When the shift in services occurs from family-centred to child-centred, it can be difficult for parents (Johnson, 2001). Family involvement is a critical component of transition planning (Bruder & Chandler, 1996; Hains et al., 1991; Johnson,

Chandler, Kerns, & Fowler, 1986). There are many ways that families can participate in their child's transition. Families may choose to gather information about potential programs, share important information about their child with new providers, or arrange for their child to have experiences that will help him or her get ready for preschool. As mentioned earlier, professionals should not assume that all families have the capacity, desire, or ability to participate in the same ways, and various factors may influence how the family participates in the transition planning (Lynch & Hanson, 2011).

Families define their roles in transition planning in a variety of ways. In some instances, one parent may take the lead in making decisions for the child. In other instances, both parents may take equally active roles. An aunt or uncle who has expertise in special education may be a major player in some families, while a single parent may elect to bring a close friend to all planning meetings. For transition planning to be successful, it is critical that professionals accept the roles that families create for themselves.

It is equally crucial that providers acknowledge and respect families' preferences based on their cultural beliefs and values. Some families may believe that professionals are the experts and that it would be a sign of disrespect to question them. At the same time, other families may be offended by communicative mannerisms (e.g., gestures or touches) that are considered to be acceptable in the mainstream culture but not in their culture.

For example, an Asian family may interpret direct eye contact as a sign of disrespect on the part of the service provider (Hyun & Fowler, 1995). Service providers who understand or recognize the influence that culture may play in a family's involvement in their child's transition will be better able to support the family in identifying their priorities for transition.

Figure 13–5 presents an outline of information that families may find helpful to share in a meeting with their child's new teachers. For many families, participation in the transition-planning process helps reduce the stress that they may be feeling regarding the change in programs. Just as transition plans should be individualized for each child, each family's role in the transition-planning process should be individualized to meet members' needs and expectations. Some families may choose to be more involved than others. As noted earlier, their involvement may be influenced by a variety of factors such as culture, history with schools, employment hours, and child care options.

Maintaining a Positive Placement Experience

The process of successful inclusion of a child with a special need may not always be a consistently smooth experience. Problems may arise if the early childhood teachers have not been part of the planning process. They may become unsure of the objectives or threatened by the developmental needs of the child, as well as by the expectations placed on them with respect to the child. This can make teachers feel inadequate or frustrated, and it may lead to a certain amount of resistance. It is important at this point to get support for the teachers. Early childhood teachers should be encouraged to obtain help in overcoming difficulties of this type when they occur. The case manager, transition coordinator, or resource teacher/early interventionist should be contacted for support and help in resolving any problems that arise.

It is important to involve all of those working with the child in developing an effective team problem-solving approach. Here are six steps to include in effective team problem solving:

1. Identify the specific issues that are of concern and state them.
2. Gather all information that has a bearing on the situation.
3. Identify and state all possible options for resolution (brainstorm).
4. Agree on the most appropriate option.
5. Agree on a specific plan of action.
6. Set up a schedule for an ongoing group review of the process.

Summary

For children with special needs and their families, a successful transition from one program to another is critical to the child's long-range progress. The number and type of accommodations made by children, families, and service providers during periods of transition, and the sustainability of these accommodations, are critical factors in a successful transition. Transition planning should involve a minimum number of disruptions for the child, the family, and the teacher, and yet sustain the child's progress.

The various perspectives of the child, family, and professionals must be considered if the accommodations that each must make are to be recognized and planned for. To increase the likelihood of successful transfer from one program to another, systematic transition planning should be a component of all inclusive early childhood programs. Planning should begin within a few weeks of a child's enrolment in the sending program and continue throughout the year and into the next program for as long as necessary. Transition planning requires a number of steps. As a starting point, representatives—one each from the sending program and the receiving program—are appointed to serve as transition coordinators. Once selected, the coordinators are responsible for visiting other programs and becoming acquainted with classroom practices and staff. The coordinators need to learn the expectations of the other programs and how they differ from their own. Next, the coordinators work with their own classroom staff to help minimize the differences between programs for the child who will be in transition.

Parents need to be included throughout the transition process. The parents and transition coordinators must discuss how to make the transition and together write up a specific transition plan. The plan should meet with the approval of everyone: parents, administrators, and teachers. At the time the child is actually transferred, careful pacing is required. Moving through changes too rapidly tends to be upsetting for any young child and especially for a young child with special needs. One recommendation is that the child's time in the new program be increased gradually.

As the child enters the new program, the receiving teacher needs to know what support services are available if needed (and wanted). Possibilities for support services include consultations with the staff from the sending program, from special service staff members in the current program, and from the family. There also may be loans of materials from the sending program and supplementary teaching in the form of teacher assistant services. It is the rare child, even one with a severe disability, who cannot be helped to succeed in a carefully selected new program. Changing from one program to another can and should be a positive experience for the child, family, and teachers. Careful, individualized planning and sufficient time are required.

Resources

ConnectABILITY

http://www.connectability.ca/en

This website offers lifelong learning and support for people who have an intellectual disability, their families, and support networks. The website provides accessible, self-directed access to valuable information and tools. It is a project of Community Living Toronto.

Provincial and Territorial Associations for Community Living

http://www.cacl.ca

The Canadian Association for Community Living is dedicated to promoting the participation of people with disabilities in all aspects of community living. This site lists all the provincial and territorial sites. Information can be accessed in English or French.

SpeciaLink Canada

http://www.specialinkcanada.org

This is the site for a Canada-wide mainstream network whose goal is to promote high-quality daycare for every child in the country, regardless of abilities.

 Access an interactive ebook and chapter-specific interactive learning tools, including flashcards, quizzes, videos, and more, in the *Inclusion in Early Childhood Programs* CourseMate. Visit NELSONbrain.com to log in, register, or purchase access.

Intervention with Specific Age Groups: Infants, Toddlers, and School-Aged Children

14

OBJECTIVES

After studying the material in this chapter, the student will be able to

- Describe the benefits of early intervention for infants and toddlers with special needs.
- Define the term *enabling environment* as related to infant and toddler caregiving.
- Explain the family's and the teacher's/caregiver's roles in promoting infant learning through sensory stimulation.
- Discuss special considerations related to working with infants and toddlers with sensory impairments.
- Discuss links between the developmental characteristics of school-aged children and effective programming.
- Identify behavioural concerns that may arise in school-age programs.
- Describe adaptations to school-age programs that promote inclusion.

KEY CONCEPTS AND TERMS

differentiated responses

early intervention

enabling environment

in-home support services

psychological balance

reciprocal relationships

responsive environment

school-age care

sensorimotor profile

sensory stimulation

CONNECTIONS

- Tyrone, a three-year-old with significant language delays, spends nine hours every day at the child care centre of a corporate building downtown where his father works.
- Leah, a toddler with Down syndrome, and her mother participate in a "Mommy and Me" exercise class three times a week.
- Sean, a four-year-old who uses a wheelchair, participates in child care, religious school, and vacation programs at his church.
- Eva, a five-year-old with autism, attends kindergarten at her neighbourhood school.

Introduction

Early intervention the provision of services to children that are showing first indications of an identifiable problem or are significantly at risk of developing a problem

This chapter focuses on two distinct age groups: (1) **early intervention** and programming for very young children (birth to two and a half years of age) and (2) intervention and programming for children (5 to 12 years old) attending school-age child care programs. Within these specific age groupings, children have great variations in developmental skill levels. Therefore, an educator's responses to infant needs may differ from those required for toddlers. For example, during the toddler years, a child shows the improving language, mental representation, and memory skills necessary for engaging with the world. Mobile, energetic, and emotionally expressive toddlers need caregivers who can sensitively guide them in self-regulation without becoming overcontrolling or withdrawing support. Healthy infant and toddler development does not "just happen," even with babies who are born full-term and are developing within culturally appropriate expectations. Infants and toddlers are actively looking, listening, and learning through mutually responsive relationships with caregivers. Similarly, the developmental profile of 6-year-old children differs from that of 12-year-olds. It is important that those working with school-aged children recognize these developmental differences when planning intervention strategies and curriculum. This chapter also focuses on particular issues that arise in the inclusion of school-aged children with special needs in before- and after-school settings.

Infant and Toddler Programs: An Overview

In-home support services services, such as development assessments and parenting support, provided in the home for infants with special needs and their families

The number of infants in need of special services is increasing (see photo, page 313). These services can be provided in an inclusive group setting, such as a child care centre; in a specialized clinic where families bring their infant or toddler for scheduled intervention sessions; or through **in-home support services**, where a professional provides support to a family for an extensive period. Guralnick (2000), after an extensive review of the early intervention system and out-of-home child care in the United States, suggested that an inclusive child care program that offers early intervention services and child care is "ideal." He stated, "The benefits that result in terms of continuity, quality and parental confidence of such an inclusive program cannot be overemphasized" (p. 28).

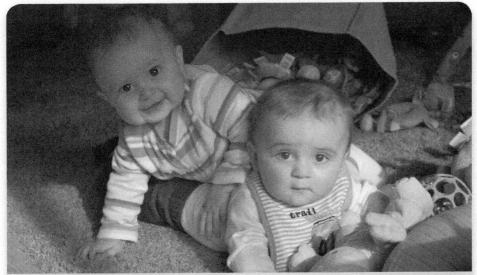

The number of infants in need of special services is increasing.

In Canada each province and territory has adopted unique approaches to providing early intervention and early childhood education and care (ECEC) services. As Guralnick (2005) noted, it is necessary for local communities to have a degree of control in decision making and service delivery. Across Canada, there is a social policy trend to link early years services and educational services. This trend has created an interest in identifying family and child needs as soon as possible in order to match them to programs that will optimize early development. Although not all provinces/territories have linked early years and educational services yet, early identification and intervention are a priority in all jurisdictions (Underwood & Frankel, 2012).

Winzer (1997) identified other benefits of early intervention:

- Relieves family stress and improves family functioning.

- Provides critical information about other services available.

- Prevents secondary disabilities, such as behaviour concerns.

- Provides a foundation for the early acquisition of developmental skills during a critical period in human development.

- Halts or prevents declines in development.*

The Importance of Enabling and Responsive Caregiving

In this section on infants and toddlers, the terms *teacher/caregiver*, *educator*, and *infant teacher* will be considered interchangeable. When discussing infants and toddlers with special needs, the term *interventionist* will also be used.

Newborns are vulnerable to negative environmental influences. Inadequate nurturing, inappropriate stimulation, or insufficient medical and nutritional care can do great damage. Some infants are more vulnerable than others; all infants, however, are vulnerable to some degree, even those who are healthy and responsive at birth. Development is at its most critical stage when infants are most dependent on others to meet all their needs. The recent findings on brain research indicate that learning

* Winzer, M. (1997). *Special Education in Early Childhood: An Inclusive Approach.* Reprinted with permission by Pearson Education Canada Inc.

occurs within the context of supportive adult–child relationships. When adults fail in their caregiving responsibilities, an infant's development is put in jeopardy. Extremely low-birthweight infants, as well as those who are medically fragile or at high risk, usually require intensive caregiving. We also know that the quality of early childhood environments influences development (Herschkowitz & Herschkowitz, 2004).

With infants and toddlers, the teacher's/caregiver's responsibilities are similar. The focus should be on providing an environment in which daily routines, play activities, and the teacher's/caregiver's responsiveness are geared to the behaviours, strengths, and developmental level of the infant or toddler. Such an environment is an **enabling environment**.

No matter how safe, sanitary, healthy, and well-supervised a learning environment may be, an infant or toddler will not thrive developmentally unless the caregiver actively engages and responds to the child (see photo, left). By its very nature, a **responsive environment** encourages and supports active exploration when adults provide individual infants and toddlers with opportunities and options for

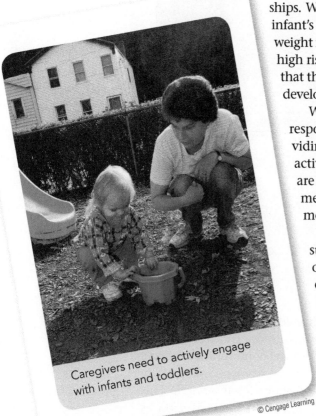

Caregivers need to actively engage with infants and toddlers.

© Cengage Learning

- gaining access to what is happening in the environment;
- making appropriate choices;
- engaging in experiences that evolve from a simple to a more complex level; and
- creating an impact on their environment.

Reciprocal Relationships with Families

Positive and candid interactions among parents and staff members—**reciprocal relationships**—are important. Staff must remember that parents are the primary source of affection and care in the child's life. Positive interaction between staff and parents can help parents feel more confident in their roles and with their child care choices (Gonzalez-Mena & Eyer, 2007). Guidelines for positive interactions with parents include

- sharing important information with parents about their children;
- demonstrating respect for a family's culture, language, and life choices;
- having appropriate information that enables teachers to answer questions about child development and available community resources; and
- responding respectfully to parents' questions, comments, and concerns.

Infant and Toddler Intervention

Children develop best when they have secure, consistent relationships with adults who are responsive (NAEYC, 2009). The goal of infant and toddler intervention is twofold: to enable infants and toddlers to explore and master their environment, and to encourage them to use their capacities and abilities in ways that are individually meaningful and productive.

Enabling environment an environment that supports a child's optimal development

Responsive environment adults actively engage with an individual infant or toddler and respond to his or her needs and sensorimotor and social exploration

Reciprocal relationships interactions between individuals in which each person gives and receives in response to the giving and receiving of the other

Sensory Stimulation

Infants and toddlers usually respond to **sensory stimulation** and social stimulation. Caregivers choose different types of stimulation and increase the levels of stimulation that can be tolerated by the child. They identify through observation the individual differences in arousal and reactivity (Goulet, 1998). Caregivers share the child's attention to and interest and delight in exploring different stimulation. An infant's or a toddler's actions are often contingent on the caregiver's responses. When the infant or toddler is overstimulated, the sensitive caregiver will reduce the stimulation and wait for the child to reorganize and refocus on other stimuli. A secure and trusting caregiver–child relationship is strengthened through the expression of positive emotions and mutual responsiveness.

Starting soon after birth, infants are learning to use their abilities to see, hear, taste, smell, and move about. These emerging skills enable them to be active participants in sharing a variety of experiences with others in their world. Toys and materials that stimulate the senses include those that encourage the infant's or toddler's developing abilities to see sights, hear sounds, touch and feel textures, and move the body in and through space.

Extensive research supports the conclusion that infants and toddlers who do not move about and explore their environment are less able to organize and represent their experiences internally. This is especially true of infants and toddlers with neuromuscular conditions affecting their balance and movement, and of infants and toddlers with visual or hearing impairments. These children, without special help, tend to engage in few exploratory moves. The family's and caregiver's/teacher's task is to provide movement experiences that are challenging, yet result in relatively few frightening falls, bumps, or otherwise unpleasant experiences. As a teacher/ caregiver helps an infant or toddler build confidence in moving about and exploring the environment, the child is likely to show increasing interest in physical activity, and may even come to enjoy "rough-and-tumble" play. It must be remembered, however, that infants should never be rocked, shaken, or swung roughly, lifted rapidly and abruptly, or thrown into the air. Infants and toddlers cannot adjust posturally to quick extremes of motion. Serious injuries to the head, brain, neck, and back may result (see photo, below).

Sensory stimulation objects and people that encourage infants and toddlers to explore their environment through seeing, hearing, touching, tasting, and smelling

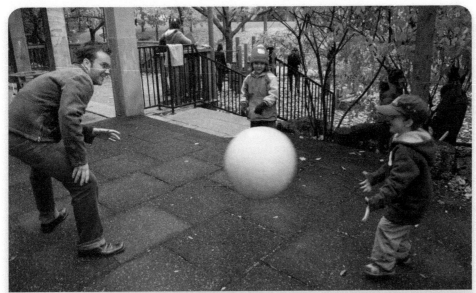

Courtesy of Ryerson Early Learning Centre

Teachers/caregivers need to provide challenging but safe movement experiences.

Integrating Sensory Modalities

Sensorimotor profile
an infant's preference for and use of one sensory modality over another for sensory exploration

Some infants and toddlers appear to enjoy all kinds of movement experiences; others may show a particular **sensorimotor profile** and be overly sensitive, sometimes in one sensory modality more than another. Still other infants or toddlers may be able to use comfortably only one sense at a time. An example is the child who likes to listen to a music box, but only if allowed to look away from the action. Great distress may occur if an adult tries to coerce such a child into listening and looking at the same time. It must be remembered, too, that how the caregiver/teacher perceives and responds to a sensation is not necessarily the way an infant or toddler will react to the same sensation. It is best, therefore, for the family or teacher/caregiver to introduce a new experience when the child is in a calm state, in familiar surroundings. Experiences that cause distress should be modified or stopped and reintroduced under different circumstances or when the child is more developmentally advanced. Responsive caregivers protect infants and toddlers from overarousal or support the child's recovery from overarousal when it does occur (Goulet, 1998).

Responding to the Infant's and Toddler's Development

Teacher/caregiver sensitivity is critical in recognizing the developmental accomplishments of the infant or toddler with special needs. Their achievements often seem so small when measured against those of healthy infants. However, the developmental gains of these infants must be viewed as joyful events. To properly appreciate these victories, teachers/caregivers need to recognize that the potential for positive development exists in all developmental areas for every infant and toddler. Teachers/caregivers need to be aware, too, that the strengthening of one area, through appropriate intervention procedures, usually contributes to development in other areas.

A major responsibility of the infant caregiver/interventionist is to appreciate all aspects of development, both evident and emerging. Infants and toddlers with special needs exhibit a wide range of competencies and developmental needs. Developmental sequences follow the same pattern for children within the same social and cultural environment. However, anything that interferes with a young child's development may reduce his or her ability to use information.

Generally speaking, one sense cannot fully compensate for another. A child who has a visual impairment may become highly skilled at identifying objects and events through touch. That information, however, is never as complete as it would be if the child were also using vision. Even when the various sensory systems appear to be intact, sensory integration may be poor. For example, the infant may hear a teacher's/caregiver's voice but be unable to orient his or her eyes or head movements in that direction. In these instances, the teacher's/caregiver's role is to provide learning experiences and intervention activities based on the guidelines outlined earlier for responsive and enabling caregiving.

Enabling the Infant to Respond and Adapt

Infants with special needs may be less responsive and less vocal. The following disturbances in behaviours commonly associated with attachment include

- delayed or infrequent smiling or vocalizing;
- tenseness, limpness, or unresponsiveness when handled; and
- little effort to get the mother's attention.

Similarly, premature and low-birthweight babies often have trouble forming attachments because of reduced physical strength or immature neurological development. It is important to recognize that lack of infant responsiveness contributes to less effective responding by others. Parents and teachers/caregivers, therefore, need to be available and ready to respond in kind when an infant initiates an interaction or responds to stimulation from the environment. For example, if an infant or toddler smiles spontaneously, the adult smiles back; if the infant or toddler smiles again in response to the adult's smile, the caregiver smiles once again and perhaps adds an affectionate pat or word.

Responding in kind may not be simple, especially when an infant's or a toddler's abilities are limited. For example, low-birthweight infants with medical complications usually are considerably less responsive than are healthy infants. Some parents of these infants may try to compensate by providing more physical and playful contacts than do parents of full-term, healthy infants (Brachfield, Goldberg, & Sloman, 1980). Parents may need to lower the number and the tempo of their reactions to match the infant's activity level, in order to avoid overstimulating the infant to the point that he or she may shut down.

Clearly, adults need to find a middle ground. In some instances, it is best to wait for the infant to make an overture and then respond at a matching level of activity. In other instances, it may be better if the teacher/caregiver watches for signs of receptiveness and then initiates a simple activity, such as smiling and gently clapping the infant's hand against his or her own hand. More often than not, infants will signal "enough is enough" by averting their gaze and then looking back when they are ready for further activity (Curry & Johnson, 1990). To meet the needs of the infant or toddler, teachers/caregivers should develop the following skills:

- general sensitivity to the infant's or toddler's need for stimulation, as well as for quiet.
- responsiveness to specific signals, such as fussing and turning away.
- talking and playing with the infant or toddler in ways that actively encourage development.

Enabling the Infant to Maintain Psychological Balance

Weak reflexes or the absence of muscle tone may interfere with an infant's or a toddler's ability to control his or her responses to the environment. Some infants and toddlers have difficulty becoming aroused, while others become too easily overaroused. For example, the predisposition to respond to the parent's or teacher's/ caregiver's face with matching facial expressions may overflow and engage the infant's entire body—the head, arms, legs, fingers, and toes. The infant is not able to dampen the intensity, so the response to stimulation involves the whole body in an undifferentiated way.

Such activity "overflow" often characterizes the behaviour of infants with special needs. Other examples include the following:

- extreme sensitivity, or marked lack of sensitivity, to everyday occurrences.
- early reflexes and behaviour patterns that persist, making it difficult for the child to initiate, stop, or redirect his or her own behaviour.

- exhaustion as a result of having to spend disproportionate amounts of energy in trying to control or direct neuromuscular activity (as in the child with cerebral palsy), or having to expend excessive energy in trying to seek out and process new learning.

Among the jobs of the teacher/caregiver is assisting the child in becoming an active participant in appropriate learning opportunities in the immediate environment. Another is communicating with the infant or toddler in ways that let the child know that his or her messages are being heard and respected.

Some caregiving strategies that may enable an infant or toddler to maintain a psychological balance include the following:

- Observe frequency patterns in arousal to and recovery from stimulation.
- Reduce situations that provoke extreme sensitivity.
- Introduce new activities when the child is most calm or alert (after a nap).
- Provide a stimulus shelter or comfort zone (an area with minimal stimulation) within the playroom.

Enabling the Infant and Toddler to Differentiate Responses

An infant or toddler with special needs may retain undifferentiated social, cognitive, and communication responses longer. In social development, for example, the infant may not show the selective interest in parents or caregivers that is seen in most two-month-olds. Unable to receive information through one or more of the senses, this infant may withdraw from his or her immediate world or overreact to it. Either response can prevent the infant from becoming actively interested in what is going on. In turn, this prevents the infant from attaining a sense of self and from forming effective relationships with others. As a result, the infant or the toddler may

- respond in a global, all-or-nothing way;
- resist changes and transitions to other activities or settings; or
- resist adaptations, extensions, and opportunities to interrelate or to combine elements and experiences.

It takes skill and insight for a teacher/caregiver to help an infant or toddler learn to modify what he or she is able to do and to accomplish differentiated responses. As a first step, the teacher/caregiver can help the child process incoming stimuli. For example, a puppet or toy that looks, feels, and sounds unusual might elicit a total approach or a total withdrawal reaction. If the infant can experience first the touch and then the sound of the object, the experience may become a manageable one. With some infants, an effort to touch the puppet still may spread throughout the child's entire body. When the child is therapeutically positioned in a manner that inhibits much of the overflow, the infant's energy can be directed at making controlled arm movements that allow the infant to successfully reach for and touch the puppet. By helping the infant inhibit some responses so that others can be functional, the teacher/caregiver has enabled the infant to differentiate and effectively use an appropriate response from among his or her outgoing responses.

Once infants and toddlers develop some strategies for controlling their responses, parents and teachers/caregivers can help them develop a greater and more varied range of behaviours. Parents and teachers/caregivers can do this by creating opportunities for the infants to seek out, explore, and manipulate

Psychological balance an infant's or toddler's ability to maintain a balance between approaching and avoiding environmental events (stimuli)

Differentiated responses an infant's and toddler's ability to differentiate simpler and more specific responses among global undifferentiated responses to stimuli whatever interests them (see photo, right). The best learning opportunities occur when the new experience is a natural outgrowth of an old and familiar one. Extensions of earlier experiences need to be gradually introduced while remaining rooted in what the infant or toddler already knows. Parents and teachers/caregivers can assist in several ways:

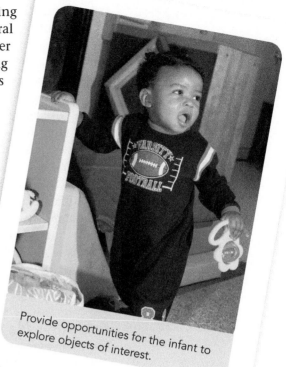

Provide opportunities for the infant to explore objects of interest.

© Cengage Learning

- Provide many slightly different opportunities for the infant or toddler to do the same thing. For example, there can be balls and blocks of many sizes, plastic cups of different shapes, chairs of different designs, and mechanical switches that are activated in different ways. If the child already walks confidently on a smooth, flat surface, this ability can be challenged by putting out a bumpy mattress to walk on. If a child with seizure disorder has to adjust to wearing a helmet for head protection, happier experiences can be offered as starters, perhaps wearing different kinds of hats in preparation for adapting to the helmet.

- Offer new experiences similar to previous experiences and using familiar materials to ease transitions. An infant or toddler may find bath time pleasant when sitting in a special seat in the bathtub. Using the same seat when introducing the child to the pool is likely to help the child adapt to being in water in a different setting.

- Change one dimension of an experience. When infants or toddlers are going outdoors to play on the grass, a teacher/caregiver can take along familiar play materials—balls, for example. As a toddler starts to play with the toys "in the same old way," the toys are likely to respond differently by not moving as freely on the grass. As a result, the toddler must internalize this new information about the toys and how differently they react in different settings. Such experiences motivate a child to explore the newly exhibited properties of balls (and other play materials) as teachers/caregivers transfer the toys from one situation to another.

Enabling Infants and Toddlers to Initiate New Responses

An infant or toddler with special needs often uses energy to maintain internal equilibrium, making it more difficult to acknowledge external events. Or, if the child should become aware of external stimuli, the awareness tends to be one-dimensional—that is, the infant or toddler addresses only one source of input while ignoring the others. Conversely, an infant or toddler may use only one sense, such as vision or hearing, to experience an object. For example, the child may be so engrossed in watching an activity that any sounds or speech accompanying the action do not register. Also, an infant or toddler may respond with one sense but not integrate the response with other sensory input. The child may look or touch, but not put the two behaviours together so as to gain more complete information. Infants and toddlers with perceptual motor difficulties, for example, may follow the movement of an object with their eyes. They may not, however, try to reach for or grasp the object as it moves out of visual range—indicating, perhaps, an inability to integrate and coordinate looking with touching.

Caregivers need to support and encourage all areas of sensory learning. They can observe infants and toddlers for a new response to stimulation and then provide opportunities for repeated practice of a skill by using similar materials. When a caregiver and a child jointly focus on stimulation, a skill may be extended and reinforced. The caregiver may move toys, particularly those desired, closer to the child to heighten his or her awareness of them. High-contrast materials (such as black-and-white combinations) help infants and toddlers with visual impairments use their residual vision. Prompting strategies that increase play behaviours include changing the presentation of a toy (e.g., turning it another way), placing a toy in the child's hands, and activating a toy and letting the child complete the task (Blasco, 2001). Ringing a bell near an object helps some infants attend to stimulation. With toddlers, frequent pairing of words and actions (e.g., "up" with the action of going up the stairs) helps them integrate different sensory stimulation.

Adapting Play and Learning Materials

Active contact with play materials allows infants and toddlers to experience some control over their environment. Hearing the chiming of a musical rattle when it is shaken or seeing a rubber toy that had been held under water float to the surface teaches the child the effects of his or her actions on the environment. All infants and toddlers, including those with special needs, need to have opportunities to manipulate objects and experience control. Remember, it is much more interesting and motivating for a child to bat a mobile or ring a bell than it is to watch as someone else bats a mobile or rings a bell.

As noted earlier, all children benefit from manipulative materials that enable them to produce some change or effect on the environment. The task of the teacher/caregiver is to make materials accessible and to figure out adaptations so that all children can explore, manipulate, and control play materials and everyday objects. Possible adaptations of materials and equipment for children with poorly developed motor skills are as follows:

- suspend toys from activity frames.
- place foam hair curlers over paintbrushes or crayons for an easier hold.
- attach toys to playboards or wall surfaces.
- place toys on a tray.
- attach objects to blankets or mats with Velcro loops (especially good for children who are not mobile).
- deflate beach balls for easier grasping, throwing, and catching.
- fit the child with a Velcro mitt and attach strips of Velcro to toys to make them more accessible.

Once play materials are accessible to the child, adaptive play goals should focus on these aims:

- increasing the duration of the child's play.
- encouraging various kinds of manipulation of play materials.
- introducing a wider range of toys and manipulative materials.
- reducing a child's dependence on prompting from the caregiver.

Times for Sharing and Learning

The daily routines of feeding, diapering, bathing, dressing, and helping an infant or toddler relax or go to sleep are prime times for a teacher/caregiver to interact calmly and playfully with the child. When an infant cries, for example, it usually is a signal that the infant needs something: food, diapering, comforting, company. Crying is usually the infant's or toddler's way of both losing control and attempting to gain control. Trust develops when the child's cries are answered in a prompt and caring way. Some infants sleep for short periods, wake often, and cry and scream (high pitched) for prolonged periods. These behaviours are hard for the caregiver to interpret and respond to, so caregivers need to be flexible and often creative in finding ways to soothe a child.

When comforting an infant or a toddler, the adult may be able to soothe with movement, sounds, sights, or touching. Rocking (gentle movement), soft singing (sounds), a favourite toy (sight and texture), or a gentle rubbing or patting (touch) will often successfully calm a baby. Sometimes an infant is signalling the need for warmth, security, or food. The appropriate caregiving response, then, may be gentle swaddling, loosely wrapping the infant in a soft blanket for a short time, being careful that circulation to limbs is not restricted. For infants with neuromuscular problems, swaddling often provides additional comfort by relieving the discomforting effect of twitching or jerking limbs or muscles. In the event that the baby is hungry, it is important that the feeding activity be made a happy and sociable time.

Feeding times may be difficult for infants with particular types of special needs. Mealtimes are likely to be less stressful if a relaxed attitude is maintained. This can be accomplished through appropriate positioning in a specially adapted chair or by seating the infant or toddler securely in the adult's lap. Certain conditions, such as cleft palate or lip, may require special feeding equipment. Children should be fed in the company of others, making mealtimes important social times (see photo, below).

Mealtime should be a social time.

Courtesy of Ryerson Early Learning Centre

Infant and Toddler Intervention: An Ongoing Challenge

As previously indicated, teachers/caregivers who work with infants and toddlers with special needs are challenged with providing a day-by-day learning environment that supports interactions between each infant and toddler and his or her world. To develop individual strengths and reduce the impact of the developmental disability or delay, teachers/caregivers should provide a variety of situations and activities that engage the child as a participant. Infants and toddlers especially need to integrate experiences across several areas of development. For this reason they often seem compelled to look at, touch, and suck on an object. Such achievements need to be viewed not as ends in themselves, but as abilities that enable the child to recognize the functions of objects and to participate in daily experiences.

Intervention for School-Aged Children

School-age care programs offered before and after school on a regular basis in various settings for school-aged children

The majority of provinces offer some licensed school-age care, and the legislation across Canada identifies licensed school-age care in very similar ways. Although the programs in various provinces and territories may differ in terms of group composition and administrative structure, a key component of all definitions of **school-age care** is that care is regulated outside school hours, for school-aged children. Across the country the ages identified are usually 6 to 12, although there is some variation. Recognized, licensed care may be found in either centre- or home-based programs (Childcare Resource and Research Unit, 2004). When educators work in these environments with school-aged children, especially those who have special needs, many components of the program must be considered. Couture and Jacobs (2001) investigated the quality of 20 Montreal school-age care programs that integrated children with special needs. They found that less than half of educators were aware that a child with special needs was joining their program, and "only six of the educators were involved in the planning process" (p. 32). This section highlights elements of a high-quality school-age care program that are necessary for the successful inclusion of children with special needs:

- an understanding of the development of school-aged children.
- effective transitions from the elementary school to the school-age program.
- intervention plans for challenging behaviours.
- communication between programming staff and families.
- programming for inclusion.
- adaptations to promote inclusion.

The Development of School-Aged Children

The development of school-aged children differs from that of preschool children in many ways. School-aged children generally have increased language and literacy skills, improved memory, and the ability to engage in more critical thinking. Children of this age are very "rule-bound," often spending more time deciding and debating the rules than playing the game. They have lots of energy that can put their more developed motor skills to good use by participating in physical challenges.

One of the key characteristics of this developmental period is the formation of strong peer relations. School-aged children need to be valued as individuals and accepted as part of a group. They need to gain self-confidence through successful completion of concrete tasks and products. They will gain self-esteem by being "good" at something and therefore need to develop a variety of skills. Teachers in school-age child care programs need to be aware of these developmental characteristics when creating an individual program plan for a school-aged child with special needs. For example, although a school-aged child with a learning disability may require additional support in learning to read and write, he or she may excel in other school-age activities.

Transition from School to a School-Age Child Care Program

The transition from elementary school to a school-age child care program may present particular challenges for some children. At the end of the day, children often come from a structured school environment in which certain expectations are established to a less structured school-age setting. A child may have difficulty adjusting to different environments and sets of expectations. Since they share responsibility for the individual child, it is essential that teachers in both the school and the school-age child care program have a collaborative relationship that provides for consistent communication of information about the child's strengths and needs and for greater consistency in expectations.

Some Canadian school districts have developed innovations in partnerships between schools and early childhood education programs. For example, the First Duty Project in Toronto is a universal early learning and care program (University of Toronto, O.I.S.E Atkinson Centre). It brings together three programs—kindergarten, child care, and parenting supports—into a single program designed to meet the learning needs of children and the child care needs of parents. Within this unified program, the kindergarten teacher and the early childhood educator work together to provide a seamless day for the children. This model is especially effective for a child with special needs as it significantly reduces the number of transitions that the child must navigate.

The transition from an elementary school to a school-age program may necessitate another accommodation for the child. Schools typically have more support services for children with identified special needs. Indeed, some children with special needs have one-on-one support in their school environment and then have to function completely independently in their after-school program. Directors and families of children in school-age programs often have to strongly advocate for additional supports for a child with special needs.

Behaviour Issues in School-Age Programs

A number of situations can contribute to increased child behaviour challenges in a school-age program. As previously noted, the demands of a transition from a preschool to a school-age environment can make it difficult for a child to cope with and manage his or her emotions, resulting, in some cases, in serious behaviour concerns that teachers feel unable to handle. Couture and Jacobs (2001) concluded that "programs of lower quality excluded children with behavioural problems more often than those of higher quality" (p. 33). Staff in a school-age program will then need to thoughtfully consider ways to help a child settle in, reduce stress, and cope with the transition. A school-aged child (and other family members) can be involved in different ways in developing strategies for coping, thus helping the child gain insight into his or her reactions to transitions. Strategies for coping may include making a change to the schedule (e.g., snack time or physical activity first), providing choices for activities, or giving opportunities to work and play alone, with one other child, or in a small group rather than a large group (e.g., circle time).

School-aged children are often more aware of physical, social, and intellectual differences. Although this presents opportunities to talk more about human differences, exclusionary behaviours among school-aged children also arise. In addition, school-aged children are forming specific peer groups that include and exclude children. Children with special needs are particularly vulnerable to the exclusionary behaviours of their peers and may react to exclusion by seeking attention in negative ways or by withdrawing. It is important for teachers of school-aged children to intervene when they observe exclusionary behaviours and work with the whole group in developing skills in empathy, problem solving, and conflict resolution. With their growing cognitive abilities, school-aged children can become advocates for others and can learn to intervene and advocate when they observe situations of bias and exclusion (see photo, below). School-aged children can also learn that advocating for a child with special needs is more positive than is overprotecting the child, which reduces independence and a sense of competency.

Communication between School-Age Program Staff and Families

In school-age programs, teachers and families have fewer opportunities to talk about the child's challenges and to develop intervention plans. Couture and Jacobs (2001) discovered that only 12 percent of the educators of school-aged children in their study had met the parents of a child with special needs before the child had been included in the program. Contact and communication with parents in a school-age program can be more difficult because older siblings in the same school may pick up children or parents may be rushed at the end of day when picking up their children. A concerted effort by staff in school-age programs that includes a variety of communication strategies needs to be made in order to build to consistent communication with families of school-aged children.

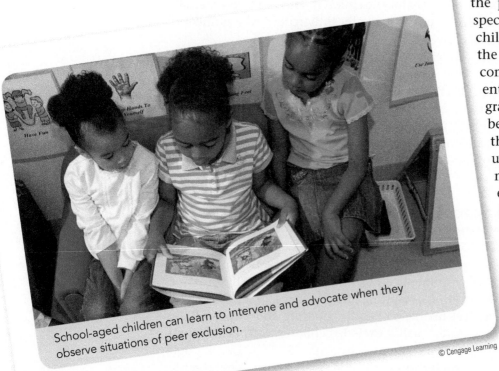

School-aged children can learn to intervene and advocate when they observe situations of peer exclusion.

© Cengage Learning

Programming for Inclusion

Curriculum in a school-age care environment should be developed based on the strengths, needs, and interests of all children. It should be focused on a choice of play, creative arts, science, and recreational activities and not exclusively on homework. Space for doing homework should be set up, but completing homework should be an option, not an expectation of the program. When planning the program, it is important to incorporate some games and activities that are cooperative and noncompetitive in nature. As school-aged children can sustain attention for longer periods, long-term projects can be planned for and implemented. Drama or dance productions, doing creative art, making videos, and writing plays are just a few examples of long-term projects in which many school-aged children enthusiastically participate. These projects should involve access to community resources that expand the school-aged child's world beyond the school and child care centre. It is essential to recognize the importance of social interactions in school-age programs and develop activities that involve working in small groups that include all children.

Adaptations to Promote Inclusion

It is essential to consistently consider adaptations for the child with special needs in order to develop programs that enable total participation. Teachers in school-age care environments need to actively promote inclusion. Inclusion doesn't just happen. It needs to be fostered. For example, when selecting teams for games, teachers may need to develop guidelines for team formation to ensure that the child with special needs is fully included. This can be done through a variety of ways:

- numbering off class participants
- organizing teams on the basis of specific colours of children's clothes, socks, shoes, and so on
- having group discussions on finding novel ways to form inclusive teams

When planning cognitive games and experiences, teachers should be aware that some children may need more visual cues, others may need more tactile ones, and still others may need verbal or written cues to maximize their participation in an activity. Playing games frequently for repeated practice, and providing the child who has difficulty following rules with an individual cue sheet that outlines those rules, are ways this can be achieved.

Outdoor play is an essential component of a quality school-age program (see photo, page 326). Adaptations will need to be made to include children who have a range of special needs. For example, a child in a wheelchair may need the support of a friend in such games as tag. Allowing the child to choose whether or not he or she needs physical assistance will help to promote the child's sense of competency, which is a key school-age developmental task.

School-Age Intervention: An Ongoing Challenge

A major concern is that there is little acknowledgment and support for children with special needs in before- and after-school programs. In addition, teachers in these programs may not have enough information and strategies to effectively support the school-aged child with special needs (Couture & Jacobs, 2001).

To include children who have a range of special needs, adaptations to outdoor activities need to be made.

Eyewire

Though there is growing support for children of kindergarten age, many programs serving older children with special needs (ages 6 to 12) have limited funding and resources. The following are needed to ensure the successful participation and inclusion of school-aged children with special needs:

- more program resources (e.g., staff, consultants, materials, equipment, and access to ongoing professional development).

- increased communication among the elementary school, school-age programs, and families.

- greater advocacy for quality inclusive school-age programs.

Summary

Social and economic factors, as well as legislation related to early intervention services, are resulting in increased numbers of infants and toddlers being cared for by individuals other than their parents. This shift away from parents' full-time care of their own infants and toddlers is generating a need for an increased number of infant and toddler teachers/caregivers/interventionists—trained individuals who are able to provide a responsive and enabling learning environment.

Providing appropriate care and promoting sound learning experiences are based on a teacher's/caregiver's knowledge of infant and toddler development. They are based also on a teacher's/caregiver's ability to implement this knowledge by providing responsive caregiving in an enabling and engaging environment.

Responsive teaching and caregiving means that each infant's or toddler's unique ways of responding are recognized, respected, and nurtured. Only by observing what an infant or toddler is doing and how the child responds to overtures from others can parents and teachers/caregivers decide how best to respond to individual abilities and needs. Experiences should not be imposed on infants or toddlers; the adult should patiently try to engage the child's active participation, as an initiator as well as a responder.

All infants and toddlers need a safe, healthy, well-supervised, and engaging environment. However, even in such an environment, developmental differences, such as sensory impairments, motor or neurological dysfunctions, and severe health conditions, can affect the child's efforts to engage positively with his or her world. The infant or toddler may experience few consistent outcomes or results to promote a sense of accomplishment and confidence. For these infants and toddlers it is especially important that parents and teachers/caregivers respond in enabling ways. Families and teachers/caregivers who delight and share in very young children's discoveries, ideas, and perspectives of the world are likely to promote the emotional well-being of children who need extra support.

Emotional support, warmth, and caring are also essential ingredients of an effective, inclusive school-age program. Educators need to recognize and value the unique developmental profiles of school-aged children. When working with school-aged children with special needs, particular issues may arise: the transition from the elementary school program to the school-age program; peer relations; and communication between those involved in the care and education of the child. Strategies for working through these issues include seeking additional resources, creating consistent intervention plans, developing interdisciplinary partnerships, and advocating for the child and family. Program adaptations that promote inclusion are necessary for quality in school-age programs.

Resources

Atkinson Centre for Society and Child Development

http://www.oise.utoronto.ca/atkinson

The Atkinson Centre is a research centre that is committed to using the best available evidence on early child development to inform public discourse, public policy, and the professional learning of those who work with young children.

Early Intervention Canada

http://www.earlyinterventioncanada.com

This organization is funded by the Max Bell Foundation and partners with McGill University and the Yaldei Developmental Centre. They provide research to create a national blueprint for early intervention service delivery to families who have children with developmental delays.

Infant Mental Health Promotion

http://www.sickkids.ca/imp

This site includes the newsletter *IMPrint*, which often focuses on supporting infants with special needs.

Kinark Child and Family Services

http://www.kinark.on.ca

This children's mental health organization provides help to children, youth, families, and communities.

Zero to Three: The National Center for Infants, Toddlers and Families

http://www.zerotothree.org

This website provides online articles, a resource list, and publications on children from birth to age three.

Access an interactive ebook and chapter-specific interactive learning tools, including flashcards, quizzes, videos, and more, in the *Inclusion in Early Childhood Programs* CourseMate. Visit NELSONbrain.com to log in, register, or purchase access.

Arranging the Inclusive Learning Environment

15

....

OBJECTIVES

After studying the material in this chapter, the student will be able to

- Explain how indoor and outdoor learning environments and program scheduling influence children's learning in an inclusive setting.
- List a number of things that teachers can do to enhance awareness of developmental differences within a learning environment.
- Describe how an emergent curriculum approach can benefit all children.
- Discuss the major issues involved in planning a program schedule for children in an inclusive setting.
- Describe how to adapt routines and transitions to ensure the full and successful participation of all children.

KEY CONCEPTS AND TERMS

bias-free materials	orderly sequences	teacher-guided learning
emergent curriculum	self-help/care	opportunities
induced incompetence	structured flexibility	

CONNECTIONS

- Tina had a congenital orthopedic problem requiring ongoing physical and occupational therapy. An IEP objective for Tina, both at home and at school, was to decrease the amount of time she spent in her wheelchair and on crutches. One aspect of the plan was to increase her tolerance for weight bearing, especially standing. Tina's therapists were delighted with the teachers' offer to arrange the classroom environment to facilitate a variety of stand-up play activities so that Tina would not be set apart from the other children.

- Gabe, a three-year-old, went to preschool at Parent Cooperative Preschool in his hometown. Each morning began with the children breaking up to form smaller circle groups with their lead teachers. Gabe often had difficulty paying attention during circle time. He would turn his back on his group, turning around to see what the other groups were doing. His lead teacher, Carrie, noticed this and began using a portable divider to provide a wall around her circle area. Gabe was better able to attend to his circle group with this new arrangement.

Introduction

The learning environments provided by early childhood programs will influence, even determine, the development of countless numbers of children. Those environments and the way they are arranged will also determine how effectively teachers will teach and the kinds of messages children will get about themselves and others. According to Swim (2006), "Taking time to reflect on the physical environment is imperative as it is considered the 'third teacher' in the classroom. In other words, the environment provides guidance to the children and adults about appropriate behaviour" (p. 101).

The Inclusive Environment

In an inclusive setting, environmental arrangements assume special importance because of the range of differences among children.

Teachers should arrange play spaces and activities, both indoors and out of doors, so that children with special needs are included easily and naturally. By doing so, teachers convey a powerful message about human values: *All kinds of children can play together and have fun.* Having fun together promotes genuine inclusion of all children. Many children in wheelchairs can join in the exuberant activity of a lively beanbag toss and other group games. Therapeutic equipment is available that is fun for all children: huge medicine balls, tumble tubs, balance beams, portable stair-climbing apparatuses, trampolines, and the like. (Specialized equipment and specific environmental adaptations will be discussed in subsequent chapters.)

Inclusive early education is based on the principle that children with special needs are first and foremost children. Their basic needs are essentially no different from those of all children, just more pronounced, as the following examples show:

- Loud and distracting noises are difficult for most children; for children with hearing impairments, such noises may be intolerable.

- Moving about safely, in an environment free of clutter, slippery floors, or rumpled rugs, contributes to the safety and security of every child; for children with limited vision or orthopedic problems, an environment free of obstacles protects against serious injury.

- Minimizing clutter and confusion enhances the ability of all young children to concentrate on the task at hand; for children with attention or learning disabilities, reducing distractions may be the only way to promote learning (see photo, right).

A well-planned learning environment is a necessary context for meeting the developmental needs of all children. It is unacceptable to provide one kind of environment for "typical" children and a different kind for children with special needs. All children need to experience a range of equipment and materials and to engage in risk-taking for their development. Indeed, the best indoor and outdoor learning environment should be based on a universal design so that all children have a variety of ways to access and participate in activities (Underwood, 2013).

Minimizing clutter and confusion enhances the ability of all young children to concentrate on the task at hand.

© Cengage Learning

Arrangements for Learning

A program setting, even the newest and most lavish, does not guarantee quality learning experiences. The physical plant may contribute to quality, but it does not ensure it. As Gordon and Williams Browne (2010) pointed out, the environment is more than a plant; it is the physical and human qualities that combine to create a space in which children and adults work and play together.

Teachers must recognize that when a child is experiencing difficulties, the first move is to step back and take a look, observing the child in the context of the daily program. Necessary changes in the environment can then be made. Almost always, it is the environment that needs fixing, not the child. Rearranging the location of learning centres, for example, changes the way children "orbit" in a room. This, in turn, changes children's interaction patterns, stimulating involvement in new areas and often bringing about positive changes in group or individual behaviour patterns.

Planning the Environment for Learning

The first step in planning an early learning environment is specifying the kinds of learning opportunities that will be offered. Most programs, including inclusive settings, plan three broad types of experiences: (1) learning through self-help/care routines, (2) learning through teacher-guided learning opportunities, and (3) learning through play-discovery learning opportunities.

SELF-HELP/CARE ROUTINES Competence in self-help/care leads to greater independence. Therefore, helping young children develop a full range of self-help/care

Self-help/care skills related to socially expected routines in early childhood settings, such as toileting, dressing, eating, cleaning up, and doing one's share of classroom chores skills is a major curriculum goal in early childhood programs. These are skills related to socially prescribed routines within early childhood settings, such as toileting, dressing, eating, cleaning up, and doing one's share of classroom chores. The goal of learning self-help/care skills holds for all children, including (and perhaps, especially) for children with special needs. Children with developmental disabilities need to learn to live as independently as possible with their disability.

Self-help/care skills are learned behaviours, which means that they can be taught. An early childhood program can be a comfortable place for children to learn self-help/care skills. Teachers are trained to help children carry out these tasks. It is an established part of the teacher's job and time commitment. For many families, already overburdened with responsibilities and stresses, teaching self-help/care skills may be just one more frustrating and time-consuming task. If their child has a developmental disability, the demands may be overwhelming. Furthermore, the resistance and stress often associated with teaching certain self-help/care skills (toileting, for example) can lead to emotional conflict between the parent and the child. It is almost as if the parent's own self-esteem is damaged if the child is not acquiring all the socially approved self-help/care skills. Teachers do not have that kind of personal involvement in the child's early mastery of self-help/care skills. They do not feel pressured to push for early achievement. Instead, whether a child has a disabling condition or not, most early childhood educators know that time and effort are saved by slowing the pace and setting realistic expectations when teaching any new skill.

Building independence During toddlerhood and the early preschool years, teachers need to systematically guide children through each step of each routine until the various skills become *automatic* and independent. Most children are striving for independence during the preschool years. They constantly watch and attempt to imitate the self-help/care efforts of older children and adults. Furthermore, they are willing to practise; in fact, they insist on practising, practising, and practising.

All children should be able to experience the joy and self-esteem that come from mastering self-help/care skills. Children, regardless of ability, feel positive about themselves when they complete a self-help/care task independently. Some children with disabling conditions are not able to verbalize their accomplishments. They may not be able to say, "Look what I did!" but their facial expressions leave little doubt as to their feelings of satisfaction.

It is true that getting about in a wheelchair, with leg braces, or with a walker can be challenging. However, use of such adaptive equipment need not prevent independence. What does interfere with independence is a lack of opportunities to learn how to manage routine matters, such as toileting, dressing, and eating.

Children with disabilities often try to do things for themselves, and these efforts often go unrecognized. Adults tend not to expect children with developmental and physical disabilities to even try to learn self-help/care skills. Also, well-meaning family members and caregivers who cannot bear to watch the child struggle may have snuffed out the earliest strivings for independence. In some instances, children with special needs become increasingly dependent because of learned dependence.

Individualizing self-help/care programs In the North American culture, children are encouraged to do for themselves as much as possible; nevertheless, teachers must be prepared to make exceptions. Some children learn self-help/care tasks early and with ease; others have varying degrees of difficulty. In addition, a child may ask for help with a task that he or she has already mastered. Children, too, have their "off" days. Like adults, they become tired or upset, or feel unwell. A child may need assistance if routines in larger groups result in overstimulation and loss of self-regulation. In addition, teachers need to take into account each family's cultural attitudes toward independence in self-help/care skills. Cultural continuity can be maintained by providing children with support while at the same time gradually reducing the amount of adult assistance.

All children can be expected to be dependent at times. They need to know that it is okay to ask for help, to say, "This is too hard. I can't do it by myself." A child should never be ridiculed or belittled for asking for help, no matter how simple the task. Children who have been helped to feel competent most of time rarely seek help unnecessarily. Usually, they will ask for assistance only when they truly feel, at the moment, that a task is too much for them to do by themselves.

Supports provided by the teacher will vary and depend on the individual child and family. These include verbal and visual reminders, periodic or partial assistance, and assistance and close supervision. The following examples illustrate teachers knowing when to help, how to help, and how much to help:

- Guide a child's arm and hand so that he or she can reach all the way down into a wrong-side-out coat sleeve. This demonstrates how to grasp the edge of the cuff, and is helping the child discover that he or she can pull the cuff through to make a coat sleeve come right side out.

- Put a rubber suction cup under the plate of a child with cerebral palsy so that the plate stays in place while self-feeding.

- Lay clothes out within easy reach of a child who is just learning to walk with crutches. When everything needed for dressing is at his or her fingertips, the child is more likely to manage happily and competently, alone.

Arranging an environment to support independence Other environmental arrangements that promote self-help/care skills, particularly for children with special needs, are appropriately sized furnishings and accessories. Hooks, washbasins, toilets, and drinking facilities that can be reached and operated by children allow children to help themselves. Children with special needs can learn to take care of many of their own needs through various environmental arrangements. Consider the following examples:

- Cork or raised tape placed along certain walls and pieces of furniture will help a child with a severe visual impairment independently find his or her way around a room.

- A prearranged comfortable and secure place to go to remove leg braces, as needed, frees a child of having to wait for an available adult.

- Large knobs or rungs on children's furniture facilitate the opening of drawers and doors.

- A child who knows how to adjust the volume on his or her hearing aid can reduce the amount of time the child is uncomfortable or not "tuned in."

- Equipment and materials in the classroom and play yard that are in good working order reduce frustrations and increase children's initiative and independence.

The last point is especially important. Few situations make a child with special needs—or anyone else, for that matter—feel more incompetent than a doorknob that spins aimlessly, a faucet that will not turn off, or a drawer that will not open. These experiences are especially devastating for children with

Induced incompetence children with special needs suffering the effects of poorly functioning equipment

developmental differences; they have to do more than their share of coping as it is. When something cannot be made to work, children often do not realize that it is the equipment and not themselves that is at fault. For the child, it may add one more frustration to accomplishing an everyday task. **Induced incompetence** is the term used to describe the effects of poorly functioning equipment on children with developmental differences.

Washroom facilities Learning to use a toilet independently is a developmental goal for most children during the early years. In designing a washroom, the following should be taken into consideration:

- Toilets and sinks should be of appropriate size and height.

- Adequate space should be provided for manoeuvring crutches or a walker, or for pulling a wheelchair parallel to the toilet or up to the sink.

- A handrail should be installed that will enable the child to steady himself or herself.

- A hollow block or small footstool should be provided for a child's feet to rest on, thereby reducing insecurity and fear of falling off the toilet.

All children should be guided in developing self-help/care skills in going to the toilet and washing and drying their hands afterward.

In programs for toddlers or children needing help with toileting, teachers need to be immediately available to the children's washroom. For preschoolers who have become fairly trustworthy in handling their toileting needs, it is best if the washroom is accessible to all activity areas. Accessibility from the outdoor play area is especially important so that children can get to the washroom in a hurry, as they often need to do. School-aged children can be expected to use a washroom out of sight of teachers, even down the hall. A teacher, nevertheless, needs to be available near the door where children leave and return.

Cubby areas Cubbies or coat hook areas in early childhood centres should be as near as possible to the outdoor exit and the washroom. This location helps children keep track of coats and mittens as they come in to use the toileting facility. If there are no distractions en route, many children can be responsible for toileting themselves during outside play periods. This arrangement may put the cubbies at some distance from the door through which children arrive and depart for home. However, this distance need not be a problem if the traffic lane from the entry door to the cubbies is free of obstacles and clutter. A child's cubby can be identified in a number of ways: a child's first language, photographs, or Braille.

Sleeping areas The sleeping area in all-day programs must be carefully planned and free of distractions. Placement of cots should

- be consistent—in the same spot every day to provide a sense of security for the child; and

- take into consideration an awareness of the specific needs of individual children—for example, a space to manoeuvre walkers or crutches independently, or a quiet corner without distractions for an active child.

Teachers can assist children in settling down for a nap in a variety of ways, depending on home experiences, including choice of sleep toy, soft music, back rub, or being rocked to sleep. Alternatives, such as quiet activities, should be provided for children who usually do not nap, and for early risers.

TEACHER-GUIDED LEARNING OPPORTUNITIES Teacher-guided learning opportunities (also referred to as large- and small-group activities, one-on-one teaching, and teacher-structured or teacher-directed activities) should be available throughout the program day (see photo, below). The teacher's intent is to support learning of skills that children need but cannot learn solely from a self-guided exploration of the environment. A teacher-guided activity might involve stories, songs, fingerplays, discussions on care of materials, demonstrations of gentleness with animals, opportunities for children to learn names of objects, basic directionality and number concepts, and so on. These activities may be formally planned learning experiences, or they may arise spontaneously out of a child's immediate interest or need (see Chapter 4 for more on incidental teaching opportunities).

Children with special needs sometimes need more teacher support in approaching and maintaining involvement in activities. They may find it hard to initiate their own play idea or gett into play with others. What they may need most is brief but frequent teacher guidance on how to join and participate in play activities. (Such methods will be discussed in Chapter 16.) They also may need teacher-guided activities related to skills that other children seem to acquire almost spontaneously. Pointing at objects might be an example. Most children need no help in learning to point; usually they have to be taught *not* to point. Children with perceptual motor problems or cognitive delays often need direct instruction in learning to point.

In arranging the location for teacher-guided activities, such as story reading or music and movement group time, a first consideration is ease of transition to and from other activity areas. Children can change activities more readily if teacher-planned interest centres and activities can be approached (and seen) from all other play areas. Furthermore, seeing that an attractive activity is starting up often serves as a cue. When a teacher wants to draw the children together for a group activity, children should be warned a few minutes ahead of time that they will need to be tidying up "in five minutes." A warning of a change can involve different communication modes, such as pictures, gestures, signs, objects, and music.

Teacher-guided learning opportunities the teacher directly supports the learning of skills during large- and small-group activities

Teacher-guided activities are interspersed throughout the program day.

Courtesy of Ryerson Early Learning Centre

Group or circle time activities should be carefully planned with close consideration given to the length of activities. A rule of thumb is keep it short! A variety of seating accommodations such as a beanbag chair or cushion may be required to help children stay focused and involved. Some children might need a fidget toy such as a squish ball or small stuffed animal to relax. At first, give all children a fidget toy and then only some children will keep it as extra support. All activities can be supported with visuals (e.g., pictures, symbols, and photographs) and props (e.g., puppets for a story, objects for a song)—really anything that aids in communication for all children and makes the activities even more intriguing and exciting.

Children still in the process of tidying up a play area may need some teacher support in completing the task before moving on to the group activity. The teacher supporting the group activity can find subtle ways to involve a child who has a shorter attention span. During music and movement large-group times, some children are not able to attend the whole time. It is then appropriate to provide the child with an alternative activity.

 DISCOVERY LEARNING Discovery learning includes child-initiated activities, a free choice of activities, and other opportunities to explore a range of learning centres set up by teachers. These should be given uninterrupted blocks of time in a well-planned play environment, both indoors and outdoors. The processes of exploration and experimentation are fundamental to early learning. It is through play that children discover their world and themselves. Play provides opportunities for children to apply their own ideas as well as the learning they have acquired in teacher-guided activities. At every developmental level, children need opportunities to play and to have access to play materials. Children with special needs, many of whom do not play of their own accord, can be helped to learn play skills. (Teaching children to play is discussed in Chapter 16.)

Very young children and some children with developmental differences do not always benefit from *large* blocks of unstructured time. They may spend too much of their valuable time unengaged or inappropriately engaged because skills are just emerging or they have a short attention span. For these children, brief teacher-structured activities are easily interspersed during free-play learning periods. Learning to point, mentioned earlier, will be used as an example:

> *Baillie needed to learn to point. During a play period, the teacher in the immediate area noticed Baillie standing about, unengaged. The teacher took her companionably by the hand, and said, "Let's go pointing" (an improvised game that Baillie enjoyed). While keeping her eye on the other children, the teacher walked around the area with Baillie for a minute or so, having her point to well-known objects. The teacher then helped Baillie point to what she would like to do next and followed up by having the teacher in that area help her settle in.*

Discovery learning areas work well when they radiate from the location of teacher-supported learning centres and activities. Where these activity centres are placed is determined by furniture, storage, and the cleanup requirements of each area. Each centre should have sufficient space to allow a group of children to play comfortably together—including a child using a wheelchair, crutches, or a walker (see photo, page 337). Teachers' selection and grouping of materials in learning centres indicate clearly how each area is to be used. Children, and especially very young children and children with developmental differences, should

Each learning centre should have sufficient space.

not be given mixed signals. For example, some children are likely to think that it must be all right to colour in the library books if crayons are left on the bookshelves. The display of materials tells the child what to expect of the material and how to use it. A broken or incomplete set of play materials should never be put out for children (For example, it is better to have no puzzles than puzzles with even one missing piece.)

Materials may need to be placed at different levels—on the floor, a wheelchair table tray, a raised table top—to allow each child access to materials independently or with assistance. Equipment and materials used and rotated should reflect the diverse needs of each child. Visual clues used to indicate play areas and expectations for behaviour should be varied: a picture, photograph, sign language version, or the child's first language. Visual displays should represent human diversity; for example, photographs and posters should show all children (boys and girls and those with and without disabilities) engaged in active play.

Including **bias-free materials** that reflect developmental differences in learning centres benefits all children (Hall & Rhomberg, 1995). When children are exposed naturally to diversity through their play environment, they will more readily respect and accept human differences (Langford, 1997).

Bias-free materials learning materials (e.g., adaptive scissors, dolls with leg braces) that reflect human differences

Example:

Karen's father was surprised when his daughter did not mention that her new friend, Lien, used a wheelchair. Karen's teachers explained that she was familiar with wheelchairs, having used one placed in the dramatic play area.

Show children appropriate uses of materials, such as crutches and Braille mats, and explain their purposes. Intervene when children are using materials inappropriately and model appropriate use. Some examples of materials to include in learning centres that foster awareness of diversity (see photo, page 338) include the following:

Creative art centre

- adaptive scissors
- left-handed scissors
- built-up handles of paintbrushes, crayons, and markers for an easier grip

Dramatic play centre

- dolls with varying abilities (with wheelchair, leg braces, crutches, eye glasses, etc.)
- communication materials, such as puppets, telephones, audio recorders (tape or mp3), mirrors, computer, Braille writer, and picture boards

Outdoor area

- wheelchair route
- bells inside balls
- brightly painted ladder steps

Emergent Curriculum

Emergent curriculum is one approach to engage children in discovery learning. Emergent curriculum, as described by Fraser (2012), is a kind of curriculum that emerges or arises out of the children's interests. In this way, the curriculum is "intellectually engaging and personally meaningful to children" (Gestwicki, 2010, p. 53). In theme-based teaching, adults decide what children will learn during a defined learning period. Sources for emergent curriculum, in contrast, can be children's play and questions, adult interests, events in the environment, developmental tasks, and cultural and spontaneous events. Interests and ideas can be extended into long-term projects (Chard & Katz, 2000) or until the children begin to show an interest in a new subject or developmental task. In the emergent curriculum approach, children are viewed as competent learners and as producers of knowledge rather than as receivers of knowledge. Collaboration between teachers and children, and among children, during the process of learning about a topic or gaining new skills is considered an important feature of emergent curriculum.

Is emergent curriculum appropriate for children with special needs? Educators using the Reggio Emilia approach in Italy believe that a special curriculum should not be developed for children with special needs (Fraser, 2012). All children in a Reggio Emilia school participate at a level that is comfortable for them and express themselves using the "hundred languages of children." Fraser (2012) wrote that educators in Reggio Emilia "believe that the image of the child as rich, strong, and powerful encompasses all children, including children with special rights, and that all children deserve to be given the support they need to reach their full potential" (p. 38).

Other educators view emergent curriculum as a way to fully motivate and engage learners. Pelo (1996) described how a group of preschool children undertook a long-term project of getting a ramp built when a child's parent could not visit the centre because it lacked wheelchair accessibility. Julovich (1998) described the change in Chad, a school-aged child who used a computer (a chin switch to pick the letters) to communicate. Julovich shifted from initiating writing activities to allowing learners choices for writing:

> Chad experienced a new power in his daily efforts to tell what he knew or thought. From then on, he wrote every day about topics of his choice. He communicated ideas that were difficult or impossible for him to express any other way. (p. 128)

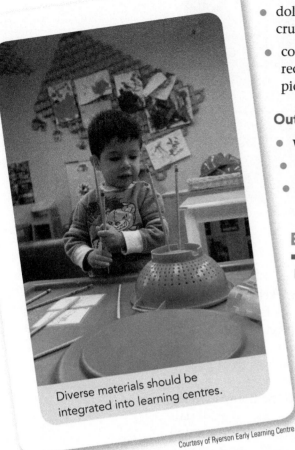

Diverse materials should be integrated into learning centres.

Courtesy of Ryerson Early Learning Centre

Emergent curriculum curriculum that is developed from a variety of sources, including children's play activities and questions, and that is personally meaningful, intellectually engaging, and socially relevant

Teachers can practise emergent curriculum in other ways, such as these:

- Observe a child's play interests and integrate IPP goals during extensions of the play interest.

- Use a problem to solve as the basis of a project. For example, a child has difficulty stepping into a swimming pool, so the child and his peers dig a hole in the sand, line it with plastic, and fill it with water. The children practise problem-solving, prosocial, and motor skills during the process of creating an alternative swimming pool. This example can be viewed in the video series *Making Friends* (Carr, 1997).

- Begin with a child's interest and create a topic or activity web.

    Example:

    Rao, a child with cerebral palsy, arrives at the centre with a small, fuzzy caterpillar in his hand. He wants to know what kind of caterpillar it is, what kind of cocoon it will make, what it eats, and what it will turn into. The other children crowd around to look at and admire Rao's find and ask questions of their own. The teacher puts aside her plans and quickly webs the questions. She asks the children where they might look for answers to their questions. The children brainstorm sources for information. They also discuss how they will care for Rao's caterpillar.

- Document learning processes through language samples, charts and graphs, creative art samples, photographs (depicting various stages of the children's activities), and videotaping. A documentation panel on the children's learning processes or a project is posted so that the children and their families can view and celebrate children's learning, competencies, and accomplishments.

Principles of Planning Early Learning Environments

Cutting across all aspects of environmental planning are certain basic principles. These include safety, visibility, ease of movement, teachers' availability, and structured flexibility. Figure 15–1 provides a listing of quality indicators for inclusive programs.

Safety

Safety in early childhood settings and play yards is a major consideration in preventing accidents and fostering independence. Independence comes about only in a safe and secure environment where children know that adults can be depended on to protect them from harm and from harming themselves. Teachers should make sure that area rugs have nonskid backing or are glued or fastened down. A skidding rug is a hazard for all children and teachers and is especially hazardous for children who have visual or orthopedic impairments. Teachers also should make sure that materials and equipment are nontoxic, free of cracks and splinters, and in good working order. It is frustrating for any child to try to steer a wheel toy that has a bent axle; for a child with emerging motor skills, it may lead to a serious accident. This can discourage the child from making

FIGURE 15-1

Indicators of an Inclusive Early Childhood Program

The following is a list that can be used by parents when looking for a program or by program staff to determine if their program is effectively including every child.

- Each children are welcomed on arrival and wished well on departure in a way that suits them.
- Parents/caregivers feel welcome and valued as an expert on their children.
- Teachers look for the reasons for a child's behaviour and teach the children appropriate ways to express their needs and feelings.
- Furniture is stable and at varying heights to meet the needs of the children.
- Floors are even and free of tripping hazards such as rugs.
- Information is presented to children in a variety of formats (e.g., visual supports, support of gestures, and eye contact).
- All areas of the classroom are accessible to all children.
- The program includes a social skills component that emphasizes kindness, empathy, and cooperative play.
- Teachers plan for and facilitate peer interaction.
- Teachers encourage children to use their language to request materials and to label items.
- Teachers give children cues before transitions and describe how to complete activities.
- Teachers use developmental observations to collect information, and use the information to plan the curriculum.
- Teachers individualize teaching and use opportunities for repetition for children who may need more time or experiences to learn new skills.
- Teachers', children's, and parents' attitudes reflect an acceptance of all children regardless of need or ability. Activities are led by the interests and enthusiasms of each child who attends.
- Pictures, equipment, and resources reflect the differing background and experiences of the children.
- The person in charge is committed to the active participation of children, parents/caregivers, team members, and others, to ensure each individual's needs are met.
- Teachers participate in ongoing training in special needs and inclusion.
- The teachers use consistent positive language in describing children, including person-first language.
- With the parents' permission, the program communicates and collaborates with other service providers working with a child (e.g., a speech therapist, an occupational therapist).

Sources: All of Us—Inclusion Checklist for Settings. KIDSactive: London. http://www3.hants.gov.uk/inclusion_checklist.pdf; Watson, A., & McCathren, R. (2009, March). Including children with special needs: Are you and your early childhood program ready? *Beyond the Journal—Young Children on the Web.*

further efforts to join in outdoor play. If the accident involves other children, avoidance of the child with special needs may follow. The children who are hurt (and their parents) usually do not understand that it is the equipment—not the child—that is at fault.

 ORDER AND ORGANIZATION Clutter and disorganization are incompatible with safety. Teachers must make sure that *everything has a place* and, when not in use, *everything is in its place.*

A child with a visual impairment needs to know that the dough and cookie cutters and rolling pins (with no potentially hurtful things mixed in) are always to be found, for example, in the lower left corner of the dramatic play cupboards. Logical arrangements contribute to the child's independence; they enable the child to put materials away when finished with them, a responsibility of every child. The ongoing *restoration* of play areas is especially important in inclusive classrooms. The child mentioned above, who is visually impaired, needs to be confident that a rolling pin that rolled off the table earlier will not be left there for him or her to fall over later.

Teachers who routinely help children restore play areas after each use provide children with valuable lessons in common courtesy, as well as regard for the physical safety of children with impairments. By the same token, regard for others also must be the concern of the child who uses special equipment. The child with an orthopedic impairment needs to learn how to position his or her crutches when they are not in use so they do not fall about, endangering others. A child who uses a wheelchair only part of the time must learn to park it in an agreed-on place, not abandon it haphazardly.

MATCHING CHILDREN AND EQUIPMENT A critical aspect of safety has to do with matching equipment and materials to the skill levels of the children in the group. Wheel toys, all oversized, for example, pose a safety hazard for younger, smaller children. They also are a hazard for children with developmental differences, who may not be able to exercise good judgment in selecting suitable equipment. In many instances, the poor judgment is simply lack of experience. Children with special needs may be overprotected by well-meaning adults concerned about their safety. These children, if they are to develop independence, must learn to take risks. Learning to take risks, however, can be accomplished only where children are protected from becoming too frightened or seriously harmed.

The type of equipment and toys can also encourage or discourage play and engagement levels of children.

If a particular child is frequently observed to engage in low levels of play, the teachers should take a look at the available activities. Are there materials at the child's play ability and level? Does the child need individual instruction to learn how to use the materials?

One final note about matching play materials with children has to do with the number of play materials available. If a classroom has only one of a very popular toy, the teachers can be sure that there will be problems with sharing. Although sharing is a critical skill for young children, teachers must find a balance between the amount of time they must intervene in "toy battles" and the best way to teach sharing. Teachers must determine that the room has an adequate number of materials so that children can use a desired toy within a reasonable amount of time. At the same time, teachers need to be sure there are not so many toys and materials that the room is cluttered or that children do not have the opportunity to learn to share or wait their turn.

SAFE OUTDOOR ENVIRONMENTS Outdoor play in a safe and carefully arranged play yard is an essential aspect of a quality program for young children. It is here that children practise physical skills, such as running, jumping, ducking, pumping, climbing, and kicking. They learn to throw, catch, and bat and to combine these skills into games. The outdoors also provides opportunities for children to learn voice and tone modulations—shouting, chanting, whistling, imitating a siren—all without causing discomfort for others.

Outdoor equipment (as well as indoor gym equipment) needs to be simple yet versatile. It should include ladders, planks, jumping boards, and simple climbing frames. There should be walking boards of various widths placed at different heights and combined with small portable climbing frames, ladders, and gangplanks with side rails. Equipment of this type can be arranged and rearranged to meet the needs of children with emerging motor skills, as well as those children with advanced skills. The arrangement in the outdoor area can be elaborate yet simple at the same time. Children just beginning to try out their gross motor coordination can be as well served as daring children in need of constant challenge.

Visibility

A major function of early childhood education is encouraging children to explore and experiment with materials and equipment. This means that children are going to be taking risks as they try out new skills; therefore, they need to be visible to teachers at all times. Some of children's experiments will work; others will not. They all provide teachers with opportunities to teach.

A six-year-old who decides to try jumping off a swing in motion, for example, presents a teaching opportunity. A teacher may make suggestions concerning speed and a jumping-off point suitable for a first attempt. Also, the teacher is alerted, ready to catch the child who does not heed suggestions or whose timing goes awry.

Visibility is especially critical in working with children with developmental disabilities who cannot always gauge the outcomes of their actions. At the first indication that a child is about to attempt something dangerously beyond his or her capabilities, the observant teacher can intervene immediately. The child's efforts can be redirected to provide encouragement for continued work on the skill, but in ways more suited to the child's skill level.

Ease of Movement

Children and teachers need to be able to move about freely. Unobstructed traffic lanes and adequate space to manoeuvre trucks and doll carriages or wheelchairs and crutches enhance movement.

Traffic lanes free of obstructions and unpleasant surprises (unmopped puddles of water on the floor, an abandoned doll carriage, or an upturned rug edge) are critical, especially for children with limited vision, as well as for those on crutches or in wheelchairs. Ease of movement within interest centres is important, too. Crowded activity areas, where children's movements are restricted, inevitably lead to conflict and aggression, as well as overstimulation for children with attention deficit hyperactivity disorder. Providing additional attractive interest centres prevents problems from arising. Small groups, of varying developmental levels, then have space to play together comfortably or side by side.

Teachers' Availability

Teachers who are readily available are the key to a safe and comfortable early learning environment. Young children are learning *something* each of their waking moments. Teachers, therefore, must be available where they are most needed throughout the program day to interact with children and facilitate learning. When children can move independently between activities, undistracted by inappropriate or unsafe activities, teachers can teach rather than police.

Offering Choice

One of the most effective and most often overlooked forms of preventive discipline is the strategy of offering choice to children. Offering choice is empowering to children as it allows them to decide such things as what they want to do. Offering choice also works effectively with children who frequently say "no" when offered only one option.

Structured Flexibility

To meet the range of developmental levels found within a group of young children, the learning environment must be well structured. At the same time it must be flexible and adaptable. Hence, **structured flexibility** is the ideal. A well-arranged environment, where rules and expectations are consistent, provides a secure yet freeing framework. Children can explore and test limits, and teachers can react spontaneously to the infinite variations in children's learning (see photo, below).

Systematic planning and logical revision of arrangements are essential to both program structure and program flexibility. Both are based on teachers' periodic assessments of their programs. One instrument discussed in Chapter 1, the SpeciaLink Early Childhood Quality Inclusion Scale, can be used for this assessment.

> **Structured flexibility**
> a well-structured early learning environment that also is adaptable to children's individual needs and preferences

Scheduling

In the inclusive setting, learning opportunities based on appropriate arrangements of space, material, and equipment are further enhanced by an organized schedule. Specific principles must be addressed when planning daily, weekly, seasonal, and year-long activity schedules for both children and teachers in an inclusive

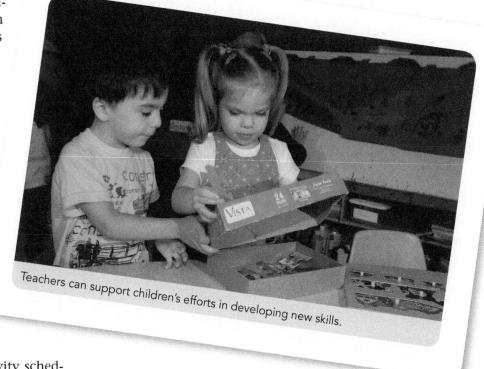

Teachers can support children's efforts in developing new skills.

© Cengage Learning

setting. Schedules vary. They are determined by the type of program, the number of teachers, and the diverse needs of the children. The big hand of the clock should not rule programs. It is the sequence of activities and allocations of ample time for children's learning needs and interests that are the critical elements. The actual number of minutes spent in stories or transitions or snack time is irrelevant.

Two major scheduling factors are individual differences among children and their changing skill levels over time.

Accommodating Individual Differences

To determine the sequence of activities, teachers must be sensitive to individual differences among children and to their special needs and preferences. Teachers should strive to maintain a global outlook of the overall plan of the day, the room setup, and the specific opportunities for learning. This view should vary during the year as teachers get to know children better and as children become more skilled in all areas of development (see photo, below). The length and type of activities and amount of outdoor time often differ from fall to winter, winter to spring, and spring to summer.

In the fall, for example, children may need longer active play periods outdoors as they adapt to new children, new adults, and a group experience. In the winter, the colder weather and bulkier outdoor clothing may limit the range of activities available to some children with special needs, such as those with cerebral palsy, spina bifida, and other conditions that may affect physical coordination.

Many activities can be brought outdoors in warm weather. Easel painting and work with clay, for example, take on entirely different dimensions when done out in the fresh air. When basic components of the program are moved out of the indoor classroom and onto permanent outdoor tables, they give teachers and children a refreshing change of pace.

Depending on the developmental skills of children in a particular setting, the following strategies can be used to adapt large-group experiences indoors and outdoors (Gould & Sullivan, 1999, p. 22):

- shorten group time.
- divide children into smaller groups.
- provide chairs for children to sit on.
- make group time optional.
- provide alternative activities for children who need to leave the group time earlier.

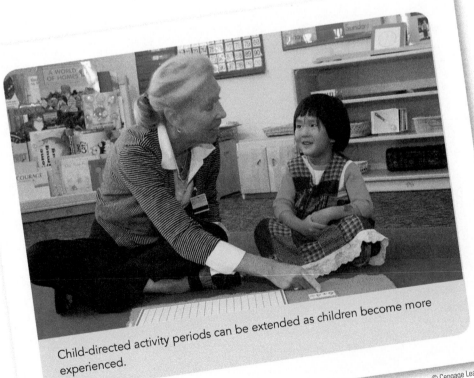

Child-directed activity periods can be extended as children become more experienced.

© Cengage Learning

Varying Activity Levels

Periods of high physical activity should alternate with periods of quiet activities. Most children are subject to a kind of *energy spillover* from active play periods. Therefore, learning experiences that require children's concentration should not be scheduled immediately following vigorous free play. A way around this is to insert a brief "cooling down" period, perhaps by spacing books at regular intervals on the circle area where a group music activity will be held. Books should always be available to children, even during free-play periods. If children are taught proper care of books from the start, their misuse during this transition activity is unlikely. As children assemble by ones and twos, they can look at books until the rest of the children have assembled and the music activity begins.

Children can be grouped in a variety of ways throughout the day: large groups, small groups, multi-age groups, and siblings together. Multi-age groups, which consist of children of varying ages and abilities, give children natural opportunities to learn a variety of skills from younger or older children. In these groups, a child with special needs can assist a younger child in learning a new skill.

Ensuring Orderly Sequences

Activity periods should generally follow predictable and **orderly sequences**. Most young children have trouble accepting any departure from what they are used to. Change in routines may be even more difficult for very young children and children with developmental differences. Children with autism spectrum disorder and attention deficit hyperactivity disorder frequently become overly attached to the daily schedule. Commonplace routines become rituals and must be held constant. Change is intolerable for some children; the unexpected may make the children extremely unsettled. All children (and most adults) feel more secure knowing what comes next.

Orderly sequences events during an activity period follow a predictable pattern

Giving Advance Notice

Children do not give up on activities easily; teachers, therefore, should give advance notice or warning well ahead of an activity change. As stated earlier, several minutes before a transition, the teacher should advise the children: "Soon it will be time to put away the blocks and get ready for snack." It comes as no shock, then, when the teacher announces a few minutes later: "Time to get the blocks on the shelf; I'll help you get started." Ample time must be allowed for children to finish each activity and accomplish each routine. All children need the satisfaction that comes with task completion. Very young children and those who move slowly or with difficulty often need additional time. Therefore, activities and transitions should be scheduled so that all children can move at their own pace, whether fast or slow. A child who has a physical disability may require additional time to get from one place to another. This need should be recognized and the child should be appropriately cued when transitions are about to occur. It is demeaning to a child's efforts, even insulting, to carry a child who, given enough time, could walk from snack to music.

Embedding Learning Opportunities in the Schedule

The challenge to teachers in a quality early childhood setting is to ensure that the children are always engaged in learning. Learning goals for children with

developmental disabilities will include their IPP goals. Teaching to meet goals can happen any time a teaching occasion presents itself, but care should also be given to ensure that goals are regularly focused on by embedding these teaching opportunities throughout the day. For example, if a child has an IPP goal of greeting familiar adults, the teacher assigned to the greeting area will be sure to focus on that goal on a daily basis. Likewise, the teacher in the dramatic play area will work on individualized play skills with the children who have those goals in their IPP. By actually targeting times in the day during which ways to reach IPP goals are to be taught, teachers can provide children with regular opportunities to practise and strengthen these skills. See Figure 15–2 for a sample schedule showing this strategy. The strategy should be balanced with other principles discussed earlier, such as teacher availability, offering choice, and structured flexibility.

Scheduled Time for Teachers

Teachers need scheduled times to carry out their own responsibilities and to have planned breaks during each session. Such time is not a luxury; it is essential. When children are present, the teacher's focus *must* be on teaching, *not* on preparing materials, *not* on cleaning up, *not* on discussing children's

FIGURE 15-2

Sample Schedule Illustrating the Integration of IPP Goals for Part of an Early Childhood Program Day

Time	Activity	Teacher Location	Goals
8:30–9:15	Arrival	Teacher 1: Check-in Area	Sam: coat removal
			Belinda: greeting
			Anna: hang up belongings
8:30–9:45	Discovery Learning	Teacher 2: Blocks/Cars	Fred: sharing
			Sarah Lynne: block building
		Teacher 3: Art Area	Tess: cutting
			Henry: expressive colour identification
9:15		Teacher 1: Manipulatives	Sam: six-piece puzzle
			Tess: bead stringing
			Anna: sorting by colour
9:45–10:00	Transition	Teacher 1: Wipe snack tables	Fred: assisting teacher with snack prep
		Teacher 2: Clean up block area	Belinda: assist with cleanup
		Teacher 3: Clean up manipulatives	Sam: hold containers for peers
10:00–10:20	Snack	Teacher 1: Break	
		Teacher 2: Group A	Sam: communication board
			Belinda: pointing
		Teacher 3: Group B	Henry: drink from cup
			Tess: picture exchange

learning needs. A block of paid preparation time should be part of a teacher's schedule. Scheduled time for frequent, even though brief, staff meetings is also important. This can be most difficult to arrange in full-day programs, but it is not impossible. Here teachers reflect and discuss the events of immediate concern and the needs of individual children. Where inclusion is the goal, even the best of teachers are significantly less effective if they do not have scheduled, uninterrupted times to talk together about children's needs and interests, staff–child relationships, and alterations in the physical setting or daily schedule.

Transitions

In a quality program, a smooth transition appears effortless. The effortlessness is deceptive, however. It is the result of considerable planning, knowledge of each child, and attention to a multitude of details. Transitions should be used for teaching and for helping children learn about their own capabilities. At no time should children be waiting about idly or in rigidly enforced silence.

The underlying principle of smooth transitions is that each child moves individually, at his or her own pace, from one activity to the next. The individual differences among children provide the gradual movement between activities for the group as a whole. Children, because they use materials with different levels of involvement, will finish cleanup at varying times. Other children, because of different levels of self-help skills, will move through the cubby area routine and into discovery learning at different times.

Some children may need to take a "transition toy" when moving from one transition to another. Other children may benefit from using transition cards or tickets that have a picture on them of the next activity (Gould & Sullivan, 1999).

An appropriate curriculum cannot be carried out unless there is an adequate ratio of teachers to children. This is especially true in an inclusive early childhood program: The ratio of children to teachers must be increased as the number of children with special needs increases.

There may be problems in some provinces and territories in which the size of the groups for young children is not legislated. In many of those provinces and territories where legislation does exist, group size may be too large for successful inclusion of children with special needs. For example, the range of differences in group size for three-year-olds varies, depending on the province or territory, from a maximum of 10 to a maximum of 25 children per group (Friendly, Halfon, Beach, & Forer, 2013).

Summary

Early childhood environments determine how well children learn and how well teachers teach. For children with developmental differences, an inclusive environment is the most suitable, with adaptations made for special needs. Teachers who provide a well-arranged learning environment communicate to children what it is that children can do in any given area. Children are less likely to transgress or behave inappropriately if the environment is well prepared.

The environment should be planned in terms of the types of learning that go on throughout the program day: self-help/care skills, teacher-guided activities, and discovery learning. Discovery learning that occurs within the emergent curriculum approach benefits all children because it focuses at a deeper level on children's competencies and interests. Teachers can arrange for activity areas that support the various kinds of learning in terms of five basic principles: safety, visibility, ease of movement, teachers' availability, and structured flexibility. Periodic assessment of all aspects of the environment is critical to advancing each child's development.

A daily schedule that is based on children's individual needs and differences furthers the benefits of the well-arranged classroom and play yard. Each segment of the daily schedule (in planned and predictable sequence) provides valuable opportunities for teaching and learning throughout the program day. All children are given advance notice when activity changes are scheduled; children with special needs often require extra advance warning and special help in dealing with departures from established routines. Regularly scheduled staff meetings, brief though they may be, allow teachers to reflect on their teaching and the children's learning and make necessary changes. Transitions are designed to enable each individual child to move at his or her own pace between program activities. Transitions characterized by large groups, idle waiting about, or rigidly enforced quiet create more misbehaviour and are detrimental to children's learning and self-esteem.

Resources

Community Living Toronto

http://www.ccdh.org/vendorimages/ccdh2008/ccdh/circle-time.pdf

This tip sheet from an Early Childhood Services Team workshop describes successful circle times, with a particular focus on supports for children with special needs.

The Project Approach

http://www.project-approach.com

This site describes how to implement the project approach, with specific examples of projects.

Reggio Emilia

http://ceep.crc.uiuc.edu/poptopics/reggio.html

Information about the Reggio Emilia curriculum approach is available at this site.

Westcoast Child Care Resources Centre

http://www.wstcoast.org

This site provides access through its Marketplace link to multicultural/anti-bias resources.

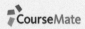 Access an interactive ebook and chapter-specific interactive learning tools, including flashcards, quizzes, videos, and more, in the *Inclusion in Early Childhood Programs* CourseMate. Visit NELSONbrain.com to log in, register, or purchase access.

Facilitating Social Development

16

OBJECTIVES

After studying the material in this chapter, the student will be able to

- Define social skills and explain their importance in the overall development of young children, especially children with developmental differences.
- Defend this statement: The degree to which parents and caregivers respond appropriately to an infant's cues may be a major factor in determining that child's social development.
- Describe the possible impact of developmental differences on early social development.
- Describe ways in which a teacher can structure an early childhood setting to foster social interactions.
- List at least 10 ways a teacher can help children with special needs learn appropriate play and social skills.
- Identify strategies teachers can use to structure peer-mediated social interactions.

KEY CONCEPTS AND TERMS

contingent stimulation	improvisational play	skill fluency
egocentric	incidental social learning	social reinforcement
environmental structuring	self-assertion	teacher-mediated interventions

CONNECTIONS

- An infant with hearing impairments smiles as her father dribbles water on her, and they both giggle.
- A child in an inclusive classroom helps a child with Down syndrome figure out how to put together a floor-sized puzzle.
- Wayne is sitting on a tricycle watching others play. A teacher approaches him with a wagon carrying Melissa, who has muscular dystrophy. "How about if I tie this wagon to your trike and you give Melissa a ride?"
- A small group of second-grade students are writing a poem together, using facts from a story they read as a class. Teddy, a student with autism spectrum disorder, needs adult support to participate as a member of the group.

Introduction

Social development occurs through each individual acquiring a wide range of skills that help people live together in a family, in a culture, and in a society. Gordon and Browne (2008) suggested four categories, called the "Four Hows," for the wide range of skills children learn in the early years: (1) *how to approach*, to get in and be included; (2) *how to interact*, through sharing and cooperating; (3) *how to deal with difference*, such as teasing, bullying, including, and helping others; and (4) *how to manage conflict* by problem solving and handling aggression. All children must learn these skills. How well they are learned depends on the quality of the interpersonal relationships in the child's everyday life. Only through interacting with others can infants and young children learn the social skills (as well as the accompanying language and intellectual skills) necessary for optimal development. Only through interacting with others can young children get feedback about their social competence.

Interpersonal relationships are reciprocal; that is, there is mutual responding or *turn-taking*. During the early months and years, social interactions depend on the child's ability to give and receive social messages. Children with special needs may find it difficult to respond to social signals, or they may give too few appropriate signals. Either situation reduces feedback and may lead to negative responses; both situations will interfere with emerging social development. It is not unusual for the social delays in children with special needs to become a greater concern than those associated with their primary disability (McLean, Bailey, & Wolery, 2004).

All children should be expected to learn acceptable social skills. Many children seem to acquire social skills spontaneously or with only brief episodes of informal coaching. Children with developmental differences often need systematic help; appropriate social behaviours may have to be taught directly, over a considerable time. How teachers can help young children acquire such a repertoire of social behaviours is the focus of this chapter. First, however, social skills will be examined from a developmental perspective.

Social Skills and Overall Development

Though discussed as an independent topic, social skills are never truly separate from other areas of development. Each influences all others. The following example illustrates the close interrelatedness of skills:

Omar ran to Aaron, who was sitting on the edge of the sandbox filling cake tins with sand.

Omar began, "Let's decorate cakes. Here are some decorations," and he poured small plastic rings into Aaron's cupped hands. Aaron replied, "Too many," handing a few back. "That's plenty."

Omar smiled at Aaron and began alternating rings around the edge of his sand cake while singing, "Now a blue one, now a yellow one."

Aaron stuck twigs into his sand cake and pulled a ring down over the top of each twig. Then he sang "Happy Birthday" several times, each time naming a different classmate.

A number of developmental skills can be identified in this play interaction. Both large and small motor skills are evident: running, pouring, catching, picking, and placing. Cognitive skills include arithmetic concepts of some, too many, and plenty, as well as colour recognition, naming colours, and understanding such concepts as *decorate* and *alternate* ("now a blue one, now a yellow one"). Memory was obvious, too, with Aaron singing "Happy Birthday" and recalling several classmates' names. Both children demonstrated good communication skills in the form of verbal exchanges, listening to each other, and smiling.

These developmental skills were in addition to, and blended with, high-level social skills:

- each child initiating his own ideas.
- following suggestions from each other.
- sharing materials.
- role-playing as cake decorators.

This exchange shows the developmental complexities that work for some children but *can be difficult* for others. In the Omar and Aaron episode, each child was helping the other to learn, and each was spontaneously reinforcing the other for a variety of skills and responses. *Spontaneous* peer reinforcement may not always happen for children with developmental differences; instead, their poorly developed play skills often lead to rejection. A negative cycle can then be set in motion. A continuing lack of skills shuts out further opportunities to learn. The lack of learning opportunities results in little positive feedback. The combination sometimes sets up emotional reactions that, as noted earlier, may cause as much developmental interference as the disability itself. It is important, therefore, that young children with (and without) developmental differences be helped to learn *appropriate* social skills (see photo, below).

It is important that all children be helped to learn social skills.

According to Shore (2003), early interactions directly affect the way the brain is wired. Good early learning programs provide the kind of meaningful activities and social stimulation that support the brain's growth through repetition and practice. This provides the brain with the patterns of social skills it needs to ensure growth.

Appropriate Social Skills: What Are They?

One definition of *appropriate social skills* is that they are prescribed ways of behaving: They are the expectations of particular social groups as to how group members will conduct themselves in private and in public. Prescriptions for what is socially appropriate vary from community to community, culture to culture, and society to society. Variations exist even within the tight circle of home, early childhood centre, and neighbourhood. Confusing choices often result, especially for young children.

Examples:

As the youngest, five-year-old Doug is given anything he wants by his parents and teenage brother when he demands something. The same demands in the neighbourhood and preschool did not pay off. Children refused to give in and ran off, leaving him shrieking.

Rebecca painted with obvious enjoyment during the first week of school. One day she began to cry, pointing to a small paint smudge on her sleeve. The teacher assured her it would wash out and that the apron protected most of her dress. Rebecca would not return to the easel, even on subsequent days. What emerged were confusing social expectations between home and school. Teachers had assured Rebecca that it was all right if paint got on clothing; at home, her parents were concerned when "good school clothes got all dirty."

Chandra spent much of her time playing in the streets with older, more aggressive children. There she learned to hit, run, dodge, grab, and kick, all social skills necessary to that particular street setting. In the preschool, these same behaviours were considered socially unacceptable. Chandra had to learn to restrain the aggressive behaviours at school but to keep them ever ready when playing in the street.

These examples, described by teachers, are from real life. They point out how difficult it is to specify what is appropriate. In each instance, children were exhibiting social skills relevant to given situations in their lives; yet they were also receiving contradictory signals about the inappropriateness of those same behaviours in another context. Most children learn to deal with such contradictions. They find ways to adapt their behaviour to the expectations of various situations (a social skill necessary, for all of us, at every life stage). Such adaptations tend to be more difficult for children with special needs. They are likely to have trouble learning to discriminate when behaviour is appropriate and when it is inappropriate.

Rather than attempting to define a term like *social skills*, it may be of greater value to list the various aspects of these skills. The major social skills to be learned during the early years relate to getting along with others:

- interacting with children and adults, in a variety of ways, at home and away from home.

- trusting and enjoying known adults outside the immediate family.
- recognizing and protesting inappropriate advances from known or unknown adults within or outside the family.
- attending to self-help/care needs at home and in public places with consideration for others.
- sometimes initiating play ideas with children and at other times following other children's leads.
- participating in group activities through listening, taking turns, and contributing to group effort.
- sometimes putting aside individual needs and interests so the needs and interests of the group may be met.
- working and playing independently as well as cooperatively; learning to be alone without feeling isolated or rejected.
- using language as the powerful social tool it is for persuading, defending, reasoning, explaining, solving problems, and getting needs and preferences attended to.

Learning social skills is a complex task involving a wide range of values, knowledge, and skills. Kostelnik, Whiren, Soderman, Stein, and Gregory (2011) described the necessary ingredients:

- *Cultural competence:* having knowledge of, comfort with, and respect for people of varying ethnic or racial backgrounds.
- *Planning and decision-making skills:* making choices, solving problems, and planning ahead.
- *Self-regulation:* having the ability to monitor ourselves, reflect on feelings, and resist temptation and peer pressure.
- *Interpersonal skills:* maintaining friendly relationships and communicating needs, ideas, and feelings.
- *Positive self-identity:* demonstrating sense of competence, purpose, and worth.
- *Social values:* exhibiting caring and demonstrating responsibility, honesty, and flexibility.

Acquiring Social Skills

Social skills are learned behaviours. Children's learning of a full range of social skills—*the socializing process*—cannot be forced or hurried. Mastering such skills is a major occupation of the developing child. Refinement of previously learned social skills and the learning of new ones continues throughout life. Figure 16–1 is a timeline of social development for the typically developing child, and it provides additional details about the sequence of development of social skills.

Temperament and Emotions

The development of social skills, as noted earlier, is influenced by home, school, community, and cultural expectations, and by the interpersonal relations within these environments. A child's emotional reactions, or more precisely,

FIGURE 16-1 Social Development Timeline (Special thanks to Gay Spitz)

Infant–Toddler	Preschooler	Primary-Age Child
Response to Other's Distress		
• Reacts emotionally by experiencing what the other seems to feel	• Begins to make adjustments that reflect the realization that the other person is different and separate from self	• Takes other's personality into account and shows concern for other's general condition
Peer Interaction		
• First encounters mutual inspection • First social contacts • (18 mo) growth in sensitivity to peer play • (2 yr) able to direct social acts to two children at once (beginning of social interaction)	• Adjustment in behaviour to fit age and behaviour of other • (3+ yr) friendship as momentary • (3–5 yr) beginning of friendship as constant	• Friend as someone who will do what you want • Beginning of friend as one who embodies admirable, constant characteristics
Social Roles		
• (10–20 days) imitation of adults • (3 mo) gurgle in response to others • (6 mo) social games based on imitation • (18 mo) differentiation between reality and pretend play • (2 yr) make doll do something as if it were alive	• (3 yr) make a doll carry out several roles or activities • (4–5 yr) act out a social role in dramatic play and integrate that role with others (mom and baby) (theory of mind)	• (6 yr) integrate one role with two complementary roles: doctor, nurse, and sick person • (8 yr) growing understanding that roles can influence behaviour (doctor whose daughter is a patient)

Source: © Cengage Learning

temperament, also exert influence (see photo, page 357). Based on differing behavioural patterns and ways of responding, Thomas and Chess (1977) described three types of infants: *easy, difficult,* and *slow to warm up.*

These personality or temperament traits may have genetic linkage. However, this is difficult to demonstrate and also relatively unimportant. What is important is that babies respond differently to what may be similar circumstances (as when they are in the same infant care program). These personal behaviour patterns appear to persist into childhood, affecting how others respond to a child. Parents and caregivers play a role in the persistence of personality traits. Behaviours that one caregiver might describe as distractible, impulsive, and hard to manage might be perceived by another caretaker as eager, active, and happy-go-lucky.

Although every child's social responses are influenced by temperament, the fact remains that all social behaviours are learned. They can be seen and heard and sometimes felt, as when one child pats or strikes another. Social skills are observable ways of behaving (see photo, page 357). Like all behaviours, they can be eliminated, strengthened, or modified. This is true even of those responses labelled *emotional*. These, too, can be eliminated, strengthened, and modified. It is through their behaviours that we know children's emotional state—that we know whether they are feeling good about themselves, sympathetic toward others, hostile, generous, or fearful.

Picture the following:

- three children jumping on a jumping board, smiling, and talking.
- two children laughing while they divide cookies.
- a five-year-old running from a snarling dog.
- two children walking together with arms entwined.

Such behaviours provide specific clues as to which children are feeling happy, frightened, or loving. They provide clues, too, as to how well the children's social skills are developing. Each of the responses was *learned* through social interactions with the child's physical and interpersonal environment. By carefully observing children's behaviours (facial expressions, bodily postures, gestures, verbalizations), we can recognize children's emotions and deal with them in ways that strengthen both their emotional development and their social skills.

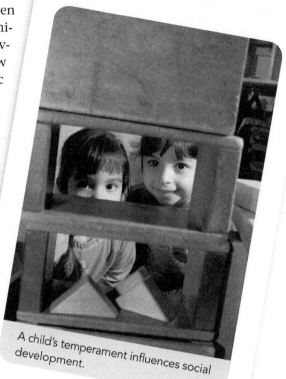

A child's temperament influences social development.

© Cengage Learning

Social reinforcement the positive and negative feedback that children receive from adults and peers that leads to further learning, either appropriate or inappropriate

Social Reinforcement

The development of appropriate social skills begins with infant bonding, attachment, and the establishment of basic trust. As the child matures, the further development of social skills depends almost entirely on the amount and type of social reinforcement available to the child when still young. All children need opportunities to interact with others in a give-and-take fashion. Most newborns *come equipped* with social behaviours that attract and hold the attention of significant adults. In the typical situation, the baby cries and someone comes and provides comfort. The baby is soothed and stops crying. The caregiver is pleased. This puts in motion a reciprocal system that is socially and mutually reinforcing for both infant and adult. Even the newborn is highly skilled at taking turns, thus promoting social interactions. Gestwicki (2014) put it this way:

> Babies are born with a predisposition to notice, interact with, and attract the attention of the people around them. Even in the first hours of life, babies react to their social world, gazing into eyes and seriously staring at faces, responding to verbal sounds, and molding their bodies to fit into the arms waiting to hold them. (p. 222)

Social skills are made up of observable behaviours.

© Cengage Learning

In *From Neurons to Neighborhoods: The Science of Early Childhood Development*, Shonkoff and Phillips (2000) listed the following key elements required of early relationships of young children:

- reliable support that establishes confidence in the adult.
- responsiveness to the child.
- protection from harm.
- affection that develops self-esteem.
- opportunities to problem solve and resolve conflict.
- support for growth of new skills.
- reciprocal interaction by which children learn the give-and-take of relationships.
- mutual respect.

ADULT RESPONSIVENESS Social reinforcement, in the form of adult responsiveness, is a crucial factor in determining how well a child's social skills will develop. When an adult responds to something an infant does by giving attention, a smile, or a kind word, or by fondling, the infant will repeat that behaviour more and more frequently. If an adult ignores the behaviour, it will happen less and less.

Contingent stimulation responding to a child in a way that prompts further learning

The process of adult reinforcement is sometimes referred to as **contingent stimulation**. The degree to which parents, caregivers, and family members respond appropriately to the infant's cues may be a major factor in determining a child's social development.

As noted in Chapter 4, when there is at least partially contingent stimulation (responding) from significant adults, infants and young children develop better. Language skills develop earlier, and children have more advanced cognitive abilities, greater self-esteem, and more durable attachments.

The Impact of Developmental Differences

A responsive early environment cannot guarantee that a child will develop necessary and appropriate social skills. Through no fault of parents or caregivers, children with developmental differences often are deprived of stimulation and reinforcement. Consider these examples:

- An infant who is deaf cannot hear the crooning, loving sounds that his or her parents make during bathing, dressing, and feeding routines. Thus, the infant does not make lively responses. The lack of responsiveness reduces the parents' efforts to interact. To further compound the situation, an infant's hearing loss often goes undetected during the developmentally crucial early months. Not realizing that their infant has a hearing impairment, parents may take the infant's lack of interest in their conversation as rejection; unwittingly, they may respond less positively to the child, as well as less often. Social reciprocity, the give-and-take of the system, goes awry. This puts the child's social development, as well as cognitive and language development, at risk.

- Infants who are blind also are at high risk for poorly developed social skills. According to Fraiberg (1974), they do not engage in the mutual gaze interactions that appear to be crucial to the attachment process between parent and child. Mothers of babies who are blind often report that they feel rejected when their infants do not look at them. Interestingly enough, Fraiberg noted that four-week-old babies who were blind did begin to smile just as the babies who were sighted did. But then, something happened. At about two months, when the sighted babies were smiling with increasing delight at their mother's face, the babies with visual impairment were smiling less frequently and more tentatively. Gradually, the mothers in Fraiberg's studies on infant blindness seemed to with draw psychologically from their babies, even though they continued to give physical care. Fraiberg's compelling example continues to hold up today.

These examples do not imply that children with developmental differences cannot learn appropriate social skills. Quite the contrary—they can and do. With the help of relevant members of the interdisciplinary team, parents learn to recognize in their infants alternative kinds of signalling and responding behaviours. An infant who is blind, for example, may begin to thrash about at the sound of the parent's approaching footsteps. The child's parent comes to value this response in the same way he or she would value a welcoming smile from an infant who is sighted. Another example is that the infant who is deaf may snuggle in when picked up. The parent learns to respond by stroking the child rhythmically—better yet, by stroking *and* singing or crooning. Though the baby does not hear the singing, it usually gives pleasure to the parent. The singing may also transmit subtle vibrations from the parent's chest or throat that further stimulate the infant's responsiveness.

Overstimulation and overresponding may also interfere with an infant's ability to make use of a responsive environment. Overstimulation often occurs among fragile infants—those who are premature or of very low birthweight. They are easily overloaded with (what are for them) too many signals coming in from the environment. Their underdeveloped nervous systems simply cannot handle the *rush* and so the infant *shuts down*, withdraws, and may become rigid or even rejecting of loving pats and cuddling. In a sense, the infant is "unavailable to its environment, becoming unable to obtain information or give feedback and, in turn, causing the parents and other caregivers to feel less competent and effective" (Bennett, 1990, p. 36). The opposite is true of the overresponding infant. In some instances, an infant with a central nervous system (CNS) disorder, for example, may have an involuntary but rigid arm extension when attempting to turn his or her head into a nursing position. The infant's strong-arming may be perceived by the parent or caregiver as rejection or obstinacy, a reaction that interferes with establishing a warm relationship.

These illustrations point out, once again, the need to identify special needs as early in infancy as possible. Early identification, followed by interdisciplinary intervention for infant and family, is a key factor in preventing other behaviours (insecure attachment, for example) that invariably compound the special needs of the child.

Guralnick (1996) developed an assessment tool called the Assessment of Peer Relations (APR) for evaluating social competence in preschoolers, which is still relevant today. This researcher identified three social tasks important to young children: (1) peer group entry, (2) conflict resolution, and (3) the maintenance of play. Teachers can use this assessment tool to determine a child's use of social strategies specific to each task. Underlying emotional, social, and cognitive processes (such as emotional regulation and shared understanding) used by the child when selecting a social strategy are then assessed. Guralnick's (2013) more recent work continues to point out how complex peer interactions are and the importance of frequent adult intervention and support, in addition to the influence of biological mechanisms and the environment.

Promoting the Development of Social Skills

In inclusive programs, teachers will encounter children who are functioning at many levels of social competence. To work effectively with these children, some of whom will have developmental difficulties and others of whom will not, teachers must have a thorough understanding of the sequence of social development during the early years. Basic to this is the development of strong affective bonds between the infant and significant individuals in the first year of life. (See child development text for additional information on sequences of social development.) As the child moves from infant to toddler to preschooler, social interactions with others increase.

A number of strategies can be used to promote social interactions among children and support the development of social skills in early childhood settings. The two main categories of strategies are as follows:

Environmental structuring teachers arrange features of the physical environment to foster social interaction

Teacher-mediated interventions teachers provide direct support to encourage children to engage in social interactions

1. **Environmental structuring:** Teachers should arrange features of the physical environment (e.g., materials, equipment, and interest areas) to foster social interaction.

2. **Teacher-mediated interventions:** Teachers should provide direct support. For example, they may prompt children to engage in social interactions.

Structuring the Environment

The materials and equipment available to children greatly influence their learning of social skills. Materials that have proven to be good socializers include the following:

- dramatic play materials
- mural-painting and collage-pasting materials (several children work on the same piece of long paper)
- vehicles, including train sets
- cooperative board games
- building blocks
- jumbo pegboards
- musical instruments
- puppets

When small groups gather, there need to be sufficient materials to go around, thus inviting each child's participation. It is also a good idea to have some duplicate materials; a child with a developmental difference then has the opportunity to use the same material as another child and so learn appropriate usage through imitation. Conversely, having too many different materials tends to promote solitary play. For example, a wheel toy for every child defeats a major goal of most programs—that of promoting sharing and turn-taking. A practical ratio is about one wheel toy to every three or four children; all kinds of inventive doubling-up games and cooperative ventures can be the result, such as wagon and tricycle trains.

Social interaction is more likely to occur when the environmental barriers among interest areas (e.g., blocks, dramatic play, and cognitive area) are reduced. Interest areas, such as sand, clay, and blocks, promote social interaction among children that ranges from early parallel and associative play to the most advanced cooperative play.

Teacher-Mediated Intervention

Play is the major avenue for early learning of every kind. Even in infancy, most children seem to play spontaneously and apparently effortlessly. In play-oriented early childhood programs, children appear to be self-propelled as they move through the curriculum. They learn new skills and practise them in the course of self-initiated play activities. They participate in group activities and join eagerly in teacher-initiated play opportunities. Almost every skill that children master is mastered through play.

Children with special needs may need more adult support in learning how to play. There have been many examples describing the delays that seem to be evident in the play of children who have hearing impairments or those with other disabilities (Pogrund & Fazzi, 2002). Children with autistic behaviours or limited cognitive skills also tend to be lacking in symbolic play skills. This may lead to inappropriate use of materials, such as hammering the cookie cutters with the rolling pin or breaking the crayons into little pieces.

In general, children with developmental differences have fewer play skills. They will often hang back, not knowing how to get into other children's play. Or, they try to gain entry in inappropriate ways—for example, crashing a truck into housekeeping play—which leads to rejection. It is essential, therefore, that children who do not know how to play be taught. Teaching children to play may seem contrary to tradition. Yet no child should be deprived of this powerful avenue for learning and the many enjoyable experiences that come with it.

If teachers view challenging behaviour as actions children use to get their needs met, they can reframe the inappropriate behaviour as an issue of skill learning or **skill fluency**. Reframing problem behaviour as a skill-instruction issue opens the door to the development of effective strategies teachers can implement in the classroom: If young children with problem behaviours are missing key social and communication skills, then a next step is to teach them those skills (Fox & Harper Lentini, 2006)!

Strategies for teaching and supporting the development of play skills include the following:

Skill fluency a child's ability to use a skill consistently and independently

- physically guiding the child to a play activity and helping him or her to settle in
- orienting the child toward the material or equipment and handing the material to the child to establish physical contact
- putting a clothespin (or some other object) into the child's hand, and moving the hand so that it is directly above the container into which the object is to be placed
- verbalizing to the child what he or she is doing: "You have a clothespin in your hand. You can drop it in the can."
- rejoicing over the smallest accomplishments: "Look at that!" or "Did you hear that! You dropped the clothespin in the can." (In the beginning it does not matter that the child is involved only because the teacher's hand is around the child's hand, manually shaping the child's response.)
- arranging for the child to be near other children in a given activity, thereby enabling the teacher to point out and describe what other children are doing and so begin to promote imitation (see photo, page 362)

Arranging for a child to work or play near another child facilitates social development.

- gradually helping other children join in activities, once the child has acquired a semblance of a play skill (e.g., two children might drop clothespins into the same can)

- providing social reinforcement for the play: "It looks as if you two are going to fill that can full of clothespins!"

- moving the child slowly but steadily toward group play by building small groups of two, then choosing three nonthreatening children who participate with the child with special needs in simple play activities, such as tossing beanbags into a box

- providing specific words if the child experiences a conflict with another child. Avoid the pat phrase "use your words," as children often need adults to guide them verbally through the process of conflict resolution.

As a child with special needs begins to play more spontaneously, teachers should continue their assistance but in a less directive fashion. For example, when helping a group of children decide where to play after music time, the teacher should review the options for each child. The child with special needs is then helped to choose after several other children have made their choices. Because the child has heard the choices reviewed several times and has heard several children choosing, making a choice becomes easier. It is helpful, too, for the teacher to pair the child who has a special need with another child who has chosen the same activity. This provides a good model for the child who is learning new skills both in locating the activity and in getting off to a good start.

Activities must be planned carefully so that children with developmental differences can experience maximum success. When a child with a severe visual impairment is participating in an art activity, the teacher might describe and physically help the child locate materials by guiding his or her hand:

"Here is the big circle to paste the little circles on. The little circles are here in the basket. Here is the paste, by your right hand. The sponge to wipe your fingers on is next to it. Corliss is working across the table from you." (This promotes the activity's social aspect.)

Courtesy of Ryerson Early Learning Centre

Along with helping the child who has developmental differences, teachers also need to help all children learn to be explicit about what they are doing in certain situations. For example, it can be disconcerting for a child who cannot see to have material moved from the rehearsed location. Yet telling the other children not to touch his or her materials can cause the child who has a special need to be regarded negatively. Instead, children can be taught the simple social skill of the courtesy (due all children) of stating what they are doing whenever they use or change another person's materials: "Kelly, I need some of your paste. I'm going to move it over here [guiding Kelly's hand] so we can share."

GENTLE INSISTENCE Children with developmental differences may lack the confidence to play and therefore avoid would-be playmates (see photo, right). These are the children who sometimes need to be gently "pushed" just to get them to try a play activity that teachers know will be of developmental benefit to them.

Teachers may need to gently "insist" that a child try a play activity that will be of developmental benefit.

© Cengage Learning

Example:

Jolene was a somewhat solitary three-year-old with cerebral palsy. An instructional objective written into her IPP by the interdisciplinary team was that Jolene learn to ride a tricycle. The physical therapist adapted a tricycle by adding a trunk support and stirrups. Jolene, however, would not get on. Teachers' coaxing intensified her resistance until just the sight of the tricycle set her to crying. The teachers were ready to give up—but not the physical therapist, who impressed on them the therapeutic value of tricycle riding for this particular child. The therapist maintained that this preschool treatment would promote more general development, as well as motor coordination, than any number of clinic sessions.

After talking it over with Jolene's parents, a plan was agreed on: One teacher would lift Jolene onto the tricycle and support (and comfort) her while the therapist put Jolene's feet in the stirrups and pulled the vehicle from the front. This they did, with Jolene crying louder and louder at first. The teacher continued to support her physically and to comfort her while the therapist moved the tricycle gently forward. Gradually, Jolene quieted.

Within a few days she stopped resisting the riding sessions. Furthermore, and much to the teachers' relief, she appeared to be enjoying the sessions. Six weeks later, Jolene was riding her specially fitted tricycle independently, in the company of other children. Giving in to Jolene's anxieties (as well as the teachers') would have meant depriving Jolene of learning a play skill central to both her mobility and her social development.

INCIDENTAL SOCIAL LEARNING As in the above instance, there are times when it is not only appropriate but even urgent to teach play skills directly. Most of the time, however, teachers can promote incidental social learning fairly easily by being alert to what goes on naturally among children. More frequently than we tend to realize, brief, positive interactions occur between children with and without special needs: smiling, handing materials, moving aside, helping to pick up the pieces of a dropped puzzle, and so on. Teachers can quietly comment about these commonplace interactions: "Martin, when you held the door open for Corey

Incidental social learning the teacher promotes social interactions as they arise naturally and spontaneously

Case Study ▪ Extra practice ▪

Simon is a three-year-old with autism spectrum disorder. Simon was supported when he attended his community preschool by a shadow aide responsible for helping facilitate social interactions with peers and classroom teachers. Simon had limited peer interaction skills. He watched his peers play. He would greet them enthusiastically upon entering his preschool. He would play chase games with them at recess. However, each day he would push or hit any peer who came close to or touched a toy that Simon wanted. The frequency of his hitting peers increased as the number of peers in the play area increased. This led to several peers being fearful of him. His shadow aide started "Friend Time."

During this time, Simon would invite a friend to join him. Initially, the shadow aide had to prompt this. Simon and the peer would go with the shadow aide to a quiet corner of the room and practise social interaction skills that Simon could use later in the classroom.

1. What social skills should the shadow aide target for teaching?

2. What types of activities do you think the shadow aide might use to facilitate these skills?

3. How might the shadow aide evaluate progress and determine success?

it was easy for him to get his wheelchair through. See how he is smiling at you?" When the teacher makes similar comments to Corey, both children are introduced to a higher level of socialization. The result may be interaction between the two.

Children's concern or anxiety about another child's developmental differences also offers opportunities for incidental social learning. A teacher may notice a child looking obliquely at the black patch over another child's eye, or witness one child showing reluctance to hold another child's malformed hand, or overhear a child expressing fear about catching the paralysis of the child in a wheelchair. The children's concerns are genuine and should not to be shushed or ignored. They provide opportunities for teachers to promote social learning and interactions. Often the teacher and the child with a developmental difference can respond together. Using the eye patch case as an example, the teacher might first acknowledge the one child's concern and then help the second child explain. If the child with the eye patch is not communicating verbally, the teacher can explain and ask for the child's corroboration: "The doctor put the patch on one eye so your other eye can learn to see better, right?" The explanation can be expanded further, depending on the interest and comfort level of both children. The teacher should always work to explain to the concerned child that "catching" developmental differences will not occur and that there are many, many things the other child can do. Often the two children can be guided into a joint activity at that point.

Educators (Derman-Sparks & A.B.C. Task Force, 1989; Derman-Sparks & Edwards, 2010) have noted that young children become aware of differences and similarities in people; they notice and ask questions about disabilities. Children are curious about what a child with a disability can and cannot do, about the devices or equipment they need, and what effect the disability might have on them. Derman-Sparks (Derman-Sparks & A.B.C. Task Force, 1989) offered some cautions about these issues:

- Do not deny differences in physical abilities; find some area in which the children are similar: "Jackie can't see as well as you can, but he likes to paint, just like you."

- Do not criticize a child for noticing and asking questions about physical differences. Use the opportunity to encourage the children to talk with one another about the disability or the eye patch.

- Do not belabour the response to children's questions; children need simple, accurate answers. Use the correct terminology for the disability or device.

- Do not lightly dismiss children's expressions of fear or anxieties about disabilities, as this may lead to rejection of the child with special needs. Help the anxious child talk about the fears, and then encourage further interactions between the two children. An inclusive early childhood program provides ways for all children to develop the ability to interact comfortably and fairly with people of various disabilities.

A child's first tentative steps toward joining a play situation are another form of incidental social learning that teachers need to note and reinforce. The child who stands and watches may be nearly ready to interact. A teacher might watch with the child for a moment or two at a time, while commenting on the activity: "It looks as if Bart is making cookies and Cami's making a pie." Another time, sensing the child's readiness, the teacher might help the child actually get into play: "Matt is bringing more cookie cutters for everybody to use." The teacher also can prompt the other children directly or indirectly.

> *Example:*
>
> *Josh, a child with Down syndrome, had a drum in his hand but was standing apart from a small group of children who were experimenting with rhythm instruments. Teacher: "It sounds as though you need a drummer in your band." (pause) Teacher: "You could ask Josh. He has a drum." If Josh joined in, the teacher could then provide reinforcement to all, as a group: "What a good band! Mary and Meg and Fouad and Josh and Karen, your music sounds really good." (It is best not to make specific mention of the children having invited Josh into the group; this could make Josh stand out unnecessarily as being so different as to need special treatment.)*

Incidental social learning can be expanded even further through play activities already in progress. Teachers need to reinforce the interaction, but subtly, to avoid distracting any child. Depending on the situation, the teacher might

- move closer, kneel down, watch with interest, but avoid eye contact to keep from interrupting the children's mutual focus;

- smile and nod if a child turns toward the teacher, but keep the focus on the activity, not the child;

- bring additional materials to extend the play, placing them close to the activity (with or without comment, depending on the situation); and

- make encouraging comments that further promote joint effort: for example, "Missy and Sam, you are building a long, long road. It looks as if it's going to go all the way to the gate!"

According to Shonkoff and Phillips (2000),

Finding settings in which children play competently with others, monitoring play to avert disasters, coaching children in what works, attributing their failures to situations and not to flaws in the children themselves, and searching for creative solutions that build on what they can do well seem to build social competence in most children. Good child care and preschool programs do these things, effectively providing universal interventions for all children who attend them. (p. 175)

SHARING AND TAKING TURNS Sharing and taking turns are the foundation for good play exchanges among children (see photo, page 366). Yet these skills

Sharing and turn-taking are the foundations for good play exchanges among children.

© Cengage Learning

are the most difficult to learn because they involve *giving up something*; giving up anything is contrary to the young child's **egocentric** view of the world. "Mine! Mine! Mine!" is the clarion call of most children at some point in their development (at least in our country). With adult support, patience, and many unpressured opportunities to learn, most children eventually cooperate when a teacher says, "Mary, two more turns around the driveway and then its Sara's turn." The teacher can say this in many different ways to each child, over the weeks and months: "Sara, watch. Mary is going around the driveway two more times; then it will be your turn. Let's count." Or, "Mary, Sara has waited a long, long time for the tricycle you were riding, so she gets a long turn, too. I'll call you when she's through."

Egocentric the child's views and thoughts focus only on his or her own perceptions

Conflict among children is avoided when the teacher structures sharing experiences carefully, monitors the situation, and helps children manage the process.

Examples:

A teacher might put out fewer but larger portions of play dough to encourage children to divide their dough with latecomers to the activity. With the teacher's help, some children (certainly not all) will be able to break off a part of their dough; when two or three children do this, and the newcomer has an adequate amount to work with, the teacher can then reinforce the act of sharing. A spinoff is that children who did the sharing have provided good models for the children not yet able to share.

Several individual baskets of coloured wooden cubes might be poured into one larger basket. The children must then share common but plentiful material. Again, the teacher must be there to guide, partly by assuring the children there is plenty for all. If one child is accused of taking more than his or her share, the teacher might suggest that each child take no more than five cubes at a time (thus teaching counting, concurrently).

A child who has great difficulty sharing may be put in charge of a plentiful but uncontested material, perhaps tickets for snacks, or for a "train ride" (chairs lined up), or tickets "just because." The tickets may be nothing more than a quantity of small squares of coloured paper—irresistible, nonetheless, to most young children. As the child passes out the tickets, the teacher can comment on how well the child is sharing his or her tickets and also might point out, "You have a lot of tickets left too."

It is the responsibility of the teacher to promote and respond to friendly interactions between two children, thereby making spontaneous sharing

somewhat easier. When two children decide to work on a puzzle together, the teacher can reinforce the friendly interaction by sitting down briefly and watching the children work. When two children are using a wagon together, the teacher may spend some time pulling them around. Teachers can also point out situations that involve friendly interactions: "Martha and Jay, you really have a long train now that you have hitched all your cars together." In addition, teachers can help children wait for a turn or a material by offering the child alternatives until the preferred material is available.

SELF-ASSERTION Some children may give up too easily or fail to defend themselves or their possessions. All children need to learn to stand up for their rights and show **self-assertion**. It is especially important that teachers find ways to help children who have special needs to fend for themselves; otherwise, some may resort to using their disability to get what they want, such as by saying, "You shouldn't take my doll because I can't walk as good as you."

The following is an example of how a teacher might help a child with severely limited vision assert her rights:

> Five-year-old Lisa, blind since birth, was playing with an interlocking floor train. Bart took one of her cars. Lisa, touching her train, realized a car was missing. She began to rock back and forth, whining and poking at her eyes. The teacher said, "Lisa, Bart has your car. Tell him to give it back. "The teacher turned to Bart: "That car is Lisa's. Be sure to hand it back when she asks you for it." By not retrieving the car, the teacher helped both children: Lisa, to learn about the rights of possession; Bart, to recognize that all children have rights that are to be respected.

IMITATION AND MODELLING Young children learn many behaviours and skills by watching other children and adults (see photo, below). Using these observations, they imitate what they have seen. For this reason, adult behaviour in interacting with, and in the presence of, children is very influential in determining the behaviours and attitudes a child will develop. Teachers of young

Self-assertion a person standing up for his or her rights and possessions

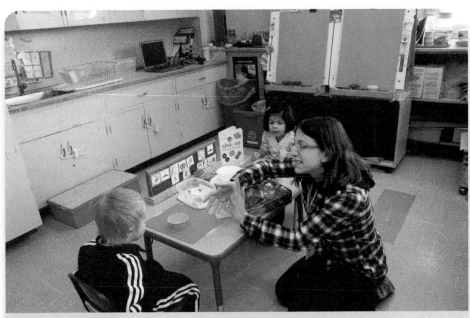

Young children learn many things by watching other children and adults.

Courtesy of Bloorview—Scarborough Site

children who model acceptance of children with special needs are helping to shape patterns of acceptance within their early childhood group. Furthermore, providing children who have developmental differences with models for appropriate behaviours, especially social behaviours, supports a major argument in favour of inclusion. It must be stressed, however, that the inclusion of all children does not automatically lead to their learning appropriate play behaviours and social skills. From the start of the inclusion movement it has been apparent that *spontaneous* social interactions among young children, with and without developmental differences, occur infrequently (Schwartz, Billingsley, & McBride, 1998). "Adding or incorporating a social skills program or social interaction strategies into an inclusive program is essential to the success of the inclusive program" (Terpstra & Tamura, 2007, p. 406). Teachers play a major role in promoting and supporting social interaction by

- arranging the environment so as to ensure interactions among all children;
- reinforcing the children, in general, for playing together; and
- reinforcing the children with developmental differences when they imitate appropriate behaviours.

Each of these practices is discussed in detail in various sections of the text. Here we stress that if children with special needs are to learn from other children, they must be involved in a wide range of play activities. Once again, the teachers—through *modelling, guiding, responding,* and *developing activities* designed specifically to facilitate play interactions through small-group experiences—play a major role in supporting the development of social skills. Such activities might include the following:

- pasting projects (collage) in which children perhaps decorate a big carton for storing sand toys.
- other art projects such as group sculpture building, murals, and papier mâché.
- tower building, so that children take turns working in small groups to add to the group effort.
- a giant-size pegboard, with children taking turns putting in pegs from their own baskets.
- a big picture book to look at together, each child pointing to a preselected character when it appears (more verbal children can tell what their character is doing).

Ensure that adults do not automatically become translators between children and peers without giving children a chance to respond. If a child asks an adult a question he or she could ask a peer, prompt that child to ask the peer.

TEACHER-STRUCTURED PEER INTERACTIONS At times, teachers may decide which children should play together in which activities. This ensures the inclusion of a child with special needs in an activity with children best suited to that child's skill levels. The grouping can be done on the basis of mutual interests, temperament, or abilities. Wagon trains (several wagons and tricycles hitched together in separate pairs), as mentioned earlier, can be introduced. This wagon-riding game (and many others that teachers can devise) allows a child who cannot walk the excitement and enjoyment of being involved—perhaps sharing a wagon ride with another child who can walk. The child with special needs is an integral part of a spirited outdoor social activity. A rocking boat also promotes closeness and interaction as children synchronize their efforts to make it rock.

A note of caution: Children who are just beginning to interact with other children should usually be paired with children who are not overly rambunctious.

Considerable research has addressed intervention strategies in which peers are taught to interact with children with disabilities in such a way that the social behaviours of the focus children are increased and improved. The socially competent peer is provided with ongoing coaching and support to promote interactions with the focus child (Dunlap & Powell, 2009). Another strategy that is not used as often by early childhood teachers, yet is a creative approach to supporting individual social development, is the use of **improvisational play** techniques ("improv"), similar to those same techniques employed by theatre performers. It is suggested that teachers can use improv as a tool to promote the social competence and inclusion of children who need support to develop their social and play skills (O'Neill, 2013). This strategy takes a playful and what might feel like a chaotic approach to building capacity in preschool children. That said, it can be quite effective in programs where consistent small-group opportunities are readily available. The following are some tips to assist with implementation:

Improvisational play includes similar techniques used by theatre performers that can be adapted to promote social development; small groups of children learn to initiate and build on one another's social cues

- Set aside time each day to play with children during choice time or centre time.

- Play with consistent small groups that include children with an array of identified play strengths and needs. Include only one child who struggles during playtime.

- Keep the play group consistent for several weeks.

- Develop key phrases and use child-friendly language that conveys that the play group is a time to get better at playing together.

- Lead selected improv games such as "Yes, and," "Mirror Mirror," and those found in improv guides (see the end-of-chapter Resources).

- Ask questions about how well the group is working together in order to help the children view themselves as creators of the group's activity and process.

Free-play and discovery learning periods are especially good times for promoting social learning through imitation and modelling (see photo, right). Teachers need to provide several interest centres and several attractive activities in which interaction is almost automatic: the water table, the dough table, the dramatic play area, a simple cooking experience. Easily conducted science and math experiences promote interactions, too, such as when a few children go into the yard together to pick up leaves to sort by size, type, or colour. The key issue is that *social interactions occur frequently and are pleasurable for all children*. Play experiences that are fun and enjoyable are likely to lead to happier and more satisfying peer relationships.

Peer mediating and peer tutoring According to Wolery (1994), peer-mediated strategies take a variety of forms, yet all have certain elements in common:

- Children who demonstrate competent social skills are taught specific ways of engaging less competent children in social interactions.

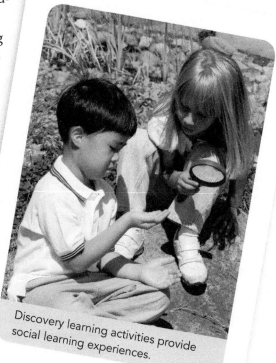

Discovery learning activities provide social learning experiences.

- Children who mediate are taught to keep trying to engage the less competent children in social interactions.

- Children with special needs and the other children have ongoing opportunities to play together and practise skills together.

- Teachers provide children with support and reinforcement for working and playing together.

As discussed in Chapter 1, other children also may act occasionally as teachers for children with special needs. Sometimes these peer-tutoring episodes occur spontaneously:

- One child helps another to rearrange and separate his or her fingers when putting on gloves.

- A child indicates which cube goes where when two children happen to be involved in sorting colour cubes for storage.

- Another child at the table shows the child pouring from a pitcher how to steady it with the other hand so as to pour slowly and prevent the juice from overflowing the cup.

Teachers also can plan child-teaching-child events. Such peer-teaching episodes are appropriate to any part of the program:

- During music, two similar instruments might be provided, with the child who can hear the music designated to help the child with a cochlear implant to recognize when and with what force to join in.

- During cognitive learning activities, the teacher could have two children work together, asking the child who is sighted to help the child who is visually impaired learn to put the wooden shapes into a form board.

- During free-play discovery learning, a teacher might ask a child with language delays to show a child wearing a prosthesis how to build a tunnel "just like yours."

In every instance, teachers should pair children carefully so as to ensure an appropriate match of skills and temperament. It is important that both children enjoy and benefit from the interaction. Never should either child feel burdened; never should either child's learning opportunities in any other area be curtailed. When carefully managed, peer tutoring should be of benefit to both children. The child with developmental differences has the opportunity to learn through play from someone who is a master at play—another child. The peer tutor practises and refines his or her own developing skills and learns a new and higher-order social skill, that of teaching or imparting knowledge. The tutor gains in self-esteem because of the increased status that comes with being a teacher. The peer tutor also gains in sensitivity in that a certain amount of nurturing is required when teaching a peer who is less able in certain areas. Furthermore, it appears that child tutors undergo positive behavioural and attitudinal changes toward the children with special needs who are being tutored (Terpstra & Tamura, 2007).

Optimal Standards for Play

Children who are learning appropriate social skills have the ability to be good models for the simple, everyday fair-play behaviours expected of children in an early childhood program. Appropriate use of materials and equipment is one example. *All children* need to learn to use community property responsibly. *No child* can be allowed to paint on the walls, crash a tricycle repeatedly, deface

Social Interaction Skills during 15-Minute Observation

Date _____ Child _____

Skill	Frequency	Notes
Observes peer		
Approaches peer		
Greets peer		
Responds to peer's greeting		
Plays next to peer with different toy (parallel)		
Play next to peer with same toy (associative)		
Plays with same toy and interacts		
Imitates peer's play with toys		
Imitates peer's play with toys and paired verbalizations		
Offers toy to peer		
Takes toy from peer		
Requests item from peer		
Takes turns back and forth		
Comments about own play		
Comments about peer's play		
Reciprocates comments about play		
Invites peer to play		
Asks peer questions		
Responds to peer's invitation to play		
Answers peer's questions		
Follows peer's instructions		
Provides peer with instructions		
Reciprocates social questions/information in an exchange		
Directs others in play		
Uses others' suggestions in play		
Offers assistance to peer		
Requests assistance from peer		
Follows peer's gestures		
Asks permission to use peer's toy		
Appropriately refuses and defends during play		
Responds to peer's refusals		
Expresses empathy		
Other		

Sources: 2008 Copyright G.E. Cowdery; © Cengage Learning

books, or waste materials. It is especially important for children with special needs to learn respect for materials and equipment—and to learn it in the company of other children, whenever possible. Otherwise, they may be viewed as unwanted playmates, disrupters of play activities, or people to be disliked or avoided. Let it be stressed, once again, that classroom rules (whatever they may be) apply to *all* children. There should be no double standards. To allow any child to repeatedly and unduly disturb or distress other children does the disturbing child a grave injustice. He or she is likely to be shunned, disliked, and excluded from play activities. Exclusion from play activities and play models closes the major avenue a teacher has for helping children learn appropriate social skills.

More Systematic Intervention Is Sometimes Required

Throughout this chapter, a lot of focus has been placed on identifying times within the day for teachers to facilitate and reinforce social and play skills. For some children, more systematic intervention and planning are required for their skills to develop. In some cases children may find the noise and activity level of the classroom too overwhelming to learn new skills and may benefit from the opportunity to practise or learn play skills with one peer in a quieter setting or corner of the room. Some children may require an additional step, such as practising a lay skill or dramatic play scenario with an adult, before inviting a peer to join. In all cases it is important for the early childhood educator to be aware of each child's abilities. Complex skills are required to succeed in a classroom setting. Figure 16–2 provides a checklist of some of the critical skills preschoolers should demonstrate. Teachers can use this checklist to determine which social skills a child might be missing. Once teachers are familiar with the various strengths and weaknesses of each child, they can work as a team to identify which skills can be taught and learned incidentally and which require more systematic intervention.

Learning to play effectively, make friends, and sustain friendships are not easy tasks, and children who do them well tend to have well-structured experiences with peer interactions starting in toddlerhood and preschool (Shonkoff & Phillips, 2000).

Summary

Children with developmental differences, like all young children, need to learn how to get along with others. To do this, they must learn appropriate social skills, which may be more difficult for children with special needs. Like all other skills, social skills are dependent on every other area of development. Nevertheless, children of all developmental levels can and do master basic social skills as prescribed by their respective families, schools, communities, and cultures.

All social skills are learned behaviours even though they are affected by individual temperament. Social development depends largely on reciprocal responsiveness between the child and significant adults, starting with the first hours and days of life. However, children with particular special needs may not be able to engage in the give-and-take typical of social interactions. For them, the entire socialization process may be difficult unless relevant members of the child's IPP team provide extra support for them and their family. Enrolment in an inclusive early childhood program can also help to advance social skills learning for children who require extra support.

Play is a major medium in early learning, especially in learning social skills. Not all children know how to play; some may even be reluctant to try. In these instances, children should be taught—using firm but gentle insistence if need be. This ensures that all children have both the fun and the incidental learning opportunities that are available only through play.

Learning social skills through imitating children who display a range of social skills is a major argument in favour of inclusion. For modelling to take place, children with and without special needs must interact. Effective social interaction often requires teacher intervention. Teachers should promote interactions among all types of children by arranging both physical and social environments. Teachers also should encourage peer tutoring (modelling and helping), which is sometimes planned but more often is incidental in occurrence. All children can benefit from peer tutoring and various kinds of peer mediation. While the majority of social skills can be taught incidentally, some children may require a more structured and systematic intervention to learn certain skills.

Resources

Improvencyclopedia

http://www.improvencyclopedia.org

This site contains numerous games, information, and strategies about improv for a range of age groups through to adulthood.

Learning Disabilities Association of Canada

http://www.ldac-acta.ca

This comprehensive website provides articles on social skills development and other issues related to learning disabilities.

Piramide

http://www.piramideapproach.com

The piramide approach to early learning encourages educators to engage in reflective practice. Educators will be better equipped to respond effectively to incidental teaching opportunities and be aware of the influence they have over a child's social response.

Second Step: A Violence Prevention Curriculum

http://www.cfchildren.org

Second Step is a social skills program that teaches children to change attitudes and behaviours that can lead to violence.

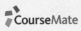 **CourseMate** Access an interactive ebook and chapter-specific interactive learning tools, including flashcards, quizzes, videos, and more, in the *Inclusion in Early Childhood Programs* CourseMate. Visit NELSONbrain.com to log in, register, or purchase access.

Facilitating Positive Behaviour (Managing Challenging Behaviours)

17

OBJECTIVES

After studying the material in this chapter, the student will be able to

- Identify possible causes of behaviour disorders.
- Identify inappropriate behaviours that are within developmental and cultural norms.
- Explain what factors determine when an inappropriate or challenging behaviour requires special attention.
- List positive strategies for preventing (and reducing) difficult behaviours in the early childhood classroom.
- Outline a plan for behavioural change for an individual child in a group setting.

KEY CONCEPTS AND TERMS

aggressiveness

antecedents and consequences

baseline

behaviour disorder (BD)

conduct disorder

data collection

difficult or challenging
 behaviour

duration

fading

frequency

functional approach

goodness-of-fit

interval

oppositional defiant disorder
 (ODD)

replacement behaviour

temperament

CONNECTIONS

- Michael is a three-year-old boy with severe seizure activity. He has made friends in his inclusive preschool classroom and is usually very happy there. He has limited receptive communication skills, and when there are unexpected changes in the routine, he often reacts with disruptive or aggressive behaviour. Through careful planning and the use of a picture schedule, Michael is learning to react more appropriately to schedule changes.

- Ginger, a five-year-old with autism spectrum disorder, has long, curly hair. She has tantrums whenever her mother attempts to brush her hair. Through practising, carefully arranging the environment, and providing Ginger with favourite toys (preferred materials) during this time, hair brushing has become a fun time for mother and daughter.

- Connor, a first-grader with limited attention during class meetings, shows increased attention and participation when he is seated in the centre front of the group.

Introduction

All young children engage in challenging and inappropriate behaviours at least once in a while (see photo, page 377). Children learn the difference between appropriate and inappropriate ways of behaving by trying out new behaviours. It is a way of learning what to do (and not do), where, and when. Almost every child has had a tantrum or an irrational fear, or has balked at being separated from a parent. Most children are sometimes moody or withdrawn, aggressive or anti-social, argumentative or oppositional. Most young children retreat or respond negatively or aggressively to situations that are new, frightening, or beyond their understanding. It is the way in which the adult responds to this behaviour that helps the child to recognize the difference between appropriate and inappropriate ways of behaving—to begin to learn new coping skills and find more effective ways of dealing with difficult emotions. Kaiser and Rasminsky (1999) summarized some findings on the importance of the early years of life. They discussed how research by neuroscientists has uncovered the extreme importance of experience in the first three years of life on the development of the brain. The experiences of the young child in this formative period create specific connections in the brain. Citing Shore (2003), they indicated,

> The more we help children refrain from their challenging behaviour, the less they're learning to use it—and the less likely that it's embedding itself in their brains. Shore (2003) continues to demonstrate the relation-ship between brain development and behaviour. If you can anticipate when and where the child will have trouble, prevent the situation from occurring, and remind him of what to do instead of waiting for him to make a mistake, you can build a new pattern. (Kaiser & Rasminsky, 1999, pp. 15–16)

More recent studies have continued to support the importance of the early years in relation to brain development and the ability to self-regulate (Gartrell, 2011). Therefore, the more we help children refrain from their challenging behaviour and help them to establish viable alternatives, the less likely it is that this difficult behaviour will become a permanent mode of coping and interacting.

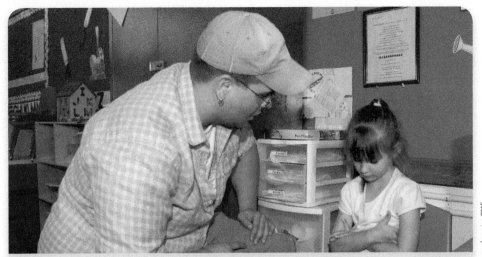

A child may exhibit inappropriate behaviours once in a while.

In this text, the term **behaviour disorder (BD)** is used to describe a child who is unable to conform to the expectations of his or her age, social, and cultural group; who seems to lack the ability or opportunity to learn or control appropriate behaviours; and who is unable to understand routine expectations. A behaviour disorder may also be the cause of secondary behaviour problems. The terms **difficult behaviour** and **challenging behaviour** are used to designate the impact a behaviour has on the people with whom the child is interacting.

Children with behavioural developmental disabilities are of major concern because they may get little positive feedback from parents, caregivers, and teachers. The frustration these children experience when they are unable to perform everyday developmental tasks often has a negative impact on their social interactions. This can result in such behaviours as tantrums or aggressive striking out at people or objects. Other children may withdraw and stop trying to relate. Adult reactions to these behaviours often unintentionally reinforce them, thus increasing the undesired behaviour, which in turn blocks the acquisition of more appropriate behaviour patterns.

Behaviour disorder (BD) describes a child who is unable to conform to appropriate expectations, who lacks the ability to learn appropriate behaviours, and who is unable to understand routine expectations

Difficult or challenging behaviour describes the impact a behaviour has on the people with whom the child is interacting

What Makes a Behaviour Challenging or Difficult?

At what point does an inappropriate, challenging behaviour become a problem behaviour? a behaviour disorder? There are no easy answers to these questions because so many factors influence a child's development. Cultural norms, parental expectations and reactions to behaviour, and environmental arrangements, such as too many distractions or too few, are some of the factors that influence a child's difficult behaviours. The range of congenital differences among children further complicates matters.

Coping with Change

Another consideration is that coping with change can be extremely difficult for some young children. Many children need adult support and understanding when they are coping with change—whether it is the birth of a new sibling, the loss of a beloved caretaker, or the initial days of attending a new school program.

For example, replacing a long-time favourite caregiver with a stranger may trigger a response of acting out or withdrawal behaviours. The reactions usually are temporary (assuming that the new caregiver is able to establish a positive relationship with the child). The child's difficult behaviours usually disappear once he or she gains understanding and confidence. A child may also exhibit inappropriate behaviours when overly tired or hungry, or when coming down with an illness. These minor disruptions are not likely to develop into fixed patterns of difficult behaviour unless they are the only way a child can be sure of getting adult attention.

Temperament

Temperament an individual's psychological makeup or personality traits; of interest to the caregiver is how temperament influences an individual's responses to different situations

Goodness-of-fit when the learning opportunities are appropriate to the child's developmental status

Another factor influencing behaviour is the **temperament** of the child. How the child's temperament does or does not blend with the temperaments of the other people with whom the child interacts may affect his or her development.

Behaviours that sometimes are viewed as inappropriate may be a reflection of the child's basic personality. Some children seem to be born with a temperament that makes them appear easy to manage, others with a temperament that makes them appear more difficult. An interesting and important aspect of this proposition is what Thomas and Chess (1986) called **goodness-of-fit**. These authors suggested that it is not the child's temperament itself that determines a behavioural outcome. Instead, it is how the child's personality characteristics match the demands of the environment, especially the expectations, as well as the temperament, of parents and caregivers. Consider, for example, a child who is active, independent, constantly curious, and into everything. This child may be seen as troublesome, a "behaviour problem," and a candidate for frequent punishment by overworked parents who hold high standards for order and routine. Conversely, energetic, creative parents might view the temperament of this active, into-everything child as highly desirable. They might go out of their way to reinforce, nurture, and respect the child's efforts at exploration and experimentation.

Young children who exhibit difficult behaviours are all too often labelled as "intellectually impaired" or "emotionally disturbed," or as having "behaviour problems." A common tendency is for adults to excuse these behaviours, explaining that the child "can't help it" or "doesn't know any better." This viewpoint is not helpful to the child, nor appropriate. All young children, regardless of their developmental level, should be supported in learning basic social requirements. Early learning environments should make every effort to provide learning opportunities for these children. Other children may come to dislike and reject them when they are not able to engage in social settings. This may result in an increased number of acting-out episodes or lead to excesses of aggression or withdrawal.

When Is Intervention Necessary?

Occasional episodes of challenging behaviours are rarely a cause for concern. However, when a behaviour or a pattern of behaviours becomes excessive, it should be considered a problem. This raises the question: How much is too much? For classroom purposes, it is useful to define excessive behaviour as behaviour that interferes seriously with a child's (or other children's) ability to engage in normal, everyday activities (see photo, right). The four-year-old who has a brief tantrum once or twice a month is not likely to be a worry. The four-year-old who has a tantrum several times every day over minor frustrations is cause for concern since this behaviour can be an obstacle to learning and to productive relationships.

Designing Interventions

Teachers, family members, and other interdisciplinary team members must work together to identify the challenging behaviour, identify the settings in which it occurs, and use this information to design interventions that all team members are comfortable with and able to implement. This process is called *positive behaviour support.* Positive behaviour support offers a strategy for understanding why a child engages in problem behaviour and looks at ways to prevent the occurrence of problem behaviour while teaching the child new skills.

Some children may need support in developing play skills.

Courtesy of Bloorview—Scarborough Site

The Center for Evidence-Based Practice (Kern, n.d.) recommended the following steps for positive behaviour support:

- *Building a behaviour support team.* This team should include the family and early educators, as well as friends and other family members who can provide support.

- *Conducting a functional behavioural assessment.* This process is described later in this chapter.

- *Developing a hypothesis.* A behaviour hypothesis articulates what is known about antecedents, behaviours, and maintaining consequences and includes a statement regarding the function or purpose of the behaviours.

- *Developing a behaviour support plan and conducting an evaluation.* After the functional assessment, a behaviour support plan is developed and behaviour is consistently evaluated.

A description of the critical features of intervention plans follows.

In their 1999 position paper, the Division for Early Childhood (DEC) in the United States listed five features critical to the identification and intervention of challenging behaviours.

1. *Comprehensive:* Team members examine a comprehensive approach that includes teaching new skills, examining the environment, and developing appropriate consequences.

2. *Individualized:* As with all areas of intervention programs, individualization is the key to success.

3. *Positive programming:* This includes teaching appropriate skills, teaching children to self-monitor, and teaching specific communication alternatives to the inappropriate behaviours.

4. *Multidisciplinary:* Extremely challenging behaviours need the input of the entire team—including the family, teachers, speech therapists, and often pediatricians and psychologists.

5. *Data-based:* Collection of data is vital to evaluating the effectiveness of any intervention plan. This is especially true because of the emotional response that challenging behaviours can trigger. Emotional responses make it hard to view changes in behaviour objectively. Data collection can also help determine environmental factors that could be influencing behaviour.

In 2013 the Division for Early Childhood (DEC), in partnership with the National Association for the Education of Young Children (NAEYC) and the National Head Start Association (NHSA), published a paper defining early childhood response-to-intervention frameworks while promoting a broader understanding and discussion. Specifically, the multitiered system used in U.S. schools was examined in relation to early childhood settings. The key elements of this framework that overlap with the principles of early childhood education are

- high-quality curriculum for all children;

- ongoing assessment and continuous progress monitoring for all children; and

- a collaborative problem-solving process.

A Functional Approach to Managing Difficult Behaviours

The best way to deal with problems or challenging behaviours—those that cause concern to teachers and families—is to prevent them (Walker, Stiller, & Golly, 1998). For there to be effective prevention, teachers and caregivers must examine their own behaviour and identify factors that might be contributing to the child's behaviour. The early childhood environment can be arranged to decrease opportunities for acting out challenging behaviours.

 Therefore, when teachers have a child with challenging behaviours in the class, they should first examine their environment to determine whether changing something could alleviate a child's problematic behaviour.

Fox, Dunlap, Hemmeter, Joseph, and Strain (2003) described a model that provides a tiered intervention framework to promote the social, emotional, and behavioural development of young children. This framework includes preventive classroom interventions as one of its tiers.

Figure 17–1 depicts the levels of the framework, the foundation of which (Tier 1) is *building positive relationships*. Building relationships is key to any effective early education program. The time spent developing a sense of security, self-esteem, and confidence with children is well spent and often requires less time implementing elaborate interventions (Fox et al., 2003). The second tier of the framework is one previously mentioned: *preventative classroom interventions*. The third tier is *social-emotional teaching strategies*. Children need to learn vocabulary related to feelings and need to be able to recognize these feelings in themselves and others. Strategies include modelling on the part of teachers and games involving vocabulary, such as "Emotions Lotto." Children also need to learn problem-solving and friendship skills, such as giving compliments, helping others, taking turns, and sharing. The final tier is *planning intensive individualized intervention*. When the lower level of the pyramid is in place, only about

FIGURE 17-1

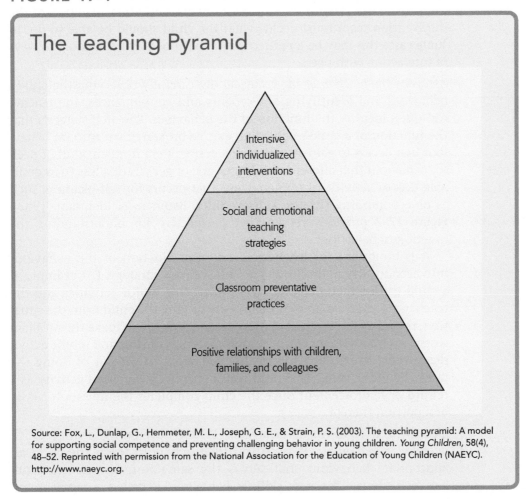

The Teaching Pyramid

Intensive individualized interventions

Social and emotional teaching strategies

Classroom preventative practices

Positive relationships with children, families, and colleagues

Source: Fox, L., Dunlap, G., Hemmeter, M. L., Joseph, G. E., & Strain, P. S. (2003). The teaching pyramid: A model for supporting social competence and preventing challenging behavior in young children. *Young Children*, 58(4), 48–52. Reprinted with permission from the National Association for the Education of Young Children (NAEYC). http://www.naeyc.org.

4 percent of children will require intensive individualized intervention (Fox et al., 2003; Sugai et al., 2000).

According to Koegel, Koegel, and Dunlap (1996), it has been well documented (Dunlap et al., 2006) that challenging behaviours have a communicative function. The task of parents and educators is to figure out what the child is attempting to communicate and to teach him or her a more appropriate way to get the message across.

A **functional approach** to behaviour management includes the following steps:

1. *Identifying the problem situation.* Teachers observe, identify, and describe the challenging behaviour. Identifying and documenting the behaviour in a designated manner will also be useful when teachers begin to gather specific information about the challenging behaviour.

2. *Assessing the child and the environment (finding out how long or how often the child demonstrates the challenging behaviour).* It is also important to know which events in the environment are contributing to the behaviour. These are known as **antecedents and consequences**, and every behaviour has them (see Chapter 11). By recording antecedents and consequences, teachers can identify patterns and gain information about why behaviour is occurring.

Functional approach examining and assessing the environment and teacher behaviour to determine in what ways they might affect a child's behaviour, then planning and carrying out an intervention, and monitoring the child's progress

Antecedents and consequences antecedents are events that come before a behaviour (in behavioural psychology, the antecedent is the stimulus that causes a response); consequences are the events that follow a behaviour

3. *Specifying an objective for the intervention.* What is the desired behaviour at home or in the classroom? Parents, teachers, and other members of the intervention team must decide what the child should be able to do. In some cases this may be a redirection of existing play behaviours or ways of interacting with peers.

4. *Assessing the function of the behaviour.* By carefully observing the child's behaviour and identifying antecedents and consequences, the teacher can often identify the function of the behaviour. Research suggests that the function of a child's behaviour can be broken down into (a) behaviour that occurs to gain attention or a desired item from an adult or peer, (b) behaviour that allows a child to escape or get out of a less than desirable task or activity, or (c) behaviour that occurs for self-pleasure, such as object spinning (Iwatta, Dorsey, Slifer, Bauman, & Richman, 1982). Figure 17–2 provides yet another perspective for understanding the function of behaviour.

   It is important for teachers to take the function of the behaviour into account when developing an intervention strategy. For example, if a child throws materials each day during fine motor activities and the teachers develop a plan that includes removing the child from the situation, they may have in fact chosen a strategy that will make the problem worse. A child who regularly throws materials during fine motor activities is most likely engaging in this behaviour to get out of doing the task. Therefore, teachers should consider using a preferred activity as a reward or reinforcement once the child completes the fine motor task, or a portion thereof.

5. *Identifying a replacement behaviour.* When developing a strategy to decrease a behaviour, it is critical for teachers to teach the child an appropriate behaviour that serves the same function as the problem behaviour. This new skill or behaviour is called a **replacement behaviour**.

6. *Planning the intervention.* Teachers need to ensure that meaningful curriculum activities, frequent positive attention, choice, and a predictable schedule are in place. This step of the process focuses on prevention. The first changes that are implemented are those that facilitate the appropriate behaviour.

7. *Implementing the plan and ensuring that it is carried out as planned.* This is the step that puts the plan into action. Teachers must make sure that everyone in the environment understands the plan and knows how to implement it. If the plan is not implemented correctly and consistently, it will not work. Teachers need to be patient. It is difficult to change behaviour, and it may take two weeks or more before significant changes can be detected in a child's behaviour. However, if teachers are consistent, change will happen.

8. *Monitoring the child's progress and continuing to monitor implementation.* The purpose of this step is to make sure the plan is working. Teachers need to collect data about the child's behaviour to determine whether the goal has been achieved. The **data collection** in this chapter focuses on monitoring the child's behaviour and determining whether a specific intervention strategy is effective. If progress has been observed, teachers may start **fading** (i.e., slowly discontinuing) some components of the intervention.

Replacement behaviour a behaviour that is taught to a child to replace an inappropriate one—a replacement behaviour should serve the same function as the inappropriate behaviour

Data collection monitoring a child's behaviour and gathering information on it; data collection is used to evaluate the success of any intervention plan and is helpful only when it is easy to do and provides an accurate picture of the child's behaviour

Fading gradually reducing prompts, cues, and physical assistance when teaching a particular skill

FIGURE 17-2

Ways of Understanding Functional Behaviour

1. "You're asking me to do something that is too difficult."

2. "I don't understand what you want."

3. "I'm bored; pay attention to me."

Source: Strain and Hemmeter (1997, p. 4), cited in Cook, Klein, and Tessier (2008).

Data Collection and Monitoring Progress

Record keeping must be designed to facilitate constant fine tuning and adjustment of program and procedures (Cook, Klein, & Tessier, 2008) when supporting children with special needs within the early learning and care setting.

Data determine whether the intervention plan is working. Data can provide information about the environment and what influences the child's behaviour. Data collection systems are helpful only when they are easy to use and provide an accurate picture of the child's behaviour.

Types of Data Collection

Three types of behaviour data are most commonly collected in an early childhood setting: frequency, duration, and interval. **Frequency** refers to the number of times during the day or a specific time the behaviour occurs (Figure 17–3). This type of data collection is used to measure behaviours that have a distinct beginning and end.

Hitting and biting are two examples of behaviours that can be effectively measured using a frequency count. **Duration** is the measure of how long each episode occurs (Figure 17–4). This measure would be used for behaviours that have a distinct beginning and end but last for at least a minute. Tantrums are typically measured this way. **Interval** measurement can often be an easier way to track behaviours and can be used for behaviours both long and short in duration. During interval measurement, a specific time of day or the entire day is broken into equal segments. The length of these intervals is determined by both the behaviour and how frequently adults can record the data. For example, teachers who want to measure a child's ability to share might divide the free-play period into five-minute segments. At the conclusion of segment,

Frequency in research, refers to the number of times during a specified period that a designated behaviour occurred

Duration measures how long an event or behaviour lasts

Interval a specified period of the day that is broken into segments to record the occurrence, frequency, and duration of a behaviour

FIGURE 17-3

An Example of a Frequency Data Sheet

	Monday	Tuesday	Wednesday	Thursday	Friday
Frequency of Hitting Peers	ЖІІ ІІІІ	ЖІ І	ІІІ	ЖІ ІІ	ІІІІ

FIGURE 17-4

An Example of a Duration Data Sheet

	Monday	Tuesday	Wednesday	Thursday	Friday
Begin Time	9:30	11:05	8:30	9:36	
End Time	9:40	11:08	8:36	9:38	
Begin Time	10:05				
End Time	10:07				
Begin Time					
End Time					

a plus sign would be placed in the interval if the child was able to share for the entire time, or a minus sign would be recorded if there was any occurrence of inability to share (Figure 17–5).

Before establishing any data collection method, a mutually agreed-on definition of behaviour must be written. This will help to increase the likelihood that all individuals recording the data are recording the same behaviour.

Collecting Data

Once the behaviour has been identified and defined, data are collected for at least three to five days before any systematic plan is made to reduce the target behaviour. This period of data collection is used to create a baseline. Baseline data provide a picture of how often or how long the behaviour is occurring. This information can be used later to compare behaviour changes when evaluating the effectiveness of the intervention. A vertical line should be drawn on the data graph to indicate the end of the baseline and the introduction of the behaviour intervention plan. Once the intervention plan is determined to be effective, data collection can be reduced or eliminated.

Some data collection methods can be time-consuming and impractical for a teacher to use. It is best to find a simple yet accurate way to measure the behaviour (see Figures 17–6 and 17–7).

Baseline data that are collected on a behaviour before a systematic plan is introduced; these data provide a base against which later behaviour can be compared

FIGURE 17-5

An Example of an Interval Data Sheet

	Monday	Tuesday	Wednesday	Thursday	Friday
9:00–9:15	+	–	+	–	+
9:15–9:30	–	–	–	–	–
9:30–10:00	–	–	–	–	–
10:00–10:15	+	+	+	+	+

FIGURE 17-6

Self-Graphing Data Sheet

20												
19												
18												
17												
16												
15												
14												
13												
12												
11												
10												
9												
8		x										
7		x										
6	x	x										
5	x	x	x									
4	x	x	x	x								
3	x	x	x	x	x							
2	x	x	x	x	x	x	x					
1	x	x	x	x	x	x	x					

An X is placed on the chart at each occurrence of the behaviour. Changes in behaviour from day to day are easily viewed using this method.

Data should be graphed and reviewed on a frequent basis. Decisions about changes in the behaviour plan should be made only after looking at the data. Data records should be saved; they can be useful in parent conferences and individual program plan (IPP) meetings.

For each of the following behaviours, strategies have been suggested for ways in which teachers might reduce or prevent the behaviour. When deciding on a strategy, teachers should consider the function of the behaviour as discussed earlier in this chapter.

FIGURE 17-7

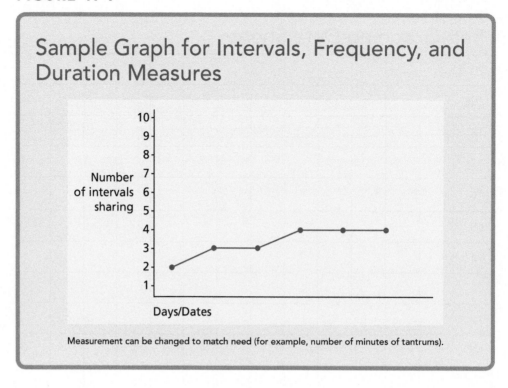

Sample Graph for Intervals, Frequency, and Duration Measures

Number of intervals sharing (y-axis: 1–10)

Days/Dates (x-axis)

Measurement can be changed to match need (for example, number of minutes of tantrums).

Disruptive, Impulse-Control, and Conduct Disorders

Conduct disorder repetitive and persistent patterns of behaviours in which the basic rights of others or major age-appropriate societal norms or rules are violated

These disorders include conditions involving problems in the self-control of emotions and behaviours. **Conduct disorder** is described by American Psychiatric Association's (APA) *DSM-5* (2013) as shown in Figure 17–8.

In an early childhood program, these behaviours seem to be fairly evenly distributed among children who have and those who do not have handicapping conditions.

Aggressiveness

Aggressiveness acting-out behaviour in which a child may hurt other children, cause disruptions by throwing objects, or behave in ways that disrupt the group

Aggressiveness, like so many other terms that we apply to children, is difficult to define. What is considered aggressive by one group of people, one parent, or one teacher may not seem noteworthy to another group, another parent, or another member of the teaching team.

Almost any child displaying continuing aggressiveness creates conflict among teachers, among parents, and among children. Often the child's problem spreads into conflict between teachers and parents, with the child caught in the middle.

Ethical issues are always at stake. Teachers have to be concerned for the safety of all the children in the group, as well as the well-being of the individual child who is displaying the aggressive behaviour.

FIGURE 17-8

APA Definition of Conduct Disorder

A. A repetitive and persistent pattern of behavior in which the basic rights of others or major age-appropriate societal norms or rules are violated, as manifested by the presence of at least three of the following 15 criteria in the past 12 months from any of the categories below, with at least one criterion present in the past 6 months: These behaviors may include:

Aggression to people and animals

1. often bullies, threatens, or intimidates others

2. often initiates physical fights

3. has used a weapon that can cause serious physical harm to others (e.g., a bat, brick, broken bottle, knife, gun)

4. has been physically cruel to people

5. has been physically cruel to animals

6. has stolen while confronting a victim (e.g., mugging, purse snatch, extortion, armed robbery)

7. has forced someone into sexual activity

Destruction of property

8. has deliberately engaged in fire setting with the intention of causing serious damage

9. has deliberately destroyed others' property (other than by fire setting)

Deceitfulness or theft

10. has broken into someone else's house, building, or car

11. often lies to obtain goods or favors or to avoid obligations (i.e., "cons" others)

12. has stolen items of nontrivial value without confronting a victim (e.g., shoplifting, but without breaking and entering; forgery)

Serious violations of rules

13. often stays out at night despite parental prohibitions, beginning before age 13 years

14. has run away from home overnight at least twice while living in the parental or parental surrogate home, or once without returning for a lengthy period

15. is often truant from school, beginning before age 13 years

B. The disturbance in behavior causes clinically significant impairment in social, academic, or occupational functioning.

C. If the individual is age 18 years or older, criteria are not met for antisocial personality disorder.

Example:

Peter, an only child whose parents worked long hours, had spent his first few years being cared for by a babysitter. He was the only child at this sitter's home. At age four, Peter's parents put him into a neighbourhood daycare centre. Peter had very little spoken language when he entered the daycare. He often became frustrated when he couldn't express his needs and feelings with words. He began to hit, kick, head-butt, and pinch when other children didn't do what he wanted. The children began to avoid him and not want to play with him. This led to an increase in the aggressive behaviour. The supervisor of the centre was worried that a child would be badly hurt, as Peter's kicking and head-butting were at times endangering children. Peter's mother was becoming concerned because he was beginning to hit and head-butt her. An early childhood interventionist was brought in to the daycare.

After observing the situation, the interventionist talked together with the teachers and Peter's parents. She concluded that a lot of Peter's behaviour stemmed not only from frustration because he was unable to express himself verbally, but also from his lack of previous experience in interacting with children in group situations. The teachers and the parents were urged to try to intervene whenever they perceived that Peter was becoming upset, to model using words, and to help Peter find simple words that would enable him to communicate his needs and feelings. It was decided that when Peter demonstrated aggressive behaviour, he should be removed from the situation and that attention would be given to the child who had been hurt. Peter would have to play on his own (something he really didn't like to do) until the teacher, through observation, felt Peter was ready to rejoin the group and play cooperatively. Before he was allowed to rejoin the group, the teacher would model for him what he could say if he was upset about something with another child, letting him know that if he was having trouble with someone he could come to her for help. She would then help him settle into a new play area. At home, a parallel process would be followed. If he struck out at his mother, he would be sent to his room to play alone (for a maximum of five minutes) until she told him he could come out.

The importance of consistency between how the home and the daycare centre handled Peter's aggressive behaviour was also stressed. Furthermore, when Peter was acting appropriately, adults worked cooperatively to focus positive attention on Peter. The parents and teachers, by sharing their concern with regard to Peter's behaviour, were able to work together to help Peter develop more appropriate behaviour. The staff had to keep in mind the safety and needs of all the children. Reducing aggressive behaviour in a group is not easy. However, with early intervention and the cooperation of a home and a daycare centre, it can be successfully accomplished, as it was in the case of Peter. Within a month, Peter's aggressive behaviour had been reduced to only infrequent outbursts. His language was improving, and, with the support of both the teachers and his parents, he was beginning to be able to use language to express his frustration and anger. He was also beginning to develop some friendships. Within three months, there were only very rare acts of aggression evident.

Young children often behave aggressively because they feel left out or do not know acceptable ways of getting into play. Children with developmental disabilities may lack the play skills or the verbal niceties that would make them desirable playmates. The teacher's responsibility is twofold.

The first responsibility is to take the initiative in helping the child acquire the necessary play and social skills. The second is to watch for the child to show approximations to more appropriate play and interact with the child pleasantly and positively at those times. When a child with a history of aggression hurts another child, it is important that the teacher turn his or her full attention to the child who has been hurt or attacked. The child who did the hurting should receive no adult attention at that time; however, that child may need to be prevented from further aggressive behaviour.

If a child continues to be frequently and severely aggressive, a qualified interventionist should be brought in to help develop an IPP. No child can be allowed to repeatedly hurt other children or to create disruption by intentionally throwing or destroying toys and equipment. With the support of the interventionist, when more positive methods have failed, time-out may need to be implemented. Time-out is a nonaggressive way to help a child learn that he or she absolutely cannot attack other children. It should be used only with children who have been identified as having an ongoing, significant behaviour problem. The use of time-out is a decision that should only be made jointly, among teachers, a behavioural interventionist from the transdisciplinary team, and the child's parents.

Provincial or territorial regulations need to be reviewed in this context. In Ontario, for example, the Ministry of Community and Social Services has regulated the use of behaviour management practices, including the use of time-out. (See the Child and Family Services Statute Law Amendment Act, 2009.) The regulation states that with extreme behaviour problems, when it is decided that a form of time-out is to be used, it should be done in consultation with the resource teacher, or a special consultant, and the parents. The procedure and process should be decided on, documented, and then clearly explained to the child (see Chapter 11).

Disruptive and Destructive Behaviours

Every early childhood classroom, at one time or another, has a child who seems bent on upsetting the program. These children interfere with teacher-directed activities and with other children's projects. Music periods are interrupted by the child making inappropriate noises, faces, and comments, or running aimlessly about the room. Books are tossed around recklessly and toys are unnecessarily damaged. The child tramples other children's sand structures, topples their block towers, soaks their clothes and hair at the water table, swears at them, or calls them names. The list of possible misdeeds is long. What early childhood teacher has not seen them all at one time or another?

Case Study ▪ Circle time in Jessica's classroom ▪

Jessica is a first-year preschool teacher who has the maximum number of children permitted by legislation. During circle time, she has divided the class into three groups. Parent volunteers assist her with the two groups she is not working with. She struggles to keep the students focused. There is at least one group that is always arguing or being disrespectful to the parent volunteers. One student in particular has been sent to the supervisor's office on a weekly basis due to her outbursts and a lack of respect.

1. What steps can Jessica take to regain control of this time of day?

2. Identify some possible approaches that fall into the strategies presented in this chapter.

3. What type of data might Jessica use to measure improvement?

NEED FOR ATTENTION Many children who behave in these ways have learned that this behaviour is a sure way of getting adult attention. These children often have low self-esteem and other stresses in their lives. Like the overly active child, they are greatly in need of large amounts of attention from important adults. These children appear to feel that when they are behaving appropriately, they are ignored (which is often the case) and when they are misbehaving, they get immediate attention (which also is often the case). Time and time again, the literature has underscored the role of educators in reducing challenging behaviours based on the proactive strategies implemented and not inadvertently reinforcing negative behaviour with too much emphasis placed on them (Fox & Lentini, 2006). Therefore, the refrain that has been heard, and will be heard again and again in this chapter and elsewhere in this text, is give attention to children when they are behaving appropriately (see photo, below).

We also must not forget the point made in the past by Kaiser and Rasminsky (1999) with regard to how important positive teacher intervention is—that through consistently supporting the young child's positive behaviour, guiding him or her, and modelling appropriate responses when he or she is having trouble knowing how to cope effectively, we can have a direct impact on the neural connections that are made in the brain, resulting in permanent and positive influences on the child's future behaviour.

We need to eliminate or at least limit the amount of unproductive time, attention, and energy that teachers and parents spend when the child is acting out. *Half as much of that time directed toward the child when not misbehaving would go twice as far toward producing a more constructive environment* (see photo, page 391). Through structured observations of the child, parents and teachers are almost always amazed when they see how much of the time the child's behaviour is appropriate and how rarely this draws adult attention. This is the first step in identifying positive behaviours and developing ways of supporting the child when he or she is acting in socially acceptable ways. It is also the time to examine problematic behaviours and develop strategies for dealing with these so that they are not reinforced.

MASTERING ROUTINES Many of the techniques for helping the overactive child apply equally to children with disruptive behaviours. Underlying causes must always be studied; part of the cause may be stresses of one kind or another. Often, the reason for a disruptive behaviour may be quite simple.

Give attention to children when they are behaving appropriately.

Many children who are disruptive have never understood or mastered classroom routines and expectations. They need to be *walked through* routines, one step at a time. For example, at the easel a child may need to be shown, and then asked to practise, how to return each paintbrush to the paint pot of its own colour. A first step may be for the teacher to remove all paint containers but two. This makes it easy for the child to "do it right." It also allows the teacher to give specific, descriptive feedback: "Great! You remembered to put the red paintbrush back in the red paint pot." Lengthy verbalizations must be avoided, or the important message will get lost. For example, teachers must not yield to the temptation to follow up with explanations about keeping the colours nice and clear for other children and so on. Such expectations can be discussed in small-group sessions, when necessary. As the child paints, the teacher can make appreciative comments, when appropriate, about the brightness of the colours or how successfully the child combined red and blue on the paper to make a new colour.

Teachers should recognize and support children's positive play.

© Cengage Learning 2015

NEED FOR REDIRECTION Disruptive acts that damage the classroom, equipment, or other children's learning experiences cannot be allowed. With most young children, simple, positive redirection is best. Statements such as "Paint stays on the *paper*," "Walk *around* Mark and Judi's block tower," or "Tricycles stay *on the path*" are all that is required. Other children, especially those with a history of disruptive behaviours, may pay little attention to subtle redirection.

When the child ignores redirection, what is often needed is a clear and firm statement about limits and expectations: "I cannot let you paint on the walls. The paintbrushes stay at the easel." If the child persists, either the material or the child should be removed, depending on the situation.

In summary, teachers should begin by observing and recording a child's behaviour and the adults' responses; then they should do everything possible to modify both the classroom environment and their own responses to the child's behaviour when nonresponsiveness occurs.

Noncompliance

Refusing to do what an adult asks, or ignoring an adult request, is a frequent and typical behaviour of many young children. This is seldom a serious or unmanageable problem unless it becomes a child's habitual way of responding to adults. In those instances the child often is labelled *noncompliant* or *oppositional*. The following three episodes, recorded in less than an hour, are characteristic of one four-year-old's habitual noncompliance, which was not being effectively dealt with:

1. Father: Michael, hang up your coat.
   Michael: No, you do it.
   Father: All right, but you pick it up off the floor and hand it to me.
   Michael: You pick it up. (Michael started playing with a truck in the cubby next to his. Father hung up the coat, said goodbye, and left.)

2. Teacher: Michael, let's pick up the blocks.

(Michael ran to his locker and sat in it, looking at a book he had brought from home.)

Teacher: Okay, Rachel, you pick up the blocks.

3. Teacher: Michael, it's time to come in.

Michael: Not coming in. (while continuing his climb to the top of the climber)

The first step in dealing with noncompliance (or any other problem behaviour) is collecting specific information through several systematic observations. The second step is consultation with parents and appropriate team members. It must be determined that the child does not have a hearing loss or a problem with receptive language. Innumerable children with these kinds of undiagnosed problems have been labelled noncompliant or disobedient (and have received undeserved punishments as a consequence). Others have been inappropriately labelled as "mentally retarded" or "emotionally disturbed" because they failed to do what they were told. The injustice is that it is often impossible for these children to follow directions without special intervention. Only after physical causes of noncompliance have been eliminated can a plan to promote more positive social behaviour be implemented.

Oppositional Defiant Disorder (ODD)

Oppositional defiant disorder (ODD) a pattern of angry/irritable mood, argumentative/defiant behaviour, or vindictiveness lasting at least six months

Oppositional defiant disorder (ODD) is defined in the *DSM-5* (APA, 2013) as shown in Figure 17–9.

A child is considered to have ODD only if the behaviour occurs more frequently than is typical in others of the same age and developmental level. To be considered as having ODD, the level of acting-out behaviour must interfere with the social or academic functioning of the child. ODD is found more frequently in boys than in girls, typically beginning before the age of eight.

Historically, the majority of people who have worked with children with ODD seemed to feel that reward and punishment was the only way in which to successfully treat this condition. Others, such as Ross Greene (1998), indicated that the cause is a combination of environmental and "brain-based" issues and that a more effective treatment is intervention. Explosions should be prevented by creating a less frustrating environment and by trying to anticipate the situations most likely to trigger an explosion so that the adults move in before it occurs. Greene pointed out that these children do not blow up purposefully; they are simply not able to express their frustrations in other ways. Greene advocated helping children to develop communication and collaborative problem-solving skills (Greene, 1998).

Current strategies believed to be effective in treating this condition include a combination of the following:

Parent management training programs to help parents and others manage the child's behaviour. Individual psychotherapy to develop more effective anger management. Family psychotherapy to improve communication and mutual understanding. Cognitive problem-solving skills training and therapies to assist with problem solving and decrease negativity. Social skills training to increase flexibility and improve social skills and frustration tolerance with peers. Medication may be helpful in controlling some of the more distressing symptom of ODD as well as the symptoms related to coexistent conditions such as attention deficit hyperactivity disorder, anxiety and mood disorders. (American Academy of Child and Adolescent Psychiatry, 2013, para. 5)

FIGURE 17-9

APA Definition of Oppositional Defiant Disorder

A pattern of angry/irritable mood, argumentative/defiant behavior, or vindictiveness lasting at least 6 months as evidenced by as least four symptoms from any of the following categories, and exhibited during interaction with at least one individual who is not a sibling:

Angry/Irritable Mood

1. often loses temper
2. is often touchy or easily annoyed
3. is often angry and resentful

Argumentative/Defiant Behavior

4. often argues with authority figures or, for children and adolescents, with adults
5. often actively defies or refuses to comply with requests from authority figures or with rules
6. often deliberately annoys others
7. often blames others for his or her mistakes or misbehavior

Vindictiveness

8. has been spiteful or vindictive at least twice within the past 6 months

Note: The persistence and frequency of these behaviors should be used to distinguish a behavior that is within normal limits from a behavior that is symptomatic. For children younger than 5 years, the behavior should occur on most days for a period of at least 6 months unless otherwise noted (Criterion A8). For individuals 5 years or older, the behavior should occur at least once per week for at least 6 months, unless otherwise noted (Criterion A8). While these frequency criteria provide guidance on a minimal level of frequency to define symptoms, other factors should also be considered, such as whether the frequency and intensity of the behaviors are outside a range that is normative for the individual's developmental level, gender, and culture.

B. The disturbance in behavior is associated with distress in the individual or others in his or her immediate social context (e.g., family, peer group, work colleagues), or it impacts negatively on social, educational, occupational, or other important areas of functioning.

C. The behaviors do not occur exclusively during the course of a psychotic, substance use, depressive, or bipolar disorder. Also the criteria are not met for disruptive mood dysregulation disorder.

One important thing to be aware of is that children with ODD tend to blame others for their behaviour and often create problems between their parents or between parents and teachers because they convince one of the parties that the other is mistreating them.

It is important to have a child suspected of having ODD referred for a complete assessment and then, with the help of specialists, develop a plan to enable the inclusion of this child within the preschool environment.

Temper Tantrums

Young children who have frequent, full-blown temper tantrums require special help. The advice often given is for adults to ignore the tantrum. Although that is good advice, parents and teachers may find it nearly impossible to carry it out. They report that they repeatedly tried ignoring the child's tantrums and "it didn't work." The reason it did not work is that most adults give in long before the child does.

A child with a history of tantrums whose outbursts are suddenly ignored may go to even greater extremes of behaviour—having tantrums of increasing fury and duration. Some children accelerate their tantrums to the point of holding their breath until they turn blue or appear to stop breathing. As a tantrum becomes more violent, the adults who are trying to ignore the tantrum get increasingly anxious; finally, they can no longer restrain their concern for the child. They go to the child and provide attention in one way or another. As this pattern is repeated, the tantrums become worse.

The child learns two damaging lessons from such experiences: (1) that it takes ever greater and more prolonged fury to break down the adults' defences, and (2) that the defences invariably do break down and the adult eventually will provide some kind of attention. This leads to deepening trouble for both the child and the adults who are involved.

Therefore, although ignoring tantrums is the surest way of ridding the child of such behaviour, most adults need help and support in carrying out such a program. Any one of several professionals on the transdisciplinary team is usually qualified and willing to work with parents and teachers in managing a child's tantrums.

Management of Tantrums

Difficult as it may be, tantrums can be handled at school. It takes careful planning among teachers, parents, and a psychologist, an interventionist, a nurse, or other member of the child's IPP team.

All the teachers in a room should be trained by a specialist on how to handle a child's tantrums. At the start of a tantrum, one teacher should take responsibility for the child who is having the tantrum. The child may need to be removed to a separate place where injury is not likely to occur and where the child is unable to break or destroy anything. Though not always available, a small, bare, carpeted room is best. The teacher should withhold all attention while the child is having the tantrum. However, the teacher (or another adult) must stay close by (immediately outside the door is preferable, unless there is a legal requirement that an adult remain in the room). When the tantrum has stopped, the teacher should wait a moment and then return the child to a play activity *with no lecturing or moralizing*. Later, the child should be complimented on how successfully he or she recovered and rejoined the group. Studies indicate that tantrums first get worse but then disappear within a week or less if adults can be totally consistent in carrying out these procedures.

The teachers in the classroom often can handle lesser tantrums without needing the help of a specialist. Like major tantrums, lesser ones will probably accelerate briefly when attention is first withheld. It is best if all the teachers have an agreed-on process for managing a child's tantrums, so as to provide consistency of procedures. The teacher(s) not involved in the management of a tantrum should focus on the rest of the children, who may become uneasy as the tantrum escalates. Teachers should reassure the rest of the class that the child having the tantrum is upset, that the teacher with him or her is caring for the child and helping him or her to calm down, and that the child will soon be all right. The teachers should then attempt to refocus the group by, for example, reading a special story or setting up an activity that will keep the other children occupied and diverted. If there is no place in which to remove the child who is having a temper tantrum, and it is evident that he or she is distracting the rest of the group, a good strategy is to take the rest of the children on a walk around the building, to the gym or library, until the tantrum is over.

Teachers and parents must recognize that tantrums always are an indication that the child is experiencing stress, anxiety, frustration, or other upset. Underlying causes must be sought and the preschool or child care program studied for changes that might be made to help the child. In the meantime, and along with the other efforts, the tantrums must be brought under control. Otherwise, the tantrums themselves prevent the child from benefiting from the changes being made on his or her behalf.

Summary of General Strategies for Supporting Positive Behaviour

The following strategies should be used to help to create changes in a child's behaviour:

- *Give advance warning.* Giving advance warning is especially important for children who may have a lower threshold for managing change. A few minutes before a transition is to occur, let the child know that "we are going inside in five minutes," or he or she has "only five more minutes before cleanup."

- *Reduce overload.* Check frequently to make sure the child is not overloaded with directions, expectations, and picky rules.

- *Give clear directions.* Make requests and give directions clearly and briefly.

- *Provide choices.* All children, and particularly noncompliant children, need to be offered, as often as possible, opportunities to make choices (e.g., "Would you like to put the cups or the napkins on the table?"). Choosing and making decisions helps a child develop a sense of responsibility and independence. It also reduces the child's feelings that he or she is always being told what to do. Adults must be careful what kinds of choices they offer young children. Whenever an adult offers a choice, the adult must be prepared to honour it.

- *Focus the child's attention.* Teachers can reduce confusion for all young children by making sure that children are paying attention before giving instructions. To capture a child's attention, follow these steps:

  1. Precede every request by speaking the child's name: "Gail, the pegs go in the basket."

  2. Get down to the child's level (the half-kneel, an almost automatic posture among preschool teachers, works well).

3. Look into the child's face and speak directly to the child. In some cases it is necessary to check the child's understanding by getting verification: "Where does the puzzle go?"

4. Demonstrate, as needed, and hold a rehearsal: "John, turn the pages like this. Now you try it."

- *Give adequate time to comply.* An instruction should not be repeated until the child has had ample time to comply. Teachers often give the instruction a second time (even a third time) while the child is gearing up, getting ready to comply with the initial request. When enough time has been given and it becomes obvious that the child is not going to comply, the direction should be offered a second time. The teacher's voice quietly conveys the expectation that the child will do it this time. The child should not be coaxed or nagged, bribed or offered a reward. Following the second request, when there is no compliance after a reasonable period, the teacher should turn away to do whatever else needs doing. The child should not be permitted to go on to another activity until the coat is picked up, the book is put away, or whatever else was requested. (See the example that follows.)

- *Show consistency and firmness.* When giving directions to children who are non compliant, teachers need to be matter-of-fact, firm, and consistent. They also must be quietly confident of their own authority. If a teacher says, "Raoul, you may go to the woodworking table as soon as your blocks are picked up," then Raoul must do just that—pick up blocks before going to woodworking. The teacher who gives this direction to Raoul should then alert the other teachers that Raoul has a job to do in the block corner before he can play elsewhere. If other children are busy putting blocks away, the teacher should push a fair share aside for Raoul to take care of. At this point, the contingency can be restated clearly and simply: "Raoul, this is your share of the blocks to put away. You can go to woodworking as soon as you finish." It is appropriate for the teacher to offer to help the child: "As soon as you get started, I will help you put the blocks away."

- *Demonstrate sound judgment.* Teachers must always remember that their behaviour serves as a model for the children in their care. The teacher who shouts at the children "Be quiet!" or who handles the children roughly is modelling the very behaviours that teachers do not want children to use. Furthermore, because consistency is important, teachers must not set a requirement that children may not be able to carry out.

When these general strategies are not enough to create changes in a child's behaviour, a functional approach should be implemented.

Evidence-Based Intervention

The Child Development Institute in Toronto has received international recognition for its SNAP program, which targets boys and girls in separate treatment programs. The program for boys

> is a family-focused, early intervention program for boys ages 6–11 who are engaging in aggressive, antisocial behaviour and/or have come into contact with the police. The program aims to prevent antisocial behaviour and reduce the chance of future conflict with the authorities through timely and effective early intervention. (Child Development Institute, n.d., para. 1)

Staff participating in the program for boys are trained in the SNAP model, which includes a highly structured group with weekly meetings, a concurrent parenting program, individual counselling and/or mentoring for boys in need, and support for teachers. The girls' program

> is a family-focused, gender-specific early intervention program for girls ages 6–11 exhibiting early disruptive behaviour problems at home, school and community. The program components are similar to the SNAP® Boys program, but there are important differences based on research and best practices for treating girl aggression. In SNAP® Girls, for example, there is greater emphasis on discussion and relationship-building. (Child Development Institute, n.d., para. 5)

The organization also provides a specialized day camp for children aged 6 to 11 years during the summer months.

Summary

This chapter has focused on a range of difficult and maladaptive behaviours that are manifested by young children. It has also provided a number of ways for teachers to work with children who have difficult behaviour. The importance of experiences and positive adult intervention on brain development during the early years has been stressed. Functional approaches to problem solving have been provided to help teachers develop some systematic ways of dealing with challenging behaviours. Emphasis has been placed on recognizing the importance of consistency between the way teachers and parents respond to a child's behaviour. It is important to remember that many of these problems experienced by young children are communicative in nature and that one of our goals is to help children to communicate and deal with their needs more effectively. Furthermore, many of the behaviours discussed are disruptive but are mainly a part of children's efforts at learning to discriminate between acceptable and unacceptable ways of responding to the expectations of their home, school, and community. Seldom are acting-out behaviours cause for serious concern, unless they become excessive to the point of threatening the child's well-being or the rights and safety of others.

Most behaviour problems can be managed through careful arrangement of the environment: materials, activities, space, routines, expectations, and adult attention—especially when adult attention is focused on all the good things each child does each day. When a child's behaviour causes damage or injury, the child must be stopped; it is unethical to do otherwise. In extreme cases, where the child has not responded to careful rearrangement of the environment, temporary use of brief time-out periods may be needed. Brief time-out periods must always be used in conjunction with other procedures, including acceptance and understanding of the child's stresses and special attention to the child's appropriate behaviours. Evidence-based programs may also be necessary when children present with extreme behavioural issues.

Resources

American Academy of Child and Adolescent Psychiatry

http://www.aacap.org

This site contains a wide range of resources for families and practitioners dealing with mental health issues.

Beyond the Journal

http://www.naeyc.org

Beyond the Journal is an online supplement to *Young Children*, the journal of the National Association for the Education of Young Children. Readers are offered a number of articles, resource lists, and other documents online that are not included in the print issue.

The Council of Children with Behavioral Disorders (CCBD)

http://www.ccbd.net

This site provides professionals with access to research, professional development opportunities, and advocacy with the aim of improving policy and practice specifically for children and youth at risk for emotional and behavioural disorders.

Health Information for Individuals and Families

http://www.health.gov

This comprehensive U.S. site includes information on children's health, behaviour, and social issues.

Mayo Clinic

http://www.mayoclinic.com

This site contains a wide range of resources related to health issues, including psychiatric and mental health disorders, for families and practitioners.

Pediatric Psychiatry Pamphlets

http://jamesdauntchandler.tripod.com

This site contains a wide range of case histories and reports on child behaviour by Dr. Jim Chandler.

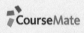 Access an interactive ebook and chapter-specific interactive learning tools, including flashcards, quizzes, videos, and more, in the *Inclusion in Early Childhood Programs* CourseMate. Visit NELSONbrain.com to log in, register, or purchase access.

Facilitating Cognitive Learning

18

OBJECTIVES

After studying the material in this chapter, the student will be able to

- Explain the concept of readiness and how to relate this to maturation and learning theories.
- Make a case against prescribed paper-and-pencil tasks in preschool programs, and describe, instead, the learning activities that should be emphasized.
- Suggest ways that teachers can help young children with developmental differences learn to focus their attention on cognitive activities.
- Describe basic cognitive functions needed by all young children.
- Identify ways that teachers can help children, including those with special needs, become involved in group cognitive learning activities.

KEY CONCEPTS AND TERMS

assistive technology

attention span

brain development

classification

discrimination

embedded learning

emerging literacy

perceptual motor skills

readiness as a learning theory

rote memorization

sensory integration

seriation

spatial and temporal (time) concepts

CONNECTIONS

● The children in Miss Ruiz's small group—Sara, Shauna, Martin, Roberto, Lamont, and Sabrina—range in age from three years and seven months to four years and eleven months. Like most early childhood educators, Miss Ruiz believes that children need to learn to recognize, name, and match colours. She considers it an appropriate developmental task and a building block in emerging literacy. Today she is using three-centimetre coloured cubes as the teaching material. Before the children arrived, she arranged individual baskets containing cubes and design cards geared to the varying skill levels of the children in her group. Martin's cubes and model designs are limited to red and blue. It is a starting task for the day's activity that will ensure his success, but can be readily extended if need be. Shauna's design cards are complex and call for many cubes of every colour. The other children's tasks with the coloured cubes vary accordingly, based on their skill levels and interests.

Emerging literacy the diverse skills that help children become successful in reading, writing, and other academic tasks

Activities labelled as *academic* or *pre-academic* tend to generate mistrust among some early childhood educators. Their concern is that the use of such terms might put a stamp of approval on developmentally *inappropriate* paper-and-pencil tasks and sanction a *pushed-down* elementary curriculum for young children. An alternative term, **emerging literacy**, has been gaining favour. In this text, we use terms such as *pre-academic*, *cognitive*, *intellectual*, and *emerging literacy* as related concepts.

Introduction

The way in which children develop is influenced by congenital factors, as well as by the postnatal environment they experience as they mature. In other words, both heredity and environment affect the process of maturation. Recent research on the way in which the brain develops provides us with further insights on how **brain development** affects cognitive growth and learning. Readiness, as a concept, attributes changes in children's skills to experience and the step-by-step learning of developmental tasks. For example, if a child has learned to recognize food, find his or her own mouth, and hold a spoon right side up most of the time, that child is in all likelihood *ready* to begin the more complex behaviour of self-feeding. In other words, children are ready to learn a new and more complex skill when they can perform and synchronize the necessary, though less difficult, skills that precede the more complex skill.

Brain development affects cognitive growth and learning; children's brains need to be stimulated for the network of connections to grow and be protected from elimination

The concept of **readiness as a learning theory** is useful when planning an inclusive program for young children. Because all children develop at different rates in different areas of development, an effective inclusive early childhood environment must be able to meet the needs of all children, regardless of how uneven their individual development may be.

Readiness as a learning theory recognizes the importance of being aware of the point at which a child has all the necessary prerequisite skills to engage in specific new learning

An inclusive early childhood program should have at its foundation child-initiated play, supported by an enriched environment that offers many opportunities for active language development and hands-on learning experiences. Learning experiences presented in the form of workbooks, prescribed paper-and-pencil tasks, and **rote memorization** (the memorizing of numbers or letters without any comprehension as to what they stand for) do not enrich learning, and they are not appropriate in any pre-academic curriculum or for any young child.

Rote memorization the act of memorizing numbers or letters without understanding them; being able to recite something that has little or no meaning for the one who has memorized it

However, most early childhood educators now accept that pre-academic activities and spontaneous play are compatible. Quality early childhood programs should include cognitive experiences, sensorimotor activities, and intellectual experiences in their daily programs.

All children, those with disabilities and those without, vary greatly in how their cognitive abilities develop. Because the process of becoming literate begins in early infancy and continues throughout the developmental years, early exposure to a range of learning, language, and communication experiences in a safe, warm, and caring environment is most conducive to the stimulation of early cognitive functioning. This chapter covers approaches and ideas appropriate for supporting cognitive development in an inclusive early childhood program.

Implications of Brain Development for Teachers of Young Children

Children's brains need to be stimulated in order for the network of connections to grow and be protected from elimination (see Chapter 5). If it is not used, the brain begins a process of discarding excess synapses after the first decade of life. Fully half have been eliminated by the teenage years. Simply stated, the growth of the brain operates on a use-it-or-lose-it principle. This knowledge is of great importance to early childhood teachers and caregivers, and to parents of young children. As the research implies, young children are biologically ready to learn. The question that arises, however, is, what best supports early brain development?

Shore (2003) wrote that a decade or more of brain research has given us some answers to these questions. She cited five major points to consider:

1. There is a complex interplay between nature (genes) and nurture (environment) in the development of the brain. *Implication:* What children experience in the first few years may influence their future intellectual functioning as much as their genetic makeup does.

2. Early care (both positive and negative) has a "decisive and long-lasting impact" on a child's ability to learn. *Implication:* A daily helping of warm and responsive care by parents and caregivers helps a child's emotional and social development and self-control.

3. The brain has a great capacity to change, but there are some critical periods (such as when developing vision, language, emotional controls) that are more crucial than others. *Implication:* Teachers and parents can learn to take advantage of the appropriate period for teaching certain intellectual tasks.

4. Negative experiences or lack of stimulation are likely to have serious and sustained effects; the parts of the brain associated with emotion (affect) seem to show the most effect. Stress has an impact on the brain's function in memory and critical thinking. *Implication:* Parents, teachers, and caregivers should nurture young children to lessen the effects of poverty and neglect on children's lives.

5. The value of timely, well-designed, and intensive intervention is of utmost importance in brain development. *Implication:* Research provides proof that early intervention reduces developmental delays and the number of children who will require special education.

Jensen (2008) summarized some additional principles of brain-based research:

- Each brain is unique; each age-level or grade-level learner should not be held to the same standards.

- Emotions run the brain; good ones create an excitement for and love of learning. Bad ones affect all attempts at learning.

- The brain is run by patterns, not by facts. We learn best with themes, patterns, and contextual experiences. The brain is poorly designed for formal instruction or rote memorization.

- Each of us learns through simultaneous styles, such as visual, auditory, and kinesthetic. We do not learn as well when tasks are linear or when information is presented out of context.

- All learning is mind–body. Posture and breathing affect learning.

- The brain is stimulated by challenge, novelty, and feedback in our learning environments.

Brain research has also had an impact on those who work with children who have developmental delays or neurological impairments. Greenspan's work (1992; Greenspan & Wider, 1997) focused on children with autism and other children with developmental delays or disabilities. Through specifically designed experiences, children developed new capacities in verbal, emotional, and social functions. Benasich and Tallal (1996) worked with infants and toddlers who had a specific language disorder. Through brain-imaging studies, early detection of an auditory-processing problem allowed the researchers to intervene at a much earlier age.

Clearly then, information about brain research is of critical importance to parents and educators of all children, no matter their abilities or disabilities.

The question arises as to whether "academic work" is appropriate at preschool age. The answer is that pure academics—rote learning, use of workbooks, prescribed paper-and-pencil tasks—are totally inappropriate with preschool-aged children. However, many cognitive and intellectual activities are embedded in spontaneous play and learning opportunities. It is up to early childhood teachers to

- support children's cognitive learning and emerging literacy;

- develop play and learning opportunities that build on children's interests and stimulate new ones;

- help children to find answers to questions;

Children need years of play with tangible objects.

© Cengage Learning

- support readiness for further information, guiding and prompting children to use the skills and information they already have in seeking answers to new questions; and
- use music and musical activities to enrich brain development in this area.

In summary, children of all developmental levels, from the most delayed to the most gifted, need activities that support their level of awareness, stimulate curiosity, and foster the urge to ask and find answers to questions. Activities that involve sensory experiences—touching, seeing, hearing, tasting, and smelling—are essential. Early childhood teachers need to create and then maintain a developmentally appropriate environment in which children are free to explore and experience materials and activities through their senses in their own way and at their own pace.

Implications and Strategies for Supporting Active Learning in the Education of Young Children

Active Learning Opportunities Should Be Embedded in the Early Childhood Curriculum

Preschools and early childhood centres are often pressured to demonstrate that children are doing more than playing, that they are learning "something worthwhile." This pressure has led to some early childhood programs emphasizing paper-and-pencil tasks and workbook exercises. *Such activities, however, represent an inappropriate and ineffectual teaching format for young children.* As Bredekamp (1997) pointed out, "Children need years of play with real objects and events before they are able to understand the meaning of symbols, such as letters and numbers. Throughout early childhood, children's concepts and language gradually develop to enable them to understand more abstract and symbolic information" (see photo, page 404). Bredekamp and Copple (2009, p. 23), in their discussion of developmentally appropriate practice (DAP), indicated that children benefit from engaging in self-initiated spontaneous play from teacher-planned and structured projects and experiences.

Preschool children are ready for academic experiences. Many of these experiences have cognitive skills learning **embedded** in them and are appropriate for young children.

Embedded learning the intentional incorporation of specific learning objectives into play and routine classroom activities

Cognitive Experiences Should Support Emerging Literacy in Young Children

The focus of early learning experiences should always be on enjoyable activities that promote children's effective use of language and the development of their social interaction skills, their emerging abilities to formulate concepts, and their interest in (and curiosity about) the world around them. The teacher's role in facilitating cognitive development is to first set the scene and then, by observing and listening, follow the children's lead.

In this text we have referred, in some detail, to an "emergent curriculum" approach that creates an ever-changing, enriched learning environment that arises out of the children's interests (Fraser, 2012). This environment should develop experiences that provide for hands-on, child-initiated, and teacher-facilitated opportunities for learning. Early childhood teachers can play an important role by guiding, encouraging, and supporting children in individual and group projects and problem-solving situations, and by helping to structure the environment to allow for expansion of children's learning.

To further support readiness and emerging literacy, early childhood teachers can advance, *indirectly* but significantly, children's anticipation of learning to read, write, and do math by writing out a child's observations, stories, or questions and reading them back to the child, helping the child to find the answers to questions, and making and then recording measurements. They can also help children keep a log by writing down what each child dictates about observed changes—for example, in a plant's growth. With these kinds of cognitive readiness activities, most children, when they reach the primary grades, are ready and eager to learn to read about, tell about, write about, and record their experiences. This type of programming reinforces the child's development in all areas and is particularly appropriate for inclusion because it enables each child, regardless of individual ability, to respond to the environment at his or her own level of development (see Chapter 15).

Skills related to concept development can be observed from infancy on, even in children with severe developmental disabilities. Children with special needs may be placed anywhere along the developmental continuum in cognitive functioning. A child who has severe motor disabilities may be advanced in some areas of cognitive development. A child with limited speech may be more cognitively advanced but unable to demonstrate his or her ability. Many children with disabilities never realize their cognitive potential; others excel far beyond their peers who have no special needs. What is important in early childhood programs is that expectations must start where the child is and work from there, step by step, focusing on planning cognitive activities that will benefit each child as an individual and the group as a whole (see photo, below).

This starting point is somewhat more difficult to find in an inclusive setting, in which teachers must be aware of a broader range of individual differences and needs in their group. Children with certain special needs, such as those with visual and hearing impairments, often need specialized guidance and encouragement in learning to use and develop all their senses and abilities to the best possible advantage. Support from a child interventionist or specialist trained in the education of children with vision or hearing deficits is recommended.

Children with cognitive delays may need more direct teaching, such as hand-over-hand guidance, when learning new concepts. For example, as the teacher

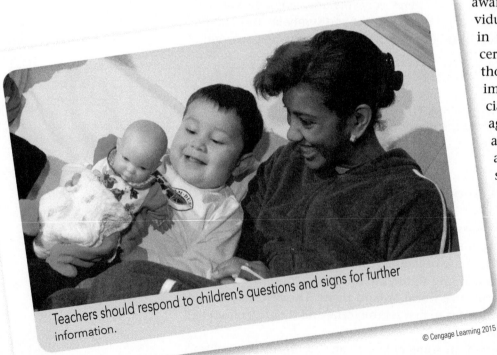

Teachers should respond to children's questions and signs for further information.

© Cengage Learning 2015

is helping a child to button a coat, the teacher might gently guide the child's hand and start to count the buttons as the task is being completed. Counting can then be expanded to other things in which the child is involved.

In cases where a child's major disability is an intellectual impairment, it is important to identify the child's current level and rate of learning in deciding what type of tasks are an appropriate match, and then to proceed with a task analysis (see Chapter 11). The length of time and number of steps into which a task is broken down depends on the individual child. It may take one child several weeks to learn what another child can learn in a day.

Assistive Technology Should Support Active Learning

For children with significant special needs, computers and other types of **assistive technology** can foster independence by providing help with communication and mobility. When technical support is provided in the classroom, teachers, with the help of specially trained assistants, can work together to plan and implement the program for a given child.

Computers have tremendous potential as teaching tools for all children if their interactions with them are monitored and supported by adults (Deiner, Dyck, & Hardcare, 2004). The value of computers in the classroom is directly related to the quality and appropriateness of the software that is used. The software market for children's programs is enormous and changing constantly (see the Children's Technology Review website listed in the Resources section at the end of this chapter). The computer is useful in supporting a child's learning when it is used as a resource for information and for finding answers to questions that develop from the children's play and exploration. It is also useful in helping to develop eye–hand coordination and may encourage practice and provide help for children who are delayed in this area of development. For children who have difficulty in expressing themselves, the computer may be able to act as an aid in helping with communication. At no time should the computer become the primary focus of the curriculum in an early childhood program. It should be treated as a useful resource in much the same way as a tape recorder might be used to collect information, record children's songs and conversations, or play music to support ongoing activities.

Assistive technology various kinds of equipment, such as a computerized Braille system or voice synthesizer, designed to facilitate learning and communication for individuals with disabilities

Necessary Skills for Cognitive Learning

Children with special needs often have difficulty acquiring readiness skills on their own. Teachers need to identify the missing skills in each child and then find ways to teach these skills, step by step.

Children may also have behaviours that will delay or interfere with learning, including the following:

- a short attention span
- a limited ability to imitate
- perceptual motor inefficiency (see photo, page 408)
- inadequate fine motor controls (eye–hand–wrist coordination)
- a limited ability to formulate concepts
- poorly developed short-term and long-term memory
- an inability to follow instructions

All cognitive skills are intertwined with one another and with all other areas of development. This interrelatedness is the essence of the *whole child* concept of development. For example, when children are recalling their trip to the zoo, all skills come into play, and even overlap, as the teacher helps the children to discuss and act out what they saw, heard, and did. This interrelatedness of developmental skills also makes a convincing argument against an academic, subject-matter approach in the education of young children.

Attention span the length of time an individual is able to concentrate on an activity or event

ATTENTION SPAN **Attention span** is the length of time an individual is able to concentrate on an activity or event. The ability to simultaneously *focus* on certain aspects of the environment and *ignore* others is essential. When working with a puzzle, a child needs to be able to focus on the frame board and the puzzle pieces while ignoring other children's play activities. As stressed in Chapter 15, children's ability (or inability) to focus their attention is strongly influenced by classroom arrangements.

> *Example:*
>
> *Three-year-old Jeri picked up a completed puzzle from the table, dumped it out, looked at it briefly, and tried to put in a piece. She then picked up a second puzzle and dumped it out also. Next, she picked up a nearby truck and ran it through the puzzle. Leaving the area with the truck, she went to the sand table. There she picked up some sifters, sifted for two minutes, and then went over to look at the fish.*

Jeri's "short" attention span can be related to activities that may have been developmentally too advanced (the puzzle she chose), an environment that was too stimulating for her (she just couldn't focus in on any one thing), and perhaps how the room was arranged, as well as the fact that no teacher stepped in to support her interest in any one area.

Teacher support is often needed when children have perceptual motor inefficiencies.

Courtesy of Ryerson Early Learning Centre

A child cannot be successful (or even interested) when materials are overly difficult or poorly arranged (the puzzle and the truck on the same table). Many children have the potential for longer periods of attention, yet they do not stay with activities because the materials are developmentally inappropriate or set up in inappropriate ways (see photo, below).

It is true that attractiveness of materials and the ways in which they are presented are important factors in determining how involved a child will become with an activity. Even so, there are children who have trouble becoming involved on their own, regardless of the attractiveness of the setting. They need help from teachers in getting started. Once their attention is engaged, however, they too learn to focus. Bailey and Wolery (1984) suggest several ways that teachers can help children focus their attention:

- providing materials that are appealing and colourful, that can be manipulated, and that have built-in feedback (true of many Montessori materials)

- offering participation as a privilege rather than a responsibility: "Children who finish putting blocks away will then be *allowed* to come to story time."

- giving children an immediate role: "Julie has the punch to punch the train tickets."

- instructing or prompting an activity: "I'll help you start a fence at this end. Where shall I put my first block?"

- identifying children's preferences for materials; preferred materials result in longer engagement

The child's ability to focus attention is strongly influenced by classroom arrangements.

© Cengage Learning

IMITATION AND MODELLING The ability to imitate is essential to all learning. Children who do not imitate spontaneously must be taught if they are to learn other developmental skills. However, the inability to imitate often goes unrecognized and so becomes the cause of continuing learning difficulties. When a child with developmental differences is enrolled in a group, an informal assessment of imitation skills should be a priority. A simplified version of a game such as "Simon Says" can tell a teacher a great deal about a child's ability to imitate. If imitation skills are lacking, initial teaching priorities should be concentrated in that area. Bailey and Wolery (1984) made the following suggestions for teaching children how to imitate:

- Imitate the child. Imitating the child's vocalizations and gestures often stimulates the child and also reinforces the child's further efforts.

- Provide models appropriate for the child's level of development.

- Provide whatever assistance is needed to help the child learn to imitate. Placing a mirror in front of the child, for example, allows the child to judge the accuracy of his or her imitations.

- If necessary, be directive in teaching the child to imitate. Physically put the child through an imitative response. For example, the teacher points to the child and says, "Marla, point to the circle," while stretching out the child's index finger and placing it on the "point to" object. An encouraging and descriptive comment follows: "Marla, look at that! You're pointing to the circle!"

- Make imitating a rewarding and playful experience; learning to imitate should be fun.

- Provide positive feedback and encouragement for approximations (first efforts) to an imitative response. When a child finally points to an object, even though it may not be the one requested, respond positively: "You're pointing to a blue truck. Good for you. Now let's find the red one and you can point to it too."

Perceptual motor skills movement generated by sensory messages, by what is seen, heard, touched, tasted, or smelled

Sensory integration the process of more than one sense working together to understand a sensory message and to translate the message into appropriate action

PERCEPTUAL MOTOR SKILLS **Perceptual motor skills** are made up of two closely related processes (see photo, below). One has to do with *understanding* sensory messages: what is seen, heard, touched, tasted, or smelled. The second is the translation of the messages into appropriate actions. Generally, more than one sense is involved in a response; this is referred to as **sensory integration**. The following are three examples of perceptual motor skills coupled with sensory integration:

- A two-year-old stops her play and turns at the sound of an engine. She looks up, moves her eyes back and forth, and then points to an airplane. This child is exhibiting integrated visual (seeing) and auditory (hearing) skills, resulting in appropriately matched motor responses of turning, scanning, and pointing.

- A four-year-old picks up a bar of cocoa butter, smells it, bites off a corner, and then spits it out while making a wry face. The child is expressing appropriate smell and taste perceptions and responding with relevant perceptual motor responses: The cocoa butter smelled like candy, and she took a bite. It tasted more like soap than candy, however, and so she spit it out while making a face indicating an unpleasant taste.

- A five-year-old, during group time, reaches into the Mystery Bag and verbally identifies unseen objects by touch.

Every preschool activity involves various forms of perceptual motor skills: climbing, jumping, riding wheel toys, watching a caterpillar creep, splashing in puddles, building with blocks, playing with table toys, painting, working with clay, colouring, cutting, and pasting. Music, stories, and dramatic play provide opportunities to pantomime, pretend, and practise the perceptual motor skills essential to everyday life.

Children with delayed perceptual motor skills often receive incomplete or distorted sensory messages. In some instances, children have become nearly immobilized because they are so distrustful of moving about; for example, children with poor depth perception are sometimes hurt and badly frightened by stepping off into unanticipated space. Children with poor directionality or who lack the ability to retain "position in space" may fear becoming lost or disoriented. Thus, children with sensory difficulties often need special activities, adapted materials, and additional support in using their intact senses.

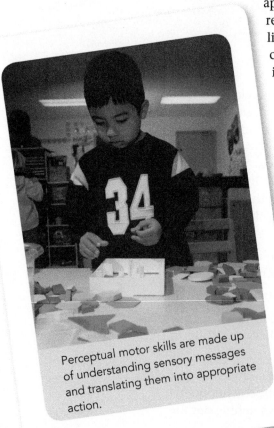

Perceptual motor skills are made up of understanding sensory messages and translating them into appropriate action.

© Cengage Learning

FINE MOTOR SKILLS Fine motor skills (eye–hand coordination; use of fingers, hands, and wrists) are closely related to perceptual motor skills. Both are important in learning self-help/ care skills, as well as in learning to use all kinds of tools: paintbrushes, hammers, crayons, markers, and eventually pencils for printing and then writing. Practice in fine motor control is embedded in early childhood activities. The same activities that enable practice of fine motor skills have important cognitive, social, and language components:

- water play: pouring, squeezing, measuring
- block building: stacking, bridging, balancing, putting away
- art activities: painting, hammering, woodworking, clay modelling, cutting, pasting, crayoning, and so forth (see photo, right)
- housekeeping: dressing dolls, pouring "tea," stirring "soup," and setting the table

Manipulative materials, sometimes referred to as *table toys*, are especially good for promoting fine motor control and perceptual motor skills simultaneously (see photo, below). Among the most useful are these:

- wooden beads and strings with metal or plastic tips
- puzzles and parquetry blocks
- picture dominoes and lotto games
- nesting and stacking cups, kitty-in-the-keg, form boxes
- pegs and pegboards, hammer-and-nail sets
- Montessori graduated cylinders and colour boards
- paper and crayons or whiteboards with markers

When appropriately matched to children's skill levels, manipulative materials ensure practice sessions that are informal and fun for all children. They also can be used successfully by children with developmental delays, because they are so readily adaptable. The following examples demonstrate how manipulative materials can be adapted by teachers to support a child with special needs:

- For fine motor skill development, wooden beads are especially useful. Offer only the largest wooden beads with a stiff wire on which to string them; a straightened coat hanger with its ends wrapped in tape works well. Also, peg handles can be attached to puzzle pieces in order to make lifting of puzzle pieces easier. Paintbrushes with large, shorter handles are easier to grasp.
- For a child who has delays in cognitive as well as fine motor development, select puzzles that have few pieces. Each piece should be a recognizable object.

Fine motor skills are a readiness skill.

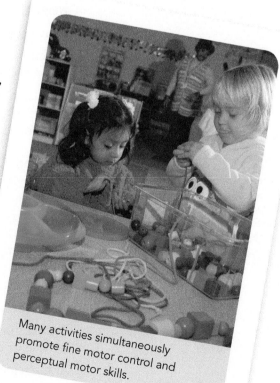
Many activities simultaneously promote fine motor control and perceptual motor skills.

- Adaptation of materials is also important. For example, when a child has mastered the simple puzzles but the next ones seem too complex, teachers need to be inventive. One suggestion is that several of the inside pieces of more difficult puzzles can be taped down from underneath with a strip of clear tape doubled back on itself. These pieces remain in the frame when the child turns the puzzle out. Less is required of the child; fewer pieces have to be replaced to complete the task, and the job is simplified because finding the fit for border pieces is usually easier. The task gradually can be made more difficult by taping down fewer and fewer puzzle pieces. The advantage to this procedure is that each time the child completes the task there is always the reward of seeing the completed puzzle.

- Nesting cups can be presented, beginning with only four or five of the larger cups, handing these cups to the child in order, one at a time. Once the child has the concept of the cups fitting into each other, the cups can be placed on the table for the child to pick up. As the child becomes more proficient in nesting cups, more cups can be added to the sequence.

CONCEPT FORMATION *Concepts* and *concept formation* are difficult terms to define without becoming overly technical. In this text, concepts will be defined as internal images or ideas (mental activities) that organize thinking. Concepts enable us to make sense out of our world. By continuously formulating new concepts, children impose order on the many things they must learn during their early years. Concepts developing in preschool-aged children include

- colour;
- texture;
- size;
- shape;
- weight;
- same versus different; and
- directionality and position in space, such as *up*, *down*, *inside*, *outside*, *on top of*, *under*, and *over*.

Skills related to concept formation include discrimination, classification, seriation, understanding of spatial and temporal relationships, memory, and the ability to follow directions.

Discrimination Concept development depends on the ability to *discriminate*. **Discrimination** is the ability to perceive likenesses and differences among related objects and events. Put even more simply, it is the ability to "tell things apart"; to specify "same or different"; and to match objects, sounds, or ideas in terms of one or more attributes (characteristics). Opportunities to practise making both simple and complex discriminations are found throughout the preschool day:

Discrimination the ability to perceive likeness and differences among related objects and events; to specify same versus different; to match objects, sounds, or ideas in terms of one or more attributes

- At music time the teacher introduces a song that asks, "Who is wearing sandals? boots? running shoes? blue socks? striped socks? no socks?"

- During story time a teacher asks children to identify how the story is the same as or different from a previous story read to the group.

- At the science table, children are asked to sort rocks by size and texture.

- A variety of sorting tasks are usually available, such as putting the yellow pegs in one compartment and the blue pegs in another.

- Unit blocks often are put away according to the size and shape drawn on the shelf.

- A patterned string of wooden beads may be presented for children to copy—a small round blue bead, a big square red bead, and then a long green bead. This is repeated several times. This task is complex in that the beads vary on three *attributes*: shape, size, and colour.

It should be noted, too, that the fine motor and perceptual motor skills are demanding. It might be that a child could make the necessary discriminations but not have the fine motor skills for stringing the beads. This is an instance in which the teacher would need to make an adaptation in materials, perhaps providing a wire rather than a string for threading the beads. A child with more severe physical limitations might participate by identifying the next bead, and another child or adult can place it on the wire.

Discrimination tasks can be adapted to fit any developmental level. For children who are functioning at a higher level, the bead-stringing task can be made more complex by introducing number concepts as well as colour, space, and shape: for example, repetitions of three small round blue beads, two large square red beads, and one long green bead. Or it can be made very simple for a child who has a developmental delay, such as alternating a square red bead with a square blue bead, or simpler yet, by having the child select and string only large blue beads (with large red beads in the basket as distracters). Adaptations for individual differences are unlimited.

Classification The process of imposing order on objects and events is another major characteristic of concept formation. This skill is sometimes described as the ability to classify. **Classification** involves the formation of categories. In other words, children learn that cats, dogs, and squirrels have certain characteristics in common: fur, four legs, a tail, and so on. On the basis of these shared attributes, the creatures all fall into the category of *animal*. Each category is then subject to further breakdown as the child's experiences broaden. *Dog* becomes a category by itself when the child learns to discriminate among different kinds of dogs—poodles, collies, Airedales, and so on. Learning to classify, like learning to discriminate, can be taught.

Classification part of concept formation in which an order is imposed on objects, or events into specific categories

Seriation Seriation is the process of arranging objects and events along orderly and related dimensions (a prerequisite skill is the ability to make fine discriminations). Examples of seriation include the following:

Seriation the process of arranging objects and events along orderly and related dimensions, for example: beginning, middle, end or small, bigger, biggest

- tall, middle-sized, shortest; eventually, "These tall ones are taller than those tall ones"

- first, last; next-to-last

- happy, sad; "saddest one of all"

Seriation experiences like those in the preceding list help children learn to make comparisons about quantities, time and space, and affect (feelings). Learning to tell about what happened in the order of occurrence is another seriation skill that many older preschoolers begin to master.

Example:

"Yesterday we went to Grandma's. We got to play in the attic. Then we had dinner but first Grandma made us wash our hands and faces 'cause we got so dirty. After dinner Grandpa read to us and then it was time to go home and I slept in the car."

Many early childhood activities lend themselves to seriation practice and to endless adaptations for children with cognitive delays. For example, children can retell a story that has just been read, or teachers can ask, "What comes next?" when reading a familiar story. Sequenced picture cards (commercial or teacher-made) are also useful. The cards tell a story when arranged in proper order: The first card may show a child digging a hole in the ground, the second shows planting a seed, and the third shows the child pulling up a carrot. For more advanced children, the series can be longer and more complex, including pictures related to watering, weeding, and sprouting. For the child with very limited seriation skills, the teacher might use just two pictures, a child climbing up on a stool and then jumping down. At first, the teacher and child can alternate placing the cards, with the teacher stating what comes first and what happens next.

Spatial and temporal relationships Learning how objects and events are related to space, to time, and to the child is another aspect of concept formation. **Spatial and temporal (time) concepts** include this grouping:

- on, in, under
- in front of, behind, next to
- in between, in the middle, second from the end
- yesterday, today, tomorrow
- soon, after a while, later, not yet

Many children seem to learn such concepts automatically. However, there are children with and without developmental differences who need direct instruction.

Spatial and temporal concepts are best taught as children themselves are moving about in space and time. For example, each child must learn to recognize his or her body-occupying-space in relationship to the body-space of others. This may not come easily and certainly it does not come early. Toddlers may "plow through" other toddlers as if they did not exist.

Active play is especially helpful in developing children's spatial awareness. Outdoors, a teacher might comment, "Hamid, you climbed so high. You are on top of the ladder box." If the child is having difficulty forming spatial concepts, the teacher should do an immediate follow-up: "Where are you, Hamid?" and wait for the child to respond. If the child does not respond, the teacher models the words "high, on top." When the child repeats the statement, the teacher corroborates: "That's right, Hamid. You are high; you are on top."

Learning to understand time is more difficult for most children. As with spatial concepts, time concepts are most effectively learned in relationship to play and everyday activities. Children understand short and more immediate time intervals most easily.

- "Time to come in *after* you run around the track two more times."
- "Snack comes *when* we finish this story."
- "We will get back *in time for* lunch."

Memory The ability to remember what previously has been experienced and learned is a skill necessary to all new learning. Two kinds of memory are required: long term and short term (being able to remember what took place some time earlier as well as what happened in the immediate past). Tasks requiring rote memorization are inappropriate for young children. Activities that encourage children to practise remembering within their everyday work and play activities

Spatial and temporal (time) concepts how objects are related to space and time and to the child are the kinds that foster learning. Developmentally appropriate activities might include the following:

- conversational questions *of interest to the child* (with teacher prompts, after a suitable pause):
  - What did you have for breakfast? ... (orange juice? cereal? anything else?)
  - Where does your kitten sleep? ... (in a basket?)
  - What was the caterpillar doing on the leaf? ... (crawling? chewing on the leaf?)
- remembering one another's names and teachers' names, and using these names appropriately
- remembering where materials are stored so as to get them out and put them away properly
- telling what object or objects have been removed in games, such as "cover the tray"
- story- and picture-reading activities, as mentioned in the discussion of seriation
- leaving the bathroom in prescribed order for the children who will be using it next

For children with cognitive, neurological, or related impairments, the teacher often can begin memory training by telling the child what comes next: "The paper towel goes in the basket." The teacher should then follow up immediately: "Where does the paper towel go?" The child has to remember only long enough to repeat the information (or comply). A child's memory system may be activated more slowly if he or she has a delay; therefore, it is important to give adequate time to respond. In teaching paper towel disposal, for example, the teacher must allow adequate time for the child's memory to become charged and produce action.

Ability to follow instructions The ability to follow instructions and carry out requests is important. Children with language, cognitive, or neurological impairments often have trouble with such tasks. Whenever a child has repeated difficulty, teachers should ask themselves the following five questions:

1. Does the child hear (or see) well enough to know what is expected?
2. Does the child have the vocabulary necessary to understand the request?
3. Does the child understand the concepts? For example, does the child understand *match* when the teacher says, "Match circles of the same colour"?
4. Is the child able to imitate the behaviours expected, as when the teacher demonstrates how to fold a piece of paper in half?
5. Are the instructions too complicated or given too rapidly? too many at one time?

Three- and four-step directions, spoken in rapid sequence, are more than most young children (let alone children who have a developmental delay) can manage. It is true that a few older preschoolers might be able to carry through on "Would you please go to the sink and wet a sponge—I think there's one under the sink or in the bathroom—and then wipe up all that messy paint on the floor and halfway up the table legs?" Many others would be completely lost.

A few might try to carry out the last step in the direction (the only thing they remember) by rubbing at the paint on the table leg.

The younger the child in age, experience, or developmental level, the simpler the directions should be. *It is important that teachers take nothing for granted about what children understand.* For very young children and for children with developmental delays, directions should be given one at a time. The process works best when the teacher gets down to a child's eye level and speaks directly to the child, and the language used is clear and free of unnecessary words or explanations.

> *Example:*
>
> *"Marty, we're going to have to get this paint wiped up. Would you go to the sink (enough of a pause to let the child start moving toward the sink) and find a sponge?"*
>
> *When Marty has the sponge in his hand, the teacher gives the next direction: "Now, wet the sponge." If the teacher wants to make sure that the child does not cross the room dripping water all the way, an intermediate instruction should be given: "Squeeze some water out of it."*
>
> *Some children might not know what the teacher expects, so the teacher says, "Like this," pantomiming how to squeeze a sponge. "Now, let's go over and wipe up the paint on the floor."*
>
> *When that is accomplished, the teacher can draw the child's attention to the paint on the table legs.*

Instructions should be accompanied by gestures—for example, pointing when asking a child to put the car on the shelf.

Most children who are developmentally ready can learn to follow instructions if they are allowed to begin with one-step directions, like those in the example above. When the child has mastered one-step directions, it is logical to move to two- and then, perhaps, three-step directions. In an inclusive setting, when teaching how to follow complex directions or instructions, it is often a good idea to pair a child without a disability with a child who has a disability.

Prerequisites for Reading, Writing, and Math

Other cognitive skills and activities are more closely associated with reading, writing, and math. The following is a list of a few skills appropriate for promoting reading, writing, and math readiness in early childhood programs:

- "Reading" a series of pictures on a page from left to right and top to bottom. (Many picture books and board games are set up to promote this kind of pre-reading visual organization in children.)

- Pencil or crayon activities that begin to show some degree of eye–hand control (scribbling large swirling circles upon circles; making the marks that children often describe as "writing"; experiencing occasional success at writing his or her own name).

- Freestyle cutting with scissors. Some children spontaneously try to "cut on the line."

- Counting a row of objects from left to right (or top to bottom, as in coat buttoning) by touching each in turn (one-to-one correspondence).

- Grouping objects in sets of two, three, or four.

- Identifying groups of objects as the *same*, *more*, or *less*.

- Recognizing that different but similar sounds are not the same. (Numerous songs, fingerplays, poems, and teacher-improvised games contribute to this learning.)

- Certain matching, ordering, and spatial relationship games and activities found in computer programs for young children.

None of these tasks is easily accomplished. They require at least minimal competence in the underlying skills discussed earlier in this chapter. However, all readiness skills can be taught, to some degree, and all can be sequenced so as to facilitate children's learning. Learning to cut on the lines is used below as an illustration of first steps in teaching a complex skill.

Julio was a seven-year-old who was highly distractible and had poorly coordinated fine motor skills. Using a pair of specially designed scissors that allowed him to put his hand over Julio's, the teacher helped Julio learn to hold the scissors and then to "cut" the air with them. Next, the teacher prepared strips of paper about 1.5 centimetres wide with heavy lines drawn across them at 2-centimetre intervals. The teacher held up a strip and instructed Julio to open his scissors. The teacher then inserted the strip between the scissor blades, in contact with one of the black lines, and said, "Cut." It was a simple matter for Julio to close the scissors. Success was immediate and evident—a cleanly cut piece of paper came off with each contact. To add interest to the task, the teacher soon switched to strips of brightly coloured paper, feeling that Julio would not now be distracted from his cutting task by the variations in colour. Julio's cuttings were put into an envelope to either take home to play with or paste into a "picture" at school.

Supporting Emerging Literacy

It is important to support a child's emerging literacy. "One of the first indications of an emerging interest in learning how to read and write is children's recognition of environmental print, in letters such as the *M* for McDonald's restaurants or words such as STOP on traffic signs" (Fraser, 2000, p. 203). Initial attempts at "writing" occur at about the same time. Children make scribbling notations on their pictures and assume that they represent a message. Sometimes their meaning becomes evident to adults.

Example:

Denise, at the age of three, began making a series of six circles in the corner of all her pictures. She told everyone that this was her name. In fact, because she was the only child "signing" her work in this way, it became unnecessary to put her name on pictures. She had created her own unique signature, and it communicated who had painted this picture.

Adult attitudes toward children's first attempts at "writing" are critical in reinforcing the child's future attempts at communicating through symbols. Children whose initial responses are greeted with enthusiasm by adults are more likely to continue to understand, practise, keep developing, and learn conventional symbols.

It can never be stressed enough how important it is to read frequently to young children. It is through early and enjoyable experiences of being read to that children become motivated to learn how to read by themselves.

Effective early literacy instruction provides preschool children with developmentally appropriate settings, materials, experiences, and social support that encourage early forms of reading and writing to flourish and develop into conventional literacy. Roskos, Christie, and Richgels (2003) broke teaching of literacy into eight specific strategies:

1. Rich teacher talk
2. Storybook reading
3. Phonological awareness activities
4. Alphabet activities
5. Support for emergent reading
6. Support for emergent writing
7. Shared book experience
8. Integrated, content-focused activities

RICH TEACHER TALK As stated previously, talking to children is the most effective way to help them develop language and to increase their vocabularies. Children should be engaged in conversations both individually and as members of groups. Conversations should include topics and vocabulary that are new and unfamiliar but interesting to the child. The teacher should expand on what the child says, providing models for more descriptive and mature statements.

STORYBOOK READING The language and illustrations of high-quality children's books depict rich stories that excite and surprise children, make them laugh, make them wonder, and make them think. Picture books should be a part of every day in the early childhood years (Strasser & Seplocha, 2010). As the *Becoming a Nation of Readers* report (Anderson, Hiebert, Scott, & Wilkerson, 1985) emphasized, "The single most important activity for building knowledge for their eventual success in reading is reading aloud to children." While the report was written three decades ago, the statement still holds true today.

Reading aloud helps children make sense of what they hear and see. By reading aloud, parents and teachers serve as reading role models. If the adult is enthusiastic about reading, then children are sure to catch their enthusiasm. Not only does reading out loud help to increase vocabulary, but also the repeated reading of favourite books builds familiarity, increasing the likelihood that children will attempt to read those books on their own.

Derry Koralek (2003) stressed the importance of reading to children of all ages. Figure 18–1 contains several of her suggested strategies for reading to young children.

PHONOLOGICAL AWARENESS ACTIVITIES Phonological awareness is the ability to hear and identify the sounds of spoken and written language. Phonemes are the building blocks of words (Strasser & Seplocha, 2010). Phonological and phonemic awareness can be increased when teachers select books that focus on sounds and are based on familiar songs. In addition to reading books, other important activities include playing games, listening to poetry, and singing songs. Activities should focus on rhyming, alliteration (words starting with the same sound), and sound matching.

FIGURE 18-1

Strategies for Reading to Children of All Ages

Babies

- Very young babies love to hear familiar voices.
- Hold the baby in your lap; make sure the baby can see the pictures.
- Play with words, sing, and make up rhymes; include the baby's name.
- Offer the baby a toy to hold and chew while listening to you read.
- Read one or two pages at a time; gradually increase the number of pages.
- Point to and name pictures in the book.
- Stay on a page for as long as the baby is interested.
- Allow the baby to help turn the pages.

Toddlers

- Toddlers feel competent when they participate.
- Read books with rhymes and predictable words they can remember.
- Read the same books again and again, if asked. A toddler will let you know when he or she has had enough of a book.
- Change your voice to fit the characters and plot.
- Find and use puppets and other props related to the story.
- Repeat interesting words and phrases.
- Stop to comment, ask questions, and look closely at the pictures.
- Encourage a toddler to join in: turn pages, name things in pictures, make sounds, repeat rhymes and phrases, and think about what might happen next.
- Talk about the pictures and point out details a toddler might miss.
- Relate the story to a toddler's real-life experiences.

Preschoolers

- Read stories with simple plots children can retell in their own words.
- Before you begin a book, read the title, author, and illustrator; look at the cover; talk about what the book might be about; suggest things to look and listen for.
- Run your finger under the text; pause at the end of sentences.
- Use information from the book to answer children's questions.
- Ask children to look closely at the pictures to help them understand the story and make predictions about what might happen next.
- Repeat interesting words and rhymes while reading a book and at a later time.
- Pause and wait so children can say the word that ends a repetitive or predictable phrase.
- Ask thinking questions, such as "What might happen next? Where did he go? Why did she do that?"

Kindergarten and School-Age Children

- Set the stage before you begin reading. Review and discuss what you read yesterday and ask about what might happen next.
- Defer questions until after you finish reading—unless the answer is critical to understanding what's happening.
- Summarize, adapt, or skip parts of books that are too far above a child's level of understanding.
- Relate a book you are reading to one read in the past. Ask the children to discuss how they are alike and how they differ.
- Provide materials and activities that let children expand their understanding of a character, historical event, or situation.
- Stop reading the book at a suspenseful point so children will be eager for tomorrow's read-aloud time.

Source: Adapted from Reading Is Fundamental and Derry Koralek, Reading Aloud with Children of All Ages. Retrieved from http://www.naeyc.org/files/yc/file/200303/ReadingAloud.pdf

ALPHABET ACTIVITIES Activities can include playing with letters, singing the ABC song and reading ABC books, pointing out letters children see in the environment, and focusing on the letters in the children's own names. Labelling areas and materials in the classroom with printed signs can further help children become familiar with the alphabet.

SUPPORT FOR EMERGENT READING Children should be encouraged to look at and read books on their own or with friends. Every classroom should provide a comfortable place to sit and read, filled with interesting and developmentally appropriate books. Functional print linked to class activities (e.g., daily schedules, helper charts, toy-shelf labels) and play-related print (e.g., signs, menus, employee name tags in a restaurant play centre) provide another opportunity for reading. Pointing out labels on snack and food items and assisting the children in reading them also provides support for the emergent reader.

SUPPORT FOR EMERGENT WRITING Children should be encouraged to use emergent forms of writing, such as scribble writing, random letter strings, and invented spelling. Do this by providing a well-stocked writing centre, which includes pens, pencils, markers, a variety of kinds of paper, and book-making materials. Teachers should demonstrate how adults use writing by writing notes in front of the children or by providing shared writing demonstrations in which the teacher writes down words dictated by a child. Writing activities connected to the classroom routine, such as signing in for attendance, signing in to enter a play centre, and providing play-related writing materials (e.g., pencils and note-pads for taking orders in the restaurant play centre) also provide another opportunity for the emergent writer.

SHARED BOOK EXPERIENCE Using big books and other enlarged texts with children enables the teacher to point to the print as it is read. The teacher can also draw the child's attention to the difference between the pictures and print, as well as how the pictures can support and add more to what the story is saying. Adults can model the skills of a good reader, including what they look for when reading, such as clues on the cover as to what the book might be about or clues in the text and pictures about what might happen next. The adult can also model the left-to-right and top-to-bottom sequence, as well as teach the components of the book, including cover page, title page, artist, illustrator, and publisher.

INTEGRATED, CONTENT-FOCUSED ACTIVITIES Teachers should take the children's lead, providing opportunities for children to investigate topics that are of interest to them. Literacy-based activities focused on their area of interest provide numerous ways for children to develop skills. Activities can include listening to and looking at books on the topic of interest, and assisting the children to gather more information about the topic through observations, questioning, and interviews. Information that is gathered should be recorded, either by the teacher or the child, depending on the child's age and ability. Play activities related to the theme should also be provided. "As a result of such projects, children's language and literacy skills are advanced, and they gain valuable background knowledge" (Roskos, Christie, & Richgels, 2003, p. 4).

Literacy teaching opportunities available for teachers of young children are endless, but they require careful planning and consideration. Teachers should examine the types of literacy activities they are providing to their students, both daily and throughout the year. Neuman, Copple, and Bredekamp (2003) have provided an easy-to-use tool to help teachers examine their curriculum and classroom environment to determine what they are doing to support children's reading and writing. "Taking Stock of What You Do to Promote Literacy" is available on the NAEYC website.

Case Study ▪ Supporting emerging literacy ▪

Selma, a preschool teacher, has observed that the recent science unit on seeds has fascinated her class. The class grew beans from seeds as part of the lesson. She wants to follow their interest and expand on it while focusing on literacy skills. She has already filled the book area with new books on the topics of seeds, growing plants, and spring. She has introduced more plants into the classroom. Over the upcoming weekend, a group of parents are building a raised-bed garden for the class to plant in. Tomorrow, in the art centre, each child is decorating the cover of a journal in which they can draw pictures of seeds and plants.

1. List additional ways that Selma can integrate her class's interest in growing seeds and plants with their emerging reading and writing skills.

2. Visit a library or look online and find some books that Selma might include in her library and read to her class.

Planning and Presenting Learning Experiences

A successful early childhood program depends on careful planning, whether the learning opportunities are informal and incidental or teacher-initiated. How the materials are presented, what child-initiated opportunities are made available, and how children are grouped also determine the success of cognitive learning activities for a child who may have special needs.

Grouping Children

An early childhood group with as many as 15 to 20 children will function most effectively if divided into three or four small groups for teacher-supported activities. The number of teachers or assistants that are available usually determines the number of groups. Group size can be increased as children become more skilled and more experienced. The closer children with developmental disabilities get to their kindergarten year, the greater is the benefit of having opportunities to work in groups, as long as the specific tasks are appropriate for the developmental level of the child. Younger children, shy children, and children with developmental disabilities continue to need more support and attention from teachers.

Group Cognitive and Interactive Activities

An overall goal for early childhood settings is to help children be interested, comfortable, and appropriately challenged. To ensure that children do participate actively in all activities, the following arrangements are suggested. These are especially important with children who have a developmental delay, are overly active, or have trouble staying on task.

SHORT PERIODS Teacher-directed activities should be limited to short periods: three, four, or five minutes. This time can be lengthened if the interest and involvement of the participating children is maintained. Activities should always be concluded *before* children lose interest.

NONTHREATENING MATERIALS AND ACTIVITIES Start with materials that children enjoy and are familiar with: crayons; simple puzzles and manipulative materials; pictures of everyday objects to talk about, match, and group. Such materials allow most children to feel comfortable and competent, right from the start.

PREFERRED MATERIALS AND ACTIVITIES Noting what materials and activities are preferred by which children is important. These can be presented several days in a row to firm up the child's comfort and competence. Preferred materials also are useful as takeoff points for increasing the complexity of learning tasks and expanding them when a child is ready.

READINESS TO EXPAND LEARNING OPPORTUNITIES If a child has become inattentive or frustrated, the teacher needs to observe the child in the context of the learning situation. Often, the problem resides not in the child but in the learning environment. Changes may need to be made in the materials or activities so they more closely match the child's interests and ability level. It is best to have additional materials immediately at hand to expand activities and create new interest.

PREPARATION Before children arrive, all materials for the daily program should be assembled and handy to the learning centres. However, teachers must remain flexible to change. If children arrive with new ideas and interests, teachers should put aside their planned ideas and pick up on the interests of the children, supporting the children's ideas on how they might explore (see Chapter 15).

Cognitive activities should be enjoyable for children and for teachers. When readiness activities are fun and developmentally appropriate, children will be eager to participate in the learning experiences. Eagerness to participate invariably promotes successful learning in children. Successful learning is also enjoyable and motivating for teachers in that it represents their effectiveness as teachers.

Summary

Stimulating learning for young children involves recognizing the children's interests and developmental levels—as well as the range of needs within the group. Programming for young children should pick up on the interests of the children and include a range of informal, pre-academic, cognitive, language, social, motor, and perceptual motor opportunities.

Readiness activities *should not* include drills and workbooks or paper-and-pencil tasks. Readiness is embedded in developmentally appropriate, child-focused activities and interactions. Promoting children's day-by-day integration of developmental skills and fostering their eagerness to learn is of prime importance in supporting cognitive activities that take place in the early childhood years.

A decade of research on the brain provides new insights into a child's early brain development. We now recognize that there is a high level of complex activity during the first few years of life. We recognize that early experiences, in partnership with the child's genes, shape the brain. Through repetition and use, the brain's network system retains early connections. By the teenage years, half of these connections are discarded. The brain's plasticity and the critical periods for learning have great implications with regard to the importance of appropriate and timely early intervention.

Readiness skills (sometimes referred to as pre-academic skills) can be taught to children if they do not occur spontaneously through the normal developmental processes. In other words, a child's short attention span or inability to imitate or follow instructions should be noted. Instead of a "wait-and-see" approach, many skills can be encouraged through step-by-step teaching. In addition to attention span, imitation skills, and following instructions, other specific readiness skills include perceptual motor and fine motor skills, memory, and the ability to formulate concepts. Readiness skills (or pre-academic learning) for reading, writing, and math skills should be inherent in an enriched early childhood program.

When learning opportunities are developmentally appropriate and interesting, provoke exploration and inquiry on the part of the children, and pick up on the children's interests, all children in the group, including those with developmental differences, should be able to participate and enjoy them, especially if teachers support the children's learning and help them acquire whatever prerequisite skills they may lack. One of the most important aspects of all activities should be that they are enjoyable to both children and teachers. Enjoyment leads to participation, spontaneous learning, and feelings of success.

Resources

The following websites offer useful resources on children's learning processes.

Canadian Child Care Federation
http://www.cccf-fcsge.ca

Children's Technology Review
http://childrenstech.com

Education Resources Information Center
http://www.eric.ed.gov

National Association for the Education of Young Children
http://www.naeyc.org

CourseMate Access an interactive ebook and chapter-specific interactive learning tools, including flashcards, quizzes, videos, and more, in the *Inclusion in Early Childhood Programs* CourseMate. Visit NELSONbrain.com to log in, register, or purchase access.

Facilitating Language, Speech, and the Development of Communication

19

....

OBJECTIVES

After studying the material in this chapter, the student will be able to

- Define language and explain how it develops.
- Explain the difference between receptive and expressive language and discuss the developmental significance of each.
- List a number of ways (including augmentative communication systems) in which teachers can help children with language delays expand their communication.
- Discuss dysfluency among young children and describe appropriate responses from teachers and parents.

KEY CONCEPTS AND TERMS

articulation

articulation errors

augmentative communication
  systems

dysfluency

expressive language

holophrastic speech

motherese

overregularization

Picture Exchange
  Communication System
  (PECS)

prelingual communication

private speech

receptive language

syntax

telegraphic speech

voice synthesizer

CONNECTIONS

- Nine-month-old Monet was eating her applesauce with apparent enjoyment. After a while, she began turning her head away each time she was offered another bite. When her mother persisted, Monet clamped her mouth shut and swiped at the spoon, sending the applesauce flying in all directions.
- Karla, almost two years old, pleaded, "Me go? Me go?" as her father picked up the car keys.
- Robin, an older four-year-old, was painting at the easel. The teacher remarked about the beautiful shade of purple he had created. Robin, the only child of a poetry professor, turned to her and said, "It's not really purple. It's more like violet; no, maybe amethyst."
- Erik, a second-grader, is very quiet in class, but when the teacher talks with him at recess or after school he speaks with great excitement about his Lego creations.

These children are "right on target" in terms of their communication skills. They are communicating effectively in a developmentally appropriate manner for their respective ages. How do the above language skills develop? How do we provide a learning environment that will ensure the optimum development of language skills? This chapter is about answering questions such as these.

Introduction

Learning their first language is a complex developmental task, yet most children accomplish it easily. As Flavell, Miller, and Miller (2001) suggested, it would be virtually impossible to prevent typically developing children from learning to talk. In fact, children seem to have fewer problems learning language than researchers do defining it. *Language* is a system that enables individuals to express ideas and communicate them to others who use the same code. *Speech* is the sounds of a language, the ability to communicate verbally. Speech depends on articulation, the ability to produce sounds distinctly and correctly.

Language—whether written, spoken, or body language—is a complicated symbol system used for communication. The *symbols* used in language are words, signs, gestures, and body movements that stand for something other than the movements themselves (that is, the symbols represent ideas). It is the mutually agreed-on meaning of symbols that enables group members to communicate with one another.

Communication is the exchange of thoughts and ideas, feelings and emotions, likes and dislikes. Although language is the major form of communication, there are other forms:

1. *Gestures and body language.* These may be used alone or with speech. Holding up a hand with fingers upright and palm facing another individual almost universally indicates "Stop."
2. *Printed words.* Books, letters, and directives allow communication without speech or one-to-one contact.
3. *Art forms.* Creative acts and products, such as music, dance, paintings, and the like, are also powerful forms of communication.

The code of every language is based on informally transmitted *rules* about grammar (word order) and word meaning (semantics). In spite of its complexity, most children acquire language with relative ease (see photo, right).

Communicating with others is the essential purpose of language, and communication functions as both a social and a cognitive activity. Allen and Hart (1984) described the interrelationship: Language serves as a social skill for interacting with others, for expressing needs and ideas, and for getting help, opinions, and the cooperation of others. It serves also as a cognitive skill for understanding, inquiring, and telling about ourselves and our world. It is for these reasons that children who have difficulty acquiring speech and language require early intervention.

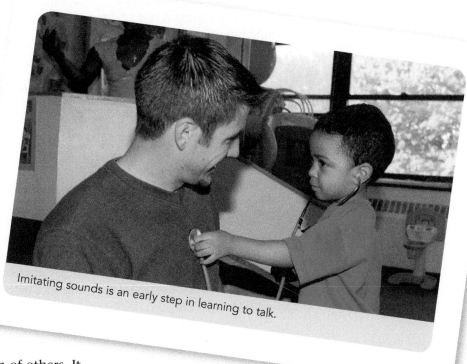

Imitating sounds is an early step in learning to talk.

© Cengage Learning

Language Acquisition

Theories about language acquisition change or become more elaborate as research reveals more about environmental input and the complex connections between the brain and language (Pinker, 2006). Here we will take a brief look at current theories about language acquisition in the very young.

The Environmental Perspective

Until a few years ago, a popular theory of language development in the young focused almost exclusively on the environment: The child learned to talk by imitating words and then receiving feedback or reinforcement (Skinner, 1957). Today, most psycholinguists dismiss the explanation as simplistic. However, we cannot discount the role of environment and the input it provides. Children have to hear—or see—the language they learn. They learn very early that language has *function*: Words help them get what they want and need. Words also promote social interactions and provide explanations and conversations about things a child is interested in (Hart & Risley, 1999).

INFANT-DIRECTED SPEECH Infant-directed speech, popularly called **motherese**, refers to the unique speech patterns that adults use with the very young. Many parents and caregivers speak more slowly and in higher-pitched voices when talking to infants. They use short sentences and a simplified, repetitive vocabulary

Motherese unique infant-directed speech patterns that adults use with the very young that usually refers to something in the immediate environment. Cooper and Aslin (1994) noted that babies only a few days old prefer to listen to motherese. In summary, the environment has adapted itself to respond to the needs of the language-learning infant.

The Imitation and Reinforcement Explanation

Children learn by imitating the speech and language habits of others. In turn, they receive feedback (reinforcement).

The Maturation or Innateness Explanation

According to this viewpoint, language is said to unfold or emerge as a part of the developmental process, with the environment playing a far less dominant role. Similarly, *constructivists* (theorists who believe that children construct their own knowledge through engagement with the environment) propose that the words a child hears will be learned if they connect with what the child is thinking and feeling (Bloom, 1995).

The Integrated Explanation

How do we put this information together as we work with infants and young children? As Bee and Boyd (2009) pointed out, explaining how children learn language is one of the most difficult challenges that face developmental psychologists. What seems most likely and more readily understood is the three-part concept suggested by Kaczmarek (1982). Language acquisition is

1. the maturationally determined mechanism for learning language (innateness);
2. the input, or quality and timing, of the child's early language experiences; and
3. the use the child makes of input and the strategies the child devises for processing spoken language and then reproducing it.

There is now general agreement that healthy newborns arrive with a potential for language. They come equipped to learn to talk, and the environment shows them how. There is no dispute that language skills are developed through participation in language activities. Early language activities, for the most part, are informal and spontaneous, occurring during daily routines, casual play, and impromptu social exchanges. Such interactions *in the everyday world* are the main ingredients of language development. When language is not developing, the child is put at great developmental risk. Failure to acquire functional communication can have long-term educational and social consequences.

Sequences in Language Acquisition

Language and speech acquisition, as in all areas of development, occur in a sequential order. They follow a step-by-step pattern from children's early primitive sounds and movements to the complex expression and fluent speech characteristics of their first language.

Prelinguistic Communication

Language development begins in early infancy, long before the first words appear. Known as the preverbal, or more accurately, *prelingual* stage, the infant's language is characterized by body movements, facial grimaces, and vocalizations. During this period of **prelingual communication**, the foundations for communicative language are established. The earliest efforts take the form of crying, then cooing, then babbling.

Prelingual communication body movements, facial expressions, and vocalizations used by infants before the first words are learned

SELF-ECHOING Infants who have been babbling for a while begin to sound as if they are having conversations with themselves. They repeat a sound several times, pause as though listening to what they have to say, and then repeat the sound again.

INTONATION Babbling soon begins to be marked by *intonation*, rising and falling variations in the pitch that resembles adults' speech.

First Words and Sentences

Major accomplishments for the child are found in making first words and then sentences. Once these are mastered, language development progresses with giant strides.

VOCABULARY As babbling increases, first "words" begin to emerge. Parents often miss out on these first words because they are hard to recognize. In the beginning, infants tend to vary the sounds. They appear to be unsure, at first, which combination of vowels and consonants to settle on when referring to a particular object or action. After the milestone of the first recognizable word, somewhere around the first birthday, new words follow slowly. Months may go by before there is a real burst in vocabulary growth. (See Figure 19–1 for additional information about sequences of language acquisition.)

RECEPTIVE AND EXPRESSIVE LANGUAGE Language is described as having two dimensions: *receptiveness* and *expressiveness*. These dimensions are interrelated but are evaluated separately.

Receptive language Receptive language refers to the words an individual understands or recognizes. Throughout life, we understand more words than we use when speaking. Although six-year-olds know approximately 14 000 words, they are likely to have many fewer words (about 2500) in their expressive vocabulary.

Receptive language language that is understood; it precedes expressive language

Expressive language Words and sentences that an individual speaks or signs come under the heading of **expressive language**. Gestures, grimaces, body movements, written words, and various art forms are included under the same heading. Expressive language takes two forms:

Expressive language spoken words or signs that individuals use in communicating with others

1. *Initiative*—the individual starts a communicative interaction with another.
2. *Responsive*—the individual answers or behaves in some way in response to another's verbal initiation.

FIGURE 19-1 Sequences in Language Acquisition

CHRONOLOGICAL AGE	LANGUAGE	SOME ACCOMPLISHMENTS
Newborn	Crying	Used to getting needs met
2 months	Cooing	Increases as parents and caregivers respond
6 months	Babbling Responds to own name	Combines consonant and vowel sounds
Around 12 months	First recognizable words Understands simple instructions	Mainly nouns
18 months	5–50 words	Still mainly nouns
24 months	250–300 words	Can name a number of common objects Uses at least two prepositions Combines words into a short sentence
36 months	1000 words	Can use three words, is able to use plurals and some past tenses Uses three prepositions About 90 percent of what the child says is intelligible
48 months	1500 words	Knows names of familiar animals Uses four prepositions Follows simple commands even for objects not in view Asks many questions 4–5 word sentence length
60 months	2000 words	Uses many descriptive words spontaneously—both adjectives and adverbs Knows common opposites Speech should be completely intelligible, in spite of articulation problems Able to repeat sentences as long as nine words Should be able to follow three-step commands given without interruptions

Source: © Cengage Learning

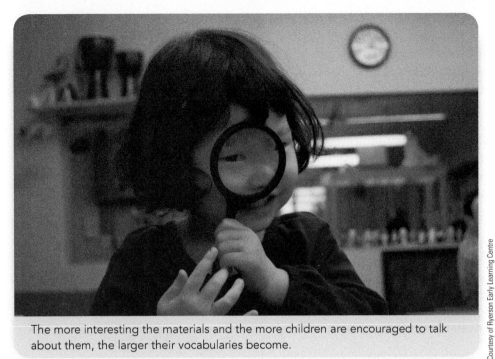

The more interesting the materials and the more children are encouraged to talk about them, the larger their vocabularies become.

A child's expressive vocabulary seems also to contain a subset of receptive vocabulary related to the materials and activities the child is engaged in at the time. The more interesting the materials and the more children are encouraged to talk about them, the larger their vocabularies become (see photo, above).

Early Sentences

Children's progress in putting words together to form sentences is as rapid as vocabulary growth during the early years. Learning to combine words in a particular order pays off. It enables the child to convey more complex thoughts. This aspect of language acquisition is known as the development of **syntax**. It has several stages, beginning with holophrastic speech.

Syntax the way in which words are put together to form phrases, clauses, or sentences

HOLOPHRASTIC SPEECH At the stage of **holophrastic speech**, the child uses a single word to convey an entire thought. The intended meaning is as unmistakable as a complete sentence. Holophrases usually occur in reference to something the child sees, hears, smells, tastes, or touches. The child's intonation or voice inflection also contributes to the meaning, as do gestures, such as pointing or looking up. The single word *doggie*, depending on context, inflection, and gesture, can be readily understood to mean

Holophrastic speech a state of speech development where a child conveys meaning with a one-word utterance

- "I want to play with this dog." (while toddling after the dog)
- "See the dog." (while pointing at a dog)
- "Where did the dog go?" (while looking outside)

During this period the child may use the same word for several objects or events. For example, *doggie* may mean *all* furry four-legged creatures; *bye-bye* often means both the absence of someone as well as someone leaving. Often, however, parents and caregivers have to work hard to figure out what the child wants. They say, "Show me," or they offer various objects until they select the "right" one.

TELEGRAPHIC SPEECH Toward the end of the second year, the child begins to speak in simple two-word sentences. These sentences convey grammatical meaning even though many words are left out. Hence the term telegraphic speech because of the similarity to the way telegrams are written. Few parents or caregivers mistake the intent of abbreviated sentences, such as "Mama's purse?" "Daddy bye-bye," "Me want," or "All done!"

These abbreviated two-word phrases are an important milestone in language acquisition. They indicate that the child is learning the word order (syntax or grammar) of the language. Without appropriate word order, words cannot convey meaning, especially as sentences get longer. Most of us would agree that without conventional word order it would take a while to figure out what the child wants.

PRIVATE SPEECH Between the ages of three and six, children often make use of a strategy of talking to themselves, frequently referred to as private speech (Herschkowitz & Herschkowitz, 2004). Private speech serves a number of important functions for children. It helps them direct their behaviour as they work things out. It helps them organize their thoughts and ideas. And it focuses their attention on what they are doing. When children master a task, the need for private speech decreases.

The Development of Language Complexity

Language acquisition progresses rapidly in children between two and five years of age. Children learn to

- use all forms of questions (e.g., *who? where? what? when? how?* and the seemingly never-ending *why?*);
- transform positives to negatives (e.g., *can/cannot, will/won't, is/isn't*);
- change verb forms, as required, to convey particular meanings (e.g., *run/ran, I will go/I went, It is raining/It has rained*);
- classify objects or animals (e.g., at first all dogs were just "dog"; now *this* dog is a collie-type of dog while *the other one* is a poodle-type of dog);
- indicate "more than one" through the use of plurals (e.g., *boy/boys, kitty/kitties, toy/lots of toys*); and
- convey ownership (e.g., *mine, hers, ours, theirs, Daddy's*).

OVERREGULARIZATIONS The years of rapid language development are characterized by several kinds of errors. Developmentally, these should be thought of as misconstructions, rather than as errors. They represent children's *best efforts* to apply the complex rules of the language to the situation at hand. Often the misconstructions occur because children are trying to regularize the irregular. This leads to overregularization (Rathus, 1988). Many children will say *digged* instead of *dug* for a while. When they say *digged*, they are relying on an earlier learning that called for adding *-ed* to a verb to indicate action in the past. These children, as yet, have no understanding of such things as irregular verbs. In a sense, *digged* is right. The child is applying the rule correctly. The child still must learn when not to apply it.

Young children also mix up and overgeneralize various forms of plurals. They may say *feets* instead of *feet, mouses* or *mices* rather than *mice, gooses* rather than *geese*. According to Rathus (1988), such *errors* aid rather than hinder language learning:

Overregularization does represent an advance in the development of syntax. Overregularization stems from accurate knowledge of grammatical rules—not

Telegraphic speech the stage in language acquisition in which children's utterances are generally longer than two words; phrases convey grammatical meaning even though many words are left out

Private speech children's strategy of talking to themselves to direct their behaviour as they work things out

Overregularization language irregularities that occur because the child is applying previously learned rules of grammar; for example, "The mouses runned"

from faulty language acquisition. In another year or two, mouses will become boringly transformed into mice, and Mommy will no longer have sitted down. (p. 277)

When such *errors* occur, adults should, without emphasis or comment, simply use the correct form—"Yes, the mice ran away." The child should not be criticized or corrected directly. Children should not be made to feel self-conscious or cute, regardless of how charming or amusing an adult may find the misconstructions. Unless undue attention is focused on the situation, these perfectly normal irregularities will self-correct in good time.

By the end of the fifth year, the development of syntax is nearly complete. Most children will be using all but one or two of the conventional grammatical structures. They will be adept at creating and using compound and complex sentences and will have a minimum of 2500 words in their expressive vocabulary.

Teachers can expect five- and six-year-olds to understand most of what is said to them, *but only if they have had exposure to the vocabulary being used*. The range and type of vocabulary is influenced by the language environment in which a child is raised. For example, a child who knows colour names may be unable to follow the directions in a colour-matching activity. Why? Because the word *match* (or the concept *match* in a task-related context) is not in the child's vocabulary.

Early Warning Signs

As in all areas of development, the rate at which children develop language varies from child to child. Children who have hearing problems will almost always demonstrate a delay in language development, as well as some mispronunciation of sounds and words once they do begin to speak. (When the model for speech is heard inaccurately or unclearly, the child's speech will reflect what he or she hears.) Children with poor muscular control of the tongue and jaw (commonly occurring in children with cerebral palsy), or who have physiological problems in the hard or soft palate in the mouth, will also have difficulties in speaking.

If an early childhood teacher feels that there is some concern about how a child's speech is developing, he or she should seek the advice of a consultant. Regardless of the cause of a speech or language delay, it is important that a child not be made to feel self-conscious in any way about his or her speech. Teachers need to develop programs that encourage and enhance opportunities for verbal interaction. Refer to Figure 19–2 (p. 446) for the Communication Checklist for children from birth to age five.

Alternative Language Systems

NONVERBAL COMMUNICATION Though the primary focus of this chapter has been on verbal skills, children's efforts to communicate nonverbally are important, too. Adults need to be aware of what children do, as well as what they say (see photo, page 434). This is especially important with children who have language difficulties or delays. A child who shrugs, scowls, smiles, flinches, or looks off into space is communicating. Teachers and parents should try to respond to such efforts as often as possible. A responsive language environment is crucial to the development of communication skills.

An essential skill for teachers is recognizing what children communicate nonverbally as well as verbally.

© Cengage Learning

Augmentative communication systems communication systems used to supplement a child's verbal language; the systems may be sign language, picture symbols, or sophisticated computer systems, such as a voice synthesizer

Voice synthesizer a computer that can produce spoken words; a type of assistive technology often used by people with severe communication disabilities

Picture Exchange Communication System (PECS) an augmentative communication system that focuses on child initiation; the child exchanges symbols and pictures to communicate desires and ideas

AUGMENTATIVE COMMUNICATION SYSTEMS Some children with severe disabilities do not acquire speech easily; others use some words but have such poor articulation that their speech is largely unintelligible. For these children, an **augmentative communication system** using gestures, signs, symbols, or pictures is helpful. These systems can be relatively simple—only a few gestures—or they can be complex, using a **voice synthesizer** connected to a computer. In most cases, an augmentative communication system is developed and introduced by the speech and language pathologist, incorporating input from the family and teacher. It is important that an augmentative communication system be used across settings. Professionals such as speech and language pathologists, special educators, or early interventionists can assist teachers and families to use the system during routines and play activities. Teachers can help the other children understand the system and use it to communicate with the child within the daily classroom activities (Hanline, Nunes, & Worthy, 2007).

When introducing augmentative communication, it is important to choose signs or symbols that occur frequently in the child's environment (Reichle, Mirenda, Locke, Piche, & Johnson, 1992): on the playground, during circle-time activities, and during free play. Using the systems across activities will improve communication skills and be useful to the child throughout the day (see photo, page 435). The **Picture Exchange Communication System (PECS)** is an augmentative communication system introduced by Bondy and Frost (1994). The system was the first to focus on the important issue of getting children to initiate a communication exchange. PECS begins by teaching a child to exchange a picture of a desired item with a "teacher," who immediately gives the object. Because no verbal prompts are used during the initial teaching, the child does not become dependent on an adult to begin a communication exchange. The system goes on to teach discrimination among symbols and then how to put them all together in simple sentences. More advanced individuals learn to comment and answer direct questions. Many preschoolers using PECS also begin developing speech. An important aspect of PECS is that it teaches the child to hand a picture or symbol to someone else. This request is difficult to ignore. Augmentative communication systems that involve the child pointing to pictures are often less effective, as an adult may not see a child pointing and thus may unintentionally

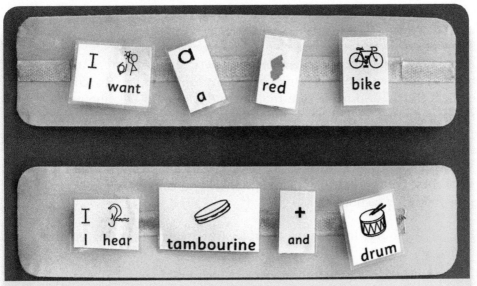

Communication boards may be activated by a pointer attached to a headband.

© Glynnis Cowdery

Case Study ■ Communicating with Tommy ■

Tommy, a four-year-old in your preschool class, uses a Picture Exchange Program to communicate. He loves building with Legos and chooses this activity on a daily basis during free play. He says one- or two-word phrases, but primarily communicates using PECS by creating a sentence strip and handing it to you, the teacher. He is able to create up to a four-word sentence—including using colours and size attributes when requesting items—for example, "I want the big,

red Lego." To date he has not communicated with the other staff in the classroom or with his peers.

1. What can you do so that he communicates with the other classroom staff?

2. What activities can you plan that will increase the opportunities for Tommy to communicate with peers?

ignore the potential interaction. Repeated episodes of being unable to communicate effectively can often lead to an overall reduction in a child's attempts to communicate.

The Teacher's Role in Facilitating Language Development

Teachers have a major role in facilitating language development in infants and young children. The foundation for building children's language and communication skills, according to Schwartz, McBride, Pepler, Grant, and Carter (1993), is the social communicative context of the environment. This means that in the inclusive classroom, teachers will engineer a social context in which people are sensitive to children's attempts to interact with others and in which the physical environment and the people in it make communication easy and enjoyable for children. In this context, teachers and children become partners who share responsibility for selecting and maintaining communicative interaction. It is most important to make sure that the environment is arranged so as to prompt both children's language and an appropriate degree of teacher responsiveness (not too much and not too little).

Creating an Inclusive Naturalistic Language-Learning Environment

To promote language development, teachers should arrange the learning environment so that every child has many opportunities to communicate. Teachers should also make sure that there is plenty to talk about (see photo, below). Activities should be arranged so that both materials and teachers are responsive to children's language efforts. The basics of arranging an effective early learning environment are covered in Chapter 15.

Teachers' skills and attitudes are discussed in Chapter 4. A brief review of a few of these concepts as they relate specifically to language acquisition appears in the following sections.

TEACHERS' ROLE In creating an inclusive language learning environment, teachers should

- provide a relaxed atmosphere in which children are allowed plenty of time to say what they want to say;

- be involved in authentic and meaningful conversations with children;

- encourage highly verbal children to learn to listen so that less assertive or verbal children have a chance to talk;

- work at being good listeners and responders;

- answer children in ways that indicate that they really are interested and genuinely want to hear more;

- respond with open-ended questions;

- facilitate many opportunities for children to communicate with their peers;

- provide duplication of complex materials so more than one child can use the same material at the same time; and

- encourage children to speak for themselves rather than have their peers speak for them.

In summary, children learn language by engaging in conversation, by using interactive communication with peers and adults. *Teachers do not need practice in talking; children do.* In an effective early learning program, talking is going on all the time, but it is the children who are doing most of the talking. Teachers are serving as facilitators, sometimes prompting, sometimes questioning, sometimes reflecting a child's thoughts back to the child (a sure signal to the child that the teacher is really listening). Children with language delays may need more adult input, prompting, and encouragement.

THE ROLE OF QUESTIONS Questions, asked or answered, are an important part of language acquisition. A child who turns away without responding when someone says, "Hi, how are you today?" quite effectively ends the exchange. If this happens frequently, teachers, family, and playmates may stop trying to communicate. The child loses out on two important sources of learning:

1. language play and practice that facilitates language acquisition (see photo, page 437)

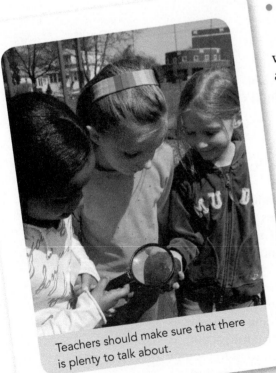

Teachers should make sure that there is plenty to talk about.

2. necessary information that most children get through everyday verbal exchanges

Teachers should ask questions *only* if they expect (and are willing to wait for) answers. If an answer is not forthcoming, the child should be helped to formulate one. It may be a simple verbalization or gesture originated by the child, or a response modelled after one the teacher provides. In any event, the child is expected to respond. All children, regardless of their speech and language skills, will soon fall quite naturally into the routine of responding if teachers' expectations are realistic and consistent.

ACTIVITIES THAT PROMOTE COMMUNICATION Children need to have many things to talk about. They need novel materials to ask questions about. They need excursions, preferably simple ones, such as a visit to the house under construction across the street, so as to practise verbal recall. They need easily managed picture books that enable them to "read" the story. Certain toddler books can even become a foundation for language learning throughout the classroom (Rosenquest, 2002). They need songs, rhymes, changes, and word play. Long-term studies show that children who participate in turn-taking games, word/sound imitation, and pretend play understand more and express themselves better (Beveridge, Loader, Northstone, & Roulston, 2002). They also need active play for prompting language of every kind. For children in need of special help with language skills, the importance of materials and equipment that require physical activity, as well as activities that stimulate social interactive play, cannot be overemphasized. The following suggestions may be helpful in promoting communication skills with children:

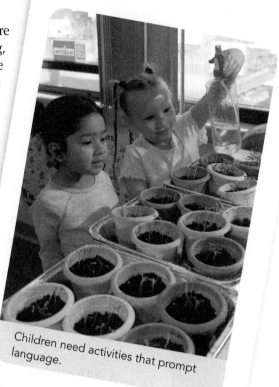

Children need activities that prompt language.

- Provide puppets and manipulative dramatic play props.

- Make homemade instruments. Try paper plate tambourines filled with rice or beans.

- Engage in fingerplays. These incorporate rhythm and children's inclination to move.

- Play "stop and go" games. Try these with music or singing.

- Make homemade puzzles. Take calendar pictures, body shapes, and so on, and cut them into pieces; then have children put them together while labelling and talking about them.

- Play "What's missing?" On a tray place several items, and have the children look at them. Then cover up the tray, or ask the children to close their eyes, and take one item away. Then ask the children, "What's missing?"

- Play matching games. These can help reinforce the concepts of same and different.

- Create weather charts. Have children cut out pictures of various types of weather conditions to use at small-group times to discuss the day's weather.

- Make photograph albums. Create albums with children focusing on children and the environment.

- Create flannel board stories. Using pictures from a book, create a flannel board story by cutting out the pieces of the story and backing them with flannel. Have duplicate copies of the story for children to follow along with or tell the story with the flannel pieces.

Learning Language and Loving It

The Hanen Centre's Learning Language and Loving It program, an evidence-based program for promoting enriched language-learning environments for young children (birth to age five), teaches educators how to facilitate language development of young children during everyday routines and activities and how to become more sensitive to the individual needs and abilities of children, responding in ways that will be most helpful to each child.

Learning Language and Loving It is grounded in the most current research in early childhood education, and has been field tested and rigorously examined using randomized controlled trials. A series of studies on the program showed that it effectively improves teacher interactive behaviour in the long term and increases children's language use.

What Participants Learn

CONVERSATIONAL STYLES In the Learning Language and Loving It program, educators learn to adapt their interaction according to the stage of language development and conversational style of each child. The following four styles are described:

1. *Sociable.* Sociable children initiate interactions constantly and are very responsive to others' initiations. If language delayed, sociable children may be slow to talk or difficult to understand, but this does not deter them from interacting with others.

2. *Reluctant.* Reluctant children seldom initiate and are often on the outside of group activities and interactions. These children may take a long to time to respond when a teacher speaks to them. Given time and opportunities, the children will interact with teachers, but peer interactions may be more difficult. If language delayed, the children's reluctance to initiate may be related to their language difficulty.

3. *Own agenda.* Children with their own agenda spend a lot of time playing alone, appearing uninterested in interaction with adults and peers. These children may initiate when they need something, but they frequently reject or ignore teachers' efforts to engage them.

4. *Passive.* Passive children seldom respond or initiate, demonstrating little interest in the objects or people around them. It can be hard to elicit a smile from them or engage them in any sort of playful interaction. If this is the child's consistent style of interaction, it reflects a developmental delay.

Identifying the conversational style of each child helps educators become aware of how the child's style of interaction may affect *their* interaction (for example, an educator may naturally be inclined to engage more with a sociable child and less with a child who does not demand attention). Being aware of this allows educators to ensure that they're providing each child in the classroom with the appropriate amount of support and opportunities to learn.

STRATEGIES TO APPLY TO DAILY INTERACTIONS To ensure that all children in the classroom receive the support they need, Learning Language and Loving It includes practical strategies aimed at

1. prevention of language delays for children at risk and second-language learners;

2. intervention for children with language delays; and

3. language enrichment for typically developing children.

Strategies include those that are child-oriented, those that promote interaction, and those that promote language development.

1. Child-oriented strategies These strategies encourage children to initiate and engage in conversational interactions so that educators can respond in ways that encourage the children's continued engagement in the interaction. Strategies include

- *Observe, wait and listen.* Observing, waiting, and listening are the keys to encouraging children to communicate. Observing means paying close attention to children in order to see exactly what they are interested in or what they are trying to communicate either verbally or nonverbally. Waiting encourages children to initiate or get involved in an activity. Listening means educators pay close attention to what children are saying so that they can respond appropriately. It is important to observe, wait, and listen with all children, but it is one of the most important strategies to use with children who are language delayed and who may be unable to keep up with the normal pace of conversation.

- *Be face to face.* In an interaction, educators should get down to the child's physical level so they are face to face. Being face to face brings the educator closer to the child, physically and emotionally, and makes the child feel the educator is really with him or her. Face-to-face contact is especially motivating for children with reluctant or own agenda styles.

- *Follow the child's lead.* Following a child's lead means picking up on the child's interests and going with them. Educators should start by being interested in what interests the child and then responding with warmth and enthusiasm to any sort of initiation from the child: a look, a smile, an offer of a toy, a gesture, a comment, or a question. Follow the child's lead includes the following four strategies, which are not used one at a time, but instead are used together in various combinations throughout an interaction:

  - *Imitate.* This means doing exactly what the child does and copying his or her actions, sounds, facial expressions, or words. Even so-called unresponsive children often become animated and interactive when they are imitated.

  - *Interpret.* Following a child's lead by interpreting his or her message means putting into words what the child appears to mean. This is a powerful way of letting children know that they have been heard and understood.

- *Comment.* Commenting in response to a child's initiation lets a child knows that this message has been received and is valued. Comments also provide children with information they can learn from.

- *Join in and play.* Join in and play means building on a child's interests and having fun. This strategy is especially helpful for children with reluctant conversational styles since it takes the focus off talking. Joining in and playing may also be the best way to encourage a child with an own agenda conversational style to engage in an interaction.

2. Interaction-promoting strategies Children need support as they gradually learn to take more turns in the back-and-forth exchange of extended interactions and conversations. These strategies encourage extended individual and group conversations between the educator and the children. They include

- *Use social routines with early turn-takers.* To make turn-taking easy for early turn-takers, educators should engage them in repetitive, predictable, fun interactions that contain clear cues as to when a child should take a turn. These interactions or "social routines," like peek-a-boo and pat-a-cake, are an important part of children's earliest social interactions.

- *Use comment and questions to cue turns.* Comments and questions followed by expectant waiting communicate the educator's interest and also cue children to take another turn. Both comments and questions should be included since children need to learn to respond to comments, not just questions, in order to become effective conversation partners. And when turns are cued with comments, children are less likely to feel that they are being "made to talk." This is especially important for children with language delays or reluctant conversational styles.

- For questions to continue the conversation, they must be developmentally appropriate and build on the child's interests. Children's understanding of questions develops over time. With infants and toddlers, start with easier to understand questions like *yes/no* questions and questions with *who? what? where?* As children develop, they will be able to answer more difficult questions with *when? why? how?* and *what if?* Test questions that have only one right answer should be avoided since they tend to stop the conversation.

- *SSCAN to interact with every child in the group.* SSCAN is an acronym for Small groups are best, Set up an appropriate activity, Carefully observe each child's level of participation and interaction, Adapt your response to each child's needs, and Now keep it going.

  - *Small groups are best.* Encouraging all the children to get involved in a interaction begin with a small group of three to five children. The smaller the group, the better able the educator will be to observe all the children and help each child become involved.

  - *Set up an appropriate activity.* The activity should interest all the children, match each child's abilities, and allow the educator and the children to be face to face.

  - *Carefully observe each child throughout the activity and adapt your response to each child's needs.* Educators should focus on each child for a few seconds to observe his or her level of involvement and interest and adapt their response to get all the children to interact with the teacher and, if possible, with each other. This includes encouraging reluctant children to interact and encouraging children who may be dominating to wait their turn.

3. Language-promoting strategies These strategies expand the child's language skills by providing language models. Strategies include

- *Say less, stress, go slow, and show for children who are just learning language.* Educators should make their language easy to understand for early language learners by shortening and simplifying their language. They should also emphasize important words, speak slowly, and talk about familiar things in the here and now.

- *Use a variety of different labels.* Labels should include not just nouns, but also action words, describing words, and location words.

- *Expand on what the child says.* When a child says something, educators should respond by using the child's words and adding some words of their own to show the child more mature ways of expressing him- or herself.

- *Extend the topic.* The purpose of extending the topic is to give children information that increases their understanding of the world. Extending becomes increasingly important with preschoolers and school-aged children who have more advanced language. Extending the topic means going beyond the here-and-now and beyond concepts such as colours, shapes, sizes, and textures. Extend the topic strategies include the following:
  - Inform with information about the past or present.
  - Explain why something is happening.
  - Talk about feelings and opinions.
  - Project into other people's lives, experiences, and feelings to help children understand the points of views of others.
  - Talk about the future.
  - Pretend and talk about imaginary things.

Speech Irregularities

Speech irregularities are common and even normal in speech development. Most children, 80 percent or more, will show some kind of articulation errors during their early years. These irregularities may not necessarily be predictive of future concerns. For a time, the ability to formulate thoughts and ideas is greater than the child's ability to pronounce words correctly or to organize the words into sentences that make sense. The irregularities that early childhood teachers are most likely to encounter are discussed in the following sections.

Articulation Errors

Articulation refers to the production of speech sounds. **Articulation errors** are part of language development and are likely to occur as young children work at mastering the complex sounds that make up everyday speech. Misarticulations usually are classified as omissions, substitutions, additions, or distortions:

- *Omissions.* Sounds are left out, often at the beginning or end of words: "That's my 'agon (wagon)," "Here's the broo' (broom)."

Articulation refers to the production of speech sounds

Articulation errors speech sounds that are inconsistent with the native language (usually a temporary developmental irregularity)

Case Study

The following is an example of how an educator may use the strategies learned in the Learning Language and Loving It program to promote the language development of all children in the classroom (Girolametto & Weitzman, 2006):

Kim had been working in the toddler room at the East End Child Care Centre for five years. She loved her job and particularly enjoyed seeing the children's enjoyment as they participated in the daily activities she planned for them. But Kim was challenged by Nathan, a two-year-old in her group who did not seem keen to interact with her or join in with the other children. He would watch the other children and appear interested in what they were doing, but he otherwise spent most of the day playing alone in the block centre or at the sand table.

Nathan's mother reported that he communicated very well at home and used about 50 to 100 words, but Kim rarely heard Nathan talk at child care. If he needed to express something important, he would sometimes come and get Kim or point to what he needed. Kim tried to encourage Nathan to talk by asking him questions about what he was doing, but Nathan typically responded with only a nod. She also urged him to "use his words," but, again, he typically just nodded or walked away.

Kim then had the opportunity to attend the Learning Language and Loving It program and was eager to see if the things she learned would help her with Nathan.

Thinking about the different conversational styles that children demonstrate, Kim suspected that Nathan fit the profile of a child with a reluctant conversational style. A child with a reluctant conversational style rarely initiates communication unless his or her need is critical but will often respond by nodding. She also began to think that her usual approach to communicating with Nathan (asking many questions and urging him to "use his words") may have been putting too much pressure on him and actually discouraging him from communicating.

Kim then identified the strategies she learned in the Learning Language and Loving It program that would be most beneficial for Nathan:

- *OWL (observe, wait, and listen). This strategy would help Kim see what Nathan is interested in so she could then follow his lead.*

- *Follow the child's lead. This strategy could be helpful for a child with a reluctant style of communication, since children are more motivated to talk and interact when the subject is one of their choosing, and when it is clear that the teacher is taking an interest in their interests.*

- *Imitate. This strategy would help to draw the child's attention to the teacher and create a fun game that the child may be motivated to continue.*

  - *Use comments and questions with expectant waiting to cue turns. This strategy would help Nathan learn to take more back-and-forth turns.*

  - *Say less and stress; go slow and show. This strategy would make Kim's language easier for Nathan to understand and imitate.*

The next day, Kim joined Nathan at the sand table. This time, instead of directing lots of questions to him, Kim took the time to OWL and noticed that Nathan liked the feeling of the sand sprinkling through his fingers. Kim then decided to imitate what Nathan was doing and also started to let the sand fall between her fingers. As she imitated Nathan's actions, she said, "The sand is falling down!" and waited expectantly. After doing this a few times, Kim was amazed when Nathan looked up at her and said "again." As Kim continued to play with Nathan and focused on following his lead, she heard more language, such as "fall down" and "dirty sand." Kim was thrilled that she had found a way to connect with Nathan and support his communication.

- *Substitutions.* Interchanging sounds, such as *b* and *v*, as in "Put the balentines on the vack seat," or replacing one sound with another: "wabbit" for "rabbit."

- *Additions.* Inserting sounds not part of a word: "warsh" (wash) or "notta now" (not now).

- *Distortions.* Deviations in speech sounds usually occur because of tongue misplacement or missing teeth, as is the case with many six-year-olds: "schwim" for "swim" or "tink" for "think."

Lisping

Rarely is lisping (pronouncing *s* as *th)* considered a worrisome problem in preschool children. Seldom does it persist. Exceptions may be those few cases where the child's lisp has been showcased by adults who think it is cute. If lisping should continue into the primary grades, parents usually are encouraged to seek consultation.

DYSFLUENCY *Stuttering* is a common word for **dysfluency** or fluency disorders. *Cluttering* is another term also used to label a fluency problem. (Both *stuttering* and *cluttering* are losing favour among developmentalists and speech and language clinicians.) *Dysfluency* better describes children's excessive repetition of particular sounds or words, noticeable hesitations between words, extra sounds, or the undue prolonging of a sound. Such speech irregularities are common. To label a young child as a *stutterer* is unwise, in part because of the self-fulfilling consequences. However, there are those few children who develop abnormal dysfluencies during the preschool or primary school years. According to Zebrowski (1995), specific features of a common dysfluency, such as stuttering, distinguish it from a developmentally typical dysfluency:

Dysfluency hesitation, repetitions, or omitted or extra sounds in speech patterns

- frequency
- type and proportion
- duration
- associated nonspeech behaviours, like excessive frustration or grimacing

Strategies for Supporting Children with Speech Irregularities

A developmentally common speech irregularity seldom needs to turn into a major problem. Teachers and parents can help to forestall such a consequence by practising preventive dos and don'ts:

- Make sure the child is getting good nutrition, adequate rest, and many more hours of active play than of television each day.

- Provide comfort, care, and support; reduce tensions as much as possible (difficult, but not impossible, even in this hurried world).

- Have fun with the child and with language; inject humour, simple rhyming activities, and simple riddles into everyday routines; music activities are also effective (such as repeating beats, echoing sounds, and filling in words in verses).

- Discipline with calmness, firmness, and consistency; avoid harshness, ridicule, or teasing.

- Offer activities in which the child can be successful and develop positive self-esteem.

- Become aware of local family literacy programs.

- Avoid correcting or nagging the child (avoid saying, "Slow down," "Take it easy," or "Think before you speak").

- Do not call attention to dysfluencies directly or indirectly; the child could become all the more tense when an adult focuses intently with exaggerated patience, a forced smile, or a rigid body, waiting for the child to "get it out."

- Avoid interrupting a child or acting hurried, as young children need plenty of time when trying to put their ideas into spoken language.

- Never compare a child's speech with another child's, especially if the comparison is unfavourable to either.

To correct a child unnecessarily undermines the child's confidence as a speaker. If children are to improve their language skills, they must keep talking. Children who fear that they will be criticized each time they speak will speak less and less; therefore, adults should avoid asking a child to repeat anything that they have understood.

Referral

The importance of not overreacting to common speech and language irregularities cannot be overemphasized (Berglund, Eriksson, & Johansson, 2001). It is important to remember that speech and language irregularities are part of development.

Adults working with young children should be aware of developmental patterns. However, if a genuine concern exists, it needs to be identified as early as possible and an intervention program put into effect immediately. The early childhood teacher may be the first to perceive a possible communication difficulty. (See Chapter 12 on the teacher's role in early identification.) Whenever a teacher is in doubt as to whether a child has a difficulty with communication, parents should be consulted and assisted to seek help, if needed. Parents often have the feeling that *something* may be wrong. Conversely, it is common for parents to become so accustomed to their child's speech that they do not realize that their child is having difficulty communicating with others. Speech, language, and hearing (audiology) clinicians who specialize in young children provide the most reliable testing and consultation.

THE REFERRAL PROCESS Consulting Figure 19–2 (pp. 446–448) may determine the necessity of referral to a speech pathologist for consultation, assessment, or therapy.

INTERVENTION Young children who are diagnosed as having specific speech and language difficulties need an individualized intervention program. For best results, the early childhood teacher and the speech and language therapist must work together. In some cases, short therapy sessions in which the child works exclusively with a speech and language therapist are provided. Therapists can promote classroom cooperation by informing teachers regularly about the goals and strategies used in the child's treatment. The particular skills the therapist is working on and the progress the child is making should also be discussed. Within a transdisciplinary approach, the therapist works with a child who is experiencing communication difficulties and with small groups of children. This provides opportunities for the child to have ongoing practice in the use of new skills and to interact with peers, who serve as language models.

The foregoing does not imply that teachers or parents are expected to become language specialists. They can, however, readily learn simple procedures for facilitating individual children's speech and language development.

Summary

Learning to speak and use the native language is the most complex developmental task mastered by infants and young children. Explaining how children do it has been the subject of thousands of research studies, as well as major, and often conflicting, theoretical formulations. In spite of disagreements about how children accomplish this difficult task, most children do, and with little apparent effort. Without specific instruction, children move through the developmental sequences in speech and language acquisition, from crying, cooing, and babbling to producing complex sentences and multisyllabic words in their first five or six years. Most speech and language irregularities come and go, and most appear to be self-correcting unless the child is pressured.

A number of young children have difficulties speaking or learning the language; some children have trouble with both. Differences may range from developmentally normal delays and dysfluencies to serious concerns requiring the services of a speech and language specialist or early interventionist. An undiagnosed hearing loss is always a possibility and needs to be ruled out first before diagnosing a language delay or impairment in a young child. A stimulating classroom environment with interesting materials and activities and support for social interaction among children, coupled with incidental teaching, has proven effective in enhancing the speech and language skills of all children at all levels of language development. Teachers' knowledge of speech and language development and their skill in observing children are essential to identifying children with language differences.

Resources

The Hanen Centre

http://www.hanen.org

The Hanen Centre is a Canadian charitable organization with an international outreach. It is committed to helping young children with (or at risk of developing) language delays learn to communicate and interact effectively.

Toronto Preschool Speech and Language Services

http://www.tpsls.on.ca

Toronto Preschool Speech and Language Services (TPSLS) is a strong network of community partners that provides community-based programs for young children with speech, language, hearing, and vision challenges.

Speech-Language and Audiology Canada

http://www.sac-oac.ca

This member-driven, national organization supports and promotes the professions of speech-language pathologists, audiologists, and communication health assistants.

CourseMate Access an interactive ebook and chapter-specific interactive learning tools, including flashcards, quizzes, videos, and more, in the *Inclusion in Early Childhood Programs* CourseMate. Visit NELSONbrain.com to log in, register, or purchase access.

FIGURE 19-2 Developmental Milestones

BY 24 MONTHS

	Yes	No
follows two-step directions—"Go find your teddy bear and show it to Grandma."	☐	☐
uses 100 or more words	☐	☐
uses at least two pronouns—(you, me, mine)	☐	☐
consistently combines two or more words in short phrases—"Daddy hat." "Truck go down."	☐	☐
enjoys being with other children	☐	☐
begins to offer toys to peers and imitates other children's actions and words	☐	☐
people can understand his/her words 50 to 60 percent of the time	☐	☐
forms words and sounds easily and effortlessly	☐	☐
holds books the right way up and turns pages	☐	☐
"reads" to toys or stuffed animals	☐	☐
scribbles with crayons	☐	☐

BY 30 MONTHS

	Yes	No
understands the concepts of size (big/little) and quantity (a little, a lot, more)	☐	☐
uses some adult grammar—"Two cookies." "Bird flying." "I jumped."	☐	☐
uses more than 350 words	☐	☐
uses action words—run, spill, fall	☐	☐
begins taking short turns with other children, using both toys and words	☐	☐
shows concern when another child is hurt or sad	☐	☐
combines several actions in play—feeds doll then puts her to sleep; puts blocks in train then drives train and drops blocks off	☐	☐
makes the beginning letter sound of most words	☐	☐
produces words with two or more syllables or beats—ba-na-na, com-pu-ter, a-pple	☐	☐
recognizes familiar logos and signs—McDonald's golden arches, stop sign	☐	☐
remembers and understands familiar stories	☐	☐

Babies like it when you:

	Yes	No
Get down to their level so they can see your face. This tells them that you're interested in what they're doing and saying. It makes it easier to interact with you	☐	☐
Repeat the sounds they make. Babies enjoy making noises, and like it when you imitate them over and over	☐	☐
Sing and laugh, especially when you are feeding, bathing, and changing them. Remember to talk to your baby throughout the day about things you do and see—"Mommy's putting on her coat." "That's a big truck."	☐	☐
Tell them the names of the objects they are looking at and playing with. Babies are interested in exploring and learning about new things, and like to hear what things are called	☐	☐

Toddlers like it when you:

	Yes	No
Let them touch and hold books while you point to and name the pictures	☐	☐
Use real words instead of baby talk—"Give me," instead of "Ta ta," or "Bottle" instead of "Baba"	☐	☐
Take the time to listen to them—they want you to hear all of their new sounds, words, and ideas	☐	☐
Give them simple directions to follow—"Go find your red boots."	☐	☐
Use lots of different words when you talk to them—opposite words like up/down, in/out; action words like running, splashing, and descriptive words like happy, big, little, clean, dirty	☐	☐
Encourage them to play with other children—at the library, play groups, and park	☐	☐
Your preschool child's speech and language development	☐	☐

Your preschool child's speech and language development

	Yes	No
Your preschool child is busy talking, exploring, and playing. All of these activities are important for his or her growth and development and for learning communication skills	☐	☐

- Your child will need well-developed communication skills when it's time to start going to school—to make friends, learn new things, and start learning to read and write. Communication skills are critical to your child's future success ...... ☐ Yes ☐ No
- You play an important part in your child's ongoing communication development. Talking, listening, and playing with your child will help to build the skills he or she needs to succeed in school and in life ...... ☐ Yes ☐ No
- About 1 in 10 children needs help developing normal speech and language skills. Without help, it's a struggle to listen and talk, it's difficult to learn to read, and it's hard to play with other children ...... ☐ Yes ☐ No

DEVELOPMENTAL MILESTONES

These developmental milestones show some of the skills that mark children's progress as they learn to communicate. If your child is not meeting one or more of these milestones, please contact your local Preschool Speech and Language Program.

BY AGE THREE

	Yes	No
understands who, what, where, and why questions	☐	☐
creates long sentences, using five or more words	☐	☐
talks about past events—trip to grandparents' house, day at child care	☐	☐
tells simple stories	☐	☐
shows affection for favourite playmates	☐	☐
engages in multi-step pretend play—cooking a meal, repairing a car	☐	☐
is understood by most people outside of the family, most of the time	☐	☐
is aware of the function of print—in menus, lists, signs	☐	☐
has a beginning interest in, and awareness of, rhyming	☐	☐

BY AGE FOUR

	Yes	No
follows directions involving three or more steps—"First get some paper, then draw a picture, last give it to Mom."	☐	☐
uses adult-type grammar	☐	☐
tells stories with a clear beginning, middle, and end	☐	☐
talks to try to solve problems with adults and other children	☐	☐
demonstrates increasingly complex imaginative play	☐	☐
is understood by strangers almost all of the time	☐	☐
is able to generate simple rhymes—"Cat-bat."	☐	☐
matches some letters with their sounds—"Letter T says 'tuh'."	☐	☐

BY AGE FIVE

	Yes	No
follows group directions—"All the boys get a toy."	☐	☐
understands directions involving if ... then—"If you're wearing runners, then line up for gym."	☐	☐
describes past, present, and future events in detail	☐	☐
seeks to please his/her friends	☐	☐
shows increasing independence in friendships—may visit neighbour by him/herself	☐	☐
uses almost all of the sounds of their language with few to no errors	☐	☐
knows all the letters of the alphabet	☐	☐
identifies the sounds at the beginning of some words—"Pop starts with the 'puh' sound."	☐	☐

Try some of these suggestions to help your child use words to solve problems, make choices, describe objects and events, and share ideas.

Three-year-olds like it when you:
- Give them different materials to encourage drawing and scribbling, including chalk, pencils, crayons, markers, fingerpaints ...... ☐ Yes ☐ No

	Yes	No
Use descriptive words such as colours and opposites (hot/cold, big/little, fast/slow) as well as action words (flying, splashing, running) when you are talking with them	☐	☐
Give them extra time to share their ideas	☐	☐
Give them choices—about what foods to eat, toys to play with, clothes to wear	☐	☐
Model correct sounds and grammar for them—child says "He wunned," and you say "Yes, he ran."	☐	☐
Read books that are predictable and repetitive—pause to give the child a chance to fill in the words and phrases	☐	☐
Play and pretend with them! They may like acting out scenes from their favourite videos, pretending to eat in a restaurant or to be a teacher or firefighter	☐	☐

Four-year-olds like it when you:

	Yes	No
Give them lots of opportunities to play with other children—at the library, the park, the Early Years Centre. Sometimes they like having just one or two friends over to their homes to play	☐	☐
Point out words in books and run your finger under words while you read to them	☐	☐
Talk about the order of events—describe what happens first, next, and last. "First we wash our hands, then we have a snack, and last we put our dishes in the sink."	☐	☐
Encourage them to tell their own stories—by asking them to tell you about their day, to describe a movie they watched, to tell you about their favourite book. Read books with rhyming words—mouse/house—and point out sounds at the start of words. "Mommy starts with the 'mmm' sound—that's the letter M."	☐	☐

Five-year-olds like it when you:

	Yes	No
Use new and more complex words—before/after, rough/smooth, easy/difficult, between/beside, same/different	☐	☐
Talk about numbers and the quantity of objects—"a lot/a little," "more/less," "one/many"	☐	☐
Ask them to predict what will happen next—"What do you think will happen when Sam opens his birthday present?"	☐	☐
Explain the reasons behind choices—"Why do we need to wear our coats today?"	☐	☐
Take turns telling each other stories using the pictures in books—children like to hear you talk and then want a turn to create their own version of the story	☐	☐
Let them help plan events. Talk about what you need to do before a birthday party, or how to get ready to go to the zoo. Ask your child "why" and "how" questions as you talk	☐	☐
Ask them to help. Your child will enjoy helping you bake cookies, set the table, sort laundry, etc.	☐	☐
Give them instructions and see if they can tell you the steps	☐	☐

Source: ©Queen's Printer for Ontario, 2010. Reproduced with permission.

Glossary

The numbers in parentheses are the page numbers in the text where the discussion of the terms can be found.

A

Accommodations—adjustments on the part of the child, family, or service providers that enable a successful transition to a new environment for the child (292)

Adaptive equipment—mobility devices, prostheses, and prescribed alterations of standard furnishings to meet the needs of children with special needs (175)

Advanced psychomotor ability—eye–hand or eye–foot coordination is at the level of a much older child, as found in some children who are gifted (133)

Adventitious deafness—deafness acquired through injury or disease after birth (108)

Advocacy—speaking and acting in support or on behalf of people or ideas (46)

Advocacy group—a group of individuals who work together for a particular cause; the Epilepsy Association works to ensure equal access, opportunity, and acceptance within society for persons with epilepsy (8)

Aggressiveness—acting-out behaviour in which a child may hurt other children, cause disruptions by throwing objects, or behave in ways that disrupt the group (386)

Amino acids—one of the chief components of proteins; amino acids are obtained from the individual's diet or are manufactured by living cells (119)

Amplification device—devices, such as hearing aids, that make sound louder and clearer for a child with a hearing impairment (146)

Anaphylactic shock—a rapid allergic reaction that can be life-threatening if not treated immediately; it is caused by an intense overreaction of the body's immune system to a trigger (194)

Anoxia—a shortage of oxygen to the brain that can cause physical damage to the brain before, during, or at any time after birth; anoxia is one of the major causes of physical and cognitive dysfunction (122, 169)

Antecedents and consequences—antecedents are events that come before a behaviour (in behavioural psychology, the antecedent is the stimulus that causes a response); consequences are the events that follow a behaviour (381)

Anxiety disorder—an extreme and lasting concern and fearfulness in certain situations, which other children their age do not experience; these commonly include separation problems, overdependence, withdrawal from social interactions, and so on (207)

Applied behaviour analysis (ABA)—a teaching approach used with children with autism spectrum disorder that involves observation, assessment, breaking skills down, and teaching skills systematically; progress is closely monitored through ongoing data collection (213)

Appreciative inquiry process—an approach that highlights the importance of open-mindedness and objectivity, curiosity, and inclusivity in observation (271)

Articulation—refers to the production of speech sounds (441)

Articulation errors—speech sounds that are inconsistent with the native language (usually a temporary developmental irregularity) (441)

Assistive technology—various kinds of equipment, such as a computerized Braille system or voice synthesizer, designed to facilitate learning and communication for individuals with disabilities (407)

Asymptomatic—showing no signs of a disease or impairment, which nevertheless may be present (120)

Ataxia—a lack of motor coordination, ataxia is characterized by poor balance and a lurching kind of walk, reflecting a lack of voluntary muscle control (170)

Athetosis—fluctuating or uneven muscle tone; muscle control that goes from one extreme to the other (either too low or too high) is typical (170)

At risk—indications (either physical or environmental) that an infant or child may develop serious problems (116)

Attention deficit hyperactivity disorder (ADHD)—behaviour that is characterized by consistently short attention span, inattentiveness, distractibility, impulsivity, and heightened levels of movement and physical activity (hyperactivity) (217)

Attention span—the length of time an individual is able to concentrate on an activity or event (408)

Auditory—refers to what is experienced through hearing (109)

Auditory brainstem response (ABR)—a procedure that measures the brain's response to high-frequency sound (146)

Auditory nerve—the nerve along which the sensory cells (the hair cells) of the inner ear transmit information to the brain (144)

Augmentative communication systems—communication systems used to supplement a child's verbal language; the systems may be sign language, picture symbols, or sophisticated computer systems, such as a voice synthesizer (434)

Autism spectrum disorder (ASD)—persistent impairment in reciprocal social communication and social interaction and restricted, repetitive patterns of behaviour, interests, or activities (209)

Autosomal recessive disorder—a gene carried by healthy parents on any one chromosome except the sex chromosomes that, if inherited from both parents, results in a child with a medical condition not present in the parents (120)

B

Backward chaining—the opposite of forward chaining; teaching starts with the last step of a learning sequence (257)

Baseline—data that are collected on a behaviour before a systematic plan is introduced; these data provide a base against which later behaviour can be compared (384)

Behaviour disorder (BD)—a chronic or pervasive challenging behaviour; describes a child who is unable to conform to appropriate expectations, who lacks the ability to learn appropriate behaviours, and who is unable to understand routine expectations (202, 377)

Behaviour modification—a system by which particular environmental events are systematically arranged to produce specified behaviour changes (242)

Bias-free materials—learning materials (e.g., adaptive scissors, dolls with leg braces) that reflect human differences (337)

Bias-free screening and assessment—selecting and administering screening and assessment tools that ensure a child is given the opportunity for optimum performance (280)

Biological insult—interference with or damage to an individual's physical structure or functioning (116)

Biological risk—infants and children whose systems have undergone some kind of biological insult, such as an accident, injury, or severe stress, are at risk for developmental disabilities (102, 116)

Blindness—vision loss severe enough that it is not possible to read print, requiring the child to be educated through the use of Braille and other tactile and auditory materials (109)

Brain development—affects cognitive growth and learning; children's brains need to be stimulated for the network of connections to grow and be protected from elimination (402)

C

Case manager—the member of the IPP team who assumes responsibility for coordination of the program and services for the child (60)

Cerebral palsy—a condition that affects muscular control; it is caused by damage to various parts of the brain. Its effects range from very mild (nonincapacitating) to moderate (involving fine or gross motor skills, or both), to pervasive (involving almost all areas of the body's physical activity) (169)

Challenging behaviour—see difficult behaviour (377)

Chemotherapy—the treatment of cancer by using drug therapy to kill cancer cells (185)

Chronic—in reference to health, a health problem of long duration and frequent recurrence (109)

Classification—part of concept formation in which an order is imposed on objects, or events into specific categories (413)

Cochlea—a snail-shaped structure in the inner ear that allows hearing to occur (144)

Cochlear implant—a device, surgically placed by opening the mastoid structure of the skull, that allows electrical impulses (sound) to be carried directly to the brain (152)

Cognitive delay—intellectual growth that does not follow the expected rate of development due to genetic or environmental conditions or a combination of both (114)

Communication and language disorders—difficulties with speaking or learning language, which can lead to serious disruptions in cognitive and social development (105)

Conduct disorder—repetitive and persistent patterns of behaviours in which the basic rights of others or major age-appropriate societal norms or rules are violated (386)

Conductive hearing loss—refers to problems in the mechanical transmission of sounds through the outer or middle ear, which in turn reduce the intensity of sound vibrations reaching the auditory nerve in the inner ear (144)

Congenital—refers to a physical condition that originates during the prenatal period (115)

Congenital deafness—deafness present at the time of birth (108)

Contingent stimulation—responding to a child in a way that prompts further learning (358)

Contractures—permanent tightening of muscles and joints (168)

Coordinated teaching—when a child with special needs is in dual placements, staff from the specialized program and those from the inclusive early childhood setting provide coordinated programming for the child (80)

Cortical/cerebral visual impairment—visual impairments originating in the brain (154)

Criterion-referenced tests—assessments that describe a child's developmental level and progress according to a prescribed set of skills, tasks, and activities (269)

Culturally competent—classroom activities, materials, and curricula that acknowledge and respect the different ethnicities that are represented in the classroom and community (53)

Culturally sensitive—classroom activities, materials, and curricula that acknowledge and respect the different ethnicities that are represented in the classroom and community (53)

Cultural mediators—individuals who help mediate between the culture of the school and the culture of the family; they share information and enhance understandings so that the family can participate fully in the assessment and education process (54)

D

Data collection—monitoring a child's behaviour and gathering information on it; data collection is used to evaluate the success of any intervention plan and is helpful only when it is easy to do and provides an accurate picture of the child's behaviour (382)

Deaf—having a hearing loss so severe that the individual cannot process spoken language even with amplification (142)

Deafblind—being both blind and deaf (142)

Descriptive praise—feedback that lets children know specifically what it is they are doing well (245)

Developmental delay—development of a skill progresses at a slower rate so that a child demonstrates the skill as a younger child would (100)

Developmental deviation—some aspect of a child's development is different from what is seen in other developing children (100)

Developmental disability—one of a range of conditions that interfere with any aspect of the normal development of the child (100)

Developmental disequilibrium—a period of inconsistent behaviour, which often follows a spurt of rapid development (82)

Developmental milestones—points at which specific skills are acquired in a fairly predictable order (99)

Developmental sequences—an ongoing process of moving step by step toward mastery of each developmental skill in every area of development (98)

Didactic materials—manipulative materials in which the child's errors and successes are self-evident—the material, not the teacher, provides the information; Montessori was the originator of many such materials (240)

Differentiated responses—an infant's and toddler's ability to differentiate simpler and more specific responses among global undifferentiated responses to stimuli (318)

Difficult behaviour—describes the impact a behaviour has on the people with whom the child is interacting (377)

Discrete trail teaching (DTT)—a teaching strategy that enables the learner to acquire complex skills and behaviours by first mastering the subcomponents of the targeted skill (213)

Discrimination—the ability to perceive likeness and differences among related objects and events; to specify same versus different; to match objects, sounds, or ideas in terms of one or more attributes (412)

Dual placements—when children with special needs spend a part of the day in a specialized program and part in an inclusive child care setting (80)

Duration—measures how long an event or behaviour lasts (383)

Dysfluency—hesitations, repetitions, or omitted or extra sounds in speech patterns (443)

Dysgraphia—difficulty with or inability to express thoughts in writing and/or to identify the written symbols of language (106)

Dyslexia—an impaired ability to read and understand written language (106)

E

Early intervention—the provision of services to children that are showing first indications of an identifiable problem or are significantly at risk of developing a problem (312)

Earmould—that part of an amplification device (hearing aid) that is fitted to the individual's ear (151)

Echolalia—describes a condition in which language is characterized by repetition of words and sentences that do not convey meaning; this condition is often associated with autism (212)

Egocentric—the child's views and thoughts focus only on his or her own perceptions (366)

Embedded learning—the intentional incorporation of specific learning objectives into play and routine classroom activities (405)

Emergent curriculum—curriculum that is developed from a variety of sources, including children's play activities and questions, and that is personally meaningful, intellectually engaging, and socially relevant (137, 338)

Emerging literacy—the diverse skills that help children become successful in reading, writing, and other academic tasks (402)

Emotional disturbances—characterized by behavioural or emotional responses so different from appropriate age, cultural, and community norms that the responses adversely affect educational performance (202)

Empowerment—planning and carrying out intervention activities in ways that pass as much control and decision making as possible on to the family (53)

Enabling environment (infancy)—an environment that supports a child's optimal development (314)

Encopresis—chronic soiling problem (209)

Enuresis—chronic wetting problem (209)

Environmental influences—the impact of environment on the development of the child (130)

Environmental risk—factors in a child's environment, such as poverty, child abuse, family beliefs, and inaccessibility of medical care, that put the child at risk for developmental disabilities (102)

Environmental structuring—teachers arrange features of the physical environment to foster social interaction (360)

Expressive language—spoken words or signs that individuals use in communicating with others (429)

F

Fading—gradually reducing prompts, cues, and physical assistance when teaching a particular skill (382)

Failure to thrive—refers to undersized infants whose bodies, for various reasons (organic, genetic, or environmental) either do not receive or cannot use the nurturance necessary for proper growth and development (61)

Family-centred service (FCS)—a set of values, attitudes, and approaches to services for children with special needs and their families. In FCS, the family works with service providers to make informed decisions about the services and supports the child and family receive. (58)

Family uniqueness—a perspective that recognizes that every family is different (53)

First trimester—the first three months of prenatal development (116)

Forward chaining—breaking a task down into a series of small steps and teaching the first step first, in contrast to backward chaining (where the final step is taught first) (257)

Frequency—in research, refers to the number of times during a specified period that a designated behaviour occurred (383)

Functional approach—examining and assessing the environment and teacher behaviour to determine in what ways they might affect a child's behaviour, then planning and carrying out an intervention, and monitoring the child's progress (381)

G

Genetic mutation—an alteration in the chromosomal materials (genes) that control inherited characteristics (186)

Genetic predisposition—a child is born with genetic characteristics that predispose them to certain abilities and/or tendencies (130)

Gifted and have ADHD—unlike most children who are gifted, these children have trouble effectively using the strategies and skills they have, and their giftedness is not recognized (135)

Giftedness—evidence of superior or unusual ability in areas such as intellect, creativity, artistic talent, physical agility, or leadership (130)

Goodness-of-fit—when the learning opportunities are appropriate to the child's developmental status (378)

H

Handicap—relates to environmental or functional demands that, when placed on an individual with a disability, cannot be met (100)

Handicappism—assumptions and practices based on physical, mental, or behavioural differences that foster differential and unequal treatment of people (7)

Health conditions—refers to the range of health problems a child might have and how these affect their growth, development, and everyday lives (169)

Health impairments—chronic or acute disorders, such as heart problems, leukemia, and asthma, that threaten a child's overall development (108)

Hearing impairment—a hearing loss that can have a delaying effect on a child's cognitive, social, and language development (108)

High risk—a high probability of developing serious problems (121)

Holophrastic speech—a state of speech development where a child conveys meaning with a one-word utterance (431)

Hydrocephalus—a condition that occurs as the result of a buildup of cranial spinal fluid in the head; if not corrected (shunted), can lead to an enlargement of the head and, ultimately, pressure on and deterioration of the brain (172)

Hyperactivity or hyperkinesis—refers to children who are highly active, energetic, impulsive, and distractible and who have a hard time waiting their turns or listening to instructions (217)

Hypertonicity—abnormally high muscle tone (170)

Hypotonicity—too little muscle tone; "floppiness" (170)

I

Immune system—that aspect of body functioning responsible for warding off diseases (190)

Improvisational play—includes similar techniques used by theatre performers that can be adapted to promote social development; small groups of children learn to initiate and build on one another's social cues (369)

Incidental social learning—the teacher promotes social interactions as they arise naturally and spontaneously (363)

Incidental teaching—using a spontaneous teaching opportunity, which is always initiated by the child when he or she asks for help, materials, or information (85)

Inclusion—children are included, with additional assistance and resources, regardless of ability in early childhood settings, educational environments, and community programs (4)

Inclusive—equitable access is offered to all children, regardless of ability (292)

Incontinence—a lack of bladder or bowel control (172)

Individual family service plan (IFSP)—similar to the IPP, the IFSP is a written plan that describes services for families with young children with special needs; it is written collaboratively with parents and describes the child's current strengths and needs (6, 59)

Individual program plan (IPP)—an approach to providing services to individuals with special needs: the process involves developing a written plan based on the child's strengths, needs, and interests; implementation and evaluation are part of the IPP process (6, 279)

Induced incompetence—children with special needs suffering the effects of poorly functioning equipment (334)

In-home support services—services, such as development assessments and parenting support, provided in the home for infants with special needs and their families (312)

Integration—children with special needs are given extra support so that they can be integrated into a regular setting and meet the existing expectations of the classroom (4)

Interdisciplinary—refers to several different professions working together on a common problem, sharing information, and exchanging roles, depending on the case (280)

Intermittent hearing loss—hearing comes and goes because of a build up of fluid caused by repeated ear infections (144)

Interval—a specified period of the day that is broken into segments to record the occurrence, frequency, and duration of a behaviour (383)

Intrinsic motivation—feelings of pleasure and personal satisfaction derived from working on or accomplishing a task, discovering something new, or solving a problem (239)

L

Learning disability—one of a number of disorders that may affect the acquisition, organization, retention, understanding, or use of verbal or nonverbal information, even though the individual is of at least average intellectual ability (thinking, reasoning, or both) (223)

Learning disorders—the name given to a group of problems that can cause children who have average IQs and reasonable adaptive functioning to nevertheless have difficulty learning to read, write, do math (202)

Learning theory—emphasizes the dominant role of environment and reinforcing experiences in all learning; social learning theory adds other dimensions—that learning also occurs through observing and imitating and that individuals can generate their own satisfactions (intrinsic reinforcement) (242)

M

Mainstreaming—children with special needs have to "be ready" for integration into the mainstream (4)

Manual prompts—when the teacher's hand is around the learner's and actually putting the learner through the motions (may also be referred to as "hand over hand") (257)

Maturation—developmentally, maturation is often defined as an internal process that governs the natural unfolding of innate ("preprogrammed") skills and abilities (238)

Mediated learning model—based on the teaching premise that cognitive and social processes are interdependent factors in all learning (92)

Medical model—an approach to understanding disabilities that individualizes and pathologizes a disability as a biological impairment, a deficit, or a dysfunction residing within the person (32)

Meningocele—a congenital protrusion of the spinal cord through the vertebrae; it is limited to the covering of the spinal cord and usually causes little or no neurological impairment (172)

Metabolic disorders—single-gene defects that cause a breakdown somewhere in the complex chemical activities needed to metabolize food (119)

Metabolize—the chemical process within living cells by which energy is manufactured so that the body systems can carry out their functions (186)

Modelling—learning by watching and imitating another's actions; also called observational learning (238)

Motherese—unique infant-directed speech patterns that adults use with the very young (427)

Multiple disabling conditions—the condition of having more than one disability (107)

Muscle tone—the interaction between the central nervous system and motor activity; the term does not mean the same thing as muscle strength; without muscle tone there is no voluntary movement (115)

Myelomeningocele—a congenital protrusion of the spinal cord through the vertebrae; paralysis and lack of sensation below the protrusion (usually the lower trunk and legs) are often the result (172)

N

Neurological—refers to the functioning of the nervous system (122)

Nonambulatory—unable to walk (256)

Nonintrusive—professionals respecting the privacy of families and not intruding into families' lives or lifestyles without an invitation to do so (256)

Norm-referenced tests—instruments that compare a child's developmental level with a normative sample of same-age peers (269)

O

Occlusion—an obstruction; as used here, something to prevent vision; an occluder is the object the examiner uses to prevent a child from seeing (usually one eye at a time) (156)

Operant conditioning—a teaching strategy in which the child's behaviour is shaped as the result of a planned response designed to reinforce a specific behaviour (242)

Oppositional defiant disorder (ODD)—a pattern of angry/irritable mood, argumentative/defiant behaviour, or vindictiveness lasting at least six months (392)

Orderly sequences—events during an activity period follow a predicable pattern (345)

Orthopedic conditions—conditions involving the bones, joints, and the associated muscles and ligaments (168)

Orthopedic impairments—developmental differences that interfere with walking or other body movements (107)

Overregularization—language irregularities that occur because the child is applying previously learned rules of grammar; for example, "The mouses runned" (432)

P

Peer imitating—young children with special needs observe and imitate more advanced skills modelled by peers (19)

Peer tutoring—one child instructing or assisting another (23)

People-first language—language that focuses on the person instead of the disability; for example, saying "a child with autism" rather than "an autistic child" emphasizes abilities rather than limitations (7)

Perceptual motor skills—movement generated by sensory messages, by what is seen, heard, touched, tasted, or smelled (410)

Perinatally—occurring or existing at the time of birth (115)

Peripheral vision—that degree of vision available at the outer edges of the eyes (160)

Perseveration—repeating the same act over and over with no discernible intention (in an obsessive, ritualistic manner) (230)

Phobias—fears that result in excessive and unrealistic anxiety about everyday happenings (207)

Pica—craving to eat nonfood substances (208)

Picture Exchange Communication System (PECS)—an augmentative communication system that focuses on child initiation; the child exchanges symbols and pictures to communicate desires and ideas (434)

Portfolio—a carefully selected collection of a child's work that is used to document growth and development (278)

Postnatally—occurring or existing after birth (115)

Prader-Willi syndrome—a genetic disorder characterized by obesity, short stature, disorders in sexual development, and a tendency toward behavioural and cognitive disabilities (193)

Precocious—the term used to describe young children who appear remarkably bright or unusually verbal and who may demonstrate outstanding talents in some specialized area, such as art, music, math (130)

Prelingual communication—body movements, facial expressions, and vocalizations used by infants before the first words are learned (429)

Prenatally—occurring or existing before birth (115)

Preorientation and mobility skills—the ability of a child who has a visual impairment to map out and travel in a room safely (159)

Preventive discipline—a child-management procedure for arranging the environment in ways that reduce the occurrence of maladaptive behaviours and increase the occurrence of appropriate behaviours (248)

Primitive reflexes—the responses the infant is born with, such as grasping, stepping, rooting, and sucking. Most of these disappear around four months of age and are replaced by similar but voluntary behaviours, as in the sucking response (170)

Private speech—children's strategy of talking to themselves to direct their behaviour as they work things out (432)

Prostheses/prosthetic devices—artificial devices replacing body parts that are damaged, missing at birth, or later removed (176)

Protein deficiency—a factor in maternal malnutrition when the mother's diet is lacking in milk, cheese, eggs, meats, and so on, which can result in premature or seriously low-birthweight babies (122)

Psychological balance—an infant's or toddler's ability to maintain a balance between approaching and avoiding environmental events (stimuli) (318)

R

Radiation—The use of high-energy penetrating rays to damage cancer cells, stopping them from growing and dividing (185)

Readiness—the point when a child has the necessary prerequisite skills to engage in specific new learning (84)

Readiness as a learning theory—recognizes the importance of being aware of the point at which a child has all the necessary prerequisite skills to engage in specific new learning (402)

Receptive language—language that is understood; it precedes expressive language (429)

Reciprocal relationships—interactions between individuals in which each person gives and receives in response to the giving and receiving of the other (53)

Reconstituted (or blended) family—each parent bringing children into a new household (54)

Refractive errors—problems, such as astigmatism, hyperopia, and myopia, caused by a minor malformation of the eye that influences the bending of light rays (154)

Regeneration—the regrowth, repair, or renewal of the spinal cord or other parts of the body (172)

Reinforcement—a general term for a consequence, an event, or a procedure that increases or maintains the behaviour it follows; high grades are reinforcement for good academic performance (243)

Reliable and valid tests—reliability relates to consistency—how accurate, dependable, and predictable a test is; validity refers to how accurately a test measures that which it purports to measure. For example, a score on a verbal IQ test for a child with an undiagnosed hearing impairment is not likely to be valid; the test does not measure the child's intelligence but rather how well the child's faulty hearing allows for interpretation of questions (265)

Renewal time—a discipline technique that gives a child the message that he or she needs some time to calm down and to gain some inner control (250)

Replacement behaviour—a behaviour that is taught to a child to replace an inappropriate one—a replacement behaviour should serve the same function as the inappropriate behaviour (382)

Residual hearing—the degree of hearing of a person who is deaf or hard of hearing (145)

Residual vision—vision remaining after disease or damage occurs to a person's visual system (156)

Resilience—the ability to "come back" after a damaging or traumatic experience (102)

Resource consultant/resource teacher/early interventionist—a professional with special training and expertise in planning and implementing developmentally appropriate programs for children who have developmental problems (61)

Respiratory distress syndrome (RDS)—a problem commonly found among premature infants because of the immature development of their lungs; it may also occur in about 1 percent of full-term infants during the first days of life (116)

Responsive environment—adults actively engage with an individual infant or toddler and respond to his or her needs and sensorimotor and social exploration (314)

Reverse integration—programs in which children without special needs participate in programs originally established for children with special needs (13)

Rote memorization—the act of memorizing numbers or letters without understanding them; being able to recite something that has little or no meaning for the one who has memorized it (402)

S

Scaffolding—a teaching and learning process in which the teacher provides decreasing levels of support while placing higher demands as the child progresses toward the goal of independent problem solving (91)

School-age care—programs offered before and after school on a regular basis in various settings for school-aged children (322)

Seizures—bursts of electrical energy in the brain that cause uncontrolled muscular movement and reduced or total loss of consciousness, as in epilepsy (187)

Self-assertion—a person standing up for his or her rights and possessions (367)

Self-help/care—skills related to socially expected routines in early childhood settings, such as toileting, dressing, eating, cleaning up, and doing one's share of classroom chores (331)

Sensitive or critical periods—a time when a child is especially responsive and able to learn a particular skill (16)

Sensorimotor profile—an infant's preference for and use of one sensory modality over another for sensory exploration (316)

Sensory impairments—difficulties in the ability to sense the environment through a specific sensory modality, such as hearing or sight (142)

Sensory integration—the process of more than one sense working together to understand a sensory message and to translate the message into appropriate action (410)

Sensory stimulation—objects and people that encourage infants and toddlers to explore their environment through seeing, hearing, touching, tasting, and smelling (315)

Seriation—the process of arranging objects and events along orderly and related dimensions, for example: beginning, middle, end or small, bigger, biggest (413)

Service coordinator—the member of the IPP team who assumes responsibility for coordination of the program and services for the child (61)

Shunting—a process for implanting a tube (shunt) into the brain to allow proper circulation and drainage of fluids from within the skull into one of the body cavities (172)

Sign language—a visual/gestural language, such as American Sign Language (ASL). Sign languages are full languages displaying the same levels of linguistic organization found in spoken languages. Sign languages include fingerspelling. (142)

Skill fluency—a child's ability to use a skill consistently and independently (361)

Social model—an approach to understanding disabilities that identifies the barriers that prevent the social inclusion of people with disabilities, and then focuses on the capacity of people with disabilities to change these barriers, with the help of others (32)

Social reinforcement—the positive and negative feedback that children receive from adults and peers that leads to further learning, either appropriate or inappropriate (357)

Spasticity—abnormal muscle tone—evident in taut muscle activity or too little muscle tone, both of which prevent fluid movements, as seen in cerebral palsy (170)

Spatial and temporal (time) concepts—how objects are related to space and time and to the child (414)

Special ability in art—an indication that a child may be potentially gifted in this area (132)

Special ability in music—an indication that a child may be potentially gifted in this area (133)

Special needs—challenges in learning and functioning in one or more areas of development and increased vulnerability to environmental and non-environmental stresses (99)

Specific learning disabilities (SLD)—a difficulty in any of the following areas: attention, memory, reasoning, coordination, communicating, reading, writing, spelling, calculation, social competence, and emotional maturation (106)

Spina bifida—the imperfect development of the spinal cord and spinal column that occurs during the first 30 days of fetal development; it can cause severe disabilities (169)

Stigmata (stigma)—an identifying mark or characteristic; a diagnostic sign of a disease or disability (118)

Strabismus—eye muscle imbalance problems, which are correctable with eyeglasses (155)

Structured flexibility—a well-structured early learning environment that also is adaptable to children's individual needs and preferences (343)

Syndrome—a grouping of similar physical characteristics (118)

Syntax—the way in which words are put together to form phrases, clauses, or sentences (431)

T

Tactile—refers to what is learned or perceived through touch (109)

Tactile sign language—sign language used by children who are deafblind (143)

Tangible reinforcers—material things that the individual likes; in children, favourite foods and drinks, toys, stickers, and so on (older children usually like money) (213)

Task analysis—the process of breaking down a complex task into smaller units so that learning can occur more easily (252)

Teachable moments—specific points when a child's level of readiness and interest come together to create the best milieu for new teaching (18, 84)

Teacher-guided learning opportunities—the teacher directly supports the learning of skills during large- and small-group activities; also called one-on-one teaching or instruction periods (335)

Teacher-mediated interventions—teachers provide direct support to encourage children to engage in social interactions (360)

Telegraphic speech—the stage in language acquisition in which children's utterances are generally longer than two words; phrases convey grammatical meaning even though many words are left out (432)

Temperament—an individual's psychological makeup or personality traits; of interest to the caregiver is how temperament influences an individual's responses to different situations (378)

Transactional relationships—the understanding that children and adults influence each other in their ongoing relationships and that both children and adults learn from these interactions; future interactions are influenced by earlier interactions (58)

Transdisciplinary—professionals sharing expertise, modelling, and instructing other team members on how to implement specific practices within the group setting (280)

Transdisciplinary team—the team that shares the responsibilities for assessment, program planning, implementation, and evaluation across members (60)

Transition coordinator—the team member who is responsible for coordinating the transition from one educational setting to a new educational setting (296)

Transition plans—the plans developed to ensure a comfortable and positive transition for the child and family as they move from one educational setting to a new educational setting (292)

Traumatic brain injury—includes injuries to the head that cause tearing of the nerve fibres, bruising of the brain against the skull, or bruising of the brain stem (110)

V

Visual acuity problems—problems in how well an individual is able to see (154)

Visual impairment—vision loss that include the following conditions: blind, partially sighted, and low vision (109)

Voice synthesizer—a computer that can produce spoken words; a type of assistive technology often used by people with severe communication disabilities (434)

Vulnerability—lack of resistance to or ability to recover from a damaging or traumatic experience (102)

W

Wedges, bolsters, and prone-boards—therapeutic positioning devices prescribed for use by physiotherapists and occupational therapists in treating children with impaired motor skills (177)

Z

Zero reject—no child is ever excluded for reasons of level or type of special need from full participation in a program or service (10)

References

Ackerman, J. P., Riggins, T., & Black, M. M. (2010). A review of the effects of prenatal cocaine exposure among school-aged children. *Pediatrics, 125*(3), 564–565.

Allen, K. E. (1974). Behavior modification principles. In J. C. Cull & R. F. Hardy (Eds.), *Behavior modification in rehabilitation settings.* Springfield, IL: Thomas, 89–129.

Allen, K. E., & Goetz, F. M. (1982). *Early childhood education: Special problems, special solutions.* Rockville, MD: Aspen Systems.

Allen, K. E., & Hart, B. (1984). *The early years: Arrangements for learning.* Englewood Cliffs, NJ: Prentice-Hall.

Allen, K. E., & Marotz, L. R. (2010). *Developmental profiles: Pre-birth through twelve* (5th ed.). Clifton Park, NY: Delmar Learning.

Allen, K. E., & Marotz, L. R. (2012). *Developmental profiles: Pre-Birth through adolescence* (7th ed.). Belmont, CA: Wadsworth.

American Academy of Child and Adolescent Psychiatry. (2013). Children with oppositional defiant disorder. Retrieved from http://www.aacap.org/AACAP/Families_and_Youth/Facts_for_Families/Facts_for_Families_Pages/Children_With_Oppositional_Defiant_Disorder_72.aspx

American Academy of Pediatrics. (2000). Clinical practice guideline: Diagnosis and evaluation of the child with attention-deficit/hyperactivity disorder. *Pediatrics, 105*(5), 1158–1170.

American Academy of Pediatrics. (2002). Use of photo screening for children's vision screening. *Pediatrics, 109,* 524–525.

American Academy of Pediatrics. (2005). Lack of transmission of human immunodeficiency virus from infected children to household contacts. *Pediatrics, 85*(2), 1115–1119.

American Academy of Pediatrics. (2010). Prevention of pediatric overweight and obesity. Retrieved from http://www.aap.org/obesity/about.html

American Association on Intellectual and Developmental Disabilities. (2013). Frequently asked questions on intellectual disability. Retrieved from http://www.aaidd.org

American Psychiatric Association. (2012, March 27). Commentary takes issue with criticism of new autism definition: *DSM-5* experts call study flawed [Press release]. Retrieved from http://www.psychiatry.org/advocacy--newsroom/newsroom/news-releases/2012-news-releases

American Psychiatric Association. (2013). *Diagnostic and statistical manual of mental disorders* (5th ed.). Arlington, VA: American Psychiatric Publishing.

Anderson, R. C., Hiebert, E. H., Scott, J. A., & Wilkerson, I. A. (1985). *Becoming a nation of readers.* Washington, DC: National Academy of Education.

Anderson, S. R., Jablonski, A., Thomeer, M. L., & Knapp, V. M. (2007). *Self-help skills for people with autism: A systematic teaching approach.* Bethesda, MD: Woodbine House.

Anderson, W., Chitwood, S., Hayden, D., & Takemoto, C. (2008). *Negotiating the special education maze: A guide for parents and teachers* (4th ed.). Bethesda, MD: Woodbine House.

Apgar, V. C., & Beck, J. (1973). *Is my baby alright?* New York, NY: Trident.

Asthma Society of Canada. (2013). About asthma: What is asthma? Retrieved from http://www.asthma.ca/adults/about/whatIsAsthma.php

AutismConnect. (n.d.). Methods and strategies: Incidental teaching. Retrieved from http://www.autismconnectmd.org/education/methods/incidental.html

Autism Speaks. (2012, June 25). Autism Speaks funds research on impact of *DSM-5* on autism diagnosis [Press release]. Retrieved from http://www.autismspeaks.org/science/science-news/autism-speaks-funds-research-impact-dsm-5-autism-diagnosis

Autism Speaks. (2014). Pivotal Response Treatment (PRT). Retrieved from http://www.autismspeaks.org/what-autism/treatment/pivotal-response-therapy-prt

Bach, M. (2002). Social inclusion as solidarity: Rethinking the child rights agenda. *Perspectives on social inclusion working paper series: Summaries*. Toronto, ON: The Laidlaw Foundation.

Bailey, D. B., & Wolery, M. (1984). *Teaching infants and preschoolers with handicaps*. Columbus, OH: Charles E. Merrill.

Baker, B., Brightman, B., & Heifetz, L. J. (2004). *Steps to independence: Teaching everyday skills to children with special needs*. Baltimore, MD: Brookes.

Bandura, A. (1973). *Aggression: A social learning analysis*. Englewood Cliffs, NJ: Prentice-Hall.

Barkley, R. A. (2005). *Attention deficit hyperactivity disorders: A handbook for diagnosis and treatment*. New York, NY: Guilford Press.

Bee, H., & Boyd, D. (2009). *The developing child* (12th ed.). Needham Heights, MA: Allyn & Bacon.

Bee, H., & Boyd, D. (2012). The developing child (13th ed.). New York, NY: Pearson.

Beers, M. H. (Ed.). (2005). Children's health issues [Electronic version]. *The Merck manual of medical information* (2nd home ed., section 23). Rahway, NJ: Merck.

Benasich, A. A., & Tallal, P. (1996). Auditory temporal processing thresholds, habituation, and recognition memory over the first year. *Infant Behavior and Development, 19*(3), 339–357.

Bennett, E. C. (1990). Recent advances in developmental intervention for biologically vulnerable infants. *Infants and Young Children, 3*(1), 33–40.

Berglund, E., Eriksson, M., & Johansson, I. (2001). Parental reports of spoken language skills in children with Down syndrome. *Journal of Speech, Language, and Hearing Research, 44*, 179–191.

Bernhard, J. K. (2012). *Stand together or fall apart: Professionals working with immigrant families*. Halifax, NS: Fernwood.

Best, S. J., Bigge, J. L., & Sirvis, B. P. (1994). Physical and health impairments. In N. G. Haring, L. McCormick, & T. G. Haring (Eds.), *Exceptional children and youth* (6th ed.). New York, NY: Merrill.

Beveridge, M., Loader, S., Northstone, K., & Roulston, S. (2002). The speech and language of children aged 25 months: Descriptive data from the Avon longitudinal study of parents and children. *Early Child Development and Care, 172*, 259–268.

Bijou, S. W. (1959). Learning in children. *Monographs of the Society for Research in Child Development, 24*(5), 25–36.

Bijou, S. W. (1993). *Behavior analysis of child development* (2nd ed.). Reno, NV: Context Press.

Billingsley, F., Gallucci, C., Peck, C. A., Schwartz, I. S., & Staub, D. (1996). But the kids can't even do math: An alternative conceptualization of outcomes for inclusive education. *Special Education Leadership Review, 3*(1), 43–55.

Blagojevic, G., Twomey, D., & Labas, L. (2007). *Universal design for learning: From the start*. Orono, ME: University of Maine. Retrieved from http://www.ccids. umaine.edu/facts/facts6/udl.htm

Blamey, P. (2003). Development of spoken language by deaf children. In M. Marschark & P. Spencer (Eds.), *Oxford handbook of deaf studies, language and education* (pp. 232–246). New York, NY: Oxford University Press.

Blasco, P. M. (2001). *Early intervention services for infants, toddlers and their families*. Needham Heights, MA: Allyn and Bacon.

Blasi, M. J., & Priestley, L. (1998). A child with severe hearing loss joins our learning community. *Young Children, 53*(2), 44–49.

Bloom, L. (1995). *The transition from infancy to language: Acquiring the power of expression*. Cambridge, England: Cambridge University Press.

Bogdan, R., & Biklen, D. (1993). Handicappism. In M. Nagler (Ed.), *Perspectives on disability* (2nd ed., pp. 69–76). Palo Alto, CA: Health Market Research.

Bohan-Baker, M., & Little, P. M. (2004). *The transition to kindergarten: A review of current research and promising practices to involve families*. Cambridge, MA: Harvard Family Research Project.

Bondy, A., & Frost, L. (1994). The picture exchange communication system. *Focus on Autistic Behavior, 9*(3), 1–19.

Boston Children's Hospital. (2011). Hydrocephalus. Retrieved from http://www.childrenshospital.org/az/Site1116/mainpageS1116P4.html

Brachfield, S., Goldberg, S., & Sloman, J. (1980). Parent–infant interaction in free play at 8 and 12 months: Effects of prematurity and immaturity. *Infant Behavior and Development, 3*, 289–305.

Bredekamp, S. (Ed.). (1987). *Developmentally appropriate practice in early childhood programs serving children from birth through age eight*. Washington, DC: National Association for the Education of Young Children.

Bredekamp, S., & Copple, C. (2009). *An activity-based approach to early intervention* (rev. ed.). Washington, DC: National Association for the Education of Young Children.

Bronfenbrenner, U. (2006). *The ecology of human development*. Cambridge, MA: Harvard University Press.

Bruder, M. B., & Chandler, L. K. (1996). Transition. In S. L. Odom & M. E. McLean (Eds.), *Early intervention/early childhood special education: Recommended practices* (pp. 287–307). Austin, TX: Pro-Ed.

Calderon, R., & Greenberg, M. (2003). Social and emotional development of deaf children: Family, school, and program effects. In M. Marschark & P. E. Spencer (Eds.), *Oxford handbook of deaf studies, language, and education* (pp. 177–189). New York, NY: Oxford University Press.

Caldwell, B. M. (1973). The importance of beginning early. In J. B. Jordan & R. F. Dailey (Eds.), *Not all little wagons are red: The exceptional child's early years*. Reston, VA: Council for Exceptional Children.

Campaign 2000. (2012). *2012 Campaign 2000 Report Card on Child and Family Poverty in Canada*. Toronto, ON: Author.

Campbell, J., Garcia-Moreno, C., & Sharps, P. (2004). Abuse during pregnancy in industrialized and developing countries. *Violence Against Women, 10*(7), 770–789.

Canadian Association for Community Living. (2011). *Inclusion of individuals with intellectual disabilities: A national report card 2011*. Toronto, ON: Author.

Canadian Council on Social Development. (2006). *The progress of Canada's children and youth, 2006*. Retrieved from http://www.ccsd.ca/resources/ProgressChildren Youth/pdf/pccy_2006.pdf

Canadian Cystic Fibrosis Foundation. (2000). *1960–2000. Proud of our progress. Confident of our future*. Toronto, ON: Author.

Canadian Diabetes Association. (2005–2009). *Kids with diabetes in your care*. Toronto, ON: Author.

Canadian Down Syndrome Society. (2014). *Celebrate being: About Down syndrome* [Brochure]. Retrieved from https://www.cdss.ca/images/pdf/brochures/english/celebrate_being_about_down_syndrome_english.pdf

Canadian Hearing Society. (2013). *Position paper on access to language and language acquisition for children*. Retrieved from http://www.chs.ca/position-paper-access-language-and-language-acquisition-children#top

Canadian Hemophilia Society. (2013). Support and education: Passport to well-being. Retrieved from http://www.hemophilia.ca/en/support-and-education/passport-to-well-being/

Canadian Human Rights Act, R.S.C., 1985, c. H-6.

Canadian Mental Health Association. (2013a). Children, youth, and depression. Retrieved from http://www.cmha.ca/mental_health/children-and-depression/#.Un5jeJTk_Dc

Canadian Mental Health Association. (2013b). Understanding mental illness. Retrieved from http://www.cmha.ca/mental-health/understanding-mental-illness/anxiety-disorders/

Canadian Stem Cell Foundation. (2013). Toward treatments: Spinal cord injury. Retrieved from http://www.stemcellfoundation.ca/en/toward-treatments/disease-summaries/spinal-cord-injury

CanChild Centre for Childhood Disability Research. (2014). About family-centred service. Retrieved from http://www.canchild.ca/en/childrenfamilies/about_fcs.asp

Carr, A. (1997). Play and relationships: Programming for inclusion. *Interaction, 10*(4), 23–24.

CAST. (2011). *Universal design for learning guidelines version 2.0*. Wakefield, MA: Author.

Centers for Disease Control and Prevention. (2011). Attention-deficit/hyperactivity disorder (ADHD). Retrieved from http://www.cdc.gov/ncbddd/adhd/treatment.html

Chaban, P., & Tannock, R. (2009, November 30). ADHD: An overview. Retrieved from http://www.aboutkidshealth.ca/En/ResourceCentres/ADHD/AboutADHD/Pages/default.aspx

Chance, P. (2006). *First course in applied behavior analysis*. Pacific Grove, CA: Brooks/Cole.

Chard, S., & Katz, L. (2000). *Engaging children's minds: The project approach*. Norwood, NJ: Ablex.

Charlesworth, R. (2014). Understanding child development (9th ed.). Toronto, ON: Nelson Education.

Cherniak, D., Grant, L., Mason, R., Moore, B., & Pellizzari, R. (2005, April). *Intimate partner violence consensus statement* (Society of Obstetricians and Gynaecologists of Canada Clinical Practice Guidelines, No. 157). Retrieved from http://www.sogc.org/guidelines/public/157E-CPG-April2005.pdf

Cherry, C. (1983). *Please don't sit on the kids*. Belmont, CA: Pitman.

Child and Family Services Statute Law Amendment Act, 2009, S.O. 2009, c. 2—Bill 103.

Childcare Resource and Research Unit. (2004). *Early childhood care and education in Canada: Provinces and territories, 2001*. Toronto, ON: Author.

Child Development Institute. (2014). SNAP® Programs. Retrieved from http://www.childdevelop.ca/programs/snap/snap-programs

Clark, B. (2007). *Growing up gifted* (5th ed.). Upper Saddle River, NJ: Merrill.

Cohen, D., & Cicchetti, D. (2006). *Developmental psychopathology: Theory and method*. New York, NY: John Wiley & Sons.

Coleman, L. J., & Cross, T. L. (2005). *Being gifted in school: An introduction to development, guidance, and teaching*. Waco, TX: Prufrock Press.

Colker, I. J. (2008). Twelve characteristics of effective early childhood teachers. *Beyond the Journal: Young Children on the Web*. Retrieved from http://journal.naeyc.org/btj/200803/pdf/BTJ_Colker.pdf

Committee on Pediatric AIDS. (2000). Educating children with human immunodeficiency viral infection. *Pediatrics, 105*(6), 1358–1360. Retrieved from http://pediatrics.aappublications.org/content/105/6/1358.full?sid=67795a9c

Conners, C. K. (1980). *Food additives and hyperactive children*. New York, NY: Plenum Press.

Conn-Powers, M., Cross, A. F., & Traub, E. K., & Hutter-Pishgahi, L. (2006, September). The universal design of early education: Moving forward for all children. *Beyond the Journal: Young Children on the Web*. Retrieved from http://www.naeyc.org/files/yc/file/200609/ConnPowersBTJ.pdf

Cook, E. R., Klein, M. D., & Chen, D. (2012). *Adapting early childhood curricula for children with special needs*. San Francisco, CA: Pearson.

Cook, E. R., Klein, D. M., & Tessier, A. (2008). *Adapting early childhood curricula for children with special needs* (7th ed.). Upper Saddle River, NJ: Pearson.

Cook, J., & Bewley, S. (2008). Acknowledging a persistent truth: Domestic violence in pregnancy. *Journal of the Royal Society of Medicine, 101*(7), 358–363. Retrieved from http://www.ncbi.nlm.nih.gov/pmc/articles/PMC2442136/?tool=pubmed

Cook, R. E., Tessier, A., & Klein, M. D. (2004). *Adapting early childhood curricula for children with special needs* (6th ed.). Columbus, OH: Merrill.

Cooper, R. P., & Aslin, R. N. (1994). Developmental differences in infant attention to spectral properties of infant-directed speech. *Child Development, 65*, 1663–1667.

Couture, M., & Jacobs, E. (2001). Integrating children with special needs in school age care programs. *Interaction, 15*(1), 32–33.

Curry, N. E., & Johnson, C. N. (1990). *Beyond self-esteem: Developing a genuine sense of human value.* Washington, DC: National Center for Education of Young Children.

Cystic Fibrosis Canada. (n.d.). What is cystic fibrosis? Retrieved from http://www.cysticfibrosis.ca/about-cf/what-is-cystic-fibrosis/

Daley, S. (2002). "Mom, will Kaelie always have possibilities?" The realities of early childhood inclusion. *Phi Delta Kappan, 84*, 73–76.

Davern, L. (2004). Home to school notebooks: What parents have to say. *Teaching Exceptional Children, 36*(5), 22–27.

Deal, A. G., Dunst, C. J., & Trivette, C. M. (1989). A flexible and functional approach to developing individualized family service plans. *Infants and Young Children, 1*(4), 32–43.

Dearing, E., Simpkins, S., Kreider, H., & Weiss, H. (2006). Family involvement in school and low-income children's literacy: Longitudinal associations between and within families. *Journal of Educational Psychology, 98*, 653–664.

Decoufle, P., Boyle, C. A., Paulozzi, L. J., & Lary, J. M. (2001). Increased risk for developmental disabilities in children who have major birth defects: A population based study. *Pediatrics, 108*, 728–734.

Deiner, P. L., Dyck, L., & Hardare, L. (2004). *Resources for educating young children with diverse abilities: Birth through 12.* Toronto, ON: Harcourt Brace.

Derman-Sparks, L., & A.B.C. Task Force. (1989). *Anti-bias curriculum: Tools for empowering young children.* Washington, DC: National Association for the Education of Young Children.

Derman-Sparks, L., & Edwards, O. J. (2010). *Anti-bias education for young children and ourselves.* Washington, DC: National Association for the Education of Young Children.

Dewey, J. (1950). *Experience and education.* New York, NY: Macmillan.

Discolo, C. M., & Hirose, K. (2002). Pediatric cochlear implants. *American Journal of Audiology, 11*(2), 114–118.

Division for Early Childhood. (1999). *Concept paper on the identification of and intervention with challenging behaviour.* Retrieved from https://www.nhsa.org/files/static_page_files/EC5FD710-1D09-3519-AD0DEF5D28FAC3CD/Concept_paper_on_Challenging_Behavior.pdf

Division for Early Childhood & National Association for the Education of Young Children. (2009). *Early childhood inclusion: A joint position statement of the Division for Early Childhood (DEC) and the National Association for the Education of Young Children (NAEYC).* Chapel Hill: University of North Carolina, FPG Child Development Institute. Retrieved from http://npdci.fpg.unc.edu/sites/npdci.fpg.unc.edu/files/resources/EarlyChildhoodInclusion_0.pdf

Division for Early Childhood, National Association for the Education of Young Children, & National Head Start Association. (2013). *Frameworks for response to intervention in early childhood: Description and implications.* Retrieved from http://www.naeyc.org/files/naeyc/RTI%20in%20Early%20Childhood.pdf

Doherty, G., Lero, D., Goelman, H., Tougas, J., & LaGrange, A. (2000a). *You bet I care! Report 2: Caring and learning environments: Quality in child care centres across Canada.* Guelph, ON: University of Guelph, Centre for Families, Work and Well-Being.

Doherty, G., Lero, D., Goelman, H., Tougas, J., & LaGrange, A. (2000b). *You bet I care! Report 3: Quality in regulated family child care across Canada.* Guelph, ON: University of Guelph, Centre for Families, Work and Well-Being.

Dokecki, P. R., Baumeister, A. A., & Kupstas, F. D. (1989). Biomedical and social aspects of pediatric AIDS. *Journal of Early Intervention, 13*(2), 99–112.

Dotsch, J. (1992). Newcomer preschool children: Their cultural and linguistic adaptation to childcare settings. *Multiculturalism, 14*(2, 3), 24–26.

Dunlap, G., & Powell, D. (2009). *Promoting social behavior of young children in group settings: A summary of research. Roadmap to effective intervention practices #3.* Tampa: University of South Florida, Technical Assistance Center on Social Emotional Intervention for Young Children. Retrieved from http://www.challengingbehavior.org/do/recources/documents/roadmap_3/pdf

Dunlap, G., Strain, P. S., Fox, L., Carta, J. J., Conroy, M., Smith, B. J., … Sowell, C. (2006). Prevention and intervention with young children's challenging behavior: Perspectives regarding current knowledge. *Behaviorial Disorders, 32*(1), 29–45.

Dunn, L. M. (1968). Special education for the mildly retarded—Is much of it justified? *Exceptional Children, 35*, 5–22.

Dunst, C. J., & Trivette, C. M. (1989). An enablement and empowerment perspective of case management. *Topics in Early Childhood Special Education, 8*(4), 87–102.

Dybvik, A. C. (2004, Winter). Autism and the inclusion mandate: What happens when children with severe disabilities like autism are taught in regular classrooms? Daniel knows. *Education Next.* Retrieved from http://educationnext.org/files/ednext20041_42.pdf

Ehlers, L. (1993). Inclusion in the lives of young children with disabilities. In S. M. Rehberg (Ed.), *Starting point: A series of definition papers* (pp. 33–43). Olympia, WA: Office of the Superintendent of Public Instruction.

Elicker, J., & Benson McMullen, M. (2013, July). Appropriate and meaningful assessment in family-centered programs. *Young Children, 68*(3), 22–26.

Elkind, D. (1981). *The hurried child.* Reading, MA: Addison-Wesley.

Epilepsy Ontario. (2013). Educate: First aid. Retrieved from http://www.epilepsyontario.org/first-aid/

ERIC/OSEP Special Project. (2001, Fall). Family involvement in special education. *Research Connections in Special Education, 9.* Arlington, VA: ERIC Clearinghouse on Disabilities and Gifted Education.

Erin, J. J. (2000). Students with visual impairments and additional disabilities. In A. J. Koenig & M. C. Holbrook (Eds.), *Foundations of education: Instructional strategies for teaching children and youths with visual impairments* (Vol. 2, pp. 721–752). New York, NY: American Foundation for the Blind.

Federal/Provincial/Territorial Ministers Responsible for Social Services. (2003). *Multilateral framework on early learning and child care.* Ottawa, ON: Government of Canada.

Feeney, S., & Kipnis, K. (2005). *Code of ethical conduct and statement of commitment.* Washington, DC: National Association for the Education of Young Children.

Feingold, B. F. (1975). *Why your child is hyperactive.* New York, NY: Random House.

Feuerstein, R., Rand, Y., Hoffman, M., & Miller, R. (1980). *Instrumental enrichment: Redevelopment of cognitive functions of retarded performers.* Baltimore, MD: University Park Press.

Flanagan, K., & Beach, J. (2010, April). *Examining the human resource implications of emerging issues in early childhood education and care (ECEC)/Communications strategy development: Inclusion.* Ottawa, ON: Child Care Human Resources Sector Council. Retrieved from http://www.researchconnections.org/childcare/resources/25276

Flanagan, K., Beach, J., & Varmuza, P. (2012). *You bet we still care! A survey of centre-based early childhood education and care in Canada: Highlights report.* Ottawa, ON: Child Care Human Resources Sector Council.

Flavell, J. H., Miller, P. H., & Miller, S. A. (2001). *Cognitive development* (2nd ed.). Englewood Cliffs, NJ: Prentice-Hall.

Fombonne, E. (2009). Epidemiology of pervasive developmental disorders. *Pediatric Research, 65*(6), 591–598.

Fox, L., Dunlap, G., Hemmeter, M. L., Joseph, G. E., & Strain, P. S. (2003). The teaching pyramid: A model for supporting social competence and preventing challenging behaviour in young children. *Young Children, 58*(4), 48–52.

Fox, L., & Harper Lentini, L. (2006, November). You Got it! *Beyond the Journal: Young Children on the Web.* Retrieved from http://www.challengingbehavior.org/do/resources/documents/yc_article_11_2006.pdf

Fraiberg, S. (1974). Blind infants and their mothers: An examination of the sign system. In M. Lewis & L. A. Rosenblum (Eds.), *The effect of the infant on its caregiver* (pp. 215–232). New York, NY: Wiley.

Frankel, E., Gold, S., & Ajodhia-Andrews, A. (2010). International preschool inclusion: Bridging the gap between vision and practices. *Young Exceptional Children, 13*(5), 2–16.

Frankel, E. B. (2004). Supporting inclusive care and education for young children with special needs and their families: An international perspective. *Childhood Education, 80,* 310–316.

Fraser, S. (2000). *Authentic childhood: Experiencing Reggio Emilia in the classroom.* Toronto, ON: Nelson Education.

Fraser, S. (2012). *Authentic childhood: Experiencing Reggio Emilia in the classroom* (3rd ed.). Toronto, ON: Nelson Education.

Freeman, B. J. (1997). Guidelines for evaluating intervention programs for children with autism. *Journal of Autism and Developmental Disorders, 27,* 641–651.

Friendly, M. (2006). *Canadian early learning and child care and the Convention on the Rights of the Child.* Toronto, ON: Childcare Resource and Research Unit, University of Toronto.

Friendly, M., & Beach, J. (2005). *Elements of a high quality early learning and child care system.* Toronto, ON: Child Care Resource and Research Unit, University of Toronto.

Friendly, M., Halfon, S., Beach, J., & Forer, B. (2013). *Early childhood education and care in Canada 2012.* Toronto, ON: Childcare Resource and Research Unit, University of Toronto.

Friendly, M., & Prentice, S. (2009). *About Canada series: Childcare.* Black Point, NS: Fernwood.

Froebel, F. W. (1911). *The education of man* (Trans. W. N. Hailmann). New York, NY: Appleton.

Gallagher, J. J. (1988). National agenda for educating gifted students: Statement of priorities. *Exceptional Children, 55*(2), 107–114.

Gardner, H. (1993). *Frames of mind: The theory of multiple intelligences.* New York, NY: Basic Books.

Garkfinkle, A. N., & Schwartz, I. S. (1998). *Observational learning in an integrated preschool: Effects on peer imitation and social interaction.* Unpublished manuscript, University of Washington, Seattle, WA.

Gartrell, D. (2011). Guidance matters. *Young Children, 66*(2), 58–60.

Gesell, A., Halverson, H. M., Thompson, B., Ilg, F. L., Castner, B. M., Ames, L. B., & Amatruda, C. S. (1993). *The first five years of life: A guide to the study of the preschool child.* New York, NY: Harper and Row.

Gestwicki, C. (1999). *Developmentally appropriate practice: Curriculum and development in early education* (2nd ed.). Albany, NY: Delmar.

Gestwicki, C. (2010). *Developmentally appropriate practice: Curriculum and development in early education* (4th ed.). Albany, NY: Delmar.

Gestwicki, C. (2014). *Developmentally appropriate practice: Curriculum and development in early education* (5th ed.). Belmont, CA: Wadsworth.

Gestwicki, C., & Bertrand, J. (2012). *Essentials of early childhood education*. Toronto, ON: Nelson Education.

Girolametto, L., & Weitzman, E. (2006). It Takes Two to Talk—The Hannen Program for Parents: Early language intervention through caregiver training. In R. McCauley & M. Fey (Eds.), *Treatment of language disorders in children* (pp. 77–103). New York, NY: Paul Brookes.

Gonzalez-Mena, J., & Eyer, D. W. (2007). Infants, toddlers, and caregivers: A curriculum of respectful, responsive care and education (7th ed.). New York, NY: McGraw Hill.

Gordon, A. M., & Browne, K. W. (2008). *Beginnings and beyond: Foundations in early childhood education* (7th ed.). Clifton Park, NY: Delmar Learning.

Gordon, A. M., & Williams Browne, K. W. (2010). *Beginnings and beyond: Foundations in early childhood education* (8th ed.). Clifton Park, NY: Thomson Delmar Learning.

Gould, P., & Sullivan, J. (1999). *The inclusive classroom: Easy ways to adapt learning centers for all children*. Beltsville, MD: Gryphon House.

Goulet, M. (1998). *How caring relationships support self-regulation: Video guide*. Toronto, ON: George Brown College.

Govindshenoy, M., & Spencer, N. (2006). Abuse of the disabled child: A systematic review of population-based studies. *Child Care, Health and Development, 33*(5), 552–558.

Greene, R. (1998). *The explosive child*. New York, NY: HarperCollins.

Greenspan, S. I. (1992). *Infancy and early childhood: The practice of clinical assessment and intervention with emotional and developmental challenges*. Madison, CT: International Universities Press.

Greenspan, S. I., & Wider, S. (1997). *Facilitating intellectual and emotional growth in children with special needs*. Reading, MA: Addison-Wesley.

Guralnick, M. (1996). *Assessment of peer relations*. Seattle: University of Washington Child Development and Mental Retardation Center.

Guralnick, M. (2013). Developmental science and preventive interventions for children at environmental risk. *Infants and Young Children, 26*(4), 270–285.

Guralnick, M. J. (1994). Mothers' perceptions of the benefits and drawbacks of early childhood mainstreaming. *Journal of Early Intervention, 12,* 168–183.

Guralnick, M. J. (2000). The early intervention system and out-of-home child care. In D. Cryer & T. Harms (Eds.), *Infants and toddlers in out-of-home care* (pp. 207–234). Baltimore, MD: Brookes.

Guralnick, M. J. (2005). *The developmental systems approach to early intervention*. Baltimore, MD: Brookes.

Guralnick, M. J. (2008). International perspectives on early intervention, *Journal of Early Intervention, 30,* 90–101.

Guralnick, M. J., & Neville, B. (1997). Designing early intervention programs to promote children's social competence. In M. J. Guralnick (Ed.), *The effectiveness of early intervention* (pp. 579–620). Baltimore, MD: Brookes.

Haines, A. H., Rosenkoetter, S. E., & Fowler, S. A. (1994). Transitional planning with families in early intervention programs. *Infants and Young Children, 3,* 38–47.

Halfon, S., & Friendly, M. (2013). *Inclusion of young children with disabilities in regulated child care in Canada. A snapshot: Research, policy and practice* (Occasional Paper No. 27). Toronto, ON: Childcare Resource and Research Unit.

Hall, N. S., & Rhomberg, V. (1995). *The affective curriculum: Teaching the anti-bias approach to young children.* Toronto, ON: Nelson Education.

Handle with Care. (2007). *Handle with Care training manual.* Toronto, ON: Hincks-Dellcrest Centre and Gail Appel Institute.

Hanline, M. F., Nunes, D., & Worthy, M. B. (2007, July). Augmentative and alternative communication in the early childhood years. *Beyond the Journal: Young Children on the Web*. Retrieved from https://www.naeyc.org/files/yc/file/200707/BTJHanline.pdf

Hanson, M. J., & Lynch, E. W. (2004). *Understanding families: Approaches to diversity, disability, and risk.* Baltimore, MD: Paul H. Brookes.

Haring, N. G., & McCormick, L. (1990). *Exceptional children and youth*. Columbus, OH: Charles E. Merrill.

Haring, N. G., & McCormick, L. (1994). *Exceptional children and youth: An introduction to special education.* Englewood Cliffs, NJ: Merrill.

Harris, F. R., Wolf, M. M., & Baer, D. M. (1964). Effects of adult social reinforcement on child behavior. *Young Children, 1,* 8–17.

Harry, B. (1992). Developing cultural self-awareness: The first step in values clarification for early interventionists. *Topics in Early Childhood Special Education, 12*(4), 333–350.

Hart, B., & Risley, T. R. (1999). *The social world of children learning to talk.* Baltimore, MD: Brookes.

Hatton, D., Anthony, T., Bishop, V., Gleason, D., Greeley, J. C., Miller, T., … Tompkins, C. (2003). *Family-centered practices for infants and young children with visual impairments* [Position paper of the Division on Visual Impairments, Council for Exceptional Children]. Arlington, VA: Council for Exceptional Children.

Hatton, D., McWilliam, R. A., & Winton, P. J. (2002). Infants and toddlers with visual impairments: Suggestions for early interventionists. Arlington, VA: Council for Exceptional Children.

Health and Welfare Canada. (1986). *Status of day care in Canada 1985.* Ottawa, ON: Author.

Health and Welfare Canada. (1990). *Status of day care in Canada 1989.* Ottawa, ON: Author.

Health Canada. (2009). Healthy living: Fetal alcohol spectrum disorder. Retrieved from http://www.hc-sc.gc.ca/hl-vs/iyh-vsv/diseases-maladies/fasd-etcaf-eng.php

Health Canada. (2010). Health concerns: HIV and AIDS. Retrieved from http://www.hc-sc.gc.ca/hc-ps/dc-ma/aids-sida-eng.php

Health Canada. (2011). *Eating well with Canada's Food Guide*. Ottawa, ON: Health Canada.

Herschkowitz, N., & Herschkowitz, E. C. (2004). *A good start in life: Understanding your child's brain and behavior from birth to age 6*. New York, NY: Dana Press.

Hershkowitz, I., Lamb, M. E., & Horowitz, D. (2007). Victimization of children with disabilities. *American Journal of Orthopsychiatry, 77*(4), 629–635.

Heward, W. L., Cavanaugh, R. A., & Ernsbarger, S. C. (2005). Educational equality for students with disabilities. In J. A. Banks & C. A. Banks (Eds.), *Multicultural education: Issues and perspectives* (pp. 317–349). Hoboken, NJ: Wiley.

Horowitz, F. D. (1987). *Exploring developmental theories: Toward a structural/ behavioral model of development*. Hillsdale, NJ: Erlbaum.

Horowitz, F. D. (1990). Developmental models of individual differences. In J. Columbo & J. Fagan (Eds.), *Individual differences in infancy: Reliability, stability, prediction* (pp. 3–18). Hillsdale: NJ: Erlbaum.

Hospital for Sick Children. (1999, July 1). Researchers pinpoint region for cystic fibrosis modifier gene [Press release]. Retrieved from http://www.sickkids.ca/AboutSickKids/Newsroom/Past-News/1999/Researchers-pinpoint-region-for-cystic-fibrosis-modifier-gene.html

Howard, V. F., Williams, B. F., & Lepper, C. (2009). *Very young children with special needs: A foundation for educations, families, and service providers* (4th ed.). Boston, MA: Pearson.

Hunt, J. McV. (1961). *Intelligence and experience*. New York, NY: Ronald Press.

Hyson, M. (2002). "Huh?" "Eek!" "Help": Three perspectives on early childhood assessment. *Young Children, 57*(1), 62–64.

Hyun, J., & Fowler, S. A. (1995). Respect, cultural sensitivity, and communication. *Teaching Exceptional Children, 28*, 25–28.

Intellectual disability (ID). (2009). In R. S. Porter, J. L. Kaplan, & B. P. Homeier (Eds.), *The Merck manual online*. Retrieved from http://www.merckmanuals.com/professional/pediatrics/learning_and_developmental_disorders/intellectual_disability_id.html

Irwin, S. H. (1997). Including all children. *Interaction, 4*(10), 15–16.

Irwin, S. H. & Lero, D. (2008). *Improving quality, enhancing inclusion: Partnerships for inclusion—Nova Scotia*. Guelph, ON: Centre for Families, Work and Well-Being.

Irwin, S. H., Lero, D. S., & Brophy, K. (2000). *A matter of urgency: Including children with special needs in child care in Canada*. Cape Breton, NS: Breton Books.

Irwin, S. H., Lero, D. S., & Brophy, K. (2004). *Inclusion: The next generation in child care in Canada*. Wreck Cove, NS: Breton Books.

Iwata, B. A., Dorsey, M. F., Slifer, K. J., Bauman, K. E., & Richman, G. S. (1982). Toward a functional analysis of self-injury. *Analysis and Intervention in Developmental Disabilities, 2*, 3–20.

Janko, S. (1994). *Vulnerable children, vulnerable lives*. New York, NY: Teachers College Press.

Janus, M., Lefort, J., Cameron, R., & Kopechanskil, L. (2007). Staring kindergarten: Transition issues for children with special needs. *Canadian Journal of Education 30*(3), 628–648.

Jaudes, P., & Mackey-Bilaver, L. (2008). Do chronic conditions increase young children's risk of being maltreated? *Child Abuse and Neglect, 32*(7), 671–681.

Jensen, E. (2008). *Brain-based learning and teaching*. New York, NY: Brain Store Incorporated.

Johnson, C. (2001). *Supporting families in transition between early intervention services and school age programs*. Boulder, CO: Colorado Families for Hands and Voices. Available from www.handsandvoices.org

Johnson, T. E., Chandler, L. K., Kerns, G. M., & Fowler, S. A. (1986). What are parents saying about family involvement in transitions? A retrospective transition interview. *Journal of the Division for Early Childhood, 11*(1), 10–17.

Jones, L., Bellis, M. A., Wood, S., Hughes, K., McCoy, E., Eckley, L., … Officer, A. (2012, July 12). Prevalence and risk of violence against children with disabilities: A systematic review and meta-analysis of observational studies. *The Lancet*. doi: 10.1016/S0140-6736(12)60692-8

Jorde, L. G., Carey, J. C., Bamshad, M. J., & White, R. W. (2009). *Medical genetics*. St. Louis, MO: Mosby.

Julovich, B. (1998). Emergent curriculum. In E. A. Tertell, S. M. Klein, & J. L. Jewett (Eds.), *When teachers reflect: Journeys toward effective, inclusive practice* (pp. 121–129). Washington, DC: National Association for the Education of Young Children.

Kaczmarek, L. A. (1982). Motor activities: A context for language/communication intervention. *Journal of the Division for Early Childhood, 6*, 21–36.

Kaiser, A. (2000). Teaching functional communication skills. In M. E. Snell & F. Brown (Eds.), *Instruction of students with severe disabilities* (5th ed., pp. 453–491). Columbus, OH: Merrill.

Kaiser, B., & Rasminsky, J. S. (1999). *Meeting the challenge: Effective strategies for challenging behaviours in early childhood environments*. Ottawa, ON: Canadian Child Care Federation.

Kalyanpur, M., & Harry, B. (1999). *Culture in special education*. Baltimore, MD: Brookes.

Kartin, D., Grant T. M., Streissguth, A. P., Sampson, P. D., & Ernest, C. C. (2002, Fall). Three-year developmental outcomes in children with prenatal alcohol and drug exposure. *Pediatric Physical Therapy, 14*(3), 145–153.

Katz, H. P. (2004). Important endocrine disorders of childhood. In R. Haslam & P. Valletutti (Eds.), *Medical problems in the classroom*. Austin, TX: Pro-Ed.

Kern, L. (n.d.). Recommended practices: Addressing persistent challenging behaviors [Fact sheet]. Retrieved from Technical Assistance Center on Social Emotional Intervention for Young Children website, http://challengingbehavior.fmhi.usf.edu/do/resources/documents/rph_pers_chall_beh.pdf

Kids Have Stress Too! (2009). *KHST! preschool program manual.* Toronto, ON: Psychology Foundation of Canada.

Kilgallon, P. (2003, December). Early childhood teachers' knowledge of teaching children with disabilities. *Australian Journal of Early Childhood, 28*(4), 9–13.

Killoran, I., Tymon, D., & Frempong, G. (2007). Disabilities and inclusion in Toronto preschools. *International Journal of Inclusive Education, 11*(1), 81–95.

Kitano, M. K. (1989). The K–3 teacher's role in recognizing and supporting young gifted children. *Young Children, 44*(3), 57–63.

Klein, M. D., Cook, R. E., & Richardson-Gibbs, A. M. (2001). *Strategies for including children with special needs in early childhood settings.* New York, NY: Delmar Thompson.

Koegel, R., Koegel, L., & Dunlap, G. (1996). *Positive behavioral support: Including people with difficult behaviors in the community.* Baltimore, MD: Brookes.

Koenig, A. J., Holbrook, M. C., Corn, A. L., DePriest, L. B., Erin, J. N., & Priestly, I. (2000). Specialized assessment for students with visual impairments. In A. J. Koenig & M. C. Holbrook (Eds.), *Foundations of education: Instructional strategies for teaching children and youths with visual impairments* (Vol. 2, pp. 103–172). New York, NY: American Foundation for the Blind.

Kohn, A. (2001). Five reasons to stop saying, "Good Job!" *Young Children, 56*(5), 24–28.

Koller, D., & Khan, N. (2013). Young children with diabetes: Emotion, knowledge and self-care. Retrieved from http://www.mydiabetesplaybox.com/files/2011/12/research-page-pdf-insert-Feb-7-13.pdf

Kontos, S., & Wilcox-Herzog, A. (1997). Influences on children's competence in early childhood classrooms. *Early Childhood Research Quarterly, 12*, 247–262.

Kopelwicz, H. S. (1996). *It's nobody's fault: New hope and help for difficult children and their parents.* New York, NY: Times Books.

Kordich Hall, D. (2000). Fostering optimism in young children. *Ideas/Interaction, 14*(3), 19–23.

Koralek, D. (2003). *Reading aloud with children of all ages.* Retrieved from https://www.naeyc.org/files/yc/file/200303/ReadingAloud.pdf

Kostelnik, M. J., Whiren, A. P., Soderman, A. K., Stein, L. C., & Gregory, K. (2011). *Guiding children's social development: Theory to practice.* Clifton Park, NY: Delmar Learning.

Kushalnagar, P., Mathur, G., Moreland, C. J., Napoli, D. J., Osterling, W., Padden, C., & Rathmann, C. (2010). Infants and children with hearing loss need early language access. *Journal of Clinical Ethics, 21*(2), 143–154.

Lamorey, S., & Bricker, D. (1993). Integrated programs: Effects on young children and their programs. In C. A. Peck, S. L. Odom, & D. D. Bricker (Eds.), *Integrating young children with disabilities into community programs* (pp. 249–270). Baltimore, MD: Brookes.

Landau, S., & McAninch, C. (1993, May). Young children with attention deficits. *Young Children, 49*–58.

Langford, R. (Ed.). (1997). *Checklist for quality inclusive education: A self-assessment tool and manual for early childhood settings.* London, ON: Early Childhood Resource Teacher Network of Ontario.

Langford, R. (2012). Innovations in provincial early learning curriculum frameworks. In N. Howe & L. Prochner (Eds.), *New directions in early childhood education and care in Canada* (pp. 206–228). Toronto, ON: University of Toronto.

Langford, R., & Kotsopoulos, S. (2008). Collaborating for inclusion: Developing a policy that works. In *Early Childhood Inclusion: Applying Lessons Learned Symposium Proceedings* (pp. 13–16). Winnipeg, MB: SpeciaLink.

Learning Disabilities Association of Canada. (2002). LD defined. Retrieved from http://www.ldac-taac.ca/Defined/defined-e.asp

Learning Disabilities Association of Canada. (2013). Official definition of learning disabilities. Retrieved from http://www.ldac-acta.ca/learn-more/ld-defined/official-definition-of-learning-disabilities

Lieber, J., Schwartz, I., Sandall, S., Horn, E., & Ashworth Wolery, R. (2003). Curricular considerations for young children in inclusive settings. *A Research-to-Practice Journal for the Early Intervention Field, 4*, 432–452.

Liptak, G. S. (2002). Neural tube defects. In M. L. Batshaw (Ed.), *Children with disabilities* (5th ed., pp. 467–492). Baltimore, MD: Brookes.

Lovecky, D. V. (1999). *Gifted children with AD/HD.* Providence, RI: Gifted Resource Center of New England.

Lynch, E. W., & Hanson, M. J. (2011). *Developing cross-cultural competence: A guide for working with young children and their families.* Baltimore, MD: Brookes.

MacKenzie, K. (Ed.). (2004). *Starting point: A resource for parents of deaf or hard of hearing children.* Toronto, ON: The Canadian Hearing Society.

Malloy, T. V. (2003, July). *Sign language use for deaf, hard of hearing, and hearing babies: The evidence supports it* (Report prepared for American Society for Deaf Children & Laurent Clerc National Deaf Education Center, Gallaudet University). Retrieved from http://www.gallaudet.edu/Images/Clerc/pdf/English%20ASDC%20summary.pdf

Markussen Linnet, K. Wisborg, K., Obel, C., Secher, N. J., Thomsen, P. H., Agerbo, E., & Brink Henriksen, T. (2005). Smoking during pregnancy and the risk of hyperkinetic disorder in offspring. *Pediatrics, 116*(2), 462–467.

Marotz, L. R. (2012). *Health, safety, and nutrition for the young child.* Belmont, CA: Wadsworth.

Marotz, L. R., Cross, M. Z., & Rush, J. M. (2009). *Health, safety and nutrition for young children* (6th ed.). Clifton Park, NY: Delmar Learning.

Marshall, H. H. (2001). Cultural influences on the development of self-concept: Updating our thinking. *Young Children, 56*(6), 19–25.

Martin, S. (2007). *Take a look: Observation and portfolio assessment in early childhood* (3rd ed.). Toronto, ON: Addison-Wesley.

Martin, S. (2010). *Take a look: Observation and portfolio assessment in early childhood* (6th ed.). Toronto, ON: Pearson.

Mason, J. A., & Herrmann, K. R. (1998). Universal infant hearing screening by automated auditory brainstem response measurement. *Pediatrics, 101,* 221–228.

Mayer, D. (2009). Disability and inclusion: Changing attitudes—changing policy. In Canadian Centre for Policy Alternatives (Eds.), *Beyond child's play: Caring for and educating young children in Canada* (pp. 159–169). Ottawa, ON: Canadian Centre for Policy Alternatives.

Mayo Clinic. (2011a). Hemophilia: Treatments and drugs. Retrieved from http://www.mayoclinic.org/diseases-conditions/hemophilia/basics/treatment/con-20029824

Mayo Clinic. (2011b). Premature birth: Complications. Retrieved from http://www.mayoclinic.com/health/premature-birth/DS00137/DSECTION=complications

McCain, M., & Mustard, F. (1999). *Early Years Study final report.* Toronto, ON: Publications Ontario.

McCain, M., Mustard, F., & McCuaig, K. (2011). *Early Years Study 3: Making decisions, taking action.* Toronto, ON: Margaret & Wallace McCain Family Foundation.

McClelland, M. M., Morrison, F. J., & Holmes, D. L. (2000). Children at risk for early academic problems: The role of learning-related social skills. *Early Childhood Research Quarterly, 15,* 307–329.

McGregor, G., & Vogelsberg, T. (1998). *Inclusive schooling practices: Pedagogical and research foundations.* Missoula: University of Montana Rural Institute on Disabilities.

McLean, M., Bailey, D. B., & Wolery, M. (2004). *Assessing infants and preschoolers with handicaps.* Columbus, OH: Merrill.

Mesch, J. (2002). *Tactile sign language: Turn taking and questions in signed conversations of deaf-blind people.* Washington, DC: Gallaudet University Press.

Meyer, D. (1995). *Uncommon fathers.* New York, NY: Woodbine House.

Mills, P. E., & Cole, K. N. (1999, June). *Mediated learning: Developmentally appropriate early childhood methods designed to facilitate inclusion.* Paper presented at the Early Childhood Special Education Summer Institute, Wenatchee, WA.

Minor, L. (2002, Summer). Effective practices in early intervention planning transitions to preschool. *See/Hear Newsletter.* Retrieved from http://www.tsbvi.edu/Outreach/seehear/summer02/planning.htm

Mitchell, S., Foulger, T. S., & Wetzel, K. (2009, September). Ten tips for involving families through Internet-based communication. *Young Children, 1*(7). Retrieved from http://www.naeyc.org/files/yc/file/200909/Ten%20Tips%20for%20Involving%20Families.pdf

Montessori, M. (1912). *The Montessori method: Scientific pedagogy as applied to child education in "children's houses"* (Trans. A. F. George). New York, NY: Stokes.

Moses, K. (1987, Spring). The impact of childhood disability: The parents' struggle. *Ways Magazine.*

MOVE International. (n.d.). Who MOVE is. Retrieved from http://www.move-international.org/about#

Mulligan, J., MacCulloch, R., Roberts, W., & Steel, L. (2009, March 9). What is autism spectrum disorder? Retrieved from http://www.aboutkidshealth.ca/En/ResourceCentres/AutismSpectrumDisorder/WhatisASD/Pages/default.aspx

Muscular Dystrophy Association of Canada. (2009). *A teacher's guide to Duchenne muscular dystrophy.* Toronto, ON: Author.

National Association for the Education of Young Children. (1988). Position statement on standardized testing of young children 3 through 8 years of age. *Young Children, 43*(3), 42–47.

National Association for the Education of Young Children. (2002). *Healthy young children* (4th ed.). Washington, DC: Author.

National Association for the Education of Young Children. (2009). *Developmentally appropriate practice in early childhood programs serving children from birth through age 8* [Position statement]. Retrieved from http://www.naeyc.org/files/naeyc/file/positions/PSDAP.pdf

National Association of Early Childhood Specialists. (2003). *Still unacceptable trends in kindergarten entry and placement* [Position statement]. Retrieved from http://www.naeyc.org.aboutpositions/pdf/Psunacc.pdf

National Fragile X Foundation. (n.d.). Prevalence: How common is Fragile X syndrome? Retrieved from http://www.fragilex.org/fragile-x-associated-disorders/prevalence/

National Human Genome Research Institute. (2011). Learning about Tay-Sachs disease. Retrieved from http://www.genome.gov/10001220

National Institute of Mental Health. (2013). What is anxiety disorder? Retrieved from http://www.nimh.nih.gov/health/topics/anxiety-disorders/index.shtml

National Institute on Deafness and Other Communication Disorders. (2002). *Cochlear implants* (National Institute of Health Publication No. 00-4798). Bethesda, MD: Author. Retrieved from http://www.nidcd.nih.gov/health/hearing/coch.asp

National Institutes of Health. (2012). What is sickle cell anemia? Retrieved from http://www.nhlbi.nih.gov/health/health-topics/topics/sca/

National Joint Committee on Learning Disabilities. (2006). *Learning disabilities and young children: Identification and intervention* [Technical report]. Retrieved from http://www.asha.org/policy

Neilson, S. L., Olive, M. L., Donovan, A., & McEvoy, M. (1998). Challenging behaviors in your classroom? Don't react—teach instead. *Young Exceptional Children, 2*(1), 2–10.

Neuman, S. B., Copple, C., & Bredekamp, D. (2003). Taking stock of what you do to promote literacy. *Young Children.* Retrieved from http://www.naeyc.org/files/yc/file/200303/PromotingLiteracy.pdf

Nipissing District Developmental Screen. (2011). *Six years of age checklist.* Retrieved from http://www.ndds.ca/ontario

Noonan, M. J., & McCormick, L. (2006). *Young children with disabilities in natural environments: Methods and procedures.* Baltimore, MD: Brooks.

Odom, S., Buysse, V., & Soukakou, E. (2011). Inclusion for young children with disabilities: A quarter century of research perspectives. *Journal of Early Intervention, 33*(4), 344–356.

Odom, S. L. (2000). Preschool inclusion: What we know and where we go from here. *Topics in Early Childhood Special Education, 20*(1), 20–27.

Odom, S. L. (Ed.). (2002). *Widening the circle: Including children with disabilities in preschool programs.* New York, NY: Teachers College Press.

Odom, S. L., Schwartz, I. S., & ECRII Investigators. (2002). So what do we know from all this? Synthesis points of research on preschool inclusion. In S. L. Odom (Ed.), *Widening the circle: Including children with disabilities in preschool programs* (pp. 154–174). New York, NY: Teachers College Press.

Odom, S. L., Vitztum, J., Wolery, R., Lieber, J., Sandall, S., Hanson, M. J., … Horn, E. M. (2004). Preschool inclusion in the United States: A review of research from an ecological systems perspective. *Journal of Research in Special Educational Needs, 4*(1), 17–49.

OECD Directorate for Education. (2004). *Canada country note.* Paris, France: Author.

O'Neill, B. (2013, July). Improvisational play interventions: Fostering social-emotional development in inclusive classrooms. *Young Children,* 62–69.

Ontario Rett Syndrome Association. (2013). What is Rett syndrome? Retrieved from http://www.rett.ca/rett-syndromertt/what-is-rett-syndrome/

Osteogensis Imperfecta (OI) Foundation. (2012). Facts about osteogensis imperfecta. Retrieved from http://www.oif.org/site/PageServer?pagename=AOI_Facts

Ozonoff, S., Iosif, A., Baguio, F., Cook, J. C., Moore Hill, M., Hutman, T., … Young, G. S. (2010). A prospective study of the emergence of early behavioral signs of autism. *Journal of the American Academy of Child and Adolescent Psychiatry, 49,* 256–266.

Paasche, C. L., Gorrill, L., & Strom, B. (2004). *Children with special needs in early childhood settings.* Albany, NY: Delmar.

Palmer, D., Borthwick-Duffy, S., Widaman, K., & Best, S. (1998). Influences on parent perceptions of inclusive practices for their children with mental retardation. *American Journal on Mental Retardation, 3,* 272–287.

Palmer, D., Fuller, K., Arora, T., & Nelson, M. (2001). Taking sides: Parent views on inclusion for their children with severe disabilities. *Exceptional Children, 64,* 457–484.

Panitch, M. (2008). *Disability, mothers and organization: Accidental activists.* New York, NY: Routledge.

Peck, C. A., Carlson, P., & Helmstetter, E. (1992). Parent and teacher perceptions of outcomes for typically developing children enrolled in integrated early childhood programs: A statewide survey. *Journal of Early Intervention, 16,* 53–63.

Pelo, A. (1996). Our school's not fair: A story about emergent curriculum. In D. Curtis & M. Carter (Eds.), *Reflecting young children's lives: A handbook for planning child-centered curriculum* (pp. 101–106). St. Paul, MN: Redleaf Press.

Petitto, L. A. (2000). On the biological foundations of human language. In K. Emmorey & H. Lane (Eds.), *The signs of language revisited: An anthology in honour of Ursula Bellugi and Edward Klima* (pp. 447–471). Mahwah, NJ: Erlbaum.

Petitto, L. A., & Maramette, P. F. (1991). Babbling in the manual mode. *Science, 251,* 1493–1496.

Piaget, J. (1992). *The origins of intelligence in children.* New York, NY: International Universities Press.

Pickard, R. E. (2002, February 6). Does early identification of deaf newborns lead to later improvements in language skills? *Journal of the American Medical Association, 287*(5), 587–588.

Pimento, B., & Kernested, D. (2010). *Healthy foundations in early childhood settings.* Toronto, ON: Nelson Education.

Pinker, S. (2006). *The language instinct: How the mind creates language.* New York, NY: Morrow.

Pogrund, R. L., & Fazzi, L. D. (2002). *Early focus: Working with young blind and visually impaired children and their families.* New York, NY: American Foundation for the Blind.

Pogrund, R. L., Fazzi, D. L., & Hess, C. L. (Eds.). (2002). *Early focus: Working with young children who are blind or visually impaired and their families.* New York, NY: American Foundation for the Blind.

Polakow, V. (1992). Deconstructing the discourse of care: Young children in the shadows of democracy. In S. Kessler & B. B. Swadener (Eds.), *Reconceptualizing the early childhood curriculum* (pp. 123–148). New York, NY: Teachers College Press.

Public Health Agency of Canada. (2013). Childhood obesity. Retrieved from http://www.phac-aspc.gc.ca/hp-ps/hl-mvs/framework-cadre/2011/index-eng.php

Rafferty, Y., Boettcher, C., & Griffin, K. W. (2001). Benefits and risks of reverse inclusion for preschoolers with and without disabilities: Parents' perspectives. *Journal of Early Intervention, 24,* 266–286.

Rafferty, Y., & Griffin, K. W. (2005). Benefits and risks of reverse inclusion for preschoolers with and without disabilities: Perspectives of parents and providers. *Journal of Early Intervention, 27*(3), 173–192.

Rafferty, Y., Piscitelli, V., & Boettcher, C. (2003). The impact of inclusion on language development and social competence among preschoolers with disabilities. *Exceptional Children, 69,* 467–479.

Rathus, S. A. (1988). *Understanding child development.* New York, NY: Holt, Rinehart, & Winston.

Ray, J. A., Pewit-Kinder, J., & George, S. (2009, September). Partnering with families of children with special needs. *Young Children.* Retrieved from http://www.naeyc.org/files/yc/file/200909/Families%20of%20Children%20with%20Special%20Needs.pdf

Reichle, J., Mirenda, P., Locke, P., Piche, L., & Johnson, S. (1992). Beginning augmentative communication systems. In S. F. Warren & J. Reichle (Eds.), *Causes and effects in communication and language intervention* (pp. 131–156). Baltimore, MD: Brookes.

Renzulli, J. S., Smith, L. H., White, A. J., Callahan, C. M., Hartman, R. K., & Westberg, K. L. (2002). *Scales for rating the behavioural characteristics of superior students.* Mansfield Center, CT: Creative Learning Press.

Rett Syndrome Research Trust. (2013). Prevalence of Rett Syndrome and related syndromes. Retrieved from http://www.rsrt.org/rett-and-mecp2-disorders/rett-syndrome/

Rice, M. L., & O'Brien, M. (1990). Transitions: Times of change and accommodation. *Topics in Early Childhood, 9*(4), 12–14.

Robinson, H. B. (1981). The uncommonly bright child. In M. Lewis & L. A. Rosenblum (Eds.), *The uncommon child* (pp. 57–81). New York, NY: Plenum.

Roedell, W. C., Jackson, N. E., & Robinson, H. B. (1980). *Re-forming gifted education: Matching the program to the child.* Scottsdale, AZ: Great Potential Press.

Roeser, R. J. (2000). *Auditory diagnosis.* New York, NY: Thieme Medical.

Rogers, K. B. (2001). *Re-forming gifted education: Matching the program to the child.* Scottsdale, AZ: Great Potential Press.

Rogoff, B. (1990). *Apprenticeship in thinking: Cognitive development in social context.* New York, NY: Oxford University Press.

Rosenquest, B. B. (2002). Literacy-based planning and pedagogy that supports toddler language development. *Early Childhood Education Journal, 29,* 241–249.

Roskos, K. A., Christie, J. F., & Richgels, D. J. (2003). The essentials of early literacy development. *Young Children.* Retrieved from http://naeyc.org/files/yc/file/200303/Essentials.pdf

Rous, B., Hallam, R., Harbin, G., McCormick, K., & Jung, L. A. (2007). The transition process for young children with disabilities: A conceptual framework. *Infants and Young Children, 20*(2), 135–148.

Rozien, J. J. (2007). Down syndrome. In M. L. Batshaw, L. Pellegrino, & N. J. Roizen (Eds.), *Children with disabilities* (6th ed., pp. 263–273). Baltimore, MD: Paul H. Brooks.

Sabrina's Law, 2005, S.O. 2005, c. 7.

Sager, E. (2010, Summer). Family and social memory: Why history matters. *Transition, 40*(2), 1–4.

Sameroff, A. J., & Chandler, M. J. (1975). Reproductive risk and the continuum of caretaking casualty. In F. D. Horowitz (Ed.), *Review of child development research* (pp. 187–244). Chicago, IL: University of Chicago Press.

Sarkar, N. (2008). The impact of intimate partner violence on women's reproductive health and pregnancy outcome. *Journal of Obstetrics and Gynaecology, 28*(3), 266–271.

Sass-Lehrer, M. (2011). *Early Beginnings for deaf and hard of hearing children: Guidelines for effective services.* Washington, DC: Laurent Clerc National Deaf Education Centre, Gallaudet University.

Saunders, J., & Espeland, P. (1991). *Bringing out the best: A resource guide for parents of young and gifted children.* Minneapolis, MN: Free Spirit.

Schick, B. (2003). The development of American Sign Language and manually coded English systems. In M. Marschark & P. Spencer (Eds.), *Oxford handbook of Deaf studies, language and education* (pp. 219–231). New York, NY: Oxford University Press.

Schickedanz, J. A., Schickedanz, D. I., & Forsyth, P. D. (1982). *Toward understanding children.* Boston, MA: Little, Brown.

Schizophrenia Society of Ontario. (2013). What causes schizophrenia? Retrieved from http://www.schizophrenia.on.ca/Schizophrenia-Psychosis/About-Schizophrenia/What-causes-schizophrenia

Schorr, E. A., Fox, N. A., van Washove, V., & Knudsen, E. I. (2005). Auditory-visual fusion in speech perception in children with cochlear implants. *Proceedings of the National Academy of Sciences of the United States, 102,* 18748–18750.

Schwartz, I. S., Billingsley, F. F., & McBride, B. (1998). Including children with autism in inclusive preschools: Strategies that work. *Young Exceptional Children, 2*(1), 19–26.

Schwartz, T. S., McBride, B., Pepler, I., Grant, S., & Carter, J. J. (1993, December). *A classroom-based curriculum for facilitating communicative independence in young children with special needs.* Paper presented at the Division of Early Childhood Conference, San Diego, CA.

Shonkoff, J. P., & Phillips, D. A. (2000). *From neurons to neighborhoods: The science of early childhood development.* Washington, DC: National Academy Press.

Shore, R. (2003). *Rethinking the brain: New insights into development.* New York, NY: Families and Work Institute.

Simeonsson, R. J., & Bailey, D. B. (2000). Family dimensions in early intervention. In S. J. Meisels & J. P. Shonkoff (Eds.), *Handbook of early childhood intervention* (pp. 428–444). Cambridge, England: Cambridge University Press.

Skinner, B. F. (1957). *Verbal behaviour.* New York, NY: Prentice Hall.

Smith, J. (2006). *Cued speech and cochlear implants: Powerful partners.* Presentation at Cued Speech 40th Anniversary Convention, Towson, MD. PowerPoint retrieved from http://www.cuedspeech.org/pdfs/Conference_2006_Cued_Speech_And_Cochlear_Implants_Jane_Smith.pdf

Snow, K. (2005). *People first language* [Position paper]. Retrieved from http://disabilityisnatural.com/

Sobsey, D. (1995). Violence against children with disabilities, an overview. *Connection: Newsletter of the Institute for Prevention of Child Abuse, 4,* 1–5.

Sobsey, D., & Varnhagen, C. (1988). *Sexual abuse and exploitation of people with disabilities: Final report* (ERDS No. ED346620). Ottawa, ON: Department of National Health and Welfare.

Spencer, P. (2004). Language at 12 and 18 months: Characteristics and accessibility of linguistic models. In K. Meadow-Orleans, P. Spencer, & L. Koester (Eds.), *The world of deaf infants: A longitudinal study* (pp. 147–167). New York, NY: Oxford University Press.

Spodek, B., Saracho, O. N., & Lee, R. C. (1984). *Mainstreaming young children.* Belmont, CA: Wadsworth.

Stapleford, E. M. (1976). *History of the day nurseries branch: A personal record.* Toronto, ON: Ministry of Community and Social Services, Ontario.

Statistics Canada. (2013). Census family. Retrieved from http://www.statcan.gc.ca/concepts/definitions/c-r-fam-eng.htm

Steinhauer, P. D. (1998). Developing resiliency in children from disadvantaged populations. In *Canada health action: Building on the legacy Vol. I. Determinants of health: Children and youth* (pp. 47–102; Catalogue No. H21-126/6-1-1997E). Ottawa, ON: National Forum on Health, Health Canada.

Stewart, K. A., & Cornell, A. (2004). Learning through the senses. In D. Gold & A. Tait (Eds.), *A strong beginning: A sourcebook for health and education professionals working with young children who are visually impaired or blind.* Toronto, ON: Canadian National Institute for the Blind.

Strasser, J., & Seplocha, H. (2010). Using picture books to support young children's literacy. In K. Menke Paciorek (Ed.), *Annual editions: Early childhood education.* New York, NY: McGraw Hill.

Streissguth, A. P., Barr, H. M., & Sampson, P. D. (1990). Moderate prenatal alcohol exposure: Effects on child IQ and learning problems at age 7½ years. *Alcoholism: Clinical and Experimental Research, 14,* 662–669.

Strock, M. (2004). *Autism spectrum disorders (pervasive development disorders)* (NIH Publication No. NIH-04-5511). Bethesda, MD: National Institutes of Health, U.S. Department of Health and Human Services.

Strock, N. M. (2006). *Attention deficit hyperactivity disorder* (NIH Publication No. l3572). Bethesda, MD: National Institutes of Health, U.S. Department of Health and Human Services.

Sugai, G. Horner, R. H., Dunlap, G., Hieneman, M., Lewis, T. J., Nelson, C. M., … Ruef, M. (2000). Applying positive behavioral support and functional behavioral assessment in schools. *Journal of Positive Behavior Interventions, 2*(3), 131–143.

Sullivan, P. M., & Knutson, J. F. (2000). Maltreatment and disabilities: A population-based study. *Child Abuse and Neglect, 24*(10), 1257–1273.

Swim, T. J. (2006). Basic premises of classroom design. In K. M. Paciorek & J. H. Munro (Eds.), *Annual editions: Early childhood education 05/06* (pp. 101–105). Dubuque, IA: McGraw Hill/Dushkin.

Teller, D. Y., McDonald, M. A., Preston, K., Sebris, S. L., & Dobson, V. (1986). Assessment of visual acuity in infants and children: The acuity card procedure. *Developmental Medicine and Child Neurology, 28,* 779–789.

Terpstra, E. J., & Tamura, R. (2007). Effective social interaction strategies for inclusive settings. *Early Childhood Education, 35,* 405–411.

Thomas, A., & Chess, S. (1977). *Temperament and development.* New York, NY: Bruner/Mazel.

Thomas, A., & Chess, S. (1986). The New York longitudinal study: From infancy to early adult life. In R. Plomin & J. Dunn (Eds.), The study of the temperament: Changes, continuities, and challenges. Hillsdale, NJ: Erlbaum.

Thurman, K. S., & Widerstrom, A. H. (1990). *Infants and young children with special needs: A developmental and ecological approach.* Baltimore, MD: Brookes.

Tourette Syndrome Foundation of Canada. (2013). Educators resources. Retrieved from http://www.tourette.ca/resources-educators.php

Tourette Syndrome Foundation of Canada. (2014). What is Tourette syndrome? Retrieved from http://www.tourette.ca/learn.php

Tozer, R. (2001). Spotlight on siblings. *Interactions, 15*(1).

Trent, S., Artiles, A., & Englert, C. S. (1999). From deficit thinking to social constructivism: A review of theory, research, and practice in special education. *Review of Research in Education, 23,* 277–307.

Turnbull, A. P., Turnbull, H. R., Erwin, E. J., & Soodak, L. C. (2005). *Families, professionals and exceptionality: A special partnership.* Upper Saddle River, NJ. Prentice Hall.

Underwood, K. (2013). *Everyone is welcome: Inclusive early childhood education and care.* Toronto, ON: Ministry of Education. Retrieved from http://www.edu.gov.on.ca/childcare/inclusion.html

Underwood, K., & Frankel, B. (2012). The Developmental Systems Approach to early intervention in Canada. *Infants and Young Children, 25*(4), 286–296.

Underwood, K., Valeo, A., & Wood, R. (2012). Understanding inclusive early childhood education: A capability approach. *Contemporary Issues in Early Childhood, 11*(4), 290–299.

UNICEF. (2012). *The right of children with disabilities to education: A rights-based approach to inclusive education.* Geneva, Switzerland: UNICEF Regional Office for Central and Eastern Europe and the Commonwealth of Independent States (CEECIS).

UNICEF Innocenti Research Centre. (2008). *The child care transition: Report card #8.* Florence, Italy: Author.

United Nations Convention on the Rights of Persons with Disabilities, 2006. Retrieved from http://www.un.org/disabilities/convention/conventionfull.shtml

United States Government Accountability Office (GAO). (2005). *No Child Left Behind Act: Most students with disabilities participated in statewide assessments, but inclusion options could be improved.* Washington, DC: Author. Retrieved from http://www.gao.gov/new.items/d05618.pdf

University of Maine Center for Community Inclusion and Disability Studies. (2014, February 27). *Learning Ideas: Universal design in pre-K and early elementary classrooms.* Retrieved from https://ccids.umaine.edu/files/2014/02/UD-Pre-K-tipsheet-022714.pdf

U.S. Food and Drug Administration. (2014). Benefits and risks of cochlear implants. Retrieved from http://www.fda.gov/medicaldevices/productsandmedicalprocedures/implantsandprosthetics/cochlearimplants/ucm062843.htm

Villeneuve, M., Catenoud, C., Hutchinson, N., Minnes, P., Perrry, A., Dionne, C., … Weiss, J. (2013). The experience of parents as their children with developmental disabilities transition from early intervention to kindergarten. *Canadian Journal of Education, 36*(1), 4–43.

Vygotsky, L. (1978). *Mind in society: The development of higher psychological processes.* Cambridge, MA: Harvard University Press.

Walker, H., Stiller, B., & Golly, A. (1998). First steps to success. *Young Exceptional Children, 1*(2), 2–7.

Warren, S. F., & Kaiser, A. P. (1988). Research in early language intervention. In S. L. Odom & M. B. Karnes (Eds.), *Early intervention for infants and children with handicaps* (pp. 89–108). Baltimore, MD: Brookes.

WebMD. (2011). Chelation therapy: Topic overview. Retrieved fromww.webmd.com/balance/tc/chelation-therapy-topic-overview

WebMD. (2012). Children's health: Dwarfism. Retrieved from http://www.webmd.com/children/dwarfism-causes-treatments

Wiart, L., Kehler, H., Rempel, G., & Tough, S. (2011, November). *Alberta Inclusive Child Care Project.* Edmonton, AB: Alberta Centre for Child, Family and Community Research. Retrieved from http://research4children.com/data/documents/AICCPFINALREPORTDecember2011pdf.pdf

Widerstrom, A. H. (2005). *Achieving learning goals through play: Teaching young children with special needs* (2nd ed.). Baltimore, MD: Paul S. Brookes.

Winzer, M. (1997). *Special education in early childhood: An inclusive approach.* Toronto, ON: Prentice-Hall.

Winzer, M. A. (2007). *Children with exceptionalities: A Canadian perspective* (8th ed.). Toronto , ON: Pearson Canada.

Wolery, M. (1994). Designing inclusive environments for young children with special needs. In M. Wolery & J. S. Wilbers (Eds.), *Including children with special needs in early childhood programs* (pp. 151–166). Washington, DC: National Association for the Education of Young Children.

Wolfensberger, W. (1972). *The principle of normalization in human services.* Toronto, ON: National Institute on Mental Retardation.

Wolfle, J. (1989). The gifted preschooler: Developmentally different, but still 3 or 4 year olds. *Young Children, 44*(3), 41–48.

Wong, W. W., & Hughes, J. N. (2006). Ethnicity and language contributions to dimensions of parent involvement. *School Psychology Review, 35*(4), 645–662.

Woods, J. J., & McCormick, K. M. (2002). Toward an integration of child- and family-centered practices of assessment in preschool children: Welcoming the family. *Young Exceptional Children, 5*(3), 2–11.

World Health Organization. (2012). Early childhood development and disability: A discussion paper. Geneva, Switzerland: Author.

World Health Organization. (2012, July 12). Children with disabilities more likely to experience violence [Note for the media]. Retrieved from http://www.who.int/mediacentre/news/notes/2012/child_disabilities_violence_20120712/en/

Wylie, S., & Fenning, K. (2012). *Observing young children: Transforming early learning through reflective practice* (4th ed.). Toronto, ON: Nelson Education.

Yeargin-Allsopp, M., Rice, C., Karapurkar, T., Doernberg, N., Boyle, C., & Murphy, C. (2003). Prevalence of autism in a US metropolitan area. *Journal of the American Medical Association, 289*(1), 49–55.

Yewchuk, C., & Jobagy, S. (1991, Winter). The neglected minority: The emotional needs of gifted children. *Education Canada,* 8–13.

Zebrowski, P. M. (1995). The topography of beginning stuttering. *Journal of Communication Disorders, 28*(2), 75–91.

Index

Note: Page numbers with b's, f's and t's refer to boxes, figures, and tables

Disability, 8b

DISC. *See* Diagnostic Inventory for Screening Children (DISC)

Discipline
  preventive, 248
  vs. punishment, 248–249

Discrete trail teaching (DTT), 213

Discrimination, 412–413

Disruptive behaviours, 389–391

Distortions, 443

Division for Early Childhood (DEC), 379–380

Dominion–Provincial Wartime Day Nurseries Agreement, 33

Down syndrome, 19, 118–119

Down Syndrome Association of Toronto, 127

Dramatic play centre, 338

Drugs, 121

DTT. *See* Discrete trail teaching (DTT)

Dual placements, 80–81

Duration measures, 277

Dwarfism, 174. *See also* Orthopedic conditions

Dysfluency, 443

Dysgraphia, 106

Dyslexia, 106

E

Early Childhood Care and Mental Health Project, 223

Early Childhood Development (ECD) Accord, 47

Early childhood educators, 46b

Early childhood programs
  chronologically age-appropriate, 10
  family-centred, 9
  full participation, 10
  indicators of, 340f
  research- and value based, 9
  transdisciplinary approach to programming, 9–10

Early childhood teachers
  specialized training for, 78–80
  training programs for, 78

Early education
  environmental arrangements, 240
  historical influences, 239–241
  learning from success, 239–240
  problem of match in, 239

Early identification
  cautionary notes, 278–279
  medical profession's role, 264–270
  observational recording techniques in, 272–278
  process in, 264–270
  screening, 264–270
  teacher as observer in, 270
  teachers' qualifications in, 270–271
  teacher's role in, 270–279

Early intervention
  benefits of, 312
  definition of, 312
  imitation, 19–20
  rationale for, 15–20
  sensitive or critical periods, 16–18
  teachable moments, 18–19

Early Intervention Canada, 327

Early interventionist, 61

Early sentences, 431–432

Earmould, 151

Eating and elimination disorders. *See also* Emotional and psychological disorders
  pica, 208
  soiling, 208–209
  wetting, 208–209

Echolalia, 212

Education Resources Information Center, 423

Educational legislation, 41–42

Egocentric, 366

Email, 67–68

Embedded learning, 405

Emergent curriculum, 86, 137, 338–339, 405

Emerging literacy. *See also* Cognitive learning
  alphabet activities, 420
  definition of, 402
  emergent reading, 420
  emergent writing, 420
  integrated, content-focused activities, 420–421
  overview, 417–418
  phonological awareness activities, 418
  rich teacher talk, 418
  shared book experience, 420
  storybook reading, 418

Emotional and psychological disorders
  anxiety, 206–207
  depression, 206–207
  overdependency, 204–205
  phobias, 207
  separation difficulties, 203–204
  shyness, 205–206
  withdrawal, 205–206

Emotional disturbances, 108, 202

Emotions and, 355–357

Empowerment, 53

Enabling environment, 314

Encephalitis, 123

Encopresis, 209

Enuresis, 209

Environmental influences, 130

Environmental structuring, 360–361

Epilepsy Canada, 198

Epilepsy Ontario, 189

Evidence-based intervention, 396–397

Expressive language, 429

External reinforcement, 244–246

Eye, structure of, 154

Eye-level materials, 180

F

Facilitator, 90–91

Fading, 258–259, 382

FAE. *See* Fetal alcohol effect (FAE)

Failure to thrive, 61

Families
  abuse of child with special needs, 55–56
  adjustment, 56–58
  census, 54
  of children with exceptionalities, 54–55
  class websites, 66–67
  communicating with, 64–68
  definition of, 53–54
  email, 67–68
  enabling and empowering of, 62
  informal exchanges, 65
  parent observations, 65–66
  partnership with, 51–71
  patterns and expectations, 53–62
  perspective on transition, 295
  reciprocal relationships with, 314
  reconstituted (or blended), 54
  support groups, 69–70
  telephone calls, 66–67
  in transition plans, 304
  two-way journal (or communication book), 68
  uniqueness of, 53
  written notes, 67

Families for Early Autism Treatment (FEAT), 233

Family life
  hearing loss and, 148
  vision impairment and, 158–159

Family-centred intervention, 9

Family-teacher partnership
  communicating with families, 64–68
  degree of participation, 63–64
  establishing trust, 64
  family support groups, 69–70
  parent feedback, 70–71
  parent participation, 63
  parent-teacher meetings, 68–69

FARE Food Allergy Research and Education, 198

FAS. *See* Fetal alcohol syndrome (FAS)

FEAT. *See* Families for Early Autism Treatment (FEAT)

Febrile seizures, 188

Feeding times, 321

Feingold diet, 220

Fetal alcohol effect (FAE), 121

Fetal alcohol syndrome (FAS), 121

Fetal development, 117f

Fine motor skills, 228, 411

First Duty Project, 323

First trimester, 116

First words and sentences, 429–431

Flemish sign language, 148

Floor coverings, 180

Floppy babies, 170

FM systems, 152

Food Guide, 194

Forward chaining, 257

"Four Hows," 352

Fragile X syndrome, 118–119

Individual family service plan (IFSP) (continued)
   family member as case manager/
      coordinator, 61
   features of, 60
   identification of needs, 60
   nonintrusiveness, 60
   program-to-program transitions, 62
   purpose of, 60
   service coordination (case management), 61
Individual program plan (IPP)
   components of, 280–287
   creation of implementation plan, 286–287
   definition of, 6, 279
   evaluation (statement of accountability),
      287
   identification of strengths, needs, and
      interests, 281–282
   long-term goals, 283
   meetings, 297
   observation and assessment, 280–281
   settings of goals and objectives, 282–286
   short-term objectives, 283–286
   team, 280
Induced competence, 334
Infant and toddler intervention
   challenges in, 322
   enabling environment, 314
   enabling infant to differentiate processes,
      318–319
   enabling infant to initiate new responses,
      319–320
   enabling infant to maintain psychological
      balance, 317–318
   enabling infant to respond and adapt,
      316–317
   overview, 313–314
   play and learning materials, 320
   reciprocal relationships, 314
   responding to development, 316
   responsive environment, 314
   sensory modalities, 316
   sensory stimulation, 315
   times of sharing and learning, 321
Infant Mental Health Promotion, 327
Infant-directed speech, 427–428
Informal exchanges, 65
Inhaler, 183
In-home support services, 312
Instructions, following, 415–416
Insulin, 186
Integration, 4
Intellectual disability, 115
Interdisciplinary, 280
Intermittent hearing loss, 144
Interpersonal skills, 355
Interval, 383
Interval data sheet, 384f
Intervention
   designing, 379–380
   early, 15–20, 312
   evidence-based, 396–397
   family-centred, 9

infant and toddler intervention, 313–322
   school-age, 322–326
   teacher-mediated, 361–370
Intonation, 428
Intrinsic motivation, 239
Intrinsic reinforcement, 244
IPP. See Individual program plan (IPP)
IQ tests, 269–270

J

Journals, 275
Joy of learning, 239
Juvenile arthritis, 174–175. See also
   Orthopedic conditions
Juvenile diabetes, 186–187
Juvenile rheumatoid arthritis, 174–175

K

Kids Have Stress Too! Preschool Program
   (KHST!), 223
Kids Have Stress Too! The Psychology
   Foundation of Canada, 234
Kinark Child and Family Services, 72, 327
Kingsley, Emily Perl, 58b

L

Labelling, 102–104
Ladder-climbing sequence, in task analysis,
   254–255
Land use, 142
Language
   complexity, 432–433
   definition of, 426
   expressive, 429
   receptive, 429
Language acquisition
   activities that promote communication,
      437–438
   alternative language systems, 433–434
   augmentative communication systems,
      434–435
   development of language complexity,
      432–433
   early sentences, 431–432
   early warning signs, 433
   environmental perspective, 427–428
   first words and sentences, 429–431
   imitation and reinforcement explanation,
      428
   integrated explanation, 428
   lisping, 443
   maturation or innateness explanation, 428
   nonverbal communication, 433
   overregularizations, 432–433
   prelinguistic communication, 428
   role of questions in, 436–437
   sequences in, 428–438, 430f
   speech irregularities, 441–445
   teacher's role in language development,
      435
Language delays, 229–230. See also
   Learning disabilities

Language development
   hearing loss and, 147
   visual impairment and, 157–158
Language samples, 276
Langue des signes québécois (LSQ), 147
l'Arche, 13–14
Lead poisoning, 123
Learned helplessness, 176
Learning disabilities
   auditory-perception difficulties, 229
   characteristics of, 223
   cognitive disorders, 230
   definition of, 223, 224–226
   indicators of fine motor difficulties, 228
   indicators of visual-sensory gross motor
      difficulties, 227–228
   language delays, 229–230
   perseveration, 230–231
   predicting, 225–227
   program considerations, 231–235
   risk indicators, 226f
   signs of, 227–231
   social skills delay, 231
   visual-perception difficulties, 228–229
Learning Disabilities Association of Canada,
   110, 234, 373
Learning Disabilities Association of Ontario,
   234
Learning disorders, 202–203
Learning experiences
   group cognitive and interactive activities,
      421–422
   grouping children, 421
   nonthreatening materials and activities,
      422
   preferred materials and activities, 422
   preparation, 422
   readiness to expand learning
      opportunities, 422
   short periods, 422
Learning Language and Loving It program
   child-oriented strategies, 439–440
   conversational styles, 438–439
   interaction-promoting strategies, 440
   language-promoting strategies, 441
   overview, 438
   what participants learn, 438–441
Learning theory, 242
Leukemia, 185
Lisping, 443
Little People of America (LPA), 174–175
Logs, 275
Low vision (partially seeing), 109

M

Mainstreaming, 4
Manipulative materials, 179, 411
Manual prompts, 257, 258
Marsha Forest Centre, 28
Math, prerequisites for, 416–421
Maturation, 238
Mayo Clinic, 398